Nonprofit
MANAGEMENT

Fifth Edition

Sara Miller McCune founded SAGE Publishing in 1965 to support the dissemination of usable knowledge and educate a global community. SAGE publishes more than 1000 journals and over 800 new books each year, spanning a wide range of subject areas. Our growing selection of library products includes archives, data, case studies and video. SAGE remains majority owned by our founder and after her lifetime will become owned by a charitable trust that secures the company's continued independence.

Los Angeles | London | New Delhi | Singapore | Washington DC | Melbourne

Nonprofit
MANAGEMENT
Principles and Practice

Fifth Edition

Michael J. Worth
The George Washington University

FOR INFORMATION:

CQ Press, an Imprint of SAGE Publications, Inc.
2455 Teller Road
Thousand Oaks, California 91320
E-mail: order@sagepub.com

SAGE Publications Ltd.
1 Oliver's Yard
55 City Road
London, EC1Y 1SP
United Kingdom

SAGE Publications India Pvt. Ltd.
B 1/I 1 Mohan Cooperative Industrial Area
Mathura Road, New Delhi 110 044
India

SAGE Publications Asia-Pacific Pte. Ltd.
3 Church Street
#10-04 Samsung Hub
Singapore 049483

Acquisitions Editor: Scott Greenan
Editorial Assistant: Lauren Younker
Content Development Editor: Anna Villarruel
Production Editor: Tracy Buyan
Copy Editor: Taryn Bigelow
Typesetter: Cenveo
Proofreader: Laura Webb
Indexer: Wendy Allex
Cover Designer: Candice Harman
Marketing Manager: Jennifer Jones

Printed in the United States of America

ISBN 978-1-5063-9686-6

This book is printed on acid-free paper.

Certified Chain of Custody
Promoting Sustainable Forestry
www.sfiprogram.org
SFI-01268

SFI label applies to text stock

18 19 20 21 22 10 9 8 7 6 5 4 3 2 1

Brief Contents

PART IV OBTAINING AND MANAGING RESOURCES

PART V SPECIAL TOPICS

Detailed Contents

Chapter 3   Theories of the Nonprofit Sector and Nonprofit Organizations   **52**

PART II   GOVERNING AND LEADING NONPROFIT ORGANIZATIONS

Chapter 4   Nonprofit Governing Boards   **80**

PART III   MANAGING THE NONPROFIT ORGANIZATION

Chapter 6   Ensuring Accountability and Measuring Performance

PART V   SPECIAL TOPICS

Chapter 16   Social Entrepreneurship and Innovation   434

Chapter 17   Governing and Managing International and Global Organizations   452

Preface

The first edition of *Nonprofit Management: Principles and Practice* was published by SAGE in 2009, the second edition in 2012, the third edition in 2014, and the fourth edition in 2017. It is striking how much the landscape of the nonprofit sector has continued to change over the years, requiring frequent updates to stay current with the state of the field in nonprofit management.Changes reflected in this fifth edition of the book include, most obviously, certain data, but also trends, new concepts and research, and new cases that have drawn attention since the fourth edition was completed. The inevitable lag between research and writing and publication often means that readers should be alert to recent changes and events that may have occurred during the process of publishing the book. Thus, even this fifth edition may have some obsolescence by the time it reaches the reader. There are reminders of this reality throughout the book, and it is recommended that students consult referenced websites and other resources on points that seem subject to change. It is, of course, impossible to know what economic conditions will prevail when this book reaches its readers. The recession that began in 2007, what some people called the Great Recession, took a significant toll on many nonprofit organizations, resulting in decreased financial resources at a time when the demand for services was increasing. Most nonprofit organizations survived the Great Recession, although the death rate was higher among smaller organizations. Even larger organizations found it necessary to reduce staff, programs, and expenditures (McKeever, Dietz, & Fyffe, 2016). A decade later, by 2017, the economy had recovered by many measures. Unemployment was low and financial markets were at historic highs. Perhaps by the time this fifth edition reaches its readers, the economy will have continued to grow. Or, perhaps, it will again have slipped into recession. In any case, some effects of the financial crisis that occurred near the end of the first decade of the current century have lingered. It produced a heightened awareness of financial uncertainty, the need for nonprofits to use resources efficiently and effectively, and the importance of achieving diverse revenue sources to weather various economic scenarios. Those lessons have brought permanent change to our thinking about the management of nonprofit organizations. It seems likely the nonprofit sector will continue to face new opportunities and challenges in the years ahead.

New to This Edition

This fifth edition includes a number of significant changes from the fourth. First, chapter topics continued from the previous edition all have been updated to reflect new data, new research, and recent events. New material, drawn from both scholarly and practitioner journals, is incorporated at relevant points throughout the book.

In response to reviewer comments as well as the evolving landscape, some topics from the previous edition have been expanded. For example, new material has been included on managing risk, social enterprise, collaborations and partnerships, and the use of social media and networks for marketing, fundraising, and advocacy. The chapter on financial management has been substantially revised to reflect new requirements for nonprofit financial statements issued by the Financial Accounting Standards Board in 2016, which became effective for years after 2017. That chapter also includes an expanded discussion of audits. The chapter on fundraising, Chapter 13, includes changes that reflect the Tax Cuts and Jobs Act of 2017, which has implications for charitable giving. That legislation also impacted nonprofits in other ways, for example, with regard to compensation. The text has been revised and updated throughout, as the new requirements are relevant to the topic.

New cases have been developed for this fifth edition, encompassing recent events and new approaches. New cases related to specific chapters include the Wounded Warrior Project, Sweet Briar College, 4-H, Housing First, the Chan-Zuckerberg Initiative, the National Audubon Society, and an expanded study of governance issues at the Hershey Trust. Cases retained from the fourth edition all have been updated to reflect new developments. The Appendix includes four cases that are comprehensive and cut across topics discussed in various chapters. Three of the Appendix cases have been updated from the fourth edition, including the New York City Opera, Share Our Strength/No Kid Hungry, and The Y. A new comprehensive case has been added, The Girl Scouts of the United States of America (GSUSA), which recounts reforms undertaken by this iconic organization and current challenges it faces. As a new feature in this edition, references are provided at the end of each chapter to cases in the Appendix that are relevant to the points discussed in that chapter, so that instructors can easily incorporate them in discussions of those chapters if they so desire.

Philosophy of This Book

A Balanced Approach

Students reading this book are likely to have varied backgrounds. Some may be undergraduates who do not yet have substantial work experience and perhaps wish to explore nonprofit management as a possible career direction. Others may be graduate students who have an interest in nonprofit careers but have not previously studied management. Still others might have studied management but may have limited knowledge of the unique values, characteristics, and circumstances of the nonprofit sector or how the management principles they know can be applied in the nonprofit environment. Yet others may be individuals with considerable experience working in nonprofit organizations who are pursuing further study to increase and broaden their understanding and professional skills.

Some students reading this book may be undergraduates taking a course that is an introduction to the nonprofit sector. Some may be enrolled in a certificate program intended to increase the skills of nonprofit professionals. Others may be enrolled in a program leading to a master's degree in nonprofit management. Some may be pursuing a master's degree in business, social work, public administration, or public policy, with a concentration in nonprofit management. Still others may be taking only one course in nonprofit management as an elective in their undergraduate or graduate degree program, seeking only a broad and general orientation to the field.

Given this diversity of backgrounds and goals often found among students taking a course in nonprofit management, a textbook that seeks to provide an overview of the field must include both theoretical concepts and practical applications; it must cover some basics as well as intellectually stimulating issues; it must be both rigorous and accessible to students of varied academic backgrounds; and it must provide both a foundation of knowledge that may serve as a springboard to more advanced study and a comprehensive overview for those students whose one experience with the field will consist of a single course.

This book strives to address all these diverse needs and interests, with the author's humble recognition that it may not succeed in meeting all of them for all students. It attempts to provide a comprehensive exposure to topics relevant to the field of nonprofit management, but it obviously must be selective in its discussion of those topics. This intended balance between comprehensiveness in topics and selectivity in their treatment may disappoint some readers. Some may find their appetites whetted but unsatisfied by the quick tour provided in some parts of the book. It is possible that others may find that some chapters include ideas they have seen before in other courses. Of course, some will find the discussion just right for their level of previous knowledge and desire for new understanding.

Students are encouraged to tailor their use of the book to their own interests and backgrounds. Readers who, for example, already have studied some of the organizational and management theories we will discuss are encouraged to read relevant sections as a refresher but to pay closer attention to material that is new to them. Those to whom the theories are new, and who find their discussion in this book to be too brief, are encouraged to explore the additional resources suggested throughout the book. In sum, it is hoped that this book may provide a kind of comprehensive menu, from which students may select the topics or approaches on which they wish to "click" for more information. Both novices and more experienced individuals may find it a foundation on which they can build, seeking appropriate avenues for further information and learning. Suggested additional readings are included at the end of every chapter. And, in all likelihood, professors also will elaborate on some topics and skip lightly over others, as they sense the tempo of their individual classes.

Focus on Charitable Nonprofits

As will be discussed in Chapter 2, the nonprofit sector encompasses an amazing array of organizations with different characteristics, structures, and purposes. This book focuses primarily on that category known as charitable nonprofits and, in particular, those that provide services, such as education and research, health care, arts and cultural programs, and social and legal services. The following chapters also will sometimes mention member-serving organizations—for example, trade and professional associations—but primarily as points of contrast with charitable nonprofits. Religious congregations make up a significant component of the overall nonprofit sector, but religion is the subsector that is the least professionalized—that is, it employs relatively few professional managers. Thus, this book does not devote significant discussion to the management of churches, synagogues, mosques, or other religious congregations. We will discuss foundations, but primarily as sources of support for service-providing nonprofits; we will not discuss the management of foundations per se. This book does not exclude, but also does not emphasize, those nonprofits that are primarily advocacy organizations, also known as social welfare organizations. While they are nonprofits, they are also different from charitable nonprofits in important ways, as we will discuss further in Chapter 2. Of course, some principles of governance, leadership, and management discussed in this book apply to all nonprofits and will be of relevance to students intending to work in any component of the nonprofit world.

Focus on U.S. Nonprofits

This book includes a chapter on nonprofits in the global environment, but it primarily addresses the management of nonprofit organizations in the United States. The American nonprofit sector is the largest in the world; it operates under unique cultural, economic, and legal circumstances. It is where most American students of nonprofit management will pursue their careers. In addition, as governments around the world seek to reduce their expenditures and devolve many functions to nonprofit organizations, many also are looking to relevant aspects of the American model in developing their own nonprofit sectors. This is evidenced by the significant number of international students who come to the United States to study in this field. Previous editions of this book are in use in countries outside of the United States and, indeed, the fourth edition was published in Mandarin by the South China University of Technology Press. Thus, even for students primarily interested in working on the international stage, an understanding of nonprofit management in the United States is both relevant and useful.

Overview of the Book

The first three chapters of this book provide an orientation to the nonprofit sector and a theoretical foundation for the more applied topics considered later. Chapter 1 provides an introduction to nonprofit management, both as a profession and as an academic field of study, and offers a justification for studying the topic as distinct from management in government or business. Chapter 2 offers a look at the structure, boundaries, and characteristics of the nonprofit sector and establishes some basic definitions. It also discusses emerging new organizational forms that may re-shape the sector in the future. Chapter 3 expands our understanding of the nonprofit sector by reviewing theories that explain its existence and its role in relation to government and business. That chapter also examines selected theories that describe the nature of nonprofit organizations and explain their behavior.

The next two chapters, Chapters 4 and 5, consider the roles and responsibilities of governing boards and nonprofit chief executive officers (CEOs) and the ways in which these two vital actors interact in leading organizations. The nonprofit governing board has functional, moral, and legal responsibilities. Nonprofit chief executives, whether titled "executive director," "president," "CEO," or something else, lead their organizations in a complex and dynamic environment that will be described. The partnership between the CEO and the board is critical to a well-operating and effective organization.

The next six chapters focus on applied aspects of nonprofit management. Chapter 6 reviews the increasing demands for nonprofit accountability and various approaches to measuring the performance of nonprofit organizations. Chapter 7 discusses the development of organizational strategy and the tools of strategic planning and strategic management now employed by many nonprofits. Strategic planning is often the first step in the larger undertaking of building the organization's capacity or its ability to achieve the goals identified in the plan; thus capacity building also is considered in this chapter. The management of risk is a topic that has gained more attention in recent years and it is discussed in a section of this chapter that is new to the fifth edition. Managing risk goes beyond the simple avoidance of liability or loss, for example, protecting against the possibility that a staff member brings a lawsuit or the building catches fire. It is a broader concept that relates to uncertainty that could affect achievement of the organization's mission. It is thus related to the development of strategy. Maintaining a process for managing risk is a component of organizational capacity (Herman, 2011).

Chapter 8 explores collaborations and partnerships among nonprofit organizations and those that cross the sectors. In addition, recent years have brought mergers of nonprofit organizations, a topic that is also considered in Chapter 8. Chapter 9 discusses both the theory and the practice of human resource management in nonprofit organizations. One of the significant differences between many nonprofits and business or government is the substantial employment of volunteers to provide the organization's core services. Management of an unpaid workforce requires an understanding of human motivation and skill in managing effective relationships between an organization's volunteers and its paid professional staff. Chapter 10 considers the management of programs for communication and marketing, essential for organizations that are highly interactive with and dependent on the world around them. This section concludes with Chapter 11, which discusses advocacy and lobbying, important activities for many nonprofit organizations that seek to bring about social change.

The next section of the book, encompassing four chapters, is concerned with the acquisition and management of resources. The securing of revenue and the management of financial resources are interrelated activities. Like many of the topics covered in this book, financial management is large, complex, and important. Chapter 12 provides a few basic concepts and directs students to additional sources from which they can obtain the more detailed understanding they may seek. This chapter has been substantially revised from the fourth edition, reflecting the Accounting Standards Update (ASU) 2016-14, issued by the Financial Accounting Standards Board in 2016. Chapter 13 discusses principles of raising philanthropic funds from individual, corporate, and foundation donors. Chapter 14 explores the subjects of social enterprise and nonprofits' earned income—that is, efforts to generate revenue through activities other than traditional philanthropy—and explains the sometimes confusing relationship between these terms. The chapter explores the myriad and growing commercial partnerships between nonprofit organizations and corporations, including cause-related marketing, sponsorships, licensing agreements, joint ventures, and others. It also considers nonprofit business ventures, the development of revenue-generating activities that provide a stream of revenue to support mission programs. Chapter 15 considers principles involved in securing and managing grants and contracts from government, a significant source of revenue for many nonprofits.

The final section of the book includes two chapters that expand our perspective. Chapter 16 examines social entrepreneurship and social innovation. Social entrepreneurship is not necessarily synonymous with the generation of earned income revenue or even with the adoption of business methods by nonprofit organizations. Nor is social entrepreneurship always synonymous with the founding of new organizations. Rather, by the definition used in this book, it includes innovations that lead to "wide-scale change at the systemic level" (Leviner, Crutchfield, & Wells, 2006, p. 89). In other words, social entrepreneurship is related to social innovation, regardless of the specific methods or financial sources that may be involved. These distinctions will be fully explored in Chapter 16. Chapter 17 looks beyond the United States to discuss the work of nonprofit organizations internationally. The Conclusion offers some of my final reflections and observations.

Students may observe that the book does not include a chapter on nonprofit law. Nonprofits are subject to a large and growing body of law at the local, state, and federal levels. However, aspects of nonprofit law are covered in the various chapters where they are most relevant rather than in a separate chapter. The book provides references to other resources for students who may want to know more. The book also does not include a separate chapter on ethics; rather, ethical issues are addressed at relevant points throughout the text, for example, in the discussion of Chapter 6 concerning accountability and in the ethical considerations in fundraising that are discussed in Chapter 13.

Attentive readers will observe that there is some redundancy among the chapters, that is, some points are repeated, at least in summary, in various locations. The author has tried to minimize redundancy, but some points are woven throughout various topics and require brief revisiting as new discussions are introduced. In addition, some professors may not assign all chapters and some repetition of key points is thus essential to complete the discussion on some topics.

Again, all the following chapters draw on the theoretical and academic literature as well as the writing of experienced practitioners and consultants. Key points are illustrated with actual cases, some drawn from the daily headlines. Students are encouraged to include the cases in their reading of each chapter, to consider the questions suggested for discussion of the cases, to consider the broader Questions for Discussion provided at the end of each chapter. The Appendix includes four cases that cut across the topics covered in various chapters but that may have particular relevance to specific chapters as well. Students also are encouraged to think about the relevance of what they are reading to any nonprofit organizations with which they may have personal experience. In addition, the daily news within the span of almost any semester or academic year includes stories that relate to nonprofit organizations and provide real-time cases that illustrate points discussed in this book.

Digital Resources

To access the resources for *Nonprofit Management,* visit SAGE's password-protected site at **http://study.sagepub.com/worth5e**. Simply provide your institutional information for verification and within 72 hours you'll be able to use your login information for any SAGE title!

- A **Microsoft® Word® test bank** is available, containing multiple-choice, true/false, short-answer, and essay questions for each chapter. The test bank provides you with a diverse range of prewritten options as well as the opportunity for editing any question and/or inserting your own personalized questions to effectively assess students' progress and understanding.

- Editable, chapter-specific Microsoft® **PowerPoint® slides** offer you complete flexibility in easily creating a multimedia presentation for your course. Highlight essential content, features, and artwork from the book.

- **Sample course syllabi** provide a suggested model for structuring one's course.

- **Video and multimedia links** appeal to students with different learning styles.

- **Chapter outlines** summarize key concepts on a chapter-by-chapter basis to help with preparation for lectures and class discussions.

- **Case activities** are designed for instructors to expand questions to students, or initiate class discussion.

- **Chapter-specific discussion questions** help launch classroom interaction by prompting students to engage with the material and by reinforcing important content.

Acknowledgments

Writing a book is a collective enterprise, even when the book has one author. Any author builds on the work of others, and this text reflects the wisdom of the many scholars and practitioners who are cited throughout it.

I am grateful to my SAGE editor Scott Greenan, who supported my undertaking this fifth edition.

I am grateful as well to the following reviewers, whose frank comments have added immeasurably to this revision:

Ann Marie Kinnell, University of Southern Mississippi

Becky J. Starnes, Austin Peay State University

Beth Gazley, Indiana University

Catherine E. Wilson, Villanova University

Chandra Commuri, California State University, Bakersfield

Christopher Klingeman, Southern Illinois University

Christine W. Cugliari, High Point University

David A. Coplan, University of Pittsburgh

Deborah Harley-McClaskey, East Tennessee State University

Eunice V. Akoto, North Carolina Central University

Jessica E. Sowa, University of Colorado Denver

John Conahan, Kutztown University

Lynn W. Clemons, Mercer University

Marilyn L. Grady, University of Nebraska-Lincoln

Marjorie Carlson Hurst, Liberty University

Robert Dibie, Indiana University Kokomo

Robert C. Teitelbaum, State University of New York, Empire State College

Sylvia Ramierz Benatti, University of the District of Columbia

Thomas L. Winter, Abilene Christian University

Tory S. Vornholt, Agnes Scott College

Dr. David Befus, Southeastern University

Patricia H. Deyton, Simmons College, School of Management

Maya Esparza, San Jose State University

Jörg Lindenmeier, University of Freiburg, Germany

Crystal Trull, University of San Diego, Leadership Studies

I have learned immensely from my students at the George Washington University, from my faculty colleagues, and from the many nonprofit executives who have participated in various classes of mine over the years. I thank them for the education they have provided me and hope that they will find this book to be a useful contribution to the field. I am grateful to my faculty colleagues, including Joseph Cordes and Jasmine McGinnis Johnson, who offered helpful suggestions for this fifth edition. I thank Cesar Villanueva and Lora Adams, graduate assistants at the Trachtenberg School of Public Policy and Public Administration during 2017–2018, for their support.

Michael J. Worth
Professor of Nonprofit Management
The George Washington University
Washington, DC

Understanding Nonprofit Management, the Nonprofit Sector, and Nonprofit Organizations

Visitor center of the Bill & Melinda Gates Foundation in Seattle. The Gates Foundation, founded in 2000, focuses its giving on world health and urban education in the United States, among other areas.

Chapter Outline

Nonprofit Management as a Profession and a Field of Study

This is a book about the management of nonprofit organizations. The topic begs two fundamental questions: Why do nonprofit organizations need to be managed? And, is management of a nonprofit organization really different from management of a business or government agency? In other words, is there really a need for a book like this, or is management a generic activity that could be learned as well from a textbook on business or public management?

Some may hold a perception of nonprofit organizations as primarily collections of well-intentioned people who struggle with minimal resources to meet human needs, without much attention to the bottom line, and with some disdain for management as an unwelcome distraction from the all-important work of delivering vital programs and services. This stereotype, if ever true, does not describe all nonprofit organizations today. Indeed, there has been a management revolution in the nonprofit sector in recent decades, and many nonprofits face management challenges no less complex than those faced by major corporations or large government agencies.

For most people, the term "nonprofit" conjures up the image of a small organization, perhaps run by a tiny band of volunteers more focused on delivering services to people in need than on building or managing an organization. Indeed, most nonprofit organizations are small, with perhaps few, if any, professional staff, but there are also others with activities that span the nation and the globe and that employ thousands of people.

Mention the word "business" and people will likely think first of a large corporation such as Wal-Mart or Apple, although, in reality, most businesses are small. But it is large business enterprises that are the focus of most management texts and MBA case studies. That is because, as in the nonprofit sector, the need for management varies with the size and scope of activity. The corner dry cleaner needs few management skills beyond basic accounting and a rudimentary understanding of how to manage a few employees. The young technology entrepreneur starting a new business in his or her parents' garage is focused not on management but on development and delivery of a product, much as the directors of small nonprofits

Learning Objectives

After reading this chapter, students should be able to:

1. Describe the differences between management in the nonprofit sector and management in other sectors.

2. Explain various approaches to the study of nonprofit organizations.

3. Describe the growth of nonprofit management as a professional field and a field of study.

4. Explain forces that have led to the professionalization of nonprofit management.

5. Classify various authors in terms of their perspective on the nonprofit sector.

are often more concerned with delivering programs than with building or managing the organization. As a company grows, requiring outside investment and employing more people, its need for professional management increases. Founding entrepreneurs are often replaced by MBAs who have formal management training. So, too, as a nonprofit organization becomes larger, it faces more complex and interesting management challenges, especially if it comes to operate in more than one location across the United States or internationally. This book includes some examples drawn from small nonprofit organizations, but it is principally about organizations that have at least some full-time paid staff, and it includes examples and cases drawn from some of the nation's largest and best-known nonprofits.

A Revolution in Management

The nonprofit management revolution of recent decades has been driven by several forces, including the introduction of competition resulting from changes in funding patterns, the growth of the sector, and increasing demands for accountability. The years since the 1980s have seen reductions in direct federal government funding for many social programs, the devolution of funding to state governments, and increased outsourcing of the delivery of social and human services by government agencies to nonprofit organizations. Nonprofits have been forced to compete for contracts against each other and, in some cases, against for-profit firms. In addition, many government benefits are now provided through voucher-type payments made directly to individuals, who are thus transformed into customers, free to purchase the services they need in the marketplace. Such customers can thus select the organizations that will provide services based on perceptions of quality and other considerations; this forces nonprofits to compete for their business. Like the competition for contracts, the competition for empowered customers has forced nonprofits to either become better managed or place their survival at risk.

But government has not been the only force driving change. Other funders, including foundations and even individual donors, have shown an increased concern with the results achieved by nonprofits through the programs they offer. This has been especially true of many newly wealthy entrepreneurs who amassed their fortunes during the technology boom of the 1990s, the thriving financial services and real estate industries of the mid-2000s, and the booming stock market and social media businesses of the 2010s. Many view their philanthropic giving as a type of investment from which they expect to see a measurable return in the form of effective programs and services. The requirement that nonprofits meet these expectations for measurable results also has increased the need for management.

In recent decades, there also has been a shift in thinking about nonprofit organizations that focuses more on the organization itself rather than merely on the programs and services it delivers. This new focus emphasizes the capacity and sustainability of organizations, ideas we will discuss later in this book. The 1990s brought searing critiques of traditional philanthropy and the management of nonprofits. Among them was a *Harvard Business Review* article by Christine Letts, William Ryan, and Allen Grossman (1997), titled "Virtuous Capital: What Foundations Can Learn From Venture Capitalists." The article essentially was an indictment of traditional foundations' grant-making practices, arguing that the short-term program grants made by most foundations were not meeting the need for investment in the long-term capacity of nonprofit organizations themselves. Letts et al. advocated an approach to philanthropy that would parallel the approach of venture capitalists to investing in companies, including a more sustained commitment to support along with the requirement that organizations meet performance standards. Bill Shore's book *The Cathedral Within* (1999), published two years after the article by Letts et al., expressed similar criticisms of traditional philanthropy. Shore argued that funders' emphasis on programs rather than building organizations was in fact preventing many successful programs from "going to scale," that is, growing to a point that they could have significant impact, because the organizations did not have the capacity to expand. Letts and colleagues, Shore, and others contributed to a change in thinking about nonprofits, shifting from the programs they offer to the strength and sustainability of the organizations themselves. It was, in the words of Jim Collins and Jerry Porras (1994), a shift of emphasis from "telling time" to "building clocks." This new emphasis on nonprofit organizational development also has been a force in increasing the demand for professional nonprofit management.

Some philanthropists have come to view nonprofit organizations as vehicles through which they can address social problems that are of particular interest and concern to them. With frustration about the persistence of problems such as poverty, despite decades of government efforts to overcome them, many entrepreneurial philanthropists believe that private philanthropy and private, nonprofit organizations offer a more promising strategy of attack. This is illustrated, for example, by the work of the Bill and Melinda Gates Foundation, which focuses its giving on world health and urban education in the United States, among other areas, and which has had significant impact by virtue of the substantial financial resources at its disposal. This conflation of national issues and concerns with the work of nonprofits has increased the importance of the sector and also has contributed to the emphasis on measurable results (Brest, 2012).

Another reality is that the dramatic growth of the nonprofit sector and its assets has simply raised the stakes. Fueled in part by a wave of philanthropy based on the growing wealth of entrepreneurs and investors, in part by the continued devolution of government programs, and in part by an increased worldwide interest in voluntary action, nonprofits now employ more people and control more resources than ever before. The nonprofit sector has become a consequential part of the American economy that cannot be ignored. Therefore, it has captured the increasing attention of legislators, the media, and others who demand that nonprofits be accountable for the assets entrusted to them and for the results that they achieve with those assets. This reflects an increased concern with accountability throughout American society, affecting government agencies and businesses as well as nonprofits. Demands for accountability and the need for systems and procedures to comply with greater scrutiny and regulation also have contributed to the need for trained managers.

In sum, if it was ever true that the typical nonprofit organization fit the image of a well-intentioned but unmanaged endeavor, nonprofit organizations today, other than perhaps the smallest, must be managed. To be otherwise is not only to risk failure in meeting society's needs and expectations, but also to place the organization's survival at risk. However, the question remains whether managing a nonprofit organization is different from managing a government agency or a business corporation. Is management generic, or is management in the nonprofit sector a distinguishable endeavor?

A Distinct Profession

Throughout most of the history of management as a recognized discipline, most theorists have advocated a generic approach, arguing that common management principles would apply equally to all organizations, whether businesses, government agencies, or nonprofits. And there remain some who are skeptical that management in the nonprofit sector is unique or that it requires particularly distinctive skills.

At an operational level, surely management in the nonprofit sector requires many of the same skills that are also important in government or business. There may not be a particularly nonprofit way of processing payroll or implementing a new information system, and indeed, many of the techniques of business management have been adopted by nonprofit organizations as well. But this book is predicated on the view that nonprofit management is different from management in the business or governmental sector in a variety of ways, including the following four.

First, as Robert Herman (2016) explains, nonprofit management requires a unique set of tradeoffs:

> A [nonprofit] chief executive, in conjunction with the board, must integrate the realms of mission, resource acquisition, and strategy. To oversimplify but phrase the issue more memorably, *mission, money, and management* are interdependent. Making progress on mission achievement depends, in part, on the potential for resource acquisition. Any mission, no matter how worthy, is likely to fail if the organization lacks necessary and sufficient resources to pursue it. Conversely, the acquisition of some kinds of resources can influence the mission. Moreover, decisions about strategies for acquiring resources must be consistent with the mission and ethical values of the organization. Actions in one realm affect the other realms. The leadership challenge is to see that decisions and actions in one realm are not only consistent with those in other realms but also mutually reinforcing. (pp. 167–168)

Managers of government agencies generally have a single source of revenue—for example, the U.S. Congress or a state legislature—and carry out programs mandated by the law. Managers in business receive revenue from the sale of products or services and have the freedom to decide what goods or services they will provide and to which customers. More sales translate into increased revenues, and activities that are not profitable can be discontinued. The same relationships do not always hold true for a nonprofit. Most nonprofits obtain resources from multiple sources and, like businesses, have considerable freedom to determine the activities in which they will engage. However, one important difference is that increased activity may strain resources rather than enhance them. That is because not all of a nonprofit's customers may pay the full cost of producing the good or service, and indeed, some may not pay at all. Judy Vredenburgh, a former executive of Big Brothers Big Sisters and the March of Dimes, describes the dilemma: "Every time we in nonprofits satisfy customers, we drain resources, and every time for-profits satisfy a customer, they get resources. That sounds very simple, but it has huge implications" (Silverman & Taliento, 2006, p. 41).

Thus, as Herman (2016) suggests, management of a nonprofit organization requires constant trade-offs among the mission, the acquisition of resources, and strategy. That distinguishes nonprofit management from the management function in the business or public sectors. Management in those sectors, while also complex, at least begins with some fixed points of clear goals and positive relationships between activities and revenues. Managing a nonprofit is more like swimming in the air, with everything variable and in constant motion.

Second, the complex relationships among a nonprofit organization's stakeholders require management that is especially skilled in negotiation and compromise, with a high tolerance for ambiguity. In corporations and in government agencies, the flow of authority from the top down is generally clear. But, as Helmut Anheier (2014) describes,

> nonprofit organizations consist of multiple components and complex, internal federations or coalitions among stakeholders … [therefore] the structure of nonprofit organizations may require a multi-faceted, flexible approach to management and not the use of singular, ready-made models carried over from the business world or from public management. (p. 328)

Jim Collins (2005) recounts a meeting between Frances Hesselbein, chief executive officer (CEO) of the Girl Scouts of the USA at the time, and a *New York Times* columnist, in which the CEO addressed this unique characteristic of nonprofit management:

[The columnist] asked what it felt like to be on top of such a large organization. With patience, like a teacher pausing to impart an important lesson, Hesselbein proceeded to rearrange the lunch table, creating a set of concentric circles radiating outward—plates, cups, saucers—connected by knives, forks, spoons. Hesselbein pointed to a glass in the middle of the table. "I'm here," she said. Hesselbein may have had the title of Chief Executive Officer, but her message was clear: *I'm not on top of anything.* (p. 9)

Nonprofit management is unique because nonprofit organizations are different from businesses and governmental entities—often reliant on the support of donors and the work of volunteers, pursuing missions derived from values and principles about which there may be disagreement, and engendering a sense of ownership and a desire for influence among multiple constituencies both inside and outside the walls of the organization itself. In this environment, a nonprofit CEO must provide leadership as well as management, a distinction we will explore further in Chapter 5. Robert Higgins, who worked as both a nonprofit executive and a venture capitalist and thus was able to observe the differences between the sectors firsthand, explains,

> In most for-profit organizations … people arrive with common goals. The board of directors may have different viewpoints, but shareholder value as a fundamental goal is something shared by the board, by the CEO, and by senior management. You start off differently in the not-for-profit world, with each board member arriving with a different set of goals and often different agendas. To manage that as a CEO is much more complex. (Silverman & Taliento, 2006, p. 38)

Third, managers of nonprofit organizations must measure their success by a **double bottom line**. A nonprofit exists to pursue a social mission, and success must be measured in terms of its ability to achieve that mission. That is one bottom line. But, in today's competitive environment, nonprofit managers also must pay close attention to the *financial* bottom line if their organizations are to survive and succeed. Some people add a third bottom line—the impact, positive or negative, that the organization has on the environment. Ask a room of people, "What's the purpose of Apple?" and some may quickly reply, "To produce electronic devices," or perhaps some will joke, "To control the world!" But both responses miss the point because Apple, like all businesses, has one clear purpose: to increase the value of the business and thus the wealth of its owners. Producing products and controlling the world are but means to that end. To be sure, many corporations today are also guided by principles of social responsibility and ethics, but social progress is not their *purpose*. Indeed, social concerns are properly viewed as constraints on the pursuit of the purpose for which every business exists: to maximize profit in order to increase the value of the owners' equity. Managers may have their own personal social goals, but if they make them a central element of the company's purpose, they will not fulfill their principal responsibility to the owners of the firm.

In contrast, a nonprofit *exists* to serve a social purpose. But, as we have discussed, in today's competitive environment, financial results also require the executive's attention—he or she must manage the double bottom line of financial and social return. And the latter may be ambiguous in its definition, even a subject of disagreement and dissension among the organization's many stakeholders, or difficult to measure.

Fourth and finally, many of the problems that nonprofit managers address are exceptionally difficult and intractable. In other words, it may be more challenging to reduce poverty, prevent disease, or improve the global environment—especially when not everyone recognizes the problem or agrees on what the solutions might be—than it is to increase the sale of attractive products that people already desire to own. To say that managing a nonprofit is inherently more complex than managing a business of comparable size is not to demean the skills of business managers or to disparage their clear focus on profit. The creativity and problem-solving skills of business leaders have built great organizations and propelled economic progress. Moreover, wealth created by the business sector helps to sustain nonprofits and make social advancement possible. But the need to manage the double bottom line, to relate to disparate and competing constituencies, and often to work against the weight of deep-seated historical and cultural barriers adds complexity to the nonprofit CEO's challenge, a challenge that is too often underestimated by some who observe the nonprofit sector from a business perspective. William Novelli, a former businessman who built the public relations firm Porter Novelli and later served as the CEO of the nonprofit AARP, explains the challenge:

> It's harder to succeed in the nonprofit world.... It may be hard to compete in the field of consumer packaged goods or electronics or high finance ... but it's harder to achieve goals in the nonprofit world because these goals tend to be behavioral. If you set out to do something about breast cancer in the country, or about Social Security solvency, it's a lot harder to pull that off. [And] it's also harder to measure. (Silverman & Taliento, 2006, p. 37)

This book is based on the premise that nonprofit management is a unique endeavor, distinguishable from management in business or government. It is necessary, however, to acknowledge that some see a convergence of management across the sectors in recent years, as both public managers and nonprofit managers are expected to be more businesslike and business managers are expected to demonstrate more responsibility toward the social and human impact of their actions (Salamon, 2012b). In addition, new types of organizations have emerged that combine characteristics of businesses and nonprofit organizations, some of which will be discussed later in this text. As we will discuss in the next section of this chapter, trends in nonprofit management education in universities have reflected the changing realities.

Nonprofit Management as a Field of Study

Students taking a course in nonprofit management today might reasonably assume that such courses have always existed. But they are a relatively recent addition to the curriculum at many colleges and universities, and scholarly research in the field, while growing, still does not approach the volume of study devoted to public or business management.

Indeed, recognition of management as an identifiable function—in any organizational setting—is relatively recent in the scope of history. While management-like functions have been performed throughout civilized history, the beginning of management as a field of study dates approximately to the development of an industrial economy in the late 19th century. Stephen Block (2001) credits an 1886 paper by the engineer Henry R. Towne as the first call for the development of management as an independent field of study with its own literature. The nation's first school of management, the Wharton School at the University of Pennsylvania, was established shortly thereafter, in 1898. The first two decades of the 20th century saw the growth of professional management societies, the publication of new books, and the introduction of additional university programs. The first doctoral dissertation in management was written in 1915. According to Block, interest in management was increased by the experience of American manufacturing during World War II, and the decades since have brought explosive growth in business management education and research, including the development of theories we will explore at relevant points in this book. But the early study of management was focused on business organizations, with attention to public management developing later. Mordecai Lee (2010) has identified some pioneering initiatives undertaken by the YMCA that may have represented the first efforts in nonprofit management education. They included the offering of a bachelor of association science degree by Chicago's Central YMCA College in 1911 and a 1935 textbook on the subject produced by the YMCA's publishing house. Notwithstanding those early efforts, interest in nonprofit management has emerged primarily within the past few decades.

As mentioned previously, until about the 1960s, most management theorists advanced a "generic approach," arguing that their theories applied equally in all types of organizations, whether businesses, government agencies, or nonprofits. As Hal Rainey (2014), a public administration scholar, emphasizes, "With some clear exceptions … the theorists repeatedly implied or aggressively asserted that distinctions such as public and private, market and non-market, and governmental and nongovernmental offered little value for developing theory or understanding practice" (p. 45). However, by the 1960s, some authors began to challenge this approach and to call for more research focused specifically on the management of public agencies. This coincided with a period of growth in the federal government and the development of master's of public administration (MPA) degree programs in universities, which for the first time emphasized management skills in government and differentiated the study of public management from the discipline of political science. The **Network of Schools of Public Policy, Affairs, and Administration (NASPAA)** was founded in 1970 and began to accredit such programs.

It is important to note that one of the well-known academic journals publishing nonprofit-related research, *Nonprofit and Voluntary Sector Quarterly*, was founded in 1972. But national attention was drawn to the nonprofit sector by an important national study conducted by the Commission on Private Philanthropy and Public Needs during the period 1973 to 1975. That commission, often called the "Filer Commission" in honor of its chair, business leader John H. Filer, issued a report titled *Giving in America* (Commission on Private Philanthropy and Public Needs, 1975), which was the most detailed study of philanthropy in the United States up to that time. The first academic center devoted to the study of nonprofits, the Yale Program on NonProfit Organizations (PONPO), was founded shortly thereafter, in 1978, and social scientists began to turn their attention to understanding the role of nonprofit organizations in economic and political life. The generic approach was beginning to yield to the view that nonprofit organizations might have unique characteristics that distinguish them from organizations in the other two sectors.

As previously discussed, the 1980s marked a turning point in public policy, with government outsourcing more of the delivery and management of social and human services to nonprofits. That development further increased the need for professional management in nonprofit organizations and captured the interest of some students previously aiming for careers in government. Public administration faculty members saw that a growing number of their students were interested in working in nonprofit organizations and responded by developing programs to teach nonprofit-specific skills (Joslyn, 2004). That decade also saw the establishment of new research centers and programs focused on the nonprofit sector, including Case Western Reserve University's Mandel Center for Nonprofit Organizations and the Center on Philanthropy at Indiana University.

Management scholars and writers turned significant attention to the nonprofit sector beginning in the 1990s. Writing in 1990, management guru Peter Drucker observed a "management boom" going on in nonprofit organizations, but he also noted the lack of recognition of nonprofit management as worthy of attention. "For most Americans," he wrote, "the word 'management' still means business management" (p. xiv). But as the nonprofit sector continued to grow throughout the 1990s and into the 2000s and 2010s, a burgeoning literature sought to adapt the theories and skills of business management to the planning, managing, and financing of nonprofits. Courses in the strategic management of nonprofits and on social entrepreneurship—a term we will discuss further later—began to appear in business schools, and new books applied the techniques used by companies and governments to the nonprofit sector (Oster, 1995; Steiss, 2003). The *Harvard Business Review* came to include occasional articles on the management of nonprofit organizations. The late 1990s brought an economic boom and a boom in the literature of venture philanthropy, social enterprise, entrepreneurial nonprofits, and business techniques applied to nonprofit organizations (Dees, 1998; Dees, Emerson, & Economy, 2001; Kearns, 2000; Letts, Ryan, & Grossman, 1999; Oster, Massarsky, & Beinhacker, 2004). The Stanford University Graduate School of Business began publishing a journal, the *Stanford Social Innovation Review*, in 2003. New textbooks focused on nonprofit management began to appear, including the first edition of this text in 2009. Online journals, blogs, and other forums related to nonprofit management, social innovation, social entrepreneurship, and related topics continue to proliferate. In 2012, the Center on Philanthropy at Indiana University became the Lilly Family School of Philanthropy, the first such academic institution in the country ("IU's Philanthropy School to Be Named for Lilly Family," 2013).

The literature of nonprofit management is drawn from three principal areas: (1) the work of social scientists who study nonprofit organizations as social and economic institutions; (2) organizational theory, theories of organizational behavior, and management theory from the business and public sectors that have particular relevance for nonprofit organizations; and (3) a rich practitioner literature that offers important understandings. This book is based on the view that a balanced and integrated approach requires drawing on all three literatures, and that is reflected in the materials presented in the chapters that follow.

Much of the nonprofit management literature is still written by or for practitioners and has a prescriptive, how-to-do-it approach. Consultants, including professionals working in for-profit consulting firms, also have made important contributions to the literature of nonprofit management. But there is a growing body of academic research, including the work of economists, sociologists, historians, and other social scientists who have developed taxonomies to identify and track the major components of the nonprofit sector; theories to explain the existence and behavior of the sector; theories describing its relationship to government and the business sector; examinations of its role and impact in the U.S. economy; and analyses of related public policy issues. The management of nonprofits also has been the focus of more applied studies drawn from the fields of public administration and business management.

Some scholars advocate defining a new academic field of "nonprofit studies" that would broaden the focus of nonprofit research beyond management (Mendel, 2014). Observing that "published scholarship on nonprofit organizations continues to cover primarily matters of interest to public management, business, social work, and other fields," Stuart Mendel (2014) argues that "nonprofit studies is approaching a tipping point [and is] ready to become an autonomous field of study" (p. 61). He also calls for a new approach to the training of nonprofit professionals that would go "beyond the management of transactional accountability" to include "the study of civil society; the dynamics of advocacy, community organizing, and public policy development; the political nature of the social sector; and the role that nonprofits play as places of employment" (Mendel, p. 62).

This book is a textbook, not a manual for nonprofit executives. But neither is its purpose to offer an entirely theoretical examination of the nonprofit sector. Although it draws on a wide range of literature, it is intended to provide a background for nonprofit management rather than a foundation for nonprofit studies. It is intended to provide students who are considering or pursuing careers in nonprofit management with a broad overview, blending theoretical and practical topics relevant to the work they do or will do. This approach incurs the risk that some pragmatic individuals may find it too academic and that some academics may find it insufficiently grounded, but it is appropriate to provide a comprehensive and useful overview of a field that is still evolving.

Concomitant with the increase in literature, educational programs related to nonprofit management have grown rapidly since the 1990s. In a 2007 report, Mirabella revealed that the number of undergraduate programs related to nonprofit management grew by 30 percent between 1996 and 2002 and by an additional 36 percent between 2002 and 2006. Indiana University was the first to offer a bachelor's degree in philanthropy and, as mentioned previously, in 2012 became the first university to establish a school of philanthropy. Recent years also have seen a virtual explosion in the availability of training for nonprofit managers and professional expertise directed toward the improvement of management practices in nonprofit organizations, including programs offered by educational institutions, regional associations of nonprofits, nonprofit infrastructure organizations, and for-profit consulting firms. Formal professional certification is available in some specialties of nonprofit management. For example, a professional specializing in fundraising can become a certified fundraising executive (CFRE) by successfully meeting criteria established by CFRE International, including an examination (see www.cfre.org for more information). And nonprofit professionals who manage volunteer programs can obtain certification from the Council for Certification in Volunteer Administration (see www.cvacert.org for more information).

Formalization of the nonprofit management curriculum in universities also has progressed. In 2001, NASPAA issued "Guidelines for Graduate Professional Education in Nonprofit Organizations, Management, and Leadership." The **Nonprofit Academic Centers Council (NACC)**, a membership association of academic centers and programs that focus on nonprofit organizations, issued its first "Curricular Guidelines for Graduate Study in Philanthropy, the Nonprofit Sector, and Nonprofit Leadership" in 2004. A second version was released in 2008 and a third version in 2015. NACC undergraduate program guidelines were developed in 2007 and revised in 2015 (Nonprofit Academic Centers Council, 2018).

The content of MPA and MPP degree programs has increasingly included nonprofit-related skills and some have proposed that even more emphasis be given to nonprofits within these programs (Cantrell-Bruce & Blankenberger, 2015). Others advocate a "nonprofit/philanthropy-first" curriculum and the development of degree programs in nonprofit management apart from those in public administration, public policy, or business. In 2017, the membership of NACC voted to proceed with a program to formally accredit academic programs with a focus on "the nonprofit and philanthropic sectors," based on its curricular guidelines. The initial effort will focus on stand-alone nonprofit management programs, rather than those that are encompassed within degree programs accredited by NASPAA or the Association to Advance Collegiate Schools of Business (AACSB). NACC announced a plan for implementation of its accreditation process, expected to launch in 2018 (Fox, 2017). Students reading this text may wish to check on the status of this initiative at the NACC website (http://www.nonprofit-academic-centers-council.org/).

In addition to the advocates of independent nonprofit management degree programs, some continue to debate whether nonprofit management should be taught in schools of business or management, in schools of public administration and public policy, or in other academic units. Some institutions have resolved the debate by establishing interdisciplinary centers, supported by more than one school. For example, at the University of Georgia, the Institute for Nonprofit Organizations operates as a component of the graduate school and offers coursework through departments of social work, political science, and management.

Many business school courses and programs relevant to the nonprofit sector are identified by the term **social entrepreneurship**. The term is used in different ways by various authors, and it is important to understand the distinctions. The literature reflects two schools of thought about the meaning of social entrepreneurship. J. Gregory Dees and Beth Anderson (2006) call these two perspectives the "social enterprise school" and the "social innovation school." Those in the social enterprise school think about social entrepreneurship as virtually synonymous with the application of business methods and the generation of earned income, that is, revenue that is received in exchange for goods and services provided, rather than as gifts. Those who belong to the social innovation school offer a broader definition of social entrepreneurship. In their view, a **social entrepreneur** is an innovator who identifies new methods and models for achieving social change. This may include the application of business principles and the pursuit of earned income, but not necessarily. These distinctions are discussed further in Chapter 14 of this text, which explores social enterprise, and in Chapter 16, which is concerned with social entrepreneurship from the social innovation perspective.

Discussion and debate on the appropriate content of programs to prepare nonprofit leaders is likely to continue. Many observers see a blurring of the nonprofit and business sectors, requiring that future nonprofit executives be trained in business skills. To some, that suggests that nonprofit management programs would be better located in business schools than in schools of public affairs and administration or in colleges of arts and sciences. But Michael O'Neill (2007), founder and former chair of the Institute for Nonprofit Organization Management at the University of San Francisco, notes that "[n]onprofits have different values, different financial systems, different laws to abide by, different people (like volunteers) to manage, and very different goals [than business organizations]" (p. 171S). He predicts that the future will see continued experimentation with regard to nonprofit programs but that business schools are unlikely to become the predominant hosts of nonprofit management programs. In addition, he predicts that despite the standards developed by NASPAA and NACC, nonprofit management curriculum is unlikely to become as standardized as the MBA curriculum.

Roseanne Mirabella and Dennis Young (2012) observe the increase in the number of business school programs focusing on social entrepreneurship and speculate as to whether the future might see convergence of the content of such business school programs and traditional nonprofit management programs, meaning primarily those offered in schools of public policy and administration. One possibility that Mirabella and Young identify is that the traditional programs may come to incorporate more courses on social entrepreneurship, while business schools come to include more emphasis on such topics as philanthropic and political skills; in other words, the programs might become more alike. Another possibility is that the traditional and business school programs remain distinct. Echoing O'Neill (2007), the authors note that the respective academic units have different cultures and, in addition, that entrepreneurship more generally "has historically not been high in the pecking order of subjects valued within business schools" (Mirabella & Young, 2012, p. 55).

In addition to the discussion about the relative desirability of business schools or other academic units as the home of nonprofit management, some call for more attention to nonprofits in the curriculum of all professional schools. There is an increasing number of collaborations and partnerships between nonprofits and government and between nonprofits and businesses—a topic that we will discuss in more detail in Chapter 8. This reality has contributed to some nonprofits becoming hybrids; that is, they include characteristics of businesses and government agencies as well as traditional nonprofit organizations. For that reason, some observers suggest that education about nonprofits should be integrated into the core curriculum of programs in business as well as public policy and administration and other professional fields (S. Smith, 2012).

Toward a Balanced Approach

The literature of nonprofit management reveals a variety of perspectives, not only on the questions and issues discussed previously, but indeed about the very nature and role of nonprofit organizations in society.

Generalization can, of course, sometimes lead to oversimplification; differences in perspective or approach are often nuanced. But students will likely observe that authors writing about nonprofit organizations and nonprofit management today reflect one of two perspectives on the purposes and role of nonprofits that are distinguishable, at least in tone and emphasis.

Some see nonprofit organizations primarily as social institutions. The services they provide are important, but nonprofits also are essential for creating civil society, pursuing social change, and sustaining the free expression of ideas and opinions in a democratic society—indeed, for preserving our most important values as a society. Process and involvement are valued nearly as much as the end results. In this view, involvement builds community and provides an important experience for the individuals involved, in addition to the benefits it may produce for other members of society. This is what Peter Frumkin (2002) calls the **expressive purposes of nonprofits**; that is, they provide an outlet for individuals to express their values and passions through their involvement with such organizations.

From this perspective, nonprofit managers often are portrayed as stewards of their organizations or servants of society. With regard to the education of nonprofit managers, those who hold this perspective usually emphasize the need to develop an appreciation of nonprofit values, an understanding of nonprofits' role in society, and a capacity for ethical decision making. In discussing charity and philanthropy, they tend to focus on their cultural and historical roots of giving and view giving as an expression of moral and religious values. They do not necessarily deny the usefulness of business methods in managing nonprofit organizations, but some do express skepticism about the possibility of measuring organizations' effectiveness against sometimes lofty missions. Some express concern that the application of business methods and business thinking holds the risk of undermining traditional nonprofit values and diminishing nonprofit organizations' unique contributions to society. They are often uncomfortable about nonprofits becoming too engaged in commercial activities or forming close relationships with business, fearing that nonprofit culture will be eroded and that organizations will lose sight of their social purposes in the pursuit of financial success. And, of course, depending on their social and political perspectives, some may even find it objectionable to see nonprofits associated with private businesses or government at all, perhaps viewing one or both of the latter as sources of problems that nonprofits are trying to correct.

From the other common perspective, nonprofit organizations are social enterprises, essentially businesses that have a social purpose. Those who hold this view do not dismiss the importance of nonprofits' social missions, nor do they necessarily deny the unique qualities and contributions of the nonprofit sector. Most give at least lip service to the idea that a business approach may not be appropriate for every nonprofit organization. However, they tend to emphasize the commonalities between nonprofit organizations and business firms and encourage the use of business principles and techniques in managing nonprofits.

Those who hold this perspective often discuss the education of nonprofit managers in terms of developing business skills. Their discussions often focus on building the capacity of nonprofits and the application of business methods, such as strategic planning, strategic management, performance management, and marketing. They often use the vocabulary of business, discussing a nonprofit organization's "competitive advantage" and "sustainability." Some criticize traditional charity and philanthropy and prefer that nonprofits rely more on earned income rather than on gifts. They emphasize what Frumkin (2002) calls the **instrumental purposes of nonprofits**, that is, the services that they provide and the needs they meet, rather than their role as vehicles for individuals' expression. They are concerned about results and the measurement of organizational performance against defined metrics. Some even support the idea of nonprofit capital markets that would allocate funds rationally to nonprofit organizations that show high performance, much as stock markets allocate investment dollars to the companies that produce the highest financial returns. Indeed, recent years have seen the initiation of new corporate forms and market-based approaches, which are addressed further in the next chapter of this book.

Again, the above characterizations of these two perspectives are oversimplified, and some writers take a moderate or blended stance between the two poles described. But it is usually not difficult to identify a particular book or article as leaning toward one perspective or the other. This text draws on literature from both approaches and strives to present a balanced and integrated understanding. Where disagreements may exist, it attempts to fairly summarize both sides of the argument. That is because this author believes that effective nonprofit management in today's environment indeed requires a balanced and integrated approach that draws upon diverse perspectives, skills, and tools.

That approach leads to the frequent use of the expression "on the one hand, but on the other hand" throughout this book. Some might prefer to know the "right answer" and learn what is the best way to lead a nonprofit organization. The philosophy reflected in this book is that there is often no one right answer and that the best way is often pragmatic and eclectic. It includes viewing a problem from multiple perspectives and drawing from various approaches selectively as situations may dictate. Students will find abundant other materials written by authors who come from one particular viewpoint or another that they may find to be especially attractive or persuasive.

Proceeding With Realism and Pride

This book is based on the view that while there is a need to improve the management of nonprofit organizations, it is a misperception to believe, as some do, that they are generically less well managed than businesses. This misperception is based in part on our society's bias toward defining success primarily in financial terms. The results of good business management are evident in bottom-line earnings, while the results of nonprofit management are reflected in progress toward a social mission, which may be less visible or easy to measure. In addition, the misperception is often reinforced when apples are compared with oranges, which may occur, for example, if someone's image of a nonprofit is as a small organization and that person's image of a business is that of a larger corporation. It may be accurate to observe that some small nonprofits are not well managed. But, it is important to note, the same is true of many small businesses, most of which fail in the first five years of their existence. It might be difficult to demonstrate that a family-run bed and breakfast is really better managed than the local homeless shelter, which would be more appropriate than comparing the shelter with a Marriott hotel.

When nonprofit organizations and companies are compared fairly, we find poor and excellent management in both. For example, the American Red Cross, one of the nation's largest nonprofits, was criticized for its management of recovery efforts following the Haitian earthquake in 2010. In the 2000s, there were highly visible scandals concerning executive compensation and expenses at American University and the Smithsonian Institution, which led to Congressional hearings and the development of new governance guidelines, discussed later in this text. In 2015, the Federal Trade Commission (FTC) alleged that James T. Reynolds, Sr., had used nearly $200 million that had been given to cancer charities that he operated to pay for personal benefits for himself, friends, and family members. The FTC characterized it as one of the largest charity scandals in history (Ruiz, 2015). However, it is fair to ask, was the Red Cross less well managed than General Motors, which required a federal government bailout? Or were ethical failures at nonprofits more egregious than those at many financial institutions in the late 2000s, which required bailouts as well? Were the allegations against Reynolds more shocking than those against Bernard Madoff, who was convicted of running a Ponzi scheme that cost investors millions of dollars? We might also ask, are Habitat for Humanity and Doctors Without Borders less innovative organizations than Facebook or Google? Is the Mayo Clinic less capable of managing risk than BP? In a sequel to his best-selling book on business management, which focuses on the social (or nonprofit) sector, Jim Collins (2005) argues that the important difference is not between business management and nonprofit management, but between mediocrity and greatness:

> Most businesses—like most of anything else in life—fall somewhere between mediocre and good. Few are great. Mediocre companies rarely display the relentless culture of discipline … that we find in truly great companies. [But] a culture of discipline is not a principle of business; it is a principle of greatness. (p. 1)

The author's purpose in making this point is to dispel any misperceptions that students may hold that nonprofit management is somehow second rate or, as implied by critical articles seen in the popular media, that incompetence and corruption are rampant in nonprofit organizations. Nonprofit managers are in general highly capable and dedicated individuals, worthy of the respect and regard of their counterparts in the other sectors of business and government. They work in organizations that are different from businesses or government, they have different purposes and goals, and they often work with fewer resources available to them, but they are not categorically less able or successful. Students pursuing education in nonprofit management should do so with a pride and confidence equal to that of their classmates who may be preparing for careers in business, government, or other distinguished professions.

At the same time, students should hold no illusions about the challenges of a nonprofit management career. Although salaries are improving, nonprofit managers are unlikely to achieve the wealth of their counterparts in business or the job security of their colleagues who hold civil service positions in the government. The pressures are significant. As Julie Rogers (2006), former president of the Eugene and Agnes Meyer Foundation, observes, nonprofit executives face a never-ending stream of advice from their boards, funders, clients, volunteers, and others: "Focus on finding dependable sources of income. Produce measurable results. Evaluate whether you are making a difference. Be strategic, not opportunistic. Build diverse boards. Spend more time on advocacy. Collaborate with other organizations" (pp. 45–46). And, too often, nonprofit managers are advised to do all this with smaller budgets, smaller staffs, less training, the ever-present threat of reduced public support, and less recognition than is provided to managers in business or government. Indeed, a 2011 study found that the complexity of the nonprofit manager's job and the multiple pressures he or she must handle frequently lead to frustration and burnout (Moyers, 2011).

However, nonprofit managers also enjoy unique rewards, including the satisfaction of knowing that they are working to advance those aspects of human life that many consider to be the most important—the arts, education, the preservation of culture, the advancement of health, the alleviation of poverty, and the development of young people. They experience the excitement of tackling some of society's most daunting problems and protecting society's most vulnerable members, making a difference in their lives and in the future of society. And they know the camaraderie and fellowship that comes from working alongside others who share their values, priorities, and commitments. For many who have dedicated their careers to working in nonprofit organizations, the value of such intangible rewards is beyond measure.

CHAPTER SUMMARY

Through most of history, management scholars pursued a generic approach, believing that management in companies, government agencies, and nonprofits shared similar principles. But nonprofit management is a distinct profession because of the unique characteristics, missions, and cultures of nonprofits. Since the 1980s, this uniqueness has been recognized in the development of research centers and academic programs focused on the nonprofit sector and nonprofit management.

There continues to be discussion about whether such programs should be located in business schools, in schools of public policy and administration, in other academic units, or established as independent degree programs. Some business schools offer programs in social entrepreneurship. The definition of that term reflects two schools of thought, called the "social enterprise school" and the "social innovation school." This distinction is discussed further in later chapters of this book. Some think that business school programs in social entrepreneurship and traditional nonprofit management programs may converge. Others note the different cultures in various academic units and predict that such programs will remain distinct. Some advocate incorporating nonprofit management topics in the core curriculum in all professional degree programs. Others advocate stand-alone degree programs in nonprofit management. The Nonprofit Academic Centers Council (NACC) has established a plan for accrediting nonprofit management programs, using curricular guidelines that it has developed. Some universities have established interdisciplinary centers for the study of nonprofits, which draw on faculty from various academic fields.

People hold two different perspectives on the purposes and role of nonprofits in society, which influence their views on how and where nonprofit leaders should be educated. Some consider nonprofits to be social institutions and emphasize their expressive purposes, that is, opportunities that they provide for people to express their values and passions through involvement. Others consider them to be social enterprises, essentially like business firms with a social purpose. They emphasize their instrumental purposes, that is, the services they provide and needs they meet. Many writers reflect a balanced understanding, but most tend to emphasize one or the other perspective. This book attempts to blend these perspectives and to provide a balanced overview of the field. This author believes that successful nonprofit management requires an eclectic approach, drawing concepts and tools from the work of scholars, practitioners, consultants, and others, as they are found to be useful in specific situations.

Although some people portray nonprofits as less well managed than businesses, that perception often is inaccurate. Small nonprofits should be compared to small businesses, which also often reveal mediocre management, and which often fail, rather than to large corporations. Many companies are innovative and well managed, and so are many nonprofit organizations. Students preparing for careers in nonprofit management should proceed with pride and confidence that their field is as distinguished as management in business or government. A nonprofit career brings challenges but also unique rewards.

KEY TERMS AND CONCEPTS

double bottom line 7
expressive purposes of nonprofits 13
instrumental purposes of nonprofits 13

Network of Schools of Public Policy, Affairs, and Administration (NASPAA) 9
Nonprofit Academic Centers Council (NACC) 11

social entrepreneur 12
social entrepreneurship 11

QUESTIONS FOR DISCUSSION

1. Should preparation for a career in the nonprofit sector emphasize management skills or a broader understanding of civil society and the role of nonprofit organizations?

2. If nonprofit management challenges are as complex as those in business, should nonprofit managers be compensated at the same levels as managers at comparably large companies? Why or why not?

3. Should nonprofit organizations be viewed principally as businesses with a social purpose, or are they inherently different from for-profit companies?

APPENDIX CASE

The following case in the Appendix of this text includes points related to the content of this chapter: Case 3 (The Y).

SUGGESTIONS FOR FURTHER READING

Books

Frumkin, P. (2002). *On being nonprofit: A conceptual and policy primer.* Cambridge, MA: Harvard University Press.

Mendel, S. C., & Brudney, J. L. (2018). *Partnerships the nonprofit way: What matters, what doesn't.* Bloomington: Indiana University Press.

Articles

Cantrell-Bruce, T., & Blankenberger, B. (2015, Summer). Seeing clearly: Measuring skill sets that address the "blurred boundaries" of nonprofit management education. *Journal of Public Affairs Education, 21*(3), 367–380.

Mendel, S. C. (2014). A field of its own. *Stanford Social Innovation Review, 12*(1), 61–62.

Mirabella, R., & Young, D. R. (2012). The development of education for social entrepreneurship and nonprofit management: Diverging or converging paths? *Nonprofit Management & Leadership, 23*(1), 43–56.

Neuhauser, D. (Ed.). (2012, Autumn). *Nonprofit Management & Leadership* (Special Issue: BenchMark 3.5 Conference on Nonprofit and Philanthropic Studies), *23*(1).

Schultz, D. (2015). The distinctiveness of nonprofits and their role in public affairs education. *Journal of Public Affairs Education, 21*(3), 305–310.

Shier, M. L., & Handy, F. (2014, October). Research trends in nonprofit graduate studies: A growing interdisciplinary field. *Nonprofit and Voluntary Sector Quarterly, 43*(5), 812–831.

Websites

Network of Schools of Public Policy, Affairs, and Administration (NASPAA): www.naspaa.org

Nonprofit Academic Centers Council (NACC): http://nonprofit-academic-centers-council.org

Andrew Carnegie's Gospel of Wealth articulated the distinction between charity and philanthropy and influenced America's tradition of giving.

Wikimedia.org

Chapter Outline

Overview of the Nonprofit Sector

America's nonprofit sector is large, complex, and diverse, including organizations very different from one another in purpose, size, and other characteristics. As J. G. Simon wrote in 1987, "The sprawling and unruly collection of animals that populate the nonprofit world—from churches to civil rights groups to garden clubs to the National Council on Philanthropy—makes this field hard to grasp and study all at once" (p. 69). And, as we will soon discover, the nonprofit sector is even more sprawling and unruly today than it was in 1987.

In this chapter, we will look at the nonprofit sector as a whole and establish basic concepts and definitions that will help bring some order to our understanding of its structure, boundaries, and characteristics. Let's start by taking a brief imaginary tour around one American city, starting from the author's office on the campus of the George Washington University, located in the Foggy Bottom neighborhood of Washington, DC, near the White House. As the nation's capital, Washington, DC, is home to a significant number of nonprofits, but the variety of organizations that we will see on our tour is typical of what we might find in any American city. A walk through this one city helps give us a sense of the complexity to be found in today's nonprofit sector all across the country.

Leaving the author's office at the university, we might walk past the George Washington University Hospital, then turn down the street and pass Western Presbyterian Church, just a few blocks from the edge of campus. We might see men and women waiting to enter the basement of the church to visit Miriam's Kitchen, an organization that provides food and services to homeless people and works to end chronic homelessness.

If we take another turn, we would walk in front of the national headquarters of the American Red Cross and past the headquarters of the National Park Service. Proceeding farther into town, we would see the headquarters of the National Geographic Society. Eventually, we might walk past the Smithsonian Institution, located in several buildings along the National Mall, which extends from the Washington Monument

Learning Objectives

After reading this chapter, students should be able to:

1. Identify various types of nonprofit organizations.

2. Explain the historical growth of the nonprofit sector.

3. Compare various terms used to identify the nonprofit sector and explain their implications.

4. Classify nonprofit organizations according to the National Taxonomy of Exempt Entities and the Internal Revenue Code.

5. Explain the differences between organizations classified under 501(c)(3) and 501(c)(4) and the advantages and limitations related to each classification.

6. Explain differences among charitable subsectors.

7. Classify organizations as purely philanthropic, purely commercial, or hybrid, depending on various characteristics.

8. Explain new organizational forms and the concept of the fourth sector.

9. Analyze cases, applying concepts from the chapter.

to the Capitol building. If we walked a loop around the Capitol, we would pass the massive buildings of the Library of Congress. Walking back toward campus over Massachusetts Avenue, we would pass the headquarters of the Cato Institute and the Brookings Institution, both public policy think tanks. Depending on our route, we might see the Phillips Collection, which is an art gallery; the Urban Institute; and Anderson House, home to the Society of the Cincinnati, which promotes interest in the Revolutionary War. Arriving back at the George Washington University, we would be tired—it would have been a long walk. Thankfully, there are a number of Starbucks nearby, so we could sit down for a cup of coffee and rest. We might be thinking about the various sights we have seen in our day and trying to identify which are nonprofits and which are not. That would not be as easy a task as it may initially seem.

We would indeed have encountered a number of nonprofits on our tour, but some may seem more nonprofit-like than others. When the word nonprofit is used, many people think first of an organization like Miriam's Kitchen. While it is located in Western Presbyterian Church, it is a separate organization. It is small and supported mostly by charitable gifts. Its workforce includes many volunteers, and it provides its services to people who pay nothing for them. Most people also probably recognize the American Red Cross as a nonprofit organization, which it is, although it is chartered by the U.S. Congress and has a mandate from government to provide services to the U.S. military and to the general population in times of disaster. Some may not think of Western Presbyterian Church or other religious congregations as nonprofits in the same way they think of the Red Cross or Miriam's Kitchen, but religious congregations are indeed a part of the nonprofit sector. So are many art galleries, such as the Phillips; research organizations, such as Brookings, Cato, and the Urban Institute; and many fraternal organizations, such as the Society of the Cincinnati.

Some organizations may seem like nonprofits, but the reality is more complex. For example, the George Washington University Hospital, which we would have passed early on in our walk, doesn't seem any different from other hospitals that are nonprofit. But it is in fact a for-profit hospital owned jointly by the George Washington University (a nonprofit) and Universal Health Services (a for-profit hospital management corporation). Although the hospital is right down the street from Miriam's Kitchen and provides services to some of Miriam's clients, as an organization, it is really more like Microsoft than Miriam's.

Some organizations display combinations of nonprofit missions and business operations. Our imaginary tour of Washington, DC, touched two of these—the Smithsonian and National Geographic. The National Geographic Society is a nonprofit organization dedicated to geographic exploration and education. But National Geographic Partners is a for-profit company that controls the iconic *National Geographic* magazine and various media entities bearing the National Geographic name. Since 2015, this for-profit business has been owned 73 percent by 21st Century Fox and 27 percent by the nonprofit National Geographic Society (Sessa-Hawkins, 2015). In 2017, it was announced that the Walt Disney Company had offered to buy various properties from Fox, including the National Geographic entities that Fox had owned (James, 2017). The National Geographic Society remains a nonprofit, with the same mission—exploration and education.

The Smithsonian Institution is a national museum and many people may think of it as a government agency. But it is a complex organization, operating in part like a government agency, in part like a nonprofit organization, and in part like an entrepreneurial business. The Smithsonian receives a significant portion of its support from federal appropriations, but it was founded through a charitable bequest from James Smithson, after whom it was named, and it actively solicits philanthropic gifts. A separate nonprofit division, called Smithsonian Enterprises, manages the business activities of the Smithsonian Institution, including retail stores, a mail order catalogue, product development and licensing, magazine publishing, an educational travel program, theaters, restaurants and other concessions, business partnerships for book publishing, and the Smithsonian TV channel. Some staff members at the Smithsonian are federal government employees, while others are supported by private sources of revenue (Smithsonian Institution, n.d.).

If the line between nonprofit organizations and for-profit businesses is sometimes difficult to distinguish, the line between the nonprofit sector and government itself is also increasingly blurry. One third of the revenue of **charitable nonprofits** (33 percent) comes from government grants and payments for services under programs such as Medicare and Medicaid (Independent Sector, 2016a). Some nonprofit organizations exist primarily as government contractors implementing government-funded programs. However, some government agencies also have begun to tap the private sector for support to supplement the funds they receive from tax revenues, including two we passed on our journey around Washington, DC—the National Park Service and the Library of Congress. Both are agencies of the federal government that are increasing their efforts to raise private funds to supplement government appropriations.

Some relationships engage all three sectors. For example, car manufacturer Subaru (a corporation) contributes vehicles to the National Park Foundation (a nonprofit organization) for use in the parks managed by the National Park Service (a government agency) (Subaru of America, 2016). Further confusing the landscape, there are for-profit companies that look, feel, and sometimes sound nonprofit-like in the way they describe their missions, programs, and goals. Some compete directly with nonprofits engaged in similar activities. Consider, for example, the following description of services offered by one organization:

- We match families with the right health care coverage so they can find a doctor in their neighborhood who speaks their language and meets their medical needs.

- We help individuals find a path to sustainable employment.

- We improve the lives of children and their families by connecting them to vital child support resources.

- We protect patients' rights through an independent and objective appeals process for health programs such as Medicare and Medicaid.

- We develop education solutions so children with special needs get the services they need to succeed, while helping school districts comply with federal requirements. (MAXIMUS, 2018)

That sounds like the description of a nonprofit organization's programs, but it is indeed drawn from the website of MAXIMUS, a large for-profit corporation that manages government programs and maintains offices in various locations around the world.

Clearly the lines between the for-profit, nonprofit, and public sectors of our society are sometimes difficult to perceive without close examination. As we will discuss later in this chapter, some have indeed become hybrids that operate in more than one sector at once. The popular image of a nonprofit organization as a small band of volunteers intending to do good, working with minimal resources, serving people in need, and sharply distinct from business and government is far from the reality of many nonprofit organizations today. To understand how we came to where we are and make sense of the "sprawling and unruly collection of animals" that is today's nonprofit sector, we will need some understanding of the history that brought us to this point—and perhaps some road maps to lead us through the "zoo" (J. Simon, 1987).

America's Nonprofit Sector: A Historical Overview

The roots of America's nonprofit sector lie in the ancient traditions of charity, philanthropy, and voluntarism. Virtually all cultures and religions include some emphasis on the importance of service to others, which includes giving or voluntary action. Kevin Robbins (2012) traces the origins of these traditions in the Western world to early Greek, Roman, and Judeo-Christian thinking.

The legal foundations of America's nonprofit sector are drawn from English law, particularly the Statute of Charitable Uses and the Poor Law, both passed in 1601. These laws clarified the relationship between the British government and the Church of England, defined the legitimate activities to be supported by charity, and established a means to make the trustees of charitable institutions accountable (Hammack, 1998). The philosophy reflected in these statutes influenced the development of U.S. law regarding nonprofits and is still reflected in American legal traditions.

Although their roots are ancient, it is in the United States that the traditions of charity, philanthropy, and voluntarism have reached their most elaborated expression. As early as 1835, the Frenchman Alexis de Tocqueville observed the unique propensity of Americans to form "voluntary associations" to address social and political objectives, which he reported in his famous book *Democracy in America* (1838). Indeed, in a young nation born in revolution against the authority of the British government, voluntary organizations and institutions provided many of the services, from schools to volunteer fire departments. A certain mistrust of government has been a pervasive and continuing aspect of American culture and has provided philosophical support for private, voluntary initiatives throughout the nation's history. As we saw in our tour of Washington, DC, there appears to be some blurring of the nonprofit sector and government in today's environment. But it is important to recognize that the blur was even greater in the earliest days of the nation, when government supported churches, and churches sponsored many of the young institutions that served communities.

The beginnings of our modern nonprofit sector lie in the early years of the 20th century. Amid the rise of great wealth resulting from the Industrial Revolution, charity and philanthropy became organized activities undertaken on a large scale. This was the time of great philanthropists such as John D. Rockefeller and Andrew Carnegie, who endowed universities, libraries, colleges, and other institutions across the nation. Carnegie's essay, popularly known as the "Gospel of Wealth," published in 1889, remains a classic statement of the philosophy underpinning the American tradition of philanthropy. Carnegie expresses the responsibility of wealthy individuals to give back to the society that has enabled their accumulation of wealth, saying, "The man who dies thus rich dies disgraced" (p. 664). Carnegie's philosophy remains deeply a part of American culture, as evidenced by many contemporary entrepreneurs and investors, such as Bill Gates and Warren Buffett, who have created charitable foundations with similar expressions of obligation. Indeed, Gates and Buffet were leaders in promoting the Giving Pledge, a commitment by some of the world's wealthiest people to use the majority of their wealth to give back to society. By 2018, the pledge had been signed by 174 individuals (Giving Pledge, 2018).

Carnegie also helped establish a distinction between the concepts of charity and philanthropy. Although the words are often used interchangeably, and philanthropy is sometimes used as the broader, encompassing term, they describe two different types of giving. **Charity** is appropriately defined as giving intended to meet current individual human needs or to alleviate current human suffering—for example, to feed the homeless or aid the victims of a natural disaster. It is emotionally driven and often impulsive, as evidenced by the outpouring of gifts made through the mail, by phone, and via the Internet within days of any natural disaster, such as Hurricanes Harvey, Irma, and Maria—as well as major wild fires in California—in 2017. The website GoFundMe (https://www.gofundme.com) provides a vehicle for individuals to respond to the critical needs of specific individuals, reflecting similar motivations.

Philanthropy, on the other hand, is a more rational form of long-term investment in the infrastructure of society, seen, for example, in gifts made to construct new hospitals, endow universities, or create new charitable foundations intended to exist in perpetuity. If the goals of philanthropists are ultimately achieved, it is arguable that the need for charity will be eliminated, since there will exist institutions prepared to meet any human needs that may arise. However, in the imperfect world of the present, both types of giving are important and complementary in their impacts.

Some writers, notably Robert Payton (1988), have defined philanthropy to encompass **voluntarism** (also called "volunteerism"), calling philanthropy "voluntary action for the public good." But most people would make a distinction. Philanthropy could involve giving money from afar, while having little or no involvement with the organization or its beneficiaries, while volunteering implies a more hands-on role.

Notwithstanding its ancient roots and long history in the United States, the concept of a definable nonprofit sector, comparable with the for-profit and governmental sectors, is of relatively recent origin, dating to the work of the Commission on Private Philanthropy and Public Needs (the Filer Commission, mentioned in Chapter 1) from 1973 to 1975. The commission's 1975 report, titled *Giving in America*, was the first to characterize nonprofits as constituting a recognizable sector of society. The Filer Commission report came at a time when the nonprofit sector was expanding, in part reflecting changes in government policy. The 1960s and early 1970s were a period of increasing government spending on social programs, starting with the Great Society programs of president Lyndon B. Johnson. In many cases, government funds were channeled to nonprofit organizations, which provided the actual services. "Indeed," Lester Salamon (2012b) observes, "much of the modern nonprofit sector as we know it took shape during this period as a direct outcome of expanded government support" (p. 22). In the 1980s, under president Ronald Reagan, federal spending for many social programs was sharply reduced. Since the 1980s, there also has been a change in the form in which federal support is provided, with important implications for the management of nonprofit organizations. The shift has been away from direct grants to nonprofit organizations and toward providing aid to individuals in the form of voucher-type subsidies. This occurred, for example, in health care, where Medicare and Medicaid reshaped the industry. And it also occurred in higher education, where government funds going directly to colleges and universities diminished, while aid directed to individual students and their families increased. This created a new generation of student consumers and transformed higher education institutions into competitive, marketing organizations. The shift also was illustrated in the welfare reform legislation of 1996, which brought competition to many areas of human services. This empowerment of individuals as consumers through direct subsidies to them has forced nonprofits to compete for customer dollars not only with other nonprofits, but also with for-profit companies that have entered fields that were previously the exclusive preserve of the nonprofit sector. For example, the for-profit firm MAXIMUS, mentioned previously, is now among the nation's largest managers of Medicaid and the Children's Health Insurance Program. Future changes in government funding, in both scale and method, are always possible and would have an inescapable impact on the nonprofit sector.

Changes in government funding also account in part for the growing commercialization of the nonprofit sector itself, the increased need for professional nonprofit management, and the demands that nonprofits demonstrate greater accountability and results. Nonprofit organizations comprise a vital and growing sector of our economy and society, but questions about their effectiveness and accountability are topics of national discussion and debate. There are even occasional challenges to the tax exemption of nonprofits, especially those that are highly commercialized.

Searching for a Common Vocabulary

The nonprofit sector is so diverse and its structure is so complex that it can be confusing, and there are various ways in which people understand it. Diverse understandings are reflected in the fact that there are multiple terms by which the sector is identified.

As Thomas Wolf (1999) points out, describing an elephant as a "non-horse" would seem to most people an unsatisfactory definition (p. 19). But the term nonprofit organization really refers to one thing nonprofit organizations do not do, rather than capturing much about what they are or the diverse programs and services they offer to society. One thing nonprofit organizations do *not* do is distribute profits to individual owners in the form of dividends or use those profits to enhance the wealth of owners through the increasing value of the enterprise.

However, it is important to dispel the common misunderstanding that nonprofits cannot earn profits. Defined as simply an excess of revenues over expenses, nonprofits can and do earn profits. Indeed, one well-known study (Chang & Tuckman, 1990) found that, contrary to what many theories might predict, nonprofit managers do try to earn profits and build up the assets of their organizations. But these profits must be retained within the organization and eventually be used to further its programs rather than enrich individuals personally. Unlike corporations, nonprofits cannot distribute their profits to individuals in the form of dividends. This nonprofit distribution requirement, also called the nondistribution constraint, is one defining characteristic of nonprofit organizations, but it is clearly not *the* defining characteristic. Indeed, by this narrow standard, the Department of Defense and the state of New York might be called "nonprofits," since they also have no stockholders or owners to whom any profit is distributed.

While the term nonprofit organization or just nonprofit is the most commonly used term for these organizations in the United States, those nonprofits that work internationally are generally known as **nongovernmental organizations**, although there is no identifiable nongovernmental sector with the same meaning as the term nonprofit sector in the United States. The term nongovernmental is one that originated with the United Nations and reflects in part the reality that many such organizations are performing government-like functions in the countries they serve and that most receive a substantial portion of their revenue from government sources. Many are like arms of government operating just outside the public sphere. Like nonprofit, the term nongovernmental defines organizations by what they are *not*—they are not government agencies. But this term seems equally inadequate. It could apply as well to profit-making companies such as Google and Amazon, which are also clearly nongovernmental in their ownership and legal control.

Alternatives to Nonprofit

While nonprofit is the term most commonly used to describe the sector, there is no shortage of alternatives that some people employ. Each alternative has its own virtues, and shortcomings as well. It is worth discussing some of these terms because each reflects a certain view and understanding of the sector.

The term **independent sector** has some prominence, since it is also the name of the principal organization representing the interests of nonprofits in Washington, DC— Independent Sector (www.independentsector.org). But the term itself raises the question of "independent from what?" Nonprofits are financially dependent on resources derived from both government and private donors and are subject to an increasing array of state and federal law, so independence would not seem to capture their essence.

Some prefer the term third sector, placing nonprofits in the universe alongside the commercial economy and government. The term is accurate in terms of size—both the business sector and government employ more people, generate larger revenues, and account for a larger share of economic output. But it also seems to imply a rank order of importance, which would not agree with the values of many people, who may consider religion, education, the arts, medical research, and other purposes served by the nonprofit sector to be among the most important of human endeavors. Furthermore, some scholars suggest that American society encompasses not three but four sectors: business, government, the nonprofit sector, and families and communities. In this broader array, it becomes more difficult to rank the sectors, except by size, in which case families and communities would come first and the nonprofit sector would be fourth rather than third.

The term **charitable sector** is sometimes used, but it is contrary to the reality that charitable gifts, while important, are not the largest source of nonprofit revenues. Nor is the term synonymous with nonprofit sector, since there are organizations that qualify as nonprofit under the U.S. tax code but that neither seek nor receive any form of charitable support. This is true, for example, of membership organizations that are funded entirely through dues and those nonprofits whose revenues may consist entirely of grants and contracts received from government. Nor does the term seem appropriate to encompass major institutions, such as Harvard University, that are nonprofit but hardly consistent with most people's understanding of a charity.

Some use the term voluntary sector. Indeed, that term is part of the title of one of the leading academic journals in the field, *Nonprofit and Voluntary Sector Quarterly*. Voluntarism is one of the foundations of the sector, and many organizations do indeed rely on volunteers, both as members of their governing boards and for at least part of their workforce. But the term does not reflect the reality that, in many nonprofits, paid staff members far outnumber volunteers. It also may perpetuate an inaccurate image of nonprofits as universally small and amateurish in their operations, when in fact many nonprofits are substantial enterprises, and professional management of nonprofits has been a growing trend.

The phrase **tax-exempt sector**, commonly used by accountants, attorneys, and other tax specialists, is similar to nonprofit. It identifies organizations entirely in terms of their status under U.S. tax law. With a few exceptions, nonprofits are exempt from paying federal income tax and generally from state and local income taxes as well. But, again, tax-exempt speaks to the legal status of such organizations and says nothing about what they actually do. As we will discuss shortly, the sector encompasses a variety of organizations with few apparent similarities aside from their tax-exempt status.[1,2]

Another term that has been proposed is **civil society sector** (Salamon, 2012a). There are many different definitions of civil society, and while "the nonprofit sector provides the organizational infrastructure of civil society," the concept itself is more abstract, including "the sum of institutions, organizations, and individuals located between the family, the state, and the market, in which people associate voluntarily to advance common interests" (Anheier, 2014, p. 9). And as Salamon (2012a) acknowledges, the term civil society sector is like voluntary sector in that it "emphasizes the citizen base" of these organizations, while most are not membership associations and many engage large paid staffs (p. 13).

In recent decades, nonprofits have come to be increasingly managed like businesses, and some undertake entrepreneurial ventures either directly, through for-profit subsidiaries, or with for-profit partners. Some people have adopted the term **social enterprise** to encompass nonprofits that have a social objective but employ commercial principles in their generation of revenue (Social Enterprise Alliance, 2017). Although the term social enterprise is generally associated with those who especially advocate organizations operating like businesses and undertaking efforts to increase revenues from commercial activities, it could be argued that the term captures the positive essence of *all* private organizations having a social purpose, perhaps better than nonprofit. Like companies, nonprofits bring together people, resources, and purposeful effort in pursuit of a mission, and they increasingly operate with plans, goals, and established criteria for success—they are indeed enterprises. But their missions relate to social purposes rather than to the enrichment of private individuals. Were social enterprise to become a general designation for all such organizations, the sector that contains them perhaps then would be called the social sector to differentiate it from business and government. Indeed, social sector has become popular among some business authors and consultants in referring to the nonprofit sector, which some define as an "industry" (McKinsey & Company, n.d.). However, this broader use of the term has not gained universal acceptance, and we generally will use the more common designations of nonprofit organization and nonprofit sector in the remainder of this book.

Noting the increasing number of organizations that operate under both nonprofit and for-profit legal forms, often called **hybrid organizations**, some authors have suggested that there may be an emerging fourth sector, encompassing organizations that blend the features and methods of both forms (Fourth Sector Network, 2017; Sabeti, 2009). Some new types of organizations have developed in alignment with this concept of the fourth sector, which will be discussed further later in this chapter. (This use of the term "fourth sector" should not be confused with the concept discussed earlier in which families and communities are considered a fourth sector of society in addition to business, government, and nonprofits.)

Size of the U.S. Nonprofit Sector

There are more than 1.5 million tax-exempt organizations in the United States that are registered with the Internal Revenue Service. That does not include religious congregations or smaller organizations that are not registered; if they were included, the total number would be about 2.2 million (McKeever et al., 2016, p. 2). These organizations serve a wide range of purposes. Some are "public-serving" and others are "member-serving," terms that will be explained further later (Salamon, 2012b, p. 7). The largest group is the charitable nonprofits, classified under 501(c)(3) of the Internal Revenue Code, numbering approximately one million (McKeever et al.). Those include many of the public-serving organizations that we all know—hospitals, museums, schools, colleges and universities, orchestras, youth organizations, and nonprofits that provide a range of human and social services. Another significant number, about 84,000, includes those classified under section 501(c)(4) of the tax code (McKeever et al., p. 3). This section of the tax code does include some large organizations that are health maintenance organizations (HMOs) or managed health plans, but the most well-known organizations in this category are distinguished by their advocacy on issues, for example, the National Association for the Advancement of Colored People (NAACP), the National Rifle Association (NRA), and the Sierra Club.

The nonprofit sector is a significant component of the U.S. economy. In 2013, nonprofits employed 14.4 million people, almost 10 percent of the workforce (McKeever et al., 2016, p. 29). In that same year, nonprofits paid $634 billion in wages, about 9 percent of all the wages paid in the United States (McKeever et al., p. 14). Nonprofit organizations that reported to the Internal Revenue Service (IRS) and were public charities had received $1.73 trillion in revenue and held $3.22 trillion in assets in 2013 (McKeever et al., p. 157). Thus, by almost any measure, the nonprofit sector has a substantial economic impact.

The nonprofit sector has grown dramatically in recent decades and years. Sixty-four percent of all public charities were created since 1990 (McKeever et al., 2016, p. 157). From 2000 to 2013, the number of employees in the nonprofit sector increased by 23 percent, compared with 5 percent growth in government and less than 1 percent in business (McKeever et al., p. 29). The growth is attributable to a variety of forces. As discussed above, they include the trend that began in the 1980s toward the devolution of federal programs to state and local governments, and outsourcing of the provision of many services to nonprofits by governments at all levels, as well as increased philanthropy. In addition, some argue, the growth of nonprofits has been fueled by a reawakening of the spirit of public service among the current generation of Americans. Events such as the attacks of September 11, 2001, and large-scale natural disasters, both in the United States and elsewhere over the past two decades, have called the nation's attention to human needs and the role of nonprofit organizations in helping to alleviate human suffering. The requirement of community service for graduation from high school has exposed a generation of young people to the idea of volunteering. Many companies also organize volunteer activities for their employees, extending the experience to more Americans and making it even more a part of American culture.

In his influential, though controversial, 1995 article, "Bowling Alone: America's Declining Social Capital," Robert Putnam discussed a decline in civic engagement among Americans, using the metaphor of his title to suggest that Americans were becoming more isolated and more involved in individual pursuits than in collective interests and activities. Yet a decade later, Putnam and his colleague Thomas Sander reported that young Americans who witnessed the events of September 11, 2001, in their adolescent years appeared to be more involved in public affairs and community life than their older siblings. As Sander and Putnam (2005) note, "We'll have to wait some years to see if this budding civic engagement blossoms, but it could prove to be the largest civic shift in the past half-century" (p. A23). It will still require time to identify what the long-term trends may be, but there is some evidence that millennials do value volunteering more than some previous generations ("More Millennials Value Volunteering," 2015). Overall, in 2014, 25 percent of Americans over age 16 volunteered and their efforts were equivalent to 5.1 million full-time employees (McKeever et al., 2016, p. 126). Trends in volunteering are discussed in further detail in Chapter 9 of this text.

Differentiating the Nonprofit Sector

As we saw from our imaginary walking tour of Washington, DC, nonprofits are a widely diverse group of organizations and institutions. Fortunately, there are ways of bringing order out of the apparent chaos by placing nonprofits into categories. Let's review some of them and see if we can gain a clearer picture of this complex arena. We will look at two ways of categorizing nonprofits according to their purposes and activities (the National Taxonomy of Exempt Entities and the Internal Revenue Service classifications): one model that categorizes nonprofits according to who benefits from their activities (public serving and member serving), and another that places nonprofits along a continuum according to the degree they are commercialized or use business principles and methods.

National Taxonomy of Exempt Entities

One way to delineate the nonprofit sector is to use the **National Taxonomy of Exempt Entities (NTEE)** Classification System (Guidestar, 2018). The NTEE divides the universe of nonprofit organizations into 26 major groups under 10 broad categories, with 600 sub-categories (Tax Policy Center, 2016). These categories are based on organizations' purposes, activities, and programs and are similar to the industry classification codes used to group for-profit companies. Box 2.1 lists the 10 broad categories in the NTEE. The complete taxonomy, including subcategories, is available on the Guidestar website (https://learn.guidestar.org/help/ntee-codes).

Arts, Culture, and Humanities	International, Foreign Affairs
Education	Public, Society Benefit
Environment and Animals	Religion Related
Health	Mutual/Membership Benefit
Human Services	Unknown/Unclassified

Source: Tax Policy Center (2016).

Similar ways of classifying nonprofits include the North American Industry Classification System (NAICS), which uses the same breakout as for the for-profit sector. The Bureau of Economic Analysis of the U.S. Department of Commerce, and some other agencies, use a definition of "nonprofit institutions serving households" (NPISHs), which excludes nonprofits that serve businesses (McKeever et al., 2016, p. 7). The fact that different classification systems are used by various agencies that collect data on the nonprofit sector accounts in part for the fact that estimates of the sector's size and impact are often not consistent.

IRS Classifications

One of the reasons that there are different definitions of the nonprofit sector is that classifications of organizations are developed with varied purposes. For the Internal Revenue Service (IRS), what is relevant is the exemption of nonprofit organizations from the corporate income tax, so the IRS places nonprofits into more than 30 categories (or "classifications") that reflect the basis for their tax exemption (McKeever et al., 2016, p. 158). As discussed previously, the very term nonprofit relates to the treatment of organizations under the U.S. tax code, so the IRS classifications are perhaps the most often mentioned. Moreover, from a practical perspective, how an organization is classified under the tax code is also of the greatest significance to those who govern and manage it, since this status dictates many of the rules by which the organization must operate. Nonprofits qualify for tax exemption under various sections of the Internal Revenue Code (IRC), depending on the nature of their principal activities.

The tax code can be complicated, as anyone who has filed his or her own personal tax returns will testify. Figure 2.1 provides a way to visualize the nonprofit sector and how various organizations are classified by the IRS. It first divides society into the three sectors: government, nonprofits, and for-profit business. The nonprofit sector then is divided into four categories: organizations that are tax-exempt under Section 501(c)(3) that are public charities; organizations that are tax-exempt under Section 501(c)(3) that are private foundations; organizations that are exempt under Section 501(c)(4), referred to by the IRS as "social welfare organizations," encompassing what many would call **advocacy organizations**, as well as others; and a variety of other tax-exempt organizations, classified under various sections of the tax code, such as labor unions, chambers of commerce, social and recreational clubs, trade associations, and others. While this latter group is tax-exempt, the organizations are not ones we commonly think about when the term "nonprofit" is used. For example, the National Football League (NFL) was tax-exempt as a trade association, under Section 501(c)(6) of the IRC, a fact that was controversial until the league voluntarily relinquished its tax exemption in

Figure 2.1   Overview of the Nonprofit Sector

Figure 2.1   Overview of the Nonprofit Sector

Private Sector (Business) | Nonprofit Sector | Government

501(c)(3) Charitable nonprofits

501(c)(4) Social welfare organizations

Includes civic clubs and advocacy organizations (e.g., Sierra Club, NAACP, NRA)

Also includes some large HMOs and managed health plans

Organizations are tax exempt, but gifts are not tax deductible.

501(c)(3) Private foundations

Tax-exempt, except for a modest excise tax on investment earnings

Most have one donor (individual, family, corporation).

Gifts are tax deductible, up to 30 percent of the donor's income (with other limitations).

A small percentage are operating foundations, but most are grant-making foundations.

File Form 990-PF with IRS.

501(c)(3) Public charities

Tax-exempt

Receive gifts from multiple sources (public support)

Gifts are tax deductible, up to 60 percent of the donor's income (with other limitations). (See Note 2)

Large organizations with gross receipts of $50,000 or more (e.g., universities, hospitals, museums) file Form 990 or Form 990-EZ, depending on size, with IRS.

Small organizations with gross receipts less than $50,000 (e.g., community theaters, neighborhood associations) file Form 990-N with IRS.

Religious congregations: registration with IRS is voluntary.

Other tax-exempt organizations

Including:

501(c)(5) Agricultural, horticultural, labor organizations (labor unions), farm bureaus, etc.

501(c)(6) Business leagues (chambers of commerce, trade associations, etc.)

501(c)(7) Social and recreational clubs (e.g., golf clubs, fraternities, sororities, etc.)

Various other small categories, including veterans organizations, cemetery companies, credit unions, etc.

Funding intermediaries

Include grant-making private foundations and public charities that receive support from the public and reallocate funds to other public charities (e.g., United Way, community foundations, institutionally related foundations)

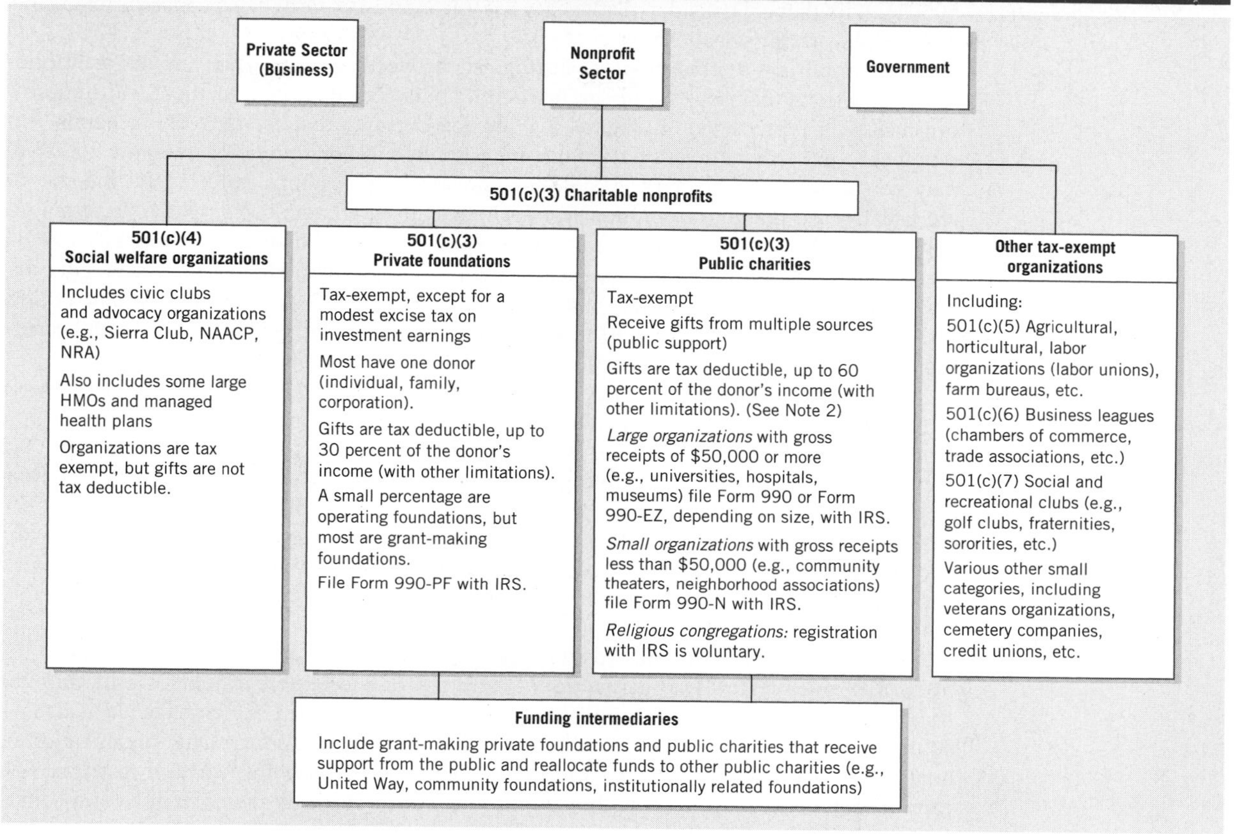

Source: Based on IRS Publication 557 (retrieved from www.irs.gov/pub/irs-pdf/p557.pdf) and various other sources reporting on the Tax Cuts and Jobs Act of 2017.

Notes: 1. Under federal tax legislation passed in 2017, called the Tax Cuts and Jobs Act of 2017, a small number of colleges and universities are subject to an excise tax on endowment income. Some nonprofits may be subject to a tax related to compensation exceeding $1 million.
2. The allowable percentage was increased from 50 percent under federal tax legislation passed in 2017. Deductions for gifts made with appreciated property, rather than cash, have a lower limitation. Some provisions of the 2017 law have expiration dates.

2015 (Strachan, 2015). Despite the wide array of organizations that are tax-exempt, most are not a focus of the discussion in this chapter or in this book, which emphasizes the charitable and advocacy organizations that most closely align with the conception of the nonprofit sector that most people hold.

Let's take a closer look at the 501(c)(3) and 501(c)(4) organizations that are the primary types discussed in this book. Although they are fewer in number than the charitable nonprofits, this chapter will first discuss the 501(c)(4) nonprofits, known to the IRS as **social welfare organizations**. Then let's return to a longer discussion of the charitable nonprofits that are the largest component of the sector.

Social Welfare Organizations

There are different types of organizations that are classified under Section 501(c)(4). A small number are health maintenance organizations (HMOs) and other medical and dental insurance plans, although they account for the major portion of the revenues in the 501(c)(4) category. In this book, we generally ignore those organizations and focus on the vast majority of 501(c)(4)s that are considered advocacy organizations, because their purpose is to advance a cause or work for social change.

It is important at this point to distinguish between two concepts: the tax exemption of organizations themselves and the tax deductibility of gifts made to them. *All* nonprofit organizations represented in Figure 2.1 are tax-exempt; that is, they are generally not required to pay federal taxes on their income, although as noted in notes to Figure 2.1, some may be subject to other taxes. In addition, organizations exempt from federal income tax are usually also granted exemption from state and local income taxes, which increases the benefits attached to this status. However, *only* those classified under Section 501(c)(3)—the charitable nonprofits—are tax-exempt themselves and *also* eligible to receive gifts that are tax deductible for the donors. Thus, the NAACP and the NRA, which are classified under 501(c)(4), are tax-exempt, but gifts made to them are not tax deductible for the donor because the NAACP and NRA are not classified as charitable organizations.

Advocacy organizations are tax-exempt—under Section 501(c)(4)—because they work, in the IRS's (n.d.-b) words, "to further the common good and general welfare of the people of a community (such as bringing about civic betterment and social improvements)." But they cannot receive tax-deductible gifts. Why are advocacy organizations different from charitable nonprofits in the eyes of the tax code? One big difference between 501(c)(3) and 501(c)(4) organizations is that the latter do not face the same limitations on lobbying and political activity that are imposed on the former. They can spend money on lobbying without limitation (IRS, n.d.-a). This is a point we will discuss in more detail in Chapter 11 of this text.

Because of the different advantages enjoyed and disadvantages experienced by 501(c)(3) and 501(c)(4) organizations, in terms of the tax treatment of gifts and the limitations on lobbying and political activity, some organizations have two arms—actually, two separately incorporated but related organizations. One organization is qualified under Section 501(c)(4) and is free to engage in lobbying without restriction. It cannot receive deductible gifts, but it can raise funds through member dues and others types of revenue. The other related organization is qualified under Section 501(c)(3) and is thus eligible to receive tax-deductible gifts. It pursues education, research, and other activities consistent with that classification.

Box 2.2 provides an example in the form of mission statements for the Sierra Club, an internationally known environmental organization, and the related Sierra Club Foundation. The Sierra Club itself is a 501(c)(4) social welfare organization that works to preserve the environment, including lobbying for environmental protection legislation. The Sierra Club Foundation is a 501(c)(3) organization that supports certain activities of the Sierra Club and other environmental programs. As its mission statement and description of its activities explain, the foundation works to "educate and empower people," activities that are consistent with the purposes allowed for 501(c)(3) organizations. Note the slight difference in the mission statement of the Sierra Club—it goes beyond educating and empowering and includes "enlisting" humanity, which suggests the possibility of building political coalitions and encouraging individuals to political action. This may seem like a subtle difference, but facing the possibility of an audit by the IRS and wishing to protect the tax status of both entities, most organizations are precise in monitoring their activities for consistency with tax law.

Charitable Nonprofits

Now let's turn to the two boxes shown in the middle of Figure 2.1—the charitable nonprofits that are public charities and the charitable nonprofits that are private foundations, both tax-exempt under Section 501(c)(3). These two groups have some characteristics in common, but in other ways, they are different.

All charitable nonprofits are not only tax-exempt but are eligible to receive tax-deductible contributions. The tax deductibility of gifts made to charitable nonprofits obviously provides a significant advantage to them in their fundraising efforts. Consider the example of an individual donor who is in a 25 percent federal tax bracket and who makes a deductible gift of $100 to a charitable nonprofit organization. He or she deducts that $100 from his or her income before calculating the income tax due. The donor's taxable income is reduced by $100, so the donor's tax bill is reduced by 25 percent of that amount, or $25. This is considered a tax savings because, were it not for the gift, the donor would have paid that amount in additional federal income tax. The out-of-pocket cost of the $100 gift is thus reduced, from $100 to $75 ($100 minus the $25 tax savings). Some view the savings as a form of tax subsidy, or tax expenditure, in the form of foregone federal revenue. And, since many states also permit the deduction of charitable gifts, the donor often has an additional savings on taxes at the state level.

The tax deduction for gifts to charitable organizations is intended to encourage charitable giving and sustain the services that such organizations provide. It should not be viewed as a tax loophole because it is intentionally provided in the law as an incentive to giving. Society has determined that the purposes nonprofits serve are to the public benefit and that if the nonprofits did not exist, those services might need to be provided by government. Being eligible to receive deductible gifts makes it easier for charitable nonprofits to raise funds, since the donors are, at least theoretically, able to give more because of the tax saving realized from the deductions. However, federal tax legislation passed in 2017, the Tax Cuts and Jobs Act of 2017, significantly increased the number of taxpayers eligible to claim a standard deduction on their tax returns, rather than itemize deductions. As a result, fewer people may benefit from the deduction of charitable gifts. Following passage of this legislation, some observers predicted that it could have a negative impact on giving, since loss of the deduction would affect the out-of-pocket cost of gifts for many taxpayers. Others argued that the tax law changes would increase incomes, permitting people to give more.

To be recognized as tax-exempt under Section 501(c)(3), an organization must demonstrate three things; in other words, it must meet three tests. First, it must be organized and operated for one or more of eight purposes: charitable, religious, educational, scientific, literary, testing for public safety, fostering national or international amateur sports competitions, and prevention of cruelty to children and animals. (Curiously, the IRC does not specifically mention health care, although it is one of the largest components of the nonprofit sector.) The term charitable may seem somewhat imprecise, but the IRS (n.d.-a) defines it to include certain specific activities:

relief of the poor, the distressed, or the underprivileged; advancement of religion; advancement of education or science; erection or maintenance of public buildings, monuments, or works; lessening the burdens of government; lessening of neighborhood tensions; elimination of prejudice and discrimination; defense of human and civil rights secured by law; and combating community deterioration and juvenile delinquency.

In addition to demonstrating that its primary purposes include one or more of those discussed above, a 501(c)(3) nonprofit must meet two other requirements. It must meet the non-distribution test, ensuring that its assets are not being used to benefit individual owners and that its managers are not being personally enriched through excessive compensation. And it must limit its political activities. A nonprofit that qualifies under Section 501(c)(3) cannot support or oppose candidates for public office, and again, it must limit its expenditures on lobbying—that is, efforts to influence legislation. The prohibition on political activity by charitable nonprofits derives from the Johnson Amendment, a federal law sponsored by then U.S. Senator Lyndon B. Johnson and passed in 1954. This issue has been controversial, especially as it relates to the freedom of religious groups. On May 4, 2017, president Donald J. Trump signed an executive order that directed the IRS to "exercise maximum enforcement discretion" with regard to the Johnson Amendment. However, despite efforts in the Congress in 2017 to repeal it, the Johnson Amendment remained law and the impact of the executive order was uncertain (Wagner, Phillip, & Zauzmer, 2017). The issue may continue to be debated in the years ahead.

Charitable Subsectors. Let's take a look at the major subsectors of the charitable nonprofits, excluding religious congregations. Bear in mind that, as shown in Figure 2.1, religious congregations are charitable nonprofits under the tax code and they are tax-exempt under Section 501(c)(3). However, as noted before, religion is a unique component of the nonprofit sector. The U.S. Constitution guarantees the separation of church and state. Gifts to religious congregations are tax deductible, but congregations are not required to register with the IRS, although some do so voluntarily. The principle of separation of church and state prevents government funds from going directly to religious congregations or to organizations that would use them for religious activities. However, congregations are to be distinguished from **faith-based organizations** that provide social services, which can receive government funds to support their secular programs. This book does not specifically discuss the management of religious congregations—for example, churches, synagogues, and mosques. Religious organizations are the least professionalized of the subsectors. Although there has been some growth in the number of church managers, the management of most congregations is still done by the clergy and volunteers.

As discussed below, the charitable subsectors differ significantly in their sources of revenue, the degree of commercialization they reflect, and the extent to which their management has been professionalized—that is, the extent to which they are run by paid staff rather than volunteers.

Arts, Culture, and Humanities. The arts and culture subsector includes museums, performing arts groups, art galleries, folk-life organizations, nonprofit radio and television stations, literary societies, arts education organizations, media and communications organizations, and arts councils and agencies. In 2013, this subsector accounted for almost 10 percent of charitable nonprofits, but only 2 percent of the sector's expenses (McKeever et al., 2016, p. 190). This sector receives substantial earned income from admission fees, gift shops, and other sources and also receives gifts from individuals, corporations, and foundations. The management of arts institutions and that of museums are specialty areas within nonprofit management, and professionals often will have attended university programs focused on these fields.

Education. Education is perhaps the subsector best known to students. It includes colleges and universities, preschool, elementary, and secondary schools, correspondence schools, libraries, parent–teacher groups, and education support organizations. Of course, most educational institutions are not nonprofits; they are entities controlled by state or local governments, including public schools and public universities and colleges.

It will not surprise students to learn that educational institutions receive a significant portion of their revenues from fees for service, including tuition. But anyone who has graduated from a college, university, or independent school knows that such institutions also actively seek gifts from alumni, parents, and other individuals who are affiliated. Educational institutions, and nonprofits with an educational mission, accounted for about 17 percent of the sector in 2013 and for more than 17 percent of all expenditures in the sector. Colleges and universities are among the largest organizations in the education subsector; while they account for just 4 percent of all education nonprofits, their expenditures account for about two thirds of the total for the subsector (McKeever et al., 2016, pp. 196–199). Higher education, in particular, is a field in which professional management has increased in recent decades. While the senior executives of colleges and universities are still predominantly drawn from the academic ranks, there has been a proliferation of midlevel management in areas such as fundraising, student services, and financial administration. Middle management has grown as colleges and universities have faced increased competitive pressures, greater governmental regulation, and the need to expand revenues through intensified fundraising and student-recruitment programs.

While for-profit education firms—for example, the University of Phoenix—have grown in recent decades, most schools, colleges, and universities remain either nonprofit or government controlled.

Environment and Animals. While the environment and the welfare of animals are important purposes, organizations working in these fields—including environmental preservation organizations, recycling programs, pollution abatement programs, animal protection organizations, wildlife preservation organizations, and zoos—constitute the smallest charitable subsector, representing only 5 percent of public charities and just 1 percent of the charitable nonprofit sector's expenses (McKeever et al., 2016, p. 201). It is also a subsector that is highly dependent on charitable gifts, with relatively few opportunities to generate income from fees or sales. It is important to note that some organizations advocating for environmental issues and animal protection are 501(c)(4) organizations, rather than charitable nonprofits under 501(c)(3). The Sierra Club was mentioned earlier as one example. Such organizations are not included in the totals stated here for this charitable subsector.

Health. The health services subsector is the largest component of the overall nonprofit sector if measured by total revenue, expenditures, or the number of employees. It includes hospitals, home health agencies, outpatient clinics, hospice programs, nursing homes, some HMOs, dialysis centers, community health centers, residential treatment programs for emotionally disturbed youth, blood banks, public health organizations, and disease organizations such as the March of Dimes and American Cancer Society.

The health subsector is huge. While health organizations account for only 13 percent of public charities, they represent nearly 60 percent of the nonprofit sector's total expenses and more than 43 percent of the sector's total assets. In 2013, the health subsector had revenue of a *trillion* dollars, higher than all of the other subsectors combined (McKeever et al., 2016, p. 205).

Health services is the most commercialized of the nonprofit subsectors; in other words, many of the organizations are businesslike in deriving most of their revenue from fees charged for services provided. It also was one of the first subsectors to become professionalized in its management—that is, to develop large paid professional management staffs rather than depend on volunteers. There are many university programs in health care management and public health, and the salaries of many professional managers in the health subsector, especially in hospitals and large medical centers, are comparable to those in private industry. It is also a field in which nonprofits compete with for-profit firms to a significant extent. In some industries—for example, nursing homes—for-profits have captured the major portion of the market. The health services subsector also has seen the conversion of some nonprofits into for-profit entities, including insurance plans, hospitals, and nursing homes.

Human Services. Human service nonprofits account for more than one third of all public charities, making it the largest subsector if measured by the number of organizations (McKeever et al., 2016, p. 205). This subsector includes what many people conventionally think about when the term "nonprofit" is used—organizations that provide job training, legal aid, housing, youth development, disaster assistance, and food distribution programs. But many of these organizations are small; together they represent only 10 percent of the nonprofit sector's total assets and 13 percent of its total expenses (McKeever et al., p. 208). Although many people might consider organizations working in these areas as among the most charitable, they are in fact substantially reliant on fees for the services they provide. About 27 percent of their revenues are fees paid by private sources and another 26 percent comes from government payments for services provided to individuals qualified for government assistance. Such organizations also receive government grants accounting for 21 percent of revenue, making them the subsector most reliant on government funds (McKeever et al., pp. 208–212). This reality reflects, in part, the devolution and outsourcing of social programs over recent decades, as mentioned earlier in this text. Dependence on government funds also makes many human service organizations vulnerable when public policy shifts and government social spending declines. They are also vulnerable, of course, to declines in giving during economic recession, just when the need for their services may be increasing. For this reason, among others, many of the efforts to diversify revenues by developing alternative sources, including business enterprises, have occurred in this subsector. It is also the focus of much of the discussion regarding the need for improved management and accountability in the nonprofit sector as a whole. While there are certainly many volunteers working in human service organizations, there also has been a trend toward more professionalized management of such organizations in recent decades. In many instances, volunteers are managed by staff who have specialized training and skills in the management of volunteer programs.

International and Foreign Affairs. The subsector of international and foreign affairs included just 2 percent of public charities in 2013 (McKeever et al., 2016, p. 212). This subsector encompasses organizations engaged with international exchange programs, international development and relief efforts, international peace and security, and human rights. Although such organizations do receive government grants, they are substantially reliant on gifts and grants from private donors, which account for 65 percent of the subsector's revenue (McKeever et al., p. 214).

Other Public Charities. A wide variety of organizations are sometimes just described as "other public charities" (McKeever et al., 2016, p. 216). They include those pursuing public and societal benefit in fields such as civil rights, community improvement, the promotion of philanthropy, and research, among other purposes. Some religious organizations that are not congregations also are included in this subsector. Together, these organizations account for 18 percent of public charities and they reflect varied patterns in terms of their sources of revenues.

Funding Intermediaries. Funding intermediaries are organizations that exist for the sole purpose of directing money to other nonprofits (Salamon, 2012a). They are tax-exempt under Section 501(c)(3) and thus gifts made to them are tax deductible to the donor. But they are also different from the organizations described in the previous sections of this text. With some exceptions, they do not themselves operate programs; rather, their role is, in a sense, to be like the bankers of the nonprofit sector, channeling private giving to other, service-providing nonprofits. Some are public charities, including, for example, United Way, the Jewish Federations of North America, and community foundations. They raise money from the public and then redistribute it to other organizations that serve their communities. Other funding intermediaries are private foundations, funding intermediaries that work under a somewhat different set of rules.

Public Charities and Private Foundations

As shown in Figure 2.1, there are two different types of charitable nonprofit organizations that are exempt under Section 501(c)(3)—public charities and private foundations. There are technical definitions of these terms established in tax law, but it is sufficient to understand that **public charities**, as the term suggests, are organizations that receive support from a relatively large number of donors or from government, that is, from the public. They include most of the nonprofits discussed in the preceding sections of this chapter. Both public charities that provide direct services, such as hospitals, and funding intermediaries that are public charities, such as United Way, generally spend a significant portion of the gifts they receive each year.

Private foundations, on the other hand, usually have only one or perhaps a few donors—often one person, one company, or the members of a family. For example, the Bill & Melinda Gates Foundation was funded through gifts from Bill and Melinda Gates, and the Ford Foundation was created through gifts from Henry Ford. It is a common misunderstanding to think that the Gates Foundation was created by Microsoft and the Ford Foundation by the Ford Motor Company. In reality, the funds used to establish the Gates Foundation were those belonging to Bill and Melinda Gates personally. Likewise, the Ford Foundation was created by Henry Ford with his personal fortune, not by the Ford Motor Company. There were over 96,000 private foundations in the United States in 2014, compared with just 78,000 in 1999 (National Center for Charitable Statistics, n.d.). That growth reflects, in part, the stock market booms of the 1990s and 2010s, which enabled many wealthy people to create foundations to manage and perpetuate their philanthropy.

Private foundations receive different tax treatment than public charities. One significant difference lies in the tax deductions allowed to individual donors for gifts to public charities and private foundations. Beginning in 2018, cash gifts to public charities are deductible up to 60 percent of the donor's income, while deductible gifts to private foundations are limited to 30 percent of the donor's annual income (Council on Foundations, 2018). In both cases, there may be additional limitations, depending on the nature of the assets used to make the gifts, and donors may be able to claim deductions for the amount exceeding those limits in later years. In addition, the investment earnings of private foundations are subject to a tax, and they face a requirement for minimum spending of their investment returns that does not apply to public charities. It is important to note that some provisions of the federal tax law passed in 2017 (the Tax Cuts and Jobs Act of 2017) are scheduled to expire in later years so students should check relevant websites for the most recent information.

What level of spending should be required of private foundations and what should be included in the definition of that spending have been sources of debate and legislation in recent years. Unlike public charities, private foundations are not permitted to engage in lobbying. Many nonprofit organizations generally prefer to be classified as public charities in order to avoid the limitations and costs that come with being deemed a private foundation. They will take care to ensure that their revenues are sufficiently diversified and that their activities are consistent with public charity status, which the IRS may sometimes challenge.

Let's add yet another complication! There are funding intermediaries that use the word foundation in their name but are in fact public charities. Some people refer to them as **public foundations**. One type, community foundations, receives gifts from members of a particular community and makes gifts to support a variety of service-providing nonprofits in that community. Another type of foundation that is a public charity is the **institutionally related foundation**. These foundations are the fundraising arms of their host or parent organizations. They are public charities because they solicit and receive gifts from the public, but unlike United Way or community foundations, which make grants to multiple organizations, this type of foundation directs its support to just *one* organization. Such foundations are commonly associated with public universities. For example, the University of Maryland Foundation raises, invests, and manages funds for the state university it serves. Some federal government entities also have affiliated foundations that seek private gifts to supplement the funds that the agency receives through public appropriations. An example of this mentioned earlier is the National Park Foundation, a fundraising entity that supports the National Park Service. And, as in the case of the Sierra Club and the Sierra Club Foundation, there are foundations associated with nonprofit organizations that do not themselves qualify to receive tax-deductible contributions.

To complicate things yet further, there are private foundations that do not make any, or many, grants to other nonprofits and that may not even have the term "foundation" in their names. For example, Colonial Williamsburg, in Virginia, and Longwood Gardens, in Pennsylvania, are legally private foundations, but all of their funds are used to support their own programs and operations. They are thus **operating foundations** rather than grant-making foundations and, with some exceptions, are not sources of financial support for other nonprofits. For these organizations, being a private foundation is a matter of status under the tax law and relates to the source of their support, but their operations may be similar to those of nonprofits that are public charities. Tax law related to private operating foundations is different in some ways from the law related to non-operating private foundations. We will consider foundations again in Chapter 13 as part of our discussion on fundraising. Students who are interested in how foundations are managed will find there are many excellent resources including books as well as the websites of the Foundation Center (www.foundationcenter.org), the Council on Foundations (www.cof.org), and Grantmakers for Effective Organizations (www.geofunders.org), among others.

Salamon's Anatomy

We now have discussed two basic ways of differentiating the nonprofit sector: the NTEE and the classifications of organizations under the IRS code. Let's look at a couple of other ways that scholars have divided up the sector. Both the IRS classifications and the NTEE identify organizations according to the principal activities in which they are engaged. Some people have sought other ways of categorizing nonprofits. A number of scholars have attempted to develop various maps to bring greater clarity to our understanding of the structure of the nonprofit sector along other lines (e.g., Gamwell, 1984; D. H. Smith, 1991; Sumariwalla, 1983; Van Til, 1988, 2000). Among them is Lester Salamon. In his book *America's Nonprofit Sector* (2012a), Salamon divides the universe of U.S. nonprofits into two broad categories, member serving and public serving, and then defines various subcategories on each side of that divide—a design he calls the "anatomy" of the nonprofit sector (p. 30).

As the term implies, **member-serving organizations** exist primarily to secure benefits for the people who belong to them or who support them through dues, membership fees, or other contributions. They include, for example, social and fraternal organizations, business and professional associations, and labor unions. In general, their sources of support and the beneficiaries of their programs are one and the same, although society may benefit indirectly—such as through the improvement of skills among members of a profession that serves the public's needs. These organizations are tax-exempt but not eligible to receive tax-deductible gifts. They are not charitable organizations (although some may have affiliated charitable foundations). Salamon's (2012a) examples of **public-serving organizations** include churches, the charitable and social welfare organizations we have discussed, as well as foundations and other funding intermediaries.[3]

Salamon's anatomy (Salamon, 2012a) provides another useful way to think about the nonprofit sector, classifying nonprofit organizations, not by the nature of their activities, like the IRS or the NTEE, but rather by who receives the principal benefit of those activities. However, while it adds clarity in certain respects, it also raises questions. For example, Salamon (2012a) puts religious congregations in the public-serving category. They surely are tax-exempt and eligible to receive tax-deductible contributions—they are 501(c)(3) organizations—but it seems possible that their activities might more directly serve their own members than the general public. As Salamon (2012a) acknowledges, "The distinction between primarily member-serving and primarily public-serving nonprofit organizations is far from perfect.... Even the member-serving organizations produce some public benefits, and the public-serving organizations often deliver benefits to their members" (p. 31). Despite some shortcomings, Salamon's anatomy has contributed to the vocabulary of the nonprofit field, and it is not unusual to hear people refer to organizations as "member serving" or "public serving."[4]

The Spectrum of Organizations

So far, we have looked at ways of differentiating nonprofit organizations according to their purposes and activities (the IRS classifications and the NTEE), according to who benefits from their activities (Salamon, 2012a member-serving and public-serving categories), and according to their sources and patterns of support (public charities and private foundations). Yet another way to differentiate nonprofits is according to the degree to which they are commercialized—that is, the extent to which they operate like businesses.

In their 2001 book, *Enterprising Nonprofits: A Toolkit for Social Entrepreneurs*, J. Gregory Dees, Jed Emerson, and Peter Economy depict a spectrum of nonprofit organizations (which they call "social enterprises"). Their spectrum is depicted in Table 2.1. Each endpoint on the spectrum represents an extreme—that is, a pure example of two alternative conditions. The spectrum encompasses every possible point in between. In the spectrum of Dees et al., the two extremes are organizations that are "purely philanthropic" and those that are "purely commercial," defined by their "general motives, methods, and goals" and their relationships with their key stakeholders (p. 15). In other words, we might think of those at the left

Table 2.1 The Social Enterprise Spectrum

	Continuum of Options		
	Purely Philanthropic	Hybrid	Purely Commercial
General motives, methods, and goals			
	Appeal to goodwill	Appeal to mixed motives	Appeal to self-interest
	Mission driven	Balance of mission and market	Market driven
	Goal is social value creation	Goal is social and economic value creation	Goal is economic value creation
Key stakeholders			
Beneficiaries	Pay nothing	Pay subsidized rates and/or a mix of full payers and those who pay nothing	Pay full market rates
Providers of capital	Make gifts and grants	Provide below-market capital and/or a mix of below-market capital, market-rate capital, and gifts	Charge market rates
Workforce	Volunteers	Accept below-market wages and/or a mix of volunteers and paid staff	Receive market-rate compensation
Suppliers	Make in-kind gifts	Provide special discounts and/or a mix of full price, discounts, and in-kind gifts	Charge market prices

Source: Adapted from Dees et al. (2001, p. 15). Used with permission of John Wiley & Sons, Inc.

endpoint of the spectrum as the most nonprofit-like and those at the right endpoint as the most businesslike. In between, at various points along the spectrum between the two extremes, are most nonprofit organizations today.

Let's walk through the spectrum of Dees et al. (2001), thinking about three organizations, including two we saw on our hypothetical tour of Washington, DC—Miriam's Kitchen and the George Washington University—and a third that is familiar to all of us, Microsoft Corporation. Even Miriam's, which is close to what most people would think of as a purely philanthropic nonprofit and thus somewhere close to the left end of the spectrum, is not entirely pure according to the criteria of Dees et al. because it does employ paid staff. But it is close enough to serve as an example for our discussion. Microsoft, most would agree, is close to a pure example of a commercial organization, at the right end of the spectrum. The George Washington University is somewhere in between—in the terminology of Dees et al., it is a hybrid that is somewhat nonprofit-like and somewhat like a business. This is true of most private colleges and universities and, in some ways, increasingly true of public universities as well.

What characterizes organizations that are purely philanthropic? As the chart by Dees et al. (2001) indicates, such organizations appeal to goodwill rather than self-interest. People engage with Miriam's Kitchen because they hold compassion and concern for homeless individuals. But few would buy the Windows operating system because Microsoft needs the money! What about universities? They appeal to mixed motives. People do feel altruistic about universities; that's why many alumni continue to make gifts long after they have graduated. But, for most students, attendance at a university is also a practical investment.

Although some may value learning for its own sake, most are likely motivated to study at least in part by self-interest, that is, by interest in their own financial and career futures.

Philanthropic organizations are mission driven. If they are purely philanthropic, then, at least theoretically, they pursue the mission with little regard for the financial bottom line. Although this image may comport with the stereotype that some may hold of nonprofits as organizations run by dedicated volunteers unconcerned with money, an example of that purest form would be somewhat difficult to find in today's nonprofit world, for many of the reasons we already have discussed. On the other hand, Microsoft is unlikely to produce software that nobody wants to buy, regardless of what social value it might serve—it is, like all businesses, market driven. What about a university? Again, most are mixed, balancing commitment to a mission with responsiveness to the market. A university may continue to offer academic programs or to support research efforts that are not profitable, indeed, that even require a subsidy, because they are important to its educational mission. But most universities also respond to the market, developing new programs and expanding others that are attracting increased student interest.

Philanthropic organizations are concerned with creating social value—that is, with improving the lives of individuals and their communities; they are not about making money for its own sake. In contrast, as we have discussed before, the principal goal of a business is to create economic value—in other words, to generate profits and increase its owners' wealth. Again, the hybrids that Dees et al. (2001) define pay almost equal attention to both components of the double bottom line, focusing on the creation of both social and economic value, or in the words of Bill Shore (1999), they may be "doing good by doing well" (p. 110).

Let's look at our three sample organizations' relationships with some of their key stakeholders—their beneficiaries (clients), those who provide them with capital funds, their workforce, and their suppliers. At purely philanthropic organizations, clients pay nothing for the services they receive, like the hundreds of homeless men and women who are served by Miriam's Kitchen. On the other end of the spectrum, people generally pay for their Microsoft software at whatever market price prevails. And hybrids? Let's consider a typical undergraduate classroom in a private university. Some students will be attending on full scholarships—they pay nothing in the way of tuition. Others, from more affluent families, may be paying the full tuition price listed in the university bulletin, while still others will be paying some portion of the listed tuition with scholarships to cover the rest. This is typical of hybrid nonprofits, including universities and hospitals, which often serve a mix of full payers and subsidized clients.

If Miriam's needs capital to expand or meet special organizational needs, it will obtain it through fundraising for gifts or grants. Microsoft will issue new stock or borrow money, paying the full market rate of interest. Hybrids often mix these methods, except, of course, that a nonprofit cannot issue stock. For example, a university may have a campaign to raise capital dollars through gifts but may also borrow funds for the construction of new buildings. Nonprofits sometimes can borrow at less than the market rate of interest, although some will also borrow at the going market rate as well.

The purely philanthropic workforce is composed entirely of volunteers. As we have discussed, this is the case for some small nonprofits, although many (including Miriam's Kitchen) have paid staff members in addition to a substantial volunteer workforce—they are not, in the terminology of Dees et al. (2001), pure. However, it is likely that almost no one volunteers at Microsoft. The company pays market wages and, indeed, competes in the marketplace for talent. Universities, as any professor will testify, are somewhere in between; professors do not work for free, but neither do they earn the salaries their talents might command in a purely commercial enterprise.

How do nonprofits obtain needed supplies? A purely philanthropic nonprofit would have all its supplies contributed; that is, it would receive them through gifts-in-kind. Miriam's does receive such gifts, although it also purchases some of the food it needs for its meal programs. However, it is doubtful that Microsoft ever receives such gifts, and it likely pays the market price for pencils as well as computers (although it may negotiate some discounts based on volume rather than the generosity of its suppliers). As a hybrid, a university may receive some gifts-in-kind, pay market price for some products, and receive educational discounts on others.

Again, it is important to emphasize that the concept of a spectrum includes various points along the line rather than two or three discrete categories, so organizations may be hybrids to a lesser or greater extent. Indeed, the reality in today's nonprofit sector is that relatively few organizations offer an example of the purely philanthropic as the chart by Dees et al. (2001) defines it. Most are hybrids to some degree, even Miriam's Kitchen. Are there examples of purely commercial organizations? Microsoft may come pretty close, but some argue that for-profit businesses are in fact becoming more nonprofit-like. While many nonprofits demonstrate increasing degrees of commercialization—that is, they are moving from left to right across the spectrum of Dees et al., many corporations are becoming more attuned to their social responsibilities, tempering their pursuit of profit at least somewhat with a concern for social value. In terms of the spectrum of Dees et al., they may be moving to the left (no political pun intended!). Because of these movements in both directions across the spectrum, some see a blurring of the nonprofit and for-profit sectors. Some celebrate it, while for others it arouses deep concern. We will return to this point in other contexts later in this text.

Emerging New Models

As our preceding discussion of the spectrum established, the blurring of the nonprofit and for-profit sectors has led to more organizations that generate revenue from both charitable gifts and business ventures and that utilize business methods and approaches in pursuit of their social missions. Some who observe the blurring of the sectors and the emergence of hybrid organizations advocate a new legal framework and a new definition of organizations. In an influential 2009 report, Sabeti describes the increasing use of business methods by nonprofits and the growing responsiveness of business to social concerns, and sees "a new class of organizations with the potential for generating immense economic, social, and environmental benefits ... emerging" (p. 2). Sabeti observes that "organizations within the three sectors [public, for-profit, nonprofit] have been evolving—or converging—toward a fundamentally new organizational landscape that integrates social purposes with business methods" (p. 2). This convergence is creating a new sector, or "fourth sector," that Sabeti thinks "can be consciously developed and expended through broad recognition and engagement" (p. 1). Julie Battilana, Matthew Lee, John Walker, and Cheryl Dorsey (2012) also note the increasing social responsibility of some corporations and nonprofits' growing pursuit of earned income. While for-profit firms create economic value and nonprofits create social value, the authors suggest that a "hybrid ideal" may emerge. As they describe, "This hypothetical organization is fully integrated—everything it does produces both social value and commercial revenue" (Battilana et al., 2012).

Figure 2.2 depicts the relationship of the emerging fourth sector to the public, private (business), and traditional nonprofit sectors. The two relevant variables are the extent to which the organization benefits society or owners and the extent to which its revenues are derived from contributed income (i.e., charitable gifts) or earned income (i.e., commercial activities). This depiction is reminiscent of Dees et al.'s (2001) spectrum, with the addition of vectors showing some of the forces at work in the convergence of the sectors. Those forces include corporations' growing concern with social responsibility, environmental sustainability, transparency, and philanthropy, among others. Government and nonprofits are likewise

Figure 2.2 The Emerging Fourth Sector

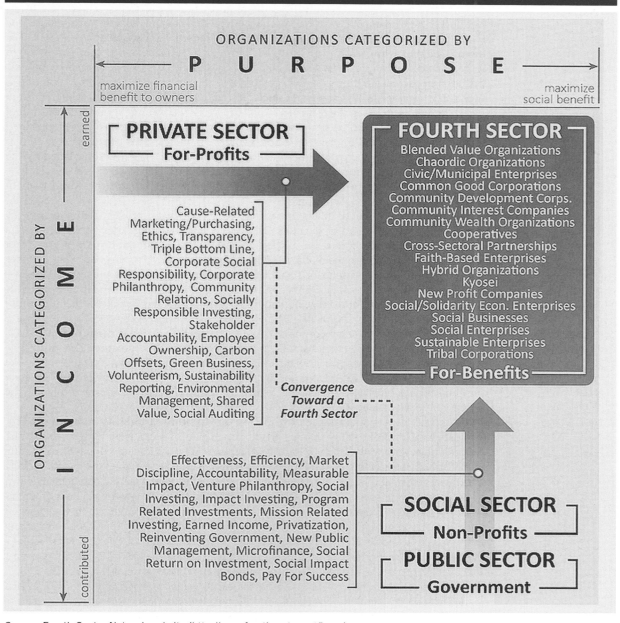

ORGANIZATIONS CATEGORIZED BY
P U R P O S E
maximize financial
benefit to owners

maximize
social benefit

PRIVATE SECTOR
For-Profits

FOURTH SECTOR
Blended Value Organizations
Chaordic Organizations
Civic/Municipal Enterprises
Common Good Corporations
Community Development Corps.
Community Interest Companies
Community Wealth Organizations
Cooperatives
Cross-Sectoral Partnerships
Faith-Based Enterprises
Hybrid Organizations
Kyosei
New Profit Companies
Social/Solidarity Econ. Enterprises
Social Businesses
Social Enterprises
Sustainable Enterprises
Tribal Corporations
For-Benefits

ORGANIZATIONS CATEGORIZED BY
I N C O M E
earned

Cause-Related
Marketing/Purchasing,
Ethics, Transparency,
Triple Bottom Line,
Corporate Social
Responsibility, Corporate
Philanthropy, Community
Relations, Socially
Responsible Investing,
Stakeholder
Accountability, Employee
Ownership, Carbon
Offsets, Green Business,
Volunteerism, Sustainability
Reporting, Environmental
Management, Shared
Value, Social Auditing

*Convergence
Toward a
Fourth Sector*

Effectiveness, Efficiency, Market
Discipline, Accountability, Measurable
Impact, Venture Philanthropy, Social
Investing, Impact Investing, Program
Related Investments, Mission Related
Investing, Earned Income, Privatization,
Reinventing Government, New Public
Management, Microfinance, Social
Return on Investment, Social Impact
Bonds, Pay For Success

SOCIAL SECTOR
Non-Profits

PUBLIC SECTOR
Government

contributed

Source: Fourth Sector Network website (http://www.fourthsector.net/learn).

being moved to change by concerns about transparency, efficiency, and the privatization of many services. These combined forces are thus moving organizations in all three sectors in the direction of the fourth sector, which, as Figure 2.2 depicts, includes various new types of organizations as well as cross-sectoral partnerships and alliances, which we will discuss further in Chapter 8.

While many nonprofit organizations have become commercialized to some extent and, as mentioned earlier, some have established for-profit subsidiaries, some people argue that emergence of the fourth sector requires new legal forms. Three new forms have received the most attention in the United States—the benefit corporation, the social purpose corporation, and the low-profit, limited liability company (L3C). The **benefit corporation** was, as of 2017, recognized in 31 states, with 7 others reported to be considering it ("State by State Status of Legislation," 2017). Social responsibility is included in the corporation's charter, granted by the state, and the benefit corporation is thus a new legal form. It is important to clarify that a benefit corporation is different from a **certified B corp**. A certified B corp is not truly a new corporate legal form, but rather a for-profit business that has been certified as following socially responsible practices and having a positive social impact while engaging in commerce. This certification is similar to the Leadership in Energy & Environmental Design (LEED) certification offered by the U.S. Green Building Council to buildings that encompass green principles. As of 2017, there were 2,140 certified B corps in the United States and around the world (Benefit Corporation Information Center, n.d.).

A benefit corporation differs from that of a regular for-profit corporation in the responsibilities of its board of directors. The benefit corporation charter permits corporate directors to sacrifice profit in order to pursue social purposes, without being concerned that shareholders might accuse them of subverting owners' interests to social goals. That provides the freedom to trade off profit for social benefit without encountering possible legal issues related to the fiduciary responsibilities of the directors. Further, the benefit corporation is required to produce an Annual Benefit Report that assesses the public benefits that it provides (Cordes, Dietz, Steuerle, & Broadus, 2017, p. 280).

The second type of new corporate form is the **social purpose corporation (SPC)**. The SPC has some characteristics similar to those of the benefit corporation. One distinctive feature is the requirement that its mission statement explicitly warn investors that the organization may put social benefits ahead of profits. That provision is intended to strengthen the protection against any shareholder efforts to bring pressure for greater profits at the expense of social benefit (Cordes et al., 2017, p. 281).

A third type of organizational form, the **low-profit, limited liability company (L3C)**, also defines a for-profit entity that has the ability to pursue social goals. The L3C was first created under Vermont law in 2008 and, by 2017, there were 1,533 such companies operating in the United States (InterSector Partners, n.d.). An L3C can accept investments and provide a financial return at a rate below what would be expected from a purely commercial entity, in order to provide social benefits. The original intent of the L3C was to facilitate program-related investments by foundations—that is, to give foundations the ability to invest a portion of their assets in grantee organizations for a modest return, possibly in addition to making outright grants. However, there is no evidence that the creation of the L3C form actually increased such investments by foundations. Indeed, there are critics who question the effectiveness of and the need for the L3C concept at all (Cordes et al., 2017, pp. 278–279).

The use of different legal forms to pursue social goals gained visibility in 2015 when Mark Zuckerberg, founder of Facebook, and his wife Priscilla Chan, announced the creation of the Chan-Zuckerberg Initiative, with an initial pledge of $45 billion (Breen, 2016). Rather than establish a traditional foundation, like Bill and Melinda Gates, Chan and Zuckerberg created an LLC. It is important to understand, however, that the organization established by Chan and Zuckerberg was a business entity (a limited liability company or LLC), not a low-profit limited liability company (L3C) that was just discussed. (See Case 2.1 at the end of this chapter, which discusses the Chan-Zuckerberg Initiative.)

The emergence of new legal forms may represent the true beginning of a fourth sector; however, as Battilana et al. (2012) discuss, there are still a number of challenges faced by hybrid organizations, including the need to obtain financing from either philanthropy or investors. Some observers predict that a new class of investors, called **impact investors**, may come to meet that need. This group includes individuals and organizations willing to accept lower rates of financial return in exchange for social benefits. As Lester Salamon (2014) argues, perhaps a better term would be social-and-environmental-impact investors, since the goal of such investors is not to have just any impact, but rather to "place equal emphasis on the financial and the social and environmental effects [such] investments are supposed to produce" (p. 15). But, as Battilana et al. report, hybrid organizations were still experiencing difficulty in raising capital as recently as 2012. Salamon (2014) likewise acknowledges that the future of the impact-investing concept remains undetermined.

In addition to the challenges of raising funds, hybrids need to face the reality that a nonprofit's customers and beneficiaries may not always be the same people, as they are in a business. As Battilana et al. (2012) observe, "For example, educational programs might increase a child's future earnings, but organizations cannot recoup the child's future wealth. For this and [myriad] other areas addressed by the social sector, integration of customers and beneficiaries may never be possible or desirable." In other words, there may always be a distinction between activities that primarily produce economic value and those that primarily advance social value.

The new legal forms discussed briefly in this chapter are not a major focus of this text, which emphasizes the management of traditional nonprofit organizations. However, even traditional nonprofits pursue earned income through commercial activities and some have become substantially commercialized. Earned income and the related concept of social enterprise are discussed in more detail in Chapter 14.

Some observers consider the increasing use of business methods in nonprofits and their efforts to develop streams of earned income to be desired, reducing their dependence on government and on gifts and increasing their effectiveness. In his influential 1999 book, *The Cathedral Within,* Bill Shore writes that nonprofits "forfeited the marketplace long ago, simply walked off the field … and chose instead to settle for the crumbs instead of the cake" (p. 205). He argues that nonprofits should begin businesses that generate revenue as a way to gain independence from philanthropic giving and government funds. "Redistributing wealth is not going to be enough," Shore says. "Creating new [economic] wealth is the only course for nonprofits and community-based organizations struggling to meet social needs" (p. 208). Shore is the founder of the nonprofit Share Our Strength, an anti-hunger organization based in Washington, DC. Consistent with his own advice, he also created Community Wealth Ventures (now Community Wealth Partners), a for-profit subsidiary of Share Our Strength. Community Wealth Partners earns revenue by advising other nonprofits and directs its profits to help support Share Our Strength's programs. Initially, its advice was focused on how to start revenue-producing businesses, but it now provides a broader range of guidance related to how organizations can affect social transformation. Share Our Strength also has established numerous partnerships with corporations, which produce revenue that is not purely philanthropic. Share Our Strength is the subject of a case study included in the Appendix of this book (Appendix Case 2).

Some observers express concern that the increasing commercialization of the nonprofit sector may lead organizations to put profit ahead of their social missions. For example, Burton Weisbrod (2004), an economist who was a pioneer in studying the nonprofit sector, cites the YMCA, which he says has "morphed into a health-and-fitness goliath" (p. 40). Observing the YMCA's increasing presence in upscale neighborhoods, where it competes with for-profit health clubs, Weisbrod questions whether it has strayed from its traditional mission of serving low-income families and asks "whether it has become overly commercialized and whether it [even] deserves tax-exempt status" (p. 43). He advocates policies to limit the commercial activity of nonprofits while creating stronger tax incentives to encourage traditional charitable and philanthropic giving. Thus, the issue of commercialization is more than philosophical; it has implications for the continued tax-exempt status of some nonprofits. We will revisit some of these issues again in Chapter 14 when we discuss nonprofit earned-income strategies. The YMCA is the focus of a case study included in the Appendix of this book (Appendix Case 3).

Commercialization and Tax Exemption

A companion to the common misunderstanding that nonprofit organizations cannot earn profits is the idea that nonprofits are *always* exempt from taxation. They are exempt from income taxation on revenues related to exempt activities—that is, activities that directly address their social missions. But revenues from activities that are not related to the mission are subject to the **unrelated business income tax (UBIT)**. An activity is unrelated and subject to this tax if it meets three requirements: (1) It is a trade or business, as defined by the IRS; (2) it is regularly carried on; and (3) it is not substantially related to the exempt purpose of the organization. The definition of "substantially related" is provided by the IRS (2016), with characteristic clarity:

> To determine if a business activity is "substantially related" requires examining the relationship between the activities that generate income and the accomplishment of the organization's exempt purpose. Trade or business is related to exempt purposes, in the statutory sense, only when the conduct of the business activities has causal relationship to achieving exempt purposes (other than through the production of income). The causal relationship must be substantial. The activities that generate the income must contribute importantly to accomplishing the organization's exempt purposes to be substantially related.

Activities carried out by volunteers; a trade or business carried out for what the IRS calls the "convenience" of clients or members; and sales of donated merchandise, for example, in a thrift shop, are specifically excluded from UBIT. So, for example, universities generally are not taxed on revenue from dining halls or other food operations since these services are provided for the convenience of students (although it may surprise students to learn this). Similarly, a university parking garage used exclusively by students and faculty would not generate unrelated business income—it is there for convenience and is therefore related to the educational mission. But a garage open to the general public might not meet that test in the view of the IRS. The Tax Cuts and Jobs Act of 2017 included changes in how organizations calculate unrelated business income. The details are beyond the scope of this chapter, but can be found on various websites that explain that legislation.

Most business activities undertaken by nonprofits are related to the mission, and the revenues generated are therefore not taxable. For example, a nonprofit that develops a business to employ individuals with disabilities is serving its mission of providing job training and rehabilitation, even though the services it provides may generate substantial revenue and even compete with the services provided by for-profit companies. But the line is not always clear. For example, one area of dispute has been gift shops operated by museums. If an art museum gift shop sells products that include reproductions of paintings in its exhibits, that could be related to its mission of educating and informing the public about art. But sales of products that are not related to the museum's collections might be regarded as unrelated and subject to the UBIT (IRS, n.d.-c).

One concern is that unrelated business activities could become a substantial part of the organization's activities. If they do—in general, if the amount of the nonprofit's time and resources devoted to the business activity exceeds that devoted to its mission (generally more than 50 percent of activities)—the nonprofit could be in danger of having its tax exemption revoked entirely. The issue of related and unrelated income is far from settled and is often an area of dispute between nonprofits and the IRS. In subsectors where commercialization has advanced the most—for example, health services—the tax exemption of institutions is a topic of continuing political debate. In other words, as a nonprofit becomes more like a commercial enterprise, moving as it were from left to right across the spectrum of Dees et al. (2001), there could come a point at which it will be deemed to have crossed over the line, ceasing to be a nonprofit at all.

Implications for Nonprofit Managers

What are the implications of increasing commercialization, the blurring of the sectors, the emergence of new legal forms, and related policy debates for the practice of nonprofit management? It seems unlikely that new organizational forms will replace traditional nonprofits in the foreseeable future but these trends are changing the landscape, making it more varied and complex. Today's nonprofit sector requires that managers be somewhat hybrids themselves. They must combine a commitment to their organization's nonprofit mission with business skills, to manage the double bottom line. They must hold an appreciation for the nonprofit sector's unique history and traditions while also understanding how to succeed in a competitive marketplace. They must be able to adapt to the social and political forces affecting their organizations while also preserving the core values and defending the special status of their organizations. In other words, as was explained in Chapter 1 of this book, nonprofit management requires a unique blend of skills, distinguishing it from management in government or the for-profit sector. Current trends suggest that the task will not become less challenging in the years ahead.

CHAPTER SUMMARY

America's nonprofit sector is large and diverse. Its roots lie in the ancient traditions of charity, philanthropy, and voluntarism; voluntary efforts were prominent in the nation's early days. But the sector's modern form is a product of 20th-century history and especially the period since the 1970s. Although nonprofit organization and nonprofit sector are the terms most commonly used, others have proposed a variety of alternative names for the sector.

The nonprofit sector is growing steadily. It includes about 1.5 million tax-exempt organizations in the United States that are registered with the Internal Revenue Service and others that are not registered. These organizations may be placed in categories according to the tax-exempt classifications used by the IRS or the more elaborated categories of the National Taxonomy of Exempt Entities (NTEE), both of which determine

categories based on organizations' principal activities. Most organizations registered with the IRS fall into two classifications. Charitable nonprofits are both exempt from income tax under Section 501(c)(3) of the IRC and eligible to receive tax-deductible gifts from individuals and other donors, with some limitations. Social welfare organizations (often called advocacy organizations) are tax-exempt under Section 501(c)(4), but gifts to them are not tax deductible because they are not limited in their expenditures on lobbying activities.

Religious congregations are charitable nonprofits under Section 501(c)(3), but they are unique in being protected by the U.S. Constitution and are not required to register with the IRS, although many do so voluntarily. Leaving aside religious congregations, charitable nonprofits are divisible into subsectors, including arts, culture, and humanities; education; environment and animals; health; human service; international and foreign affairs; and other organizations, including those that provide public and societal benefit. These subsectors show significant differences in their sources of revenue and the extent to which their management has been professionalized. Also important are funding intermediaries, which generally do not operate programs but rather receive gifts that are directed to other nonprofit organizations. They include public charities, such as United Way, and private foundations. Private foundations are charitable nonprofits, but they are not public charities and thus are subject to different rules under the tax code. There are public charities that use the term "foundation" in their name, but they are not classified as private foundations because they raise money from multiple sources.

In addition to the NTEE and IRS classifications, nonprofits may be defined as member serving or public serving. Another way to classify organizations is on a spectrum defining the extent to which they are purely philanthropic or purely commercial. Many nonprofits today are said to be hybrids. They are not purely philanthropic or purely commercial but fall somewhere between those two extremes. This is because they demonstrate a mixture of philanthropic and commercial motives, methods, and goals, and their relationships with their stakeholders demonstrate a mix of philanthropic and business characteristics. Many nonprofits have become more commercial at the same time that some businesses are expressing more concern about social goals. Some see the emergence of hybrid organizations as the beginning of a fourth sector alongside government, business, and traditional nonprofits.

Some business organizations are incorporated as benefit corporations; their charters require social responsibility. Others have been certified as B corps, a designation given to for-profit businesses that follow socially responsible practices in conducting their activities and report on their social impact. The social purpose corporation is another new legal form, which requires the board and management to agree on social purposes. The low-profit, limited liability company (L3C) is a legal form of organization that was first defined in law in Vermont and now exists in other states. Its initial purpose was to facilitate program-related investments from foundations.

Challenges to hybrid organizations include the need to raise funds from either or both philanthropy and financial investors. Investors willing to accept lower financial returns in exchange for social benefits are known as impact investors, but their future importance remains undetermined. Blurring of the sectors pleases some and concerns others, who fear that nonprofits will drift away from their social missions. In this environment, nonprofit management requires a unique combination of commitment, knowledge, and skills.

NOTES

1. The terms nonprofit and tax-exempt are not strictly synonymous, since there are some for-profit entities—for example, certain partnerships—that are also not required to pay income tax, and there are organizations that are required to pay taxes but do not distribute profits to owners (Hopkins, 2005). In addition, "nonprofit" is a status conferred by the charter that an organization receives from its state, while the conditions for tax exemption are defined under tax law.

2. It is a fine but important distinction to understand that the IRS does not "grant" tax exemption to nonprofit organizations. If they meet appropriate criteria, they are tax-exempt under the law. The IRS merely "recognizes" that status conferred by the law (Hopkins, 2005).

3. There is a distinction between religious congregations and nonprofit organizations that are faith-based but provide social services to their communities without regard to religious affiliation.

4. Although we do not focus on member-serving organizations in this book, students who are interested will find a rich array of resources, including those available through the American Society of Association Executives (www.asaenet.org), a professional association comprising trade and professional association managers, which is based in Washington, DC.

KEY TERMS AND CONCEPTS

advocacy organizations 28

benefit corporation 42

certified B corp 42

charitable nonprofits 21

charitable sector 25

charity 22

civil society sector 25

faith-based organizations 32

hybrid organizations 26

impact investors 43

independent sector 24

institutionally related foundation 36

low-profit, limited liability
    company (L3C) 42

member-serving organizations 37

National Taxonomy of Exempt
    Entities (NTEE) 27

nongovernmental organizations 24

operating foundations 36

philanthropy 23

private foundations 35

public charities 35

public foundations 36

public-serving organizations 37

social enterprise 25

social purpose corporation
    (SPC) 42

social welfare organizations 29

tax-exempt sector 25

unrelated business income tax
    (UBIT) 44

voluntarism 23

CASE 2.1 The Chan-Zuckerberg Initiative

Mark Zuckerberg was the first member of his generation, a millennial, to become the CEO of a Fortune 500 company, Facebook. In 2015, Zuckerberg and his wife, Priscilla Chan, announced that they would dedicate 99 percent of their shares of Facebook stock to changing the world. But they would not pursue that goal by establishing a private foundation, following the example of Bill and Melinda Gates and other technology entrepreneurs. Their innovative approach "rocked the philanthropy world" (Baird, 2015).

The Chan-Zuckerberg Initiative would be dedicated to "advancing human potential and promoting equal opportunity" (Chan-Zuckerberg Initiative, 2017), but it would not be a charitable nonprofit. Rather, it would be created as a for-profit limited liability company (LLC). Chan and Zuckerberg would transfer their shares of Facebook stock to the new company. They would not receive an immediate tax deduction, as they would were their personal assets transferred to a foundation. But the LLC would have more flexibility than a nonprofit entity. The new company could change its purpose at any time and would not be required to provide as much transparency as a private foundation (White, 2015). It also would be able to engage in activities that would not be permitted, or that would be more difficult to accomplish, under a nonprofit structure. The LLC could make charitable gifts, but it also would be able to make private investments in for-profit activities, raise private equity, hire lobbyists, become involved in political campaigns, and participate in political debates (Cordes et al., 2017).

Some people welcomed Chan and Zuckerberg's decision as a positive development, noting advantages of the double bottom line approach over traditional philanthropy. In this view, the LLC is better, since it can earn profits and reinvest them into other activities with social benefits, unlike a foundation grant that is "gone for good." If the LLC invests in companies that provide social benefits, those companies may fail, but that is better than maintaining traditional charities, "which can keep going, even if they are not very effective at their work, as long as they are good at raising money from donors" (Lenkowsky, 2015).

But others expressed concerns. Unlike a foundation, the Chan-Zuckerberg Initiative would face no requirement that it give away a percentage of its funds each year. Although Chan and Zuckerberg said that they would use the assets for social good, there was no assurance that they would actually make gifts from the LLC in the future; perhaps they would just run it as a business for their own benefit. Unlike a foundation, the LLC would not have transparency. Some expressed concern about the implications of such consequential resources not being subject to greater accountability to the public. One critic wrote, "This lack of oversight and the ability to freely use funds to affect public policy invisibly become toxic when combined with the growing concentration of wealth in the hands of a small slice of the American public" (Levine, 2015). Another wrote that "such philanthropic approaches smack of colonialism" and even questioned whether the Chan-Zuckerberg pledge posed "a threat to democracy" (McCambridge, 2015b).

Other commentators saw the creation of the Chan-Zuckerberg Initiative as an example of generational change and said that the criticisms reflected "a way of thinking about capital as outdated as telegrams and rotary phones" (Baird, 2015). From this perspective, the Chan-Zuckerberg approach represents the end of "two-pocket thinking," meaning that individuals work to earn profits in one component of their life and then seek to accomplish social change by engaging in philanthropy as a separate activity. The merging of these goals was said to be consistent with the worldview of millennials and an innovation that could be as transformative as the development of Facebook itself (Baird, 2015).

Questions Related to Case 2.1

1. How do you evaluate the arguments for and against the Chan-Zuckerberg Initiative? Does it hold more promise of accomplishing social change than traditional nonprofits or does its lack of transparency and accountability grant too much control to its founders?

2. How does the Chan-Zuckerberg Initiative relate to the social enterprise spectrum and to the fourth sector, concepts discussed in this chapter?

3. Do you think millennials hold a different worldview about philanthropy from those of other generations? If so, why do you think that is the case?

CASE 2.2   A Double Bottom Line: Ben & Jerry's

In 1978, Ben Cohen and Jerry Greenfield made a $12,000 investment and opened an ice cream company, originally called Ben & Jerry's Homemade. Their goal was to make a profit and also pursue a social mission. As Greenfield expressed it, "We measured our success not just by how much money we made, but by how much we contributed to the community. It was a two-part bottom line" (Folino, 2010). Some people called this approach "Ben & Jerry's double dip" (Page & Katz, 2012).

The company grew through the 1980s and 1990s and remained committed to the social mission of its founders. With the creation of the Ben & Jerry's Foundation in 1985, the company gave 7.5 percent of its pretax profits to community-oriented projects. Its operations emphasized environmental sustainability, and it followed enlightened employment and community-relations policies.

By 1984, the company was in need of capital for expansion and undertook a public stock offering. This meant that it now had public shareholders (Folino, 2010). By 1999, the stock had fallen from $34 to $17, and some observers said that Ben & Jerry's management style did not include the discipline that investors demanded (Caligiuri, 2012). Pressure began to build to do something that would satisfy critical shareholders. In 2000, Ben & Jerry's announced that it was being acquired by Unilever, a large multinational corporation.

The new owners offered assurance that Ben & Jerry's would remain committed to its social mission and that it would operate as an autonomous unit of Unilever, with its own board, including the founders. Unilever made a substantial gift to the Ben & Jerry's Foundation and pledged to continue its social commitment while also making the company profitable (Hayes, 2000).

Since 2000, Ben & Jerry's has continued to follow many of the principles of its founders, who also have personally supported many political and social causes. However, some critics have claimed to observe compromises with regard to the company's social values, even before the sale to Unilever, driven by the need to earn a profit. For example, one wrote that "much of Ben & Jerry's tie-dyed approach to life has vanished, replaced by a philosophy in which balance-sheet priorities have gained the upper hand" (Hayes, 1998). Others cited the decision to discontinue some products that were deemed unprofitable as proof that the social mission had been de-emphasized (Page & Katz, 2012).

It was reported that cofounder Ben Cohen and some members of Ben & Jerry's board had opposed the sale to Unilever. However, some argued that Ben & Jerry's board had no choice but to sell the company to the highest bidder, which was Unilever. This was based on the legal responsibility of a public company board of directors to maximize returns to shareholders. Some offered the case as evidence that a traditional business corporation model is "inhospitable, if not outright hostile" (Page & Katz, 2012) to the pursuit of social goals. This understanding of the Ben & Jerry's case is advanced by some who advocate the need for new corporate forms, such as the benefit corporation, that would permit corporate directors to weigh social goals equally with profits to shareholders. However, other legal scholars argue that corporate law did not require the sale. Some critics have speculated that the sale was dictated by the founders' desire to "cash out" (Page & Katz, 2012).

In 2012, Ben & Jerry's became the first wholly owned subsidiary of a multinational corporation to become a certified B corp, a step that was supported by Unilever (Field, 2012). B Corps are required to produce an annual impact report, which scores the company on the criteria of environment, treatment of workers, customers, community, and governance. Ben & Jerry's 2017 report showed a total score of 100, compared with the median of 55 (B Lab, 2017). An explanation of the criteria and scoring methods is available on the B Lab website (https://www.bcorporation.net/community/ben-and-jerrys).

Questions Related to Case 2.2

1. In your opinion, is it realistic for a public, for-profit corporation to remain committed to social purposes, or will the demands of shareholders and investors for maximum profit inevitably win out over time?

2. Depending on your answer to question 1, are the new legal forms discussed in this chapter required in order to permit a double bottom line approach?

3. Do the rating criteria for B Corps, summarized in the Ben & Jerry's case (and further discussed on the B Lab website), cover everything that should be considered or are there additional criteria that you would add?

QUESTIONS FOR DISCUSSION

1. If you had $25 to give today to any nonprofit organization, which one would it be? Now, imagine that you are 75 years old and have $1,000,000 to give to an organization at the event of your death—that is, through your will. Which one would it be? Do your answers reflect a difference between charity and philanthropy?

2. If you were the president of an independent (nonprofit) college or university, what things would you consider in making a decision on a possible tuition increase, which might enhance your bottom line but possibly work against your mission of providing educational opportunity?

3. Should gifts made by individuals to a nonprofit organization that receives the largest portion of its revenues from fees for services be fully tax deductible, partially tax deductible, or not deductible at all? Explain your answer.

4. Suppose a nonprofit organization operates a business that is related to its mission, such that revenue is not subject to the UBIT, but it competes directly with a for-profit business nearby that must pay taxes. For example, think about a nonprofit bookstore that is near another bookstore run by private owners as a for-profit business. Is that unfair competition with the for-profit businesses? Should the nonprofit be taxed just to level the playing field? Why or why not?

SUGGESTIONS FOR FURTHER READING

Books

Hopkins, B. R. (2013). *Starting and managing a nonprofit organization: A legal guide* (6th ed.). Hoboken, NJ: Wiley.

Lane, M. J. (2015). *The mission-driven venture: Business solutions to the world's most vexing social problems.* Hoboken, NJ: Wiley.

Ott, J. S., & Dicke, L. A. (Eds.). (2016). *The nature of the nonprofit sector* (3rd ed.). Boulder, CO: Westview.

Salamon, L. M. (Ed.). (2015). *New frontiers of philanthropy: A guide to the new tools and new actors that are reshaping global philanthropy and social investing.* New York, NY: Oxford University Press.

Articles/Book Chapters

Battilana, J., Lee, M., Walker, J., & Dorsey, C. (2012, Summer). In search of the hybrid ideal. *Stanford Social Innovation Review.* Retrieved from http://www.ssireview.org/articles/entry/in_search_of_the_hybrid_ideal

Brest, P., & Born, K. (2013, Fall). When can impact investing create real impact? *Stanford Social Innovation Review.* Retrieved from http://www.ssireview.org/up_for_debate/article/impact_investing

Cordes, J., Dietz, N., Steuerle, C. E., & Broadus, E. (2017). New ways of creating social value: Hybrids. In E. T. Boris & C. E. Steuerle (Eds.), *Nonprofits and government: Collaboration and conflict* (pp. 263–290). Lanham, MD: Rowman & Littlefield/ Urban Institute Press.

Miller, C. (2016, July 1). Millennials and hybrid legal structures are here to stay. *Stanford Social Innovation Review.* Retrieved from https://ssir.org/articles/entry/millennials_and_hybrid_legal_structures_are_here_to_stay

Websites

Alliance for Nonprofit Management: www.allianceonline.org/

Aspen Institute Program on Philanthropy and Social Innovation: www.aspeninstitute.org/policy-work/nonprofit-philanthropy

B Corporation: www.bcorporation.net

Fourth Sector: www.fourthsector.net

Independent Sector: www.independentsector.org

Urban Institute Center on Nonprofits and Philanthropy: https://www.urban.org/policy-centers/center-nonprofits-and-philanthropy

The freedom of speech, religion, assembly, and petition, enshrined in the First Amendment of the U.S. Constitution, have supported voluntary action by nonprofit organizations on issues such as civil rights, women's rights, and the environment. Nonprofits often have focused public attention and helped create changes in social attitudes that paved the way for eventual legislation.

iStock/diane39

Chapter Outline

Theories of the Nonprofit Sector and Nonprofit Organizations

In this chapter, we will discuss some theoretical views of the nonprofit sector and nonprofit organizations, as a foundation for consideration of more applied management topics in later chapters. We will first examine some macro theories advanced by scholars from various disciplines. These theories attempt to explain the nonprofit sector as a whole, addressing questions such as why the nonprofit sector exists at all in the United States; what role it plays in American society; and what relationship it has to the other two sectors, private business and government. In the second section of the chapter, we will consider some micro theories—that is, theories that attempt to explain nonprofit organizations as individual units. These will include concepts drawn from organizational theory that help explain why nonprofit organizations look and behave the way they do, how they make decisions, and how they are different from both public and for-profit organizations.[1]

Explaining the Nonprofit Sector

Theories that seek to explain America's nonprofit sector have been developed by economists, sociologists, historians, political scientists, psychologists, social psychologists, anthropologists, and scholars in other disciplines. As we will discuss, some theories are at odds with others, and each theory has its advocates as well as critics. Some prominent theories are discussed in this chapter and are summarized in Box 3.1. This chapter provides just a sample of the most prominent theories, rather than an exhaustive overview.

Nonprofit Theory Across the Disciplines

Historians explain the existence of America's nonprofit sector as largely a result of historical forces and events. As noted in Chapter 2, the growth of America's nonprofit sector closely parallels the development of the nation itself. The nation was founded in rebellion against the authority of the British monarch, and skepticism toward government is deeply embedded in American political attitudes. Moreover, many American towns

Learning Objectives

After reading this chapter, students should be able to:

1. Summarize key theories from various disciplines that explain the nonprofit sector.

2. Define public, private, and common goods and the role of nonprofit organizations in providing them.

3. Summarize key theories explaining the behavior of nonprofit organizations.

4. Explain factors influencing the organizational structure of organizations.

5. Analyze cases, applying concepts from the chapter.

History	The nonprofit sector reflects voluntary traditions of early America, changing social needs arising from various historical movements, and the tax structure as it has evolved throughout U.S. history.
Sociology	Involvement in nonprofits helps socialize individuals, reinforce norms and values, and develop social capital. Nonprofits are mediating structures that help people interact with large bureaucracies, such as government and business.
Political science	Nonprofits exist to accommodate diversity, undertake social experimentation, provide freedom from bureaucracy, and address minority needs.
Economics	Nonprofit organizations fill gaps left by market failure and government failure. (There also is voluntary failure, often attributable to the inability of nonprofits to secure adequate resources.) Some nonprofits arise because of action on the supply side, that is, social entrepreneurs or donors who are motivated to solve a problem or promote a cause. Because clients or consumers may not have full information about the products or services offered (information asymmetry), they may prefer nonprofit providers because of greater trust.
Interdisciplinary	Lohmann's theory of the commons defines common goods as a separate category, distinct from private and public goods. At least some nonprofits exist to provide common goods to groups of individuals who share an interest in them.

and cities developed before local governments did, and vital services often were provided by voluntary associations, including volunteer fire departments, libraries, schools, and hospitals. In the small towns of early America, people came together to meet common needs and provide for the poor, their voluntarism often reflecting religious convictions. Religion played an important role in colonial America, and missionary and charitable organizations were often founded by a religious congregation. The freedoms of speech, religion, assembly, and petition, enshrined in the First Amendment to the U.S. Constitution, also have created a hospitable environment for voluntary action throughout the nation's history, especially for organizations seeking social change. For example, the civil rights and women's rights movements focused public attention on injustices and helped create changes in social attitudes that paved the way for legislative action. Nonprofits have taken the lead in raising environmental concerns that are now receiving attention from governments and international agencies around the world.

As the nation grew, movements such as urbanization, industrialization, and immigration increased the need for nonprofit organizations to serve diverse populations. The evolution of U.S. law further supported the growth of the nonprofit sector. The income tax was introduced in 1913, and Congress approved tax deductibility for gifts to certain nonprofits four years later (Arnsberger, Ludlum, Riley, & Stanton, 2011). Changes in public policy, including the expansion of government social programs in the 1960s and 1970s and their reduction and devolvement in the 1980s and 1990s, also have shaped today's nonprofit sector. In sum, historians explain today's nonprofit sector as a consequence of America's unique past, critical historical movements and events, and policies that tended to reinforce the sector's development and growth.

Theories advanced by sociologists, who focus on relationships between and among people in groups, also offer important insights on the nonprofit sector. Sociologists' theories describe how involvement in nonprofits helps socialize individuals, reinforce norms and values, and develop "social capital," creating "interpersonal bonds of trust and cooperation and counteracting loneliness and isolation" (O'Neill, 2002, p. 42). Their theories emphasize "the roles of community networks of individuals, groups, and organizations and the importance of community elites and influentials for nonprofits" (Ott & Dicke, 2016, p. 183). Sociologists also discuss nonprofits as mediating structures, operating as buffers between individuals and the larger institutions of government and business. Berger and Neuhaus, in their influential book, *To Empower People: The Role of Mediating Structures in Public Policy* (1977), argued that in our complex society, people need organizations like nonprofits to provide such interfaces. Political scientists have looked at nonprofit organizations with respect to their role in supporting democratic traditions and in terms of power relationships between citizens and government. They have identified four major functions that nonprofits perform in relation to government:

1. *Accommodate diversity:* Nonprofits give voice to groups with differing values, beliefs, and practices that cannot be fully accommodated within government, with its obligation to treat all citizens equally.

2. *Undertake experimentation:* Nonprofits can undertake research and development (or "R&D") for social programs. In other words, nonprofits can begin new programs on a smaller scale and incur greater risk than government can with public funds. New programs developed by nonprofits that prove to be successful then may provide models and eventually be incorporated into larger government efforts.

3. *Provide freedom from bureaucracy:* Nonprofits may be able to respond more efficiently and quickly to new needs because they do not have the large bureaucracies that characterize government.

4. *Attention to minority needs:* Government's priorities must be consistent with those of the majority of voters. There may not be political support for programs to meet the needs of minority groups that do not possess sufficient political power. Nonprofits fill such gaps created by political realities (Douglas, 1983, 1987).

Economists have made significant contributions to theories of the nonprofit sector, but as Ott and Dicke (2016) note, "Nonprofit organizations provide an interesting challenge for mainstream economic theory" (p. 106). Economists analyze the working of markets in terms of the variables of supply and demand and based on certain assumptions about human nature that nonprofits, at least on the surface of things, would seem to defy. How can we explain labor markets in which people work without compensation or the seemingly irrational act of giving away one's money?

The Failure Theories

Let's start by defining a few terms before we discuss economic theories of the nonprofit sector. Some key concepts include private goods, public goods, externalities, and free riders.

By *goods*, economists mean what we conventionally think of as goods—that is, products that are things—but they also include services and intangible benefits, such as our enjoyment of a symphony, the knowledge we acquire through education, and the solace we may gain from participation in religious services.

Working on the principle of supply and demand, the market is an efficient mechanism for regulating the production and distribution of what are called **private goods**—that is, products or services that we buy and consume as individuals, with no significant impact on others. These would include, for example, the clothing and food that we buy and consume, as well as the services that we personally receive, such as haircuts or personal training sessions at a health club. With a private good, the person who pays also gains the full benefit of the good. Unless you choose to lend your friend your shirt or share your fries, enjoyment of the good is all yours and society is not significantly affected by your consumption of it. The market works well for private goods, because we as consumers vote with our dollars. In other words, we buy the products we like and allow others to sit on the shelves; ultimately, the latter will disappear from the market. The market thus determines—very efficiently and effectively— what private goods are produced and who consumes them.

But some goods have what economists call **externalities**: Very simply, their consumption affects other people, either negatively or positively. For example, your new barbeque grill may bring great pleasure to you and your cookout guests, but its smoke may annoy your neighbors. The smoke is a negative externality. On the other hand, if you beautify your yard, the shrubs and flowers you purchase and plant may create a positive externality for your neighbors—an improved neighborhood and perhaps enhanced property values.

Some goods create so many positive externalities that it is not possible to confine the benefits to an individual purchaser. For example, if you were to hire a private contractor to pave your street, your neighbors also would benefit from a smoother ride but without paying for it. You would be paying the full costs of such improvement, even though your neighbors would benefit as well. In other words, there would be a disconnect between the cost that you would incur and the portion of the benefit you would receive. Your neighbors might say "thanks," but you might perceive the situation as unfair.

In situations like that—the privately funded street paving—those who benefit without paying are known as **free riders**. They benefit from your expenditure at no cost to them— you are paying the fare, and they are just riding along for free! Who would be willing to spend his or her resources under such circumstances? Well, just about nobody, so the market is not a very good mechanism for ensuring that such goods will be produced at all. Therefore, when there is a potential problem with free riders, we as a society may decide that the good should be provided by government; in other words, we treat it as a public good.[2] This is clearly a fairer way to provide **public goods** than leaving their production to the market. In this way, because everyone (or a large group of people) benefits, everyone is forced to pay for these goods through the tax system.

To sum it up, then, if the purchaser is able to capture all the externalities, it makes sense to have a product provided through the free market—to treat it as a private good. But if the externalities are so great that the good also will benefit many others who do not pay—the free riders—then the market is unlikely to provide it, and it should be provided as a public good.

Market and Government Failure

One problem is that, in some situations, the market does not work effectively or efficiently. Economists call this **market failure** (Hansmann, 1987; Weisbrod, 1975, 1988). There are various reasons why the market may fail. For example, there may be a type of market failure that economists call **contract failure**, essentially a breakdown in the ideal or typical relationship between a buyer and a seller. This may occur when there is **information asymmetry**, meaning a situation in which the seller has more information about the product than does the purchaser, undermining the economic assumption that exchanges occur with complete knowledge on both sides of the deal.

Information asymmetry might be especially likely to occur in the case of complex or intangible products. For example, it is difficult for a person to judge the actual quality of the education or medical care he or she is receiving (Young, 2016a). Moreover, in some cases, the purchaser may actually be a different person from the one who is receiving the service— for example, parents who pay the tuition fees for their children's college education or adult children who pay for parents' nursing home care. In these instances, it may be difficult for the purchaser to obtain accurate information, even from the consumer, about the actual quality of the good or service being provided. The market also does not work well for people who are poor or belong to groups that face discrimination, since they may not have the resources with which to purchase what they need or may face other barriers.

In situations where the market does not work, government often steps in to fill the gap. But there also may be **government failure**. This is meant to imply not that government is incompetent, but rather that there are political, structural, and systemic reasons that may prevent the government from filling the gaps left by the private market.

Among those reasons is the fact that government must by its nature respond to the needs and demands of the majority. Weisbrod (1975, 1988), who is credited with introducing the public-goods theory of nonprofits, discusses the concepts of "demand heterogeneity" and the "median voter." In the simplest terms, **demand heterogeneity** means that in a diverse society such as the United States, there may not be universal agreement about what goods and services government should provide. Various groups may want different kinds or different amounts of some goods. The **median voter**, that is, one of the typical voters who comprise the largest single bloc, may not support some of the governmental activity that other groups may favor.

Government may be unable to provide services that some may desire but that are politically controversial—for example, family planning services for poor women. Or the problem may not yet be recognized as relevant to the majority—as, for example, AIDS in the first years of the pandemic in the early 1980s—and thus not command the attention of government.

Government also might fail to fill the gaps left by the private market because the time horizon of elected officials is often short; they need to focus on issues of current concern to the electorate and on policies that can show progress within their terms in office. They may not be able to find political support for undertaking solutions to problems or issues that require many years to come to fruition. For example, some people do not accept the idea of global warming, and others do not think much about it because its most serious implications seem far in the future. It is not a problem that the market can easily address, and while public awareness of the problem is growing, until quite recently, there has not been a political consensus for strong government action and the subject remains controversial.

Finally, government agencies are of necessity often large and bureaucratic; as a result, they may not have complete information, especially on local problems, and their size may make it difficult to undertake quick action. Their perceived bureaucracy also may inhibit individuals from interacting with them, thus limiting government's ability to meet needs and leaving gaps that are unaddressed by either the market or government. Who can fill such gaps?

Nonprofits as Gap Fillers

In the context of the failure theories, nonprofit organizations are essentially gap fillers—they fill the gaps left by market failure and government failure, providing the goods and services that the other two sectors, for whatever reasons, could not. As Howard Berman (2010) explains, the nonprofit sector (what he calls the "community sector") is "society's solution for filling the gap between the needs of various communities and the aggregate of what the public sector is enabled to do plus what the private sector is willing to do" (p. 191).

For example, maybe the market has failed because of information asymmetry: Individuals just do not have complete information or lack the ability to understand or judge the quality of the good they seek to purchase. In such circumstances, they may choose to receive services from a nonprofit. Students may choose to enroll at a nonprofit (or public) university rather than a for-profit school. Adult children may prefer to entrust their aging parents' care to a church-sponsored nursing home rather than one operated by a for-profit company.

They may do so because they believe that the non-distribution constraint removes the motive to exploit consumers, because they believe that nonprofit leaders are driven more by altruistic motivations than are for-profit managers, or because they do not trust for-profit providers for some other reason. This thinking, known as the **trust theory** of nonprofits, has been developed over the past three decades by various scholars, including Hansmann (1987), who is often credited for it.

As we have noted, sometimes government is simply too constrained by its size and complexity to respond quickly, especially in situations that may affect only a small group of people or a single community. For example, while the federal or state governments may respond to major disasters, nonprofit relief organizations like the Red Cross or Salvation Army may be more nimble in responding to the needs of victims in smaller, local disasters, such as an individual house fire or local flooding (Salamon, 2012a). It is important to note, however, that economists also identify a third failure—**voluntary failure**—which may occur if nonprofits are simply unable to obtain the resources necessary to meet the need (Anheier, 2014, p. 201).

Nonprofit organizations also provide a buffer between individuals and large government agencies, which people may find difficult to access. For example, organizations that serve immigrants, the mentally ill, and the homeless help them to access government programs that may provide benefits—a task that some would find daunting on their own (Young, 2016b). In these instances, nonprofits are also gap fillers, filling the gap between people and the information and services they need.

In essence, the failure theories' explanation of the existence of nonprofits is parallel to the vocabulary issue we discussed in Chapter 2. Just as the term nonprofit connotes what such organizations are not, the failure theories explain their role by what others do not do; that is, nonprofits serve needs that the private market and government, for various reasons, do not meet. Although they enjoy wide support, the failure theories leave unanswered questions: How do we explain industries in which both nonprofits and government provide services (e.g., education)? Or in which nonprofits and for-profits compete side by side (e.g., in health care)? Moreover, some critics dismiss the failure theories as missing the unique and positive realities of nonprofit values, motivations, and contributions to society (Ott & Dicke, 2016). For example, Lohmann (1992), whose theory we will soon discuss, mentions activities such as worship, contemplation, help, inquiry, self-expression, and other purposes served by the nonprofit sector, arguing that "any theory of economics that reduces [such] goods to the basic categories of production, consumption, and exchange is reductionist and misleading" (p. 62).

Supply-Side Theories

Before we conclude our discussion of economic theories, it is important to consider other approaches that go beyond the failure theories and explain the existence of the nonprofit sector based on supply-side forces. In economics, a **supply-side theory** explains events based on the motivations of and incentives given to those who produce a good or a service rather than on the motivations of those who have the capability and desire to consume it—which constitutes demand. In other words, supply-side theories look at the *push* side of the market rather than the *pull*.

Supply-side nonprofit theorists observe that many nonprofits are, either currently or historically, outgrowths of religious congregations, motivated by faith rather than primarily economic incentives. Thus, we cannot explain them by market forces alone; rather, we need to consider what is known as the **entrepreneurship theory** of the nonprofit sector. This theory attributes the existence of nonprofit organizations to the vision and initiative of individuals who have created and built them. Such individuals are often motivated by religious zeal or strong secular values of idealism and social justice (James, 1987; Rose-Ackerman, 1996; Young, 1983). Indeed, a study by Child, Witesman, and Braudt (2014) found that individuals who create new organizations with social purposes base their choices about whether to establish a nonprofit or for-profit on their moral and philosophical values as well as pragmatic business judgments related to the advantages of various corporate forms. It is important to note that this entrepreneurship theory of nonprofits is not synonymous with social entrepreneurship, as that term is commonly used. However, supply-side theories are implicit in much contemporary writing about social entrepreneurship. For example, Ashoka (n.d.-a), an organization that provides support for promising social entrepreneurs around the world, points to the power of such individuals to lead fundamental change:

> Social entrepreneurs are individuals with innovative solutions to society's most pressing social, cultural, and environmental challenges. They are ambitious and persistent, tackling major issues and offering new ideas for systems-level change.

Supply-side explanations complement the theories of market and government failure by defining nonprofits as more than gap fillers. They suggest that nonprofits exist not just to pick up the pieces left behind by the market and government, but also as organizations different from business and government that are driven by vision and values. We will return to a more detailed discussion of social entrepreneurship, defined as innovation, in Chapter 16 of this text.

Theories of Altruism and Giving

Some scholars offer theories to explain the nonprofit sector based on the motivations underlying altruism and philanthropic giving. We consider them at this point in the text because their perspective is similar to that of the supply-side theorists. That is, they focus not on those who consume the goods and services that nonprofits provide (the demand side), but rather on those who supply the funds to support the work of nonprofits. Theories related to altruistic behavior and giving predate the nonprofit theories of economists and continue to be a focus of scholars. They are drawn from the work of philosophers, theologians, and legal scholars as well as psychologists, social psychologists, and other social scientists.

Marilyn Fischer (2000, pp. 10–12) calls the nonprofit sector the "gift economy" because it is often supported through voluntary gifts and donors do not receive a quid pro quo, as they do when they purchase a product in the marketplace. Rather, the benefit of their gift payment goes to others, who are served by the organization's programs. But theorists who focus on charitable and philanthropic giving raise the following questions: Do people really make gifts based on altruism or is giving a social exchange, in which the donor receives benefits that include warm feelings and recognition? And what influence do tax benefits play in the motivation of individuals to make gifts? In other words, is charitable and philanthropic giving always motivated by ideals, or do donors also expect to receive some benefits for themselves?

Research provides evidence for mixed motives, both altruistic and self-interested (Worth, 2016, pp. 68–69). As Schervish (2009) argues, we do not necessarily need to subscribe to "either the elegant framework of rational choice theory or the civilized framework of altruism" (p. 36). In other words, a donor may give for a combination of reasons, some altruistic and some pragmatic. We will consider donor motivations again in Chapter 13 of this book when we discuss philanthropic fundraising.

Theory of the Commons: An Interdisciplinary Approach

Roger Lohmann's *The Commons,* published in 1992, presents an interdisciplinary theory of the nonprofit sector that offers a different perspective and introduces some new vocabulary with which to discuss the sector. Lohmann challenges the economists' failure theories directly.

Lohmann (1992) uses the term commons in various ways. In some contexts, commons refers to nonprofit organizations themselves. But used more abstractly, the commons comprises a "protected space for the collective expression of what people find most important in their lives" (Van Til, 1992, p. xi) or "an economic, political, and social space outside the market, households, and state in which associative communities create and reproduce social worlds" (Lohmann, 1992, p. 59).

In his **theory of the commons**, Lohmann (1992) argues that common goods are a third category, alongside private goods (provided through the market) and public goods (provided by government). Nonprofits are not just making up for the failure of the market and government—they are not just gap fillers. Rather, they produce a distinctive third kind of good—common goods. How are common goods different from private and public goods? Unlike private goods, common goods cannot be consumed alone by an individual. But neither are they of interest or benefit to all people, like public goods. As Lohmann (1992) explains,

> Whereas a private good benefits only the individual who consumes it and a public good benefits all of society, common goods benefit (or are of interest to) all the members of the particular commons but possibly not those beyond. This helps explain how organizations that may hold entirely opposite positions or goals can coexist. The "good" of one common may be viewed as a "bad" by members of another common, but the existence of the commons fosters social and political pluralism. (p. 18)

Lohmann's (1992) theory is not universally accepted, and indeed, he has offered concessions, clarifications, and modifications in subsequent writing (e.g., Lohmann, 2015). Economists in particular take issue with his criticisms of their theories. For example, Dollery and Wallis (2003) write that, "compared to sociological and other non-economic theories of the voluntary sector, economic theorizing represents a rather rare success story in the conceptual analysis of voluntary organizations" (p. 34). While Lohmann's theory offers useful insights, his concession that traditional economic theories *do* apply to nonprofits that rely substantially on earned income is a significant one, especially since earned income is the predominant source of revenue for the sector overall and for many of its largest organizations. His examples of commons include many organizations that would fit Salamon's (2012a) member-serving category—for example, associations of bird-watchers or car collectors and amateur athletic leagues—rather than the commercialized nonprofits that are an increasingly large component of the sector. But, like the supply-side economic theorists and those who identify altruistic motivations of donors, he succeeds in arguing that the failure theories do not provide a complete explanation for the nonprofit sector and in establishing the importance of shared values and purposes among those who participate in the sector's work.

Changing Definitions of Private, Public, and Common

Now that we have established the concepts of private, public, and common goods, how can they be applied to better understand today's nonprofit sector and explain some of the changes that we already have observed—for example, commercialization within the nonprofit sector and the shifting roles of government?

Clearly, if private goods benefit only their consumers, then they should be paid for by the individuals who use them. Public goods benefit everyone, and payment is thus compelled from all through the tax system. And common goods, because they are of interest or benefit only to members of the particular commons, should be funded by members of that particular commons. Most would agree on these simple rules, but there is often disagreement on the details and debate about whether certain goods should be considered private, public, or common. None are likely to disagree that military defense is a public good to be provided by government or that a soft drink is a private good that should be paid for by the individual who consumes it. And most would agree that religious worship fits Lohmann's (1992) concept of a common good, that churches, synagogues, and mosques should be sustained by adherents of their respective faiths collectively rather than through appropriated public funds. But for other goods, there may be disagreement, and public attitudes may change over time.

For example, where should we place health care? In many nations, it is considered a public good, to be provided to everyone through government programs. In the United States, health care has the characteristics of private, common, and public goods. Government programs support health care for some members of society, so we regard it at least in part as a public good. But nonprofit hospitals are supported in part through philanthropic gifts from members of the community they serve, as if they are common goods. Some analysts call for greater privatization of health care, in the belief that giving consumers more control will increase efficiency, reduce unnecessary treatment, and bring down costs. So some regard medical care as primarily a private good, at least in part. These viewpoints were evident in the debates in the U.S. Congress and across the country that preceded passage of the Patient Protection and Affordable Care Act in 2010 and that have continued since. These debates will likely continue in one form or another because they reflect fundamentally different philosophies about the nature of health care as a good.

Historically, K–12 education has been considered a public good in the United States, based on the belief that an educated citizenry is of benefit to all of society because it is essential to a successful democracy and a healthy economy. In early U.S. history, higher education was a private good. But beginning with the founding of the land grant universities in the mid-19th century and until recent decades, higher education was increasingly treated as a public good. State support of public universities, the establishment of community colleges, and federal assistance to colleges and universities and their students sought to make higher education more like K–12, accessible and affordable to anyone with the ability to succeed—like a public good. Indeed, some do argue that a college should be free, the same as K–12 education. But in the past three decades, higher education has come to be considered more like a private good, with government support for higher education declining in many states, and students and their families being expected to shoulder an increasing portion of the cost. In other words, opinion has swung more to the view that higher education is primarily an investment made by an individual and his or her family, with the benefits accruing mostly to that individual in the form of higher income. However, government support continues and, indeed, many education loans are government subsidized, so higher education is also viewed as a public good. It is also a common good, since educational institutions are supported in part through contributions from individuals who share an interest in them, like religious congregations.

Most people today probably think of highways as a public good, but in the nation's early days, it was not uncommon for roads to be developed by private interests. There have been private toll roads built in some states in recent years, with the tolls going to provide a return to investors (Mildenberg, 2013). The spread of EZPass, which permits drivers to automatically pay tolls through a transponder mounted on their vehicles, is perhaps a step toward a system in which the consumption of highways, bridges, and tunnels will increasingly be charged to users like a private good. And what are we to make of the Blue Ridge Parkway Foundation (www.brpfoundation.org), a "professional fundraising organization" established to help fund projects to improve a road owned and operated by the National Park Service? Are roads public, private, or common goods? When national parks that were previously free start to charge admission fees, it represents some movement of the good they provide from the public toward the private sphere. And when foundations are created to raise funds for the support of public parks, it begins to give them characteristics more like those of common goods. When a performing arts center that is primarily supported through audience fees and philanthropic gifts receives a government grant, it has moved from somewhere between private and common to a position that is some blend of private, common, and public. Again, we find that boundaries are not always clear, definitions are not always fixed, and thinking can change over time.

Lohmann (1992) suggests that public support for what are in reality common goods is often provided in response to "appeals by various leisure classes for tax-supported patronage of particular common goods valued by those leisure classes" (p. 187). He explains that such appeals are often based on the argument that there is an indirect benefit to society. For example, advocates for greater public support of higher education might argue that there is a benefit to all citizens in having well-educated leaders, although the students who attend universities may be the primary beneficiaries of the education they receive there. Similarly, arts patrons might advocate for public support of the arts because they provide an indirect benefit to society, not just to those who participate as their patrons. Lohmann disputes such arguments, saying that such claims are "demonstrably untrue, simply by virtue of the fact that many people never even attend artistic performances" (p. 186).

As attitudes of the public and its political leaders change over time, goods may come to be viewed as more public, more private, or more common—in varying combinations—and the roles of business, government, and nonprofits will evolve to reflect that new philosophical and political landscape. The debate about the proper nature of certain goods and services has been taking place since the founding of the United States and is likely to continue. It is a central issue in differing political views and affiliations.

Explaining Nonprofit Organizations

The theories we have been discussing so far in this chapter are macro theories—they attempt to explain why nonprofit organizations exist and what role they play in our society. We now will shift our discussion to micro theories, theories that look inside nonprofit organizations and attempt to explain why they behave the way they do and make the decisions they make—how we can understand them as organizations. This discussion will include a look at the characteristics of nonprofit organizations, a review of some concepts from the field of organizational theory, and principles related to the structure and culture of nonprofit organizations. There is a rich literature in the fields of organizational behavior and organizational theory, but historically, much of the theory has been generic, meaning that its originators apply it to all forms of organization, whether business, government, or nonprofit. Recent decades have produced a considerable literature specifically addressing the distinctive features of nonprofit organizations. Given this extensive and diverse literature, our discussion of theories is of necessity selective.

Characteristics of Nonprofit Organizations

As we saw in Chapter 2, the nonprofit sector encompasses an array of organizations and institutions that are very different from one another. Is it possible, then, to identify some characteristics that are associated with what it means to be a "nonprofit"? In his book, *America's Nonprofit Sector: A Primer* (3rd ed., 2012a), Lester Salamon identifies five qualities that define nonprofit organizations: They are organizations (that is, they are organized entities), they are private (as opposed to governmental), they are non–profit distributing, they are self-governing, and they are noncompulsory (p. 15). Let's discuss these qualities one at a time.

Organized Entities

There are loose and informal groups of people who undertake voluntary efforts similar to the programs of nonprofits, but the organizations that we will consider in this book are generally chartered as formal organizations. Most are incorporated under state law and enjoy the same benefits as business corporations—that is, status as a legal person in and of itself, separate from the individuals who may control it.

Private

Although nonprofit organizations have a commitment to public service, they operate in the private sector rather than as agencies of government. Many receive government funds, and indeed, government funds make up the largest source of revenue for some. Some authors use the term nonprofit agencies, implying that they are essentially like units of government. However, it is important to be clear that the control of nonprofit organizations lies outside the sphere of government, and they have considerable autonomy to set their own strategies, design their own programs, pursue revenues through multiple means, and select those who will benefit from their services.

A government agency, by contrast, is generally obligated to provide services to anyone who qualifies, or as Wolf (1999) describes it, they have "a requirement of equity" (p. 20). The requirement may be specifically defined—for example, people making below some level of annual income or people over a certain age—but the agency is required to provide services to anyone who meets those criteria, within the limits of resources appropriated to it. Nonprofit organizations may receive government funding that requires them to provide specific services to qualified individuals as a condition of accepting the funds. However, in general, they have both the liberty and the challenge of defining their own constituencies, deciding the services to be offered, and deciding which funding they will or will not accept. Both government agencies and nonprofits may have missions, but government agencies also face mandates, which most nonprofits do not.

Non–Profit Distributing

As we already have discussed, nonprofits, by definition, do not distribute any excess of revenues over expenditures to benefit individual owners. Any profit that a nonprofit organization generates must be reinvested in the organization itself or its programs, rather than be used to pay dividends to owners or investors. This requirement is indeed one of the primary criteria for being recognized as a nonprofit organization and any violation of it could be a cause for the Internal Revenue Service (IRS) revoking recognition of the organization's nonprofit status. It is also required that compensation to employees of the organization be reasonable, so that managers are not being enriched as if they were in fact owners of the enterprise. Indeed, nonprofit executive compensation is an area of potential abuse that has received increasing attention from Congress and the IRS in recent years. The standard of reasonableness does not mean that nonprofit executives must be paid low salaries; in fact, in some fields, nonprofit salaries are comparable with salaries for similar jobs in the for-profit sector. It does require, however, that nonprofits justify the compensation paid to their executives, to ensure that they are receiving payment in exchange for the services they provide to the organization rather than a share of profits disguised as salary or benefits. The federal tax law passed in 2017, called the Tax Cuts and Jobs Act of 2017, maintained the standard of reasonableness, but with the new requirement that nonprofits pay an excise tax on the amount of compensation above $1 million paid to any of its five highest-paid employees. (Meiksins, 2018).

Self-Governing

Nonprofits are self-governing, which is another way of saying that they are not controlled either by the government or by individual owners. Control of the nonprofit lies with a board of directors, which may be identified as a board of trustees or by some other term. The board is a group of individuals who have overall responsibility for ensuring that the organization serves its nonprofit mission and uses funds in accordance with that mission and the law. The board also has responsibility for the overall welfare of the organization itself.

Noncompulsory

As Salamon (2012a) notes, "participation in [nonprofits] is not a function of birth or required by law or official sanction" (p. 16). It is noncompulsory; that is, it is voluntary. Although many nonprofits employ significant numbers of paid staff, they are rooted in the tradition of voluntarism. Most—though not all—members of nonprofit governing boards are volunteers, who serve without compensation. Moreover, many organizations also engage substantial numbers of service volunteers in delivering their programs. Even nonprofits that employ significant numbers of staff often had an earlier period in their histories when volunteers were the predominant workforce, and the values of inclusion and openness to varying opinions often remain important components of their cultures. Indeed, nonprofits can be somewhat unruly forums of debate about even basic questions of values, mission, and priorities.

Public Benefit

In an earlier edition of his book, Salamon (1999) identified a sixth characteristic of nonprofit organizations: They are of public benefit. However, in his 2012(a) revision, he reconsiders that term, arguing that it may not be appropriate to include this as a characteristic that defines all nonprofits, since "public benefit" may be a subjective concept. People may not agree on exactly what it means. Most people would likely agree on the public benefits that are provided by some nonprofits. For example, few would argue with the benefits of feeding the hungry, eliminating drunk driving, or fighting drug addiction. In other instances, however, definition of the greater good will vary between those who advocate opposite sides of a controversial issue. For example, there are organizations that hold pro-life or pro-choice positions. Some advocate prayer in public schools, while others emphasize the separation of church and state and oppose school prayer. Some citizens see environmental organizations as accomplishing important public benefits, while others may see them as extremist roadblocks to economic progress. However, such organizations are nevertheless tax-exempt, because they advance a free and open debate, a value presumably shared by those on all sides of an issue in a democratic society. From that perspective, providing a public benefit perhaps might be considered a sixth common characteristic that defines all nonprofit organizations.

A nonprofit's purpose is stated in broad terms in its charter and is elaborated in its mission statement. The **mission statement** is a guide to every action taken by the organization and is the principal standard against which its performance should be measured. Amending a charter is a complex process, but the mission of an organization is more easily changed. Indeed, consideration of the mission is usually among the first steps undertaken in an organization's planning process.

The mission is so central to all nonprofit organizations that these entities are said to be **mission driven**. The mission is their purpose, and accomplishing it is their overriding goal. This commitment to a mission is a fundamental difference between nonprofit and for-profit organizations, and one of the reasons why nonprofit management is a distinctive professional field. We will consider mission statements in further detail in Chapters 6 and 7, which discuss measuring performance and strategic planning, respectively.

As noted previously, government agencies also have missions, to which the individuals who work in them are often highly dedicated. But government agencies are ultimately controlled by elected officials, who must respond to the wishes of the majority. They can only support programs according to what is politically feasible—that is, those favored by a majority of the voters. This is not to disparage the practice of politics, or to imply that politicians do not have personal convictions, but merely to state the reality that if officials do not meet the expectations of the majority over time, they will be replaced by others whose programs are more reflective of the majority's preferences. Thus, political viability is in a sense an ultimate test as fundamental to the purposes of government as profit is to business (Wolf, 1999).

Nonprofits stand somewhere between business and government. They are driven neither by the need to maximize profit nor by the need to meet the expectations or desires of a majority, but rather by achievement of the missions for which they exist. Like businesses, some nonprofits can and do generate profits. But, by definition, the generation of revenue is the means to the end of achieving the purposes stated in their charters and fulfilling the social purposes expressed in their mission statements.

The characteristics of nonprofit organizations identified by Salamon (1999, 2012a) help explain *what* they are. Now let's look at some concepts and theories that explain *why* nonprofit organizations look and behave the way they do.

Nonprofits as Open Systems

To many people today, the word **bureaucracy** provokes negative images of a slow-moving, complex, unresponsive institution—perhaps a government agency like the motor vehicle department or even a large university. But in the early years of the 20th century, the sociologist and economist Max Weber advanced the idea of a bureaucracy as an ideal model. Characterized by rules and a formal hierarchy of positions, he thought a bureaucracy to be especially capable of efficiency and effectiveness. For decades after Weber's pioneering work, his concept of a bureaucracy remained central in organizational theory, and other scholars expanded on his work, studying issues such as the span of manager control, the roles of managers, and other questions based on his idea of organizations as machine-like entities. Later scholars, such as Barnard, Simon, Cyert, March, Lewin, Maslow, McGregor, Argyris, and others, began to chip away at Weber's principles by placing more emphasis on human needs, motivations, and incentives rather than on formal organizational structures, eventually leading to development of the **human relations school** of management (Rainey, 2014, pp. 34–37). But Weber's concept of a bureaucracy, operating with formal structures, rules, and machine-like precision, probably still comports with many people's image of how an organization works.

Theories based on Weber's concept of bureaucracy usually focus on internal dynamics and on the behaviors of individuals within the organization. Beginning in the 1960s and 1970s, however, thinking about organizations began to shift toward viewing them as systems and analyzing their ability to adapt to different circumstances, or contingencies, in the external environment facing them. A landmark book by Daniel Katz and Robert Kahn (1966) presented a classic description of organizations as open systems that is still often cited. Widely read books authored by Peter Senge (1990, 1994) describing "learning organizations" also were based on systems theory. This shift in attention from the internal mechanics of an organization's operation to studying the effects of pressures and constraints brought to bear on the organization by the social context in which it exists was a profound change.

The simplest system includes inputs, a transformative process that acts on the inputs—that is, changes or manipulates them in some way—and the outputs resulting from that process. Systems also include feedback loops. Feedback enables the system to adapt to changing circumstances—that is, to learn and alter its behavior accordingly. In their ability to learn and adapt, systems are less like machines and more like living organisms. Indeed, some theorists study systems using principles drawn from the study of living organisms. For example, **population ecology** is an approach taken by some sociologists to explain the birth and death of organizations. They analyze organizations in terms of population density— that is, the number of organizations occupying particular niches—and the competition for resources among them. Population ecologists see some organizations as being selected in a Darwinian competition for scarce resources. They tend to place less emphasis on the ability of organizations to survive by adapting to environmental changes than do some other theories—for example, the resource dependence model we will consider soon (Aldrich, 1999).

Systems theorists make a distinction between closed and **open systems**. A system is closed or open depending on the extent to which it interacts with and is influenced by the environment in which it exists. A totally closed system would be one that is entirely self-sufficient and impervious to influences from its environment. It is difficult to conceive of an example of this extreme situation; no organization is insulated against all impact from outside. But some government agencies may be relatively closed. For example, those that provide essential services and have relatively reliable appropriations may enjoy a high degree of autonomy in determining their own policies and procedures. A nonprofit that has a large endowment and thus can rely on investment earnings for all its operating support, not requiring revenue from donors, government, or fees for service, also might operate as a relatively closed system. This could describe private foundations, for example, and indeed, foundations sometimes have been criticized for being insufficiently responsive to the world outside.

Most nonprofit organizations, however, are open systems. They are dependent on and interact frequently with their external environments. This is true because of their dependence on external resources, their social missions, and the involvement of volunteers at various levels of the organization.

As we have discussed, most nonprofit organizations have voluntary cultures. This has important implications for how they work. Individuals *choose* to be associated with a nonprofit. This is obviously true of service volunteers, people who perform the organization's work for no compensation and are free to stay or leave as they see fit. But it is often true that even paid staff of nonprofits have a voluntary attitude, meaning that they are motivated as much by the nature of the work and the organization's mission as by the pay, and often see themselves as performing a service. Even organizations that are highly commercialized or that rely primarily on government contracts have a "long history, deep traditions, and cultures steeped in voluntaristic values" (Ott, 2012, p. 250).

Most nonprofit governing boards are composed of volunteers, who may be drawn from constituencies served by the organization or from among its donors and who, in some cases, may have worked their way up through the ranks to join the board after having served as volunteers in delivering the organization's programs. The nonprofit board plays a boundary-spanning role; that is, its members are a part of the organization and represent the organization to the outside world, but they also are representatives of the outside world who bring the views and desires of the organization's stakeholders to bear on the organization and its management. The boundaries between "inside" and "outside" the organization may be fuzzy and permeable. Volunteers often work alongside paid staff, and communication flows back and forth across the formal boundaries of the organization. Volunteers providing the organization's services and also sitting on its governing board bring their own views and values to the board's discussions, and since they are not bound by the constraints of paid employment, they can be forcefully outspoken. Thus, communications both within the organization and between the organization and its external environment often do not follow the paths and patterns of formal authority.

Nonprofits serve a public purpose, and as such they are subsidized through tax exemption and—in the case of charitable nonprofits—the tax deductibility of gifts. They often serve as contractors to government in the delivery of public services. For those reasons, they are subject to the scrutiny and opinions of government officials as well as the media, recipients of their services, and the general public. Unlike businesses, which have the relatively simple and clear goal of generating profits, nonprofits often have ambiguous goals, and there is often lack of agreement on how achievement of the goals should be measured. This leaves plenty of room for debate and discussion, which are not easily contained within the organization's walls. In sum, most nonprofits are very open systems, interacting with their external constituencies and needing to adjust to changes in their environment all the time.

Resource Dependence

Expanding on the open systems theory, Pfeffer and Salancik's (1978) **resource dependence theory** explains the behavior of organizations in terms of their dependence on external constituencies—for revenue, information, and other resources. Although the theory has been around for 40 years, it is still widely cited and applied in research on nonprofit organizations.

According to this theory, we can understand the choices and behavior of organizations less by studying their internal structures and dynamics than by focusing on their interdependencies with external organizations and individuals who hold power over them by virtue of the resources they provide. For example, if a nonprofit receives most of its funding from government, the government will be able to impose its policies on that organization. An example of this can be seen in higher education, where government support was leveraged to require that colleges and universities provide equal support for men's and women's athletic programs (Pfeffer, 2003). An organization that is highly dependent on a single foundation or a major individual donor also loses some of its autonomy and must respond to the priorities or demands of those who provide it with needed resources.

Goal Displacement

One significant risk of resource dependence is what is called **goal displacement**—that is, actions taken by the nonprofit to alter its goals and activities to satisfy the contributor of funds. This sometimes occurs not as a result of overt demands by funders, but in more subtle ways, when an organization expands its programs and activities into areas that may be appealing to donors or when it avoids activities that may alienate donors. Responsiveness to the interests of funders may lead an organization in directions inconsistent with its mission, but this is not necessarily insidious in its result. For example, Mirae Kim, Sheela Pandey, and Sanjay Pandey (2017) studied nonprofit performing arts organizations. They found that organizations primarily dependent on local governments, foundations, and corporate donors are more likely to provide free attendance for lower-income people, whereas those deriving most of their revenue from market sources, mainly ticket sales, were less likely to do so. Many people would view access to the arts as a benefit to society, but the finding reinforces the idea that what we can observe about the behavior of organizations may be explained at least in part by where they get their money.

Resource Dependence and Performance Measurement

Resource dependence helps explain some recent trends and issues in the nonprofit sector, including efforts to make nonprofits more accountable for performance. Government funders, foundations, and other substantial donors can impose performance standards on nonprofits that receive their support and establish the achievement of certain goals as conditions for future support. The extent to which organizations are constrained by such requirements depends on how important the resources of a particular funder are. For example, United Way was a leader in advocating the use of outcome measures as a method for evaluating nonprofit effectiveness (something we will explore further in Chapter 6). To the extent that individuals made unrestricted gifts to United Way, permitting it to allocate those funds to specific organizations, United Way held considerable influence over those organizations and could require that they follow its approach to measuring effectiveness. However, individuals began to designate their United Way gifts to specific organizations and to bypass United Way entirely to support organizations directly, including through online giving. As giving patterns changed, United Way had less ability to influence those organizations. The trend toward designated gifts made organizations less dependent on United Way and thus reduced United Way's ability to influence their priorities and policies. Indeed, United Way responded to these changing patterns with a significant transformation in its own approach, which is discussed in Case 5.2 in Chapter 5 of this text.

Internal Impact of Resource Dependence

An important insight from resource dependence theory is that external resource dependencies also can affect power relationships and structures within the organization. As Pffefer (2003) explains, "The people, groups, or departments inside organizations that ... manage important environmental dependencies, and help the organization obtain resources, [hold] more power as a result of their critical role" (p. xiii). Consider, for example, an organization that depends primarily on charitable gifts for the largest portion of its revenues. The person who raises such money—perhaps the chief executive or a fundraising professional—will hold power within the organization because he or she delivers so much of the revenue on which it depends. Requests for increases to the fundraising budget or perhaps a higher salary for the chief fundraising officer are likely to be favorably received. Alternatively, think about a commercialized nonprofit that derives most of its revenue from fees for services. Gifts may be less important to the organization, and hence its fundraisers may have less internal clout. For example, they may have a more difficult time gaining approval of increased budgets. Such an organization is more dependent on fee-paying consumers or clients than on donors, and internal power thus may lie more with those who are experts in marketing or customer relations.

How does dependence on government funds affect a nonprofit organization? In her classic article on this topic, Froelich (1999) argues that "the most pronounced effects of government funding involve changes in internal processes and ultimately in the structures of nonprofit organizations" (p. 256). For example, she points to studies showing that the government's "dense web" of regulations and required accounting and reporting have altered the internal structure of arts organizations. She calls government "the primary force driving out the technical experts in arts management in favor of professional arts administrators, many of whom know little about the art forms they are managing" (p. 261). The same is true of health care institutions that depend on government reimbursements for the services they provide. Hospitals were once managed by physicians, but today most are managed by health care management professionals who have specialized training and skills.

The influence of resource dependence on an organization's internal structure, processes, and culture is so great that over time nonprofits may indeed become more like those very organizations that are their principal sources of revenue. For example, nonprofits that are primarily government contractors may become bureaucratic and develop a culture that is similar to that of government agencies. In contrast, those that receive a high percentage of their revenues through fees for service and other business activities may come to exhibit the characteristics of entrepreneurial business firms.

Organizations Adapt to Resource Dependence

Organizations use a variety of strategies to try and maintain their autonomy—that is, to resist external pressure on their decision making. They may try to make changes to accommodate to the external demands, perhaps by undertaking internal reforms, or they may try to alter the environment in a way that ameliorates the demands (Pfeffer & Salancik, 1978). For example, when in 2004 the nonprofit sector was threatened with new federal legislation to curb perceived abuses, the organization Independent Sector responded with both proposals and guidelines for self-regulation of the sector and with intensive lobbying efforts aimed at forestalling the proposed new federal legislation (Independent Sector, 2007).

Managing Resource Dependence

A hallmark of resource dependence theory is the idea that "although organizations [are] ... constrained by their situations and environments, [they have] opportunities to *do things* [italics added] ... to obtain, at least temporarily, more autonomy and the ability to pursue organizational interests" (Pfeffer, 2003, p. xii). In other words, organizations need not be helpless captives of their funding sources. They can make strategic choices that enable them to manage resource dependence in a way that maximizes their autonomy.

One way to reduce resource dependence and thus maintain more autonomy is to diversify the sources of revenue. For example, an organization that is highly dependent on gifts may decide to develop a revenue-producing business to reduce its reliance on donors. Or an organization that relies on the support of one government agency or foundation may focus on broadening its base of individual donors. The goal is to reduce dependence on any one source of revenue in order to achieve the autonomy needed to determine its own mission, programs, and measures of effectiveness. However, some research has suggested that the increased commercialization of nonprofits in recent years may reflect increased competition for revenue among organizations, rather than efforts to manage resource dependence in the face of declining philanthropic or government support (Kerlin & Pollak, 2011).

Isomorphism

Resource dependence suggests that some nonprofits may become more like their primary funders. Other scholars see a tendency for organizations in the same field to become more like each other as a result of facing similar influences from their environments. Called **isomorphism**, this concept is drawn from the work of organizational scholars who use **institutional theory**.

Like resource dependence and population ecology, institutional theory represents "a continuation and extension of ... open systems conceptions" (Scott, 1995, p. xiv). It recognizes the importance of an organization's environment and emphasizes the constraints placed on it by rules, expectations, norms, and values. Institutional theory describes organizations' efforts to gain legitimacy by embracing the norms, values, beliefs, and mores prescribed by the environment in which they exist.

Walter Powell and Paul DiMaggio (1991) describe three types of isomorphism— coercive, mimetic, and normative—and we can find examples of all three at work in the nonprofit sector. *Coercive isomorphism,* as the term implies, is forced on organizations. This pressure might come, for example, from laws, government regulations, accrediting bodies, or accounting rules established by the Financial Accounting Standards Board. There also are several standards of nonprofit behavior that have been established by watchdog organizations, such as the Better Business Bureau's Wise Giving Alliance and Independent Sector. Such standards do not have the force of law, but they can nevertheless be coercive, since the media attention given to organizations that do not meet them may have a negative impact on giving and other sources of support. In other words, nonprofit organizations, particularly those in the same field, might tend to become more alike over time simply because they are forced to play by the same sets of rules.

Mimetic isomorphism refers to the tendency of organizations to mimic each other—that is, to look to the example of similar organizations for models to be adopted. Many nonprofit organizations today engage in benchmarking, a practice we will discuss more fully elsewhere in this book. "In benchmarking, an organization that has defined an opportunity for improved performance identifies another organization … that has achieved better results and conducts a systematic study of the other organization's achievements, practices, and processes" (Letts et al., 1999, p. 86). Through this approach, organizations try to identify the best practices of other organizations they consider to be similar to them, and thus learn ways to improve their own operations. It is not surprising that this leads eventually to different organizations in the same field doing things in much the same way.

Normative isomorphism arises when organizations are influenced by the same standards of professional practice. For example, doctors follow the same ethical codes, so some things will be done the same way in all hospitals; social service organizations will reflect the norms of the social work profession; and university professors' similar understandings about academic freedom will affect the way in which all colleges and universities operate.

Explaining Nonprofit Organizational Structures

Isomorphism creates a tendency for organizations to become more alike, but we can observe that there are also often differences. For example, some organizations are relatively bureaucratic and centralized, with everyone following tightly prescribed policies and procedures sent down from the top. Others are more entrepreneurial and flexible, with decisions being made closer to the action in the field. What explains such differences?

As we already have discussed, some of the explanation lies with resource dependence. Structure is influenced by the organization's principal sources of support. For example, those that are dependent on just a few sources of support may operate with more centralized managements, to achieve consistent communication with funding sources and ensure compliance with funders' requirements. Those that have more broad-based public support may be more decentralized, to tap the involvement and support of larger numbers of volunteers and local donors.

But a nonprofit's structure also is influenced by other variables, including the task environment it faces. The **task environment** includes the nature of the goods or services it provides; the type of technology it uses; the degree of uncertainty it faces in its environment; the complexity of its environment; the dynamism or rate of change in its environment; whether its units are tightly or loosely coupled, that is, in what time, proximity, and sequence they must interact as they produce the organization's product or service; and whether the interactions are complex or linear, that is, "the extent to which interaction sequences in operations are well known, predictable, unambiguous, and recoverable among operational units" (Anheier, 2014, p. 287). In simplest terms, how an organization is structured may depend in part on whether the work it does is straightforward, follows some clear set of procedures, and is predictable, or whether it often faces complex, unique, and messy situations that cannot be well predicted in advance.

Let's consider an example that illustrates this idea. One of the nation's largest nonprofits, the American Red Cross, engages in two principal activities—blood services and disaster relief. It collects blood, processes and stores it, and provides it to hospitals and other medical facilities as needed. It also responds to natural disasters, providing immediate relief to victims in the form of food, shelter, and other help. Handling the blood supply requires precision, and it needs to be done one way. Disasters are different. Of the almost 70,000 disasters to which the Red Cross responds annually, the majority are local, including incidents such as house fires, hazardous material spills, and transportation accidents. The timing and nature of events are unpredictable—each situation is different and requires a somewhat different, tailored response. Blood services and disasters thus present different task environments, and the Red Cross organizes itself differently for each of these activities.

In local disasters, most services are provided by local chapters, which operate in a somewhat decentralized manner with the support of local donors and volunteers. In this area, there is relatively loose coupling between the national office and local chapters. Blood services were once more decentralized, but the Red Cross reorganized its blood services in the 1990s in the face of growing national concern about HIV infection. This reorganization created a more centralized structure and additional bureaucratic policies and procedures. In other words, the organizational structure changed when the nature of the task was changed by HIV. Following Hurricane Katrina in 2005, the Red Cross's disaster relief services also were reorganized, to reflect the new task environment presented by the seemingly more frequent incidence of catastrophic disasters affecting large geographic regions as well as the potential for terrorist incidents that have regional or national implications. Because the nature of the task had shifted, the organization needed to develop a structure consistent with the changed reality.

Organizational Culture

Any of us who has experience with organizations—as employees, as volunteers, as students, or in any other capacity—knows that formal structures and written rules often do not fully account for "the way things work around here." There are unwritten rules of behavior that govern things such as what people wear (suits or jeans), how people address each other (by first name or formal title), whether personal phone calls and e-mails can be received during working hours, whether or not people who work together also socialize outside the office, and many other realities of day-to-day organizational life. These realities often are controlled not by formal policies, but rather by **organizational culture**.

Scholars long have studied the subject of organizational culture, but the "topic [of culture] really came alive in the management literature" following the publication in the 1980s and 1990s of popular business books that emphasized the importance of culture in successful corporations (Rainey, 2014, p. 354). Peters and Waterman's book, *In Search of Excellence,* published in 1982, focused the attention of corporate managers on the idea of corporate culture and inspired additional research.

The lesson of Peters and Waterman (1982) was simple: Great companies that produce excellent results have core values that are widely shared; in other words, they have strong cultures. In their 1994 book, *Built to Last: Successful Habits of Visionary Companies,* James Collins and Jerry Porras identified several characteristics that were associated with successful business corporations. Like Peters and Waterman, they found that culture was important. Successful companies have core values that are widely understood and often codified; they undertake efforts to protect the core values; they have a shared understanding of "purpose" that goes beyond the maximization of profit; and they demonstrate strong, "cult-like" cultures that are often perpetuated through promotion from within.

Culture is a word that is frequently used in everyday conversation, and most people probably have a reasonably accurate understanding of what it means. But organizational scholars offer precise definitions. For example, Edgar Schein (2016) breaks culture down into three categories: (1) *artifacts and creations*—for example, logos, symbols, ceremonies, rituals, and words used in conversations; (2) *basic values*—the less observable understandings of "how things are done around here," for example, who communicates with whom within the organization and in what manner, what external relationships are important, and so forth; and (3) *basic assumptions*—for example, how people see things, their personal theories about human nature, and expectations about whether people in the organization should be entrepreneurial and aggressive or compliant and passive.

It may be an oversimplification to speak of an organization's culture, as if it is coherent and uniform throughout. Most organizations, except perhaps the smallest, will include various subcultures—that is, groups of individuals "who share strong values about basic beliefs with some, but not all, of the other members of the organization" (Clegg, Kornberger, & Pitsis, 2005, p. 277). For example, executives may have different values and beliefs than do rank-and-file staff or volunteers. Staff members may have values derived from their professional cultures; for example, doctors and nurses working in hospitals may be influenced by professional norms not shared by professional hospital managers. University development officers may have more favorable views of business than do their academic colleagues who interact with businesspeople less frequently. The leadership and staff in the national headquarters of a nonprofit organization may see things quite differently from those who work in the local chapters. In hybrid organizations, like those we discussed in Chapter 2, there may be cultural differences between staff who provide mission-related services and those who are engaged in the revenue-producing business ventures of the organization.

Is there something that can be called "the nonprofit culture," some set of values and beliefs that runs commonly and consistently across the nonprofit sector? A number of authors assert that there is. We mentioned earlier in this chapter that many nonprofits, even those that may be largely dependent on earned income and paid staff, have "long history, deep traditions, and cultures steeped in *voluntaristic values* [italics added]" (Ott, 2012, p. 250). Christine Letts and colleagues (1999) describe a "service culture" in nonprofits, stating that

> organizational issues hold little appeal for the several types of nonprofit employees who populate much of the sector.... [M]any nonprofit employees develop a "just do it" attitude that places more value on service than on the analysis and measurement needed to improve organizational performance. (p. 33)

Letts et al. (1999) also observe a "cooperative [rather than competitive] nature" in nonprofit workplaces and nonprofit professionals who see their work as "artistry" that is diminished by performance measurement (pp. 33–34). Frumkin and Imber (2004) claim that

> many nonprofit employees, and even some donors and volunteers, are uncomfortable with the language and practices of business and may be skeptical of the values and motives of people trying to introduce business concepts ... [and that] the sector overall ... seems to have a bias towards small organizations, local autonomy, and consensus-driven decision making. (p. 70)

The fact that culture exists and is an important aspect of understanding organizations is well supported and resonates with our own experience as individuals. However, as we have discussed, the nonprofit sector is diverse and complex, so it may not be a simple matter to describe a universal nonprofit culture. In addition, the blurring of the for-profit, governmental, and nonprofit sectors may be changing the culture of at least some organizations. The working of isomorphism may not be constrained to organizations within the same sector: Nonprofit hospitals may become more like for-profit hospitals. Nonprofit museums may become more like for-profit entertainment venues. Human service organizations may become more like competitive service businesses. As discussed in Chapter 2, nonprofits are adopting the methods and vocabulary of the marketplace; becoming more businesslike at the same time that some corporations are emphasizing missions, vision, and values; and implementing more socially responsible policies. In essence, some nonprofits may be developing more corporate-like cultures, while some corporations are becoming more nonprofit-like in theirs. In this changing environment, it may be increasingly unrealistic to describe a distinctive nonprofit culture that is universally characteristic of all organizations across the entire sector.

CHAPTER SUMMARY

Scholars in various disciplines have developed theories to explain the nonprofit sector as a whole and the behavior of individual nonprofit organizations. Theories drawn from economics surround the concepts of public goods and private goods, externalities, and free riders, and explain nonprofits as gap fillers that compensate for the failures of the market and government. Other theories address the supply side and explain nonprofits in terms of social entrepreneurship; the contributions that nonprofits make to freedom, pluralism, and joint action; and motivations for altruism and giving.

Lohmann's interdisciplinary theory of the commons explains nonprofits as providers of common goods, a third category of goods alongside private and public. The definitions of what is private, public, or common may change over time, reflecting current philosophical and political trends.

According to Salamon (2012a), nonprofit organizations exhibit five defining characteristics: (1) They are organizations (organized entities, rather than informal groups of people), (2) they are private, (3) they are non–profit distributing, (4) they are self-governing, and (5) they are noncompulsory. A sixth characteristic may be that nonprofits provide a public benefit (Salamon, 1999). Not all may agree with the definition of that term, since some nonprofits advocate contradictory positions. But encouragement of debate may be considered generally a public benefit in a democratic society. These characteristics have implications for how nonprofits behave as organizations. Their purposes are stated in their mission statements. The mission is so central to nonprofit organizations that they are said to be mission-driven.

Organizational theorists discuss nonprofits as open systems that respond to the pressures and constraints presented by their environments. Their behavior reflects their resource dependence, and nonprofits face the risks of goal displacement and loss of autonomy if they are too dependent on one or a few sources of funding. Most attempt to manage resource dependence by diversifying the sources of support and remaining committed to their missions.

Isomorphism describes the tendency of organizations in the same field to become alike. This may result from external pressures, the inclination of organizations to adopt each other's practices, or the commonalities of professional codes practiced by the organization's staff members. The organizational structure of a nonprofit also may be determined by the task environments it faces.

An organization's culture—the informal rules about "the way things are done around here"—has received increased emphasis in management literature over the past three decades. Some authors describe an identifiable nonprofit culture, but the much-noted blurring of sectors may be reducing the cultural differences, especially between nonprofits and business firms.

NOTES

1. There is a distinction between the terms *organizational behavior* and *organizational theory*, although most books on management blend the two fields and some consider organizational theory to be the larger, encompassing field. Scholars of organizational behavior generally focus on the behavior of individuals or groups in organizations, often drawing on the disciplines of psychology and social psychology. Their interest is often in questions related to topics such as motivation, work satisfaction, and leadership. Organizational theory, which is usually based on sociology, is more concerned with the organization as a whole, considering topics such as organizational culture, environment, structure, and effectiveness (Rainey, 2014).

2. Economists make a distinction between pure public goods and quasi-public goods. The distinction involves the characteristics of non-excludability and non-rivalry. The discussion here is generally referring to quasi-public goods. For simplicity, they are just called public goods in this text.

KEY TERMS AND CONCEPTS

bureaucracy 65

contract failure 56

demand heterogeneity 57

entrepreneurship theory 58

externalities 56

free riders 56

goal displacement 67

government failure 57

human relations school 65

information asymmetry 56

institutional theory 69

isomorphism 69

market failure 56

median voter 57

mission driven 64

mission statement 64

open systems 66

organizational culture 71

population ecology 66

private goods 55

public goods 56

resource dependence theory 67

supply-side theory 58

task environment 70

theory of the commons 60

trust theory 58

voluntary failure 58

CASE 3.1   The Smithsonian Institution and the Catherine B. Reynolds Foundation

The Smithsonian Institution, an educational and research institution in Washington, DC, is best known for its 19 museums and 7 research centers. It is an unusual hybrid of federal government agency and nonprofit institution. It was chartered by Congress as a charitable trust in 1846, in response to a bequest from the Englishman James Smithson, who left a gift to the United States of America to establish an institution "for the increase and diffusion of knowledge among men." But the Smithsonian is administered by the federal government, and courts have held that it is legally part of the federal government. More than two thirds of its workforce are employees of the federal government, while others supported by private funds are known as "trust fund employees." Although significant governance reforms were undertaken in 2007, in 2000 the Smithsonian was governed by a 17-member board of regents, including officials of the federal government and private citizens. The secretary of the Smithsonian is the paid chief executive, who is appointed by the board of regents.

Throughout most of its history, the Smithsonian relied on ample funding from the U.S. government. But beginning in the 1980s, federal funds failed to keep pace with the Smithsonian's needs. Faced with a change in its environment, the Smithsonian "didn't exactly turn on a dime," and battles over the influence of private donors over the content of exhibits led to subsequent "knock-down, drag-out funding fight[s]," centered in particular on one of the Smithsonian's most prominent components, the National Museum of American History (Thompson, 2002).

By 2000, federal funds were only sufficient to cover the Smithsonian's core budget, including salaries. Private funds needed to be raised for new exhibits, and some standing exhibits had become dated. Deferred maintenance on the Smithsonian's extensive physical facilities had allowed many to deteriorate. Recognizing the need for change, the board of regents reached outside the scientific and museum communities for a new secretary—the title of the chief executive officer—someone who could bring business methods and private resources to bear on the Smithsonian's mounting problems. Lawrence Small, appointed by the board of regents as the new secretary in 2000, came from a background in banking and finance rather than science or museum management. Small noted the deteriorating condition of the Smithsonian's facilities and the continuing decline in federal funds, and he committed himself to "a vision that involves two M's: modernization and money," with most of the money to come from more aggressive fundraising in the private sector (Thompson, 2002, p. 22).

Small had met Catherine B. Reynolds, a Washington-area entrepreneur who controlled a large foundation bearing her name. She shared Small's view that the National Museum of American History needed to be updated, and in May 2001, she announced a gift of $38 million from her foundation to support a project on which she and Small had agreed: a 10,000-square-foot "hall of achievement" exhibit, intended to portray the lives of eminent Americans. Small and Reynolds had agreed that the selection of individuals to be portrayed would be determined by a special advisory committee of 15 people, with 10 being appointed by the Reynolds Foundation. *The Washington Post* reported that the contract between the Reynolds Foundation and the Smithsonian provided that if the committee could not agree, the dispute would be resolved not by the curatorial staff, but by the secretary himself ("Museums and Money," 2001).

Upon learning the terms of the gift, the museum's staff erupted in anger, writing directly to the Smithsonian Board of Regents saying that the obligations Small had made to the Reynolds Foundation "breach[ed] established standards of museum practice and professional ethics" (Thompson, 2002, p. 26). The story caught the attention of the news media, resulting in a flurry of stories representing the museum curators' views and a *New York Times* editorial asking "what is the curatorial rationale for a permanent exhibit that seems to open the door for commercial and corporate influence at one of the capital's keystone institutions" ("Gifts That Can Warp a Museum," 2001). The American Historical Association, including prominent historians among its members, joined the debate in support of the museum staff's views. Museum staff began to post "Dump Small" stickers in elevators, on bulletin boards, and on their own lapels (Sciolino, 2001b). A series of meetings were held between the curators and Ms. Reynolds to try and reach a common understanding, but they did not resolve the differences.

At least two issues were central to the controversy. The first was a difference in philosophy about the meaning of history and the purpose of museums. Historians and museum curators believed that the purpose of museums was to educate and that the study of history should not focus on the personal stories of "great" men and women. Rather, they argued that the teaching of history should focus on broad historical forces and movements, often portrayed in exhibits through their impact on the lives of everyday people. They believed that the purpose of a museum was to encourage people to think critically about history, not to inspire people personally. As one curator expressed it, "We are not a great man/great woman place.... This museum is about context, about putting people and events in place within the social fabric" (Thompson, 2002, p. 18). But Ms. Reynolds held a different view of history and the purpose of the museum's exhibits—it should be to inspire young people by portraying the lives of famous Americans and extolling the virtues of entrepreneurship in achieving success. "The foundation was created out of a very entrepreneurial business," Ms. Reynolds said, "and that is the spirit and culture we want to apply to the philanthropic world" (Sciolino, 2001c).

The second, and broader, issue was the question of who should control the content of museum exhibits—professional historians and museum curators, or donors. To what degree should private donors have a say in museum exhibits to be developed with the money they are voluntarily giving? One scholar asked, "Will the Smithsonian Institution actually allow private funders to rent space in a public museum for the expression of private and personal views?" (Thompson, 2002, p. 16). Scholars accused Small of "selling" the museum to wealthy donors, with jeopardizing the "integrity and authority" of professional curators, and with having "[pre-empted] the issue of control" by reaching an agreement with the Reynolds Foundation without adequate consultation with his own staff (Sciolino, 2001c).

Small responded, saying that "government funding cannot do it all" and pointing out that the idea of private donors—who had something to say about how their money would be used—was not exactly new. After all, the Smithsonian Institution had been founded with James Smithson's gift! Small said, "We make no apologies for seeking private support to develop programs or facilities that the public wants and benefits from." He argued, "In all cases, we retain intellectual control while demonstrating to donors that their money can be spent productively and prudently. Does that mean we don't consult them? Of course we do. But the Smithsonian regents and staff control, without limitation or question, the Smithsonian activity" (Small, 2001, p. A25).

In February 2002, Ms. Reynolds canceled the bulk of her foundation's pledge to the Smithsonian, saying merely that she felt the exhibit would not adequately portray "the power of the individual" (Lewis, 2002, p. 16). But important questions remained, for the Smithsonian and generally for other organizations. Like the Smithsonian, others have long relied on relatively ensured sources of revenues, perhaps the government, a single foundation, or some other generous source. Many find themselves now needing to pursue new and more diversified sources of financial support. The questions that need to be addressed clearly go beyond the specific one raised by the Reynolds Foundation's gift to the Smithsonian, that of how history should be portrayed and who should decide. There are more generic questions: What trade-offs are appropriate, realistic, and necessary for institutions and organizations striving to meet their financial needs and develop new sources of revenue while preserving their traditional missions and values? And how can chief executive officers (CEOs) meet expectations for their leadership in such a time of change?

Additional Sources: Cash (2002); Sciolino (2001a).

Questions Related to Case 3.1

1. How are the concepts of open and closed systems reflected in the case of the Smithsonian Institution and the Catherine B. Reynolds Foundation?

2. How does the theory of resource dependence relate to the case of the Smithsonian Institution and the Catherine B. Reynolds Foundation?

3. What cultures were at play in the case of the Smithsonian Institution and the Catherine B. Reynolds Foundation, and how did the interplay of cultures influence the controversy and the outcome?

CASE 3.2 The National Trust for Historic Preservation

The National Trust for Historic Preservation is a private, nonprofit membership organization dedicated to saving historic places and revitalizing America's communities. Having been chartered by Congress in 1949, the trust became known for its ownership and operation of historic properties and its annual list of America's Most Endangered Historic Places. It also provided educational programs, issued grants to support local preservation projects, and joined court cases in support of preservation laws and causes. In 1982, it filed its first case as a plaintiff—against the U.S. Army Corps of Engineers. And, in 1994, it became the leader in the successful effort to prevent development of a Walt Disney theme park near the Manassas National Battlefield Park, in Virginia, which pitted the trust against powerful business interests.

The trust had continued to receive an annual unrestricted appropriation from Congress since its founding, and by 1995, government funds accounted for $7 million of its $35-million total budget. The balance came from private sources, including income from a modest endowment of about $33 million (Adelman, 2005; Kennicott, 2009). But the trust's efforts were often controversial with members of Congress, and the annual appropriation process required the trust to lobby vigorously on its own behalf to maintain government support. The 1995 budget cycle was especially bruising. While the trust ultimately received its full appropriation, it was a close call, with one congressional committee voting to cut it in half (Adelman, 2005). Richard Moe, who had been appointed president of the trust in 1993,

reached a decision. "We decided [that] persuading Congress is [too] consuming an effort—and chancy," Moe recalls. "Rather than be full-time lobbyists [on our own behalf], we wanted to lobby for others—for the National Park Service, tax credits, preservation policies. We wanted to be in control of our own destiny" (Adelman, 2005). Congress agreed to guarantee limited support for a three-year transition, and the trust committed to going without unrestricted federal appropriations thereafter. The pressure was on.

The trust reduced staff, cut some programs, launched a strategic planning effort, and started a capital campaign. It developed new revenue streams through partnerships with corporations and entrepreneurial programs, such as Historic Hotels of America, which provides the trust with a fee from reservations placed through it with qualified hotels nationwide. It also initiated new donor programs, including organized trips to historic landmarks for major individual benefactors and intensified foundation fundraising (National Trust for Historic Preservation, 2008).

Freedom from federal support and a more diverse structure of revenue enabled the National Trust to pursue a more expansive agenda and increase its effectiveness as an advocate for historic preservation. Following Hurricane Katrina in 2005, the trust worked to protect 37,000 historic structures in New Orleans. It opened a New Orleans office, completed demonstration projects, and lobbied Congress for $40 billion in grants to be funded through state preservation officers to help people rehabilitate their homes. And it fought the U.S.

government in court to prevent federal funds from being used for demolition of substantial parts of the Mid-City Historic District (Kennicott, 2009; McDill, 2006). The work of the National Trust for Historic Preservation gradually expanded the understanding of "preservation" from saving buildings to a more holistic approach of protecting entire neighborhoods, towns, communities, and the environment. Furthermore, it changed the thinking of the business community. "Preservation is much more widely accepted today than it was fifteen or twenty years ago," Moe said in 2009. "Developers don't look at demolition as the first option as a rule, they look at the possibility of adaptive reuse and renovation" (Kennicott, 2009, p. C12).

Stephanie Meeks succeeded Richard Moe as president and CEO in 2010 and developed a plan for the trust's continued transformation. The federal appropriations that the trust had received in its earlier era were designated for the preservation of its historic properties. The change in funding and a new definition of the trust's mission called for a new model of operating the historic properties it controlled: co-stewarding with locally based nonprofit organizations. Under a 10-year plan, called Preservation 10X, the sites would become locally governed and financially self-sufficient. That would require engaging market forces, including more partnerships with corporations (National Trust for Historic Preservation, 2014).

The National Trust also would expand its advocacy in order to make preservation a "movement" and to engage more Americans in appreciation for the nation's architectural heritage (National Trust for Historic Preservation, 2013). In 2011, the trust launched a capital campaign and announced a new program called National Treasures, through which it would identify significant threatened places across the country and take action to save them. In 2017, the trust announced a new campaign to raise $25 million to preserve historic sites important to African American history (Lovejoy, 2017).

As Meeks explained, the trust's impact would expand beyond the preservation of buildings to encompass impact on people: "Our work often focuses on the built environment and landscapes. As we move forward for the next fifty years, I believe we need to keep expanding our horizons. As we keep working to save historic buildings, let's also think beyond them … to culture, and communities, and people. We tend to think of our successes in terms of places saved. And that is so important. But just as important—perhaps even more important—are why these places matter—the many lives we touch because of our hard work" (Meeks, 2015).

Additional Source: Lubell (2005).

Questions Related to Case 3.2

1. How does the case of the National Trust for Historic Preservation reflect the concept of resource dependence discussed in this chapter? How does it reflect the interaction between sources of revenue and priorities?

2. Think back on (or read again) the discussion in Chapter 2 about the functions that nonprofit organizations perform with regard to government. How does the case of the National Trust for Historic Preservation reflect those various roles?

3. Considering the evolution of the National Trust's activities, which might not have been possible to undertake under its previous funding model?

4. How might an increased reliance on local organizations and market forces to operate historic sites affect the National Trust's priorities in the future?

QUESTIONS FOR DISCUSSION

1. Should higher education be considered a private good, to be paid for by those who benefit from it? Or should it be considered a public good, available as a right to all citizens (like K–12 education)?

2. Should health care be considered a public, private, or common good?

3. If you were responsible for placing an older family member in an assisted-living community, would you prefer to select one that is nonprofit or one managed by a for-profit company? Or would it not make any difference to you? Why?

APPENDIX CASE

The following case in the Appendix of this text includes points related to the content of this chapter: Case 3 (The Y).

SUGGESTIONS FOR FURTHER READING

Books

Ott, J. S., & Dicke, L. A. (Eds.). (2016). *The nature of the nonprofit sector* (3rd ed.). Boulder, CO: Westview.

Ott, J. S., & Dicke, L. A. (Eds.). (2016). *Understanding nonprofit organizations* (3rd ed.). Boulder, CO: Westview.

Salamon, L. M. (2015). *The resilient sector revisited*. Washington, DC: Brookings Institution.

Articles

Liu, G. (2017, August 1). Government decentralization and the size of the nonprofit sector: Revisiting the government failure theory. *The American Review of Public Administration, 47*(6), 619–633.

Salamon, L. M., & Toepler, S. (2015, December). Government–nonprofit cooperation: Anomaly or necessity? *VOLUNTAS: International Journal of Voluntary and Nonprofit Organizations, 26*(6), 2155–2177.

Witesman, E. M. (2016, August 1). An institutional theory of the nonprofit: Toll goods and voluntary action. *Nonprofit and Voluntary Sector Quarterly, 45*(4), 97S–115S.

Governing and Leading Nonprofit Organizations

Working successfully with the board is critical to an executive's effectiveness. Since in most cases the CEO is appointed by and reports to the board, it is also essential to his or her professional survival.

iStock/PeopleImages

Chapter Outline

Nonprofit Governing Boards

The governing board of a nonprofit organization holds ultimate responsibility for ensuring that the organization serves its mission and for the overall welfare of the organization itself. In addition, as we discussed in Chapter 3, the board plays a critical boundary-spanning role in the open system of a nonprofit organization, connecting the nonprofit to its community and constituencies, often including important sources of financial support. Understanding the board's responsibilities and role and knowing how to work with the board is an essential skill of effective nonprofit managers, especially chief executive officers (CEOs). This chapter will discuss the nature and responsibilities of governing boards, some characteristics of effective boards, and some challenges faced by nonprofit boards today. It also will consider the important question of the relationship between the board and the organization's CEO. Before we get started, it is important to clarify some terminology.

The boards we are concerned with here are those that have a legal responsibility for governing their organizations—they are **governing boards.** Nonprofit organizations may have various groups that are called boards but that do not have such responsibilities, for example, advisory groups that may contribute their expertise to the organization and help raise funds but that do not hold any legal authority for its governance. Some advocate that such groups be called councils rather than boards, to keep that distinction clear (Worth, 2017a). We will discuss advisory councils later in this chapter, but it is important to recognize that while such groups may play an important role in the organization, they are not governing boards and they are therefore not a principal focus of this chapter.

Nonprofit organizations may use different terms to identify their governing boards. Most nonprofits are chartered as corporations, and members of the governing board are directors of the corporation under the law. Thus, many organizations use the term **board of directors** to identify them. Educational, cultural, and medical institutions often use the term **board of trustees.** Other organizations may use the terms board of governors, governing council, or something else to describe their governing boards. This book generally

Learning Objectives

After reading this chapter, students should be able to:

1. Describe various types of boards.

2. Explain the advantages and disadvantages of various types of boards.

3. Explain the governing board's legal and functional responsibilities.

4. Summarize prominent models of the board–CEO relationship.

5. Summarize theories regarding board behavior.

6. Explain the roles of the board chair, governance committee, and board professionals.

7. Identify board best practices.

8. Analyze cases, applying concepts from the chapter.

uses the generic term, governing board, except when discussing the board of a specific organization, in which case it maintains the name that organization uses.

In many cases, the person who heads the board is called the president of the organization, and the paid staff person who manages the organization is called the director or executive director. Some nonprofits—especially universities, hospitals, and major arts and cultural institutions—have adopted corporate terminology, calling the head of the board the chair and the paid executive the president. Others have adopted another corporate term, chief executive officer, or just CEO, to identify the top paid staff person. This chapter refers to the top board officer as the chair and the paid executive of the organization as the CEO.

One more point before we begin our discussion: The previous two chapters have drawn primarily from the academic literature, but this chapter relies significantly on the practitioner literature as well. Although the body of academic research on nonprofit boards is substantial, an influential literature on the topic has been developed by practicing nonprofit managers and consultants who work with boards and CEOs. Most of it describes what boards do or prescribes practices that boards should follow. Thus, this chapter draws on both academic and practitioner literature, including the work of some authors who are academics but also provide applied advice to boards.

Types of Governing Boards

Nonprofit governing boards are not all the same. For one thing, they differ in the way their members are selected. This may have important implications for how they operate and what agendas, priorities, and pressures members may bring to their work on the board. Different types of boards also may interact differently with the organization's CEO. For anyone working in a nonprofit organization, especially as a CEO or other senior executive, understanding how individuals come to be sitting at the governing board table is essential to understanding and working successfully with the board. Working successfully with the board is not only critical to the executive's effectiveness, it is also essential to his or her success, since in most cases the CEO is appointed by and is evaluated by the board. Table 4.1 summarizes types of boards and some of the advantages and disadvantages of each, which are discussed in the following paragraphs.

Elected Boards

Some boards are elected by the membership of the organization. This is common in member-serving and advocacy organizations. The methods used to elect the governing board vary; for example, some elections are conducted by mail or online and others are conducted at an annual meeting. Depending on the political and cultural environment within the organization, elections may be contested, and some individuals may, in effect, campaign for seats on the board. In other cases, a nominating committee of the existing board presents recommended candidates, who are often approved in a pro forma vote (that is, as a formality) by the membership.

Having an elected board may result in uncertainty about who will govern the organization from one year to the next—the outcome of elections is not always assured, and this may present a challenge to the CEO. What the board expects of the CEO may change; alliances and factions on the board may develop and shift; and the board's values and priorities may be dynamic, as political and philosophical crosscurrents among the membership find their way into the boardroom. The controversy that surrounded the election of the Sierra Club's board in 2004 provides an interesting illustration.

Table 4.1 Types of Boards

Type of Board	Advantages	Disadvantages
Elected governing boards	Help ensure that the organization and the CEO will be responsive to members' needs and priorities	Division among the membership may create disagreement on the board. Turnover on the board may make it difficult to sustain focus on long-term goals and plans. Skills of board members may be uneven, since personal popularity or positions on issues may influence election.
Self-perpetuating governing boards	Can maintain continuity of culture, priorities, goals Can craft the board membership to gain needed skills Can select members who are helpful in fundraising	May become unrepresentative of the community or constituency May become too stable to respond to changes in the environment May become too passive and yield too much authority to the CEO
Hybrid governing boards (often including appointed, self-perpetuating, ex officio)	May combine the responsiveness of elected boards, the stability of self-perpetuating boards, and accountability to an appointing authority—for example, a sponsoring church	Different interests and loyalties of board members may lead to a stalemate. Ex-officio members may not be fully committed to the organization.
Advisory councils	May be a vehicle for gaining expert advice on technical matters and/or for engaging more people as advocates and donors	If roles and responsibilities are not clearly defined and understood, may intrude on areas in which only the governing board has authority.

In 2004, anyone could join the Sierra Club with a $25 dues payment, and all members were eligible to vote in the election of the board. (That was an unusually low threshold for voting eligibility. Many organizations limit those eligible to vote to members who have been active for a certain period of time.) The Sierra Club's board included 15 members, and five seats were open for election that year. Individuals who were strong advocates for more restrictive U.S. immigration began to organize and encourage people sympathetic to their views to join the Sierra Club. Their goal was to have their sympathizers elect new board members who would change the club's position on the immigration issue. Within three months, 30,000 people became new members of the Sierra Club, compared with only 22,000 the previous year. Some of these new members had been organized by the anti-immigration candidates who were seeking election to the board. The election was contentious. Some described the outsiders' efforts as a "hostile takeover" and accused them of pursuing "the greening of hate." Others portrayed their efforts as addressing needed reform in the club's operation and claimed that their election would increase the club's effectiveness (Greene, 2004).

The insurgents did not prevail, but the Sierra Club case illustrates the potentially tumultuous environment that may be created when governing boards are elected by an organization's membership. To be the CEO of such an organization requires a high tolerance for discussion, debate, and uncertainty. In addition, the membership terms of an elected board tend to be relatively brief, and turnover on the board may make it difficult to sustain its focus on long-range goals and plans. Doing so requires considerable repetition of presentations and discussions, to maintain consensus among the changing membership of the board. It may be difficult to motivate members of an elected board to make gifts or engage in fundraising, since the ability and inclination to do so have not been criteria in their selection. The skills of board members may be uneven, since their personal popularity or their positions on certain issues may have been considerations in their election. However, elections do help ensure that the board will be representative of the constituency the organization serves and that the organization and its executive will be responsive to members' views and priorities. Elected boards are less likely than the next type, self-perpetuating boards, to become stale, uninvolved, or homogeneous in their membership.

Self-Perpetuating Boards

Most charitable nonprofits have **self-perpetuating boards**. New members of a self-perpetuating board are selected by the existing members of the board, who identify and enlist individuals according to criteria established by the board itself. When a new nonprofit organization receives a charter, it must identify the original, founding members of the governing board; many states mandate a minimum of three (Blackwood, Dietz, & Pollack, 2014). Those individuals then have the authority to develop bylaws, which specify the total number of members of the board. The original board members then may select others to join them, up to the maximum permitted under the bylaws (which, of course, the board retains the authority to change). As individuals leave the board or complete their terms of service, the remaining members select others to take their seats, and this cycle continues as long as the organization exists.

In contrast to a board elected by the membership, a self-perpetuating board creates a relatively stable situation for the organization and its CEO. Although the bylaws of many boards do limit the number of terms that members may serve, self-perpetuating boards tend to have longer terms than elected boards, and the board's membership changes more slowly. Thus, the board's policies and culture may reflect continuity, reinforced by the tendency of its members to select successors who generally share their values and views. Indeed, in some cases, strong or long-serving CEOs may gain significant influence in the selection of board members, in effect choosing their own bosses.

One advantage is that a self-perpetuating board can craft its own membership, selecting individuals specifically to bring needed skills or augment its strength in areas important to its work. Many boards maintain an inventory of the expertise and connections represented among their members and make a systematic effort to identify and recruit new members to fill any identifiable gaps. For example, if someone with financial expertise is needed, the board can seek out such an individual and recruit him or her to join the board in order to add those skills. A social service organization may try to find someone with professional social work experience who can help the board evaluate program recommendations from its staff. If the organization desires to increase the amount of support it receives from corporations, the board can identify and recruit corporate executives who may be helpful in that regard.

But these advantages of the self-perpetuating board are accompanied by some potential weaknesses as well. One is that the board may come to be unrepresentative of the constituency or community the organization serves. If the existing members of the board do not recognize the importance of diversity, they may continue to select new members who are just like them, drawing on their own business and social circles to fill board openings. Over time, the organization could become out of touch and be unable to adapt sufficiently to changes in its environment. Another risk is that a self-perpetuating board may become too stable in its membership and too complacent. There have been cases in which self-perpetuating boards, without the scrutiny that comes from the broader constituency of the organization, have been too lax in their oversight of their CEOs or even the behavior of their fellow board members, with disastrous results for the organization.

Appointed and Hybrid Boards

A third way in which board members may be selected is through appointment by some authority outside the organization. This is the typical model for public organizations; for example, the boards of state universities are usually appointed by the governor of the state. Few nonprofits have totally appointed boards, but some do have a number of appointed members. This is sometimes the case in nonprofit organizations that are affiliated with a religious congregation, which may have board members appointed by a church authority. Colleges and universities may have board members appointed by an alumni association. Organizations that work closely with government may have some board seats held by individuals who are appointed by a governmental authority. Boards also may have some seats that are held **ex officio**—that is, designated to be held by the individual who holds a certain office or position. For example, the vice president of the United States and the chief justice of the Supreme Court serve as ex-officio members on the Board of Regents of the Smithsonian Institution. An organization's CEO often holds a seat on the board in an ex officio capacity, which may come with or without a vote.

Other boards are hybrids, perhaps with some members being elected, some appointed, some self-perpetuating, and some serving ex officio. For example, a nonprofit that provides health services to underserved populations and that meets certain other requirements may become a Federally Qualified Health Center. That status brings certain benefits, including eligibility for enhanced reimbursements from Medicaid and Medicare for the medical care the organization provides. But this status also has an impact on the organization's governing board, since the law requires that a majority of board members be active, registered users of the health center and representative of the population served. Other members may be selected through another process and on the basis of other criteria, but the requirement regarding a majority of clients establishes a hybrid board and reduces flexibility in composing the board's overall membership (Rural Assistance Center, 2014).

Hybrid boards may represent the best of both worlds, encompassing an elected component that helps keep the organization responsive to its constituencies; a self-perpetuating component that provides stability, continuity, and perhaps financial support; and an appointed component that ensures the organization's accountability to a parent organization or government. However, hybrid boards also can present challenges. For example, if elected, appointed, and self-perpetuating members hold different views or agendas, stalemate may result. Ex officio members may not always feel a real commitment to the organization and its mission, having just landed on the board by virtue of some other position they hold. If this is the case, they may not fully participate in the work of the board or develop a full understanding of the organization and its work.

Advisory Councils

As mentioned earlier in this chapter, many nonprofit organizations and institutions have a variety of groups that may be called boards or councils but that do not have legal responsibility or authority for governance of the organization. In this book, we call such groups **advisory councils**.

There are various reasons why a nonprofit organization may create advisory councils, and the membership of a council will reflect its purpose. For example, it may be desirable to create a group of experts who can provide substantive advice on the organization's programs. A nonprofit providing human or social services may benefit from an advisory council of experts in the field, who can offer professional guidance and help to evaluate programs. Some may have advisory councils that include current or former clients, who provide feedback on the effectiveness of programs from that perspective. Professional schools in universities often have advisory councils that provide the dean and faculty of the school with advice regarding what skills are most needed by employers of their graduates, helping to shape the curriculum.

In other cases, advisory councils are established, at least in part, as a strategy for engaging more people who may become advocates or donors and who may assist in fundraising. Members of such a council augment the fundraising support that the governing board can provide. Sometimes, advisory councils also serve as a vehicle for engaging individuals who may eventually serve on the governing board, providing them with an opportunity to learn more about the organization and become better known to members of the governing board before they are invited to join it. Some individuals may prefer to serve on an advisory council rather than the governing board, desiring to make a contribution to the organization without assuming the formal responsibilities that come with service on a board of directors or board of trustees. Advisory councils also may be valuable as a sounding board for the CEO. Since the CEO does not report to the council and the council has no authority to formally evaluate the CEO, they may provide an opportunity to test new ideas and engage in brainstorming in an open manner before the CEO brings proposals directly to the governing board.

Some advisory councils may be formally established in an organization's bylaws, but others are informal, really just a group of individuals assembled by the CEO (or some other manager, for example, the director of a program or center) to bounce ideas and gain help with fundraising. However, even with advisory councils that are appointed by the CEO, it is often recommended that the council's role be formalized with guidelines that define its responsibilities, the limits of its activity, terms of service, and the manner of election or selection of members (Worth, 2017a). Since advisory councils do not have a formal role in governance, most do not need to be mentioned in legal documents, such as bylaws. But a written statement of the council's role may help to prevent an evolution of its role that could come into conflict with the authority of the governing board. For example, during a search for a new CEO, an advisory council may meet with candidates and make recommendations to the governing board. In other instances, the council's advice may relate to the organization's programs, and its opinions may affect the thinking of the governing board. In such cases, the council may have influence, but it needs to be clear that the governing board is the only entity that has authority (Worth, 2017a).

Our discussion in the balance of this chapter is focused on governing boards, that is, the boards that have legal responsibility for the organization and its programs.

The Governing Board's Responsibilities

Now that we understand different types of boards and how their members come to sit at the table, exactly what are their responsibilities? To whom are they accountable for meeting those responsibilities? The answers are not always simple.

As Bruce Hopkins (2003) describes it, nonprofit governing board members are "fiduciaries of the organization's resources and guardians of its mission" (p. 1). The board is accountable, that is, answerable, "for everything the organization does and how those things are accomplished" (Howe, 2002, p. 30). In the corporate world, it is clear to whom the directors are accountable and for what. Members of the corporate board of directors are the agents of the owners (the principals), and their responsibility is to direct and monitor the activities of management in the interests of the owners. Those interests also are quite clear—the maximization of economic value, consistent with sustainability of the business and the values of the owners. There are, of course, boards in the public sector as well. Most of them also have an identifiable constituency whose interest they serve; for example, a city council is accountable to the citizens of the city who elected them. But with nonprofits in the private sector, it is not always so clear to which owners the governing board is accountable.

Perhaps the owners of a member-serving organization are the members—it is primarily their interests that the organization exists to serve. But suppose the organization is a professional association that also sets standards for practice and certifies members of the profession. It may be primarily a member-serving organization, but doesn't the public— especially individuals served by members of the profession—also have some interest at stake? Who owns a charitable nonprofit, chartered to pursue a mission in the public interest? Are the owners the donors who support the organization through their philanthropy, the clients served by the organization, or perhaps the general public? If it is the general public, how can the board serve its interests when there may not be consensus about what the public interest means? Lacking the simple measure of results that the bottom line provides to business, by what standards should a nonprofit's effectiveness be evaluated, and who should determine those standards? Without clarity or agreement about who owns the organization, it is difficult to answer those questions. This creates an environment in which the board's responsibilities and role may be the subject of discussion and debate.

The Governing Board's Legal Responsibilities

Some governing board responsibilities are unambiguous; they are defined by law. Most laws affecting nonprofit boards are state laws, enforced by state attorneys general and state courts. However, the federal government, and specifically the Internal Revenue Service (IRS), has gained increasing power in recent years.

A landmark case in 1974 is often cited as providing the most definitive statement of nonprofit board responsibility. In that case, *Stern v. Lucy Webb Hayes National Training School for Deaconesses and Missionaries* (usually known as just "The Sibley Hospital Case"), parents of children who had been patients at the hospital alleged that members of the board of directors had mismanaged the hospital's assets and had placed hospital funds in accounts at banks in which they had personal financial interests. The parents claimed that hospital charges were unnecessarily high because of actions by the board. That claim provided their legal standing to bring the suit. Judge Gerhard Gessell found that the directors had not engaged in fraud or benefitted personally from their actions, but that they had breached their fiduciary responsibility to the hospital. He required that the board adopt a new policy and, in his decision, he articulated the standards of legal responsibilities of nonprofit boards that are still applied. Those responsibilities are summarized as the duties of care, loyalty, and obedience.

Care, Loyalty, Obedience

The **duty of care** in this context means paying attention and exercising due diligence in monitoring the organization's finances and supervising the actions of its management. Board members who do not attend meetings, who sleep through meetings, who do not read board materials, or who vote without understanding the issues are guilty of a lack of care. Included within the concept of care is the requirement that members of the board act in a prudent manner in managing the organization's finances—for example, by ensuring that any endowment assets are invested in a diversified portfolio to minimize risks. This does not mean that the board will necessarily have violated its responsibilities should it make the wrong investment decisions and the organization's assets decline, but merely that it should exercise common sense and not lose money as a result of recklessness, indifference, or failure to seek appropriate advice.

The **duty of loyalty** means that members of the board put the interests of the organization above their own personal financial interests or that of another organization with which they may also have a formal relationship. Individuals cannot use their position on a nonprofit board to enhance their own businesses or financial position. Closely related to the concept of loyalty is that of **conflict of interest**. A conflict of interest may arise, for example, when the board has to vote on whether to give a business contract to a company that may be wholly or partly owned by a member of the board itself or that perhaps may employ a board member's relative. Or a conflict could exist if the board is voting to enter some kind of partnership with another nonprofit, and one of the voting members serves on both boards. Conflicts of interest are not unusual, especially in smaller communities, where there may not be much choice about which suppliers or contractors the nonprofit can use and where prominent business leaders who own those businesses may serve on multiple nonprofit boards. Conflicts of interest are not illegal per se, but it is important how the board deals with them. Well-managed boards have formal conflict-of-interest policies that describe the procedures to be followed. Such policies usually require that potential conflicts be disclosed and that the board independently determine whether any business transaction that gives rise to the conflict is disadvantageous to the organization.

A legal concept related to conflict of interest is that of **private inurement**. Anyone who is an insider—generally any board member or officer of the organization—cannot unreasonably benefit from the organization's funds. This is related to the non-distribution constraint that was previously discussed. Nonprofits cannot use their profits to benefit owners, nor can they pay unreasonable amounts to board members or executives, which might have the same effect as sharing the profits with them—that is, giving them financial benefits as if they were owners. For example, a board can pay its CEO a salary and other compensation that is reasonable in exchange for his or her services, but anything exceeding a reasonable amount may be illegal private inurement. Likewise, an organization can do business with a company owned by a board member, but only if the payment is appropriate for the goods and services received. As mentioned previously, the federal Tax Cuts and Jobs Act of 2017 retained the standard of reasonableness overall, but imposed a tax on nonprofits that pay salaries exceeding $1 million under certain circumstances.

The **duty of obedience** requires that the board make sure that the organization is complying with the law and, in addition, that any decisions or actions taken are consistent with the organization's mission and governing documents, including its charter. Following the law may seem a simple charge, but ensuring that the organization does not drift from its mission may require greater vigilance, especially if that drift may bring with it some unanticipated risks.

Intermediate Sanctions

In general, if a board member carries out his or her duties faithfully and prudently, he or she is unlikely to be found personally liable for any losses that the organization may incur. Just making a mistake, or even a bad decision, is not in itself a violation of the board's responsibilities, provided that one has met the standards of care, loyalty, and obedience in making it. However, the risks to individual board members are somewhat higher today than they were prior to 1996, when federal legislation was passed providing the IRS with the authority to impose **intermediate sanctions**—that is, financial penalties to punish individuals who engage in or permit improper transactions.

Prior to the passage of intermediate sanctions, virtually the only weapon available to the IRS in dealing with a nonprofit board that violated its fiduciary responsibilities was to drop the atom bomb by revoking the organization's tax-exempt status. Facing an all-or-nothing situation and reluctant to take a drastic step that might essentially impose a death sentence on the organization—and bring harm to its clients—the IRS had few options. Intermediate sanctions provided a fly swatter alternative to the atom bomb of revoking tax-exempt status by permitting the IRS to impose penalties on individual board members or officers who engage in an **excess benefit transaction**, meaning one in which "a person's level or type of compensation is deemed to be in excess of the value of the person's services" (Hopkins, 2005, p. 219). The intermediate sanctions legislation and the regulations that the IRS has issued pursuant to it are complex and beyond the scope of our discussion here, but in summary, the penalties can involve return of the excess benefits received as well as additional penalties. Because it made the possibility of IRS action more than a remote threat, the passage of intermediate sanctions was a wake-up call to nonprofit boards.

Sarbanes-Oxley Act

Following corporate governance scandals in the early 2000s, including the demise of two major companies, Enron and WorldCom, Congress passed the **Sarbanes-Oxley Act** in 2002. Sarbanes-Oxley placed new requirements on the governance of publicly traded for-profit corporations. Only two provisions of Sarbanes-Oxley apply as well to nonprofit organizations: those regarding the destruction of documents and protection for whistle-blowers. However, Sarbanes-Oxley served as another wake-up call for nonprofit boards, and many nonprofits have voluntarily adopted some or all of its provisions (Williams, 2006). In addition, some state laws—for example, the California Nonprofit Integrity Act of 2004—have incorporated Sarbanes-Oxley–type requirements. Sarbanes-Oxley will be discussed again, in more detail, in Chapter 6 of this book, which discusses nonprofit accountability in a broader framework.

In 2004, the organization Independent Sector created a **Panel on the Nonprofit Sector** in the wake of several controversies involving nonprofit governance. The panel issued reports in 2005 and 2007, offering over 150 recommendations and 33 principles for good governance and ethical practice by nonprofits, many of which reflect Sarbanes-Oxley–like practices (Independent Sector, 2007). The principles were revised in 2015 to include new points addressing the need for organizational codes of ethics; whistle-blower policies; risk tolerance and mitigation in response to technological advances; earned income ventures undertaken by nonprofits; transparency and privacy; executive compensation; overhead costs; and fundraising using online platforms, mobile giving, social media, and crowdsourcing (Independent Sector, 2015). In addition to Independent Sector's principles, various state associations of nonprofits also have established standards and codes of best practices. Most encompass the practices of governing boards but also address practices in other areas. A fuller discussion of such standards can be found in Chapter 6 of this book.

Form 990

In 2009, the IRS introduced a revised version of **Form 990**, which nonprofits having at least $50,000 in annual revenues are required to file. The revised 990 included a number of changes, such as a new Part VI (see Figure 4.1), which requires "yes" or "no" answers to questions specifically addressing the practices of nonprofit boards. In effect, what had previously been a financial report was changed into a financial and *governance* report. To be clear, while all organizations that are required to file Form 990 must complete Part VI, the policies and practices described are generally not required by the Internal Revenue Code. That fact is even stated clearly in the heading for Section B of Part VI on the 990 form (IRS, 2013). And again, not all provisions of Sarbanes-Oxley apply to nonprofit organizations. But the questions included in Section B of Part VI of Form 990 inquire about practices that are strikingly consistent with its provisions. The IRS (2013) implies that providing the right answers may be well advised:

> In general, the policies and practices described in Part VI are not required by the Internal Revenue Code. However, organizations are required by the Code to make

Figure 4.1   IRS Form 990, Part VI

Part VI   **Governance, Management, and Disclosure** *For each "Yes" response to lines 2 through 7b below, and for a "No" response to line 8a, 8b, or 10b below, describe the circumstances, processes, or changes in Schedule O. See instructions.*
Check if Schedule O contains a response or note to any line in this Part VI . . . . ☐

Section A. Governing Body and Management

			Yes	No
1a	Enter the number of voting members of the governing body at the end of the tax year . .	**1a**		
	If there are material differences in voting rights among members of the governing body, or if the governing body delegated broad authority to an executive committee or similar committee, explain in Schedule O.			
b	Enter the number of voting members included in line 1a, above, who are independent .	**1b**		
2	Did any officer, director, trustee, or key employee have a family relationship or a business relationship with any other officer, director, trustee, or key employee?	**2**		
3	Did the organization delegate control over management duties customarily performed by or under the direct supervision of officers, directors, or trustees, or key employees to a management company or other person? .	**3**		
4	Did the organization make any significant changes to its governing documents since the prior Form 990 was filed?	**4**		
5	Did the organization become aware during the year of a significant diversion of the organization's assets? .	**5**		
6	Did the organization have members or stockholders?	**6**		
7a	Did the organization have members, stockholders, or other persons who had the power to elect or appoint one or more members of the governing body?	**7a**		
b	Are any governance decisions of the organization reserved to (or subject to approval by) members, stockholders, or persons other than the governing body?	**7b**		
8	Did the organization contemporaneously document the meetings held or written actions undertaken during the year by the following:			
a	The governing body?	**8a**		
b	Each committee with authority to act on behalf of the governing body?	**8b**		
9	Is there any officer, director, trustee, or key employee listed in Part VII, Section A, who cannot be reached at the organization's mailing address? *If "Yes," provide the names and addresses in Schedule O*	**9**		

Section B. Policies *(This Section B requests information about policies not required by the Internal Revenue Code.)*

			Yes	No
10a	Did the organization have local chapters, branches, or affiliates?	**10a**		
b	If "Yes," did the organization have written policies and procedures governing the activities of such chapters, affiliates, and branches to ensure their operations are consistent with the organization's exempt purposes?	**10b**		
11a	Has the organization provided a complete copy of this Form 990 to all members of its governing body before filing the form?	**11a**		
b	Describe in Schedule O the process, if any, used by the organization to review this Form 990.			
12a	Did the organization have a written conflict of interest policy? *If "No," go to line 13*	**12a**		
b	Were officers, directors, or trustees, and key employees required to disclose annually interests that could give rise to conflicts?	**12b**		
c	Did the organization regularly and consistently monitor and enforce compliance with the policy? *If "Yes," describe in Schedule O how this was done*	**12c**		
13	Did the organization have a written whistleblower policy?	**13**		
14	Did the organization have a written document retention and destruction policy?	**14**		
15	Did the process for determining compensation of the following persons include a review and approval by independent persons, comparability data, and contemporaneous substantiation of the deliberation and decision?			
a	The organization's CEO, Executive Director, or top management official	**15a**		
b	Other officers or key employees of the organization	**15b**		
	If "Yes" to line 15a or 15b, describe the process in Schedule O (see instructions).			
16a	Did the organization invest in, contribute assets to, or participate in a joint venture or similar arrangement with a taxable entity during the year?	**16a**		
b	If "Yes," did the organization follow a written policy or procedure requiring the organization to evaluate its participation in joint venture arrangements under applicable federal tax law, and take steps to safeguard the organization's exempt status with respect to such arrangements?	**16b**		

Section C. Disclosure

17   List the states with which a copy of this Form 990 is required to be filed ▶ -

18   Section 6104 requires an organization to make its Forms 1023 (or 1024 if applicable), 990, and 990-T (Section 501(c)(3)s only) available for public inspection. Indicate how you made these available. Check all that apply.

☐ Own website   ☐ Another's website   ☐ Upon request   ☐ Other *(explain in Schedule O)*

19   Describe in Schedule O whether (and if so, how) the organization made its governing documents, conflict of interest policy, and financial statements available to the public during the tax year.

20   State the name, physical address, and telephone number of the person who possesses the books and records of the organization: ▶

publicly available some of the items described in Question 18 of Part VI.... The IRS will use the information reported in Part VI, along with other information reported on the form, to assess noncompliance and the risk of noncompliance with federal tax law for individual organizations and across the broader exempt sector.

The State of Governance

In light of the requirements of law and best practice we have discussed, what is the state of nonprofit governance today? In a 2010 study, Amy Blackwood et al. (2014) found that a majority of nonprofits are compliant with many, but not all, of the principles covered by Form 990 questions. More than 60 percent of organizations had an audit conducted by an independent accountant, a formal review process for executive compensation, and a written conflict of interest policy. However, less than half of the organizations surveyed had whistle-blower policies or document retention and destruction policies, ironically, the only two provisions of Sarbanes-Oxley that do apply to nonprofit organizations. Not surprisingly, practices varied among organizations depending on certain characteristics. Larger organizations were more likely than smaller ones to follow all of the best governance practices. Health care institutions were the most likely to do so and arts institutions the least likely. Nonprofits that received government funds and older organizations were more likely to follow best practices than were others. In comparing their findings to some earlier studies, Blackwood et al. concluded that "The adoption of good governance practices certainly is on the rise" and speculated that IRS initiatives "may very well be creating a more effective culture of governance in the nonprofit sector" (p. 14).

The Governing Board's Functional Responsibilities

The law primarily dictates the things nonprofit boards *cannot* do—fail to exercise care, place its own members' individual interests above those of the organization, or lead the organization in directions inconsistent with its mission and the law. But what is it exactly that boards *should* do?

A number of authors have offered lists of a board's functional responsibilities—that is, job descriptions listing the duties that boards should perform (see, e.g., BoardSource, 2010; Ingram, 2015). Most lists are similar on the principal activities in which the board should be engaged, although there are often differences among the experts with regard to the division of specific tasks between the board and the organization's CEO. The following responsibilities are common to most board job descriptions, although, as we will see later, some authors express contrary views.

Appoint, Support, and Evaluate the CEO

Although the CEO may serve as an ex officio member of the board, that person is generally appointed by the board and serves at the pleasure of the board, subject, of course, to any contractual terms that may be negotiated at the time of appointment. However, having appointed the CEO, the board also has a responsibility to support that individual. This includes acting as a sounding board for the CEO to discuss ideas and problems and also coming to his or her defense when pressures arise from within or outside the organization. If the board's response to every criticism of the CEO's actions is to challenge him or her or to take the side of the critic, the board will quickly undermine the CEO's ability to be effective, and it is unlikely to attract or retain a strong executive. But the board also is responsible for setting expectations for the CEO, monitoring his or her performance against those expectations, and providing the executive with performance evaluations. Of course, if expectations are regularly not met, the board also has the responsibility of dismissing the CEO and beginning a search for a successor.

The relationship between the governing board and the CEO is complex, and it is a topic that generates its own considerable literature. The subject is of such importance that we will return to a more thorough discussion of it shortly.

Establish a Clear Institutional Mission and Purpose

Establishing the organization's mission is the responsibility of the board. Although the organization's charter states its purposes in broad terms, the board can and should periodically review its mission; indeed, doing so is often the first step in the process of strategic planning.

Approve the Organization's Programs

Although experts advise boards to avoid becoming involved in the details of management, most think that the board should approve the programs undertaken by the organization to meet its responsibility for ensuring adherence to the mission and protecting the organization's financial viability. For example, the board of a liberal arts college would need to consider whether establishing a business school would be consistent with its mission, the implications for the college's financial resources, and the ability of the college to maintain its academic standards and reputation in light of such an expansion of its programs. The board of an organization serving dinners to homeless people would need to consider any extension of its activities to provide medical services or housing. Because such decisions relate directly to the mission, which is the responsibility of the board, they cannot be delegated to the CEO or the staff.

Ensure Sound Financial Management and the Organization's Financial Stability

Protecting the organization's assets is, of course, central to the board's legal responsibility as fiduciary. Most boards approve annual budgets and receive regular reports of the organization's financial status. Most organizations engage outside auditors and many boards also have separate audit committees that meet with those outside auditors (Blackwood et al., 2014).

Some authors say that board members' responsibility to ensure the organization's fiscal soundness implies an obligation to provide their own financial gifts and actively engage in fundraising. Indeed, except perhaps for the debate about the appropriate relationship between the board and the CEO, no subject commands more ink, or more lung power, than the role of the board in giving and raising philanthropic funds. Of course, not all boards are expected to provide their personal financial support to the organizations they serve. Boards of member-serving organizations often have no significant responsibility for fundraising, since the largest portion of revenue may come from dues, subscriptions, or meeting fees. Organizations that are primarily or entirely dependent on revenue from government contracts and grants also may not place emphasis on the board's fundraising role. But in most charitable nonprofits, the board is expected to play a significant role in providing and soliciting philanthropic funds.

There are divergent views on whether board members should be required to give or raise a specific minimum amount, and the question raises some complicated issues. Some boards require a minimum personal gift from each board member. However, if this requirement is substantial, it may make it more difficult to achieve appropriate diversity among the board membership without making exceptions to the policy for those who may bring important skills and qualities but do not possess financial capacity. Then again, making such exceptions may introduce the perception that there are two classes of board members—those who give and those who don't. If that perception exists, those who cannot provide financial support may too readily defer to those who are known to be important sources of support to the organization. On the other hand, if the minimum is set so low that all board members can meet it, it can have the effect of converting an intended floor into a ceiling. In other words, some board members who have the financial ability to give more than the minimum may come to see the minimum as all that is expected of them, foreclosing the possibility of larger gifts. Such a situation may leave the organization with less total revenue than it might otherwise receive (Worth, 2016, pp. 135–136).

Some boards do not set a minimum for personal giving by board members but adopt what is often called a **give-or-get policy,** requiring that each board member either give personally or solicit gifts from others to total the minimum amount. However, this may also establish a standard that some board members may find difficult to meet, especially if they are not involved in business or professional circles that provide access to wealth. Furthermore, it raises the risk that board members may solicit gifts without coordination with the organization's staff, creating a potentially chaotic situation that could alienate donors. An alternative to setting minimums for board giving and getting is to simply establish the expectation that each board member will give and participate in fundraising proportionate to his or her capacity to do so. If that standard is firmly embedded in the culture of the board, then conscience and the judgment of peers may motivate the board to its peak fundraising performance without the risks inherent in defining specific minimum amounts. Whatever approach is taken by individual boards, the subject of the board's responsibility for giving and fundraising is on the agenda for discussion at many nonprofit organizations today (Worth, 2016).

Establish Standards for Organizational Performance and Hold the Organization Accountable

The board should define the standards by which an organization's effectiveness in achieving its mission is to be evaluated. Establishing standards to judge whether the organization is effectively employing the resources entrusted to it in pursuit of its mission is a fundamental aspect of the board's responsibility to those who provide financial support, to the society that grants the organization exemption from taxation, and to those whose needs its programs serve.

Some authors see the role of nonprofit boards as especially important because many nonprofits do not face the same market discipline that business firms do. As John Carver (2006) explains, "Without a market to summarize consumer judgment, [a nonprofit] organization literally does not know what its product is worth.... In the absence of a market test, *the board must perform that function*" (p. 15). Christine Letts, William Ryan, and Allen Grossman (1999) elaborate on this point:

> Compared to their for-profit counterparts, nonprofit boards carry a much bigger burden in demanding and supporting performance.... [In the for-profit world,] both boards and management can use market feedback to assess how well they are performing: customers, investors, and creditors all make evaluations that eventually show up in the bottom line.... In contrast, the nonprofit board must often substitute for many of the feedback systems available in the marketplace. Nonprofit clients very often do not have a choice of providers, and are therefore unlikely to signal dissatisfaction by "voting with their feet." [Funders of nonprofits] may signal dissatisfaction by withdrawing their support, but are much less likely to play the affirmative role of a shareholder activist or institutional investor. (p. 133)

For these reasons, Letts et al. (1999) argue that "nonprofit boards are more vital [than for-profit boards] in ensuring performance and accountability" (p. 132).

How do the activities of actual boards compare with the functional responsibilities identified by experts? In 2012, Grant Thornton conducted a survey of nonprofit boards and asked what activity or responsibility was the "most important focus" of the board in the preceding year. Of those responding, 27 percent identified strategic planning, 22 percent fundraising, 19 percent "ensuring effective programs," 9 percent "management performance," 5 percent protecting the organization's "reputation," 3 percent the "economy/recession," 3 percent "cash management," 2 percent "investment management," and 2 percent "enterprise risk management" (p. 4).

The Board and the CEO

Young, small nonprofit organizations often have a **working board.** In those situations, volunteer members of the board have a hands-on role and perform all of the organization's operations, from raising funds, to balancing its bank accounts, to making decisions about its programs. But as the organization grows and a professional is hired to serve as its executive officer, the division of responsibilities and functions between the board and that staff leader becomes a central consideration.

The relationship between the governing board and the organization's CEO is the subject of an extensive literature, reflecting divergent views. The questions addressed in this literature go well beyond who does what. They include fundamental assumptions about the nature of nonprofit governance and leadership.

At the heart of the matter is the question of who leads the nonprofit organization. In some organizations, the CEO may be dominant, with the board playing a passive role. The CEO proposes and the board disposes, often with little discussion or debate. As noted earlier, the CEO may even come to influence the selection of board members, in effect choosing his or her own bosses. This situation could arise in any organization, but it is especially common in organizations led by their founders, a special case we will discuss further in Chapter 5.

The realities of many organizations may enable CEOs to gain the upper hand. Boards are composed of "part-time amateurs," while the organization's staff, including the CEO, are "full-time professionals" (Chait, Holland, & Taylor, 1996, p. 3). In other words, the CEO may know more about the organization and its programs than do the lay trustees, especially if its programs involve highly technical services, and board members may be reluctant to show their ignorance by questioning. Large boards pose a special challenge in this regard. Individual board members may be unwilling to risk embarrassment by challenging a CEO's proposals in front of a large number of other board members, or they may assume that others on the board are well-informed and just go along with what appears to be a consensus. The CEO may control access to information about the organization, and indeed, the CEO may be the only one who knows what information actually exists. He or she may determine what information reaches the board and develop the agenda of matters that the board will even get to consider. In sum, it may be possible for a CEO to manipulate the board, orchestrate board meetings, and relegate the board to the role of a rubber stamp for his or her initiatives.

The danger in such a scenario is that the CEO could lead the board and the organization in directions that are inappropriate or risky and that the board may not be able to meet its responsibilities for ensuring adherence to mission, fiscal soundness, and optimum performance. For example, in 2002, the Washington, DC, community was shocked by allegations that the long-serving executive director of the United Way of the National Capital

Area (UWNCA), Oral Suer, had received as much as $1.6 million in improper payments, including non-reimbursed cash advances, payment for vacation and sick leave time that he had in fact taken, and reimbursement for travel and entertainment that were personal rather than related to United Way business. Those improper payments were alleged to have occurred over the period of 27 years that Suer was employed at the UWNCA (Wolverton, 2003). The UWNCA's board had 45 members, and some observers attributed the abuses to the board's large size and the fact that the executive director had maintained tight control over communication with the board and among its members. One former employee of the organization told the *Chronicle of Philanthropy,* "This was definitely a 'clapper' board. They listened to staff members tell wonderful stories about how much money we were raising, and they applauded instead of asking tough questions" (Wolverton, 2003, p. 27). Others cited the organization's internal culture, which made it difficult for the board to meet its fiduciary responsibilities. One board member said that the board met only four times a year, a total of eight hours, and that the large board discouraged her from speaking. She said that she didn't have the phone numbers of the other board members, so she was unable to follow up with them after meetings. When she tried to obtain the numbers, a secretary at UWNCA told her that the numbers were confidential (Wolverton, 2003).

An alternative scenario, in which the board micromanages the organization and usurps the authority of the CEO, is no better. Such a board is likely to find it difficult to attract or retain a strong chief executive and may find itself making decisions about details outside its expertise. What most experts recommend is neither of these extreme scenarios but rather a partnership between the board and the CEO in the leadership of the organization. There are, however, different views on exactly how this partnership should be constructed and should operate.

Various authors have addressed the subject of the board–CEO relationship. A comprehensive review would be beyond the scope of this chapter, but let's compare the thinking of three authors who are widely cited and whose different approaches highlight the major issues. First, we will look at John Carver's **policy governance model,** described in his 1990 book *Boards That Make a Difference* and in subsequent editions published in 1997 and 2006. Carver draws a clear line between the board's responsibility for *policy making* and the executive's responsibility for *implementation* and provides what he calls an "operating system" to ensure that the distinction is maintained. Next, we will review the concept of **governance as leadership,** described by Richard Chait, William Ryan, and Barbara Taylor (2005) in their book of that title. The book was sponsored by **BoardSource,** an organization that provides research, education, and assistance to nonprofit organization boards. Chait et al. (2005) challenge Carver (1990, 1997), writing that "governing is too complicated to reduce to simple aphorisms, however seductive, like 'boards set policies which administrators implement'" (p. 5). Instead, they advocate a leadership role for the board that blurs the distinction between policy and implementation and focuses the attention of both boards and CEOs on "what matters most." And, finally, we will consider the research of Robert Herman and Dick Heimovics (2005), who argue that the most effective CEOs are those who accept the reality of their "psychological centrality" in the organization and provide **board-centered leadership,** working to "develop, promote, and enable their boards' effective functioning" (p. 157). Following the original work by Herman and Heimovics, Herman has continued to discuss their findings in additional writings (e.g., Herman, 2016).

Carver's Policy Governance Model

According to John Carver (2006), boards should be the leaders of the organization, "not by invading territory best left to management but by controlling the big picture, the long term, and the value laden" (p. 6). But his diagnosis of the prevailing reality is bleak. He observes boards mired in the trivial, largely reactive to staff initiatives, and absorbed in reviewing and rehashing actions the staff has already undertaken (Carver, spp. 19–20). Carver argues that board committees are often organized in a way that leads to this condition. Committee responsibilities often coincide with those of senior managers; for example, there may be committees on finance, fundraising, program evaluation, and other areas of the organization's operation overseen by professional staff. In many cases, the staff prepares materials for meetings of the relevant committee and influences what items the committee considers. This structure pulls the board's attention into the details of each of the management silos. Board members thus become either super managers or just advisers to the professional staff. This prevents them from staying focused on big-picture matters such as mission and goals. As Carver writes, "Our tradition of board work encourages boards to derive their agendas from staff-based divisions of work. This common board practice is tantamount to classifying a manager's functions on the basis of his or her secretary's job areas" (p. 46).

Carver (2006) calls for a clear distinction between the work of the board and that of the management staff, and he argues that the board should lead the organization, focusing its attention on establishing policies. But this does not mean the kinds of policies that boards often discuss, such as personnel policies, which really reflect the work of management and are related to implementation rather than leadership of the organization. The board should make policies that reflect the board's values and the interests of the "moral owners" of the organization. In Carver's (2006) model, boards lead by developing and maintaining policies in four areas:

1. *Ends to be achieved:* Ends policy statements describe what the organization is to achieve and "could be called results, impacts, goals, or outcomes as well as ends, each title having its own connotations" (p. 48). The broadest ends statement would be the organization's mission. More specific ends policies might address more detailed goals—for example, those related to products, consumers, and costs.

2. *Means to the ends:* In Carver's model, means statements are expressed in terms of "executive limitations"—that is, boundaries that the CEO may not cross in pursuing the ends established by the board. For example, the broadest statement of policy in this area might be that the CEO may not violate the law. More detailed limitations might address more specific constraints, perhaps levels of cost and debt that may not be exceeded. Carver argues that by stating executive limitations in negative terms— that is, by prescribing what executives may *not* do—the board preserves maximum flexibility for the CEO. Subject to the constraints that the board has explicitly stipulated, the CEO is free to determine the best methods for achieving the ends that the board has established, without the board's inappropriate involvement in operations.

3. *Board–staff relationship:* Policy statements in this area clearly delineate the responsibilities of the board and the CEO, defining what decisions are delegated to the CEO and which ones are retained by the board. This category of statement also includes specific criteria for monitoring and evaluating the CEO's performance. Carter argues that one benefit of such clarity is that it addresses the common concern about board members communicating directly with other staff within the organization or with other volunteers. "In a formal sense, the CEO role insulates the staff from the board and the board from the staff. However, the insulation does not rigidly prohibit contact between board and staff members. On the contrary, those very human connections are never problematic if the formal roles are clear" (p. 161).

4. *Process of governance:* This fourth category of policy addresses the board's own role and operation, clarifying which owners it represents and defining its own "job process

and products"—for example, the procedure through which new board members are elected (p. 51).

A board practicing Carver's (2006) model would be driven in its meetings by the need to develop and maintain its policy manual. When issues arise, the first questions to be addressed would be to which category of policy the issue belongs, whose issue it is, and whether it is addressed by an existing policy—if not, a new policy needs to be adopted, eliciting discussion and debate. Carver argues that this approach steers boards away from the mundane, from show-and-tell presentations by staff, and from merely rubber-stamping the staff's recommendations. According to Carver, following the policy governance approach leads the board toward discussions that are focused on the long term and rooted in the board's values and perspectives (p. 129).

Chait, Ryan, and Taylor: Governance as Leadership

Now let's examine a different approach, the governance-as-leadership model proposed by Chait et al. (2005). Chait et al.'s 2005 book has gained wide visibility in the nonprofit sector, in part because of its sponsorship by BoardSource, which bases its board training programs largely on this model. A 2013 book by Cathy Trower provides a "practitioner's guide" that offers practical guidance to boards for implementing Chait et al.'s (2005) recommendations.

Chait et al. (2005) agree with many of Carver's criticisms of the way boards operate today. Boards are not leading their organizations. They are reactive to staff initiatives. They structure their work in a way that draws them into managerial details and routine technical work. Indeed, these authors argue, things are turned upside down. Boards are so mired in operational details that they are, in effect, *managing* their organizations. Meanwhile, CEOs are articulating missions, beliefs, values, and cultures—in essence *leading* their organizations and engaging in activities that "closely resemble conventional notions of *governing*" (Chait et al., 2005, p. 3). As the authors explain,

> In theory, if not in practice, boards of trustees are supposed to be the ultimate guardians of institutional ethos and organizational values. Boards are charged with setting the organization's agenda and priorities.... Boards are empowered to specify the most important problems and opportunities that management should pursue. If this logic holds, as we contend, then many nonprofit executives are not only leading their organizations, but ... they are actually governing them as well. (p. 3)

> With sophisticated leaders at the helm of nonprofits, a substantial portion of the governance portfolio has moved to the executive suite. The residue remains in the boardroom. This surprise twist in the story line suggests that the real threat to nonprofit governance today may not be a board that micro*manages* but a board that micro*governs,* while blind to governance as leadership. (pp. 4–5)

But while their diagnosis of board problems is similar to Carver's (1990, 1997, 2006), Chait and his colleagues (2005) offer a quite different prescription. Instead of drawing sharp lines between policy and implementation, clearly dividing the role of the board and that of the CEO, they call for breaking down the barriers and focusing the attention of both the board and the CEO on the critical issues facing the organization. In other words, the question should not be, "Is this an issue of policy or implementation?" Rather, the question should be, "Is the issue at hand important or unimportant, central or peripheral?" (Taylor, Chait, & Holland, 1999, p. 62).

In their book, Chait et al. (2005) define a new model, which they call "governance as leadership," based on three "modes" of governance in which a board may be operating at any given time—the **fiduciary mode**, the **strategic mode**, and the **generative mode**:

1. *The fiduciary mode:* When the board is operating in this mode, it is concerned with the "bedrock of governance," that is, with matters such as stewardship of tangible assets, faithfulness to mission, performance accountability, and obedience to law—in other words, generally addressing its legal responsibilities.

2. *The strategic mode:* When operating in the strategic mode, boards go beyond their basic fiduciary responsibilities and "create a true strategic partnership with management," addressing matters such as the organization's long-term directions and goals (p. 69).

3. *The generative mode:* A board in generative mode is engaged in generative thinking—that is, the creative, out-of-the-box thinking in which visionary leaders often engage. It relates to values and judgments, encompasses "sense making" (essentially, coming to understand things in new ways), and may result in insights that lead to paradigm shifts. The authors say that generative thinking is a necessary foundation for setting direction and goals and thus an essential activity of leadership.

Chait et al. (2005) observe that most boards work only in the fiduciary and strategic modes and therefore are not participating in leadership of the organization. However, "when trustees work well in *all three* [italics added] of these modes, the board achieves governance as leadership" (p. 7). Thus, rather than maintaining a clear distinction between what is the board's territory and what is the CEO's, Chait et al. (2005) propose that boards and CEOs focus together on what matters most, moving together among the three modes as appropriate to address the issues at hand. Setting goals, and thus using generative thinking, cannot be a task for the CEO or the board alone but rather must be a *shared* activity:

> Because we resolutely regard this [generative thinking] as shared work, we cannot offer what the board-improvement field so often promises trustees and executives: a set of bright lights that neatly divide the board's work (policy, strategy, and governance) from the staff's (administration, implementation, and management). It simply makes no sense to reserve generative work for boards when leaders are vital to the process, or to reserve for leaders work that belongs at the heart of governance. Generative work demands a fusion of thinking, not a division of labor. (Chait et al., 2005, p. 95)

Simply stated, Carver (1990, 1997, 2006) envisions the board and the CEO on opposite sides of the table, one clearly labeled "policy" and the other "implementation." Chait and his coauthors (2005) envision a three-sided table, each representing one of the modes discussed previously. The board and the CEO sit together on one side but move around the table to the other sides, depending on the nature of the business to be considered at the time.

Herman and Heimovics: Psychological Centrality and Board-Centered Leadership

In Carver's (1990, 1997, 2006) approach, boards lead their organizations. Chait et al. (2005) describe a model for leadership shared by the board and the chief executive. In 2005, Robert Herman and Dick Heimovics provided a third perspective, which Herman has continued to explore in more recent writing (Herman, 2016). Based on their research concerning effective nonprofit CEOs, Herman and Heimovics offer a pragmatic approach, concluding that CEOs should lead but that their leadership needs to be board centered and designed to support the board in meeting its governing responsibilities.

The **purposive-rational model** of organizations, based on Max Weber's theory of the bureaucracy, conceives of the board as the top of a hierarchy and the CEO as merely its agent. Indeed, Herman and Heimovics's (2005) review of the normative literature on nonprofit boards finds that most research has been based on that model and thus "has advanced a heroic ideal for nonprofit boards" (p. 155). However, they apply the **social-constructionist model** and explain that "official or intended goals, structures, and procedures may exist only on paper. Actual goals, structures, and procedures emerge and change as participants interact and socially construct the meaning of ongoing events" (p. 156). Regardless of what the organizational chart or the conventional view of organizations may suggest, Herman and Heimovics find that the reality in most organizations is that of **executive psychological centrality.** In other words, it is the CEO who is actually seen as responsible for the organization's success or failure. Herman and Heimovics interviewed CEOs, board chairs, and other staff members and found that all of them saw the chief executive as "centrally responsible for what happens," including both successful and unsuccessful events (p. 156). This does not imply that the CEO holds more formal authority than the board or that the CEO is indeed the central figure in the life of the organization. "Psychological centrality" means that he or she is *perceived* as responsible, even by members of the board.

If this is the reality, then what do Herman and Heimovics (2005) recommend that CEOs should do? They do *not* recommend that CEOs become autocrats or demote their boards to rubber stamps, but rather that they take a leadership role to ensure "that boards fulfill their legal, organizational, and public roles" (p. 156). In exercising board-centered leadership, CEOs take responsibility for "supporting and facilitating the board's work." In doing so, they engage in six behaviors that Herman and Heimovics observed among the effective, board-centered executives they studied (p. 158):

1. Facilitating interaction in board relationships

2. Showing consideration and respect toward board members

3. Envisioning change and innovation for the organization with the board

4. Providing useful and helpful information to the board

5. Initiating and maintaining structure for the board

6. Promoting board accomplishments and productivity

Herman and Heimovics (2005) conclude that not only are the CEOs who have developed these board-centered leadership skills effective in their roles, but they also have hardworking, effective boards. "The board-centered executive is likely to be effective because he or she has grasped that the work of the board is critical in adapting to and affecting the constraints and opportunities in the environment" (p. 159). In a study of "high-impact nonprofits," Leslie Crutchfield and Heather Grant (2012) draw a similar conclusion, writing that while "many leaders try to minimize their interactions with their board, or they perpetually fight with them … great nonprofit leaders have a positive relationship with the board. They share leadership to advance the larger cause" (p. 201).

But, what is the reality? Do most nonprofit CEOs provide board-centered leadership as Herman and Heimovics (2005) and others recommend? The 2011 *Daring to Lead* study (Moyers, 2011) suggests that many are not doing so. The majority of CEOs responding to the study reported spending less than 10 hours per month on board-related activities. Moyers (2011) speculates that "perhaps executives fail to see the immediate benefit of spending more time with the board, since the activities on which the largest number of respondents said they need to spend more time—marketing and fundraising—produce tangible results" (p. 5). But, paradoxically, nonprofit CEOs who do spend more time on the board report more satisfaction with board performance, which is consistent with the conclusions of the earlier research by Herman and Heimovics (Moyers, 2011, p. 6).

Explaining Board Behavior

The recommendations of Chait et al. (2005), Carver (1990, 1997, 2006), and Herman and Heimovics (2005) suggest how things *should* be. But how do governing boards actually behave? Where do they focus their attention? And how do they define their relationship with the CEO? And what determines the patterns that we can observe? These questions have been the subject of research by various scholars, who have proposed contingency approaches; in other words, they argue that how boards behave depends on the internal and external conditions they face.

Patricia Bradshaw (2009) identified five "board configurations," determined in part by the external circumstances that the organization faces. For example, organizations facing an external environment that is simple and stable tend to follow something similar to Carver's policy governance model, in which the board is "more formalized, hierarchical, and bureaucratic" (Bradshaw, p. 69). Boards that face an external environment of uncertainty and turbulence, but that also have a simple array of stakeholders, adopt an "entrepreneurial/ corporate configuration." That is less formal and may include more overlap of board and staff roles (Bradshaw, p. 70), perhaps something more like the environment implied by Chait et al. (2005). Those facing a stable environment but a complex constituency adopt a constituency/ representative configuration, in which the board includes representatives of various groups or associated organizations (Bradshaw, p. 69), perhaps something like the hybrid model discussed earlier in this chapter. Organizations that must address turbulence and uncertainty in their environments as well as complex, decentralized constituencies may exhibit what Bradshaw calls an "emergent cellular configuration." That includes a flatter structure that is dynamic and fluid, without clear roles and lines of authority, and with participants often demonstrating a commitment to alternative or "nonmainstream" ideologies (Bradshaw, p. 70). And, of course, some boards illustrate variations on these four basic configurations. The existence of these models reflects the reality discussed in Chapter 3, that nonprofit organizations are open systems, highly influenced by the environment that surrounds them.

In 2010, Francie Ostrower and Melissa Stone studied boards and also took a contingency approach, looking at both internal and external variables. They found that boards at larger organizations are more focused on financial monitoring than on external roles (p. 912). Boards without a professional CEO are more likely to monitor programs and services than those that have a professional CEO in place (p. 912). Boards with women as members are more attuned to external roles and boards with members who also serve on corporate boards tend to focus more on financial oversight (p. 913). Larger boards are more involved in fundraising than are smaller boards, perhaps, as Ostrower and Stone speculate, because the board has been made larger in part as a fundraising strategy (p. 913). An interesting—and likely controversial— finding is that "having the CEO as a voting member of the board undermines the governance role of the board" (Ostrower & Stone, p. 913).

Managing Nonprofit Boards

In earlier times, an invitation to join a nonprofit board might have been construed as primarily a social opportunity. Although boards had legal responsibilities, in the days before Sarbanes-

Oxley, Form 990, and charity watchdogs, many could operate informally and comfortably, without too much attention to their effectiveness, any expectation that their work would be scrutinized by outsiders, or perhaps any great understanding of the board's role. But developments discussed in this chapter have changed the environment, requiring that the board's activity and performance be actively monitored and managed.

Role of the Chair

The board chair is the individual responsible for leading the board. In addition, the chair is responsible for board process and board tasks. With regard to the former, it is the chair's responsibility to build the board into a team and to establish its culture. The chair also is primarily responsible for identifying the tasks that the board will undertake, that is, setting its agenda. In practice, identifying the board's tasks is often a responsibility shared with the CEO and committees of the board (BoardSource, 2010).

There sometimes can be tension arising from confusion about the respective roles of the board chair, the board, and the CEO (BoardSource, 2010). Carver (2006) emphasizes the point that only the full board can make decisions and take action; in other words, the chair leads the board but does not hold full authority for the organization. The CEO is appointed by the board, not by the chair, and the CEO reports to the board, not to its chair as an individual. In other words, as Carver (2006) explains, the board chair and the CEO are more like colleagues than supervisor and subordinate. Nevertheless, the board chair is often the board's principal liaison to the CEO, and it is important that the two individuals establish and maintain "a professional relationship with clear boundaries" (BoardSource, 2010, p. 88).

Governance Committee

In years past, many boards—primarily those that were self-perpetuating—had a standing committee charged with identifying possible new board members and with recommending candidates for election by the full board. Usually called the nominating committee or committee on nominations, this group functioned essentially as the board's talent scout; its responsibility was primarily to assure that individuals selected to join the board would be compatible with the board's culture and, perhaps, bring the capacity to provide personal financial support and help with fundraising. In most well-managed boards today, the relatively simple task of the nominating committee has been expanded and the committee has been renamed as the governance committee, or by some similar term, reflecting its larger role. As BoardSource (2010) explains:

> Rather than focusing on nominations for annual elections [like a nominating committee], the governance committee works year-round to guarantee that the board takes responsibility for its own development, learning, and behavior; sets and enforces its own expectations; and allots time, attention, and resources to understanding its stewardship role. The governance committee does not run the board, but it makes it possible for the board to be well-run. (p. 63)

The responsibilities of the governance committee encompass that of identifying potential new members, like the traditional nominating committee, but also a broader process of board development, which generally includes nine steps: identify the board's needs in terms of skills, knowledge, connections, and perspectives; identify and cultivate the interest of prospective board members to meet those needs; recruit new board members; provide new members with orientation, both to the board and to the organization; involve board members in appropriate committee and task force assignments; educate the board, both with regard to the organization's mission and programs and to best governance practice; evaluate the board as a whole as well as individual members; rotate members through term limits; and celebrate exemplary board performance (BoardSource, 2010, pp. 100–101).

Periodic self-evaluation is a best practice recommended by BoardSource (2010) and others. The governance committee initiates board evaluations, which typically use surveys, sometimes conducted by an outside consultant. Some boards also require the evaluation of individual members, which may include self-evaluation and/or evaluation by peers. This is commonly undertaken when an individual member is being considered for election to a new term (BoardSource, 2010, p. 269).

Board Professionals

Overall management of the board is a responsibility of the board chair, and perhaps a governance committee, working in cooperation with the CEO. Other members of the organization's staff also may be involved in supporting board committees; for example, the chief financial officer may work closely with a finance committee and the chief development officer with a development or fundraising committee of the board. When such circumstances exist, most authors, notably Carver (2006), emphasize the importance of maintaining clarity with regard to reporting lines and the authority of individual board members. For example, the chief financial officer, chief development officer, and other senior staff members may provide staff support to their respective board committees and their chairs and develop close relationships with them, but those officers report to the CEO, not to the committee chairs. In addition, the committee chairs have no authority to direct staff of the organization. Their committees may develop recommendations to the full board, which the full board may adopt and transmit to the CEO, who may in turn delegate responsibility to other senior staff (Carver, 2006). Of course, in many cases personal relationships may lead to a situation in which not all communication and influence follow such formal lines. (Remember our earlier discussion about the informal hierarchies that exist in many nonprofit organizations.) But if the appropriate roles of the board, individual board members, and staff members are not respected, there is the potential for undermining the CEO and creating tension within the organization.

In some large organizations with large boards, a senior staff member is charged explicitly with supporting board development activities. This is a responsibility that is sometimes assigned to the chief development officer, since that individual often enjoys close relationships with board members, especially if the board is engaged in fundraising and includes important donors. In other cases, the organization's general counsel may play this role, in light of his or her knowledge regarding the legal requirements of governance. The individual may also be titled **corporate secretary** and have responsibility for the maintenance of the organization's official documents and records. Some institutions, notably colleges and universities, have a senior staff officer for whom supporting the board is a full-time job. The Society for Corporate Governance was founded in 1946 and includes board professionals in the corporate and nonprofit sectors (www.governanceprofessionals.org/about/aboutus). Reflecting the growing prevalence of such positions in higher education institutions, the Association of Governing Boards of Universities and Colleges (AGB), maintains a program for board professionals and sponsors an online network and conferences for members (agb.org/agb-board-professionals). Governing board management is thus emerging as an identifiable subspecialty of nonprofit management.

Nonprofit Board Effectiveness

"So," students may be wondering at this point in the chapter, "what's the bottom line?" Are most nonprofit boards effective or not? What are the characteristics of effective boards?

What is the right way to define the relationship between the board and the nonprofit CEO? What is indeed the best model for governance, and what are the best practices that boards should follow?

Critics of Board Performance

In answer to the question of how nonprofit boards are doing, there is no shortage of negative commentary extending over decades. For example, in 1996, Chait, Holland, and Taylor reported that "after 10 years of research and dozens of engagements as consultants to nonprofit boards, we have reached a rather stark conclusion: effective governance by a board of trustees is a relatively rare and unnatural act" (p. 1). Writing a decade later, Carver (2006) essentially agrees, asserting that "the problem is not that a group or an individual *occasionally* slips into poor practice, but that intelligent, caring individuals regularly exhibit procedures of governance that are deeply flawed" (p. 18). Nearly a decade after Carver's observation, Ryan, Chait, and Taylor (2013) report continuing concerns, writing that "the board is widely regarded as a problematic institution. And it's not just the occasional nonprofit financial implosion or scandal that's troubling. All institutions, after all, have their failures. Perhaps more worrisome is the widespread sense that underperforming boards are the norm, not the exception."

Such criticisms cannot be ignored, but it may be prudent to question the evidence behind such sweeping statements. Some are based on experience rather than research. Some are reported by consultants who are called on to work with troubled boards and whose samples therefore may be somewhat self-selecting. Moreover, some assessments may reflect the values and views of the assessor about what nonprofit organizations and their boards should be like.

In a study published in 2017, BoardSource surveyed the opinions of board chairs and nonprofit CEOs regarding the performance of their boards. The results were more nuanced than the realities portrayed by the harshest critics. Boards were described as performing well with regard to fundamental responsibilities, including understanding of the mission and providing financial oversight. Survey respondents did see room for improvement with regard to external responsibilities, including fundraising, advocacy, community building, and outreach (BoardSource, 2017, p. 28).

In sum, the evidence suggests that it is unreasonable to argue that board failure is the norm. However, it is reasonable to believe that the performance of boards and their members can be improved and to continue the search for best practices in nonprofit governance.

The Search for Best Practices

Various researchers have attempted to identify behaviors that are associated with effective nonprofit governing boards—that is, to identify those practices that, if followed, will lead to effective governance. BoardSource (2018) assembled a panel of experts to address the question. Their consensus produced the following "twelve principles of governance that power exceptional boards":

1. *Constructive partnership:* Exceptional boards govern in constructive partnership with the chief executive, recognizing that the effectiveness of the board and chief executive is interdependent. They build this partnership through trust, candor, respect, and honest communication.

2. *Mission driven:* Exceptional boards shape and uphold the mission, articulate a compelling vision, and ensure the congruence between decisions and organizational

values. They treat questions of mission, vision, and core values not as exercises to be done once, but as statements of crucial importance to be drilled down and folded into deliberations.

3. *Strategic thinking:* Exceptional boards allocate time to what matters most and ensure the congruence between decisions and core values.

4. *Culture of inquiry:* Exceptional boards institutionalize a culture of inquiry, constructive debate, and engaged teamwork that leads to sound and shared decision making.

5. *Independent-mindedness:* Exceptional boards are independent-minded. When making decisions on behalf of the organization, board members put the interests of the organization above those of the chief executive, themselves, or other interested parties.

6. *Ethos of transparency:* Exceptional boards promote an ethos of transparency and ethical behavior by ensuring that donors, stakeholders, and interested members of the public have access to appropriate and accurate information regarding finances and operations.

7. *Compliance with integrity:* Exceptional boards govern with full recognition of the importance of their fiduciary responsibilities, developing a culture of compliance through appropriate mechanisms for active oversight.

8. *Sustaining resources:* Exceptional boards ensure that the organization's resources are balanced with its strategic priorities and capabilities. Individual board members extend the reach of the organization by actively using their own reputations and networks to secure funds, expertise, and access.

9. *Results oriented:* Exceptional boards track the organization's advancement toward mission and evaluate the performance of major programs and services.

10. *Intentional board practices:* Exceptional boards make form follow function when it comes to their own operations. To provide stable leadership to the organization, they invest in structures and practices that transcend individuals and thoughtfully adjust them to suit changing circumstances.

11. *Continuous learning:* Exceptional boards embrace the qualities of a continuous learning organization, evaluating their own performance and assessing the value that they add to the organization.

12. *Revitalization:* Exceptional boards energize themselves through planned turnover, thoughtful recruitment, and intentional cultivation of future officers.[1]

BoardSource's 12 principles of governance (2018) offer an attractive description of an exceptional board and reflect the consensus of a distinguished panel of experts assembled to develop them. But it is nevertheless primarily a compilation of practitioner wisdom rather than science. And there remains no single definition of board effectiveness. This is so in part because there is no single standard for defining the effectiveness of nonprofit organizations. As John Carver (2006) notes, the variables chosen for measurement in some research studies seem to imply

that effectiveness in governance is to be judged by whether board members are more fulfilled, challenged, or involved; the CEO is happier or the board is less meddlesome; the board raises more funds; grant revenues are increased; committees are more active; or the board chair perceives the CEO to be meeting his or her objectives. (p. 337)

The link between such variables and the effectiveness of boards—or organizations—remains elusive. BoardSource's 2017 survey found that 93 percent of board chairs think that the board has a positive or very positive impact on the organization's performance. That view is also held by 81 percent of CEOs (BoardSource, 2017, p. 44). As BoardSource acknowledges, its findings report perceptions, which are subjective and lack "objective validation" (p. 44). Some academic authors have addressed that point. In a 2002 review of the literature on nonprofit effectiveness, Robert Herman and David Renz conclude that "[board] effectiveness is whatever significant stakeholders think it is, and there is no single objective reality." Calling the concept of best practices "somewhat of a holy grail," they advise nonprofit boards and CEOs to take a skeptical view of "one right way" prescriptions:

> Many sources that claim to offer "best practices" for NPO [nonprofit organization] boards or management provide little or no basis for their assertions. *The evidence from our … study does not support the claim that particular board and management practices are automatically best or even good (that is, that using them leads to effective boards and organizations).* We prefer to talk in terms of "promising practices" to describe those approaches that warrant consideration.

> Not only is there no "silver bullet" (i.e., one practice that ensures board effectiveness)—there is no "silver arsenal." In the context of other research, we support the assertion that boards (perhaps with facilitative leadership from their chief executives) need to identify those processes that are most useful to them. Boards should not use a practice just because other boards, experts, or consultants say it is useful. They should ask some key questions: Does the practice fit this board's circumstances? Does the practice actually help the board reach good decisions? Does the practice contribute to the organization's success? (Herman & Renz, 2002, pp. 6–7)

In a subsequent review, Renz and Herman (2016) reaffirm their previous expression of caution. They acknowledge that "recent research clearly adds further support for the conclusion that (in at least in some ways), board effectiveness is related to organizational effectiveness" (p. 280). But, they add, "there is much more to learn" (p. 280) and reiterate that "the promise of best practices should be viewed with skepticism" (p. 283). The authors conclude, as in earlier writing, that "the evidence does not support the claim that any particular board and management practices … automatically … [lead] to increased effectiveness for boards and organizations" (p. 283).

The skepticism expressed by Herman and Renz (2002, 2008) and Renz and Herman (2016) about best practices should not be interpreted as saying that boards are unimportant or that the literature on governance has nothing to offer and should be disregarded. Rather, their conclusions are consistent with the philosophy expressed in Chapter 1 of this text: There is often no right answer, and the best way is often pragmatic and eclectic. This includes viewing a problem from multiple perspectives and drawing from various approaches selectively as the situation may dictate.

The Challenge of Nonprofit Governance

Serving as a member of a nonprofit board today is an interesting and challenging assignment. Nonprofit boards are buffeted by strong crosscurrents emanating from virtually all their constituencies. The forces of law, media scrutiny, and more demanding funders are pushing them to do a better job of governance. At the same time, the financial pressures facing many nonprofits in light of diminished government support, increased competition for philanthropy, and the rising needs and expectations of their clients are leading to greater emphasis on their responsibilities to serve as the organization's advocates, protectors, and fundraisers. As the brief review in this chapter reveals, the literature of nonprofit governance includes an abundance of advice, but some of it is inconsistent, even contradictory. Today's boards are being exhorted not only to raise money and promote the organization, but also to be more aggressive in monitoring its performance. They are told to develop independent sources of information about the organization's operations but to stay focused on the big picture and not meddle in operations, to maintain a clear line between themselves and their CEO but not to forfeit their responsibility for leadership.

Nonprofit boards are expected to be Janus-like—that is, like the Roman god of doorways and arches, who was said to have two faces and be able to look outward and inward at the same time. Nonprofit organizations are open systems, with vaguely defined and often porous boundaries. The board is positioned on that boundary, between the organization and its external environment. From that position, the board is expected to look inward, fulfilling its fiduciary responsibilities on behalf of the membership or society. It is a kind of watchdog, responsible for ensuring that the organization is accountable for the resources entrusted to it, for assuring that those resources are used effectively in pursuit of its mission, and for representing the interests and viewpoints of the owners, whoever they may be.

But board members are also expected to be looking outward in order to meet their responsibilities to the organization itself and advance its interests. This is especially true for boards of charitable nonprofits, which may depend at least in part on philanthropic support. Because they are often leading citizens themselves, board members bring credibility to the organization in the broader community and authenticate its worthiness to receive support. They serve as its ambassadors and advocates, increasing its visibility and reputation within their own social and business circles. They protect the organization against inappropriate intrusions on its autonomy by government, donors, or other external forces. Further, they have a responsibility to ensure the organization's financial strength and sustainability, which many accomplish in part through giving or helping secure financial resources. These dual responsibilities—to society and to the organization itself, looking inward at the same time as looking outward—can sometimes be complex and competing. As Chait et al. (1996) explain,

> Boards constantly wrestle with when to be "product champions" and when to be studied neutrals—whether to stand and cheer like rabid partisans when the President of the United States delivers the State of the Union address or to remain seated and stone-faced like the Supreme Court justices. (p. 3)

As Table 4.2 suggests, the complex responsibilities of boards may imply somewhat different ideal qualities in the individuals selected to serve, depending on which set of responsibilities is emphasized—a possible trade-off between what is often called "wisdom" (shorthand for the skills and judgment needed to govern well) and "wealth" (meaning the ability to give or obtain funds and other external resources). To fulfill their fiduciary responsibilities, boards must include individuals of integrity, and at least some will need to have specialized knowledge in finance and perhaps in professional fields related to the organization's programs and services.

But to advance its reputation, protect its interests, and secure funds, a nonprofit also needs board members who are individuals of stature in their communities, perhaps having influence with governmental officials or other regulators, and who have either the wealth to be significant donors or access to other individuals, foundations, or corporations that can provide financial support. Of course, there may be individual candidates for governing board service who are possessed both of wisdom and of wealth—that is, who are equally well suited to meet their responsibilities for governing the organization and for serving as its external advocates and fundraisers. But not all individuals may be strong in all the requisite qualities.

Table 4.2 The Board's Sometimes Competing Responsibilities

To society:	To the organization:
Accountability for resources and results	Advocacy and authenticity
Adherence to mission and law	Protection of autonomy
Representation of community needs	Fiscal stability and sustainability
Indicated board member qualities:	**Indicated board member qualities:**
Integrity	Stature
Expertise on programs and finances	Influence
Knowledge of community/clients	Wealth or access to wealth

Boards attempting to craft their membership and faced with selecting a new member to fill an open seat may indeed face a dilemma regarding which qualities should be emphasized (Worth, 2005).

Likewise, in deciding on which issues to focus its limited time and attention, a board may face either-or choices between the tasks associated with governing and those associated with advancing the organization, its interests, and its resources. Today's environment presents increasing pressure on boards to do all things better—to be better stewards and better fundraisers and to become more engaged with the organization's planning, programs, and effectiveness while also giving and raising more funds to support its work. The proper trade-offs between wealth and wisdom and how to balance the sometimes competing demands are questions prompting discussion—and some anxiety—in many nonprofit boardrooms today.

CHAPTER SUMMARY

The governing board holds ultimate responsibility for the nonprofit organization. There are various types of boards, including those elected by the organization's membership; self-perpetuating boards; boards appointed by some outside authority; and hybrids, which may include elected, self-perpetuating, appointed, and ex officio members. Each of these types offers advantages but also introduces risks for the organization and the board.

The governing board's fiduciary responsibilities are defined in law and include the duty of care, the duty of loyalty, and the duty of obedience. Since the passage of intermediate sanctions in 1996 and the Sarbanes-Oxley

Act in 2002, there has been increased scrutiny of nonprofit boards by federal and state governments, the media, and other organizations. Under intermediate sanctions, nonprofit board members can face individual penalties for violating their fiduciary responsibilities, and many boards adopted new conflict-of-interest and disclosure policies in response to that legislation. Although Sarbanes-Oxley applies primarily to publicly traded corporations, many nonprofit organizations have voluntarily adopted some or all of its provisions, and some have been encompassed in legislation passed by states. Independent Sector's Panel on the Nonprofit Sector issued 33 principles for good governance in 2007 and a revised version was released in 2015. Some provisions reflect Sarbanes-Oxley–like requirements. Some state associations of nonprofits also have established standards for best governance practice that are used as the basis for accreditation programs. Implementation by the IRS of a revised Form 990 in 2009 further focused the nation's attention on nonprofit accountability and the responsibilities of boards. Some questions on Form 990 also reflect Sarbanes-Oxley–like principles, which will be considered further in Chapter 6 of this book.

Functional responsibilities of boards have been defined in the literature and include appointing, supporting, and evaluating the CEO; establishing a clear institutional mission and purpose; approving the organization's programs to ensure consistency with its mission and financial prudence; ensuring sound management and financial stability; and establishing standards by which the organization's performance will be evaluated. Some people view the board's responsibility to ensure the organization's financial stability and sustainability as implying an obligation on the part of board members to give from their personal resources and actively engage in fundraising. Some boards have policies requiring that members give or raise a minimum amount, but others rely on a culture that encourages members to participate as appropriate to their capacities.

The relationship between the governing board and the CEO is the subject of a substantial literature. In some organizations, especially those managed by a founder, the CEO may be a dominant figure, and the board may be largely reactive to the executive's initiatives. Most experts call for a partnership between the board and the CEO but differ on how that partnership should be designed. Three experts discussed in this chapter include John Carver (2006), whose policy governance model suggests a clear separation of roles, defined in policies established by the board related to ends, means, board–staff relationships, and governance process. Chait et al. (2005) propose a model they call "governance-as-leadership," in which the lines between the responsibilities of the board and the CEO are broken down and both work together in focusing on the most critical issues and questions facing the organization. Leadership is shared, particularly when both engage in generative thinking. The research of Robert Herman and Dick Heimovics (2005) revealed that in reality both board members and

the chief executive see the CEO as primarily responsible for the organization's success or failure, a condition they call "executive psychological centrality." They advise CEOs to accept that reality and practice board-centered leadership, not usurping the responsibilities of the board but rather supporting and facilitating its work.

The recommendations of Carver (2006), Chait et al. (2005), and Herman and Heimovics (2005) are prescriptive, but some scholars have sought to explain why boards are configured and operate the way they do. Some have taken a contingency approach, suggesting that boards are varied according to the internal and external realities that they face.

Responsibility for managing the governing board lies primarily with the chair, working cooperatively with the CEO. In recent years, more boards have established a governance committee, which has responsibility for the overall development of the board, including the enlistment of new members, board member orientation and education, and the evaluation of the board and individual members. Some large organizations with large boards have established a senior staff position to support board activity and the role of the board professional may be an emerging new subspecialty of nonprofit management. However, it is important to remain clear that staff members report to the CEO, not to the board or its officers, and that authority lies only in the full board rather than individual members.

In today's environment, there is considerable emphasis on the effectiveness of nonprofit governance. A 2017 survey by BoardSource revealed that the majority of nonprofit CEOs were at least somewhat satisfied with their boards' performance, although the CEOs reported that boards do better in some areas than others. BoardSource and others have identified best practices of effective boards, but research by Herman and Renz (2002, 2008), revisited in later work by the same scholars (Renz and Herman, 2016), suggests that there may be no one right way that works for every organization.

Nonprofit boards today face conflicting pressures. They are expected to do a more effective job of governing but also become more active in generating financial support for the organizations they serve. The appropriate trade-offs between the wealth and wisdom needed to meet these sometimes competing priorities are a matter of current discussion and debate in many nonprofit boardrooms.

CASE 4.1   Sweet Briar College

Founded in 1901, Sweet Briar College, in Virginia, had provided higher education to generations of women by 2015. With a campus of 3,250 acres in the foothills of the Blue Ridge Mountains, complete with a stable, boathouse, and 18 miles of trails, the college long had enjoyed strong loyalty among its alumni (Stolberg, 2015).

Members of the Sweet Briar community were shocked when the Board of Trustees announced abruptly in March 2015 that the college would be closed at the end of the academic year. Although the college had an $84-million endowment, the board explained that it would not be sufficient to meet the institution's future financial needs (Anderson & Svrluga, 2015). Enrollment had declined to just 532 students on campus. Much of the endowment was restricted to specific purposes and could not be accessed to meet general operating expenses. The board said there was no other decision that could be reached (Stolberg, 2015).

Opposition to the board's decision came swiftly from students, faculty, and alumnae. A group of alumnae created a group called Saving Sweet Briar, demanding that the college remain open and that the board and president step down. Some challenged the integrity of the board's decision, noting that it had amended its bylaws just days before the closure vote to permit a smaller number of trustees to make decisions ("More Scrutiny of Decision to Close Sweet Briar," 2015). The attorney for the county in which the college was located asked the court to block the closure and appoint a special fiduciary to prevent the existing board

and president from misusing the college's remaining assets (McCambridge, 2015a).

The college had been founded through the will of Indiana Fletcher Williams. Those opposing the closure argued that the board was violating its fiduciary responsibilities under the terms of his will. One court ruled against them on that point, saying that Sweet Briar was in fact a corporation, so the law governing trusts did not apply. That decision was quickly overturned by the Virginia Supreme Court, which ruled that trust law could indeed be applied and sent the case back down to the lower court to handle. However, the Supreme Court's decision did not resolve the underlying question of whether the board could close Sweet Briar. Meanwhile, what might have been the last commencement had taken place, it was the beginning of summer, and time was running out. Sweet Briar's faculty and current students did not know whether the college would reopen in the fall or not and no freshmen class had been enrolled for the new academic year (Svrluga, 2015).

The Attorney General of Virginia initiated an effort to negotiate a solution, which the court approved in late June 2015. Under the terms of the court order, all of the current board members resigned and were replaced. Phillip Stone, who had successfully led another college through financial difficulties, was selected to become the new president at Sweet Briar. The court permitted the new board to use $16 million of restricted endowment funds to meet operating costs for the next year (Stolberg, 2015). Alumni pledged $12 million in new resources and announced a campaign to raise an additional $120 million (Stolberg, 2015). Sweet Briar would live at least for one more year.

The college's advocates cheered the agreement and the court ruling. The hashtag #SaveSweetBriar was replaced with #WeSavedSweetBriar. But many of the 87 professors had accepted jobs elsewhere and many students also had transferred to other institutions. Some former board members remained convinced that they had made the right decision (Stolberg, 2015). The college's future remained perilous.

Only 240 students enrolled for the fall 2015 semester and the 2015–2016 academic year was one of budgetary constraint and rebuilding. The efforts to close had been costly, requiring the college to spend $30 million on severance payments to faculty and staff and to meet other obligations. Alumni gave over $10 million in unrestricted gifts, the largest amount in the college's history, helping to meet the additional costs and permitting the restricted endowment funds to remain untapped (Svrluga, 2016). But there were significant remaining challenges. The curriculum would need to be restructured, in order to better address student and donor interests. Increased fundraising would be essential. And the enrollment would need to grow substantially to make Sweet Briar financially viable over the long run (Locke, 2015). In 2016, one year after the college's near death, President Stone observed that some people called the saving of the college a "miracle." He credited the work of alumnae, but also noted that more hard choices would lie ahead (Stone,

2016). Meredith Woo was appointed as president of Sweet Briar in 2017, replacing Stone, and the college announced a significant restructuring of its curriculum and tuition pricing (Biemiller, 2017).

Reflecting on the near closing, lawyer Michael Peregrine notes that the Sweet Briar board was not found to have done anything illegal. Indeed, the court had praised the board's "principled determination" in reaching its decision to close the college (Peregrine, 2015). Nevertheless, despite the board's legal actions, "everything blew up" (Peregrine, 2015). What lessons can be learned from that experience by other nonprofit boards? Peregrine (2015) offers several. For one, due diligence matters. The board must be able to prove that it followed a well-structured process in reaching its decisions and it is important for the board to "document everything" (Peregrine, 2015). Boards need to be clear about the law that applies to them, a point illustrated by the confusion about whether trust or corporate law was relevant to the responsibilities of Sweet Briar's board. Perhaps most significantly, boards cannot expect that their deliberations and decisions will remain within the boardroom. If they make controversial decisions, they will "feel the heat" from stakeholders. Social media will amplify the criticism and quickly engage many more people. Public officials and the courts will not be reluctant to become involved. Given this new environment and the example of Sweet Briar, this likely will not be the last in which a board's decisions are challenged from outside (Peregrine, 2015).

Questions Related to Case 4.1

1. Although the Sweet Briar College board was not found to have acted illegally, which of the legal responsibilities of boards discussed in this chapter were most relevant to its actions in deciding to close the college?

2. Should the board of Sweet Briar College have taken actions earlier to avoid the financial pressures that led

it to consider closure? If so, what actions might the board have considered?

3. Do you think that boards are more likely to face more external scrutiny and pressure regarding their decisions in the future? If so, what accounts for that change?

CASE 4.2   The Hershey Trust

Milton Hershey was the founder of the Hershey Chocolate Company, which is now known as Hershey Foods, the maker of Hershey's Milk Chocolate, Hershey's Kisses, and other products with which all Americans are familiar.

Hershey and his wife, Catherine, did not have children of their own. In 1909, they founded a school to educate poor male orphans, created a charitable trust to support the school, and appointed nine trustees to manage the trust for the school's benefit. In 1918, after his wife's death, Hershey gave his entire personal fortune, consisting mostly of stock in the company, to the Hershey Trust to support the Milton S. Hershey School. The school today enrolls a diverse student body of about 2,000 low-income young men and women on a residential campus in central Pennsylvania. The students do not pay tuition or other fees, since the trust receives revenue from its interest in the food company each year to support the school's operation (Milton S. Hershey School, 2014).

By 2001, the Hershey Trust had grown to over $5 billion, most of which was stock in Hershey Foods. Indeed, the charitable trust owned a controlling interest in the company, and company stock was 56 percent of the trust's assets (Gadsden, 2002). With 6,200 employees, the company was the largest employer in its hometown of Hershey, Pennsylvania (Scully, 2009).

However, in 2002, the trustees of the Hershey Trust were concerned by the lack of diversification in the trust's investments and by the increasing competition from other companies. Fearing that the food company's decline could endanger the school's future, they proposed selling the trust's controlling interest. Wrigley, best known for its chewing gum, was prepared to buy it for $12.5 billion (McCracken & Brat, 2009).

The Hershey, Pennsylvania, community strongly objected to the sale, fearing the loss of jobs and a negative impact on the local economy. Under Pennsylvania law, the state attorney general oversees charitable trusts. The attorney general at the time, Mike Fisher, sided with the community and petitioned the state court to block the sale, arguing that it "could have profoundly negative consequences" for the Hershey region. The court agreed, and the sale was stopped. The Pennsylvania legislature later passed a law affirming the court's decision (Larkin, 2002). Some argued that the attorney general and the court had overstepped their authority and had dangerously altered the law regarding the fiduciary responsibilities of charitable trustees. They might now be required to make their decisions not only in light of the interests of the trust's beneficiaries, but also in consideration of local political and economic pressures (Larkin, 2002).

The food company's position continued to decline after 2002. By 2009, Hershey Foods had suffered years of stagnating revenue and a slumping stock price, which reduced the assets of the trust and thus the revenue of the school. In addition, a wave of mergers in the food industry was presenting increased competition from large multinational producers. Meanwhile, Hershey was finding it difficult to grow its business outside of the United States and derived only 10 percent of its revenue from overseas (Wachman, 2009).

The food industry was consolidating. Mars merged with Wrigley in 2008 and, in 2009, Kraft made a bid to take over the famous British candy brand, Cadbury (Scully, 2009). The trustees of the Hershey Trust were deeply concerned by this new challenge to Hershey Foods. They knew the law would not permit them to *sell* the company, but they considered making an offer to *buy* Cadbury. Kraft had offered $16.5 billion for Cadbury, and Hershey would need to offer more. Hershey was only half the size of Cadbury and a fraction of Kraft's size. Buying Cadbury would require borrowing massive amounts of money. It was reported that differences arose between the views of the company's board and management, on the one hand, and the board of the charitable trust, on the other. The company's board and management were concerned that such borrowing would cause the company's credit ratings and stock price to decline, raise the cost of future borrowing, and hurt profits. The charitable trustees were concerned that failing to buy Cadbury would mean that Hershey would find it even more difficult to compete internationally in the future and that the long-term interests of the trust and the school would be jeopardized (Wachman, 2009).

Throughout January of 2010, there was daily speculation in the financial media about a possible Hershey counteroffer for Cadbury. But, on January 22, Hershey announced that it would not proceed and Kraft announced that Cadbury had accepted its revised offer of 11.9 billion British pounds ($19.4 billion). Kraft and Cadbury combined would become the largest candy company in the world ("Hershey Loses Taste for Cadbury," 2010). But this was not the end of the story—neither for the Hershey Trust nor for the food industry.

In 2012, Kraft decided to split its company into two, spinning off its snack business under the new corporate name Mondelez International (Strom, 2012). The industry remained competitive in the following years. By 2016, Mondelez was under pressure from investors to do something that would increase its profitability (Berk, 2016). The stock of Hershey Foods was much higher than it had been in 2002. The assets of the charitable Hershey Trust had reached $12 billion (Fouad, 2016) and its income from its holdings in the chocolate company totaled $160 million every year (Solomon, 2016). But the food company's performance had lagged since 2013 and there were once again reasons for the company and the Trust to be concerned

(Solomon, 2016). Meanwhile, at the Hershey Trust, there were serious problems that were unrelated to the food industry or the price of the Hershey company's stock.

Since the 1990s, there had been controversies surrounding the Hershey Trust's governance practices and its complicated interrelationships with the for-profit entities it controlled. Some observers criticized the salaries paid to directors of the trust, real estate acquisitions that appeared to benefit individuals with connections to the trust's board, and other practices (Eisenberg, 2011). The board had reached agreements with the Pennsylvania attorney general in previous years, requiring it to undertake reforms. But in 2011, the attorney general launched another investigation. Although the investigation concluded that the trustees had not violated their fiduciary responsibility, the board of the Hershey Trust agreed to undertake further reforms related to board compensation, conflict of interest, the process for selecting board members, and the process for considering acquisitions (Peregrine, 2013).[2]

Three years after the 2013 agreement, the attorney general's office was not satisfied with the trust's progress in implementing the changes and ordered it to remove three board members and reduce board members' pay. ("Critics Question," 2016) In-fighting among board members gained public attention, leading one journalist to observe, "Some serious behavioral issues have convulsed the Milton Hershey School. But the problem isn't the students. The problem is the adults in charge" (Segal, 2016). In the midst of this turmoil, Mondelez made its move.

In July 2016, Mondelez offered $23 billion for Hershey Foods, knowing that the decision ultimately would be made by the board of the Hershey Trust, which was mired in controversy and change (Solomon, 2016). Mindful of the events that had unfolded in 2002, when community opposition had sunk the previous attempted takeover of Hershey, Mondelez offered reassurances. It would move its headquarters from Illinois to Hershey, Pennsylvania, and the combined company would keep the Hershey name (Solomon, 2016). The Hershey board rejected the offer, demanding a higher price. Mondelez increased its original offer, but Hershey would not come down from the price it previously had demanded, which was still more than Mondelez was willing to pay. Mondelez CEO Irene Rosenfeld eventually said she saw "no actionable path forward" (Frost, 2016). In other words, the deal was dead.

Some observers said it would have been difficult for the Hershey Trust board to accept an offer while it was mired in its own turmoil (Gasparro & Cimilluca, 2016). As one stock analyst explained, "The trust was always a wild card" (Frost, 2016). But others pointed to the inherent challenges in the structure of interrelated Hershey entities and their unique place in the community. Perhaps Mondelez's commitments to stay in Hershey were necessary to have any hopes of making a deal, but the costs of keeping those commitments also may have made it impossible for Mondelez to offer a higher price (Solomon, 2016). Perhaps the "triple approval process" was just too complex (Solomon, 2016). The sale would have required agreement by the board of the food company, the board of the Hershey Trust, and the attorney general of Pennsylvania, three parties that were bound to have different perspectives and agendas (Solomon, 2016). The company board cares about earnings; the Trust has all the money it needs and wants to retain its position in the community; and the attorney general is concerned about keeping the jobs and economic benefits in the state (Solomon, 2016). As Solomon (2016) concludes, "Perhaps [Hershey] is a jewel to be treasured, one that should be exempt from the laws of economics and today's hyper-market efficiency. And perhaps it should stay that way."[3]

Questions Related to Case 4.2

1. Why might the board of Hershey Foods and the trustees of the Milton S. Hershey Trust sometimes hold different views and priorities? To whom and for what are they responsible?

2. Should boards of nonprofits be concerned only with following the intention of donors and serving the interests of those who directly benefit from the nonprofit's assets, or should they also consider the impact of their decisions on local communities?

3. What concerns might the trustees of the Milton S. Hershey Trust have held about their own legal responsibilities throughout the events described in the case? In other words, which laws might potentially have created liability for members of that nonprofit board?

QUESTIONS FOR DISCUSSION

1. If you were a nonprofit CEO, how would you describe the ideal board for which to work?

2. If you were the chair of a nonprofit board, how would you describe the ideal relationship between the board and the CEO from your perspective?

3. Should boards be held responsible for the results achieved by the organizations they govern or is that primarily the responsibility of the CEO and staff?

NOTES

1. Reprinted with permission from *12 Principles of Governance That Power Exceptional Boards*, a publication of BoardSource ©2018. For more information, call 1-877-892-6273 or e-mail learningcenter@boardsource.org.

2. Governance issues at the Hershey Trust have been discussed extensively in articles in the *Philadelphia Inquirer* (http://www.philly.com/), the *Chronicle of Philanthropy* (www.philanthropy.com), and a book (Fernandez, 2015).

3. The food industry remained dynamic in 2017, when it was reported that Hershey Foods might consider a bid to buy Nestle's U.S. confectionary business (Hirsch, 2017). In December 2017, Hershey bought Amplify Snack Brands (LaMonica, 2017). Students interested in events that may have unfolded after this case study was written will find articles on the Web. They may find it interesting to consider such events in light of the governance structure and other issues discussed in this case study.

APPENDIX CASES

The following cases in the Appendix of this text include points related to the content of this chapter: Case 1 (New York City Opera); Case 4 (The Girl Scouts of the United States of America).

SUGGESTIONS FOR FURTHER READING

Books/Reports

BoardSource. (2017). *Leading with intent: A national index of nonprofit board practices*. Washington, DC: Author.

Gazley, B., & Kissman, K. (2015). *Transformational governance: How boards achieve extraordinary change*. San Francisco, CA: Jossey-Bass.

Ingram, R. T. (2015). *Ten basic responsibilities of nonprofit boards* (3rd ed.). Washington, DC: BoardSource.

Trower, C. A. (2013). *The practitioner's guide to governance as leadership: Building high-performing nonprofit boards*. San Francisco, CA: Jossey-Bass.

Worth, M. J. (2017). *Advisory councils in higher education*. Washington, DC: Association of Governing Boards of Universities and Colleges.

Websites

Association of Governing Boards of Universities and Colleges: http://www.agb.org/

BoardSource: http://www.boardsource.org/

Daring to Lead: http://daringtolead.org/

Independent Sector: http://www.independentsector.org/

The deep commitment of a leader, as evidenced by his or her willingness to sacrifice and suffer for the cause, confers a charismatic appeal. Clara Barton founded the American Red Cross and led the organization for 23 years.

Wikimedia.org

Chapter Outline

Executive Leadership

Chapter 1 of this text discussed why nonprofit management is a distinctive undertaking, different in important ways from management in the for-profit sector or in government. Among these differences were the need for nonprofits to integrate mission, the acquisition of resources, and strategy; the complex relationships among a nonprofit organization's stakeholders (including volunteers) that require negotiation and compromise and demand that executives possess a high tolerance for ambiguity; and the need to manage a double bottom line of financial results and social impact.

These differences may not directly affect the work of everyone employed at a nonprofit organization. For example, there is no particular nonprofit way of processing bills or payments, programming computers, or maintaining physical facilities. Many who work in the nonprofit sector are engaged in such technical work, and their skills may be readily transferable across the for-profit, nonprofit, and governmental sectors. Even those who provide the services of a nonprofit organization may not perform their functions in any unique way. For example, a doctor working in a nonprofit, for-profit, or government hospital will follow the same medical protocols; a counselor working with clients recovering from drug or alcohol addiction may use the same treatments whether working in a nonprofit organization or a state-managed entity; and teachers in private and public schools may teach a similar curriculum. Where the unique characteristics of nonprofit management come together with the greatest significance is in the position of the chief executive officer (CEO). The CEO is a position requiring unique skills in both management and leadership, which this chapter explores. In this examination, we will draw on the theoretical literature of leadership as well as the practitioner literature produced by consultants, other experts, and nonprofit CEOs themselves.

The CEO's Job

What do nonprofit chief executives actually do? In other words, what is the job description? Of course, because no two organizations are exactly the same, the CEO's job may

Learning Objectives

After reading this chapter, students should be able to:

1. Describe the responsibilities of nonprofit CEOs.

2. Contrast leadership and management.

3. Summarize prominent leadership theories related to nonprofit organizations.

4. Describe the characteristic behaviors of successful nonprofit CEOs.

5. Explain founder syndrome.

6. Identify steps in the process of change.

7. Analyze cases, applying concepts from the chapter.

vary widely from one to another. In some, fundraising may be an important expectation, while in others it is not. In organizations that have mostly paid professional staff, the skills required of a CEO may be different from those needed to lead an organization that relies on volunteers for a substantial portion of its workforce. Also, as discussed in Chapter 4, the type of governing board with which the chief executive works may greatly influence the types of challenges that he or she may face. While recognizing these inevitable differences, Richard Moyers identified 10 basic responsibilities of the nonprofit chief executive in a 2013 publication for BoardSource:[1]

1. *Commit to the mission:* The CEO must understand the mission, keep the mission prominently in mind when making decisions, and guard against mission drift.

2. *Lead the staff and manage the organization:* The CEO has direct responsibility for hiring, training, developing, and motivating the staff; developing an organizational structure that suits the organization's work; and ensuring that day-to-day operations and programs are effective and efficient.

3. *Exercise responsible financial stewardship:* While the governing board has overall responsibility for ensuring the organization's financial soundness, it is the chief executive who must manage its assets, revenues, and expenditures on a day-to-day basis and ensure that controls are in place to protect the organization against fraud or waste.

4. *Lead and manage fundraising:* The CEO's responsibility for fundraising will vary from one organization to another and is shared with the governing board. In charitable nonprofits, the CEO's direct engagement in fundraising, planning fundraising programs, and managing the fundraising staff may consume a substantial portion of his or her time and energy.

5. *Follow the highest ethical standards, ensure accountability, and comply with the law:* Again, the governing board may set policies (remember Carver's executive limitations discussed in Chapter 4) that establish standards and procedures to ensure legal and ethical behavior. However, it is the chief executive who needs to put these policies into practice in the organization's daily life and set an example through his or her own behavior.

6. *Engage the board in planning and lead implementation:* Planning for the organization's future is a shared responsibility of the board and the CEO, but the reality in many organizations requires that the chief executive take a significant role in initiating the planning effort, providing the resources for planning, and defining issues and questions for the board to deliberate.

7. *Develop future leadership:* In many organizations, the CEO plays a role in developing the leadership of the board, both informally and often as a member of the board's nominating committee. There is also an increasing emphasis on the importance of the CEO's preparing for possible staff departures by developing a bench of qualified successors and, indeed, for preparing the way for a smooth transition when he or she may leave the chief executive's position.

8. *Build external relationships and serve as an advocate:* Some research considered later in this chapter emphasizes that effective chief executives are those who are externally oriented—who are constantly alert to opportunities and threats in the external environment and engaged in building external partnerships for their organization.

9. *Ensure the quality and effectiveness of programs:* The board may set the standards by which the effectiveness of programs is to be evaluated, but the CEO must ensure that the right questions are asked and the right data collected so that a process of evaluation and continuous learning is a part of the organization's ongoing work.

10. *Support the board:* Just as the governing board has a responsibility to support its CEO, the CEO has a reciprocal responsibility to support the board. Moreover, as we discussed in Chapter 4, research suggests that effective CEOs are ones who practice board-centered leadership.

Two realities are evident in Moyer's list of CEO responsibilities. One is the number of areas in which the chief executive shares responsibility with the governing board regarding mission, financial stewardship, fundraising, accountability, planning, performance standards, and the work of the board itself. This explains why the relationship between the CEO and the board is so complex and why so many experts have focused on delineating the CEO and board responsibilities in each area.

The second observation that emerges from a review of the CEO's responsibilities is that they involve both managing and leading. The CEO is responsible for ensuring that financial management systems are in place, for the hiring and evaluation of staff, and for monitoring the quality and effectiveness of programs. But chief executives are also expected to be external spokespersons for their organizations, able to articulate the mission and make a persuasive case for financial support; to be capable of motivating both paid staff and volunteers to high performance; and to hold a vision and strategy for the organization's future, which, working together with the board, they translate into a plan for the organization's advancement and growth. These latter tasks require something beyond management: They require that the CEO be a leader.

Management and Leadership

Although people may use the words interchangeably, leadership and management are not the same thing. **Management** is generally concerned with day-to-day operations, with making things work. It emphasizes policies, procedures, rules, and processes. Management is transactional; the manager provides rewards in exchange for the work contributions of others or imposes sanctions (punishments) on those who do not meet the requirements of their assignments. A manager is often concerned primarily with maintaining a smooth operation, that is, keeping the machine running and avoiding breakdowns, rather than with change.

Leadership is more about purpose, vision, and direction—that is, more about the "where" and the "why" rather than the "how." In a widely quoted statement, Warren Bennis and Burt Nanus (1985) suggest a moral element to leadership: "Managers are people who do things right and leaders are people who do the right thing" (p. 21). Leadership is interactive; that is, it is a process, and it involves a relationship between the leader and the people who are led. There can be no leaders without followers, and both play a part in the process of leadership. Leaders are focused on change, and that change is not directionless; leadership involves moving people toward the achievement of some defined goals. Some of the differences between leaders and managers are summarized in Table 5.1.

Sometimes, the roles of leader and manager are performed by different people; indeed, some argue that the two roles require different personal qualities or skills rarely found in the same individual. At other times, one person may have the responsibility both for leading the organization and for managing its affairs—for example, the CEO of a small nonprofit. But the functions of leadership and management are different and executives who perform both need to be able to switch from one role to the other as the needs of the organization and the occasion may dictate. Indeed, some people observe that founders of nonprofit organizations often exhibit strong qualities of leadership but sometimes may be unable to provide the management the organization needs as it grows, leading to the problem known as founder syndrome, discussed later in this chapter.

Table 5.1 Managers and Leaders Compared	
Managers	**Leaders**
Concerned with mastering routines	Concerned with vision and judgment
Adopt impersonal or passive attitudes toward goals	Active and visionary about the future
Excel in problem solving and work design	Seek out opportunities and take risks
Work with people in carefully controlled ways	Passionate about their work and likely to cause turbulence
See themselves as conservators or regulators of organizations	See themselves as agents of change

Source: Based on Denhardt, Denhardt, and Aristigueta (2016, p. 191).

In larger organizations, CEOs often play the leadership role and delegate management responsibilities to subordinates, such as a chief operating officer. It is possible for a CEO to delegate management to others, but only the CEO can provide leadership to the entire organization. Leadership of the organization is not a responsibility that can be delegated.

All organizations need both leadership and management to be successful in the long run. It is conceivable that an organization—whether a for-profit business, a government agency, or a nonprofit organization—can survive for a time with only good management. But to thrive and grow, an organization also needs leaders who define vision, articulate direction, set goals, and influence others to achieve these together.

Nonprofit organizations especially need leadership. The reasons are rooted in their characteristics, which we have discussed in earlier chapters. Corporations and government agencies generally have well-defined missions, straightforward measures of performance, and revenue that is derived from either appropriated funds or quid pro quo transactions with customers. In contrast, nonprofits are values based and mission driven. There is not always consensus about mission or about appropriate ways of measuring performance against the mission. Financial and other resources are often bestowed voluntarily. Leadership is essential to develop consensus about mission and performance and to articulate a vision that gains and holds the commitment of volunteer board members, service volunteers, donors, and others. Leadership is central to the role of a nonprofit CEO. A lack of leadership by the CEO will eventually, and inevitably, lead to the organization's drift, decline, and failure.

Overview of Leadership Theories

We have established that leadership is critical in nonprofit organizations. Now let's turn our attention to understanding it by looking at some fundamental questions. Are leaders born or made? If they are made, what specific knowledge or skills do individuals need to acquire in order to be strong leaders? What is it that successful leaders actually do—in other words, are there specific behaviors that are associated with effective leadership? These are questions that long have been asked, and there is a substantial body of research that has sought to provide answers.

It is important to remember two points as we review some of the well-known leadership theories. First, most of the theories are generic; that is, theorists intend them to apply to leadership in all types of organizations, not just nonprofits. And second, as in our earlier discussion of governing, there may be no one right theory of leadership that is applicable in every situation, at all times. Some of the more prominent theories are identified in Table 5.2.

Table 5.2 Summary of Selected Leadership Theories

Theories	Representative Author(s)	Summary of Concepts
Trait theories	Stodgill (1948)	Leadership is explained in terms of inherent characteristics of individuals.
Skills theories	Katz (1955)	Leaders possess specific technical, human, and conceptual skills.
Leadership style (behaviors)	Blake and Mouton (1985)	Leaders engage in specific behaviors, including some that are task oriented and some that are human oriented. The mix of these behaviors defines a leadership style.
Situational theories	Hersey and Blanchard (1969)	Based on leadership styles; different situations call for a different leadership style, and the leader needs to adapt.
Contingency theories	Fiedler (1967)	Certain styles of leadership, including the mix of task-oriented and human-oriented behaviors, may be effective in some situations and not in others. Three important variables that define the situation are leader–member relations, the task structure, and position power of the leader. Contingency theories match leadership styles to particular situations.
Path-goal theory	Evans (1970)	Focuses on the motivations of employees and efforts to enhance performance and satisfaction
Leader–member exchange theory	Dansereau, Graen, and Haga (1975)	Emphasizes interactions between the leader and followers
Servant leadership	Greenleaf (1977)	Leadership is related to the leader's values and commitments; servant leaders see themselves as serving others.
Transformational leadership	Burns (1978)	Leaders develop a relationship with followers and tap into their values in order to enable them to grow, both morally and in terms of their levels of motivation.
Charismatic leadership	House (1976)	Leaders perceived as charismatic are those who engage in certain behaviors, including advocating a vision, sacrificing in pursuit of the vision, exhibiting confidence, and engaging in persuasive appeals rather than exercising formal authority.

An Evolution in Thinking

Leadership theory has evolved over the decades. Among the earliest theories were the **trait theories**, which explain leadership in terms of the innate characteristics of individuals who are leaders. They are essentially "great-man-or-woman theories," which hold the qualities of leadership to be fundamental aspects of an individual's personality. In the past, some have looked to physical characteristics to explain why certain people are leaders; for example, physical height and a resonant speaking voice—essentially male qualities—were once considered intrinsic to leadership, although they would not explain Clara Barton, Indira Gandhi, or Mother Teresa! Other trait theorists have pointed more to elements of personality, character, or psychology. For example, in 1948, Ralph Stodgill studied leaders and found them to be better than the average person in terms of intelligence, alertness, insight, responsibility, initiative, persistence, self-confidence, and sociability. Since it is difficult for individuals to change their intelligence or personalities, trait theories imply that leaders are born, not made; that is, leadership is not something that can be taught or learned (Northouse, 2016, p. 19).

The trait theories, however, do not seem to provide the whole answer. For that reason, in about the middle of the 20th century, theorists began to take a different approach, developing **skills theories** of leadership. Skills theories hold that it is not the innate qualities of individuals, such as physical appearance or even intelligence, that make them effective leaders. Rather, there are specific skills that effective leaders possess; in other words, effective leadership depends less on what the leaders are and more on what they are able to do. For example, in 1955, Daniel Katz suggested that effective leadership depends on the leader possessing skills in three areas: technical (knowledge of the job, profession, or task), human (the ability to work with people), and conceptual (the ability to understand ideas and principles). A skills theory is the assumption underlying most leadership training or development programs.

Beginning in the 1950s, leadership researchers started to move beyond studying the traits and skills of individual leaders and toward looking at what it is that leaders actually do—that is, they considered whether it was possible to identify specific behaviors associated with effective leadership. Among the most famous of leadership studies that followed this approach were those conducted at The Ohio State University. These studies identified two basic types of leader behaviors: **task behaviors** (actions that relate to the work to be done) and **relationship behaviors** (actions that focus on the feelings of subordinates). At about the same time, similar studies conducted at the University of Michigan identified essentially the same categories, which researchers there labeled **production orientation** and **employee orientation**. The ways in which leaders mix task and relationship behaviors can define a leadership style (Northouse, 2016, pp. 72–73).

Among the theorists who analyzed leadership styles are Robert Blake and Jane Mouton (1985), who developed the well-known **managerial grid**. This grid is based on different combinations of task and relationship behaviors and defines four styles. Organizations that are high on production (task) and low on relationships are said to have authority-obedience management. Essentially, they are dictatorships, although they may be productive. Those high on relationships and low on concern for production are described as having country club management. They may be great places to work, but they get little or nothing accomplished. Organizations that are low on both concern for people and production exhibit impoverished management. These would be dreadful places to work, and most people likely would not stay long in such an uninspiring environment. The ideal type, showing high concern for both people and production, is called team management (Northouse, 2016, pp. 74–75). It is likely that most readers can imagine situations, or perhaps have even experienced ones, in which each of these styles is practiced.

It might seem obvious that what may be an effective leadership style in one situation may not be so under different circumstances. But the idea that effective leadership behavior might depend on the situation was a new approach in the late 1960s and early 1970s. Building on the concept of leadership styles, the **situational theories** emphasized the fact that different styles might be more appropriate in certain situations than in others, that is, that leaders might need to adapt their styles to the environment in which they were working.

Contingency theories take situational theories one step further and provide a way of matching leader styles to defined situations. In other words, the most effective style of leadership is *contingent* on the situation. Different situations might call for different combinations of task-oriented and relationship-oriented behaviors. But what defines a "situation"? And exactly what differences between situations are relevant to determining the right leadership style (Northouse, 2016, p. 94–96)?

One of the best-known contingency theories is the one developed by Fiedler in 1967. According to Fiedler, the situation may be favorable or unfavorable to the leader, depending on three variables: leader–member relations (e.g., the degree of trust, cooperativeness, and friendliness between the leader and followers), the task structure (whether the job to be done is clear and specific or ambiguous and uncertain), and the position power of the leader (i.e., the formal position of authority the leader holds). The most favorable situation is when all three variables are high, and the least favorable is when all three are low, but there can be moderately favorable situations that show some combination of favorable and unfavorable conditions. According to Fiedler's findings, task-oriented leaders do best when conditions are very favorable or very unfavorable, while relationship-oriented leaders do best in the intermediate circumstances.

Contingency theories add a level of sophistication beyond the trait, skill, and behavior theories of leadership. They begin to explain why some styles of leadership may be successful in certain circumstances and not in others. Imagine, for example, a situation in which a nonprofit chief executive is facing the need to mobilize staff and volunteers to provide relief to victims of a natural disaster. The urgency of the situation makes everyone inclined to be cooperative. Let's also assume that the executive is trusted and well liked by the staff and volunteers. The task is clear and unambiguous: It is to provide food, clothing, and shelter to the victims as quickly as possible. These circumstances—cooperativeness, trust, a clear task, a leader with formal authority—would be a situation that Fiedler's (1967) model would define as favorable to the leader. A task-oriented style likely would be most effective. The important thing would be to get the job done, and there would be little need to concentrate on relationships among people, which are already good. But imagine a different situation, one in which an acting executive director has been on the job for just a few months while a search for a permanent director is proceeding. This person leads an environmental advocacy organization and is trying to mobilize volunteers to support critical environmental legislation by contacting their elected representatives. The task seems clear and specific. However, the person's position of power is weak because of the acting status, and he or she may not have been in the role long enough to have gained the trust and friendship of the staff and volunteers. In Fiedler's theory, this situation is intermediate in its favorableness to the leader, who likely would need to devote considerable attention to nurturing his or her relationships with the volunteers and staff to mobilize them to action; in other words, the leader would need to emphasize relationship behaviors more than task behaviors.

Although not a theory per se, one approach to leadership that has gained a following and spawned a number of books is that of servant leadership, advanced by Robert Greenleaf (1977). Greenleaf argues that leadership begins with the leader's values and commitments and that moral leaders are more concerned with serving others than with meeting their own self-interest. Servant leaders exhibit honesty, integrity, character, and spirit. Rather than trying to impose their will on others, they listen, empathize with others, and focus on relationships, approaching the position of leader as a type of stewardship of the organization, with the goal of social improvement (Denhardt et al., 2016, pp. 198–198).

Our discussion of leadership theories in this chapter is limited, but various scholars have taken approaches that depart from the theories discussed above. For example,

path-goal theories emphasize how leaders can adapt their behaviors to motivate followers and enhance satisfaction and performance (Northouse, 2016, p. 115). **Leader–member exchange theories** view leadership in terms of interactions between leaders and followers (Northouse, 2016, p. 137). Students interested in knowing more about these approaches may wish to pursue additional reading suggested at the end of this chapter.

Transformational Leadership

A 1978 book by political scientist James MacGregor Burns, titled simply *Leadership,* had seminal influence on thinking about the topic and offered insights that may be of particular relevance to leadership in the nonprofit sector. First, Burns made a distinction between transactional leadership and transformational leadership. **Transactional leadership** is an exchange process, in which the leader exchanges rewards or punishments for the behaviors of others: If you come to work, you will get paid; if you don't, you won't. If you miss work too often, you will be fired. Thus, transactional leadership is essentially like management, as that term was defined previously in this chapter. In contrast, **transformational leadership**, as the name implies, is leadership that *changes* people. According to Burns, transformational leadership inspires and enables people to grow, both morally and in terms of their levels of motivation. It empowers individuals to go beyond self-interest and pursue goals that are in the common interest. Transformational leaders accomplish this by developing a relationship with followers and tapping into their personal values in a way that matches them to the values of the organization. They motivate followers not based on rewards and punishments, but by appealing to these shared values and ideals.

Let's consider a simple example that might illustrate transactional and transformational approaches. Tom is the CEO of a nonprofit organization that delivers meals to housebound older people. He is addressing a meeting of his staff, and he is concerned that some have been showing up late for work, delaying the delivery of meals to clients. One way to approach the issue would be for Tom to say something like,

> I've noticed that I am the first one here in the morning. Some of you don't show up until an hour later. As a result, some meals are being delivered late. If this continues, I will need to consider docking the pay of staff who report late and firing people if it continues. I will expect to see you all here at 6 a.m. tomorrow morning.

However, taking a different approach, Tom might say something like,

> I am concerned. I know that some of our clients wait for their meals to be delivered and that in fact their contact with our volunteers may be the high point of their days. When I see that we are late in getting the meals out the door in the morning, I cannot help but worry about a lonely older person, perhaps a little hungry, who is left waiting because maybe we had other things to do that morning. I know you share my concern about that. I know our clients appreciate everything you can do to make sure we are meeting their needs—and on time—because they count on us.

Which approach is more likely to result in staff arriving earlier? The first is purely transactional: You do (or do not do) this and I will do (or not do) that. The transactional approach may be effective in the short run; after all, staff members rely on their paychecks. But the effects of Tom's speech may wear off in a few days unless he repeats it and his threats are backed up. That will require his continuing intervention, possibly undermining his relationships with the staff over time. The second approach has tones of transformational leadership. It appeals to shared values rather than the promise or threat of consequences.

It may move staff members to change their behaviors by affecting changes in their own heads and hearts. If accomplished, such change will likely be more lasting and powerful than the tools of a more transactional style.

Burns's book inspired work by other scholars, who adopted, expanded, and refined his ideas. One prominent leadership scholar, Bernard Bass (1985; Bass & Avolio, 1994), developed a more comprehensive model of transformational leadership. He differed slightly with Burns on some points. For one, Bass emphasized that transformational leaders also use transactional techniques in that they do provide goals and rewards for reaching them. This is not a problem as long as they do not overemphasize these techniques, especially those that are negative. Rewards may be more consistent with transformational leadership than are punishments. In other words, there may be times when the hypothetical CEO Tom may find that some staff members do not respond adequately to his values-based approach and will indeed need to be subject to "transactions" (Rainey, 2014, pp. 350–351).

Most of the leadership theories summarized in this chapter describe a leader's relationship with subordinates. But what is significant about the concept of transformational leadership is that it also offers an approach to leading organizations—especially those that are values based and mission driven. A nonprofit chief executive must lead more than the members of his or her paid staff. Among others, the CEO must also at times lead donors, volunteers, and even members of the board.

Think back to the earlier example of Tom speaking to members of his staff. The transactional approach, using rewards and punishments to change behavior, might be effective with the staff, at least in the short run. But how could that approach be effective in motivating individuals to give or members of the board to increase their efforts in fundraising, or in inspiring volunteers to work longer and harder? Would not those goals be better accomplished by identifying how the values of those individuals coincide with those of the organization and appealing to those values in a way that the desired behavior is dictated from within their own hearts?

In *Good to Great and the Social Sectors*, a sequel to his best-selling book on companies (2001), Jim Collins (2005) observes how nonprofit leadership is unique, and he describes two types (or styles) of leadership that have similarities to Burns's transactional and transformational approaches. **Executive leadership** exists when the leader has the power to simply make decisions. **Legislative leadership** is a style that "relies more upon persuasion, political currency, and shared interests to create the conditions for the right decisions to happen" (Collins, 2005, p. 11). Nonprofit executives often do not have the formal power of corporate CEOs. They generally do not have the financial resources with which to offer significant monetary incentives. Indeed, some of their workforce is not paid at all, and even those who are may be motivated as much by their commitment to the mission as they are by their financial needs. Rather than lead through rewards and punishments, nonprofit executives must use the less raw, but considerable, power of ideas, persuasion, inspiration, and relationships to lead others—and their organizations—in the directions they wish them to pursue. Collins (2005) also observes that effective nonprofit leaders are those who practice Level 5 leadership, the top level of a hierarchy he defines. Such leaders are "ambitious first and foremost for the cause, the movement, the mission, the work—*not themselves*—and they have the will to do *whatever* it takes to make good on that ambition" (p. 11). Collins (2005) argues that in the nonprofit sector, a leader's "compelling combination of personal humility and professional will is a key factor in creating legitimacy and influence" (p. 11).

Charismatic Leadership

The idea of charisma is one that is familiar to most people. When asked to name a leader, people often will mention the names of political figures, such as Ronald Reagan, Martin

Luther King, Jr., Barack Obama, or Eleanor Roosevelt. When asked what makes all these individuals unusual, some inevitably will use the term charisma. The prominence of Burns's (1978) concept of transformational leadership has led to an increasing interest in **charismatic leadership**, which remains an active area of research today. Some debate whether transformational and charismatic leadership are the same, different, or overlapping concepts, but fine distinctions need not concern us here. The two types of leadership are, at the least, related.

There is debate about the nature of charisma. Is it based on personal characteristics of the leader—is it some kind of "right stuff" that some people just have and others do not? Or is charisma defined by behaviors that can be learned? Some argue that theories of charismatic leadership really represent a retreat to the earlier trait theories. But Bass and other scholars have identified specific behaviors that may cause followers to attribute the characteristics of charisma to the leader. In other words, a leader is someone who behaves in certain ways that cause others to see him or her as charismatic (Bryman, 1992).

What are some of the behaviors that may cause others to see a leader as charismatic? Here are some that researchers have identified (Rainey, 2014, p. 352):

- *The leader advocates a vision that is different from the status quo but still acceptable to followers.* Leadership is about change, but not change so radical as to alienate potential followers. Martin Luther King, Jr., advocated an end to segregation and racial discrimination. This represented not only a change from the status quo in America in the 1960s, but also a change that King's followers, and eventually the nation, came to accept as morally compelling. Rather than call for violent revolution, King advocated nonviolent means, remaining within the boundaries of what his followers and sympathizers could find acceptable.

- *The leader acts in unconventional ways in pursuit of the vision.* King led boycotts and marches. Nelson Mandela spent 27 years in jail in protest against South Africa's inhumane system of apartheid. Neither brought about change merely by giving occasional speeches or by other more conventional means.

- *The leader engages in self-sacrifice and risk taking in pursuit of the vision.* Mandela sacrificed 27 years. Mother Teresa lived a life of poverty among the poor. King ultimately gave his life. The deep commitment of a leader, as evidenced by his or her willingness to sacrifice, even suffer, for the cause compels attention and confers a charismatic appeal. "By showing unswerving dedication to the vision, making personal sacrifices, and engaging in unconventional behavior ... [charismatic leaders] inspire their followers to transcend their self-interests for the sake of a collective goal" (Choi, 2006).

- *The leader displays confidence in his or her own ideas and proposals.* Perhaps the undoing of Jimmy Carter as president of the United States (he was not reelected to a second term) was a speech he gave to the nation in which he acknowledged his own shortcomings as president and described the nation's mood as discouraged. (This speech is often referred to as Carter's "malaise" speech, although he did not use that word.) In contrast, Ronald Reagan's optimistic vision of "morning in America" was an important factor in his election to the presidency in 1980, although many opinion polls showed that a majority of Americans disagreed with his specific positions on issues. Similarly, it was Barack Obama's optimistic assurance of "yes, we can" that inspired many of his supporters in 2008. And Donald Trump's promise to "make American great again" was attractive to some people who were dissatisfied with the condition of the country in 2016. Charismatic leaders command our following, partly because they appear so certain that their course is right.

- *The leader uses visioning and persuasive appeals to influence followers, rather than relying mainly on formal authority.* Martin Luther King, Jr., never held public office. But the words "I have a dream" created a vision of a different America that inspired millions and changed the nation more dramatically than most presidents of the United States have ever been able to do.

- *The leader uses the capacity to assess context and locate opportunities for novel strategies.* Charismatic leaders read the moment; that is, they can take the temperature of their times and followers and create opportunities to demonstrate their cause in dramatic and novel ways. In 1987, Ronald Reagan stood yards from the Berlin Wall and addressed himself to the leader of the Soviet Union saying, "Mr. Gorbachev, tear down this wall!" It was a dramatic moment, which Reagan must have known would resonate with people on both sides of the wall at that point in history. Just over two years later, the wall was gone, not entirely as a result of Reagan's speech but rather as the culmination of historical forces that were gathering strength. However, Reagan understood the context and used the opportunity of his visit to the wall to dramatize the issue. Many years later, then-presidential candidate Barack Obama spoke to a large and enthusiastic gathering in Berlin, signifying in a visual way that he intended to pursue a policy approach to Europe that would represent change and improve U.S. international relationships.

To the above list of behaviors of charismatic leaders, James Fisher (1984), who writes about the use of charismatic leadership by college and university presidents, adds the idea of social distance. He suggests that to be perceived as charismatic, the leader cannot permit himself or herself to be too familiar. Consistent with the military's long-standing rule that officers are not to fraternize with enlisted personnel, leaders may be friendly, but not too much so. They can be congenial but never silly. They can socialize with subordinates (or board members or donors) but never stay too long or drink too much. If charisma is something attributed to leaders, as psychologists suggest, it may be that we prefer just a bit of mystery and to believe that they are just a little different from us.

Although they play an important part in contemporary leadership theory and research, the ideas of transformational leadership and charismatic leadership have their critics. Some raise academic issues, saying that charisma is too ill defined to measure or analyze. Others say the idea of charismatic leadership is really just a newer version of the "great man/great woman" theory of leadership. (Remember the issue from our case in Chapter 3 about the Smithsonian's National Museum of American History and the Catherine B. Reynolds Foundation?) Still others raise substantive concerns about the risks of charismatic leadership to organizations: For example, the power of charismatic leadership may be abused, or an organization dependent on a charismatic leader may be vulnerable if that leader leaves, retires, or dies (Northouse, 2016, pp. 164–165).

The Effective Nonprofit CEO

If leadership is so vital to the success of the nonprofit organization, what do we know about what makes an effective nonprofit CEO? We have discussed some major theories of leadership, but what evidence do we have of what actually works best in the nonprofit sector?

As with the topic of governing boards, much of the literature on nonprofit executive leadership is prescriptive. In other words, "It tells more about how to lead and much less about how leaders actually go about their business" (Dym & Hutson, 2005, p. 6). And, as is the case with governing boards, a significant portion of the literature on nonprofit leadership has been written by consultants or reflective practitioners and is practitioner oriented in its approach.

Empirical research focused specifically on nonprofit leadership is growing. But research on effective nonprofit leadership faces challenges. One problem is how to define it; this is bound up with the larger issue of how to define an effective nonprofit organization. As in measuring the effectiveness of the nonprofit board, the idea of CEO effectiveness is also socially constructed, and the definition of what constitutes an effective nonprofit CEO may vary according to the perceptions of the organization's diverse constituencies.

Indeed, a common method that researchers have used for identifying effective nonprofit leaders is based on perceptions. Nonprofit executives or perhaps opinion leaders, such as foundation officers and academics, are asked to identify those CEOs whom they deem to be most successful or effective. The characteristics of these CEOs are then compared with those of another group of CEOs who were not named. But this method is problematic and raises the question of how the nominators are defining "effective." Those identified as effective may simply be the most visible or popular in their fields. Charismatic leaders may be favored over others of different styles because they are often highly visible and have magnetic personalities. Or the executives identified by their colleagues as being effective might have been those who had been active as presenters at professional conferences or as authors, perhaps demonstrating their knowledge about nonprofit leadership, but not necessarily bearing any relationship to their performance as leaders of their own organizations. Furthermore, it is not always clear whether survey or interview respondents are describing how things are, how they believe they should be, or how they think they should respond.

Many studies based on surveys of perceptions reflect what seem to be trait or skills theories of leadership. For example, nonprofit CEOs interviewed by Mike Hudson (2005) identified openness and honesty as the most important qualities of effective nonprofit chief executives. In another study, nonprofit sector opinion leaders identified passion and commitment, vision, integrity, trust, and credibility (Light, 2002). Similar traits are also mentioned in the practitioner-oriented literature—integrity and trust (Pidgeon, 2004), vision, initiative, openness, and responsiveness (Howe, 2004).

Some research studies and the practitioner literature have also identified skills associated with effective nonprofit leadership. They commonly identify interpersonal skills, communication skills, delegation skills, staff management skills, the ability to articulate and write a message, and the ability to raise funds (Howe, 2004; Light, 2002; Pidgeon, 2004). Kevin Kearns, Jonathon Livingston, Shelley Sherer, and Lydia McShane (2013) interviewed 20 nonprofit CEOs, who reported that "interpersonal skills, especially communication and trust building" were most commonly employed in their leadership (p. 712). Many of the skills identified are, of course, generic and would seem to be useful to leaders in any organization. The skills unique to nonprofits (e.g., fundraising) are essentially technical, and others mentioned are more related to management than to leadership.

Some authors do describe behaviors of effective nonprofit CEOs, but most of this literature is prescriptive. It tells us what CEOs should do to be effective, and it often emphasizes areas on which the chief executive should focus his or her time and attention. Five areas are frequently mentioned, and these are discussed below.

Focus on Mission

The importance of staying focused on the mission is emphasized by almost all authors on the topic of effective nonprofit CEOs. The mission is the nonprofit's reason for existence, and the CEO should use it as a guide for every decision. Many nonprofit boards include leaders from the business community, who may sometimes find it attractive to direct the organization toward activities that are financially lucrative but that may distract it from its primary mission. Staff may sometimes propose activities that would be "nice to do" but that may not advance the mission directly. The CEO can use the mission as a shield against such pressures from the staff or board, to explain, justify, and give coherence to his or her actions.

Focus on the Board

Many authors emphasize the importance of the CEO's relationship with the board. Chapter 4 discussed the research of Robert Herman and Dick Heimovics (2005), who identified board-centered leadership as the behavior distinguishing effective CEOs from others. As they report in their research findings,

> Analysis showed that executive leadership in relation to staff and in relation to the board are independent and distinct factors. Effective and comparison executives differed little in leadership with their staffs. The most important finding was that the effective executives provided significantly more leadership to their boards. (p. 157)

Focus on External Relationships

Effective nonprofit leaders are those who are not excessively focused on internal management. They are not obsessed with policies and procedures and the day-to-day activities of their subordinates. Rather, they "delegate much of the management of internal affairs and focus on the external" (Herman & Heimovics, 2005, p. 159). Practical strategies for enhancing external impact may involve developing an informal information network, including contacts in government, other nonprofits, foundations, and professional associations, to supplement hard data with soft information about emerging trends and practices in the field.

Fundraising is an important aspect of the external activity of many nonprofit CEOs, and indeed, its importance is growing as government support for many programs has been reduced. While the opinion leaders and nonprofit CEOs interviewed by Light (2002) mentioned fundraising as an important skill, it is surprising how seldom it is addressed in much of the nonprofit leadership literature.

Share Leadership and Empower Others

In their study of high-impact nonprofits, Leslie Crutchfield and Heather Grant (2008, 2012) determined that effective nonprofit CEOs share leadership with others. This sometimes includes having two people in top positions, with complementary skills—for example, someone who is good at outside relationships and another who specializes in internal operations. It also includes developing a team of leaders within the organization, that is, having bench strength and empowering members of the leadership team.

In a review of the literature on shared leadership, Robert Routhieaux (2015) identifies important trends in nonprofits, including pressure on funding sources, the growing emphasis on collaborative efforts, generational changes in the nonprofit workforce and leadership, and the increasing demand for accountability. Consistent with the conclusion of Crutchfield and Grant (2008, 2012), Routhieaux suggests that "organizations that have already developed a culture of shared leadership might be able to respond to [these trends] more effectively and efficiently" (p. 144).

Focus on Key Roles and Priorities

In their well-known work on leadership, Nanus and Dobbs (1999) address the question of where the nonprofit CEO needs to direct his or her attention—their answer: almost everywhere. They define four quadrants in which the CEO may focus and operate at any given time—inside the organization, outside the organization, on present operations, and on future possibilities. They identify six roles defined by these four areas and argue that the effective CEO needs to be proficient in *all* of them. When the CEO combines an internal perspective with attention to present operations, he or she is acting in the role of "coach," guiding staff and others who are performing the organization's work. Looking inward but with a view to the future, the CEO is playing the role of "change agent." When CEOs are focused outside the organization but concerned with present operations, they are performing as "politicians" and as "fundraisers." And when CEOs are focused externally and looking to the future, they are performing as "visionaries" and "strategists."

Herman and Heimovics (2005) urge nonprofit CEOs to stay focused on key "goals or outcomes [that are] crucial"; that is, they advise nonprofit CEOs to "know your agenda" (p. 160). A well-managed organization may have goals derived from a formal process of strategic planning, but effective executives have their own short list of priorities—a few key things they wish to accomplish. Those priorities may be drawn from the plan or be supplemental to it. Rather than scatter their attention and efforts across a broad list of goals, CEOs will be more successful if they can limit their priorities to a few critical initiatives that will define their leadership of the organization and focus their own attention and that of others on those items. Mim Carlson and Margaret Donohoe (2003), both former nonprofit executives and now consultants, agree, advising, "Don't let a list of priorities exceed five items, and three is better" (p. 33).

Board members, donors, and even staff may not be thinking about organizational goals all the time and they face innumerable distractions in their own personal and professional lives. For that reason, it is important for the CEO to keep the short-listed goals constantly in front of them and to ensure that they have the same information and perspective as the CEO. This may lead them to share his or her understanding of what the priorities are and why. Leaders also need to simplify the priorities and "lay a bread-crumb trail" to key decisions through communication and small actions that lead the way to larger changes. This is a way of preparing the board and others, so that when changes need to be made, they will not seem to come out of the blue. The leaders will have prepared their constituents for change, one step at a time (Herman & Heimovics, 2005, pp. 160–161).

Use the "Political Frame"

In their insightful and practical research on nonprofit executives, Herman and Heimovics (2005) find that effective CEOs are distinguished from others by their use of a "political frame." Indeed, they say this is a finding of their research in which they have particular confidence.

The concept of frames was developed by Lee Bolman and Terrence Deal (2003). A frame is a perspective or a way of seeing and understanding things—like seeing the glass either half empty or half full. Bolman and Deal (2003) identified four frames that leaders may use. Some may view their organizations through a structural frame, focusing on structures and formal relationships. Or they may use the human resources frame, emphasizing interpersonal relationships and worker morale. A third frame is the symbolic frame, through which a leader may see events, rituals, and stories as central to his or her work.

When leaders use the political frame, that does not mean that they see things in terms of partisan or elective politics, but rather that they recognize the inevitable interplay among the organization's important constituencies. The political frame is a perspective through which the CEO sees and understands the environment in terms of the pressures brought by various constituencies that compete, bargain, and negotiate over the allocation of resources. Leaders using this frame will be sensitive to external forces that might affect the organization and, therefore, devote their time and effort to maintaining relationships and influencing various competing constituencies. All leaders may use all of the frames at particular times. What

Herman and Heimovics (2005) found was that effective nonprofit CEOs use a political frame substantially more than others who were identified as less successful (p. 165).

Right Person, Right Place, Right Time

In a book focused on leadership in the nonprofit sector, but with more generic applications as well, Barry Dym and Harry Hutson (2005) argue that nonprofit executive effectiveness results from having the right person in the right job at the right time; in other words, it is necessary to have a good fit between the leader and the needs of the organization at the time.

They propose an alignment model that seeks to integrate the major leadership theories, that is, to provide "an overarching conceptual framework that brings the theories together, or at least describes how the theories relate to one another" (Dym & Hutson, 2005, p. 36). The leader's fit with the organization involves traits as well as skills, leadership style as well as situation. In other words, there is no one right theory, but all have relevance in the context of the right time and place. Invoking many of the major leadership theories in one paragraph to describe their concepts of fit and alignment, Dym and Hutson write,

> If one were to align a leader who is determined and communicates well and whose personality and behavior (style) fit well with the organizational culture, who understands how to structure the organization's future and light up the pathway to success, who communicates frequently with direct reports and makes staff followers feel supported and understood, and who holds high standards in a way that is sensitive to both individual and group psychological needs—if someone were to see such alignment, what would be witnessed is effective leadership. (p. 345)

Dym and Hutson (2005) provide an **alignment map** (see Table 5.3), summarizing the components on which they say alignment must be achieved. It encompasses the characteristics of the individual as well as characteristics of the organization and of the community or market that the organization serves. All three must be aligned to produce a perfect fit. Thus, for example, a charismatic leader with an extroverted personality might be a good fit for an advocacy organization that is working to gain public awareness and change public policy, but such an individual might not be a good fit as a director of a museum, university, or think tank, where a more collegial, participative style might be more readily accepted. An executive director who does not speak Spanish and has little understanding of Hispanic/Latino culture would not be a good fit as the executive director of an organization that serves primarily Hispanic/Latino clients. A leader who comes from the business world—or even from a different type of nonprofit organization—might find it difficult to be effective

Table 5.3 Dym and Hutson's Alignment Map

	Leader	Organization	Community/Market
Basic nature	Character and style	Organizational type	Patterns and norms
Underlying principles	Personal values	Organizational culture	Larger culture
Means available	Individual skills	Organizational resources	Economy and industry
Purpose and direction	Personal objectives	Mission and strategy	Community needs and market demands

Source: Dym and Hutson (2005, p. 93).

in a nonprofit organization that has an established culture different from that with which he or she is familiar. An organization that encourages self-empowerment among its clients would not be aligned with its mission if its own leadership behaved in autocratic ways. In other words, for a CEO to be effective, his or her traits, styles, skills, and values need to be in sync with the organization and its constituencies. Too much dissonance may diminish the CEO's ability to lead or even, in the case of a bad fit, result in his or her eventual departure.

However, according to Dym and Hutson (2005), alignment is a two-way process. It may involve change by the leader and by the nonprofit itself: "Leaders must ... align themselves to organizations by adapting themselves to the organization's structure, process, culture, and strategy—and by aligning the organization's to fit their style. Both processes are necessary for effective leadership" (p. 100). But, they advise, alignment should not be perfect and some tension is desirable. "A fit that is too perfect leads to stagnation.... Close but imperfect fit combines the smooth functioning we associate with efficiency and effectiveness with the flexible adjustment to change we associate with creativity" (Dym & Hutson, p. 67).

Founder Syndrome

As Dym and Hutson (2005) discuss, one leadership style may be appropriate at one point in an organization's history and another at a different time. The idea that the organization's need for leadership might change over time derives from life-cycle theories of nonprofit organization development, which describe specific stages through which organizations naturally evolve.

For example, charismatic leaders are often seen leading an organization in its early stages, where the vision and inspiration of a committed founder drive volunteers and early generation staff members to exceptional effort. However, as the organization matures, it may require a different kind of leader—one "who feels comfortable in and supported enough by the stable organization to begin to implement long-term growth projects" (Dym & Hutson, 2005, p. 89). In other words, as the organization grows, adds staff, develops systems, and expands its programs, there will be an increased need for professional management, and the charisma of the founder may no longer suffice. (We will discuss organization life cycles in more detail in Chapter 8.)

There are many examples of nonprofit organizations founded by visionary and charismatic individuals who became the first executive directors. The founder attracts and inspires dedicated and loyal volunteers, donors, and staff. The board may consist of individuals recruited by the founder, who generally acquiesce to his or her authority and charisma (Block & Rosenberg, 2002). But at some point, as the organization grows and its needs for professional management, formal systems, and a more deliberate approach increase, the founder may not possess the required management skills or may be unable to adjust his or her vision of the organization to the new reality. He or she may prefer the entrepreneurial culture of the early organization.

The founder is likely to have a deep dedication to the organization and its cause—it may be the founder's life, and he or she may expect staff to make similar personal sacrifices. Founders often have task-oriented styles and are described as difficult and demanding by their subordinates. Like a controlling parent, the founder may have become accustomed to making all the decisions and may resist any initiative from the board or staff to be more independent. That style might work in the early days when the staff and board comprise a small number of loyal followers who share the founder's enthusiasm, but it may become less tolerated as the organization comes to require a larger staff of technical specialists and professional managers. Passion may no longer be an adequate substitute for rational decision making.

But the founder's psychological identification with the organization—after all, it's the founder's baby—may make it impossible for him or her to accept a more democratic, team approach. The situation becomes more stressful as staff turnover increases, management errors begin to mount, systems spin out of control, and the board feels increasingly torn between its loyalty to the founder and its responsibility to the organization. The board may begin to add more outsiders, people who are not personally selected by the founder and who bring more professional skills. These outsiders have less loyalty to the founder, and the balance begins to shift, increasing tension between the founder/executive director and the board: The organization is suffering from what is commonly called **founder syndrome**.

The arrival of founder syndrome in the life of the organization poses a challenge, even a crisis. Eventually, some crisis or event may trigger an explosion, resulting in the dismissal of the founder. Board members and staff loyal to the founder may leave amid bitterness, while others scramble to save the organization. Often the founder will be replaced by a professional manager, who then faces the challenge of rebuilding and developing new relationships. Or if the crisis is not resolved, the founder's departure may precipitate the organization's decline into turmoil and eventual death. Dym and Hutson (2005) portray the ugly scene:

> There is a declining certainty about the organization's original purpose. People wonder whether they were naïve to think they could accomplish so much in the first place. They question whether they can survive without being more realistic about their goals, their methods, and the people they trust. As doubt creeps in, people grow more conservative, more cautious. They see problems where before they mainly saw solutions. They begin to invest less of themselves—their hopes and dreams, their willingness to risk, and their time. Or they begin a somewhat frenzied and exhausting alternation of investing more and less. (p. 118)

If the transition from the founder to a professional manager is traumatic and risky for the organization, following the founder also can be a challenging assignment for the new CEO. It may be that the board, perhaps feeling guilty over its dismissal of the founder as executive director, has allowed him or her to remain as a member of the board—an unfortunate decision that may provide a platform for the founder to criticize and undermine the new executive. In other cases, the founder may be retained as a consultant or perhaps in an honorific position to engage in fundraising and other external tasks. But, under these arrangements, unless the founder has exceptional wisdom and grace and the new executive shows unusual understanding and sensitivity, the situation is likely to remain volatile for some time, continuing to burden the organization and distract it from pursuit of its mission.

Of course, there are enlightened and wise founders, who recognize their own limitations and their organization's changing needs. In this situation, founder syndrome really does not exist, since there are many options for providing both the leadership and management that the organization requires. For example, the founder may take on more of an external role, delegating much of the day-to-day management to others, perhaps an associate director, chief operating officer, or executive vice president. But, in such a scenario, it is also essential for the founder to avoid end runs around the new operating officer by staff, who may have been hired by the founder, and to support and reinforce the operating officer's authority and control.

Executive Transitions

Every nonprofit will eventually face the need to replace its CEO. Indeed, the subjects of executive transition and **succession planning** have gained increased urgency as the nonprofit sector prepares for a significant transfer in leadership. The baby boomers, who have risen to the top ranks in many sectors, are reaching retirement age, suggesting that there will be significant turnover in CEO positions (McKee & Froelich, 2016).

Of course, not all transitions occur because of a predictable event, such as a retirement. In some cases, the need for a change is first recognized by the board, and the current CEO needs to be persuaded—or forced—to step down. As we have discussed, this can be especially difficult when the chief executive is a charismatic founder of the organization, but the involuntary departure of any CEO is a difficult and potentially wrenching experience for an organization. In other situations, the CEO may initiate the change. This may occur for several reasons. The CEO may receive a better offer from another organization or perhaps just feel burned out and want a change of scene. For some CEOs, there comes a point when they feel that their major goals for the organization have been accomplished and that it is just time to move on to something new. This may occur at the completion of some major effort, for example, a successful fundraising campaign, or on reaching some milestone, such as 10 years of service (Weisman & Goldbaum, 2004). For the board, there is a difference between an anticipated departure, such as retirement, and one that comes as a surprise, such as when the CEO receives an unanticipated job offer that is just too good to turn down. In the first instance, the board has time to prepare for the transition; in the second, some boards may be caught unprepared to make one of the most critical decisions they will ever face.

In business corporations, it is not unusual for chief executives to come up through the ranks. They are often individuals who have worked in the company for a long time, are steeped in its culture, and are knowledgeable about its products and markets. Indeed, as a corporate executive approaches retirement, it is not unusual for there to be an heir apparent who has been groomed for the top position for years. For example, Apple CEO Steve Jobs had selected Tim Cook, then Apple's chief operating officer, to be his successor as CEO when his own health began to decline, and he knew that a transition eventually would need to occur. Many nonprofit boards work in the same way with regard to their own membership; bylaws often include limits on how long the board chair can serve, and thus, the transition in leadership is predictable and planned. There is often a vice chair of the board or even a chair elect, who is well prepared to take over the job in a smooth transition. However, a significant majority of nonprofits do not have a succession plan with regard to the CEO position (McKee & Froelich, 2016).

When the time does arrive to appoint a new CEO, most are recruited from outside the organization. This is frequently because the organization is thinly staffed and tightly budgeted and cannot afford the luxury of a number-two executive with the capability to be the CEO (Froelich, McKee, & Rathge, 2011). The lack of an internal candidate for the chief executive position might also exist if the organization is still led by a founder who may not have provided others with the opportunity to learn and grow sufficiently to be prepared for leadership. And, of course, boards sometimes hold the view that someone from outside may bring new ideas and create greater change than an individual who has been working in the organization for a long time. Thus, nonprofits may appoint as CEO an individual who is a virtual stranger—not someone whom they have known or have had the opportunity to get to know in more junior positions before advancing him or her to the top office. In these circumstances, the selection of a new CEO may carry some risk that the wrong person will be selected, with potentially serious consequences for the effectiveness and stability of the organization.

In order to minimize the risk, the selection of a new CEO must be rooted in the organization's own understanding of itself—its mission, its values, its vision, and its goals. The process cannot be rushed, and it is often about far more than just finding someone qualified for the job. To define who may be the right person in the right place at the right time, the organization must have a clear understanding of its past, its purpose, its constituencies, and its aspirations. A full discussion of the search process is beyond the scope of this text, but there is a growing literature on the subject and many excellent resources are available, through BoardSource, CompassPoint (www.compasspoint.org), and other organizations. As competition for management talent has intensified, professional executive search firms also have come to play a larger role.

Although, again, most nonprofits do not have a succession plan for the CEO position (McKee & Froelich, 2016), there is an expanding literature on the topic and a growing consensus on the desirability of such preparation. Boards are advised to ensure that such internal planning is occurring and also to remain aware of leaders in other similar organizations whom they might try to recruit should the need arise (Weisman & Goldbaum, 2004). And, the need for succession planning goes well below the top level of management. Other staff members, for example, program directors or even key volunteers, may need to be replaced and there may not always be advance warning. Communication, documentation, and cross-training of staff in the responsibilities of each other's jobs can minimize disruption during the period of transition after someone leaves the organization. This work is primarily a responsibility of the CEO, but boards should assure that such preparation is in place.

Leading Change

Leadership often involves change. Indeed, James Kee and Kathryn Newcomer (2008) observe that "some ... argue that leadership is inherently change-oriented—that the function of management is to protect and nurture the status quo, while the function of leadership is to continually examine better ways of doing things" (p. 23).

There are a number of prominent change theories and models. Kee and Newcomer (2008) propose a taxonomy of change models, placing some well-known theories into the categories of **leader-centered**, **follower-centered**, and **change-centered** leadership, each of which has advantages and disadvantages (p. 23). While arguing for "a model of change leadership that engages other stakeholders in a 'whole systems' approach to the change process," Kee and Newcomer acknowledge that "the dominant advice in the literature on change management is that ... leaders ... must overcome resistance to change through a variety of top-down approaches" (p. 32).

Indeed, one of the best-known authors on change, John Kotter (1996), describes a top-down approach. Kotter's model is based on business corporations, which is why some scholars find it less than ideal for nonprofit organizations. However, elements of it may be adapted to the nonprofit setting. One hallmark of the model is its emphasis on the importance of organizational culture—the shared values, attitudes, feelings, beliefs, rituals, habits, codes of conduct, and other such characteristics of an organization—invisible rules that may support or hinder an initiative for change.

Kotter (1996) describes eight common mistakes that leaders trying to implement change are prone to make and proposes a parallel eight-step change process to avoid them. According to Kotter, efforts at transformational change in an organization often fail because leaders allow too much complacency; that is, they do not engender a sufficient sense of urgency about the need for change. For example, in a mature organization, decline may be gradual, and future threats may not be visible to most people. As long as the operating budget is balanced, there is no negative publicity or scandal, and staff positions seem secure, most people may be content to continue with business as usual and not be receptive to changes that would disrupt their worldviews or routines.

Leaders often fail to develop what Kotter (1996) calls a "powerful guiding coalition" in support of change. In other words, they too often try to drive the change alone without first developing a critical mass of allies—perhaps including key staff members, members of the board, and others—who share their commitment to the need for change. Leaders sometimes underestimate the power of vision. They try to bring about change through a series of actions—incremental changes, perhaps small modifications to procedures, reorganizations of staff, or modest enhancements to fundraising or communications programs. These are steps along the way that may appear unconnected to those who do not see or understand the larger vision toward which they are intended to lead. Leaders may try to operate behind the scenes, without adequately painting the picture of what the future will be like. In that case, they are unlikely to build the steam necessary to propel real and lasting change in the organization. The inertia of current culture and practice may be just too strong to overcome with an incremental approach.

Too often, change leaders undercommunicate the vision, perhaps relying on routine communication vehicles such as newsletters, annual reports, and other publications. They may assume that everyone in the organization carefully reads and considers such publications—or takes them seriously—and is thus sufficiently aware of the plan for change and shares the leader's commitment to it, when in fact this may not be true.

Kotter (1996) says that leaders may fail because they do not create "short-term wins"— that is, set intermediate goals that can be achieved and reassure followers that the ultimate longer-term changes can be successfully reached. Setting some achievable short-term goals and celebrating their attainment can be an essential tactic to retain the commitment of staff and volunteers to a long-term change process and prevent frustration and inertia from bringing it to a halt midstream.

But there is also the risk of declaring victory too soon. Change may have occurred on the surface, but leaders err when they do not stay with the program long enough for the changes to "sink down deeply into the [organization's] culture" (Kotter, 1996, p. 13). Only by anchoring the changes in the organization's culture can the leader pursuing change ensure that the board and successive generations of management will also adhere to new ways of doing things. As Kotter explains,

> Smart people miss the mark here when they are insensitive to cultural issues. Economically oriented finance people and analytically oriented engineers can find the topic of social norms and values too soft for their tastes. So, they ignore culture—at their peril. (p. 15)

Kotter (1996, p. 21) offers an eight-step change process that avoids each of the potential mistakes. To ensure that the momentum for change is not overwhelmed by the inertia of existing culture and practices and to make certain that the change is real and permanent, the leader should follow the steps sequentially, not moving on to the next until the previous has been solidly accomplished:

1. Establish a sense of urgency

2. Create a guiding coalition

3. Develop a vision and strategy

4. Communicate the change vision

5. Empower broad-based action

6. Generate short-term wins

7. Consolidate gains and produce more change

8. Anchor new approaches in the culture

What is the essential ingredient of successful change? Kotter (1996) argues that it requires 70 to 90 percent leadership and just 10 to 30 percent the skills of management. "Leadership defines what the future should look like, aligns people with that vision, and inspires them to make it happen despite the obstacles" (p. 26). But leadership may be in short supply when an organization needs it to drive essential change. Kotter describes a life-cycle theory of business firms that is reminiscent of the nonprofit life cycles we discussed earlier. Companies start as entrepreneurial businesses, then grow and achieve a position of market dominance. As size and dominance increase, control becomes most important, and management predominates over leadership. However, that can produce a bureaucratic, inward orientation that causes managers to become complacent about performance. The situation requires change, Kotter writes, but the forces of complacency and inertia make change difficult, requiring "sacrifice, dedication, and creativity." These cannot be engendered through coercion but instead require "leadership, leadership, and more leadership" (Kotter, p. 31).

CHAPTER SUMMARY

The position of CEO in a nonprofit organization is different from similar positions in government or the business sector, for reasons that relate to the distinctive nature of nonprofit organizations themselves. While every organization, regardless of sector, requires capable management in order to be effective, nonprofits especially need CEOs who can exercise strong leadership. This is true because they are organizations based on values and driven by their missions, which mobilize commitment and support by appealing to a shared vision.

Theorists have defined leadership in terms of individual qualities, skills that leaders possess, behaviors that successful leaders exhibit, and interactions between leaders and followers. Most contemporary theories recognize that effective leadership may be contingent; that is, it may depend on the circumstances, including human relationships, the nature of the task, and the formal position of the executive.

James MacGregor Burns (1978) offered a definition of transactional leadership that sounds very much like management. The transactional leader rewards or punishes others in exchange for the work that they perform and emphasizes rules, policies, and procedures to ensure that things are done right. Burns introduced the concept of transformational leadership, in which the leader enables individuals to experience their own moral and motivational growth by appealing to values that they share with the organization. This text suggests that transformational leadership may be especially appropriate in organizations that often attract the participation of people motivated by commitment to their values-based missions. The concept of charismatic leadership is frequently observed in the founders of nonprofit organizations. They are individuals who inspire others to extraordinary effort through the model of their own commitment and their articulation of a vision, among other behaviors.

Various scholars and practitioners have tried to define the effective nonprofit CEO. Some reflect trait theories or skills theories of leadership, while others have described the behaviors of effective chief executives. The behaviors most often identified involve the CEO focusing his or her attention on the mission, the board, external relationships, and a few key priorities while understanding the political reality of competition among constituencies for the organization's resources. A framework offered by Dym and Hutson (2005) seeks to integrate various leadership theories and describe how effective leadership arises when the individual, the organization, and its community or market are aligned—in other words, when the right person serves in the right place at the right time.

Some organizations will face a significant challenge when a CEO leaves the organization, either voluntarily or through a forced transition. Although the majority of nonprofits do not have a succession plan, the importance of such preparation has received greater attention in the recent literature of nonprofit management and is considered by many to be a best practice. Most new nonprofit CEOs are appointed from outside the organization rather than from the existing staff, which is different from most business corporations. When the time comes to appoint a new CEO, the board should base the search firmly in the organization's mission, values, vision, goals, and aspirations.

Leadership often involves change, and some authors argue that this is inherently so. There are various theories of change leadership, including those that are leader-centered, those that are follower-centered, and those that are change-centered. Each has its advantages and disadvantages, and the model selected should be appropriate to the organization. One common principle is the importance of anchoring changes in the organization's culture.

NOTE

1. Reprinted with permission from *The Nonprofit Chief Executive's Ten Basic Responsibilities* (2013, 2nd ed.) by Richard L. Moyers, a publication of BoardSource. For more information about BoardSource, call 800-883-6262 or visit www.boardsource.org. BoardSource ©2013. Content may not be reproduced or used for any purpose other than that which is specifically requested without written permission from BoardSource.

KEY TERMS AND CONCEPTS

alignment map 129
change-centered 133
charismatic leadership 124
contingency theories 121
employee orientation 120
executive leadership 123
follower-centered 133
founder syndrome 131

leader-centered 133
leader–member exchange theories 122
leadership 117
legislative leadership 123
management 117
managerial grid 120
path-goal theories 122
production orientation 120

relationship behaviors 120
situational theories 121
skills theories 120
succession planning 131
task behaviors 120
trait theories 120
transactional leadership 122
transformational leadership 122

CASE 5.1 A Change in Leadership at Habitat for Humanity

Habitat for Humanity International is an ecumenical, faith-based nonprofit dedicated to eliminating substandard housing and homelessness. Habitat constructs, renovates, and repairs houses with the assistance of volunteers and partner families, who then purchase the homes with affordable loans. It works in 1,400 communities in the United States and 70 countries and has helped 9.8 million people secure affordable, dependable shelter (Habitat for Humanity International, 2017). Habitat has been hailed as one of the most successful nonprofits and as "one of the most dramatic examples of social entrepreneurship … that blends commercial and social methods to generate much of the cash, labor, and materials needed to construct its programs" (Dees, Emerson, & Economy, 2001, p. 12).

Habitat was founded in 1976 by Millard Fuller, who led the organization as its CEO for many years. Fuller had acquired wealth before the age of 30 and then dedicated himself to a life of service. While he was the CEO of Habitat, Fuller accepted an annual salary of only $15,000, declined raises, and lived for 23 years in a modest house without air-conditioning (Bixler, 2005). Fuller was widely praised as a visionary, and his commitment attracted volunteers and donors to Habitat, including former president Jimmy Carter, who became one of the organization's most prominent advocates.

But by the early 2000s, issues began to arise between Fuller and Habitat's board. As Fuller approached the age of 70 in 2004, he sought to extend his service as CEO until 2005, when Habitat would complete construction of its 200,000th house. But the board began to plan for transition and appointed a former board chairman as managing director. Although Fuller retained the title of president and chief executive officer, he was said to have complained that the board's decision forced him into a figurehead role (Pierce, 2004).

One board member observed that a gradual change had occurred in the composition of the board, saying, "There was a movement to start engaging board members who had some 'juice'—people who were powerful in different fields and were well connected" (Pierce, 2004, p. 15). The changing board became critical of Fuller for undertaking some projects without its approval (Pierce, 2004), and Fuller became critical of the board, saying, "I've always seen Habitat for Humanity as a movement.... There's a certain mentality on the board now that wants to change it into an organizational bureaucracy" (Jensen, 2005, p. 26).

In January of 2005, the board fired Fuller and his wife, who also had held a position at Habitat, and appointed an interim CEO. The interim CEO explained the situation saying, "The strength of vision and ego that was so important for the beginning and initial growth of Habitat are not what we need today to provide the structure for what has become a large, far-flung operation" (Jewell, 2005, p. 24). Fuller spoke out against the board's action, saying trustees were not committed to the faith-based nature of Habitat and just wanted to replace him with a "high paid bean counter" (Jewell, 2005, p. 24).

Some Habitat for Humanity affiliates, volunteers, and donors spoke out in opposition to the board's action and in support of Fuller. Fuller created a new organization, which he called Building Habitat. He later changed its name to the Fuller Center for Housing, after Habitat for Humanity filed a lawsuit alleging infringement of its trademark (Wilhelm, 2005). Habitat for Humanity undertook a search for a new CEO and eventually hired Jonathon Reckford, a former businessman with Goldman Sachs and Best Buy. Following his designation as the new CEO, Reckford met with Fuller. After the meeting, Fuller said, "I was not prepared to like the guy, but I did" (Wilhelm, 2005).

Reckford committed the organization to continued growth but said that it needed to "build the platform" for that growth and determine the right organizational structure and ways of maximizing effectiveness (Wilhelm, 2005). He expanded Habitat's mission to include neighborhood revitalization and disaster relief. The organization responded to the Indian Ocean tsunami in 2004 and Hurricane Katrina in 2005 as well as the U.S. housing market collapse in 2008 (Chipman, 2015). Habitat increased its advocacy efforts to help low-income families obtain loans for housing and increased its own earned income through the sales of recycled building supplies at its ReStores. The number of families engaged with Habitat increased from 25,000 per year when Reckford took over to 300,000 in 2014 (Chipman, 2015).

Reflecting on the controversy that had surrounded the transition in leadership from Habitat's founder, one nonprofit scholar observed, "Habitat for Humanity [was] much bigger than one man, and that speaks of Mr. Fuller's success" (Minor, 2005). Fuller passed away in 2009 at age 74.

Questions Related to Case 5.1

1. Which theory or theories seem to best describe the career of Millard Fuller at Habitat for Humanity?

2. In what ways is the story of his departure an example of founder syndrome?

3. If this case is indeed a case of founder syndrome, do you think Fuller could have avoided it, or had the organization evolved in a way that was just inconsistent with his values and experience?

4. Thinking about the characteristics of nonprofit organizations discussed in Chapter 3, what changes in his or her style might someone with a background in business need to consider when moving into a leadership position in a nonprofit organization?

Case 5.2   Challenge and Change at United Way

In 1887, Denver became the first city to establish a united organization to raise funds in order to meet community needs. Other cities adopted the idea, creating organizations that were commonly called the Community Chest, later becoming known as United Way (United Way of America, n.d.-a). By 2003, there were more than 1,400 local United Ways, raising almost $4 billion to support a broad range of nonprofits in their communities (Wolverton, 2003). Local United Ways are independent nonprofit organizations. In the United States, the national office provides support and assistance to local United Ways, and the local organizations are required to meet certain standards in order to use the name.

In 1995, the president of the United Way of America, then the national umbrella organization, was convicted of stealing funds for personal use, eroding public confidence. Another blow came in 2001, when the CEO of the United Way of the National Capital Area, the local chapter serving the Washington, DC, region, was charged with similar abuses. But larger forces also were at work, presenting challenges to the United Way and its model. By 2003, the amount of gifts to United Way that were designated for specific nonprofit organizations had risen 13 years in a row (Ogden, 2008). That approach to giving denied the United Way the ability to select recipient nonprofits, reducing its influence. More donors were bypassing the United Way altogether to make gifts directly to nonprofits that interested them. Some were questioning the continued relevance of the United Way model, which raised funds through workplace fundraising campaigns and provided support to a wide variety of nonprofit organizations. Both individual and corporate donors were becoming more interested in the impact of their gifts and less interested in giving to a fund that would benefit any nonprofit organization that qualified ("Brian Gallagher," 2007). In addition, an economic recession in 2003 had led to a significant decline in workplace giving by employees, which accounted for 66 percent of United Way revenues, and support for United Way from corporations, which comprised the balance (Wolverton, 2003). Brian Gallagher, who had worked in local United Way chapters for 20 years, had been appointed as the new president and CEO of the United Way of America in 2002. He recognized the urgent need for change.

Gallagher raised a basic question about the mission of United Way: Was it to raise funds or to have an impact on communities? "We are in the business of changing people's lives," he concluded, "Fundraising is a strategy." He explained, "We had forgotten to connect with donors as customers and to combine community interests and corporate interests because we were so focused on raising money in the workplace using a monopoly position" (Boston Consulting Group, 2011).

Gallagher committed to undertaking a significant transformation. Although the idea had preceded Gallagher's presidency, he began to promote a plan in which United Way would move from being just a fundraising organization to one that would focus its resources and be measured by its impact on communities. But it would not be easy to accomplish such change in an organization with so many decentralized and independent components, each of which supported a wide range of local nonprofits that depended on the funds. Supported organizations would be worried about the possible loss of United Way support, and local United Way organizations might remain committed to the old model.

Gallagher brought together local United Way leaders from across the country to discuss the new model. About half were receptive to the proposed new approach, but the other half wanted to remain primarily fundraising organizations (Wolverton, 2004). Gallagher focused the discussion on the question about the mission, helping to build greater consensus (Boston Consulting Group, 2011). He also hired new people for the national staff who were less committed to the old way of thinking. He surveyed United Way professionals in various communities to learn what issues concerned them and consulted experts from think tanks, foundations, and government to identify the most pressing social problems facing the country (Ogden, 2008). Gallagher created new channels to increase communication among local United Ways, including webinars and other online tools, so that they could exchange ideas on best practices ("Brian Gallagher," 2007).

"United Way has a theory about how to create changes of this magnitude," Gallagher wrote. "It begins with declaring *bold goals*. When the stakes are high, Americans will rise to the occasion" (United Way of America, n.d.-b). But some resisted the new vision, including some employees both at local United Ways and the United Way of America (Wolverton, 2004). Gallagher knew that change would take time and require a shift in his organization's culture. "Your field of vision has to be really wide," he explained, "and you have to be willing to take risks. You have to be flexible and adjust as you go" (Boston Consulting Group, 2011).

Six years later, in 2008, United Way of America adopted a 10-year plan reflecting the new approach. It would emphasize the health, education, and finances of working families and be focused on achieving three Goals for the Common Good by 2018: cut in half high-school dropout rates across the United States, cut in half the number of families with working parents who don't earn enough to cover the family's basic expenses, and increase by one third the number of Americans who are healthy and avoid risky behaviors (Schwinn, 2008).

Rather than distributing funds widely, United Way would focus on organizations that were achieving progress toward the three goals and would hold them accountable for specific performance metrics (Schwinn, 2008). Gallagher recognized that United Way could not do it alone and sought to establish partnerships with other national nonprofits, including the YMCA and Boys and Girls Clubs of America. United Way also would increase its advocacy efforts to encourage government to spend money on the three priorities (Schwinn, 2008).

Charities that had traditionally received United Way support continued to be concerned that they would be shut out of the new program. Gallagher stated that many could still qualify for United Way support, but they would need to adopt a different approach as well: "Activity is not going to be enough anymore, [for example,] saying we served 200,000 seniors last year. The question is what are we doing to increase the financial stability of seniors?" (Schwinn, 2008). A tracking system would be established for local United Ways, which would report data to United Way of America so that progress toward the goals could be measured at a community level (Ogden, 2008).

In 2009, United Way of America merged with United Way International to form United Way Worldwide. Brian Gallagher became CEO of the new organization and turned his attention to promoting the impact model internationally. In 2012, Stacy Stewart became the new president of United Way USA, the national organization in the United States. There remained work to be done. Stewart identified her challenges to include the need to continue building the United Way culture; to achieve cooperation among the many local United Ways, while maintaining local flexibility; and to encourage donors to designate their gifts for one of the three community impact priorities (Donovan, 2012). In 2017, Stewart went on to become president of the March of Dimes and Mary Sellers became the U.S. president of United Way Worldwide. Sellers committed herself to continued change, including adapting new fundraising channels, such as mobile giving, and increasing opportunities for young people to become involved as volunteers (Aschbrenner, 2017).

Questions Related to Case 5.2

1. Which theory or theories seem to best describe the leadership of Brian Gallagher at United Way?

2. In what ways does the process for change that Brian Gallagher implemented at United Way reflect Kotter's model?

3. If you had been the CEO of a nonprofit organization that had been receiving United Way funds, how would you have prepared for the changes that Brian Gallagher led?

4. What advice would you give to Gallagher's successors about how to keep the change process moving forward?

QUESTIONS FOR DISCUSSION

1. Are leaders born or made? Can anyone learn to be a leader or does it require some innate qualities or characteristics of the individual?

2. Could one individual be a great leader in government, a corporation, or a nonprofit? Why or why not?

3. Is leadership necessarily moral? Was Hitler a leader even though he was evil? Why or why not?

4. Who are some contemporary leaders that you would identify as charismatic? Think about individuals in the nonprofit sector, business, and government. How do they exhibit the behaviors of charismatic leaders identified in this chapter?

APPENDIX CASES

The following cases in the Appendix of this text include points related to the content of this chapter: Case 1 (New York City Opera); Case 4 (The Girl Scouts of the United States of America).

SUGGESTIONS FOR FURTHER READING

Books

Collins, J. (2005). *Good to great and the social sectors: A monograph to accompany* Good to Great. New York, NY: Harper.

Denhardt, R. B., Denhardt, J. V., & Aristigueta, M. P. (2016). *Managing human behavior in public and nonprofit organizations* (4th ed.). Thousand Oaks, CA: Sage.

Dym, B., Egmont, S., & Watkins, L. (2011). *Managing leadership transition for nonprofits: Passing the torch to sustain organizational excellence.* Upper Saddle River, NJ: FT Press.

Northouse, P. G. (2018). *Introduction to leadership: Concepts and practice* (4th ed.). Thousand Oaks, CA: Sage.

Articles

Bernstein, R., Buse, K., & Bilimoria, D. (2016, June). Revisiting agency and stewardship theories: Perspectives from nonprofit board chairs and CEOs. *Nonprofit Management and Leadership, 26*(4), 489–498.

McKee, G., & Froelich, K. (2016). Executive succession planning: Barriers and substitutes in nonprofit organizations. *Annals of Public and Cooperative Economics, 87*(4), 587–601.

Websites

Center for Creative Leadership: http://www.ccl.org/leadership/index.aspx

Daring to Lead: http://www.daringtolead.org

Managing the Nonprofit Organization

PART

III

Accountability requires not only that the resources entrusted to the nonprofit not be misused, but also that they be used to the maximum benefit in pursuing the organization's mission. However, this component of accountability turns out to be the most complex, since there is not always consensus on how results should be measured.

iStock/simarik

Chapter Outline

Ensuring Accountability and Measuring Performance

Nonprofit organizations enjoy considerable autonomy in defining their missions, setting their own goals, and crafting their own strategies for achieving those goals. They are private organizations, but they are granted charters to serve purposes that society has deemed to be of public benefit. The organizations are exempt from taxation, and donors are permitted deductions for gifts made to charitable nonprofits to further those purposes. Tax exemption and the tax deductibility of gifts represent foregone government revenue and therefore are regarded by many as a form of tax subsidy; in other words, to some extent, nonprofits are working with the public's money. That gives society an interest in ensuring that they are *accountable* for their use of the resources entrusted to them and that those resources are indeed being directed toward the pursuit of their social missions. But what exactly is society entitled to expect?

The question is a little like asking, "What is a good student?" Does one qualify just by attending all classes, turning in papers on time, and showing up for exams—that is, by not breaking any of the rules of the course? Or is a good student someone who studies hard and seeks help from the professor when something is not clear—in other words, someone who shows exemplary student behavior? Does being a good student require earning good grades? Do grades accurately reflect what a student may have learned in a course, or is it possible that a better measure would be to compare what he or she knew or could do at the beginning of a course with what he or she knew or could do at the end, maybe basing the label of good student on some measure of value added? As we will see in this chapter, similar questions arise when we consider ideas such as the accountability, effectiveness, and performance of nonprofit organizations.

Defining and Ensuring Accountability

To be accountable essentially means being required to answer, to take responsibility, for one's actions. Perhaps the narrowest

Learning Objectives

After reading this chapter, students should be able to:

1. Define the concepts of accountability, effectiveness, and performance.

2. Explain current mechanisms for ensuring the accountability of nonprofit organizations.

3. Summarize the major points included in prominent standards for nonprofit accountability.

4. Describe various approaches to measuring organizational performance.

5. Explain the pros and cons of various approaches to measuring organizational performance.

6. Create a basic logic model for a program.

7. Identify appropriate performance metrics related to an organization's mission.

8 Analyze cases, applying concepts from the chapter.

concept of **accountability** for a nonprofit would require merely following the law—for example, obeying the non-distribution requirement, avoiding conflicts of interest, treating staff without discrimination, and filing IRS reports as required. But that might seem to be a minimal standard to expect. Perhaps we might look for something more, not just following the law but also going beyond the requirements of law to follow best practices in governing and managing the organization—in other words, doing the right things as well as not doing things that are wrong.

But does even a definition of accountability that expects nonprofits to do the right things really go far enough? For example, the board may meet regularly, the budget may be invariably balanced, the staff may be happy and motivated, and there may be a written strategic plan, but that does not ensure that clients are recovering, the symphony is achieving artistic excellence, or public attitudes on the environment are being changed. Thus, perhaps, accountability needs to include more than just avoiding transgressions and exhibiting model behavior. It may need to encompass demonstrated effectiveness in achieving the purposes for which the nonprofit exists. That requires not only that the resources entrusted to the nonprofit not be misused, but also that they be used to maximum benefit in pursuing the organization's mission. As we will see, however, this component of accountability turns out to be the most complex, since there is not always consensus on how results should be measured, or even on how they should be defined.

To whom are nonprofits accountable? Organizations are accountable in three directions: upward to donors, funders, and government; downward to the clients or communities they serve; and internally, to staff and to their own missions (Ebrahim, 2016, p. 104). Which is most relevant depends on the mission of the organization. For example, a membership organization is primarily accountable to its members, whereas a service organization must be accountable to its clients and the community it serves. The question of to whom nonprofits must account has gained more precise answers in recent years, as governments have increased their reporting requirements and a variety of other entities have cast the light of transparency on nonprofit behavior.

Concern about the accountability of nonprofit organizations has a long history. As early as 1918, the National Charities Information Bureau was created to educate the public about nonprofit organization behavior in order to reduce the incidence of charity fraud. But concern about accountability became heightened in the 1990s and 2000s. In 1992, the widely publicized misuse of United Way funds by the man who was then president, William Aramony, for which he was convicted and served jail time, shocked the nation. Again after September 11, 2001, accusations that some charity fundraising appeals were misleading and questions about the use of the funds given to help victims of the terrorist attacks further undermined the public's confidence in the integrity of the sector. Controversies at the Nature Conservancy, American University, and other organizations in the mid-2000s captured the attention of the media as well as the U.S. Congress and further heightened concern about accountability in the nonprofit sector. Members of the U.S. Congress held hearings, and there was discussion of passing new legislation to regulate the nonprofit sector. The sector responded by developing voluntary principles for accountability, including the Independent Sector principles, first issued in 2007 and revised in 2015. Some states also responded by passing new legislation regulating nonprofits chartered within their jurisdictions and various state associations of nonprofits adopted codes and standards that have been implemented by some organizations. For example, standards developed by the Maryland Association of Nonprofits (now called just Maryland Nonprofits) are discussed later in this chapter.

The broader definition of accountability, including the requirement to produce results, also has become more pronounced with the growing impact of donors who view their gifts as social investments and demand specific evidence of the impact of their support. For these reasons, the topics of accountability and **performance** are intrinsically linked today, and this chapter explores both.

Mechanisms for Accountability

There are three principal mechanisms by which nonprofits are held accountable: the rule of law, self-regulation, and transparency—that is, holding nonprofit behavior up in clear view for donors, the media, and others to see. In addition, Ebrahim (2016) identifies two "process mechanisms," namely public participation, which can occur in various ways, and adaptive learning, in which the organization itself engages in reflection and analysis of its work (pp. 113–114). Table 6.1 summarizes these mechanisms and provides some examples.

Requirements of Law

Chapters 3 and 4 covered some of the legal requirements facing nonprofits, so we need only review a few key points here. Nonprofits must comply with laws at both state and federal levels. State governments grant nonprofits their charters, and state attorneys general and state courts have the authority to take action against law-breaking nonprofits. This can include the removal of board members who violate their fiduciary responsibilities and possibly even revoking of the organization's charter. Most states also have laws regulating the behavior of nonprofits in specific areas—for example, requiring that they be registered in order to solicit gifts from the general public.

Table 6.1 Mechanisms for Accountability and Examples	
Mechanism	**Examples**
Requirements of law	Sarbanes-Oxley Act Pension Protection Act of 2006 State laws IRS regulations
Self-regulation	Independent Sector Principles for Good Governance and Ethical Practice (2007, 2015) Accreditation bodies in education and health care State nonprofit association standards and voluntary accreditation programs
Transparency	Form 990, available on GuideStar and other websites News media scrutiny Charity watchdogs and raters (*U.S. News & World Report* rankings, Better Business Bureau Wise Giving Alliance, Charity Navigator) GreatNonprofits (www.greatnonprofits.org)
Process mechanisms (Ebrahim, 2016)	Members of the public communicate with the organization or are involved in its programs (e.g., as volunteers) The organization creates opportunities internally to reflect on the mission and learn from experience

At the federal level, regulation of nonprofits is carried out primarily by the Internal Revenue Service (IRS) Division on Tax-Exempt and Government Entities. The IRS has the authority to impose intermediate sanctions or to revoke an organization's tax exemption, eliminating its ability to raise tax-deductible gifts and subjecting it to the requirement to pay income taxes itself. Nonprofits that receive federal funds above certain amounts are also subject to additional rules with regard to their use of the federal dollars. Organizations with revenues greater than $50,000 (except religious congregations) are required to file an annual Form 990, 990-EZ, or 990-PF with the IRS. As discussed in Chapter 4, beginning in 2009 (with filing of the Form 990 covering 2008), the IRS introduced a revised form that greatly expanded the information required. The revised 990 includes questions related to governance as well as finances and programs. (See Figure 4.1 for the Form 990, Part VI questions related to governance.) Since 2008, even small nonprofits that are not required to file Form 990 are required to electronically file Form 990-N, also known as the **e-Postcard**. It includes minimal information that essentially reflects the organization's existence, without the data encompassed by Form 990.

In 2002, as noted in Chapter 4, Congress passed the Sarbanes-Oxley Act, responding to corporate governance scandals. While Sarbanes-Oxley (or "SOX," as it is commonly called) pertains primarily to publicly traded corporations, two of its provisions—those regarding protection for whistle-blowers and destruction of documents—also apply to nonprofit organizations. Some states, including California, have passed legislation directed at nonprofits that essentially incorporates Sarbanes-Oxley–type requirements (Nonprofit Integrity Act, 2004). Many nonprofits have voluntarily adopted Sarbanes-Oxley provisions as a way to assure their donors that they are operating with high integrity, transparency, and sound governance. In addition, questions included in Part VI of Form 990 imply that nonprofits should comply with some Sarbanes-Oxley practices, even if not required to do so by law.

Principles of good governance and ethical practice, such as those established by the Panel on the Nonprofit Sector, also include many points consistent with Sarbanes-Oxley. These developments clearly have pushed the definition of accountability beyond just "do no wrong"; it now includes adherence to best practices in governance and ethical behavior. Using the "good student" we discussed at the beginning of the chapter as a metaphor, nonprofits are now expected to do more than just not be absent from class and miss paper deadlines; they are also expected to demonstrate that they have done their homework, have studied, and have engaged in other activities defined as good-student behaviors.

The federal **Pension Protection Act of 2006**, as its title implies, is principally focused on the reform of pensions, but it also contains a variety of provisions that affect the nonprofit sector. They include, among others, changes in the law regarding charitable giving, tighter regulation of certain types of nonprofit organizations, greater communication between the IRS and state authorities regarding action taken against nonprofits, and the requirement that nonprofits with unrelated business income make public their Form 990-T (Johnson, 2006).

As discussed elsewhere in this text, the Tax Cuts and Jobs Act of 2017 included provisions that may affect some nonprofits, although it was not directly related to accountability. The law raised the standard deduction, lowered individual income tax rates, and increased the amount of estates exempted from federal taxation. Some people predicted that such changes could affect the amount of charitable giving. The law also imposed a few new requirements that apply directly to a relatively small number of nonprofit organizations and institutions. One change related to the calculation of unrelated business income, a topic that is discussed in more detail elsewhere in this text. Other provisions impose a tax on endowment income at a small number of colleges and universities with high endowment-per-student and on nonprofits that pay more than $1 million in compensation to their highest-paid five employees (National Council of Nonprofits, 2018b).

This text does not include a complete discussion of laws affecting nonprofit organizations. Moreover, regulations change frequently and the law may change at any time. Students will find the websites of Independent Sector (www.independentsector.org) and the National Council of Nonprofits (www.councilofnonprofits.org) to be an excellent sources of up-to-date information on new or pending legislation.

Self-Regulation: Standards and Accreditation

If the nonprofit sector would prefer not to be burdened by increased government regulation, then the alternative is to develop more effective mechanisms for self-regulation. In 2004, concern about nonprofit accountability prompted the Finance Committee of the U.S. Senate to hold hearings and consider proposals for significantly increased regulation of the nonprofit sector at the national level. At the committee's request, Independent Sector convened a Panel on the Nonprofit Sector to develop recommendations. The panel's report was presented to the Congress in June 2005; it suggested increased enforcement of existing state and federal law, increased reporting by nonprofits, and some additional legislation. But its emphasis was on the importance of maintaining the sector's independence and on its capacity for self-regulation (Independent Sector, 2005). The Panel on the Nonprofit Sector's recommendations and 33 principles for good governance and ethical conduct were published by Independent Sector in 2007 and revised in 2015. They are organized into four broad areas: legal compliance and public disclosure, effective governance, strong financial oversight, and responsible fundraising (Independent Sector, 2015).

There are a number of well-known standards of practice in addition to the Independent Sector principles, some of which are the basis for **accreditation** of nonprofits by various authorities. There is a long history of accreditation of educational and health care institutions. For example, schools and colleges are accredited through regional associations. Individual institutions engage in self-studies according to a process defined by the accrediting body and are evaluated through intensive visits by teams from peer institutions. Professional schools within universities have separate accrediting mechanisms; for example, law schools are accredited by the American Bar Association, business schools by the Association to Advance Collegiate Schools of Business, and public affairs schools by the Network of Schools of Public Policy, Affairs, and Administration. Health care organizations, including hospitals, nursing homes, health care networks, and other service providers, are accredited by the Joint Commission. Although educational accreditation is voluntary, accrediting bodies are recognized by the U.S. Department of Education, and accreditation is required in order to be eligible for certain government funds. Likewise, accreditation of health care organizations is voluntary, but the power of government creates a significant incentive, since status as an accredited health care provider is required in order to be eligible to receive certain government reimbursements, an essential source of revenue for many organizations.

In the broader nonprofit sector, the accreditation of organizations is a relatively recent concept, having its origins in the development of accountability standards and definitions of best practices by state associations of nonprofits and others. As one example, Maryland Nonprofits (previously known as the Maryland Association of Nonprofits) developed Standards for Excellence in nonprofit management that are well regarded and have become a model. These standards are presented in Table 6.2. They essentially describe recommended best practices—that is, a set of guides for behavior that reflect a consensus about how well-managed and accountable nonprofits should operate.

Maryland Nonprofits established the Standards for Excellence Institute, which offers a voluntary accreditation program nationwide to nonprofits that wish to demonstrate adherence to its standards (Standards for Excellence Institute, 2014). Similar to the accreditation process in educational and health care institutions, the process requires that the organization complete an application, pay a fee, and be approved by a team of trained peer reviewers. Organizations that successfully complete the process are entitled to use of a Standards for Excellence Seal in their solicitations and other materials (Standards for Excellence Institute, 2014).

Table 6.2 Standards for Excellence®: An Ethics and Accountability Code for the Nonprofit Sector (2nd edition, 2014)

PREAMBLE

America's nonprofit sector serves the public interest and plays an essential role in our society and economy. Hard at work strengthening communities across the nation, nonprofits enrich our lives in a variety of ways by creating a broad array of benefits to society in fields such as charitable, religious, scientific, economic, health, cultural, civil rights, environment, and education.

Public investment and confidence drive the success of nonprofit organizations. Individuals, corporations, foundations, and federal, state, and local governments add value to the services that nonprofits provide by investing time, resources, and funds.

The Standards for Excellence Institute aims to raise the level of accountability, transparency, and effectiveness of all nonprofit organizations to foster excellence and inspire trust. The Standards for Excellence code (Standards, or code) provides a framework and step-by-step guidelines to achieve a well-managed and responsibly governed organization.

The code builds upon the legal foundations of nonprofit management, governance, and operations to embrace fundamental values such as honesty, integrity, fairness, respect, trust, compassion, responsibility, and transparency. The code consists of six Guiding Principles in 27 topic areas with specific performance benchmarks that characterize effective, ethical, and accountable organizations. The Institute helps the nonprofit sector operate in accordance with the Standards for Excellence code by providing educational resources, assistance, and a voluntary accreditation process.

The Standards for Excellence Institute encourages all nonprofit organizations to adopt the Guiding Principles of the Standards for Excellence code. By implementing the performance benchmarks in the code, nonprofit organizations will meet the highest ethical standards for effective service in the public interest.

MISSION, STRATEGY, AND EVALUATION

Guiding Principle:

Nonprofits are founded for the public good and operate to accomplish a stated purpose through specific program activities. A nonprofit should have a well-defined mission, and its programs should effectively and efficiently work toward achieving that mission. Nonprofits have an obligation to ensure program effectiveness and to devote the resources of the organization to achieving its stated purpose.

A. Mission and Impact

1. A nonprofit should have a mission statement that is a clear and formal statement of the organization's purpose as defined and approved by the board of directors. The organization's activities should be consistent with its stated purpose.

2. A nonprofit should be able to articulate how its mission is supported by a statement of the organization's vision and strategic goals.

B. Planning Strategically

1. Nonprofits should engage in ongoing long- and short-term strategic planning activities as necessary to determine the mission of the organization, to define specific goals and objectives related to the mission, and to evaluate the success of the organization's programs toward achieving the mission.

2. A nonprofit should periodically revisit its mission (i.e., at a minimum every 5 years) to determine whether the need for its programs or services continues to exist. In light of societal changes and critical strategic issues, the organization should evaluate whether its programs should be modified, expanded, or discontinued to meet the mission.

C. Organizational Evaluation

1. A nonprofit should engage in organizational evaluation to ensure that all financial resources and human capital are being used toward fulfilling its mission.

D. Program Evaluation

1. A nonprofit should have defined, cost-effective procedures for evaluating, both qualitatively and quantitatively, its programs and projects in relation to its mission. These procedures should address programmatic efficiency and effectiveness, outcomes for program participants, and the relationship of these outcomes to the cost of achieving them. Evaluations should include input from program participants, and should monitor the satisfaction of participants.

2. Evaluations should be candid, and should be used by leadership to strengthen the organization's effectiveness, and, when necessary, be used to make programmatic changes.

E. Strategic Partnerships

1. Nonprofits engaging in strategic partnerships and formal alliances with other organizations should do so within the context of a board-approved policy outlining the goals and parameters of such partnerships. Depending on the type of strategic partnership, nonprofits should ensure that proper due diligence has been followed and that agreements, memoranda of understanding, or similar documentation have been thoughtfully reviewed and considered.

LEADERSHIP: BOARD, STAFF, AND VOLUNTEERS

Guiding Principle:

Nonprofits depend upon effective leadership to successfully enact their missions and programs. Effective leadership consists of a partnership between the board and management, each of which plays an essential role. Understanding and negotiating these shared and complex elements of leadership is essential to the organization's success. A nonprofit's employees and volunteers are fundamental to its ability to achieve its mission.

Board members are in a position of trust to ensure that resources are used to carry out the mission of the organization. An organization's board leadership should consist of volunteers who are committed to the mission and who demonstrate an understanding of the community served. An effective nonprofit board should determine the mission of the organization, establish management policies and procedures, assure that adequate human and financial resources are available, and actively monitor the organization's allocation of resources to effectively and efficiently fulfill its mission.

Nonprofits should also have executive leadership which carries out the day-to-day operations of the organization, ensures financial and organizational sustainability, and provides adequate information to the board of directors. An organization's human resource policies should address both paid employees and volunteers and should be fair, establish clear expectations, and provide meaningful and effective performance evaluation.

A. Leadership and Governance

1. Governance and Fiduciary Responsibility
   - The board should be composed of individuals who are personally committed to the mission of the organization and understand their roles as fiduciaries in performing the legal duties of a governing body.
   - The board should establish and periodically review the bylaws and policies to ensure the effective governance and management of the organization.

2. Executive Supervision, Performance, and Compensation
   - The board should appoint the chief executive, set the executive's compensation, and annually evaluate the executive's performance. In cases where a designated committee performs one of these responsibilities, the decision should be ratified by the full board.
   - The board is responsible for supporting the functions of the executive, granting sufficient authority, and helping to ensure his or her success in managing the organization.

(Continued)

Table 6.2   (Continued)

3. Board Effectiveness
- The board is responsible for its own operations, including periodic (i.e., at least once every two years) evaluation of its own performance.
- The board should have stated performance expectations and hold board members accountable for attendance at meetings, participation in fundraising activities, committee service, and involvement in program activities.
- The board should establish a rigorous board development strategy for recruiting and selecting new members and ensuring that the board has an appropriate mix of talent, connections to the community, and diversity.
- Board policies should include limits on the number of consecutive terms a board member may serve. The board is responsible for the orientation, education, and (where appropriate) the removal of board members.
- New board members should receive an introduction to the Standards for Excellence code.

4. Succession Planning and Leadership Development
- The board, in partnership with the executive, should engage in coordinated succession planning and leadership development to ensure a thorough process for recruiting and developing new board, executive, staff, and volunteer leaders.

5. Board Member Independence
- Board members of public charities should serve without compensation for their service as board members. They may be provided reasonable reimbursement for expenses directly related to performing their board service.
- The board should have no fewer than five (5) independent and unrelated directors. Seven (7) or more directors are preferable.
- When an employee of the organization is a voting member of the board, the board is responsible for ensuring that the employee will not be in a position to exercise undue influence.

6. Board Meetings
- The board should meet as frequently as needed to fully and adequately conduct the business of the organization. At a minimum, the board should meet four (4) times a year.
- Board agendas should be strategically structured around decision making in a way that facilitates efficient, effective, and engaging meetings. Accurate minutes reflecting board and committee actions should be kept and distributed to all board and committee members.
- Committees with decision-making authority should report any committee actions or decisions to the full board. Those decisions must be reflected in the board minutes.

B. Leadership and Operational Management

1. Functions of the Executive
- The executive is responsible for the day-to-day management and operations of the organization. The executive should be committed to the mission of the organization and have the skills necessary to manage the paid and volunteer talent, and financial resources of the organization.

2. Supporting the Board
- The executive should support the board's policy and oversight function by providing accurate and timely information and resources to the board.
- The executive should periodically prepare for the board an overview of the compensation structure of the organization and the value of volunteer investments in the organization.

3. Organizational and Financial Sustainability
- The executive should consider what human (staff) and financial resources are necessary for organizational sustainability and mission fulfillment. The executive should also assist the board in planning for the organization's future.

4. Managing Employees and Volunteers
- Staff and volunteers should be recruited, screened (including required background checks), selected, trained, supervised, evaluated, and recognized appropriately. Staff and volunteers should be oriented to their positions, the organization, and the Standards for Excellence code, and should be provided with appropriate professional development opportunities.

C. Diversity, Equity, and Inclusion

1. Organizations that incorporate diversity, equity, and inclusion efforts into their work and as part of their missions are more effective in engaging and serving people across different cultures, backgrounds, and abilities. Nonprofit leaders should actively assess their policies, plans, procedures, as well as board and staff composition, to ensure that they are inclusive. Leaders should establish and implement an organization-wide strategy or plan that addresses gaps identified in the assessment and promote a culture that demonstrates practices of diversity, equity and inclusion for board, staff and volunteers, and program participants.

LEGAL COMPLIANCE AND ETHICS

Guiding Principle:

Nonprofits enjoy the public's trust, and therefore must comply with a diverse array of legal and regulatory requirements. Organizations should conduct periodic reviews to address regulatory and fiduciary concerns. One of leadership's fundamental responsibilities is to ensure that the organization governs and operates in an ethical and legal manner. Fostering exemplary conduct is one of the most effective means of developing internal and external trust as well as preventing misconduct. Moreover, to honor the trust that the public has given them, nonprofits have an obligation to go beyond legal requirements and embrace the highest ethical practices. Nonprofit board, staff, and volunteers must act in the best interest of the organization, rather than in furtherance of personal interests or the interests of third parties. A nonprofit should have policies in place, and should routinely and systematically implement those policies, to prevent actual, potential, or perceived conflicts of interest. In this way, ethics and compliance reinforce each other.

A. Maintaining Legal Compliance

1. Nonprofits must be aware of and comply with all applicable federal, state, and local laws. This may include, but is not limited to complying with laws and regulations related to IRS filing requirements, governance, human resources, licensing, financial accountability, taxation, valuation of in-kind gifts, unrelated business income, document retention and destruction, related entities, data security, accessibility, fundraising, lobbying, and advocacy.

2. Nonprofits should periodically conduct an internal review of the organization's compliance with known existing legal, regulatory, and financial reporting requirements, and should provide a summary of the results to the board of directors.

B. Required Public Disclosures

1. Nonprofits should have at least one designated representative who is responsible for ensuring that the organization is complying with both the letter and the spirit of federal and state laws that require disclosure of information to the public.

C. Reporting Misconduct and Whistleblower Protection

1. Organizations must provide employees, board members, and volunteers a confidential means to report suspected impropriety or misuse of organizational resources. Organizations should have in place a policy prohibiting retaliation against persons reporting improprieties.

D. Conflicts of Interest

1. Nonprofits should have a written conflict of interest policy and statement. These should be applicable to board members and staff, as well as volunteers who have significant, independent decision-making authority regarding the resources of the organization. The policy and statement should be executed by covered individuals, both at the time of the individual's initial affiliation with the organization and at least annually thereafter.

The conflict of interest policy should identify the types of conduct or transactions that raise conflict of interest concerns, should set forth procedures for disclosure of actual or potential conflicts, and should provide for review of individual transactions by the uninvolved members of the board of directors. The conflict of interest statement should provide space for the board member, employee or volunteer to disclose any known interests that the individual, or a member of the individual's immediate family, has in any business entity which transacts business with the organization.

(Continued)

Table 6.2 (Continued)

E. Ethics

1. Nonprofits should ensure that they have an explicit and clear set of ethical principles and, as appropriate, operational or program standards that have been discussed by their board and staff and that are transparently clear to all stakeholders.

2. In rendering its programs or services, a nonprofit should act with the utmost professionalism and treat persons served with respect.

3. Nonprofits should provide an effective procedure for problem solving or reporting grievances, including but not limited to, legal or ethical misconduct by the organization's employees and volunteers. The procedure should include actions for addressing and resolving complaints effectively.

4. Nonprofits should have policies in place that protect the confidentiality and privacy of personal information.

FINANCE AND OPERATIONS

Guiding Principle:

Nonprofits should have sound financial and operational systems in place and should ensure that accurate records are kept. The organization's financial and non-financial resources must be used in furtherance of tax-exempt purposes. Organizations should conduct periodic reviews to address accuracy and transparency of financial and operational reporting, and safeguards to protect the integrity of the reporting systems.

A. Financial Budgeting, Reporting, and Monitoring

1. The board should annually approve the organization's budget and the organization should be operated in accordance with this budget.

2. The organization should periodically assess the organization's financial performance in relation to the budget. A nonprofit should create and maintain reports on a timely basis that accurately reflect the financial activity of the organization. Internal financial statements should be prepared at least quarterly, should be provided to the board of directors, and should identify and explain any material variation between actual and budgeted revenues and expenses.

3. The board should annually review the percentages of the organization's resources spent on program, administration, and fundraising.

4. For nonprofits with annual revenue in excess of $500,000, the annual financial statements should be subject to audit by a Certified Public Accountant. The board should hire the auditor. The full board should approve the audited financial statements and receive a copy of the management letter (if any). The board should monitor the implementation of the recommendations of the management letter, if applicable.

B. Internal Controls and Financial Policies

1. Nonprofits should have written financial policies that are adequate for the size and complexity of the organization. These policies should address investment of the assets of the organization, internal controls, purchasing, and unrestricted current net assets.

C. Personnel Policies

1. A nonprofit should have written, board-approved personnel policies and procedures that govern the work, actions, and safety of all employees and volunteers of the organization. The policies should cover the basic elements of the relationship (e.g., working conditions, telecommuting [if applicable], employee benefits, vacation, and sick leave). The policies should address orientation to the organization, employee evaluation, supervision, hiring and firing, grievance procedures, employee growth and development, and confidentiality of employee, client, and organization records and information.

D. Administrative Policies

1. A nonprofit should have written, board-approved administrative policies that are periodically reviewed by the board. At a minimum, these policies should address issues such as crisis and disaster planning, information technology, communications, and social media.

E. Risk Management And Insurance

1. Organizations should make every effort to manage risk and periodically assess the need for insurance coverage in light of the organization's activities and its financial capacity. A decision to forego general liability insurance coverage or Directors and Officers liability insurance coverage should be made only by the board of directors. The decision should be reflected in the minutes for the meeting at which the decision was made.

RESOURCE DEVELOPMENT

Guiding Principle:

The responsibility for resource development is shared by the board and staff. Nonprofit organizations depend on an array of sources of financial support. An organization's resource development program should be maintained on a foundation of truthfulness and responsible stewardship. Its resource development policies should be consistent with its mission, compatible with its organizational capacity, and respectful of the interests of donors, prospective donors, and others providing resources to the organization.

A. Resource Plan

1. Nonprofits should have a resource development plan in place. This plan should outline a framework for ensuring appropriate financial resources for the organization, and a reasonable process to evaluate cost effectiveness of all resource development activities. Ideally, the resource plan should include diversified income sources to avoid dependence on a single source. The resource development plan should be board approved, regularly reviewed, and in accordance with the organization's budget.

2. A nonprofit's fundraising costs should be reasonable over time. On average, over a five-year period, a nonprofit should realize revenues from fundraising that are at least three times the amount spent on conducting them. Organizations whose fundraising ratio is less than 3:1 should demonstrate that they are making steady progress toward achieving this goal, or should be able to justify why a 3:1 ratio is not appropriate for their organization.

B. Sources of Income

1. When determining what types of income sources are pursued by a nonprofit to meet its mission, the organization should carefully consider the income source's impact on the population served, its demographics, and overall mission alignment. The organization should also assess these sources of income for feasibility and any associated risk.

C. Fundraising Activities

1. Solicitation and promotional materials should be accurate and truthful and should correctly identify the organization, its mission, and the intended use of the solicited funds.

2. All statements made by the nonprofit in its fundraising appeals about the use of a contribution should be honored.

3. Solicitations should be free from undue influence or excessive pressure, and should be respectful of the needs and interests of the donor or potential donor.

D. Donor Relationships and Privacy

1. Nonprofits should respect the donor's right to determine how their name and contact information is used, including providing opportunities to remain anonymous, request that the organization curtail repeated mailings or telephone solicitations from in-house lists, and have their names removed from any mailing lists which are sold, rented, or exchanged.

(Continued)

Table 6.2 (Continued)

2. Nonprofits must honor the known intentions of a donor regarding the use of donated funds.

E. Acceptance of Gifts

1. An organization should have policies in place to govern the acceptance and disposition of charitable or in-kind gifts that are received in the course of its regular fundraising activities. These policies should include procedures to determine any limits on individuals or entities from which the organization will accept a gift, the purposes for which donations will be accepted, the type of property which will be accepted, and whether to accept an unusual or unanticipated gift in light of the organization's mission and organizational capacity.

F. Fundraising on Behalf of the Organization

1. Resource development personnel, including both employees and independent consultants, should not be compensated based on a percentage of the amount raised or other commission formula.

2. When using the services of a paid professional fundraising consultant, organizations should only use the services of professional solicitors and fundraising consultants who are properly registered with the appropriate state authorities.

3. Organizations should exercise control over any staff, volunteers, consultants, contractors, other organizations, or businesses that are known to be soliciting contributions on behalf of the organization.

PUBLIC AWARENESS, ENGAGEMENT, AND ADVOCACY

Guiding Principle:

Nonprofits should represent the interests of the people they serve through public education and public policy advocacy, as well as by encouraging board members, staff, volunteers, and stakeholders to participate in the public affairs of the community. When appropriate to advance the organization's mission, nonprofits should engage in promoting public participation in community affairs and elections. As such, they should communicate in an effective manner to educate, inform, and engage the public.

A. Educating and Engaging the Public

1. Information about the organization's mission, program activities, finances, board members, and staff should be easily accessible, accurate, and timely (i.e., updated at least annually).

2. Nonprofits should provide a meaningful opportunity for the public to communicate with a representative of the organization.

3. Nonprofits should assure that any educational or advocacy information provided to the media and policy-makers, or distributed broadly, is factually accurate and provides sufficient contextual information to be understood.

B. Advancing the Mission through Public Policy and Advocacy

1. Nonprofits should have a written, board-approved policy on advocacy defining the process by which the organization determines positions on specific issues.

2. Working independently and in partnership, nonprofits should strive to influence public policies that affect the organization's ability to achieve its mission.

C. Engaging in Lobbying and Political Activity

1. In promoting public participation in community affairs, charitable nonprofits must be diligent in assuring they do not participate or intervene in any political campaign on behalf of or in opposition to any candidate for public office.

Source: Reprinted with permission of the Standards for Excellence Institute, a project of Maryland Nonprofits.

Transparency

In addition to the force of law and the desire to comply with voluntary guidelines, nonprofits also may be motivated to accountability by public scrutiny. Some disclosures are required by law and many organizations publish additional material in annual reports and other documents. As discussed earlier, Form 990 provides information that may be considered by donors, the news media, and others and that may reveal an organization's divergence from accepted best practices. Donors have online platforms on which they can provide their own reviews of organizations (e.g., greatnonprofits.org/). In addition, there is an increasingly influential array of charity watchdog organizations that proactively examine nonprofit organizations, applying their own standards. They are not really examples of self-regulation because some undertake their evaluations with or without the cooperation of the organizations on which they focus. They are an important force in creating increased transparency, and they have influence because of the visibility they enjoy, but they are also often controversial.

For example, among the best known may be the ratings of colleges and universities and hospitals by *U.S. News & World Report,* which have been shown to influence students' choices about where to attend college and patients' decisions about where to receive medical care. Such ratings surely do not have the force of law, but they are powerful. A negative ranking poses a significant potential threat to an organization, since publicity may deter potential customers, chill giving, or even invite scrutiny from government. And yet, many educators and hospital administrators do not agree that the standards by which *U.S. News* determines its rankings are appropriate or indicative of quality.

One well-known charity watchdog that operates at the national level is the Better Business Bureau (BBB) Wise Giving Alliance. Formed in 2001 through a merger of the National Charities Information Bureau and the Better Business Bureau's Philanthropic Advisory Service, the Wise Giving Alliance focuses its attention on the largest nonprofits in the United States. Since the BBB has a long history and an established reputation as an organization that acts to protect consumers against unethical business practices, its standards for nonprofits are among the best known and most widely cited in the news media.

The BBB undertakes investigations of an organization based on complaints or inquiries from the public (in the long-established tradition of consumers reporting businesses to the BBB). Nationally soliciting charities also may request a review in order to ensure compliance and may be eligible to use a "BBB national charity seal" in their promotional and solicitation materials. While the Wise Giving Alliance does not rate organizations, it does report whether they meet or do not meet its various standards, which are available on its website (http://www.give.org/). The BBB Standards for Charity Accountability are based on best practices; that is, they prescribe what accountable nonprofits should do in the areas of governance and oversight, measuring effectiveness, finances, fundraising, and informational material. They require that organizations have a mechanism for measuring results that involves the governing board, but it is important to note that they do not prescribe the specific standards that organizations must apply. The BBB standards require that organizations "have a board policy of assessing, no less than every two years, the organization's performance and effectiveness and of determining future actions required to achieve its mission." And the organization must submit "to [its] governing body, for its approval, a written report that outlines the results of the aforementioned performance and effectiveness assessment and recommendations for future actions" (Better Business Bureau Wise Giving Alliance, n.d.). In other words, the BBB standards emphasize process and accountability, but they are not about setting specific standards of effectiveness or performance, aside from a couple of key financial ratios, which we will discuss soon. The BBB standards thus reflect what Adam Eckerd calls the "conformance model" of nonprofit accountability. In other words, an organization meets or does not meet the standards, but there is no better or worse above that threshold. In this approach, nonprofits cannot be ranked or compared (Eckerd, 2015). Many nonprofit organizations have accepted the idea of best practices, adhere to one or another of the recommended standards, and have sought some type of accreditation or certification. It may be that in addition to the potential threat of negative publicity, the widespread acceptance of voluntary standards reflects, as Light (2000) suggests, institutional theory at work. Enunciated standards become a part of the conventional wisdom of what constitutes ethical or sound practice and are increasingly adopted by organizations that seek recognition for being consistent with the norms of the subsector or profession within which they operate.

But questions remain: Does doing the right things ensure that the organization is effective in accomplishing its mission? Or that it can be described as a high-performing organization? Is there some mechanism that automatically leads from best practices in governance and management to a successful nonprofit organization? Robert Herman and David Renz (2008) advise caution on this question:

> The popularity of "best practices" attests to the hope of finding a pot of gold at the end of the search. One key assumption of the best practices approach is that a particular technique or process that works well in one setting can and should be incorporated into other different settings. This may be true for certain rather common administrative functions, particularly those that must comply with externally mandated standards such as the adoption of procedures to ensure adequate internal controls. However, in many instances a practice that enhances effectiveness in one organization may be a poor choice for another. (p. 411)

In a 2015 study, Kellie Liket and Karen Maas surveyed both the academic literature and nonprofit managers and found that they agreed on 26 practices that they believed to be related to organizational effectiveness, including some related to transparency; to the focus, strategy, and board of the organization; and to the organization's programs. But in reflecting on their findings, they also sound a note of caution, writing, "due to the absence of consensus on the concept and measurement of [organizational effectiveness], it is not possible to empirically validate the recommended set of practices." In other words, it is difficult to determine what leads to effective organizations when there is not agreement on how effectiveness should be defined or measured. Let's take a look at some approaches to doing so.

Measuring and Managing Performance

If doing the right things does not guarantee that the organization is effective in achieving its mission, then we need some standards by which to evaluate results. But how should results be defined, and how should they be measured? The subject has been the focus of national conversation in recent years, but there are still differences in view and a somewhat inconsistent vocabulary in the field. Distinctions among terms and concepts are important.

For example, there may be a difference between the performance of a nonprofit's programs and the performance of the organization as a whole. Let's first consider the performance of programs.

Although some people may use the terms interchangeably, it is useful to distinguish between **performance measurement** and **performance management**. Performance measurement "tells what a program did and how well it did it" (Tatian, 2016). Like taking your temperature, it reveals conditions at a point in time. Performance management is more like wearing a fitbit to monitor the situation on a *continuous* basis. In other words, it is "the process of defining, monitoring, and using objective indicators of the performance of organizations and programs to inform management and decision making *on a regular basis* [italics added]" (Poister, Aristigueta, & Hall, 2015, p. 1). There are a growing number of resources available to help nonprofits develop performance management systems, including software and online tools. (For one example, see the Performance Imperative Organizational Self-Assessment; Leap of Reason Ambassadors Community, 2018).

Evaluation goes beyond performance measurement to determine the "program's effect on the people, families, or communities it is serving, that is, whether a program is producing results or having an impact" (Tatian, 2016). Program evaluation is a method that many nonprofits use to determine whether specific programs are effective in achieving results. As one prominent text on the subject explains, a program is defined as "a set of resources and activities directed toward one or more common goals, typically under the direction of a single manager or management team" and program evaluation is "an assessment that compares actual with intended inputs, activities, and outputs" (Newcomer, Hatry, & Wholey, 2015, p. 34). Authors differ on whether performance management and program evaluation are different, complementary, or essentially the same thing (Poister, 2015). But program evaluation and performance management are often different in practice. Program evaluations often are conducted by outside experts, using social science methods. The results are used to make decisions about the design of programs in the longer term. Performance management is usually handled by the organization's staff and informs real-time adjustments in programs as they are operating.

But is a nonprofit with high-performing programs automatically a high-performing organization? Or should the latter determination include such questions as whether the organization as a whole is effective in achieving its mission, is financially sound (recall the double bottom line concept discussed in Chapter 1), and is capable of learning and adapting to change, among other considerations? Of course, for a small nonprofit with a single program, the distinction may not be very meaningful. For larger, more complex organizations with broad missions, however, the difference may be significant. For example, a university might have a very effective basketball team, one that frequently wins championships, but it may not be a very effective university overall. Or it might be academically sound but suffer from financial challenges that threaten its long-term strength.

Some use the terms organizational effectiveness and organizational performance synonymously. Others define an organization's performance as broader than effectiveness, with the former measuring achievement against mission and the latter encompassing "other concepts such as efficiency, productivity, or quality" (Baruch & Ramalho, 2006, p. 41). For example, let's consider a nonprofit that meets the needs of clients. That could define an effective organization. But if the organization loses money every year, the staff are miserable, and management is always just skirting the law, it would be hard to say it is high performing as an organization. Being effective may be necessary to be high performing, but it is not necessarily sufficient.

It is also important to distinguish between **effectiveness** and **efficiency**. As Kathleen Kelly (1998) explains it, efficiency is "a measure of the proportion of resources used to produce outputs or attain inputs–cost ratios," whereas effectiveness "is measured by comparing the results achieved with the results sought." As Kelly further observes, "Although efficiency may help an organization be more effective, the two concepts are not interchangeable" (p. 428). Indeed, some argue that an emphasis on efficiency may in fact work against the effectiveness of organizations by discouraging investment in capacity, a topic that will be discussed in greater detail in Chapter 7.

There are various approaches that have been devised to assess effectiveness and performance. In this chapter, we consider some of the most commonly discussed: financial ratios, benchmarking, outcomes, the balanced scorecard, social return on investment, and blended value.

Financial Ratios

In the business world, financial data and ratios are the principal ways to measure a company's performance and strength. A company's earnings, earnings per share, stock price, and the ratio of stock price to earnings (the P:E ratio) are important variables that investors consider. Some have applied a similar approach to nonprofit organizations. The advantages of using financial indicators are that the data are objective, readily available, and easily compared, across either the nonprofit sector or particular subsectors. For nonprofits, these data are available on Form 990, and they are easy to access and compare.

What are some of the financial ratios that a nonprofit might produce? A 2004 study by the Urban Institute and Harvard's Hauser Institute (Fremont-Smith & Cordes, 2004) looked at 10 monitoring organizations that use financial ratios and found a variety of measures being applied, including variations of the following:

- The ratio of program expenses to contributed income

- The ratio of fundraising expenditures to private support received—that is, the cost of raising a dollar

- The percentage of total expenditures (or income received from contributions) applied to charitable programs or activities

- The percentage of total expenditures applied to fundraising and administration (overhead)

- Accumulated cash and asset reserves in relation to operating budget

Until 2011, one of the prominent charity raters, Charity Navigator, based its ratings exclusively on financial ratios. In response to widespread commentary on the limitations of such ratios, Charity Navigator expanded its methodology to consider accountability and transparency in addition to financial ratios. The latter are assessed based on data from Form 990 and organizations' websites. A mathematical formula is used to calculate an overall score, which is then compared with the scores of other organizations. The formula used to calculate the scores changes from time to time; for example, a change was made in 2016—that resulted in a shift in scores for about 27 percent of organizations (Stiffman, 2016b).

Unlike the BBB Wise Giving Alliance, which rates nonprofits according to whether they meet or do not meet its standards, Charity Navigator ranks nonprofits using a system of stars, like those used by Morningstar to rank mutual fund performance (Charity Navigator, 2017a). This is what Eckerd (2015) calls the "optimization model," in contrast to the conformance model used by BBB. In other words, under Charity Navigator's model, some nonprofits may be rated as doing better than others, not just meeting a threshold of acceptable practice.

Beginning in 2015, Charity Navigator started working to add a third component to its methodology, going beyond financial ratios and accountability criteria to incorporate results. Development of this new methodology, which was labeled Charity Navigator 3.0, was still in process at the time of this writing (Lindsay & Stiffman, 2017). Charity Navigator stated on its website that impact data would be included in its ratings within the next five years and that their system would be expanded to provide nonprofits with tools to track their impact (Charity Navigator, 2017b). Students may wish to consult the Charity Navigator website to check on the progress of this initiative (www.charitynavigator.org).

Despite their limitations as indicators, two of the variables most emphasized by those who use financial ratios to assess charities are the cost of fundraising and the percentage of expenditures that go for overhead rather than for programs and services. These ratios are so well known and easy to calculate that they have become popular shorthand for some donors, who may prefer to support low-overhead nonprofits that do not appear to spend too much on fundraising. As mentioned above, while the BBB standards do not in general emphasize financial ratios, they require that an organization's spending on fundraising be no more than 35 percent of the funds raised. However, the BBB also permits an organization to offer a justification for higher ratios. Charity Navigator does not set an absolute limit, but fundraising costs are one element in the formula by which it ranks organizations. As shown in Table 6.2, the Standards for Excellence developed by Maryland Nonprofits establish a 3:1 ratio for fundraising costs (i.e., expenditures should be no more than about 33 percent of gift revenue), but like the BBB, they also permit some flexibility, suggesting that organizations not meeting that standard may provide a justification (Standards for Excellence Institute, 2014).

The percentage of total expenditures directed toward program-related activities, rather than overhead or fundraising, is viewed by some as a measure of an organization's efficiency in delivering its services. Too low a percentage may even be seen as a potential red flag, suggesting that management is deriving excessive compensation or other benefits from the organization or that fundraising has replaced mission as the organization's highest priority. For example, the BBB standards require that at least 65 percent of expenditures be devoted to programs but, again, they allow that organizations not meeting that standard may provide an explanation (Better Business Bureau Wise Giving Alliance, n.d.).

Indeed, organizations that spend too much on overhead or fundraising may be making inefficient use of donor funds or perhaps may be spending too lavishly on salaries and other overhead costs. Very high fundraising costs may suggest the possibility of inefficiency, or even unethical or fraudulent behavior. But, critics argue, rating organizations based on their overhead and fundraising costs may create perverse incentives. For example, this approach could simply encourage organizations to engage in creative accounting to allocate costs to programs rather than administration. Insisting on low fundraising costs also may place young organizations at a disadvantage. They often need to invest substantial amounts in developing a database of regular donors that will ultimately produce continuing revenue at lower costs. Moreover, low fundraising costs may not be realistic for an organization that advocates unpopular causes or lacks a constituency of major donors (Fremont-Smith & Cordes, 2004).

Other critics argue that "the fundraising efficiency standard is not a measure of efficiency at all. [Rather,] it documents the sunk costs associated with cultivating donors" (Hager & Flack, 2004, p. 3). In other words, looking at just this year's fundraising costs ignores the substantial amounts that the organization may have spent in earlier years to develop relationships with donors who now make larger gifts, lowering the per-dollar cost of fundraising today.

Still others argue that program-spending ratios are just not a measure of organizational effectiveness, and indeed, that emphasizing low administrative cost may even work against building effective organizations by encouraging them to "value thrift over excellence." Trying to maintain a low ratio may cause an organization to invest too little in "good governance, planning, compliance and risk management, collection of data for service performance evaluations, and staff training" (Hager & Flack, 2004, p. 4).

Financial ratios do provide one perspective on the operations of an organization. If they are widely divergent from accepted practice, they may indeed suggest something wrong. And, as a practical matter, high fundraising costs may be viewed suspiciously by some donors. However, despite their ease of use, these ratios may not present the complete picture. Indeed, the shortcomings of such ratios have become part of the national dialogue concerning the nonprofit sector. In a 2010 book, Dan Pallotta, founder of the fundraising firm Pallotta TeamWorks, argues against the use of the overhead ratio for evaluating organizations and their fundraising efforts (Pallotta, 2010). Pallotta's 2013 TED Talk, titled "The Way We Think About Charity Is Dead Wrong," arguing the same point, has gained millions of views on YouTube and focuses further attention on the topic (Pallotta, 2013). In December 2013, the leaders of GuideStar, Charity Navigator, and the Better Business Bureau Wise Giving Alliance issued a joint "Letter to the Donors of America," urging that overhead ratios be kept in appropriate perspective. The authors note that, "At the extremes the overhead ratio can offer insight: it can be a valid data point for rooting out fraud and poor financial management." But, they add, "In most cases … focusing on overhead without considering other critical dimensions of a charity's financial and organizational performance can do more damage than good" (Overhead Myth, 2013).

Other observers agree that an exclusive focus on financial ratios can have negative consequences. As Mark Hager and Ted Flack (2004, p. 4) caution, "the undue emphasis on financial ratios diverts attention and resources from the development of more meaningful measures that address performance against mission and program objectives." For this reason, there has been an increasing emphasis on outcomes measurement, which many consider a source of more meaningful data related to achievement of the nonprofit's mission. This is an approach that will be discussed further later in this chapter.

Benchmarking

If simple financial measures applied to all nonprofit organizations are potentially misleading, perhaps a more accurate picture may be obtained from comparing data from organizations that are similar in their mission, size, location, and other characteristics. Comparing similar organizations is at the heart of benchmarking.

As Theodore Poister et al. (2015) note, the term benchmarking is often misused. Some organizations set goals for future years in their strategic plans and then measure their progress by looking at targets, which they call "benchmarks." But in its proper definition, benchmarking involves *comparisons* among organizations, either at the macro (whole organization) or at the micro (program or function) level. Benchmarking involves collecting data from multiple organizations in order to "gauge [an organization's] performance against other similar organizations … to see how its performance stacks up against counterpart programs elsewhere" (Poister et al., p. 382). For example, an organization might look at statistics on client outcomes across a group of organizations providing services to individuals with similar problems or compare its patterns of gift revenues with those of similar organizations. This macro approach, called **statistical benchmarking**, or comparative performance measurement, may be a useful technique in strategic planning and may help highlight strengths or weaknesses of an organization that require further analysis. It is not really a tool for evaluating the whole organization, although some assume that "a thorough program of benchmarking will 'roll up' to provide a good indicator of how well the organization is doing overall" (Murray, 2010, p. 447).

Another approach to benchmarking, what Poister and colleagues (2015) call **corporate-style benchmarking**, "focuses directly on so-called best practices or [organizations] that are high performing" (p. 386). The purpose of this type of benchmarking is to identify the most effective or efficient methods of performing specific functions and seeing how the subject organization compares with the best. The organization conducting the benchmarking then would intend to adopt those practices in order to increase its own performance.

Letts et al. (1999), early advocates of benchmarking in the nonprofit sector, argue that it "bridges the gap between great ideas and great performance" (p. 86) and that the nonprofit culture of openness and sharing may make it a more feasible approach for them than for competitive businesses. However, like the use of financial ratios, benchmarking also has its shortcomings and critics. For one, it requires a larger investment of time and effort than comparing financial ratios, which are readily available from Form 990. Second, there is no way to really know whether the practice being studied is related to an organization's overall effectiveness. For example, how does the amount of time required to process the payroll relate to whether it is an effective organization? In addition, it is often difficult to identify the specific indicators on which the best practice is to be compared. For instance, what number best indicates how many clients have recovered from an illness or addiction? Should recovery be declared shortly after the client completes a treatment program or only after some period of time has passed? It is also often tricky to identify which organizations can really be considered alike. For example, nonprofits in different cities may face very different funding environments and more or less favorable markets for volunteers and staff. There also may be methodological issues, for example, concerning the availability and reliability of comparative data (Poister et al., 2015).

Benchmarking is a useful tool, but perhaps more for examining specific program or administrative functions than for evaluating the effectiveness or performance of an organization. Moreover, since the selection of peer organizations is often complicated by local factors, benchmarking may be better used as a tool for learning than for evaluating. If used (or perceived) as a technique for evaluating the performance of specific departments or staff, it also may come to be manipulated; that is, individuals may try to game the system by selecting peer organizations with which they think they may have the most favorable comparisons.

Outcomes

Financial ratios and benchmark data may provide some insights into a nonprofit's performance, but mission is the heart of the matter. It is the very purpose for which a nonprofit exists. Thus, the most important indicators of effectiveness should be related to its success in accomplishing that mission. As Brian Gallagher, president of the United Way of America, expressed it in 2005,

> Financial accountability is just table stakes. You *have* to get that right first. But, ultimately, the American public should hold our sector accountable for delivering on our missions.... We should be asked to report concrete results that are tied directly to our missions, not just the level of activity we produce.

The outcomes approach to measuring program effectiveness has gained wide acceptance, in part through the early efforts of the United Way of America during the 1990s. It also has been adopted by many foundations and government agencies for measuring their grantees' effectiveness. Venture philanthropy funds and foundations that have adopted concepts from venture philanthropy also have placed an emphasis on the measurement of outcomes. Mario Morino, the founder of Venture Philanthropy Partners, a venture philanthropy organization based in Washington, DC, has been a visible proponent of outcomes. Another organization that he founded, Leap of Reason, provides extensive materials and education on the topic (Leap of Reason, n.d.).

Again, it is important to define terms and concepts. Table 6.3 summarizes some of the important definitions that many authors use when discussing outcomes.

The United Way outcomes model is illustrated in Table 6.4, which highlights the key variables: inputs, activities, outputs, and outcomes. **Inputs** are the resources dedicated to the program, including money, staff, volunteers, facilities, equipment, and supplies, as well as the constraints

Table 6.3 Basic Definitions Related to Outcomes

Theory of Change—how we effect change

The overarching set of formal relationships presumed to exist for a defined population, the intended outcomes that are the focus of the organization's work, and the logic model for producing the intended outcomes. A theory of change should be meaningful to stakeholders, plausible in that it conforms to common sense, doable with available resources, and measurable.

Logic Model—what we do and how

The logically related parts of a program, showing the links between program objectives, program activities (efforts applied coherently and reliably over a sustained time), and expected program outcomes. A logic model makes clear who will be served, what should be accomplished, and specifically how it will be done (i.e., written cause-and-effect statements for a given program design).

Inputs—what resources are committed

The resources—money, time, staff, expertise, methods, and facilities—that an organization commits to a program to produce the intended outputs, outcomes, and impact.

Outputs—what we count

The volume of a program's actions, such as products created or delivered, number of people served, and activities and services carried out.

Outcomes—what we wish to achieve

Socially meaningful changes for those served by a program, generally defined in terms of expected changes in knowledge, skills, attitudes, behavior, condition, or status. These changes should be measured, be monitored as part of an organization's work, link directly to the efforts of the program, and serve as the basis for accountability.

Indicators—what we use to stay on course

Specific, observable, and measurable characteristics, actions, or conditions that demonstrate whether a desired change has happened toward the intended outcome. Also called "outcome indicators" or "predictive indicators."

Impact—what we aim to effect

To slightly oversimplify, the results that can be directly attributed to the outcomes of a given program or collective of programs, as determined by evaluations that are capable of factoring out (at a high level of statistical probability) other explanations for how these results came to be.

Editorial Note: These definitions were adapted from the *Glossary of Terms* of the Shaping Outcomes Initiative of the Institute of Museum and Library Services, Indiana University and Purdue University Indianapolis; *The Nonprofit Outcomes Toolbox: A Complete Guide to Program Effectiveness, Performance Measurement, and Results* by Robert Penna; and the *Framework for Managing Programme Performance Information* of the South African government. The definitions were informed by distinguished reviewers who provided valuable insights.

Source: Morino (2011, p. 9).

Table 6.4 United Way Program Outcome Model

Inputs	Activities	Outputs	Outcomes
Resources dedicated to or consumed by the program, e.g., money, staff and staff time, volunteers and volunteer time, facilities, equipment, and supplies Constraints on the program, e.g., laws, regulations, funders' requirements	What the program does with the inputs to fulfill its mission, e.g., feed and shelter homeless families, provide job training, educate the public about signs of child abuse, counsel pregnant women, create mentoring relationships for youth	The direct products of program activities, e.g., number of classes taught, number of counseling sessions conducted, number of educational materials distributed, number of hours of service delivered, number of participants served	Benefits for participants during and after program activities, e.g., new knowledge, increased skills, changed attitudes or values, modified behavior, improved condition, altered status

Source: United Way of America (1996).

imposed by the external environment. (Some models refer to resources rather than inputs, although the meaning is similar.) Activities are what the program does—for example, tutoring children, feeding the homeless, or providing job training. **Outputs** are the direct products of the activities and are often relatively easy things to measure—for example, the number of children tutored, the number of homeless fed, and the number of individuals trained in employment skills. But measuring outputs does not make the connection to the program's goals, which are generally to change in some way the individuals it serves and to make a lasting difference in their lives. **Outcomes** are the changes that occur in the individuals as a result of their participation in the program—for example, new knowledge, expanded job skills, or a better position in life.

Outcomes may be measured immediately after the individual completes the program (initial outcomes); after a longer period has elapsed, say a few years (intermediate outcomes); and after an even longer period of time (long-term outcomes). Thus, it may be found that students who participate in an after-school tutoring program improve their grades, but are they still succeeding academically two years later? Do they go on to complete college in larger numbers than students who do not participate in the program? Are they more likely to be employed a decade after their participation in the program? Obviously, measuring outcomes over the longer term can require considerable effort and expense, perhaps involving the tracking of former clients and follow-up surveys. That can be difficult for organizations that serve clients who are highly mobile and difficult to reach—for example, homeless people.

But measuring outcomes is not quite the same as evaluating programs. In other words, it is one thing to establish that outcomes have occurred, but evaluating the program requires determining that these outcomes were in some way related to the program. That requires developing a sound and plausible **logic model**, that is, a theoretical explanation of the links all the way through the process from inputs to outcomes. As John McLaughlin and Gretchen Jordan (2015, p. 64) explain, "A logic model is a plausible and sensible model of how a program will work under certain environmental conditions to solve identified problems." The logic model is related to a theory of change, which is "a more detailed description of the theoretical basis for a program and the assumed causal mechanisms that are needed to produce desired ends. The logic model is a condensed version of theories of change" (Hatry, 2014, p. 12).

Figure 6.1 depicts the logic model of a program offering tutoring to at-risk teens. It shows how the organization believes the process works. To justify using school graduation rates as an outcome measure for its program, the organization would need to explain how the

Figure 6.1   Logic Model of At-Risk Teen Mentoring Program

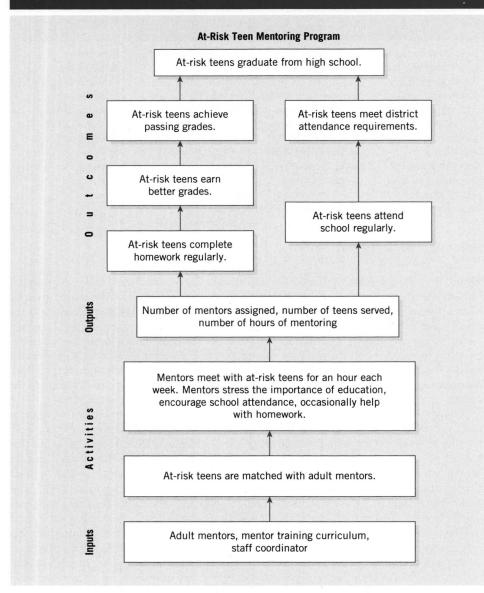

At-Risk Teen Mentoring Program

Outcomes

At-risk teens graduate from high school.

At-risk teens achieve passing grades.

At-risk teens meet district attendance requirements.

At-risk teens earn better grades.

At-risk teens attend school regularly.

At-risk teens complete homework regularly.

Outputs

Number of mentors assigned, number of teens served, number of hours of mentoring

Activities

Mentors meet with at-risk teens for an hour each week. Mentors stress the importance of education, encourage school attendance, occasionally help with homework.

At-risk teens are matched with adult mentors.

Inputs

Adult mentors, mentor training curriculum, staff coordinator

Source: United Way of America.

mentoring experience *causes* students to complete their homework and attend school more regularly and how homework and attendance affect graduation rates. Otherwise, the rate of students' graduation from high school cannot be a useful indicator of the tutoring program's outcome. One obvious problem in developing such logic models is how to identify the external influences that can cause the outcome in addition to the activities associated with the program. This becomes more of an issue the higher up in the model one ascends. For example, students' grades and graduation rates may be positively affected by the tutoring program, but they also could be affected—either positively or negatively—by students' experiences at home or in the community where they live. As Poister et al. (2015), emphasize, "Developing valid indicators of program effectiveness is often particularly challenging because the desired outcomes are somewhat diffuse, only tenuously connected to the program, or affected by numerous other factors beyond the program's control" (p. 131).

One obstacle to measuring outcomes is the loftiness and vagueness of many mission statements. For example, the mission of one organization serving the needs of older people is to enable them "to live with dignity and independence." One educational institution includes as a part of its mission "fostering a love of learning." But how are the outcomes of "dignity" or "love of learning" to be defined or measured? And if they are defined and measured and found to exist, how can the organization be sure that its programs are indeed what created them? In other words, what is the organization's *impact* on the measured changes, since there are many factors that influence the lives of older people and students? Sometimes it is necessary to identify more easily obtained intermediate indicators that the logic model suggests may be proxies for the outcomes desired.

An instructive example is provided by the experience of The Nature Conservancy (TNC) in the 1990s. TNC was struggling with the question of how to measure its performance against its ambitious mission, which was to promote biodiversity on the Earth by preserving land necessary for species to survive. For 50 years, it had measured its success by looking at two figures that were readily available, the amount of money it raised and the quantity of land this money enabled it to protect—what became known as "bucks and acres." But these two measures really reflected the *means* TNC was using, not the *ends* it was committed to achieving. They were inputs, but not outcomes. If the mission was ultimately to preserve biodiversity on Earth, how could TNC be sure that the means it was employing—the acquisition of money and land—was indeed having an impact on the achievement of that purpose (Sawhill & Williamson, 2001)?

Possibly a better measure of TNC's effectiveness in achieving its mission might have been to count the number of species existing on the planet each year—to measure biodiversity. That would be an outcome. But even if it were practical to take an annual global inventory, the number continues to decline every year, despite TNC's efforts, for reasons way beyond TNC's control. The impact of its programs is small compared with all the other forces affecting the survival of species on Earth. Indeed, using that figure as an indicator of effectiveness in achieving the mission would doom TNC's performance to be assessed as a continual failure because that figure inevitably declines. Moreover, it would be meaningless as a measure of the outcomes of TNC's own efforts.

After considering the problem, TNC adopted a family of measures, including the number of species existing on land it *controls*. Easier to count than all the species on the entire planet, and more reflective of TNC's own efforts, this intermediate number could provide a realistic and feasible proxy for the organization's impact on the Earth's overall biodiversity. This approach thus requires developing

> micro-level goals that, if achieved, would *imply* success on a grander scale; indicators of goal achievement that can be measured with a feasible level of effort, and that arguably are affected by the organization's efforts rather than other extraneous and uncontrollable factors. (Sawhill & Williamson, 2001, p. 23)

The challenge is greater for some organizations than for others. Let's consider an organization with the simple mission of "providing a hot meal every day to homeless people." It is perhaps hard to improve on a simple count of the number of meals served—and perhaps a measure of the food's temperature—as a way to measure effectiveness in delivering that straightforward and uncomplicated mission. Those are outputs, not outcomes, but they may be all the organization really needs to know. But take a more complicated mission, say that of the American Cancer Society (2017): "The American Cancer Society's mission is to save lives, celebrate lives, and lead the fight for a world without cancer." Unfortunately, many variables affect the incidence of cancer and cancer death rates—individuals' lifestyles, environmental factors, and the availability of medical care, among others. If lives are saved, it may be difficult to attribute that positive result to the leadership of the American Cancer Society alone. Just measuring the national cancer rates, whether they are found to be increasing or declining, would not tell the American Cancer Society much about the effectiveness or ineffectiveness of its efforts to eliminate cancer. But research has demonstrated that screening and educational programs are effective in reducing cancer incidence and mortality; thus, the American Cancer Society can make a sound theoretical link between the effectiveness of its screening and educational programs, which can be more easily evaluated, and achievement of its larger mission, the prevention and eventual elimination of cancer (Sawhill & Williamson, 2001). Obviously, however, the validity of any micro-level indicator as a measure of effectiveness toward achievement of a broader mission depends on the soundness of the logic model behind it—that is, the chain of theoretical reasoning that explains exactly how the organization's efforts led to the desired larger result.

It must be emphasized again that the outcomes model does not necessarily incorporate other important aspects of organizational performance. For example, it is possible to conceive of an organization that is delivering effective programs but whose sustainability as an organization over the long run is imperiled by financial imbalances. It could also be possible to achieve positive program outcomes, but at a very high cost; in other words, the organization could be very inefficient. Moreover, measuring program outcomes does not tell us anything about the organization's ability to learn and adapt to change.

Focusing on outcomes provides a different understanding of "efficiency" than the simple version encompassed in the emphasis on low "overhead," discussed earlier. As Harry Hatry (2014) explains,

> Performance measurement of efficiency has traditionally used indicators of the form: "average cost (or number of FTEs) per unit of output." However, "true" efficiency is reducing costs without sacrificing service quality. A more important indicator is to relate cost to the amount of outcome achieved. The performance measurement is then "average cost per unit of outcome." (p. 21)

How are nonprofit CEOs actually choosing between overhead and outcomes in measuring the effectiveness of their organizations? In a survey of CEOs of international nonprofits, George Mitchell (2012) found that most defined the effectiveness of their organizations in terms of outcomes, while a minority thought about it in terms of maintaining low overhead. But, like Hatry, Mitchell (2012) argues that the two perspectives are related, since the definition of efficiency would need to include outcomes as well as the costs incurred to produce them. In other words, considering outcomes gives efficiency a different, and more appropriate, meaning than if we are looking at overhead alone.

Can outcomes be benchmarked, that is, compared across organizations? Obviously, that would not be practical or useful if the organizations are in different sub-sectors and have very different missions. In 2004, the Urban Institute and the Center for What Works undertook a project to identify a common set of outcomes and outcome indicators that nonprofits could use to inform practice and that could be practical to implement in defined program areas. The project team selected 14 separate program areas based on their missions, the outcomes sought, and potential outcome indicators for tracking progress toward those program areas' missions. The first step was development of an outcome sequencing chart, essentially a logic model, to explain how outcomes would ultimately lead organizations in each area to fulfill their missions. The chart was then applied to the 14 program areas: adult education and family literacy, advocacy, affordable housing, assisted living, business assistance, community organizing, emergency shelter, employment training, health risk reduction, performing arts, prisoner reentry, transitional housing, youth mentoring, and youth tutoring. The project's 2006 report also included a generic "nonprofit taxonomy of outcomes" as a guide for organizations in program areas in which specific indicators had not yet been developed (Lampkin, et al., 2006). But comparing outcomes, even among organizations in similar fields, may be misleading to the extent that their missions are somewhat different, even if in nuanced ways.

Balanced Scorecard

Financial ratios may be an indication of organizational performance, but they do not measure whether the organization's mission has been achieved. Outcomes measure effectiveness against mission, but may not provide insight on broader organizational performance. Benchmarking may be useful as a learning tool, but it has shortcomings as a method of evaluating performance, as discussed above. The **balanced scorecard**, and variations on the concept, has been adopted by some nonprofit organizations as a tool for monitoring indicators across various dimensions. Like other models, it has its strengths and weaknesses.

The balanced scorecard is a concept developed by Robert Kaplan and David Norton (1992) as a way for businesses to obtain, as the term suggests, a balanced perspective on performance by combining financial data with other considerations. It has since been adopted by many nonprofit organizations and government agencies as a way to combine financial ratios and other data in measuring organizational performance. The balanced scorecard looks at an organization from four perspectives:

1. *The financial perspective,* including financial performance indicators

2. *The customer or client perspective,* including measures of customer satisfaction

3. *The internal business perspective,* including measures of operational efficiency and quality

4. *The innovation and learning perspective,* including measures of the organization's ability to adapt to changes in the environment (Murray, 2010, p. 446)

Rob Paton (2003) offers a variation of the balanced scorecard designed specifically for nonprofits, which he calls the **dashboard**. Indeed, the terms balanced scorecard and dashboard are often used interchangeably (Poister et al., 2015). Paton's model seeks to answer two fundamental questions: Does it work? In other words, "do the different activities, services, and programs achieve broadly the results intended?" (Paton, 2003, pp. 139–140). And is the organization well run? Paton notes that there may be a relationship between how well run an organization is and the effectiveness of the programs it delivers, but that the two are separate matters and both need to be measured in order to obtain a complete picture of the organization's performance:

A valuable and innovative service may be provided by an organization that is inefficiently administered, or even by one whose funds are being discretely embezzled; and a well-administered organization with excellent morale may be delivering high-quality programs to clients whose needs are slight compared to those of the client group originally envisaged. (p. 140)

Paton's (2003) dashboard thus looks at the organization from five perspectives, encompassing short-, medium-, and long-term measures:

1. *Current results:* Monthly checking against key targets—for example, a summary of achievements, a finance report, and a marketing report

2. *Underlying performance:* Annual reviews of the appropriateness and cost-effectiveness of programs and support functions—for example, service outcomes, business outcomes, and external comparisons

3. *Risks:* Monitoring of the ways the organization may be put in jeopardy—for example, by a liquidity crisis, legal or procedural noncompliance, or a breakdown in key relationships

4. *Assets and capabilities:* Annual reviews of capacity to deliver future performance—for example, physical and financial assets, external reputation and relationships, and expertise and process knowledge

5. *Change projects:* Regular reports on projects intended to bring about improvements in the organization that the board and the CEO are supervising directly (p. 142)

Many nonprofit organizations have developed some version of a dashboard to provide an overview of performance to executives and the governing board. It often includes key variables and graphics displays on a single page that provides a comprehensive snapshot of the organization at a point in time, change compared to previous periods, and progress toward goals. The dashboard often summarizes key indicators with regard to both program outcomes and financials.

In recent years, there has been an increase in the availability of tools to help nonprofits track and report their performance in a consistent manner. For example, in 2012, the BBB Wise Giving Alliance, GuideStar USA, and Independent Sector launched Charting Impact, an online tool that is provided through GuideStar and offers a common report format for nonprofits to use (Independent Sector, 2017a). The report is organized around five key questions:

1. What is your organization aiming to accomplish?

2. What are your strategies for making this happen?

3. What are your organization's capabilities for doing this?

4. How will your organization know if you are making progress?

5. What have and haven't you accomplished so far?

There are also various commercially available software products that nonprofits use to monitor their activities and outcomes. Tools for developing dashboards are widely available on the Web, for example, at the site of the National Council of Nonprofits (2018a).

The balanced scorecard and similar approaches have critics, too. For example, Marshall Meyer (2002) notes that the balanced scorecard really measures very different things—for example, financial results and customer satisfaction, numbers that must be looked at alongside each other rather than combined. It does not provide a single measure of an organization's performance. He suggests instead the idea of identifying correlations between measures. For example, do good financial results always go along with customer satisfaction? If so, there is no need to measure customer satisfaction directly, since it can be assumed from the financial results.

Social Return on Investment

The concept of the double bottom line has been mentioned earlier in this text. It refers to the need for nonprofit managers to look to both their organization's financial performance as well as the social impact of its programs. In 1996, the Roberts Enterprise Development Foundation (now known simply as REDF), a venture philanthropy fund based in San Francisco, pioneered the concept of **social return on investment (SROI)** as a way to put a dollar figure on—that is, to monetize—the social value created by an organization. The idea was to add social return to financial return in order to generate a single number—in dollars—that could be used as an indicator of the organization's performance and value.

As a venture philanthropy fund, REDF approaches giving as a form of investing in a select group of social enterprises that have a social mission. And, like other investors, REDF seeks to measure the return on its investments. Financial return is easy to understand: If you invest $100,000 and receive $200,000 back, that's a 100 percent return on your investment. But how do we measure the less tangible social benefits created by a nonprofit's programs? SROI provides a method for measuring those social benefits in dollar terms so that they can be compared with expenditures to produce a single number as simple to understand as the rate of return on a philanthropic investment.

REDF's SROI methodology evolved from **benefit–cost analysis** (also called cost–benefit analysis), a technique drawn from applied economics and most often used to evaluate government programs. As Stephanie Cellini and James Kee (2010, p. 494) define it, "cost-benefit analysis … identifies and places *dollar values* on the costs of programs [and weighs] those costs against the *dollar value* of program benefits [italics added]." The advantage of this approach is that it produces a ratio that can be used to compare programs against programs. But putting a dollar value on social benefits—that is, monetizing them—can be a challenge. As an example, let's consider a program that offers job training, helping people move from welfare to work. The benefits may include the new income taxes paid by the people who become employed, savings through lower welfare costs, less need for homeless shelters, and perhaps savings in the cost of policing as fewer people are on the streets. These benefits can be given a dollar value and summed to find the SROI in the nonprofit's job-training programs. But that does not include, for example, the very real benefits of reduced fear and social tension resulting from the decrease in crime. Though real, they are hard to measure, especially in dollar terms. Moreover, costs are incurred to support the program today, but many of the benefits may not be realized until far into the future. For example, one benefit of an after-school tutoring program that helps young people complete high school may be their higher wages after graduation. That is, at least theoretically, easily stated in dollar terms. But increased education also may lead to healthier and happier lives through their lifetimes, although this is hard to capture and harder to monetize. In addition, SROI and similar approaches face what Alnoor Ebrahim and V. Kasturi Rangan (2010, p. 8) call the "thorny issue of causality." That is, benefits may reflect the influence of other variables beyond the program that is being evaluated.

SROI has been adopted by a number of organizations, especially social enterprises that worked with REDF and other venture philanthropy funds. However, REDF no longer uses SROI exclusively as its measure of an organization's social performance. A 2008 report by Carla Javits acknowledges the shortcomings of the approach:

- The SROI analysis process is resource intensive;

- Engaging the practitioner is essential and time consuming;

- Metrics are important, but metrics aren't everything;

- SROI is a good tool, but SROI isn't everything. (p. 2)

In a 2015 article, Laurie Mook, John Maiorano, Sherida Ryan, Ann Armstrong, and Jack Quarter reiterated some of the common criticisms of SROI and proposed a **stakeholder impact statement** as an alternative approach to integrating financial and social impact data (Mook et al., 2015).

Blended Value

The concept of **blended value**, defined by Jed Emerson (Blended Value, n.d.), builds on the idea of social return on investment by adding a third component—impact on the environment. With the increasing focus by nonprofits on financial results and the growing corporate concern about social responsibility, many observers note a blurring of the nonprofit and for-profit sectors; in other words, they argue that nonprofits and business firms are becoming more alike and that it should therefore be possible to define some common measures of performance that could be applied to all organizations across the sectors, including nonprofit, for-profit, and hybrid enterprises. Blended value is advanced as the answer. Simply defined,

> Value is what gets created when investors invest and organizations act to pursue their mission. Traditionally, we have thought of value as being either economic (and created by for-profit companies) or social (and created by nonprofit or non-governmental organizations). What the Blended Value Proposition states is that all organizations, whether for-profit or not, create value that consists of economic, social and environmental value components—and that investors (whether market-rate, charitable or some mix of the two) simultaneously generate all three forms of value through providing capital to organizations. The outcome of all this activity is value creation and that value is itself non-divisible and, therefore, a blend of these three elements. (Bibb, Fishberg, Harold, & Layburn, n.d.)

Is there a sound rationale for this concept? Yehuda Baruch and Nelson Ramalho (2006) analyzed a variety of scholarly articles, some reporting research on nonprofits and others reporting on for-profits. They found some common ground in the measures that those various studies used to measure organizational effectiveness. However, as they observed, "all measures seemed to correspond to broadly diffused concepts" (Baruch & Ramalho, p. 58). In other words, organizations in different sectors can be compared using similar measurements, but only at a very high level and in very general terms. Corporations and nonprofits do have characteristics in common, since both are organizations, but limiting the study of effectiveness to their common characteristics may require a level of generalization that is simply not informative. For example, both dogs and cats might be evaluated by their effectiveness in winning their owners' hearts, as well as eating, drinking, and sleeping. But none of these qualities would be related to their effectiveness in catching mice or guarding a junkyard, tasks for which cats and dogs are generally superior, respectively.

In the past, corporations have worked to maximize economic value, while nonprofits have tried to maximize social value—that is, to increase SROI. However, the blended value theorists say, value should be thought about as having three components: economic value, social value, and environmental value (Blended Value, n.d.). Both companies and nonprofits should be measured by how much of all three they create—in total. Thus, companies may create considerable economic value, but through socially responsible behavior they may also create some social value. For example, companies earn profits for their owners but also create jobs for the less well-off. Nonprofits may score high as creators of social value and lower than companies in creating economic value, but many now operate revenue-generating enterprises, and they may also earn profits and contribute to the economies of their communities. Both companies and nonprofits may affect the environment, in positive or negative ways. In other words, the blended value advocates call for "breaking down the silos" and developing a single measure to evaluate for-profits and nonprofits in terms of the total benefits, or value, that they create (Blended Value, n.d.). The concept of **shared value** is closely related to that of blended value and has gained wide discussion. Its advocates encourage companies to measure their results in terms of social impact as well as financial profit and to place shared value in the center of what they do rather than at the margin (Porter & Kramer, 2011).

Although the use of blended value to measure organizational performance across the nonprofit and business sectors is intellectually intriguing, there are several challenges to its wider acceptance. For one, there are some critics who challenge the very concept of corporate social responsibility, one of the silos across which blended value measures would be built (Karnani, 2010). There are strong incentives for corporations to maximize financial returns, including the ratings of financial analysts and the pressure of shareholders seeking to maximize the financial returns on their investments. And, of course, there remain the inherent difficulties of defining and measuring social impact in both sectors.

However, work continues on innovative concepts similar to blended value and on the idea that social enterprises might be valued and receive investments much like for-profit companies. The concept of blended value is the foundation of **impact investing**. As the term implies, impact investing involves "investments made into companies, organizations, and funds with the intention to generate measurable social and environmental impact alongside a financial return" (Global Impact Investing Network, n.d.). Reflecting the view that market mechanisms based on impact investing might bring about a more efficient allocation of capital to nonprofit activities than do traditional grants and giving, in 2008, the Rockefeller Foundation awarded a grant of $500,000 to develop a **social stock market** to be based in London. "The market would allow investors to trade shares in projects that seek to preserve the environment, such as clean technology, and that promote health care, aid for the poor, or other social goals" ("Rockefeller Foundation Gives $500,000," 2008). By 2015, the idea was also being implemented, with variations, in several other countries, including Brazil, Canada, Kenya, Singapore, and South Africa. Each operates somewhat differently, but the common ultimate goal is to connect impact investors with companies that serve a social mission. In 2015, challenges to their further development included the need for consistent certification of social purposes and techniques for establishing the valuation of companies that pursue both financial and social goals (Chhichhia, 2015).

Performance Measurement: The Continuing Debate

The proliferation of approaches to measuring the performance of nonprofit organizations has proved frustrating to many. Some have cited the complexity of academic approaches and the demands on staff time and attention to compile and analyze data. Some have questioned to what extent the data compiled are actually used in the operation of many organizations. And some scholars have even concluded that systemically measuring impact in the nonprofit sector is impossible (Lampkin et al., 2006).

Students may remember from Chapter 4 that David Renz and Robert Herman (2016) raised questions about the relationship between board best practices and organizational effectiveness. Indeed, Renz and Herman argue for a social constructionist approach to understanding the effectiveness of organizations overall, writing that "organizational effectiveness is not a single reality but rather a more complicated matter of addressing different interests and expectations" (p. 276). In other words, an effective organization may be one that is perceived as such. As Renz and Herman explain, "effectiveness *is* whatever [the organization's] relevant multiple constituencies or stakeholders judge it to be" (p. 277). In other words, the definition of effectiveness is socially constructed and it may not be realistic to understand it as a "single objective reality" (Renz & Herman, p. 270).

And yet, despite reasons for caution about any particular definition of effectiveness, demands for performance data from nonprofit organizations are unlikely to abate. Management inherently involves the strategic allocation of resources to achieve and improve results. A complete disregard for results achieved as a result of resources expended would be not only irresponsible and unacceptable to those who provide those resources, but it would also be, by definition, non-management. Nonprofit managers are confronted with sorting through an array of options and selecting the measures and methods that will meet both their own need for useful management information as well as the expectations of funders, watchdogs, and regulators. There continues to be a debate both about the appropriate methods to be applied and the emphasis that should be given to efforts to measure results.

One concern is the amount of time and effort devoted to measuring effectiveness and whether indeed the effectiveness of organizations with limited capacity may be compromised by the effort required to compile, analyze, and report data. Some argue that nonprofits could eventually reach a condition of analysis paralysis, consumed with measurement to the preclusion of action. Clearly, it is important—especially for very small organizations—to keep things simple and not become distracted by monitoring too many, complex indicators of performance. An additional problem is that multiple funders may require an organization to "count different things or count similar things differently," increasing the burden even more (Newcomer, 2008, p. 37).

A more philosophical concern is expressed by Paton (2003), who sees a risk of developing "disconnected managerialism," a situation "where modern discourse and methods are conspicuous (and may even play well externally), but they do not impact the main work, except as noise and a burden" (p. 161). In other words, if nonprofit managers work to the numbers, there is the risk that the numbers will gain more importance than the vital work their organizations are committed to performing. That is, too much emphasis on measuring performance could create a "Dilbert world," in which the passion and commitment of the professional staff and volunteers are replaced by caution, even skepticism, which might undermine the nonprofit culture and its traditional strengths. Striking similar themes, William Schambra (2013) decries what he calls the "empire of empiricism," and laments,

> Long gone are the dark ages when grants might have supported some young, passionate activist who wanted to start a movement from scratch; some professional disenchanted with the established procedures, yearning to try a different but purely experimental approach; some cause that probably was never going to succeed, but was worth supporting nonetheless because it was simply just and right. All such grants would have been based on mere feelings, on hunches, on subjective moral or religious preferences. None of them could have specified the precise dosages needed to inch the arrow along from clearly understood cause to clearly predicted effect.

A number of experts who strongly advocate performance management also recommend a holistic and reasonable approach. For example, Lynn Taliento, Jonathan Law, and Laura Callanan (2011), who are with McKinsey & Company, a consulting firm that works with nonprofits, recommend that organizations include constituents in designing assessment programs, assess for the purpose of learning and applying findings to action, apply rigor with reason, be practical and not try to do everything, and create a learning culture.

Failure to measure performance is the antithesis of managing and is unacceptable in the environment in which nonprofit organizations exist today. However, practical good sense is required. It may be, as Paton (2003) suggests, that the appropriate position for nonprofit managers is a middle ground between ignoring the need for measuring performance and making it the purpose of the organization. As Paton writes, "In considerable measure they are obligated to support measurement and performance improvement—to object can easily appear self-serving and irrational." On the other hand, "they are fully entitled to have misgivings" (p. 164). The middle position, which Paton finds to be the "proper one," is to be "realistic about the range of possibilities,"

> to engage constructively with measurement while being very alert to its limitations and misuse, and to approach the performance agenda positively while also being fully aware that every valid and useful method can also become an occasion for goal displacement by being pursued inappropriately or excessively. (p. 165)

CHAPTER SUMMARY

There is an increasing demand that nonprofit organizations be accountable—that is, responsible for their actions. For some, this has a narrow meaning of following legal and ethical requirements; others include the requirement that nonprofits follow recommended best practices in governance and management. A still broader definition includes the responsibility to demonstrate that the organization is achieving results, that the resources entrusted to it are used not only ethically and legally but also efficiently and effectively.

Accountability is enforced by state and federal laws, but the nonprofit sector also has established methods for self-regulation. These include standards of best practice and programs through which nonprofits can gain accreditation or certification indicating their adherence to such standards. **Charity watchdogs and raters**, private organizations that evaluate nonprofits according to their own standards, also have influence because of the visibility their ratings command. Transparency, that is, the easy public availability of Form 990 and other sources of data, also has enabled donors to become a force for accountability. Members of the public communicate with the organization or are involved in its programs (e.g., as volunteers), providing another mechanism for accountability. Some organizations also create opportunities internally to reflect on the mission and learn from experience.

It is necessary to distinguish among program effectiveness, organizational effectiveness, and organizational performance. Effectiveness relates to achieving the mission, but performance is a broader concept that also includes financial results and other variables related to the overall organization. There is also a difference between managing the performance of programs, which is an ongoing process, and program evaluation, which commonly is defined as an in-depth study undertaken once or periodically. In evaluating effectiveness and performance, some emphasize financial ratios, including the percentage of expenditures devoted to programs rather than overall management and fundraising. But it is important to distinguish efficiency from effectiveness, with the latter related to accomplishment of the mission rather than merely minimizing costs. Some argue that an undue emphasis on efficiency could undermine effectiveness, by causing organizations not to invest in capacity.

Among other approaches to evaluating performance is benchmarking, which compares organizations with others with similar characteristics, but this may be a technique better suited to learning than to evaluation. Another approach that has gained wide acceptance among many funders and nonprofit organizations is outcome measurement. This approach requires developing a logic model that links inputs to activities, to outputs, and to outcomes, the latter representing changes in the people who are served by the program. Outcomes may be measured immediately following completion of the program, over an intermediate term, or over the long term. Long-term measurement may be difficult and costly. The Urban Institute and the Center for What Works have developed **common indicators** for nonprofits working in specific fields as well as universal core indicators that might apply to all nonprofit organizations. There are websites and commercially available software packages that enable nonprofits to monitor programs and measure outcomes.

The balanced scorecard seeks to integrate internal, external, and program variables to provide a comprehensive picture of an organization's performance. Many organizations using a balanced scorecard approach prepare a dashboard, a simple and often graphic portrayal of key variables that is used to monitor and communicate performance. Some venture philanthropists and scholars have adopted the tools of benefit–cost analysis and social return on investment (SROI) to measure social impact. Others have developed concepts of blended value, incorporating financial, social, and environmental impacts, which they would apply to both nonprofit and for-profit entities. The concept of blended value is the basis for impact investing and recent establishment of social stock markets.

All methods of measuring nonprofit performance offer advantages as well as disadvantages. There is a continuing debate about the best methods to use and the appropriate emphasis to give to measurement. Nonprofit managers must be committed to performance measurement but should not become focused on it to the detriment of delivering their mission's programs. But the failure to measure results altogether is an abdication of management responsibility. There are a growing number of online tools available that offer nonprofits standardized indicators and formats for measuring and reporting results.

KEY TERMS AND CONCEPTS

accountability 144
accreditation 147
balanced scorecard 167
benefit–cost analysis 169
blended value 170
charity watchdogs and raters 173
common indicators 173
corporate-style benchmarking 160
dashboard 167

effectiveness 157
efficiency 157
e-Postcard 146
impact investing 171
inputs 161
logic model 163
outcomes 163
outputs 163
Pension Protection Act of 2006 146

performance 144
performance management 157
performance measurement 157
shared value 171
social return on
   investment (SROI) 169
social stock market 171
stakeholder impact statement 170
statistical benchmarking 160

CASE 6.1 The Wounded Warrior Project

When wounded veterans began arriving home from Iraq in 2003, John Melia remembered his own experience as a Marine who had been shot down off the coast of Somalia in 1992. He began visiting returning Iraq War veterans in military hospitals, giving them backpacks with basic personal items they would need. The backpack project grew and Melia expanded the services to include sports programs, employment help, and other assistance to veterans. As the programs grew, he hired additional staff, including Steven Nardizzi, who had been an executive in a small nonprofit that also served veterans. By 2009, the project Melia had started, employed about 50 people, and raised $21 million in revenue. Melia and Nardizzi began to disagree about the pace of the organization's

growth and the economy was in a recession, presenting new fundraising challenges. Melia resigned and Nardizzi became the CEO of the Wounded Warrior Project (Phillips, 2016a).

Nardizzi's model was not that of traditional veterans' organizations, which often were similar to fraternal organizations or advocacy nonprofits. Under his leadership, the Wounded Warrior Project would adopt a business mindset, focusing on growth and on metrics to measure the performance of programs and staff members. "I look at companies like Starbucks," Nardizzi said in one interview, "that's the model" (Phillips, 2016a). Soon after taking over as CEO in 2009, he doubled spending on fundraising and continued to increase it in following years (Phillips, 2016a). The organization expanded its programs to 22 locations and stepped up promotion. Fundraising soared and the Wounded Warrior Project became a well-known brand, with "its logo emblazoned on sneakers, paper towel packs, and television commercials that [ran] dozens of times" (Phillips, 2016a).

By some measures, the Wounded Warrior Project's spending on overhead, including fundraising and management, had reached 40 percent of its revenues in 2014, drawing the attention of charity watchdog organizations (Phillips, 2016a). Some former staff members also became critical, claiming that the emphasis on fundraising and performance metrics had begun to eclipse the commitment to the organization's mission. Some claimed that performance metrics were unrealistic and that numbers reported by the organization were misleading. For example, some said that veterans were being placed in low-paying jobs that were nevertheless counted just to meet the organization's employment targets. They argued that meeting the organization's goals had become more important than the impact of its programs on the well-being of veterans. Some former employees also were critical of what they deemed excessive spending (Phillips, 2016a).

At the beginning of 2016, the Wounded Warrior Project was hit with criticism from multiple news media and charity watchdogs. The *New York Times* and CBS News ran stories citing lavish spending on events and travel, including a staff meeting in 2014 that brought 500 Wounded Warrior employees to the five-star Broadmoor hotel in Colorado (Phillips, 2016a). The organization's alumni events, which included trips to wine festivals, casino nights, and visits to resorts, also were criticized as too lavish (Sandoval, 2017). Nardizzi argued that the expenditures were legitimate and that a growing organization must invest in fundraising in order to build the capacity to achieve its mission (Phillips, 2016b). The board initiated an independent investigation. The resulting report challenged some of the data cited by news media, arguing, for example, that 94 percent of the travel and conference costs were in fact incurred in connection with providing services to veterans and their families, not luxury travel by the staff (Hrywna, 2016). Senator Charles Grassley, chair of the Senate Judiciary Committee and a member of the Senate Finance Committee, also launched an investigation (Sandoval, 2017). Dan Pallotta, founder of the Charity Defense Council, established to refute criticisms of nonprofits, came to the defense of the Wounded Warrior Project and wrote to Grassley to express his views (Stiffman, 2016a).

In March 2016, the board dismissed Nardizzi and the organization's chief operating officer, Al Giordano (Chuck, 2016). Former military officer Michael Linnington was appointed as CEO in June, charged with rebuilding the organization's reputation (Hrywna, 2016).

Was the Wounded Warrior Project indeed guilty of excessive spending or was there a "knee jerk reaction" to the accusations without sufficient examination of the facts (Sandoval, 2016)? Opinions were divided. One issue involved the different approaches taken by prominent charity watchdog organizations in calculating overhead. Accounting standards permit nonprofits to allocate some costs between fundraising and programs. For example, the costs of a mailing that asks for a gift but also includes educational materials may be split between those two functions, with the educational portion considered program related. The Better Business Bureau Wise Giving Alliance does not count the portion allocated to program as overhead, but others, including Charity Navigator and Charity Watch, consider it differently (Sandoval, 2016). These different definitions result in different numbers for overhead being reported. For example, in 2016, the Wounded Warrior Project claimed that 75 percent of its expenditures were for programs; Charity Navigator reported 61 percent; and Charity Watch calculated program expenditures at 54 percent (Sandoval, 2016). Another question that was raised is to what extent overhead is an important number to consider and how organizations should communicate about the subject.

In discussing the Wounded Warrior controversy, some argued that the most important metric for a nonprofit organization is not overhead but what is achieved. As one nonprofit CEO told the *Chronicle of Philanthropy*, "If I can go to a donor and say 'You gave me $10 and I spent the $10,' I expect a thank-you from that person. But imagine if I go to that person and say 'You gave me $10 and I turned it into $100, and with that $100, I achieved the following outcomes in the area you care about.' That is a much more powerful conversation" (Sandoval, 2016). Some people said the biggest mistake made by the leadership of the Wounded Warrior Project was insensitivity to how overhead spending might appear. As one expert said, "It is not good enough to say that 'overhead is a stupid metric,' which it is. You have to accept that while it is a stupid metric, it is the metric that many people focus on" (Sandoval, 2016). Others said that the organization could have responded to critics more quickly with more detailed explanations and that Nardizzi's known hostility to the charity watchdog organizations was not helpful (Sandoval, 2016).

In 2017, the report of Senator Grassley's investigation was released. It concluded that the Wounded Warrior Project had indeed engaged in "inappropriate spending" and had "inaccurately reported" some expenses. It also concluded that the organization had taken steps to remedy the problems and to implement best practices. The organization responded to the report saying that it had overhauled its procedures on travel, replaced some board members, and adjusted its programs to better serve veterans. It disagreed with the report's finding that it had inaccurately reported program costs and said that it would continue to calculate overhead following IRS accounting rules, as it had before (Sandoval, 2017).

Questions Related to Case 6.1

1. Are the issues and questions raised in the Wounded Warrior Project case related to the concepts of accountability, performance, or both? How are those concepts related to this case?

2. Think back on the responsibilities of governing boards discussed in Chapter 3. How do they relate to the case of the Wounded Warrior Project?

3. Accounting rules permit nonprofits to allocate some costs between fundraising and programs; for example, the costs of a mailing that solicits gifts but also advocates for a cause may be apportioned between those two functions. Some people defend this practice while others say it is misleading to the public. What is your opinion?

4. This chapter discusses the view of Renz and Herman (2016) that nonprofit effectiveness is socially constructed, that is, it may be defined by what people perceive about the organization. How does that relate to the case of the Wounded Warrior Project?

CASE 6.2   Youth Villages

Youth Villages was founded in Memphis, Tennessee, in 1986 through the merger of two campuses that provided residential treatment to young people with emotional or behavioral issues. In subsequent years, the organization expanded, eventually opening offices in 20 states and the District of Columbia. As it grew, Youth Villages also expanded its programs beyond residential treatment to include intensive in-home services, treatment foster care, adoption services, community-based services, transitional living services, family-based care for children with developmental disabilities, and specialized crisis services. Each year, Youth Villages serves more than 22,000 children (Youth Villages, 2017).

By offering a continuum of services, Youth Villages aims to help children overcome their challenges and live at home. If a child must receive help beyond his or her own home, residential treatment is provided in the least restrictive setting for the shortest amount of time possible, with transition to a group home or foster home if necessary before returning home. The adoption program helps to find permanent homes in cases where it is not possible for children to return to their birth families (Youth Villages, 2017).

Youth Villages' model, called "Evidentiary Family Restoration," reflects five core tenets: (1) The program treats families as well as children simultaneously; (2) outcomes are measured long term; (3) the program continues in the community, with children being kept with original families or adoptive families, keeping out-of-home placements temporary; (4) highly intensive services are delivered 24/7 by maintaining low caseloads and trained, accountable staff; and (5) programs are research based, data driven, and accountable to children, families, and funders (Youth Villages, 2017). Youth Villages reports that 86 percent of young people who complete the program are living successfully two years later (Youth Villages, 2016).

The use of performance metrics is a central feature of Youth Villages' approach. As CEO Pat Lawler explains, "Youth Villages' goal always has been to provide the best services for children and families. That's one of the reasons we started collecting data.... It was all about getting better outcomes for kids" (Lester, 2016, p. 32). The organization established its own research department in 1994, which collects and analyzes data from all youth who have participated in its programs for at least 60 days. The youth are tracked at 6, 12, and 24 months post-discharge, and Youth Villages has amassed one of the largest outcome datasets in the country. In addition, the organization has formed research partnerships with an array of scholars and academic institutions to study its data and refine its outcome evaluation process.

In addition to outcome data, day-to-day operations are tracked through a performance management system, which is focused on several core indicators related to program and organizational performance. Initially, the performance management system used off-the-shelf software, but now uses a more complex system in order to track the various core indicators, which include

- Actual number of children being served versus projections

- Data on staff turnover

- Physical interventions required

- Serious incidents, such as runaways

- Perceptions of Youth Villages' programs by children served and their families

- Financial performance, measured by the margin of revenue over expenses

- Compliance with regulatory guidelines and best practices

- Success in moving children to less-restrictive environments, including returning to their families, group homes, or independent living (Lester, 2016)

Youth Villages' results have attracted the attention and support of national funders. The Edna McConnell Clark Foundation has invested more than $36 million in the organization since 2004 and helped Youth Villages receive an additional $25 million from 11 other funders who were participating in Clark's Growth Capital Aggregation Pilot (GCAP) program, which ran from 2007 to 2012. Youth Villages and other organizations receiving the investments were permitted to draw down funds for growth capital only if they achieve agreed-upon performance milestones, which include securing reliable, renewable funding. In 2015, Blue Meridian Partners, which is affiliated with the Clark Foundation, committed $200 million over 11 years to make programs based on the Youth Villages model available to nearly all young people in the country in need of such services, both through expansion of Youth Villages' programs and partnerships with other organizations (Edna McConnell Clark Foundation, 2017).

Additional source: Author's personal communications with Sarah Hurley, Ph.D., Managing Director of Data Science, Youth Villages, Memphis, TN.

Questions Related to Case 6.2

1. How are the concepts of effectiveness, efficiency, and organizational performance reflected in the Youth Villages case?

2. Which of the approaches to measuring and reporting performance discussed in this chapter are illustrated in the case of Youth Villages?

3. If Youth Villages were to apply the social return on investment (SROI) approach, what would be some of the cost savings to society that might be calculated (i.e., the social benefits in dollar terms)?

4. How does the view of Renz and Herman (2016) that effectiveness is socially constructed relate to the case of Youth Villages?

QUESTIONS FOR DISCUSSION

Below are the mission statements of three organizations, describing their purposes. All are involved in education. Based on these statements,

1. How are their missions different?

2. What metrics would you use to measure their effectiveness?

3. Could some or all use common indicators, or would the indicators need to be varied in light of their distinctive missions?

- The SEED Foundation is a national nonprofit that partners with urban communities to provide innovative educational opportunities that prepare underserved students for success in college and beyond (https://www.guidestar.org/profile/54-1850819).

- [The District of Columbia College Success Foundation] provide[s] a unique integrated system of supports and scholarships for underserved, low-income students to finish high school, graduate college and succeed in life (http://www.dccollegesuccessfoundation.org/dc/meet-csf).

- College Summit transforms the lives of low-income youth by connecting them to college and career. In low-income communities across America, College Summit creates a team of high school students who lead their peers to and through college (https://www.guidestar.org/profile/52-2007028).

APPENDIX CASES

The following cases in the Appendix of this text include points related to the content of this chapter: Case 3 (The Y); Case 4 (The Girl Scouts of the United States of America).

SUGGESTIONS FOR FURTHER READING

Books

Clark, C., & Emerson, J. (2014). *The impact investor: Lessons in leadership and strategy for collaborative capitalism*. San Francisco, CA: Jossey-Bass.

Morino, M. (2011). *Leap of reason: Managing to outcomes in an era of scarcity*. Washington, DC: Venture Philanthropy Partners. (Full text available for download at http://leapofreason.org/)

Newcomer, K. E., Hatry, H. P., & Wholey, J. S. (2015). *Handbook of practical program evaluation* (4th ed.). Hoboken, NJ: Wiley.

Pallotta, D. (2010). *Uncharitable: How restraints on nonprofits undermine their potential*. Lebanon, NH: Tufts University Press.

Poister, T. H., Aristigueta, M. P., & Hall, J. L. (2015). *Managing and measuring performance in public and nonprofit organizations* (2nd ed.). San Francisco, CA: Jossey-Bass.

Solomon, L. M. (Ed.). (2014). *The new frontiers of philanthropy*. New York, NY: Oxford University Press.

Articles/Report

Brest, P. (2010, Spring). The power of theories of change. *Stanford Social Innovation Review*. Retrieved from http://www.ssireview.org/articles/entry/the_power_of_theories_of_change

Clarkin, J. E., & Cangioni, C. (2016). Impact investing: A primer and review of the literature. *Entrepreneurship Research Journal*, 6(2), 135–173.

Hatry, H. P. (2014). *Transforming performance measurement for the 21st century*. Washington, DC: Urban Institute.

Websites

Balanced Scorecard Institute: http://www.balancedscorecard.org/

BBB Wise Giving Alliance: http://www.give.org/

Blended Value: http://www.blendedvalue.org/

GuideStar: http://www.guidestar.org/

Independent Sector (Principles): https://www.independentsector.org/principles

Leap of Reason: http://leapofreason.org/

Nonprofit Finance Fund: https://www.nonprofitfinancefund.org/

PerformWell: http://www.performwell.org/

REDF: http://www.redf.org/

Standards for Excellence Institute: http://www.standardsforexcellenceinstitute.org/dnn/

Urban Institute: http://www.urbaninstitute.org/

Strategic planning begins with where the organization is, defines some new places where it wants to be, and develops a plan to get there, all in the context of its mission and values and the realities of the environment in which it operates.

iStock/christophertdumond

Chapter Outline

Developing Strategy, Building Capacity, and Managing Risk

Nonprofit organizations are driven by their missions. Those who work in them, as staff or volunteers, also are often motivated primarily by their passion for the social purpose that the organization serves. But, as discussed in Chapter 6, society increasingly demands that nonprofits be accountable for the use of the resources entrusted to them. While passion for the cause is essential, nonprofit organizations also must apply tools of rational management. This chapter discusses some tools that a nonprofit can use to develop a strategy for achieving its goals, create a strategic plan, and build the organizational capacity needed to deliver its mission.

Understanding Strategy

Some people may hear the term strategy and think it is synonymous with strategic planning. But there is a difference; let's consider an example. In 1989, Robert Egger was managing nightclubs in Washington, DC. His fiancée persuaded him to join her in a volunteer program that passed out food to the city's homeless from trucks that toured the streets and parks. This gave him an understanding of the prevalence of hunger and a new idea. Egger began to think about how homeless people were trapped in their situation because they lacked the ability to gain employment. And he thought about the tons of food that were wasted every day by restaurants, hotels, and caterers throughout Washington. He put these two realities together, which led him to found DC Central Kitchen (www.dccentralkitchen.org). The organization collects surplus food, processes and repackages it, and today provides more than 5,000 meals a day to shelters and other facilities throughout the area, while also providing job training to homeless people who work in the kitchen and eventually move on to jobs in the food service industry. The kitchen also operates various revenue-generating businesses that help to provide employment and fund its programs. Egger (2002) didn't start out with a strategic plan. He didn't have a written document that described the details of how he would proceed. But he had a winning strategy. Egger later went on to found LA Kitchen in California, which follows many of the same models.

Learning Objectives

After reading this chapter, students should be able to:

1. Define strategy, strategic planning, and strategic management.

2. Describe the key steps in the strategic planning process.

3. Explain the pros and cons of strategic planning.

4. Explain various approaches to developing an organization's strategy.

5. Define organizational capacity.

6. Describe models for capacity building.

7. Identify capacity building appropriate to an organization's point in its life cycle.

8. Identify types of risk facing nonprofit organizations.

9. Analyze cases, applying concepts from the chapter.

Management scholars and consultants have offered many definitions of **strategy**, and there is not agreement on exactly what it is or how to develop it. It may be articulated in a plan, that is, a written document, or it may be more intangible, perhaps no more than an idea or an approach to reaching a goal. Strategy is focused on the long term, not on the day-to-day, or as Michael Allison and Jude Kaye (2015) write, "It is concerned with the longer-term course that the ship is steering, not with the waves" (p. 7). Developing strategy does not necessarily require any particular process or result in any written document at all. It does require creativity and a different way of seeing reality. In this chapter, we will look at the process of **strategic planning**, but it is important to keep in mind that "strategic thinking, acting, and learning are more important than any particular approach to strategic planning" (Bryson, 2016, p. 241). The distinction is important because a strategy without a plan to implement it may be no more than wishful thinking, and some plans may be ineffective because they are not based on any clear strategy.

Kevin Kearns (2000) identifies three approaches to formulating strategy for an organization. The first is the visioning approach. This approach begins with the leader's vision and then works backward to determine "what strategies, tactic, actions, and resources are needed to achieve it" (pp. 31, 41). This approach has its advantages and may be the only realistic way to go in a new or young organization or one facing a crisis, situations in which formal strategic planning may not be useful or appropriate. But it can be risky as well. The leader's vision may not always be 20/20. Relying on the leader's vision may leave the organization open to external threats that the optimistic leader just can't or won't see but that are real. It is an approach to formulating strategy, but it may become increasingly inadequate as the organization grows and becomes more complex—in other words, as the risks become greater.

Another approach to developing strategy that Kearns (2000) describes is the incremental approach. Strategy evolves out of experience as the organization goes along, one decision at a time, buffeted by bargaining and the push-and-pull of its constituencies. This may be a pragmatic accommodation to the complexity of many nonprofits' environments and their diverse constituencies, and it may produce an organization that is flexible and open to new opportunities. But it may also produce an organization that keeps moving to who knows where. It is not strategic planning, and indeed, some would question whether an organization operating this way has a strategy at all (p. 44).

The third approach to developing strategy is what Kearns (2000) calls the analytical approach, one in which "you use logic and in-depth analysis to improve the strategic fit between your organization and its environment" (p. 32). This approach is what most people have in mind when they say strategic planning. But, as we will discuss later in this chapter, some observers challenge the suitability of the analytical model in today's fast-paced environment and recommend alternative approaches.

Strategic Planning and Strategic Management

Strategic planning is more than a strategy; it is a *process* that produces a product—a strategic plan—that puts meat on the strategy and points the way to implementing it. John Bryson (2016), a widely cited author on strategic planning, explains, "We can use strategic planning to help us think, act, and learn strategically—to figure out what we should want, why, and how to get it" (p. 242). While Bryson emphasizes the need to achieve clarity about the organization's mission and set priorities, Allison and Kaye (2015) point to the value of the strategic planning process in building consensus about the priorities that are identified: "Strategic planning is a systematic process through which an organization agrees on—and builds commitment among key stakeholders to—priorities that are essential to its mission and are responsive to the environment" (p. 1).

Strategic planning begins with where the organization is, defines some new place where it wants to be, and develops a plan to get there, all in the context of its mission and values and the realities of the environment in which it operates. Today, most nonprofit organizations except the newest and smallest engage in some form of strategic planning—both because they find it an effective tool and because many funders, including foundations, regard it as an essential badge of a well-managed organization.

Strategic planning is not to be confused with what is sometimes called long-range planning, a term that was more commonly used in the past. Long-range planning really involves projecting trends and data into the future—that is, estimating what is going to happen based on certain assumptions. In contrast, strategic planning is goal oriented and action oriented—its purpose is to change the future rather than merely predict it.

A strategic plan is likewise not the same as a business plan, which is discussed in Chapter 16. Although some nonprofits use a business planning approach in a broader context related to the whole organization, most business plans are developed for specific programs, initiatives, or ventures to be undertaken by the organization. Business plans build on the decisions made in strategic planning, but they are more focused on implementation and financial elements, typically including detailed projections for revenue and expenses over at least three years. Strategic planning is also not the same as **operational planning**, which, as the term suggests, relates to the actions necessary to implement the strategic plan.

Strategic management is a concept that was developed in the business world and that has been applied to government and the nonprofit sector. As Jack Koteen (1997) acknowledges, the term "does not possess an exact, universally accepted definition" (p. 25), but he offers at least a description:

> Strategic management emphasizes an ongoing process that integrates strategic planning with other management systems ... [it] seeks to use and merge all necessary approaches and resources to reach strategic goals ... it embraces the entire set of managerial decisions and actions that determine the long-run performance of an organization. (p. 21)

In other words, strategic management is an integrated approach to managing the organization that is based on the strategic plan and includes the entire cycle of strategy formulation, implementation, and evaluation. The goals of the strategic plan drive decisions on managerial matters such as program design, budgeting, organizational structure, human resources development, and evaluation. The goals provide "guidelines to direct resources and talent into the highest priority activity" (Koteen, 1997, p. 27). Strategic management thus links strategy and implementation.

The Strategic Planning Process

Every doctor defines infection in the same way, and every lawyer knows what a tort is. But the vocabulary of strategic planning is unsettled. That is to say, various experts use different terms to mean the same thing. For example, some say "purpose" instead of "mission" and use the terms "goal" and "objective" in different ways, sometimes interchangeably. Some say "programs," and others say "activities." There is also no universally accepted planning process, although most models include the same essential concepts. For example, some experts recommend that development of the organization's vision should occur early in the process, while others say the vision should be defined toward the end of planning after more discussion has taken place. Written strategic plans also are organized in various ways. Allison and Kaye (2015) are right to say that "It doesn't really matter what you call certain concepts, as long as everyone in your group uses the same definitions" (p. 17). But the proliferation of terms requires that planners establish clarity about the concepts and not become distracted by differences in terminology. Table 7.1 summarizes the definition of strategic planning terms as they are used in this text and some alternative terms that are commonly used in various planning models.

There are various models for strategic planning. The **Harvard policy model**, developed at the Harvard Business School by various scholars over a period of decades, is the most commonly mentioned and is the inspiration for several well-known variations. In practice, most strategic planning models are a hybrid of various approaches, which is appropriate because the planning process needs to be tailored to fit each specific situation. A basic, generic strategic planning model is depicted in Figure 7.1 and includes the steps common to many models:

- Plan to plan—that is, determine the process, the players, and their roles.
- Clarify the organization's mission, vision, and values.
- Assess the situation—that is, scan the external environment and the organization's internal realities.
- Identify the strategic issues or strategic questions that need to be addressed.
- Develop goals, strategies, and objectives.
- Write and communicate the plan.

Table 7.1　Summary of Strategic Planning Terms

Term	Meaning	Other Commonly Used Terms
Mission	The reason the organization exists; the starting point for strategic planning	Purpose
Vision	Description of an ideal future, either for the organization (internal vision statement) or of society (external vision statement)	Vision of success
Values	Principles the organization holds as the most important	Guiding principles
SWOT analysis	An inventory and analysis of the organization's strengths and weaknesses and of opportunities and threats (SWOT) posed to the organization by the external environment	Environmental scan
Strategic issues	"The fundamental policy questions or critical challenges affecting the organization's mandates, mission and values; product or service level and mix; clients, users or payers; cost, financing, organization, or management" (Bryson, 2016, p. 251)	Strategic questions
Goals	Directions that the organization will pursue with respect to the strategic issues	Strategic goals Strategic directions Objectives Strategic objectives
Strategies	Actions that the organization intends to take to achieve its goals	
Objectives	Specific, quantified targets that represent steps toward accomplishing the goals	Goals

Figure 7.1   Basic Strategic Planning Model

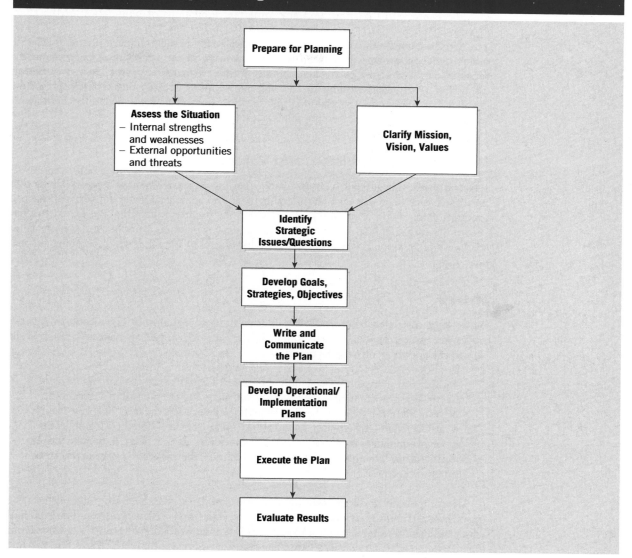

- Develop operational and implementation plans.
- Execute the plan.
- Evaluate results.

Planning to Plan

It is important to have a plan for planning, that is, to identify what process will be used, who will participate, and what information will be needed to inform the planning. There needs to be agreement among the participants on points such as the purpose of the effort; the steps in the process; the form and timing of reports that will be issued; the role, functions, and membership of any group or committee empowered to oversee the effort; the role, functions, and membership of the strategic planning team; the commitment of the resources necessary for proceeding with the effort; and any important limitations or boundaries for the effort (Bryson, 2016, p. 245).

Some organizations use an outside consultant to guide their strategic planning process; others prefer to manage it themselves. Some plan an off-site retreat at some point in the process—perhaps a day or weekend in which the participants devote extensive time to discussion of strategies without the normal interruptions of daily business. Up-front time devoted to planning for the planning will be well spent if it avoids misunderstandings or wasted motion during the planning process itself.

Defining Mission, Vision, and Values

Effective planning begins with consensus about basics—mission, vision, and values. Discussion on these basics often can take considerable time, and some pragmatic individuals, eager to jump into identifying issues and goals, may find the exercise frustrating. But experience has shown that neglecting to create a solid foundation for planning by achieving consensus on the basics of mission, vision, and values will likely lead to a breakdown in planning at some later stage.

Mission

As we have discussed before, **mission** is everything to a nonprofit organization—it is the reason the organization exists, and it must be the starting point for its planning. James Phills (2005) speaks eloquently to this point:

> Mission is the psychological and emotional logic that drives an organization. It is the reason why people get up in the morning and go to work in a nonprofit.... Mission [defines] the social value that the organization creates. The key feature of social value—whether it is spiritual, moral, societal, aesthetic, intellectual, or environmental—is that it transcends economic value. Thus, it is inextricably linked to fundamental human values, which are the basis for intrinsic worth or importance. (p. 22)

It is important to distinguish mission from mandates. Mandates are functions that the organization is required to perform, perhaps by its charter or law. For example, a college may have a charter that requires it to enroll only women students. Although it is a nonprofit organization, the American Red Cross has mandated services that it is required to provide to the government under its congressional charter. If the organization faces mandates, it will need to be clarified at the outset and incorporated in the plan. These are givens. But, in general, nonprofit organizations have fewer mandates than do public agencies and thus have considerable freedom to design their own futures; this may include redefining their missions.

There are different philosophies about mission statements. Some prefer fairly simple statements that are almost like a slogan—they capture the essence of the organization's purpose in a sentence. But many mission statements say not only what the organization does, but also, at least briefly, how it does it. One study suggested that nonprofits should develop mission statements that include the activities of the organization and "include words that highlight specific accomplishments" (Pandey, Kim, & Pandey, 2017). But Kevin Starr argues for brevity—mission statements that are brief and to the point: "A verb, a target population, and an outcome that implies something to measure—and we want it in eight words or less" (Starr, 2012a). Some organizations develop briefer mission statements and separate statements of their vision and values, while others include some components of vision and values in their mission statements, either explicitly or implicitly. Box 7.1 provides a sampling of three mission statements that reflect somewhat varied approaches.

We might think that an organization's mission should be relatively unchanging. Indeed, a performing arts organization is not likely to one day alter its mission statement to address environmental issues or the welfare of animals. But there are often changes that require a rethinking, or at least a restatement of the mission. For example, you may recall Miriam's Kitchen, the Washington-based organization serving homeless people, which we passed in our hypothetical walking tour back in Chapter 2. Miriam's began as a breakfast program, and its mission was once simply to provide a healthy meal each day to homeless men and women. But as its programs evolved, it began to offer case management services to its clients and expanded medical services and other programs. Its work came to include more advocacy, and it focused its efforts on securing more supportive permanent housing. Over time, the scope of its purposes and activities had changed, and it became essential to consider a mission statement that reflected the new reality. In 2012, the statement was changed to say "Our mission is to end chronic homelessness in DC with the values of dignity, belonging and change" (Miriam's Kitchen, n.d.). This broader statement of mission encompassed what Miriam's was actually doing but did not represent a complete departure from its original purposes.

Saying that the mission can change is not to suggest that organizations should simply expand their programs and then change their mission statements to fit. But, inevitably, programs and missions often will evolve as the organization grows and expands its capabilities. Revisiting the mission is really asking the questions, "What business are we in?" and "What are we really trying to accomplish?" Getting to the right answer sometimes requires adopting a new perspective. There is always a trade-off between keeping the mission sufficiently broad and keeping it sufficiently focused. There is a risk in going to extremes in either direction. Too narrow a mission statement may be too constraining, making it

Box 7.1 Mission Statements

Big Brothers Big Sisters

Provide children facing adversity with strong and enduring, professionally supported one-to-one relationships that change their lives for the better, forever. (www.bbbs.org)

City Year

City Year's mission is to build democracy through citizen service, civic leadership and social entrepreneurship. It is through service that we can demonstrate the power and idealism of young people, engage citizens to benefit the common good, and develop young leaders of the next generation. (www.guidestar.org/organizations/22-2882549/city-year.aspx#mission)

Special Olympics

Special Olympics transforms lives through the joy of sport, every day, everywhere. We are the world's largest sports organization for people with intellectual disabilities: with more than 4.9 million athletes in 172 countries—and over a million volunteers. (www.specialolympics.org)

impossible for the organization to grow or expand. But a statement that is too broad may become meaningless and open the door to **mission creep**—a gradual evolution away from the organization's purposes into ancillary activities that may eventually result in an organization that is very unfocused.

Vision and Values

Most organizations clarify their **vision** and **values** in the first phase of strategic planning. The vision statement is a description of an ideal future. Some vision statements describe the future of the organization itself; these are **internal vision statements**. For example, the Boy Scouts of America envisions the future of its impact as an organization: "The Boy Scouts of America will prepare every eligible youth in America to become a responsible, participating citizen and leader who is guided by the Scout Oath and Law" (Boy Scouts of America, 2017b). Other vision statements paint a picture of the ideal world that the organization is striving to shape; they are **external vision statements**. For example, Teach for America's vision is that "one day, all children in this nation will have the opportunity to attain an excellent education" (Teach for America, 2017). Some experts suggest that developing a vision statement should come later in the strategic planning process, not at the beginning, believing that planners need to go through other phases of planning before they are able to develop a consensus about their vision of the future either internally or externally (Bryson, 2016, p. 259). But many models call for developing the vision along with the mission and values as an early step in planning. Values are those principles that the organization holds most important. For example, an arts organization might value the artistic quality of its work the highest, or perhaps might be more concerned with the diversity of its audience. As mentioned above, sometimes values are implicit in the mission statement, and other times they are stated separately. Sometimes values are identified as guiding principles, fundamental assumptions, or by some other term.

Taken together, statements about mission, vision, and values establish a foundation for the strategic plan and provide a lens through which everything is viewed in order to develop goals for the organization's future.

Assessing the Situation

As discussed in Chapter 3, nonprofits are open systems; that is, the boundaries between the organization and its environment often blur, and changes or pressures originating in the environment will have a profound impact on what the organization is able to do and how it needs to go about doing it.

Strategic planners need to collect information in two arenas—within the organization and outside it. There are various methods available for analyzing internal and external conditions, but the most commonly used is the **SWOT analysis**, a method that comes from the Harvard policy model noted earlier. In this approach, the organization itself is surveyed to identify strengths (S) and weaknesses (W), and the external environment is examined to discern opportunities (O) and threats (T). The ultimate purpose of the exercise is to develop a comparison between the organization's own strengths and weaknesses and the opportunities and threats facing it in the external environment, in order to identify strategic issues that need to be addressed.

Strengths and weaknesses of the organization may be analyzed in terms of assets or competencies. That is, what resources does it have or lack, and what does it do well or poorly? The analysis of strengths and weaknesses may use some of the tools of a capacity assessment, discussed later in this chapter. As a result of this analysis, the organization will identify its **competencies** and **distinctive competencies**. A competency is an ability that the organization has, something it can do well. A distinctive competency is one that other organizations cannot easily replicate (Bryson, 2016, p. 251). The organization's weaknesses might be viewed in terms of resources that are lacking or the organization's ability to perform in certain areas. For example, identified weaknesses might include inadequate facilities, insufficient staff, poor fundraising performance, or a chronic inability to meet performance objectives.

The external (or environmental) scan is a distinctive feature of strategic planning. Its purpose is to identify opportunities and threats facing the organization, which might encompass things such as demographic trends or trends in philanthropy, grant making, or government funding. The scan may include a **stakeholder analysis**, to identify the characteristics, values, perceptions, expectations, and concerns of stakeholders, including clients or customers, donors, and relevant government officials. Another approach that is sometimes applied considers political, economic, social, and technological factors in the environment that may affect the organization—it is commonly called a PEST analysis, an acronym derived from the four factors that are considered And it is essential to undertake an analysis of the positions and programs of competitors or partners offering similar services.

It is important to focus on factors that are relevant to the organization, in other words, to be selective. For example, there may be national trends that are affecting human service organizations, but are all of them relevant to an organization in Chicago? Do national birth rates really provide useful insight for an organization that serves children in a city with a large and growing immigrant population? Not being selective in looking at the environment can cause the process to just bog down and overwhelm the planners with too much information.

Part of the environmental scan requires research on other organizations. Kearns (2000) suggests looking at three categories of organizations—those that offer related programs and services, those that offer similar programs and services, and those that offer substitutable programs and services (pp. 54–55). So, for example, an organization that is involved in addiction counseling would need to be alert to trends affecting hospitals, government agencies that fund addiction counseling programs, and homeless services organizations that may be sources of referrals. Organizations that offer similar programs or services in other locations or markets may be relevant, too. An addiction counseling program in Boston should examine trends affecting similar organizations in Baltimore and Los Angeles, since they may also face similar situations. Other types of nonprofits also need to scan what is happening with regard to their competitors. Colleges need to know which other institutions recruit students in the same high schools. And museums need to know at which other cultural institutions their patrons may be spending their time. Some may resist the idea of competition among nonprofit organizations, but it is a reality that many, if not most, need to address in their planning.

As an example, Table 7.2 shows the hypothetical results of a simple SWOT analysis that might be conducted by the planners for an urban theater. The theater has strengths, including a good reputation for quality performances and a capable artistic director. It faces opportunities presented by the gentrification of the downtown area by college-educated people and the city's plans to develop an arts district, offering the potential for larger audiences. But lack of any staff dedicated to marketing is a weakness and possibly an obstacle to capitalizing on that opportunity, as is the small and outdated facility. It is important to remember that strengths and weaknesses apply to the organization itself, while opportunities and threats come from the outside. Sometimes keeping that clear requires making some careful distinctions. For example, the theater's reliance on one principal donor and lack of fundraising capacity is a *weakness*. The possibility that the donor might lose interest, or perhaps suffer financial reversals that would make continued support impossible, is a *threat*. The outdated facility is a weakness, but the possibility that the artistic director or actors may find more attractive

Table 7.2 SWOT Analysis for an Urban Theater	
The Organization (Internal)	**The Environment (External)**
Strengths: Reputation for quality performances Capable artistic director Good location near downtown	Opportunities: More college-educated people living downtown New restaurants opening nearby City's plan to develop an arts district in our neighborhood
Weaknesses: Facility too small and outdated No staff dedicated to marketing or fundraising Overdependence on one major donor	Threats: Competition from other organizations Loss of key major donor Artistic director and/or actors may no longer be willing to work in old facility

opportunities elsewhere is a threat. Competition from other theaters that may have better facilities and a stronger base of financial support also is a threat to this organization.

Identifying Strategic Issues

Drawing on the information available from the environmental scan and guided by the organization's own mission, vision, and values, the next step in strategic planning is to identify the key **strategic issues** (sometimes called strategic questions) facing the organization. Strategic issues are "the fundamental policy questions or critical challenges affecting the organization's mandates, mission and values; product or service level and mix; clients, users or payers; cost, financing, structure, processes, and organization, or management" (Bryson, 2016, p. 251). The strategic issues or questions define areas in which the organization needs to take action. This could mean taking defensive action to protect against threats, or it might mean developing new initiatives to grow, expand, or improve in order to seize opportunities presented by the environment. There is a need to set priorities by separating issues into categories. For example, Bryson (2016) classifies strategic issues into four types:

1. Issues that go to the heart of the organization's core business and which may involve "a fundamental change in products or services, customers or clients, service or distribution channels, sources of revenue, identity or image, or some other aspect of the organization"

2. Issues that require an immediate response and therefore cannot be handled in a routine way

3. Issues that are on the horizon and likely to require some action in the future and perhaps some action now

4. Issues that require no organizational action at present but that must be continuously monitored (pp. 253–254)

There are various approaches to the identification of strategic issues. Bryson (2016) summarizes nine: the direct approach, the goals approach, the vision-of-success approach, the indirect approach, the oval-mapping approach, the livelihood scheme, the alignment approach, the tension approach, and the systems analysis approach (pp. 255–256).

A discussion of each of these approaches is beyond the scope of this text, but students may wish to consult Bryson's writing for a detailed discussion.

Sometimes the identification of strategic issues is complex and controversial. But sometimes the situational assessment readily reveals the strategic issues or questions facing the organization; they just "fall out" of the analysis of strengths, weaknesses, opportunities, and threats. For example, some strategic questions the urban theater described in Table 7.2 would need to consider may be rather obvious:

- How can we address the weakness presented by our outdated facility?

- How can we capitalize on the opportunities presented by our changing neighborhood?

- How can we address the weakness and threat posed by our high dependence on a single donor?

- How can we retain our respected director and continue to attract good actors, in order to maintain our quality and remain competitive?

Setting Goals

Goals are directions that the organization will pursue with respect to the strategic issues that it has identified. In the context of strategic planning, they are sometimes also called strategic goals. Koteen (1997) divides goals into three types: those addressed to program thrusts, that is, those that go to services that the organization provides; those addressed to institutional concerns, matters that need to be addressed to build a more effective organization (i.e., capacity, culture); and financial goals, which, of course, have to do with resources (p. 126). We will discuss capacity building further at a later point in this chapter.

Goal statements are stated in broad terms and do not need to be quantifiable. (Keep in mind that some planning models describe these broad statements as objectives, strategic objectives, strategic directions, or by some other term.) **Goal statements** generally use action verbs—words such as increase, improve, enhance, ensure, strengthen, expand, develop, sustain, encourage, or initiate. For example, three simple goals for the urban theater might include

- Improve our physical facility

- Increase our visibility and reputation

- Expand (or diversify) our sources of revenue

The goal statements articulate broad directions but do not state how they will be accomplished. For example, the theater intends to improve its facility, but the goal statement does not say exactly how. It will increase its visibility and reputation and expand its revenue sources, but the goal statements do not explain how those changes will be accomplished or by when. Nor do the goal statements include the measures by which success will be defined. That comes later.

Developing Strategies

Once goals have been established, the planners next need to determine strategies to achieve them. Developing strategies is, of course, the heart of the strategic planning process. This is when the organization determines what it will do to address the strategic issues that it has identified as a result of its SWOT analysis and to achieve the goals that it now has established.

As with goals, there are three levels of strategies: **organizational strategies**—broad directions and those that relate to mission, vision, trends, competitors, partners, and market position; **programmatic strategies**—related to the programs and activities implemented to achieve specific outcomes; and **operational strategies**—those "aimed at enhancing ... administrative efficiency, preparedness, and execution" (La Piana, 2008, p. 26). David La Piana's model of planning (p. 25) portrays the three categories as a pyramid, with organizational strategy at the top (to be addressed first), programmatic strategies at the middle level (they come next), and operational strategies at the bottom of the pyramid (to be addressed last).

To continue with the case of the urban theater, some strategies that the planners would consider to address their goals might include the following:

- Renovate and expand our facility.

- Build marketing partnerships with neighborhood restaurants.

- Gain increased attention in the media.

- Expand our presence on the Web and in social media.

- Strengthen our fundraising programs.

Portfolio Analysis

Various scholars have developed core or generic organizational strategies that nonprofits might follow with regard to its programs. For example, Kearns (2000) identifies four strategies: growth, retrenchment, stability, and collaboration. These would seem to be virtually exhaustive of possible strategies in the broadest sense. But strategic planners need to develop more specific strategies with respect to programs, activities, and the goals that they have identified. Strategies might include developing new initiatives, building new partnerships, expanding current programs, or decreasing or even eliminating others.

As noted earlier, strategic planning is a tool developed in the business world that many nonprofits have adapted to their environment. There are additional tools that have been adapted from business that can be usefully applied in the two steps that are at the heart of the strategic planning process—the identification of strategic issues and the development of strategies to address them. Because these concepts were developed in the business sector, the vocabulary they use—terms such as competitive advantage and profitability—may sometimes seem strange in the nonprofit sector. But with appropriate adjustments in our understanding of the terminology, many of the concepts can be useful in nonprofit strategic planning.

One useful tool for identifying strategies is **portfolio analysis**, a technique used by business firms to determine if their various programs, products, and services are in line with their goals. Portfolio in this context does not mean a collection of investments in stocks and bonds, as most people might understand the term, but rather the array of programs and services that an organization offers. Portfolio analysis places various programs into categories—the cells or boxes of a matrix based on some set of variables considered most relevant.

Perhaps the best-known version of portfolio analysis in business is the growth-share matrix developed by the Boston Consulting Group. It is used to evaluate company products or services based on the rate of growth in a particular market and the share of the total market that their products and services represent (Kearns, 2000). In its original form, this model may not be of great value to many nonprofits, which may be concerned about the growth of markets (i.e., growth in need for services) but are often less concerned with their market share. But others have developed variations that offer a better fit to the nonprofit environment and can be useful tools in the strategic planning process.

Jeanne Bell, Jan Masaoka, and Steve Zimmerman (2010) offer a "matrix map" to help nonprofits identify generic strategies for their programs, which these authors call "strategic imperatives" (p. 75). As shown in Figure 7.2, they place programs in one of four quadrants, defined by the two variables of profitability and impact. Programs that are high in impact and profitability (upper right quadrant) are "stars." The strategy should be to invest in these programs and grow them (p. 79). Programs in the lower left quadrant are neither profitable nor have high impact on achievement of the mission. The best strategy would be "stop," that is, to close them down or give them away to another organization (p. 83). Programs in the upper left quadrant are high on impact but unprofitable. Bell et al. call these programs "hearts," that is, they go to the heart of the mission (p. 85). Because they advance the mission, a nonprofit would want to keep these programs operating, but it would be important to manage their costs so that they do not place an unsustainable drain on resources. The bottom right quadrant of the matrix includes programs that are profitable but do not have much direct mission impact. This might include the organization's fundraising programs or earned-income activities that make money but do not relate directly to the mission. Bell and coauthors suggest that the best strategy for these activities would be "water and harvest, increase impact" (p. 90). For one thing, it is possible that the "money trees," if watered and harvested, may subsidize some of the "hearts" (p. 90).

The matrix map offered by Bell et al. (2010) provides a way to think about strategies for programs based on the two variables of impact and profitability. Another portfolio analysis model, developed by I. C. MacMillan (1983), also suggests core strategies that an organization might pursue. It is somewhat more complex. It goes beyond the variables of profitability and impact and looks at each of the organization's programs or services according to three criteria:

1. The organization's competitive position with regard to the program, which might be strong or weak. Again, competition may not be a comfortable concept for many nonprofits—it is a concept drawn from the business world. But another way to interpret this is to think about whether the organization can claim superiority over other organizations in its ability to deliver the program. In other words, does the

Figure 7.2 Matrix Map: Strategic Imperatives for Programs

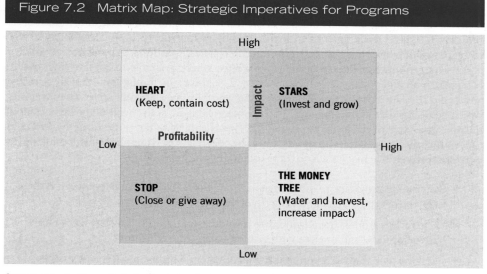

Source: Adapted from Bell, J., Masaoka, J., & Zimmerman, S. (2010). *Nonprofit sustainability: Making strategic decisions for financial viability.* San Francisco, CA: Jossey-Bass, pp. 75–95.

organization have resources, skills, advantages of location, or other advantages that make it the best organization—or potentially the best—to provide this program or service?

2. The attractiveness of the program to the organization, which might be high or low. In other words, to what extent does the organization really want to offer this program or service? It is important to understand that this assessment would not be based solely on profitability. It reflects a variety of criteria, including its fit with the mission, its potential for attracting resources, and others.

3. The extent of alternative coverage, that is, similar services offered by other organizations, which might be high or low. In the business world, this question would be whether there are many competitors in this market. But a nonprofit may look at it as a question of whether there are other options available to people who need the service.

Because there are three variables to be considered, each of which may be high or low, a matrix depicting this model is three dimensional; that is, it has width, length, and height. The space is divided up into eight cells, or eight scenarios, that exist with regard to each program considered. MacMillan (1983) suggests a strategy for each scenario. Table 7.3 summarizes the eight scenarios. It also shows the generic strategy recommended by MacMillan for each, using terms taken from the business vocabulary, as well as a description of each situation in ordinary language—that is, in the words that a group of nonprofit planners might actually use in their conversations.

MacMillan's (1983) matrix does provide a nonprofit with a way of recognizing patterns that may help clarify thinking about each specific program and also about the relationship of its portfolio to its mission as an organization. As Kearns (2000) observes, if an organization finds that all its programs fall into scenarios 1 to 4, that is, encompassing just those that are highly attractive, that may suggest it is drifting away from addressing the most hard-core social problems in favor of those that are the most lucrative, perhaps in terms of paying customers or the ease of raising gifts. This might cause some concern about its adherence to mission.

On the other hand, if all its programs fall into scenarios 5 to 8—scenarios in which the programs are relatively unattractive, perhaps because they are tangential to the mission or difficult to support in the long term—Kearns (2000) speculates that the organization may just be responding to the availability of short-term funding for some programs, running the risk that it will be stuck with them if the funding evaporates (p. 126). MacMillan (1983) recommends that an organization try to build a balanced portfolio of programs in which it has a strong competitive position, in other words, where it is able to achieve high quality compared with other organizations (scenarios 1, 2, 5, and 6), including some that are attractive and some that are not. In simplest terms, the portfolio may include some moneymakers, which help subsidize other programs that lose money but are at the heart of the organization's mission (the "soul of the agency" programs). This is similar to the point made by Bell et al. (2010) that the "money trees" may subsidize the "hearts." Applying MacMillan's thinking, an organization would achieve such an ideal balance of programs by

- Giving up programs to other organizations that can do them better, even if they may be attractive financially and in other ways;

- Encouraging other organizations to abandon programs in which it has a clear advantage and can operate with greater quality and efficiency;

- Making sure that all its programs are consistent with its mission and strategy;

- Considering partnerships or collaborations with other organizations, a subject we will consider in more detail in Chapter 8.

Table 7.3 MacMillan Scenarios

Scenario	Competitive Position	Program Attractiveness	Alternative Coverage	Suggested Strategy (MacMillan)	The Situation in Ordinary Language
1	Strong	High	High	Aggressive competition	We're the best at this, or we easily can be, and we really want to do it. There are a lot of other organizations offering the same thing, but we're going to compete head-on and try to persuade them to yield this program to us.
2	Strong	High	Low	Aggressive growth	We're the best at this or we easily can be. We really want to do it. And, there is almost nobody else doing it. It's an open road—let's invest in this program and grow it quickly before others start to compete with us.
3	Weak	High	High	Aggressive divestment	We would really like to continue offering this program, but we are just not good at it and probably never will be. There are a lot of others doing it and they are a lot better than we are. Let's just get out and let them have it.
4	Weak	High	Low	Build strength or sell out	We would really like to do this, and there are few others who do it. But let's be realistic, we just aren't very good at it. We either need to invest in this program to make it good or find some other organization that can do it better and is willing to take it on.
5	Strong	Low	High	Build up best competitor	We're the best at doing this, but it is just not attractive to us to do it any longer. We don't want to let people down who rely on this program, but there are other organizations that do the same thing. Let's talk to the next-best organization and help them take this over from us.
6	Strong	Low	Low	Soul of the agency	We are the best and almost the only organization doing this. We're really known for it. It's not that attractive to us in many ways—for one thing, we lose money on it. But a lot of people depend on us and have nowhere else to go. We just have to find a way to keep it going.
7	Weak	Low	High	Orderly divestment	This is just not an attractive program for us, and we're not that good at it either. A lot of other organizations offer the same thing. No rush, but let's gradually direct people elsewhere and phase this program out.
8	Weak	Low	Low	Joint venture	We're not very good at this, and we really don't want to do it. Some people need the program, but not that many. We're stuck with it for now, but let's see if we can find another organization that's willing to partner with us in this area, so we can focus on our higher priorities.

Setting Objectives

Objectives are specific, quantified targets that represent steps toward accomplishing the goals. (Again, remember that in some models, these objectives statements are called goals.) Objectives are often stated in the form of "Increase (something) from (some number) to (another number) by (deadline)." The statement could, of course, also use "decrease," "reduce," or some other verb that implies a change in the value used to define the objective. This form is useful in communicating not only what the objective is, but also how ambitious it is—it enables any reader of the plan to see exactly what rate of change is anticipated and the date by which it is to be achieved.

Let's pick up with the example of the urban theater that we have been discussing. Given the goals and strategies that its plans have identified, one objective might be: "Increase the number of major donors from one to ten within three years." Another might be, "Double the number of visits to our website from x to y within the next year." For new activities, objectives need to be stated differently, and in some cases, a numeric objective may not be appropriate—just accomplishing something may constitute achievement of the goal, although a deadline should be included. For example, the theater might establish objectives such as "Retain an architect by June 1 to begin planning for renovation of our facility," "Appoint a marketing director within three months," "Appoint a director of development within six months," "Establish promotional partnerships with six neighborhood restaurants by the beginning of the next season," "Create a Facebook page within three months," and "Obtain five positive media reviews in the next season."

There need not be a one-to-one correspondence between objectives and goals—that is, achievement of an objective might well address more than one goal. Quantifiable objectives create the bridge from strategy to implementation by setting specific targets to be achieved. Operational plans then can be developed to spell out in detail exactly what will be done, when, and by whom in order to achieve the objectives in the strategic plan.

Writing the Strategic Plan

Strategic plans are, almost by definition, written documents. The written plan records the decisions reached and the goals, strategies, and objectives to be pursued. Usually, it is best if one or two people do the actual writing, but the draft is often used to stimulate wider discussion throughout the organization and its constituencies. Eventually, the governing board should take formal action to adopt the plan as the organization's policy.

The length of the written plan varies. Some plans may be no more than a few pages, summarizing mission, vision, values, and core strategies, and including a list of programs and objectives. Others may run 50 pages or more and include appendices with supporting data.

Once the written plan has been completed, it is important to use it as a tool for communication throughout the organization. The audience may include board members, staff, volunteers, clients, funders, other organizations, the news media, and the public (Allison & Kaye, 2015, p. 188). One of the benefits of strategic planning is that it helps build wide consensus and common understanding about mission, vision, values, goals, and strategies. That benefit is sacrificed if it remains a document available only to a select few in management or so voluminous that few are likely to read it. As Allison and Kaye emphasize, "The more concise and ordered the document, the greater the likelihood that it will be used and be helpful in guiding the organization's operations" (p. 188).

Developing an Operational Plan

Once the strategic plan is in place, there remains the job of developing a detailed operational plan—that is, a plan for implementation. This will include identifying specific tasks to be completed, establishing a timeline for their completion, assigning responsibility for each task, identifying the resources that will be needed—human and financial—determining the right organizational structure, identifying what information systems will be required, defining measures by which the completion or success will be determined, and other operational details. As explained earlier, some organizations combine the strategic and operational plans in one document, but developing them requires separate processes, usually with different individuals involved. Whereas board members and representatives of other constituencies may be involved in developing the strategic plan, the detailed work of producing an operational plan generally needs to be done primarily by the staff.

Benefits and Limitations of Strategic Planning

Strategic planning in some form is practiced by most nonprofit organizations today. However, it is important to recognize that strategic planning has its critics. One criticism was mentioned briefly earlier in this chapter: Strategic planning is not synonymous with and does not inevitably produce strategy. The risk is that traditional strategic planning may produce a list of goals, but not anything bigger (La Piana, 2008). Richard Chait, William Ryan, and Barbara Taylor (2005) reinforce this point, writing that "disillusionment with strategic planning has escalated." They observe that in too many plans, "dreams trump reality," that is, they include "blue sky" goals without addressing existing barriers to their achievement (p. 57).

Others point to the amount of time and effort that is required by the traditional strategic planning model, arguing that it may prove frustrating to the organization's staff and distract them from management of current programs. Indeed, when strategic planning is mentioned, some people will resist, or perhaps groan, based on previous negative experiences—the long meetings spent debating every word in the mission statement, the weekend retreats filled with team-building exercises. Strategic planning should not become the purpose of the organization, which is to say, it should not become an all-consuming activity.

Planning cannot just be about putting a report on the shelf. It needs to be a continuous part of the organization's way of operating, and the plan itself needs to be a living document that is revisited and adjusted in light of experience and the changing environment. La Piana (2008) argues that a process requiring perhaps 6 to 12 months to complete may put the organization "on hold" for too long, causing it to defer decisions, miss emerging opportunities, and fail to respond to pressing current needs while awaiting the outcome of the planning process. In addition, strategic planning usually occurs on a fixed cycle, perhaps every three years, which may be too infrequent for the fast-changing environment that most nonprofits face. La Piana (2008), who is a consultant to nonprofit organizations, proposes a continuous, "real-time" strategy development model that he characterizes as a "planning-doing cycle" (p. 19). In other words, instead of undertaking planning in a process that is "long, discrete, and separated from the external environment," La Piana recommends that nonprofits engage in "ongoing strategic thinking and acting in the context of the environment on a much shorter cycle" (p. 19). Consultants Dana O'Donovan and Noah Rimland Flower (2013) also call for flexibility: "The approach we developed in working with our clients ... is what we call adaptive strategy. We create a roadmap of the terrain that lies before an organization and develop a set of navigational tools, realizing that there will be many different options for reaching the destination. If necessary, the destination itself may shift based on what we learn along the way."

Strategic planning is not a panacea for every organization's problems at every point in its existence or under all circumstances. As mentioned earlier, it may not be a useful thing to undertake in a new organization, especially one guided by a charismatic, visionary leader. Likewise, strategic planning may not make sense for an organization that is in a state of crisis. What's the point of taking time to debate the mission or scan the environment when the roof is caving in, the creditors are at the door, or the executive director has just resigned and the staff are scrambling to keep things afloat until a new CEO can be found?

Strategic planning is not a substitute for leadership. Unfortunately, some organizations may try to make it so. Perhaps confused and out of ideas, board members or managers may say, "What we need is a strategic plan." They hire a consultant, go through a series of meetings and retreats, and end up with a document that is as lifeless and unimaginative as the paper it is printed on. Planning may provide a road map for implementing a vision, but it is not the vision itself. The plan can only lead to success if it is used as a tool of leadership toward achievement of the vision.

Despite its critics and its limitations, strategic planning offers many benefits. It forces the organization to think about its mission and to confront basic questions about where it stands, what it does, and where it wants to go. It requires that the organization look beyond itself to the environment around it and see itself in the context of broader trends and forces, including the society, economy, and other organizations. It provides a basis for rational decision making, rather than relying on guesswork or intuition. It may help to build consensus and understanding about mission, vision, values, and goals throughout the organization. And, when properly executed, it may produce strategies that can help guide a nonprofit toward achievement of its mission. And it may provide a foundation for building the organization's capacity to achieve its mission.

Building Organizational Capacity

As discussed in Chapter 2, interest in building the **capacity** of nonprofit organizations increased partly as a result of several books and articles that received wide attention in the late 1990s. They noted the problem of inadequate nonprofit capacity and laid the blame on traditional models of grant making, which emphasized short-term support for programs and required that organizations maintain low overhead expenses, preventing investment in their own capacity (e.g., Letts et al., 1997; Shore, 1999). These authors advocated shifting the focus to building strong organizations that could support, sustain, and expand effective programs to a scale that could have meaningful impact (Shore, 1999).

Such critiques influenced the thinking of some funders, who began to shift some of their focus from program grants to providing support for capacity-building initiatives. That was central to the approach of some venture philanthropy funds that originated in the 1990s, which adopted the methods of venture capitalists in business, who emphasize building a company for long-term sustainability. **capacity building** became a movement in the first half of the 2000s, with an explosion of articles, books, and conferences dedicated to the subject. A significant body of literature on the topic dates from that period. But by 2004, foundation funding to support nonprofit capacity-building efforts began to decline (Jensen, 2006). In addition, the recession that began in late 2007 shifted the priorities of many nonprofits—and funders—toward sustaining essential programs, further reducing funds available for capacity building. However, in 2009, capacity building received a new boost when the U.S. Congress passed the Edward M. Kennedy Serve America Act, which included a Nonprofit Capacity Building program to provide grants for organizational development to small and mid-size nonprofits. By 2012, interest in capacity building was growing again and 30 percent of funders had increased their support for such activities within the previous two years (Raynor, 2014). Grantmakers for Effective Organizations, an organization that has foundations as its members, stated in 2014 that "capacity building support [is] here to stay" (Raynor, 2014). However, the availability of external funds to support capacity building always has been and remains modest compared with the total of philanthropic giving, and most capacity-building efforts are undertaken by nonprofit organizations using their own internal resources.

Defining and Understanding Capacity

Exactly what is an organization's "capacity"? Paul Light (2004b) offers a succinct, but expansive, definition: Capacity is "everything an organization uses to achieve its mission, from desks and chairs to programs and people" (p. 15). What is capacity building? Letts, William Ryan, and Allen Grossman (1999) call it simply a process to "develop, sustain, and improve the delivery of a [nonprofit's] mission" (p. 4). But these brief definitions are like saying that life encompasses everything that happens and that eating sustains it. They do not really offer enough for us to have a clear understanding of either term. That requires that we go inside the black box of capacity to look at its component parts and observe some specific activities that it comprises.

It is no more meaningful to think about an organization's capacity as an indivisible quality than it is to think about a person's capacity in that way. For example, your capacity for study may be different from your capacity for athletics or for singing, so we would need to think about your capacities in the plural—that is, break capacity down into different categories or elements. Having done so, we could then consider what activities you might need to undertake in order to increase your capacity in areas that need improvement—perhaps some tutoring to improve your study skills, weight training to enhance your athletic prowess, and singing lessons. Fortunately, various authors have identified components of nonprofit organization capacity in much the same way, in categories.

Although they offer somewhat different lists, there are many similarities in the elements they include. Mike Hudson (2005) divides capacity into internal and external elements, writing that building organization capacity is about systematically investing in developing an organization's internal systems (e.g., its people, processes, and infrastructure) and its external relationships (e.g., with funders, partners, and volunteers) so that it can better realize its mission and achieve greater impact (p. 1). When the term capacity is used, many people first think primarily about the internal elements. That is understandable. For example, if we think about individuals' capacities—like studying, swimming, or singing—we are really talking about the skills or talents they possess. We are perhaps less inclined to think about their relationships with others as elements of their capacity as individuals. But, as discussed before, nonprofit organizations are open systems and are resource dependent. Their relationships with the external world—including other nonprofits, the media, government, and donors and other funders—are critical to their survival. Establishing and strengthening these relationships may thus be important aspects of capacity building, equal in importance to developing their internal structures, systems, and skills.

Internal and external are still two very broad categories. Paul Connolly and Carol Lukas (2002) offer a more comprehensive framework that helps deepen our understanding. The elements of capacity they identify include (1) the organization's mission, vision, and strategy; (2) its governance and leadership; (3) its ability to deliver programs and ensure the impact of its programs; (4) its strategic relationships—that is, the important external relationships that are critical sources of revenue or that may present constraints on the nonprofit's activities; and (5) its internal systems and management—its human resources; financial management systems; technology and information systems; facilities; plans for managing risk; programs for volunteer recruitment and management; and working relationships among its managers, staff, and volunteers. Connolly and Lukas's list reminds us again that capacity encompasses almost everything a nonprofit organization has or does.

Letts et al. (1999) break down the concept of capacity in a different way, describing three types of capacity an organization may possess: **program delivery capacity**, **program expansion capacity**, and **adaptive capacity**. They say that most nonprofit organizations are familiar with the first two, but it is "adaptive capacity that makes an organization not only efficient but also effective" (p. 20). As the term implies, program delivery capacity grows out of the organization's knowledge of a specific field—for example, education, the environment, or public health. Its capacities include the skills of its staff, who are recruited for their professional expertise. If this is the only capacity the organization possesses, "the organization is little more than a convenient venue where programs are implemented" (p. 20). As an organization expands its program, possibly to multiple sites, it needs to develop additional capacities, including payroll and financial systems, fundraising, and staff with supervisory skills. But, Letts and her coauthors argue, it is the third capacity—adaptive capacity—"that an organization needs to be sure it is delivering on its mission" (p. 21). This includes the ability to learn as an organization and identify ways to improve, to change in response to client needs, to create new and innovative programs, and to create an environment that is motivating to staff and volunteers (p. 23). Letts et al. draw on models developed in the business sector that they say can be adapted to build the capacity of nonprofits, and they emphasize the need to develop a "culture of performance."

As the discussion in this section demonstrates, the definition of capacity is so broad that it may seem difficult to distinguish capacity building from simply managing the organization. It may help for us to look at some specific processes and activities that nonprofits actually undertake when they say they are engaged in building capacity, which we will do in the next section.

Capacity Building in Action

An organization beginning a capacity-building initiative might use one of a number of tools that are available to evaluate its various capacities and identify areas of weakness that might need to be addressed. The consulting firm McKinsey & Company (2001, 2013) has developed a guide for assessing organizational capacity and a capacity assessment tool (OCAT). The Organizational Capacity Assessment Tool is available on an open-access basis to any nonprofit organization (mckinseyonsociety.com/ocat/). Nonprofit managers, staff, board members, and others can use it to rate the organization's current status on each element of capacity, assigning a score of 1 where there is a clear need for increased capacity, a 2 when there is a basic level of capacity in place, a 3 if there is a moderate level of capacity, and a 4 if there is a high level of capacity on the element being evaluated. When the instrument is completed by various people within the organization, the combined scores help identify areas in which there is consensus about the need for improvement. The tool could be used as a part of the SWOT analysis described earlier in this chapter as a part of the strategic planning process, since it would help to identify organizational strengths and weaknesses.

Having identified areas of its capacity that need to be strengthened, exactly what actions might an organization undertake? There is a large toolbox available, with tools designed to address almost any need. Capacity building often includes efforts to strengthen the organization's leadership, including the governing board and the CEO. As discussed in Chapters 4 and 5, there are a variety of tools for assessing and improving the skills of boards and CEOs and for developing policies designed to improve their performance. Board development activities might include, for example, board self-assessments, retreats, and establishing a governance committee of the board to focus on the board's own responsibilities, structure, and operation. There are a number of ways in which organizations invest in their executive leadership. Participation in professional associations and activities enables CEOs to learn from the experiences of their peers. There are a wide variety of formal leadership training programs available. Some organizations support their CEOs by retaining an executive coach, a practitioner of a field that has grown into a distinguishable profession in recent years. Having a plan for executive transition is a recommended practice for well-managed nonprofit organizations, and the existence of such a plan is indeed an element of capacity (Kibbe, 2004; Light, 2004b).

Establishing a system for performance management, as described in Chapter 6, would add to an organization's program delivery capacity. Strengthening fundraising and partnerships, perhaps developing strategies for increasing earned income, improving facilities and systems, and enhancing staff and volunteer skills are all important purposes of capacity building. Undertaking a campaign, which will be discussed in Chapter 12, may be an important capacity-building activity that will provide the funds needed for improving physical facilities and strengthening the organization's financial base. Strengthening internal management systems and functions, including human resource management, volunteer programs, financial systems, and operating procedures and policies, is commonly included in capacity-building initiatives.

A Model for Capacity Building

We now have an understanding of the various elements of capacity and the broad array of activities that can be undertaken to enhance capacity in each area. But where do we start? How do the elements fit together, and where should an organization begin to address its capacity in a holistic way?

In its work for Venture Philanthropy Partners in 2001, McKinsey & Company developed a comprehensive capacity framework that helps answer these questions. That framework was revised in 2013 and is shown in Figure 7.3 (McKinsey & Company, 2013). Other models

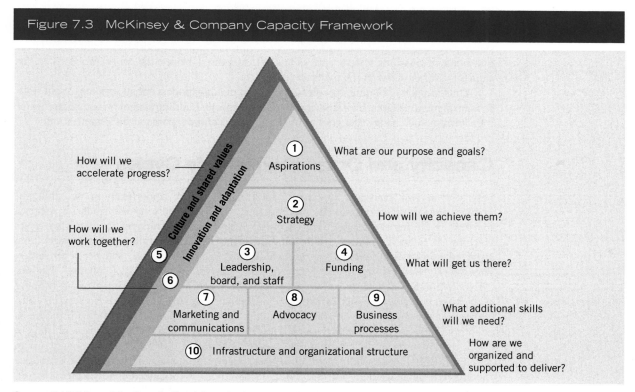

Figure 7.3 McKinsey & Company Capacity Framework

Source: Exhibit from "The Organizational Capacity Assessment Tool (OCAT): 2.0", Oct 2013, McKinsey & Company, www.mckinsey.com. Copyright ©2018 McKinsey & Company. All rights reserved. Reprinted by permission.

have been developed, some of which offer variations on the McKinsey tool (Despard, 2017). McKinsey defines nonprofit capacity in a pyramid of 10 essential elements. These elements include some of the items identified earlier in this chapter, but their depiction in the framework of a pyramid implies relationships among them and suggests a process for capacity building. McKinsey & Company's pyramid also highlights the importance of an intangible but powerful force that affects every aspect of capacity and efforts to strengthen it—the organization's culture and values.

In McKinsey & Company's (2013) model, capacity building is a process, in which the 10 elements are addressed sequentially, beginning at the top of the pyramid. Like strategic planning, it begins with "aspirations," which encompass mission, vision, and values. At the next level of detail are the organization's strategies, and then its leadership and funding—in other words, the questions descend from purposes to how they will be achieved, to the resources that will be needed to get there. The organization's skills and organizational structure come further down in the pyramid and thus would be considered only after the high-level elements had been addressed.

In the McKinsey (2013) framework, all 10 elements are surrounded by, or embedded within, the shell called culture and shared values. Culture affects all the elements and provides the overall environment in which capacity-building efforts may be undertaken. McKinsey & Company (2001) calls it the "invisible thread that runs throughout the entire subject of capacity building" (p. 63).

It may be tempting to initiate capacity building near the bottom of the pyramid, perhaps by looking at business processes, staff resources, and organizational structure. Indeed, that may be what many people think about first when capacity is mentioned. These are areas in which many organizations have some deficiencies, and they often affect the daily work of its staff, so there is a high awareness of them. They are concrete and specific and thus easy for people to get their heads around. But McKinsey & Company (2001) emphasizes the importance of following a process that begins at the top of the pyramid and works down, stating that its capacity-building work with nonprofits has been most successful when larger questions of mission, vision, and values are addressed before the work proceeds to the elements farther down in the pyramid (p. 15).

Thus, capacity building may mean more than making modest enhancements to staff skills or management systems. Like strategic planning, capacity building also may require disruptive transformational change that goes to the basic values and purposes of the organization.

Capacity and Organizational Life Cycles

Let's look at two examples of capacity building in action, undertaken in two different organizations under very different circumstances. Wendy Kopp founded Teach for America in 1989, recruiting recent graduates from top colleges and universities to spend two years teaching in schools serving low-income students before beginning other careers. She attracted hundreds of talented young men and women to her cause, and her organization grew rapidly. But five years later, Teach for America was "on the verge of collapse" (Hauser, 2003). While Kopp's energy and charisma were sufficient to keep the organization running and growing for a time, its lack of organizational structure, management systems, and comprehensive fundraising strategies eventually left it in debt and struggling with problems of communications and morale (Hauser, 2003). After considering the possibility of closing, in 1995, the organization launched an effort to achieve stability. "They … implemented a plan to build a diverse and sustainable funding base, to concentrate on core activities, to introduce much-needed management processes, and to strengthen the [organization's] culture" (Hauser, 2003). It worked. By 2016, Teach for America had programs in 53 regions, 46,000 alumni, and had served 410,000 students (www.teachforamerica.org).

Rubicon Programs, a California-based organization that helps low-income people gain independence and self-sufficiency, did not face a crisis like Teach for America. Rather, its goal in 1994 was to further develop its already successful programs and increase their impact. With support from the Roberts Enterprise Development Fund (now REDF), Rubicon built a measurement system to track client outcomes. The new system made it possible not only to serve more clients and better match programs to their needs but also to accurately report outcomes to funders, and it "fundamentally reshaped the organization's performance culture" by making management and staff focus on social impact. By 2000, Rubicon had quadrupled its staff, achieved financial self-sufficiency, and increased the number of people served from 800 to 4,000 (McKinsey & Company, 2001, pp. 55–56). Since 2000, Rubicon has continued to refine its system and to expand its impact. In 2016 alone, it helped more than 670 people find jobs (www.rubiconprograms.org/index.html).

Teach for America and Rubicon programs offer examples of nonprofit organizations at different places in their histories, one struggling to survive and the other aspiring to greater scale and effectiveness. But both represent examples of capacity-building efforts that helped lead to stability, growth, and recognition for performance.

A number of authors have advanced **life cycle** models describing how organizations grow, mature, and may eventually decline. Many are similar and include the same basic stages, identified by different terms (see, e.g., Adizes, 1999; Carlson & Donohoe, 2003; Stevens, 2001). Let's look at one life cycle model of nonprofit organizations, developed by Judith Sharken Simon (2001) and summarized in Table 7.4.

As Table 7.4 suggests, an organization begins as an idea, a dream, often in the mind of its founder. Once chartered as a formal organization, it still resonates with the enthusiasm of the founder and a small group of founding board or staff members, who work to frame its programs, establish some structure, and chart its direction for future growth. Like an adolescent, it may sometimes seem to be in chaos, but raw energy and commitment drive it forward. Once a foundation has been established, the organization may grow as rapidly as an adolescent. It adds new programs, raises more funds, hires more staff, and becomes more

Table 7.4 Life Stages of Nonprofits

Organizational Life Stage	Description of Organization
Stage I: Imagine and inspire	The organization has not yet been founded; it is still an idea or a dream. This stage is characterized by enthusiasm, energy, and creativity.
Stage II: Found and frame	The organization is created and begins to frame its program. There is still great enthusiasm and energy.
Stage III: Ground and grow	The organization is building its foundation and growing. There is an emphasis on accountability, but rapid growth can be challenging to management.
Stage IV: Produce and sustain	The organization is mature and stable. It may be on autopilot. There is the risk of becoming stale, and maintaining momentum is a concern.
Stage V: Review and renew	The organization revisits its mission and programs and undertakes change. Minor changes may take it back to Stage IV. Major changes may take it back to Stage II. Returning to one of the earlier stages then may lead to renewed and continued growth.

Source: Based on Simon (2001).

systematic in its approach. It will place greater emphasis on measuring results and ensuring accountability as it approaches maturity. Just as with individuals, organizational maturity has its risks. The organization may be stable, its programs churning along in an effective way, its systems operating so well that it runs almost on autopilot. But there is the risk of complacency, bureaucracy, stagnation, and decline.

Simon's (2001) concept of **life stages** is a more optimistic one than some models depict. For example, in Susan Stevens's (2001) model, the final stage is "terminal"! In Simon's model, the organization proceeds from an idea to existence as a mature organization and then has the capacity to renew itself and return to an earlier stage of growth. But there are threats at every stage. A new organization may not have sufficient resources or skills to survive past its childhood. It may be unable to raise enough funds; attract enough volunteers or staff; or keep pace with the competition offered by older, more established organizations in its field. The organization's leadership may not be able to manage the period of rapid growth. For example, Chapter 5 discussed the risk of founder syndrome, in which a founding CEO is unable or unwilling to step aside when the organization's growth demands a different set of management skills. Systems and skills may lag behind the demands placed on them by expanding programs, and quality may deteriorate. Chaos may reign, and the organization may collapse during this period.

John Brothers and Anne Sherman (2012) describe nonprofit life cycles in terms of an arc, depicting a rise and then a decline. Some high-arc organizations may proceed through the life stages rapidly, perhaps growing too quickly in the early stages and then facing a precipitous decline. Others are low arc, that is, their rise is slower and more deliberate; the conditions for potential decline arise more slowly, providing more time to adjust and avoid the worst case (p. 9).

If the organization survives to the stage of maturity, it may be in danger of losing its edge. A mature organization might not have the energy and innovativeness of its early years. It may become a lumbering bureaucracy. Its staff could just be going through the motions. It might not confront the need for change. It may be unprepared to respond to changes in its environment, to the loss of a key source of support, or to shifting patterns of community needs. If it does not move to the stage of "review and renew," it may stagnate, decline, and eventually expire (Simon, 2001).

This suggests that a focus on capacity is important at every stage of an organization's life but that the elements of capacity that are most relevant may be different in each stage. A young organization may need to be concerned primarily with honing its mission, developing its core program, securing funds, and ensuring accountability (Brothers & Sherman, 2012, p. 7). A growing organization may need to devote attention to its infrastructure, for example, its human resources and IT systems (p. 7). A mature organization may be primarily concerned with its "impact expansion," focusing capacity building on its external capacities, such as fundraising and advocacy (p. 7). A mature organization facing potential decline may need to return to its aspirations in order to renew the enthusiasm and energy of its earlier years, revive growth, and ensure its continued relevance and survival (Simon, 2001).

In a study of 318 nonprofits, Light (2004b) discovered that the types of capacity-building activities undertaken do vary according to the organization's size and age. He found that younger organizations are more likely than older ones to develop collaborations with other organizations and undertake organizational assessments but are less likely to focus their capacity building on media relations, reorganization, team building, leadership development, or the implementation of new information or personnel systems (p. 60). Older and larger organizations in Light's (2004b) study were more likely to "behave like weight-conscious organizations: They adopt capacity-building approaches designed to counter bureaucratic encrustation," including reorganization, team building, leadership development, changes in their personnel systems, staff training, and program evaluation (p. 60). Strategic planning also is more likely to be used by older and larger nonprofits than by younger and smaller ones and is an approach that may enable them to break out from a stage of maturity and potential stagnation to a period of renewed growth.

Capacity Building Evaluated

Like strategic planning, capacity building offers many benefits, but it is also important to note its limitations. Does it work? In a 2013 study of nonprofits that received support under the federal government's Compassion Capital Fund Demonstration Program, Amy Minzner, Jacob Klerman, Carrie Markovitz, and Barbara Fink (2014) found that capacity-building efforts had indeed increased the capacity of the organizations that participated. But some people raise a more fundamental question: Does capacity building really affect an organization's effectiveness or impact? A positive answer may seem intuitive. How could improved governance, strengthened leadership, better systems and facilities, more highly trained staff, and an adaptive culture *not* lead to the more effective delivery of programs and a better performing organization? Indeed, some scholars have proposed theories for examining the link between capacity and outcomes. But Minzner et al. concluded in 2014 that there had been "virtually no work" on finding evidence of such a link (p. 550). Light (2004b) concludes that greater capacity does lead to increased effectiveness. He acknowledges that it may be difficult to measure effectiveness directly but argues that increased effectiveness will be reflected in perceptions, trust, and confidence in the organization. However, his evidence of the link between capacity and effectiveness is based on the perceptions of nonprofit employees who participated in his study. He acknowledges that "perceptions are always affected by self-interest" but nevertheless concludes that "given the lack of objective data for measuring nonprofit capacity and effectiveness, perceptions will have to do for now" (p. 15).

Others remain somewhat skeptical. Based on their research, Lewis Faulk & Mandy Stewart (2017) conclude that general capacity building has a positive impact on some aspects of organizations, but more targeted efforts did not show the same benefits. In their study of high-impact nonprofits, Leslie Crutchfield and Heather Grant (2012) also question the appropriate emphasis to be placed on capacity, writing that "textbook strategies like relentless fundraising, well-connected boards, and effective management are necessary … [but] they are hardly sufficient" (pp. 35–36). They explain that some of the organizations identified in their study as those with high impact are, indeed, not especially well managed or focused on internal capacity. Rather, they are "satisfied with building a 'good enough' organization and then spending their time and energy focused externally on catalyzing large-scale systemic change." Crutchfield and Grant conclude that "Great organizations work *with and through others* to create more impact than they ever could achieve alone" (p. 36). We will look more closely at nonprofits' collaboration and partnerships with others in the next chapter.

Managing Risk

An important element of capacity that has received increasing attention in recent years is the organization's ability to systematically manage risk. As Melanie Lockwood Herman (2011) defines the concept, risk is "a measure of the possibility that the future may be surprisingly different from what we expect" (p. 5). **Risk management** requires identifying scenarios that could negatively impact the organization and then devising policies and controls to either prevent those events from occurring or to provide a plan of action if one does occur.

We usually think about risk in terms of unexpected negative events. For example, a major donor or sponsor could withdraw support, precipitating a budget crisis or that costs of a program might exceed projections for some unforeseen reason. An organization dependent on government funding might be impacted by budget cuts, or earned income revenues might decline if the economy goes into a recession. A decline in the overall economy and the stock market also could adversely affect gift revenue and the value of endowment. Unfortunately, there is always the risk of financial fraud and abuse by a volunteer or executive. A volunteer, client, or staff member may be treated unfairly or unethically. That could have negative consequences for the organization's reputation and, in addition, that person might bring legal action that would result in a financial payment. And, of course, there are the risks that most people would think about when the term is mentioned—the building could burn down or someone could slip and fall on the sidewalk, creating liability.

Herman (2011) emphasizes that while nonprofit boards and CEOs often think about such negative risks, they may often fail to prepare for a positive surprise. Remember that risk means simply a variation from what was expected, so it could go in either direction. In this broader view, risk is perhaps better thought about as uncertainty. For example, suppose the organization receives an unexpected large bequest or an unprecedented inflow of funds, such as the $115 million that the ALS Association received from the Ice Bucket Challenge in 2014 (ALS Association, 2017)? Will it have a plan for how to absorb and effectively use the windfall? And how will it handle the possibility that regular donors might stop giving because they think all of the organization's needs have been met? Herman (p. 9) writes that boards and CEOs need to consider and prepare to address possible future events from three perspectives: direction (meaning negative or positive); probability (that is, how likely it is to occur); and magnitude (in other words, how serious its impact is likely to be).

The most common risks that concern nonprofit organizations generally fall into one of four categories:

- People: Board members, volunteers, employees, clients, donors, and the general public

- Property: Buildings, facilities, equipment, materials, copyrights, and trademarks

- Income: Sales, grants, and contributions

- Goodwill: Reputation, stature in the community, and the ability to raise funds and appeal to prospective volunteers ("A primer on risk management," 2007)

Some of these specific areas of risk are discussed in greater detail in other chapters of this text where they are most relevant. For example, Chapter 4 describes risks that members of nonprofit governing boards may incur in connection with their fiduciary responsibilities. Chapter 9 includes a discussion of human resource management and policies intended to prevent violations of employment law and employee rights as well as risks associated with the engagement of volunteers. Most risks have some financial implications and some are particularly related primarily to the management of financial resources. Chapter 12 includes further consideration of financial policies and controls that well-managed organizations adopt.

In the context of this chapter's focus on strategy and capacity, two points are essential to a broader understanding of risk management. First, risk management should not be an afterthought, but rather a "discipline for dealing with uncertainty" (Herman, 2011, p. 32). A disciplined approach to risk management could include establishing risk management goals, creating a risk management committee or task force, and establishing a risk management plan (Herman, 2011, pp. 33–34). In other words, risk management involves an important component of organizational capacity.

Second, while many people likely think of risk as synonymous with specific events, Herman (2011) emphasizes that a nonprofit should take a broader view—risk is the possibility that the organization will not achieve its mission. Risk management is not just about *avoiding* risk. Rather, as the term suggests, it is about *managing* risk in a thoughtful and proactive way. David O. Renz ("From Risk Management to Risk Leadership," 2017a) argues that nonprofit boards are often too "risk averse," which may cause them to "continue operations in program areas beyond the time when they are really delivering the greatest value to and for the stakeholder and client communities they exist to serve" (p. 16). That may seem like a safer course than moving to new or innovative programs, which may entail more risk but also may better serve clients' needs. He suggests that discussion of risk needs to be part of strategic planning. And, rather than regard risk as something to be avoided altogether, or left to management, boards should consider what is acceptable risk, as part of the generative mode of governance discussed in Chapter 4. Renz (p. 17) maintains that the central question should be "are [we] preparing to address the risks that could be problems, and are [we] preparing to *take the risks* [italics added] that might position [our] organization more effectively and successfully for its next generation of service?"

In a special issue of their magazine devoted to the subject, the editors of *Nonprofit Quarterly* suggest that risks may be viewed on a continuum ("Sorting Nonprofit Risk and Uncertainty," 2017). At one end are predictable risks. For example, losing a major funder, having a CEO resign, or having a fire in the headquarters building are things we know could happen and we can be prepared, perhaps by diversifying funding sources, developing an executive succession plan, and maintaining insurance. Other risks are unpredictable, for example, something like 9/11 or Hurricane Harvey in 2017, bringing about devastation and turmoil that most could not imagine. It is difficult for any organization to fully prepare for such eventualities, but maintaining a network of funders and other partners may at least provide resources to which an organization can turn should something unpredictable occur ("Sorting Nonprofit Risk and Uncertainty," 2017, p. 11). Between the two extremes, in the middle of the continuum, are risks that may be inherent to the work that nonprofits do—addressing challenging problems in a time of change, even working to bring about such change, without the guidance of any established models or history. As the *Nonprofit Quarterly* editors suggest, "Sometimes the uncertainty in a space like that is overwhelming and must be balanced by hope, informed by as much information about variables and models as can be mustered, and sometimes by a sense that there is nothing else to be done" (p. 12).

CHAPTER SUMMARY

Strategy is an abstract concept that may simply mean a direction or a new, innovative approach to getting from one place to another. It may arise from a leader's vision, incrementally from smaller decisions the organization makes one at a time, or from a formal analytical approach such as strategic planning.

Strategic planning is a process that many nonprofit organizations have adopted from the business world. It is a useful tool for organizations in designing their futures but may not be appropriate in every situation. Strategic management is a broader concept that links the goals of the strategic plan to decisions on managerial matters such as program design, budgeting, organizational structure, human resource development, and evaluation.

There are many different models for strategic planning, and most organizations practice a hybrid of different approaches. One well-known version is the Harvard policy model, on which many alternative models are based. Most start with clarification of the organization's mandates, mission, vision, and values. The opportunities and threats presented by the external environment are compared with the organization's internal strengths and weaknesses (the SWOT analysis) in order to identify strategic issues or questions on which the planners need to focus. Broad goals are then established, and strategies, programs, and objectives are developed to achieve them. Operational plans are written to set specific timetables and accountability for the achievement of the objectives according to the plan.

With appropriate modifications in vocabulary, tools that businesses use to analyze their competitive environment may be adapted to help nonprofits identify strategies. Bell et al. offer a matrix that can help identify strategic imperatives based on the profitability of a program and its impact on achievement of the mission. A portfolio analysis model developed by MacMillan suggests generic strategies under scenarios defined by the organization's strengths or competitive position, the desirability of various programs, and the extent to which other organizations are providing similar coverage.

Some critics of strategic planning argue that it may lead to setting goals but not a strategy, that it is time-consuming and may distract the organization from current opportunities and problems, and that its periodic nature does not permit an organization to be responsive and flexible in real time in a fast-changing environment. Strategic planning is not a panacea for all problems. It may not be appropriate for some organizations at some points in their history, and it cannot substitute for vision or leadership. But, properly executed, strategic planning can bring many benefits.

A nonprofit organization's capacity includes all of the resources it uses to pursue its mission. An organization's capacity is not an indivisible quality; rather, there are various elements of capacity—or capacities—that it might concentrate on strengthening. These elements include internal systems as well as external relationships and more abstract qualities of the organization, such as its culture and capacity for innovation. There are tools for identifying components of capacity that need to be strengthened and models for undertaking such activity. One such model, provided by McKinsey & Company, emphasizes the importance of beginning with "aspirations" (mission, vision, and values) before proceeding to examine such elements as strategies, financial resources, business processes, and organizational structure. The McKinsey framework also emphasizes that capacity building occurs in the overall context of an organization's culture.

Some theorists describe life cycles of nonprofit organizations. The type of capacity building that is needed differs at various stages. Whether capacity building increases organizational effectiveness remains a debated question and some researchers advocate spending more time and energy on catalyzing large-scale systemic change by working with others.

Risk management has become an important area of nonprofit management. Although many people may think about risk in a narrow way as the potential for legal or financial liability, judgements about how much risk to accept is related to the broader question of how to achieve the mission. Management of risk should be formalized and is an important component of an organization's capacity.

KEY TERMS AND CONCEPTS

CASE 7.1 New Hope Housing Strategic Plan 2013–2018

The following is a summary of the 2013–2018 strategic plan of New Hope Housing (2017), a nonprofit organization in Northern Virginia, founded in 1977, that provides shelter, transitional, and permanent housing for homeless families and single adults.

INTRODUCTION

New Hope Housing has demonstrated over 35 years of innovative and award-winning programs and services assisting homeless families and individuals in our northern Virginia community. Our founders saw a need and responded, opening the first homeless shelter in Fairfax County, Mondloch House, in 1978. Since that beginning, New Hope Housing has added programs and services, always in response to needs in the community.

New Hope Housing continuously assesses its programs and services, evaluating how best to focus its future work for greatest impact. In recent years New Hope Housing has been deeply involved in collaborative efforts across northern Virginia jurisdictions striving to end and prevent homelessness. As these efforts are underway, new approaches are developed, and greater emphasis placed on prevention, rapid re-housing and housing-first approaches, New Hope Housing has reevaluated the priorities for its future work. These priority areas, outlined here, will guide the work of the agency over the next four-to-six-year period. The Strategic Plan 2013–2018 presents the principles that ground the agency's work, the assumptions that underlie the plan, and the strategic directions going forward.

GROUNDING PRINCIPLES

Vision: The vision we work for is a home and bright future for every man, woman and child in our community.

Mission: New Hope Housing provides homeless families and individuals shelter and the tools to build a better life.

Our Core Values:

- We renew hope that homelessness is solvable.
- We welcome all, including the unwelcome.
- We treat each person with dignity and respect.
- We believe that a competent and dedicated staff is critical to our mission.

- We are effective stewards of the human and financial resources entrusted to us.
- We are a community-based organization.

Planning Assumptions:

- We will continue to be an organization focused on ending homelessness among both families and single adults in our community.
- We will continue to serve persons who are difficult to serve and/or underserved persons with extremely low income, persons with disabling conditions, persons with violent criminal records, and others who are therefore less likely to receive services as readily through other agencies.
- We will focus any new program development primarily within the footprint of existing programs and services—southeastern Fairfax County, the City of Alexandria, the City of Falls Church, and Arlington County—to maintain a geographically cohesive service area.
- We will focus on assisting persons at imminent risk of homelessness to remain housed, on reducing time spent in shelter, on "rapid re-housing" of persons who are homeless, on the "housing first" approach in serving chronically homeless persons, and on providing ongoing services to these individuals and families once they are housed.
- Government sources of funding will remain static or decrease. Long-term planning for major new activities must consider how new revenue can be secured, including increased private support.

STRATEGIC DIRECTIONS

Strategic Direction A: New Hope Housing (NNH) will demonstrate leadership in developing and implementing effective approaches in moving homeless persons quickly to stable housing.

- Implement and evaluate the impact during FY2014 of the Emergency Solutions Grant rental subsidy program in the City of Alexandria.
- Reduce time in shelter by 5% annually, from 2011 baseline through 2016.

- o Next Steps Family Program; FY2011 baseline, 142 days

- o Alexandria Community Shelter, Families; FY2011 baseline, 121 days

- o Eleanor U. Kennedy Shelter; FY2011 baseline, 76 days

- o Alexandria Community Shelter, single adults; FY2011 baseline, 57 days.

- Increase exit to permanent housing from shelter and transitional housing from 15.5% to 25% for single adults and from 50% to 60% for families by the end of FY2016.

Strategic Direction B: New Hope Housing will work to increase the number of permanent supportive housing for underserved homeless populations.

- By end of FY2015, place 90% of chronically homeless adults with Bridging Affordability I subsidies in permanent supportive housing (PSH) or permanent housing without subsidy.

- By the end of FY2018 add at least eight beds of PSH for chronically homeless single adults in the City of Alexandria and six beds in Fairfax County.

- Advocate for passage of a residential studio unit (RSU) amendment to the Fairfax zoning ordinance, using Mondloch Place as an example of a successful RSU.

Strategic Direction C: New Hope Housing will work to raise awareness of homelessness in our community and promote our efforts to address it. We will advocate for policies that strive to end homelessness in the communities we serve.

- Promote New Hope Housing's core mission, vision, and values in our community through advocacy.

- Encourage board members to deepen their connection to NNH's mission through volunteerism and advocacy.

  - o Work with New Hope staff to provide board members with regular opportunities for volunteerism and advocacy.

- Organizationally strengthen the Advocacy Committee to create "advocates" among board members.

- o Implement curriculum for each board member to deliver short mission pitch for NHH.

- o Seek opportunities for board members to present to civic organizations, faith communities, and prospective funders.

- Implement advocacy plan for local governments where NHH operates.

  - o Fairfax County focus

  - o Alexandria City

  - o State and federal as appropriate

- Develop PR/marketing plan for NHH by 12/31/13.

  - o Hire a communications director by 12/31/13.

  - o Social media

  - o NHH operation areas (Fairfax/Alexandria)

Strategic Direction D: New Hope Housing will optimize its effectiveness and viability.

- Emphasize staff support, development, and recognition.

  - o Raise staff salaries in FY2015 and beyond.

  - o Continue employee recognition program.

  - o Reinstate tuition reimbursement in FY2015. Reinstate 5% contribution on 403(b) by FY2016.

- Prepare for leadership change/succession.

  - o Develop plan of action for future leadership succession, and provide proposed plan to the board by June 2014.

  - o Develop an annual leadership and professional development plan for identified staff by FY2015.

- Evaluate the organization's infrastructure and develop steps for strengthening in accord with findings.

  - o Review, update, and standardize all position descriptions by the end of FY2014.

  - o Develop measurable outcomes for board review (dashboard) by December 31, 2014.

- Ensure the financial stability and sustainability of the organization.

  o Meet annual fundraising budget.

  o Develop revenue projections by each April for the following fiscal year. Resource development committee responsibility.

  o Assess staffing needs for resource development by the end of FY2014. Implement by December 31, 2014.

  o Increase the number of individual donors at the President's Circle level ($1,000) or above, from 51 in FY2011 to at least 100 by the end of FY2015.

  o Develop a prospecting strategy for deeper penetration for major donors.

  o Develop a case statement by September 1, 2014.

Approved by the New Hope Housing Board of Directors, 2013

Source: New Hope Housing website (http://www.newhope-housing.org/about/strategic-plan/).

Questions Related to Case 7.1

1. What might have been the strengths, weaknesses, opportunities, and threats identified in the process that developed the plan for New Hope Housing; in other words, can you work backward from the plan summary to determine what the SWOT analysis might have revealed?

2. What are the strategic issues or questions identified by the planners for New Hope Housing?

3. What are the goals and strategies in this plan, consistent with the vocabulary used in this chapter?

4. How are New Hope's assumptions about the environment reflected in its strategic priorities? Are there any strategic directions you might add, based on the assumptions?

5. Which elements of capacity described in the McKinsey & Company capacity-building framework are reflected in the strategic plan of New Hope Housing?

6. What are some of the risks that New Hope Housing should address in its planning?

QUESTIONS FOR DISCUSSION

1. One organization that all students will have some knowledge about is their own college or university. What are the strengths, weaknesses, opportunities, and threats that you see facing your college or university? What strategic issues do you suggest for your institution?

2. Suppose a nonprofit organization's strategy requires that it phase out a program on which few people rely, but those people are vulnerable and no good substitute exists. How might the organization proceed with its plan in an ethical and humane manner?

3. Select an organization that you know well—maybe you work there, have been a volunteer, or just follow it on Twitter. What do you think is the organization's strategy, as that term is discussed in this chapter? What are the principal risks that it needs to address in its risk management plan?

APPENDIX CASES

The following cases in the Appendix of this text include points related to the content of this chapter: Case 1 (New York City Opera); Case 2 (Share Our Strength/No Kid Hungry); Case 3 (The Y); Case 4 (The Girl Scouts of the United States of America).

SUGGESTIONS FOR FURTHER READING

Books/Brochure

Bell, J., Masaoka, J., & Zimmerman, S. (2010). *Nonprofit sustainability: Making strategic decisions for financial viability.* Hoboken, NJ: Wiley.

Brothers, J., & Sherman, A. (2012). *Building nonprofit capacity: A guide to managing change through organizational life cycles.* San Francisco, CA: Jossey-Bass.

Bryson, J. M. (2017). *Strategic planning for public and nonprofit organizations: A guide to strengthening and sustaining organizational achievement.* San Francisco, CA: Jossey-Bass.

Crutchfield, L. R., & Grant, H. M. (2012). *Forces for good: The six practices of high-impact nonprofits* (Rev. ed.). San Francisco, CA: Jossey-Bass.

Herman, M. L. (2011). *Ready or not: A risk management guide for nonprofit executives.* Leesburg, VA: Nonprofit Risk Management Center.

McKinsey & Company. (2013). *The organizational capacity assessment tool (OCAT): 2.0* [Brochure]. Retrieved from https://mckinseyonsociety.com/downloads/tools/OCAT/OCAT_brochure_v6.pdf

Articles

Bilich, T. (2016, July 13). A call for nonprofit risk management. *Stanford Social Innovation Review.* Retrieved from https://ssir.org/articles/entry/a_call_for_nonprofit_risk_management

Chen, C., & Bozeman, B. (2012, March). Organizational risk aversion: Comparing the public and non-profit sectors. *Public Management Review, 14*(3), 377–402.

Websites

Alliance for Nonprofit Management: http://www.allianceonline.org/

The Bridgespan Group: http://www.bridgespan.org/

Grantmakers for Effective Organizations: http://www.geofunders.org/

La Piana Consulting: http://www.lapiana.org/

Nonprofit Risk Management Center: https://www.nonprofitrisk.org/

Venture Philanthropy Partners: http://venturephilanthropypartners.org/

Pressures to collaborate and merge are unlikely to abate as nonprofits face an increasingly competitive environment and there is a nationwide focus on performance and accountability.

iStock/courtneyk

Chapter Outline

Collaborations, Partnerships, and Mergers

As we discussed in the previous chapter, the purpose of strategic planning and capacity building is to increase the effectiveness of a nonprofit organization in achieving its mission. But, as Leslie Crutchfield and Heather Grant (2012) conclude, "Building an organization is only part of the story. [High-impact] *nonprofits work with and through other organizations—and they have much more impact than if they acted alone*" (p. 128). In this chapter, let's shift our attention from the effectiveness of individual organizations to focus on the effectiveness of the nonprofit sector as a whole and how it may be enhanced through collaboration—between and among nonprofit organizations as well as across the nonprofit, public, and business sectors. We will also look at what might be considered the ultimate form of collaboration—the merger of two or more nonprofit organizations.

First, we need to clarify some terms and concepts and establish some boundaries for our discussion. The vocabulary surrounding this topic is not always consistent (McLaughlin, 2010). For example, it is not unusual to see the terms collaboration and partnership used interchangeably to describe any relationship in which two or more organizations are working together in some way. But some authors make a distinction between these concepts, with partnership meaning something more formal than collaboration. For example, if one day, you and your neighbor work together to rake leaves from a small park that adjoins both of your properties, that is collaboration. If you agree that you will regularly take turns raking the park, that arrangement may be more like a partnership, especially if for some reason you decide to formalize it in a written agreement.

As John Forrer, James Kee, and Eric Boyer (2014) explain, collaborations involve "the voluntary linking of organizations … in a common effort that involves a sharing of information, resources, activities, capabilities, risks and decision-making aimed to achieve an agreed to … outcome that would have been difficult or impossible to achieve by one organization acting alone" (p. 9). Both collaborations and partnerships involve a mutuality of interests and responsibilities. As Derick Brinkerhoff and Jennifer Brinkerhoff (2011) explain,

> Mutuality refers to mutual dependence, and entails the respective rights and responsibilities of each actor

Learning Objectives

After reading this chapter, students should be able to:

1. Define various types of relationships between and among nonprofit organizations.

2. Explain the potential advantages and disadvantages of various types of nonprofit collaboration.

3. Identify conditions that may enhance or diminish the likelihood of successful nonprofit collaborations or mergers.

4. Define various types of cross-sector collaboration.

5. Identify conditions that may enhance or diminish the likelihood of successful cross-sector collaboration.

6. Explain the advantages and disadvantages of various types of cross-sector collaboration from the perspective of managers in the nonprofit sector.

7. Identify circumstances affecting the success or failure of collaborations.

8. Analyze cases, applying concepts from the chapter.

vis-à-vis the others. Embedded in mutuality is a joint commitment to the partnership's goals, and their alignment to be consistent with each partner organization's mission and objectives. Mutuality also means some degree of equality in decision-making, as opposed to domination of one or more partners. All partners have an opportunity to influence their shared goals, processes, outcomes, and evaluation. (p. 4)

Some authors use additional terms to define relationships between and among organizations, making even finer distinctions than the one between collaboration and partnership. Thomas McLaughlin (2010) calls the simplest type of collaboration affiliations and identifies those that are more complex as alliances, which he considers to be basically synonymous with networks (p. 51). He uses the term merger to describe an integration of corporate entities. As Figure 8.1 depicts, La Piana Consulting (2018) calls simple relationships collaborations, but uses the terms alliances and strategic restructuring to encompass more

Figure 8.1 The Collaborative Map

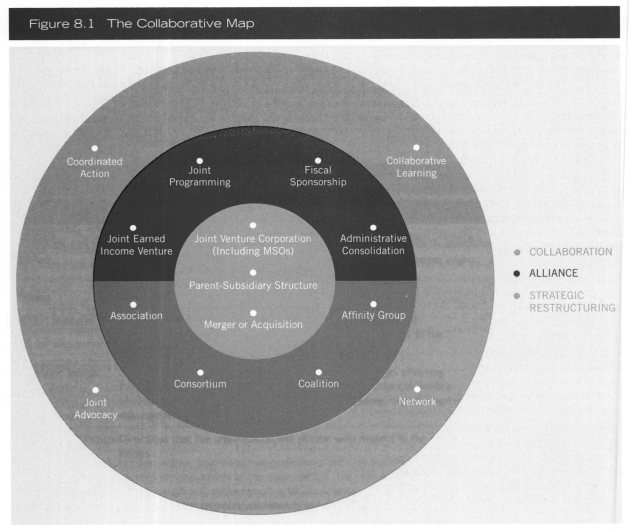

Source: La Piana Consulting (2018). *The collaborative map.* Retrieved from http://lapiana.org/insights-for-the-sector/insights/collaboration-and-strategic-restructuring/collaborative-map. Used with permission.

complex relationships, including mergers. We'll return to discuss this model in more detail shortly.

To keep things simple, except where finer distinctions are relevant to the particular point under discussion, this chapter just uses **collaboration** as a generic term to mean separate organizations working together and **merger** to mean the corporate integration of one or more nonprofits.

In addition to collaborating with each other, many nonprofits also have relationships with the government and with for-profit companies. Again, it is important to maintain some clear definitions. For example, if the government simply contracts with a nonprofit to provide a specific service, that is not collaboration. The government is a **principal** and the nonprofit is its **agent**, serving the government's interests and purposes. In collaboration, the relationship is that of a principal to a principal, since power, decision making, and risk are shared (Forrer et al., pp. 31–32). As H. Brinton Milward and Keith Provan (2016, p. 232) note, "The idea behind contracting is exactly the opposite of collaboration—competition, where two or more organizations are forced to compete for the contract." However, Forrer et al. note that, in contrast to "classic or traditional" contracts, which entail principal–agent relationships, some contracting between government and nonprofits does have characteristics of collaboration, since there is a "mutual dependence in the relationship" (p. 59).

Nonprofits may have a variety of relationships with corporations; four basic types include **philanthropic collaborations**, **strategic collaborations**, **commercial collaborations**, and **political collaborations** (Galaskiewicz & Colman, 2006). Some nonprofits also have **operational relationships** with companies, for whom they may serve as a supplier or a source of labor (Sagawa & Segal, 2000). This chapter discusses collaboration among nonprofit organizations and also cross-sector collaborations in which nonprofits, businesses, and government work together. Corporate philanthropy is discussed as a separate topic in Chapter 12. Discussion of commercial and operational relationships between nonprofits and corporations is deferred to Chapter 13, which considers nonprofit earned-income strategies.

Growing Interest in Collaboration

Just as capacity building became a movement in the 2000s, much of the national dialog about the nonprofit sector in the 2010s has emphasized the need for collaboration. This is true for various reasons. For one, the number of nonprofit organizations has grown rapidly in recent decades, with the number of public charities growing 19.5 percent between 2003 and 2013 (McKeever, 2015). This trend has prompted some to say that there are too many nonprofits competing for the same limited funds, with too few having the capacity to grow to scale or effectively meet the needs of society or their clients. Some have called for mergers among nonprofits in order to reduce the duplication of services and to create larger, stronger organizations with the capacity to make a greater impact. For example, McLaughlin (2010) argues,

> the plain fact is that having an excess number of nonprofit organizations actually weakens the collective power of the entire field. Organizations that should be serving a mission must instead spend disproportionate amounts of resources worrying about how they are going to fund it, manage it, and perpetuate it. (p. xvi)

McLaughlin also argues that most models of service delivery now have been well established and that there is less need for program innovation than in the past. "Innovation," he says, "is shifting to the way those programs are managed" (p. xv).

Prominent among the advocates of mergers in the nonprofit sector are funders, including foundations, a number of which have provided grants to support collaboration and mergers. But some people say that foundations also have been part of the problem, because they prefer to support new initiatives rather than provide ongoing, core support to organizations. Critics also cite cases in which foundations have responded to mergers by reducing their grants—using the merger as an "exit strategy"—rather than by providing adequate support to the combined entity (Gammal, 2007, p. 51).

As discussed later in this chapter, there are significant obstacles to mergers and, indeed, their number has not increased significantly, even in periods of economic difficulty (Milway, Orozco, & Botero, 2014). And not everyone is enthusiastic about the need for mergers. Some observers say that small organizations may stay in closer touch with their communities and are likely to provide more personal service than their larger, more bureaucratic counterparts (Gose, 2005). Others argue that competition in the nonprofit sector is as beneficial as in others, "providing checks and balances and protecting vulnerable populations from being exploited" (Gammal, 2007, p. 50).

David La Piana (2010), a consultant who works with nonprofits and an author, agrees that there are inefficiencies in the sector, but he argues that they often can be reduced through collaborations between and among existing organizations, obviating the need for mergers. He calls the claim that there should be fewer nonprofits "too simplistic," arguing that the pressure on funders occurs not because there are too many nonprofits, but rather because there are too few dollars available to meet community needs (p. 28). He advocates the establishment of various relationships in which nonprofits can work together to increase efficiency, without merging. While the number of nonprofit mergers has remained relatively modest, collaborative relationships have become the norm. In a 2010 survey, 81 percent of organizations reported that they were engaged in some form of collaboration (Milway et al., 2014). Let's take a look at some of the relationships that may be involved.

A Continuum of Relationships

Relationships between and among organizations may be placed along a continuum, from informal cooperation to more formal arrangements and, eventually, possible merger. A simple way to think about the continuum is the **3C model**—cooperation, coordination, collaboration. (Simonin, Samali, Zohdy, & Laidler-Kylander, 2016). Organizations may begin by informally cooperating, then proceed to coordinating their activities, and eventually progress to collaborative endeavors. Each step involves greater engagement and commitment. McLaughlin (2010) describes a similar continuum, with the amount of integration defined by the extent to which the relationship affects organizations' corporate structures, their operations or programs, the distribution of responsibility within them, and their economics or business models (p. 49). He calls his model the "C.O.R.E. Continuum" (p. 49). Movement across this continuum is accompanied by increasing integration of the organizations, which depends on "the nature and the intensity of the commitment that two or more nonprofits must make to each other in order to collaborate using their chosen model" (McLaughlin, 2010, p. 49).

Figure 8.1 portrays a somewhat more complex continuum, developed by La Piana Consulting (2018) and identified as "The Collaborative Map." The outer circle encompasses simple collaborations, for example, belonging to a common network, collaborative learning, coordinated action, and joint advocacy. Such relationships do not disturb the autonomy of the participating organizations and may not be permanent arrangements. Somewhat more complex relationships, which La Piana Consulting (2018) calls alliances, include **administrative consolidations**, **joint programming**, **joint earned income ventures**, and others. Such relationships are more than ad hoc; they require a commitment to the future and generally will involve written agreements. Decision making is shared by the participating organizations, but these are still relationships between or among organizations that remain separate corporations. La Piana places such alliances in two categories: "1) those that involve doing some part of your nuts-and-bolts business together (such as programming, administration, or revenue generation), and 2) those that are really more about working together to have an impact on the field, for example through advancement of a social change agenda or work to strengthen organizations with a particular issue or geographic focus" (La Piana Consulting, 2018).

In the center of the map is **strategic restructuring** These relationships go beyond collaboration and alliances and require "a structural change or the creation of a new entity" (La Piana Consulting, 2018). In other words, these relationships involve a change in corporate structure or control of the participating organizations. We might be inclined to think of **corporate integrations** as being synonymous with mergers, but not all go that far. They may involve **joint venture corporations**, the creation of **management service organizations (MSOs)** that support one or more nonprofits, and **parent–subsidiary structures**. These types of relationships imply reduced autonomy for participating organizations, since at least some decision making is transferred from the individual nonprofits to another corporate entity, but the organizations still maintain their separate charters and identities. Of course, in the case of a merger, there is a change in control and structure that usually involves the total dissolution of one or more of the former organizations (La Piana Consulting, 2018).

Sometimes, but not always, one thing may lead to another. Collaboration between two organizations eventually may lead toward the center of the map, involving more formal relationships and perhaps ultimately a merger, just as dating may lead to engagement and eventually to marriage. For example, two organizations might begin simply by sharing information and referring clients to each other. As they come to know each other better and develop mutual trust, things might progress to sharing office space, consolidating administrative functions, developing joint programs, or undertaking joint ventures. Each step toward the center of the map implies less autonomy for each of the separate organizations and greater integration of their interests and operations. Eventually, the organizations may proceed to merge, giving up their separate identities to operate as a single, larger organization. As with relationships between individuals, some nonprofit collaborations may work well and others may break down at some point along the way, for a variety of reasons that we will discuss soon.

Exploring Collaborations and Mergers

Let's look at a few examples to gain a sense of the nature of the relationships that some nonprofits have developed and see how they fit on the collaborative map just described:

- Two environmental organizations, the River Revitalization Foundation and Friends of Milwaukee's Rivers, were both operating from inadequate space, so they decided to pursue the idea of sharing larger quarters. Their efforts eventually led to the renovation of a facility to create space for eight environmental organizations. Although the organizations remain independent, the sharing of space provides financial benefits as well as an office environment that has improved employee morale (Wasserman, 2005, p. 13).

- The Chicago Youth Centers (CYC) serve children from age three through their school years. Another organization, Family Focus, serves younger children, from birth to age three, in the same geographic area. In addition to sharing some infrastructure, the two organizations were able to coordinate their programs. Family Focus refers children to CYC, providing a "continuum of care from birth through school years." The steady flow of clients from Family Focus also saves CYC recruitment costs, freeing up resources to be devoted to its programs (Stengel, 2013).

- In 2008, the Kentucky Opera and the Louisville Orchestra considered an outright merger but realized it would be difficult. Instead, they decided to combine their administrative responsibilities. Initially, they relocated their back-office operations to a shared space; subsequently, they merged functions such as phone, box office, reception, marketing, and finance. Now two other organizations share the same finance operation. By 2011, the Kentucky Opera marked its second consecutive year with a budget surplus, achieved in part through reduced costs resulting from its collaboration with the other groups (Berkshire, 2011).

- In 2011, the Allston Bright Community Development Corporation and Urban Edge, both Massachusetts organizations that manage low-cost housing projects, created a third corporate entity to manage their combined properties, saving costs and freeing both organizations to focus on the needs of their respective local communities (Berkshire, 2011).

- When a county hospital closed in Milwaukee, many low-income patients lost their source of dental care. They began to visit other clinics, which were soon overloaded. The Madre Angela Dental Clinic was established as a new entity to meet the need. It is a collaborative effort of three hospitals in Milwaukee, Marquette University, several local nonprofits, and volunteers. An advisory board of representatives from participating organizations oversees the clinic, and the role of each is spelled out in written agreements (Wasserman, 2005).

- The Cancer Wellness Center, Wellness House, Cancer Support Center, and Wellness Place are four independent nonprofits in the Chicago area that provide support to breast cancer patients. They are sufficiently far apart that they do not compete for patients, but they had been competing for corporate and foundation support, and each of them lacked sufficient visibility to gain referrals of patients from the area's major hospitals. They began cooperating to increase their combined visibility, then after a decade created a consortium to present themselves to the public as a single entity. Finally, they created a fifth nonprofit, the Cancer Health Alliance of Metropolitan Chicago, that promotes and helps support all four organizations (Haider, 2007).

- Three geographically contiguous hospice providers in the Chicago area faced increasing competition from for-profit companies in the field. They merged in 2015 to create JourneyCare, now the largest provider in Illinois. The merger produced efficiencies, increased impact, and strengthened competitive advantage (Haider, 2017).

The examples above illustrate various points on La Piana's (2018) collaborative map: eight organizations sharing space while remaining independent; two organizations cooperating to serve clients; four organizations maintaining independent programs but merging their back-office operations; two organizations creating a third organization to provide management services; three organizations collaborating to offer a new service; four organizations creating a fifth to pursue shared goals; and three organizations merging to become one. Each step entails a reduction in the autonomy of individual organizations and increasing entanglements among them; in other words, some organizations are living together as roommates, others have become partners, and some are getting married.

Drivers of Collaborations and Mergers

Collaborations and mergers among nonprofit organizations may offer benefits to society, nonprofit clients, and the sector as a whole, but what are the potential gains for the organizations themselves? In other words, what might motivate an organization to seek a relationship with another?

Think back on some of the organizational theory we discussed in Chapter 3. Scholars working from many of the theories we reviewed have offered explanations of nonprofit collaboration consistent with their theoretical perspectives. For example, scholars who work from the resource dependency theory point to resource constraints and the need for organizations to reduce uncertainty in their environments. Those who follow institutional theory explain collaboration in terms of the need for organizations to develop a shared response to problems and to achieve legitimacy (Sowa, 2009). Building on these multiple theoretical approaches, Jessica Sowa conducted a study of 20 collaborations among nonprofits in the field of early child care and education and concluded that the motivations to collaborate were indeed complex, including both anticipated benefits in providing services as well as expected benefits to the individual organizations.

Some authors have identified specific **drivers** of collaboration, that is, forces that may make organizations more inclined to pursue this option. The drivers may be internal or external (Yankey & Willen, 2005). **External drivers** arise from changes in the environment. They might include, for example, increased competition for clients or resources (such as competition for diminished giving and government funding in an economic recession); shifting priorities or demands of private or government funders (who may require collaboration or merger as a condition of continued support); or political changes that could adversely affect a group of organizations, making it advantageous for them to work together to protect their interests.

Internal drivers arise from conditions within an organization. They may involve financial, managerial, and programmatic considerations. For example, a collaboration or merger may enable organizations to reduce overhead costs, increase purchasing power, or perhaps gain better access to loans. Managerial considerations may include the ability to gain access to specialized talent by working with a partner. Merging organizations, or at least consolidating some functions, may make it possible to recruit a more experienced CEO or CFO (chief financial officer) and to pay a more competitive salary. Drivers that are programmatic in nature relate to organizations' ability to enhance or expand their services through collaboration or merger; in other words, they relate to delivery of the mission (Yankey & Willen, 2005). Mendel (2016) also identifies as internal drivers "the passion for collaboration by a nonprofit's key executive" (Mendel, 2016).

Adding another perspective, Dan McCormick (2001) explains an organization's proclivity to collaborate or merge in terms of three driving forces—liability, viability, and survivability (p. 8). Regarding liability, he offers the example of an environmental organization that had acquired land in order to preserve it but found itself burdened with debt it could not manage. Its solution was to merge with a larger organization with a similar mission that could absorb that liability. Although it ceased to exist as an independent organization, its mission of preserving the land was achieved. Another situation that might encourage a collaboration or merger is the diminished viability of an organization, which McCormick defines as "a condition in which your organization may be alive, but [is] not having a positive impact on its mission" (p. 9). Such an organization may be characterized by stagnant fundraising, high staff turnover, and perhaps a gradual erosion of financial position. An organization may decline to the point that its very survivability becomes questionable. That could result from significant financial problems, scandal or controversy, or a change in the environment that makes the mission no longer relevant—for example, discovery of a cure for the disease that the organization existed to combat. This may lead to what McLaughlin (2010) calls a "rescue merger" (p. 26), in which an organization is forced to merge whatever assets remain with those of another, stronger nonprofit as the only alternative to closure. As McCormick (2001) notes, the position at which an organization stands along the continuum—liability, viability, survivability—determines its bargaining power in entering any collaboration or merger it may seek (pp. 11–12).

Obstacles to Collaboration and Merger

Each of the examples of collaboration we considered earlier is one of success, but not all efforts turn out so well. Let's look at some that did not and then consider some of the obstacles and pitfalls that can prevent or complicate such undertakings.

- In 1999, a total of 25 prominent child, youth, and family organizations created the National Call to Action, a collaborative effort to eliminate child abuse by 2020. The relationship started well, but "conflicts over trust and turf ultimately undercut the process" (Kirkpatrick, 2007, p. 46).

- A proposed merger between Operation Smile and Smile Train was cancelled in 2011. Both organizations had the same purpose—providing surgery to correct facial deformities—but pursued different strategies. One sent doctors from the United States to perform surgeries around the world, while the other focused on training local doctors in other countries. Both doctors and donors raised issues about how the combined organization would operate, and the boards voted to stay independent (Sataline, 2011).

- Family Eldercare and Meals on Wheels, both in Austin, Texas, started discussing a merger in 2009. It seemed a natural step, since both groups provided services to older people. But as discussions ensued, it became obvious that the two organizations had very different plans. Family Eldercare wanted to expand its services into the suburbs and to work with people who are disabled. Meals on Wheels wanted to focus on serving low-income seniors within the city. In addition, a judge expressed concern that a merger might endanger Family Eldercare's guardianship program, which managed financial affairs for older people. The two boards decided to end their merger discussion (Sataline, 2011).

- In 2012, Sanford Health, headquartered in South Dakota, and Fairview Health Services, based in Minnesota, began to discuss the possibility of a merger. Fairview included the University of Minnesota Medical Center, which it controlled from a previous merger in 1997. Both entities had substantial assets, about $3 billion each. They were interested in the possibility of a merger in light of changes in the health care environment and the need for hospitals to become larger, integrated systems; in other words, external drivers. When the talks became public, the Minnesota attorney general and some state legislators raised objections. There were a variety of issues, including concerns that nonprofit assets in the State of Minnesota might be transferred to an out-of-state entity. Some were concerned about the implications for the medical costs that patients might face and the implications for medical education in Minnesota. Faced with mounting opposition, Sanford Health announced in 2013 that it was discontinuing the exploration of a merger with Fairview (Wyland, 2013).

As discussed previously, collaborations may be easier to pull off than mergers, since the latter imply a loss of autonomy for the participating organizations. But collaborations and mergers both face some built-in obstacles of which we need to be aware. What differentiates successful from unsuccessful relationships between and among nonprofit organizations? What are some of the obstacles that need to be overcome and pitfalls to be avoided? What are some conditions that may favor a successful relationship? And what may cause some to never get off the ground or eventually crash? Let's look at some of the variables that are involved.

Motivations

As discussed earlier in this book, there is a fundamental difference between for-profit and nonprofit entities. While business corporations may be socially responsible, their primary purpose is to increase the wealth of the owners, whereas the primary purpose of a nonprofit is to achieve its social mission. The shareholders of a corporation thus have a clear and specific interest in the organization, focused on its long-term financial performance. They will evaluate potential partnerships and mergers based on their expected impact on the bottom line. Although some corporate mergers turn out to be colossal mistakes, such failures usually reflect miscalculations about the future of the business rather than confusion or disagreement about purposes or goals.

The stakeholders of a nonprofit do not have a financial interest in the organization and thus evaluate potential relationships by different, more complex criteria. Volunteers and staff may highly value the social relationships surrounding their involvement with the organization and see a potential collaboration or merger with another entity as uncomfortably disruptive and be concerned that a loss of autonomy may reduce their own role. Some volunteers may view the organization as existing in part for their benefit as well as that of clients and may highly value the opportunity that serving as a volunteer provides to express their own social conscience. Even members of the governing board may be reluctant to disrupt existing relationships in the short run, even if there may be financial benefits to the organization in the long run. Both volunteers and staff are usually very committed to the mission and may place less importance on the potential financial or competitive advantages to be gained through collaboration. And, as McCormick (2001) explains, "Mission is an emotional issue. [Nonprofit organization] mission statements are about service and attention to causes, unlike most for-profit counterparts, whose mission statements talk about financial security and market leadership" (p. 6). As some of the examples mentioned at the beginning of this section illustrate, nonprofits may be very committed to their own theories of change, believing that their approach to problems is more appropriate than that of other organizations. Since, as discussed earlier in this text, nonprofit organizations are rooted in values, the commitment of some stakeholders to a particular philosophy may outweigh their concern with efficiency or financial strength.

Culture

In the previous chapter, we discussed the importance of culture. An organization's culture is usually a strong force, and the integration of two or more cultures can be a complex undertaking. As Mendel (2016) observes, successful partnerships require "alignments in operational culture" between or among the partners.

Let's look at an example of a merger in which an alignment of cultures was required and also was not easily achieved. Denise Gammal (2007) describes a merger between the Davis Street Community Center and San Leandro Community Counseling, in California. Davis had practiced a "holistic social welfare model." Counselors met clients off-site and worked to help families deal with a wide range of issues, not just psychological ones. Community Counseling had a "traditional psychotherapeutic model," in which patients came to the office for counseling by psychologists holding PhD degrees. After the merger, the Davis people expected the Community Counseling staff to go out to meet clients, which they resented, while members of the Community Counseling staff were concerned about patient confidentiality and the qualifications of some Davis staff. The merger ultimately survived, but only after most of the original counselors had left and the organization had spent over $100,000 on staff training and development (p. 50).

Language is closely related to culture. For example, the very word merger may carry negative connotations in the nonprofit sector because of its association with the highly publicized consequences of corporate mergers. Influenced by what they hear or read about mergers in the commercial sector, people may tend to focus on what may be lost in a merger—the organization's identity, social relationships, possibly even jobs (McLaughlin, 2010). A study of successful mergers conducted by Northwestern University's Kellogg School of Management, Mission + Strategy Consulting, and eight Chicago-based foundations concluded that how the new relationship was framed affected whether it was ultimately successful. Terms such as "takeover," "deal," or even "merger" could elicit negative feelings. Describing the proposed change as a "combination of equals," a "union of affiliates," or by some other term that may have less negative connotations is more likely to lead to success (Haider, 2017).

Egos

Kirkpatrick (2007) quotes the words of one nonprofit executive: "For all the cause-related work we do … there's a great deal of ego involved in 'my way' of solving the problem" (p. 46). Egos may be a problem, especially if one or more of the organizations is led by a founder whose personal identity may be bound up with that of the organization he or she leads. But as the words of the executive quoted above suggest, the issue may be more than a matter of personal pride. Even nonprofits that pursue similar missions may practice different philosophies or methodologies that they believe to be right and to which volunteers and staff may be strongly committed. For CEOs conditioned by a competitive environment, it may be psychologically difficult to approach any relationship without instinctively protecting the interests of their own organization. For example, in describing the failure of the National Call to Action, one observer recounted that things were going well until "the heads of the [collaborating] national organizations waltzed in. All they wanted to know was 'What's in it for me?' 'How much money do I get?' 'How much money will this take away from my bottom line?'" (Kirkpatrick, p. 46).

Brand Identity

The loss of a nonprofit's unique brand identity can be an obstacle to a merger, especially if an organization has existed for a long time and its name is well-known in its community. In a business merger, loss of a brand name is a concern because it is known to customers. In a nonprofit merger, loss of the name may be an emotional issue that causes reluctance among the board, staff, and members of the community who are loyal to the existing organization (Milway et al., 2014). But if the negotiators recognize the barrier that brand loyalty may present, it may be possible to develop strategies for preserving brand identities. For example, New York's Hillside Family of Agencies has merged nine nonprofits that serve youth, but operates them as business units that maintain the name of the former nonprofit, including Crestwood Children's Center, Snell Farm Children's Center, and Hillside Children's Center (Milway et al., 2014). Failure to respect existing brands may doom a merger despite strong logic behind it.

Community or Political Objections

Potential mergers may be met with objections from community and political leaders. This sometimes may be based on loyalty to an existing organization's identity or to concerns about the implications for services, accountability, and control. Some state attorneys general may raise questions about transferring nonprofit assets, which may be subject to conditions established by donors, whose interests they are responsible for protecting. As illustrated in the case of Sanford Health and Fairview Health Services, "when a business decision becomes a political issue, played out in the media, business considerations become overwhelmed by politics and public opinion" (Wyland, 2013).

Costs

Collaborations and mergers may increase efficiency in the long run, but developing formal relationships also may require the investment of substantial resources. There are the time and opportunity costs of internal analyses and meetings between the potential collaborators. There may be additional legal and accounting fees and other out-of-pocket expenses. If a merger is undertaken, there will be costs involved in the integration of management and information systems, the development of new printed materials, possibly relocation to new facilities, and continued staff development to meld the merged organization together. Full integration may take three years or more and cost more than anticipated (Gammal, 2007). And, as Katie Smith Milway and colleagues (2014) observe, there is a dearth of funding available to meet the costs of due diligence in advance of a merger or the costs of implementation once a merger has been undertaken. The authors' review of foundation grants revealed only $5.3 million given in support of merger activity in 2011 (Milway et al., 2014).

If the relationship does not work out, exit costs also can be high. Moreover, although both organizations should engage in analysis and due diligence before combining, there have been cases in which unforeseen or undiscovered liabilities or problems came back to haunt the new organization after the merger (Yankey & Willen, 2005). What if an attempt at collaboration is not working? Art Taylor (2017), president of the Better Business Bureau Wise Giving Alliance, advises nonprofits to "build rigorous feedback loops" and "fail fast." In other words, if "the project is not achieving expected outcomes, decide quickly if adjustments can salvage it. If not, take the learnings and end the project."

Conditions for Success

Despite the obstacles, successful collaboration and mergers do occur. What are the conditions under which successful relationships are most likely to evolve? The literature offers consistency on several points.

Driven by Mission

Relationships undertaken primarily to advance the mission are more likely to be successful than those undertaken solely for financial reasons or as a response to pressure from funders. Or, as Gammal (2007) expresses it, "in the nonprofit sector, as in the world of human courtship, money is not the right reason to merge. But mission may be" (p. 51). There may be financial benefits to be gained through a relationship, but the most successful are those driven by the opportunity to expand their service in pursuit of a common mission.

Commitment From Top Leadership

The egos of CEOs and board members can be obstacles to successful collaboration, and their commitment to the effort is a necessary condition for success. The configuration of leadership in a merged entity is a particularly sensitive issue. This will involve board leadership positions, the CEO, and managers at other levels. Some board members may have served in anticipation of ascending to leadership positions in the future, a route that now may be blocked by the integration of boards. Unless the board as a whole strongly supports the new relationship, such personal ambitions can become stumbling blocks. Staff will have loyalties to their CEOs or other managers and may undermine the relationship if they perceive that their leaders feel reluctant or skeptical about the change (McCormick, 2001).

Trust

As in human relationships, successful collaboration between or among nonprofit organizations must be built on a foundation of trust. An atmosphere of trust helps "lower the barriers between individuals and organizations, foster the growth of possible relationships, discourage hidden agendas, and promote good-faith negotiations" (Yankey & Willen, 2005, p. 270). The absence of trust is likely to bring all the obstacles to successful collaboration up to maximum strength. It will exacerbate fears about the impact of collaboration or merger on individual positions and careers and cause some to question the shared commitment to mission. Open communication is, of course, a core element of trust. This includes the sharing of objective data and disclosure of liabilities or problems that could surface in later phases of the relationship. Trust may be greater between organizations that have had a previous relationship with one another, that have had successful collaborations with others, that are part of the same professional or information network, and that have linkages at the level of the governing board (Guo & Acar, 2005).

Relatedness

McCormick (2001) says that "mergers appear to work better when the parties involved can find an initial connection built on some tangible relationship" in one of four categories of relatedness: mission, constituency, organization or structure, and geography (p. 21). Although his principles apply to mergers, they could apply as well to any level of collaboration.

Creating a relationship may make sense if two or more organizations have compatible missions and may be illogical if the missions are very different. For example, it might be difficult for an organization focused on women's health to merge with one concerned with men's health; their expertise would likely be related to different diseases, and their funding sources would likely be those with a particular interest in one gender or the other. But a health organization seeking to extend its programs into schools might find it useful to collaborate or merge with an educational organization (McCormick, 2001).

Compatibility of services and competencies may provide a basis for collaboration or merger. In other words, if each organization is good at some things but not others and the potential collaborator can fill in the gaps, both organizations may find collaboration to provide an attractive opportunity to expand the range and quality of services they offer. On the other hand, if their competencies are much the same and they traditionally have been competitors, this variable may offer a hindrance rather than an incentive (McLaughlin, 2010).

Organizations that serve the same or similar constituencies may have rather obvious opportunities to combine efforts, but as McCormick (2001) emphasizes, **constituency relatedness** needs to be considered in broad terms. Thus, two advocacy organizations that lobby the same individuals or agencies may find it beneficial to combine efforts, since "in seeking political clout, bigger is definitely better" (McCormick, p. 25). So, for example, two nonprofits that lobby for environmental legislation, each having a million members, might get more attention from Congress by presenting themselves under one banner representing two million member voters. They might work together in lobbying, even though their programs might be quite different.

Geographic proximity may suggest the potential for collaboration or merger, perhaps eliminating confusion among clients or donors. Such relationships also may be a strategy by which a nonprofit can extend its reach into new markets, perhaps contiguous cities, towns, or regions (McLaughlin, 2010). In sum, collaborations and mergers that have a natural logic to them are more likely to succeed than those that are forced or contrived.

Process

Research indicates that successful nonprofit collaboration requires sufficient time to develop and that following the right process is critical. Indeed, "the process through which the [relationship] is developed and operationalized has a significant impact on the likelihood of its success" (Yankey & Willen, 2005, p. 269). Trying to consummate a relationship too quickly may result in insufficient attention to the concerns of some constituencies or to potential pitfalls that may be lurking.

Various scholars have described a process for the development of relationships through stages. While their vocabulary differs, most identify the following steps:

- Self-examination on the part of at least one organization, sometimes conducted in connection with a strategic planning process

- A decision to explore the possibility of collaboration

- Identification of potential partners, perhaps using the four criteria of relatedness discussed above

- Initial contacts between representatives of the organizations, perhaps initially limited to the CEOs or selected board members

- Efforts to assess the degree of mutual interest

- A feasibility assessment, which includes the full sharing of information by both organizations and due diligence by both to avoid any future surprises (McLaughlin, 2010)

- Negotiation and the development of agreements

- Implementation (Yankey & Willen, 2005)

Especially if the goal is a merger, the organizations involved in the process may engage consultants as facilitators and advisers. A consultant can bring objectivity, a steadying influence, and experience in other similar situations. The use of a consultant may be especially important if one of the organizations involved has a vacancy in the CEO position and members of the board are reluctant or unable to be involved directly in negotiations (McLaughlin, 2010).

Collaborations and Mergers Within National Nonprofits

The discussion in this chapter so far has emphasized collaboration or merger between or among nonprofit organizations that previously were legally independent. The latter are called **intermergers**. Combining units within a single corporate entity—for example, the consolidation of local chapters of a national organization—is called **intramergers** (McCormick, 2001, p. 2). Many of the same principles apply in either case.

National nonprofits with local chapters follow one of two principal organizational forms, which will affect the ease or difficulty with which collaborations and mergers may be undertaken. Some exist as a single corporation under one charter; chapters are essentially local branches or offices of the national organization. For example, the American Red Cross is a single organization governed by a single national board, and local chapters are accountable to the national office. Chapter assets are owned by the national organization, and chapter executives ultimately report through channels to the national president.

Other nonprofits are federations; local chapters have separate charters and are governed by independent boards. They may be required to follow prescribed policies and practices developed by the national office for the right to use the organization's name and logo, and they may pay dues to the national office in exchange for services provided to the chapters, but they also have considerable autonomy. This is the structure of a number of national disease-related organizations—for example, the Crohn's and Colitis Foundation, the American Lung Association, and the Arthritis Foundation. That is also the structure of some human services and environmental organizations, including Goodwill Industries.

Mergers of chapters within a federated organization are, of course, not intramergers but rather intermergers, since the local organizations have independent charters. Lacking the authority to impose mergers, the national office may face significant resistance that is difficult to overcome. For example, several affiliates of the American Lung Association severed their ties with the national organization in 2007 over their displeasure with a plan to consolidate 78 state and local affiliates into 11 regional organizations. Some adopted new names to be free of control by the national association (Schwinn, 2007).

Another example is provided by the Girl Scouts of the United States of America, a federated organization that reduced the number of its local councils from 315 to 122 between 2003 and 2011. As the then-CEO Kathy Cloninger describes, "[The process is] very messy. It can't but impact the culture and some people leave and new people are coming in, so it's pretty chaotic" (LaBarre, 2006, p. 50). The Girl Scouts of the United States of America is discussed in more detail in a case in the Appendix of this book.

While national nonprofits that operate under a single corporate charter, like the American Red Cross, have the formal authority to bring about collaboration and mergers among their chapters, there nevertheless may be obstacles similar to those complicating such efforts among independent organizations. Issues about turf, ego, culture, and the allocation of resources are still relevant.

Individuals may be more inclined to support organizations with which they are involved and that have impact they can observe in their own lives. For a national organization endeavoring to consolidate its local or regional chapters, the challenge is to gain the efficiency and effectiveness that consolidation may offer, while preserving the willingness of local volunteers and donors to participate and continue providing financial and other forms of support.

Transparency and policies on the sharing of revenue between national and local offices can help create incentives for cooperation and make the system work to the best advantage of all component entities. Nevertheless, such efforts often meet with resistance. Local chapters may be concerned that the national office will encroach on their traditional donors or alienate them through excessively aggressive contacts. Some in the national office may be concerned about sharing information on major donor prospects with their local colleagues based on a presumption that they are not as skilled in fundraising. Others may be concerned that the centralization of donor records will be a first step toward greater control by the national office that will eventually undermine their autonomy in other areas (Wallace, 2005).

But systems have been devised to address these potential problems. For example, Habitat for Humanity appointed major gift officers to work in local chapters with a dual responsibility to raise funds for the chapters as well as for Habitat for Humanity International. The historical mistrust of local chapters toward the national office was overcome in part by developing a centralized database to which the fundraisers would post contact reports of their visits as well as their strategies for developing other prospects. That enabled both the national office and the local chapter to be fully aware of what the gift officers were discussing with prospects and how their efforts were divided between the two levels of the organization. In addition, both the national office and local chapters participated in the selection of the major gift officers (Wallace, 2010a).

Pressures for nonprofits to collaborate and merge are not likely to abate. Continued encouragement from funders, increased competition for resources, and the nation's focus on performance and accountability are likely to make complete independence less tenable for smaller and decentralized organizations and to increase the potential benefits to be gained through collaboration. However, as cases discussed in this chapter illustrate, there is also a need to ensure that relationships between and among organizations are well considered and that mission remains paramount. Those driven *exclusively* by financial considerations may find that the human and financial costs ultimately exceed the gains and that missions may be diluted or lost, to the detriment of the organizations and society.

Cross-Sector Collaboration

As Forrer et al. (2014) observe, "Nothing is simple. No aspect of modern society is the domain of any single sector. None" (p. xi). The complexity of problems, interconnectedness of communities in a wired global community, and limited resources have combined to increase interest in collaboration across the public, for-profit, and nonprofit sectors in order to address social needs and issues.

A Continuum of Cross-Sector Collaboration

Forrer et al. (2014) define **cross-sector collaborations (CSCs)** as "the interaction of two or more of the three organizational sectors" and depict a range of possible relationships along a continuum, similar to the continuum of relationships between nonprofits that we discussed earlier in this chapter. Writing from the perspective of public administrators, the authors define positions along the continuum in terms of the degree of government control over the goods and services provided. Of course, from the nonprofit perspective, the continuum reflects the extent to which organizations maintain their autonomy or share responsibilities and risks with partners in other sectors.

As depicted in Figure 8.2, on the left side of the continuum, goods and services are provided totally by government. They are likely to be public goods, as we discussed in Chapter 3. On the right side, goods and services are provided entirely by the business and nonprofit sectors, perhaps subject only to government regulation. Again reflecting on our discussion in Chapter 3, they are probably private or common goods. In the middle are a variety of arrangements defined by varying degrees of government control and the autonomy of the private and nonprofit actors involved. As we move from left to right, the private and nonprofit collaborators "are [increasingly] not treated as agents of the government but as principals deserving of a voice in production decisions" (Forrer et al., 2014, p. 16).

As mentioned earlier in this chapter, when one entity contracts with another, that is not necessarily a collaboration, since the issuer of the contract may be a principal that is simply hiring an agent to perform some specific function. That might be the case, for

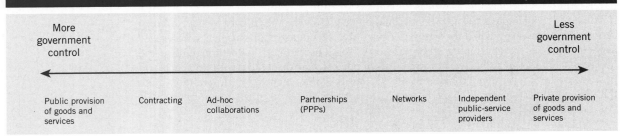

More government control

Less government control

| Public provision of goods and services | Contracting | Ad-hoc collaborations | Partnerships (PPPs) | Networks | Independent public-service providers | Private provision of goods and services |

Source: Adapted from Forrer et al. (2014, p. 15).

example, if a government agency contracts with Goodwill Industries to provide janitorial services in its office building. The relationship is pretty simple, the service provided is rather straightforward, and the government can easily determine whether it is receiving the service for which it paid. But, Forrer et al. (2014) argue that some contracts are "relational"—they are **collaborative contracts**—since they require the ongoing interaction of the parties (p. 59). This is especially true when the solutions to a problem cannot be easily specified in advance and the principal and agent must communicate about adjustments to the services as the needs of the people being served are identified and understood. This is often the case, for example, when the purpose of the relationship is to address social issues, such as public health, poverty, or homelessness. Government contracts and grants and the implications for nonprofits that receive them are discussed further in Chapter 14.

Moving farther right on Forrer et al.'s (2014) continuum, government may engage in **ad hoc collaborations** with nonprofits or for-profit firms. As the term ad hoc implies, these relationships are short term. One might occur, for example, in response to a natural disaster, in which government agencies might collaborate with the nonprofit Red Cross as well as corporations such as Federal Express and Home Depot, which have the means to supply the stricken areas with urgently needed supplies. These relationships are collaborations rather than purely contractual relationships, since the parties involved are likely to maintain considerable independence to decide their own activities. There may or may not be contracts involved, and if there are, they are likely to be of the collaborative nature that Forrer et al. (2014) describe. Indeed, research undertaken by Beth Gazley (2008) found that "government agencies and nonprofit organizations interact in myriad ways, both formally and informally" (p. 142).

In the middle of the continuum are partnerships, commonly referred to as **public–private partnerships (PPPs)**; Forrer et al., 2014). As explained earlier in this chapter, the term partnership implies a formalized relationship that is not ad hoc, with the parties sharing power as well as risks (Forrer et al., p. 86). A partnership between government and a for-profit or nonprofit entity is undertaken differently from a traditional contractual relationship. In contracting, the government usually conducts a competitive process, in which the low-cost provider is advantaged. However, the government is likely to choose a partner because of its unique capabilities rather than just cost. One example is the federal government's partnership with the United Way of New York City (UWNYC) to distribute assistance following the terrorist attacks of September 11, 2001. The UWNYC was not in competition with other potential partners; it was judged by the government to be the only organization capable of providing the needed service (Forrer et al., p. 86).

Forrer et al. (2014) describe **networks** as "collaborative, not bureaucratic, structures that involve autonomous organizations, often responsive to a broad range of nongovernmental stakeholders, while also working independently with both government and other network participants" (p. 113). In other words, members of networks may work collaboratively in some ways and independently in other ways, with a common focus on the same issues but with none exerting control over the other members. And, finally, near the right side of the continuum are **independent public-service providers**—nonprofit organizations that may provide public services and sometimes work with government, but that determine their own priorities and operate with autonomy outside of government control (Forrer et al., p. 140). They include, for example, quasi-governmental organizations such as federally funded research laboratories and fundraising entities that work with government agencies, such as the National Park Foundation.

Advantages and Disadvantages of CSCs

Writing from the perspective of public administrators, Forrer et al. (2014) identify a number of advantages and disadvantages of various CSCs. As relationships move from left to right across the continuum (depicted in Figure 8.2), public managers are likely to be concerned about their decreasing ability to control the services provided or to assure outcomes. But the tradeoffs may include "greater efficiency, more innovation, greater targeted service, and the growth of the private sector" (Forrer et al., p. 21). Of course, nonprofit managers may hold their own concerns about their increasing entanglement with government and possibly corporate partners. Collaborating with government and/or the for-profit sector entails a sacrifice of autonomy, the potential for mission drift, and possible negative reactions from donors and other established funders. But the tradeoffs may include enhanced resources and capacity with which to increase mission impact. Business managers also may have concerns about collaborating with government or nonprofits, but find such relationships helpful in enhancing their company's image and advancing their own definition of **corporate social responsibility** (Forrer et al., p. 34).

There may be increased risks to all parties resulting from the reduction of autonomy and control. Public administrators may face less certainty in being able to account to their principals (elected officials and the public). For-profit managers may face similar concerns in accounting to their shareholders and nonprofit managers to their boards and other constituents (Forrer et al., 2014, p. 22). But the risks of collaboration may be accompanied by strategic benefits to leaders in all three sectors, including the following:

1. Deliverables and outcomes: This might include enhancing operations, attaining goals, or achieving better overall results.

2. Increased capacity and competence: This might result in greater capacity for individuals, the organization, or the community.

3. New resources and opportunities: This might lead to new funding, opportunities for new markets or program areas, and the potential for further cross-sector collaboration (Forrer et al., 2014, p. 41).

As mentioned previously, Forrer et al. (2014) write from the perspective of public administrators. Other scholars adopt a "nonprofit first" approach in their research, meaning that they examine partnerships from the perspective of the nonprofit organizations involved. Those nonprofit-oriented authors caution that models coming from public administration scholars may not fully account for the unique circumstances of nonprofits (Mendel, 2016). They may not fully acknowledge the importance of aligning nonprofit cultures, the drive of participating nonprofits to fulfill their missions, and the "'just right balance' of enlightened organizational self-interests that tends to move collaboration or partnership to successful outcomes" (Mendel, 2016). As discussed in Chapter 3 of this text, nonprofits have defining characteristics as organizations and face unique circumstances with regard to their governance, funding, and missions, making them different from government agencies and for-profit businesses. That may create a unique perspective on partnerships that public administrators who are interacting with nonprofits need to understand and consider.

Obstacles and Conditions for Success

The obstacles to successful cross-sector collaboration and the conditions for success are quite similar to those discussed earlier in this chapter with regard to collaborations between and among nonprofit organizations.

Nonprofits, businesses, and government agencies have different incentives, motivations, legal constraints, and cultures. Nonprofit managers think about benefits for their clients; public administrators think about the public interest; and the first responsibility of corporate managers is to their shareholders. Leaders in the three sectors may use different vocabularies and even suspect the values of those in other sectors. Individual egos and organizational identities can be equally powerful in all three sectors and may impede the sacrifice of control and identity that collaboration requires. Relationships between government and nonprofit organizations may raise political issues, with the potential to become visible in the media. And collaborations may involve costs, requiring the investment of resources that are diverted from other activities that the collaborators might otherwise devote to their individual efforts. All of these realities can present obstacles.

What conditions may lead to success? Again, positive conditions are similar to those discussed earlier with regard to collaboration among nonprofits. Forrer et al. (2014) identify trust among the collaborators as a fundamental requirement, but also note the need for governance and accountability structures to measure respective contributions. As with collaborations between or among nonprofits, the chances for success may be enhanced by following a careful process in exploring and implementing the relationship. And, finally, successful collaborations require an approach to leadership by individuals in all sectors that goes beyond traditional notions of hierarchy and control and that is characterized by "systems thinking." It requires a perspective that goes beyond a job description and includes "viewing one's role within a wider structure of collaboration" (Forrer et al., p. 241).

Achieving Collective Impact

Now let's take a look at an example of cross-sector collaboration that has gained considerable attention and discussion. The concept is called **collective impact**.

In 2006, community leaders in Cincinnati became alarmed by the disappointing statistics on the school failures of students in Ohio and Kentucky. Ohio ranked 42nd out of 50 states on the number of young people earning bachelor's degrees, and Kentucky ranked next to last, at 49th place (Bridgespan Group, n.d.). Conversations about how to address the situation began among the former president of the University of Cincinnati, the former CEO of KnowledgeWorks (an education foundation), and the superintendent of Cincinnati's schools (Bridgespan Group, n.d.). Eventually, more than 300 leaders, including individuals from the public sector, private business sector, and nonprofit sector, joined the dialogue (Kania & Kramer, 2011). This cross-sector collaboration eventually became known as the Strive Partnership (http://www.strivepartnership.org/).

The leaders recognized that just addressing one point on the education continuum, for example, early childhood education or college access, would not be enough to solve the overall problem. It would require a comprehensive and coordinated approach and would require that various organizations put aside their individual agendas to focus on shared objectives. While individual organizations had missions and expertise related to one aspect of education, greater impact could be achieved by collaborating to provide young people with support "from cradle to career" (Bornstein, 2011). This approach encompasses five critical life stages: early childhood, adolescence, early adulthood, and transition from high school or postsecondary training to the workforce (Bridgespan Group, n.d.).

A highly influential 2011 article in the *Stanford Social Innovation Review* by John Kania and Mark Kramer gained attention for the term that describes Strive's approach: collective impact. Kania and Kramer (2011) are affiliated with the consulting firm Foundation Strategy Group (www.fsg.org), which advises some collective impact initiatives. The authors argue that even a high-performing nonprofit can have only "isolated impact" and that no one organization—or sector—can meet the challenges presented by complex, entrenched social problems by working alone. Moreover, such problems have no predetermined solutions and can only be addressed by multiple organizations developing consensus about possible strategies and acting in a coordinated manner. Collective impact is different from routine cross-sector collaboration, since it "envisions an even higher standard of collaboration that requires long-term commitment and consensus from all" (Carson, 2012a).

As summarized in Box 8.1, Kania and Kramer (2013) identify five conditions essential to successful collective impact partnerships, including participation by all sectors within a community; measurement of results by common, agreed-upon indicators; mutually reinforcing activities; continuous communication among the partners; and a centralized coordinating infrastructure with dedicated staff providing support to the entire initiative. The creation of a dedicated **backbone organization** is a hallmark of collective impact that distinguishes the approach from some other cross-sector collaborations. In addition to these five conditions, collective impact requires shifts in mindset, including the inclusion of people who have directly experienced the social problem, recognition that relationships are as important as data, accepting that structure is as important as strategy, and understanding that sharing credit is as important as taking credit (Kania, Hanleybrown, & Juster, 2014). In other words, the experts on collective impact reinforce a point mentioned earlier in this chapter with regard to collaboration more generally: Successful collaboration requires that nonprofit leaders adopt a perspective that goes beyond their own job descriptions.

Initially, the Strive Partnership was managed by a steering committee but later appointed an executive director and other full-time staff, who managed collaborative work, engaged

Box 8.1 The Five Conditions of Collective Impact

Common Agenda	All participants have a shared vision for change including a common understanding of the problem and a joint approach to solving it through agreed-upon actions.
Shared Measurement	Collecting data and measuring results consistently across all participants ensures efforts remain aligned and participants hold each other accountable.
Mutually Reinforcing Activities	Participant activities must be differentiated while still being coordinated through a mutually reinforcing plan of action.
Continuous Communication	Consistent and open communication is needed across the many players to build trust, assure mutual objectives, and create common motivation.
Backbone Support	Creating and managing collective impact requires a separate organization(s) with staff and a specific set of skills to serve as the backbone for the entire initiative and coordinate participating organizations and agencies.

Source: Kania and Kramer (2013).

in advocacy, and maintained communication among the partner organizations (Bridgespan Group, n.d.). By 2011, kindergarten readiness in the Cincinnati schools had increased by 9 percent; fourth-grade reading and math scores had increased by 7 and 14 percent, respectively; and graduation rates for students from local urban schools had increased at both the University of Cincinnati and Northern Kentucky University (Bornstein, 2011). Based on such results, similar partnerships were created in other U.S. communities as well as in Canada, Australia, Israel, and South Korea (Kania et al., 2014). In 2010, Strive's experience gained the attention of the White House Council for Community Solutions, which created tools to help additional communities pursue the approach (Nee & Jolin, 2012). By 2017, the initial partnership in Cincinnati had evolved into a national network of 70 similar initiatives serving 8.2 million students (StriveTogether, 2017).

Collective impact does face skeptics. For example, Emmett Carson (2012a), CEO of the Silicon Valley Community Foundation, argues that collective impact may be difficult to achieve even under ideal conditions and "in some cases, may undermine key values of the nonprofit sector." Carson further observes that solutions to complex problems will require a long-term approach and questions whether all parties in a collective impact partnership will be able to persist. He asks, "Can a mayor afford to be engaged in an effort that will take years to reach consensus? Will her successor be equally committed to the initiative? Will business leaders believe that a multiple-year process just to develop the strategy is a productive use of their time?" Moreover, Carson (2012a) asks whether it is realistic to think that nonprofits with distinctive values can readily sign on to consensus solutions without sacrificing their purposes and offending their donors; for example, if the issue is family planning, there are likely to be nonprofits that advocate very different approaches. Carson sees a downside if foundations focus their support on nonprofits participating in collective impact: It could prevent other organizations from exploring innovative approaches that do not coincide with the consensus of the collective impact partners (Carson, 2012b). And, finally, Carson argues, the idea of collective impact is still relatively new and has not generated strong evidence to prove its long-term effectiveness (Carson, 2012b).

In a 2016 article, consultant Tom Wolff acknowledges that Kania and Kramer's (2011, 2013) articles on collective impact "created a remarkable revolution in government and foundation approaches to community coalition building," and that they "bring fresh eyes to the work of collaboration." But, he argues, their model is flawed. Wolff (2016) offers specific criticisms of collective impact, including the following: It is a top-down business approach that does not meaningfully engage people in the community. It does not include the policy and system changes that other models have demonstrated are required to bring about community change. It does not address social justice issues. It is based on a few case studies, not "research" and it does not reflect the experience of the "thousands of coalitions" that preceded Kania and Kramer's 2011 article (Wolff, 2016). Its assumption that coalitions will find funding for backbone organizations is unrealistic. It emphasizes the leadership of the backbone organization but does not address the importance of building broader leadership within the coalition. Kania and Kramer's five conditions are an over-simplification of reality (Wolff, 2016). Wolff also points to research (e.g., Flood, Minkler, Lavery, Estrada, & Falbe, 2015) that identifies weaknesses in the collective impact model. Kania and Kramer (2016) responded to Wolff's 2016 article, explaining that the collective impact model had evolved since their original 2011 article in areas that address many of his points, especially with regard to equity and community engagement.

In the midst of strong advocates as well as critics, Carson (2012b) reaches a nuanced conclusion regarding collective impact, which may apply as well to collaborations more broadly:

> The job of every nonprofit and foundation is to make difficult decisions based on vision, mission and values. If other entities share those perspectives, collaboration—and

perhaps some form of collective impact—is possible and desirable. But to come together on any other basis undermines the very reason for the nonprofit sector's existence. Sometimes, the hardest thing to do is to say no to the crowd, especially when they are your friends and colleagues.

That view is generally consistent with the philosophy of this book—that nonprofit managers should maintain a balanced approach, remaining open to new ideas and innovation, but also keeping their organizations' distinctive missions central and exercising caution with regard to any proposed one-right-way solutions.

CHAPTER SUMMARY

With the growth in the number of nonprofits in recent decades, there has been an increased emphasis on collaboration and mergers among nonprofits, in order to reduce inefficiencies and increase the capacity and impact of the sector overall. Funders, including government bodies and foundations, have been visible among those calling for such consolidation. However, some observers argue that funders have contributed to the problem and that small nonprofits may better provide more personal attention to clients.

It is not unusual to see the terms collaboration and partnership used interchangeably to describe any relationship in which two or more entities are working together in some way. But others make finer distinctions, and the vocabulary in the field is not consistent. Partnerships generally involve more formal relationships than collaboration, which may be ad hoc. Nonprofits have relationships with government and with corporations. Relationships with corporations include philanthropic collaborations, strategic collaborations, commercial collaborations, political collaborations, and operational relationships.

Contracts are a type of relationship that nonprofits may have with corporations or with government. Traditional contracts are not collaborations; they are principal–agent relationships. Some may be considered collaborative contracts, if decision making is shared between the two parties.

Collaboration between and among nonprofits occurs along a continuum; it may include informal collaboration or more formal relationships, in which the organizations are legally committed to each other.

Some organizations create additional corporations to provide services or to pursue new ventures, yielding some of their autonomy to these new entities. A merger joins two or more organizations and includes a change in legal control. There are intermergers, combinations of previously independent organizations, and intramergers, which are consolidations of chapters or units within a single legal entity, usually a large, national nonprofit. Some national nonprofits are a single corporate entity, while others are federations of independent local organizations. Intramergers can be a complicated matter in either type of organization.

Obstacles to collaboration and merger include the distinctive motivations of nonprofit entities; organizational cultures that may be resistant to change; the egos of the individuals involved, especially founders; concerns about brand identity; community or political concerns; and the costs, in time and money, of the study, planning, and negotiations required. Successful collaborations and mergers are driven primarily by mission, rather than just financial benefits. Other conditions needed for success include support from the board and CEO, an appropriate process, trust, and relatedness. Relatedness means that there is a logic to the relationship based on mission, constituency, organization or structure, or geography. Using language that frames the combination as positive is better than using terms with negative connotations, such as takeover or deal.

Pressures to collaborate and merge are unlikely to abate as nonprofits face an increasingly competitive environment and there is a nationwide focus on performance and accountability. It is important that mission remain paramount and that such relationships not be based entirely on potential financial gains.

Cross-sector collaborations involve organizations from two or more of the three sectors—government, business, and nonprofit. Such relationships also lie along a continuum. From the perspective of public administrators, points on the continuum are defined by the degree to which the government relinquishes control. Nonprofit managers may view various relationships in terms of the degree to which they relinquish autonomy. In addition, nonprofits are concerned with the need to align cultures, the drive to achieve their missions, and an appropriate balance of organizational self-interests, which may lead to a perspective different from that of their public-sector partners.

Cross-sector collaboration may bring benefits to all parties, but leaders in all three sectors may have concerns about risks and performance. For nonprofits, collaborating with business or government may increase resources and capacity, but also bring challenges of accountability to stakeholders and possible mission drift. Obstacles to successful cross-sector collaborations and the conditions necessary for success are similar to those related to collaboration between and among nonprofit organizations. Such relationships require leaders to think beyond their own jobs and view the wider structure of society.

One approach to cross-sector collaboration that has gained wide attention is known as collective impact. It includes participation by all sectors within a community, with a focus on common goals, measurement of results by common indicators, decision making based on data, a centralized coordinating infrastructure with dedicated staff, and continuous communication among the partners. As with other aspects of nonprofit management, there is continuing debate about the effectiveness of such initiatives. Nonprofit managers should be open to new concepts and models, but keep dedication to their missions as a central focus.

KEY TERMS AND CONCEPTS

3C model 218
ad hoc collaborations 230
administrative
   consolidations 218
agent 217
backbone organization 233
collaboration 217
collaborative contracts 230
collective impact 232
commercial collaborations 217
constituency relatedness 226
corporate integrations 219
corporate social responsibility 231

cross-sector collaborations
   (CSCs) 229
drivers 221
external drivers 221
independent public-service
   providers 231
intermergers 228
internal drivers 221
intramergers 228
joint earned income
   ventures 218
joint programming 218
joint venture corporations 219

management service organizations
   (MSOs) 219
merger 217
networks 230
operational relationships 217
parent–subsidiary structures 219
philanthropic collaborations 217
political collaborations 217
principal 217
public–private partnerships
   (PPPs) 230
strategic collaborations 217
strategic restructuring 219

CASE 8.1 N Street Village and Miriam's House

Like many American cities during the 1960s and 1970s, Washington, DC, experienced declining population, economic challenges, and growing social problems, as many middle-class families and businesses moved to the suburbs. In addition, in 1963, Congress passed the Community Mental Health Center Act, leading to the deinstitutionalization of people who were mentally ill. There were inadequate services available to assist that population, a situation that led to an increase in the number of homeless people on urban streets. Riots followed the assassination of Martin Luther King, Jr., in 1968, leaving burned-out stores on streets that had been commercial corridors, accelerating economic decline and the flight of middle-class families. By 1970, the area near 14th and N Streets, Northwest, in the Logan Circle neighborhood of Washington, was a dystopian scene, known primarily for prostitution, drug dealing, and the visibility of homeless people.

In 1970, Pastor John Steinbruck and his wife, Erna, arrived at Luther Place Memorial Church, in the midst of the troubled neighborhood. By 1972, an interfaith organization called ProJeCt (standing for Protestant, Jewish, and Catholic) was distributing food and clothing in the area. Other organizations were created to provide housing for homeless women. With leadership by the Steinbrucks, those and other efforts led to the founding of N Street Village in 1973. Its mission was "[to empower] homeless and low-income women to claim their highest quality of life by offering a broad spectrum of services and advocacy in an atmosphere of dignity and respect" (N Street Village, n.d.-a).

Services expanded in the decades that followed, and by 2014, what had begun with housing provided with sleeping mats on the floor of the church and food served in a parking lot had evolved into an organization providing a comprehensive continuum of care for homeless and low-income women, including a day center, health and wellness programs, and shelter and housing (N Street Village, n.d.-a).

From its founding in 1973, NSV experienced periods of growth as well as periods of crisis. Mary Funke, who had a background in counseling and education, was appointed as executive director in 2004 and immediately faced a financial crisis. She recognized that urgent action would be needed, but also that the current crisis was deeply rooted in long-term problems, which would require more complex planning and change. Funke implemented emergency

measures, including budget cuts, staff reductions, and intensified fundraising. She also put in place new policies and practices intended to provide long-term stability, including performance measurement, strategic planning, strengthened governance, and a leadership succession plan (N Street Village, 2011). She also worked with the board and staff to create a culture of accountability and performance. By 2006, N Street Village was meeting its goals and its financial situation had been stabilized. It applied for the Washington Post Award for Excellence in Nonprofit Management. The staff benchmarked other organizations, developed the application as a team, and succeeded in winning the competition (Kee & Newcomer, 2008).

Despite N Street's improved management and financial position, it could not escape the impact of the serious economic downturn that began in 2007, which some labeled the Great Recession. Overall philanthropy declined and foundation giving in the Washington region dropped 8 percent just from 2008 to 2009. Meanwhile, the recession was increasing the need for NSV's services. Funders were encouraging grant recipients to do more with less and to seek partnerships with other nonprofits (Tomassoni, 2011).

In 2010, Mary Funke was followed as executive director by Schroeder Stribling, in a planned succession. Stribling was a social worker with a background in mental health programs, who had served as director of programs at NSV since 2003 and deputy executive director since 2008. Faced with the economic crisis, Stribling implemented a hiring freeze, reduced some employee benefits, and was forced to use some funds from the organization's reserves. She warned the board that if the financial environment did not improve, NSV might be forced to cut programs, despite the growing need for services. As she reports, "The stress was really tremendous during those times" (Small, 2012). The board approved a strategic plan to deal with the continuing economic downturn, including the pursuit of partnerships with other nonprofits serving low-income women (FitzGerald, 2013; Small, 2012).

Meanwhile, the recession also was having an impact at Miriam's House.[2] Miriam's House had been founded in 1996 to provide transitional housing for women living with HIV and AIDS. The founder, Carol Marsh, had retired as executive director in 2010 and was followed by Sam Collins. Like Stribling, Collins walked right into the economic maelstrom. Just prior to his arrival, Miriam's annual revenue had declined from $800,000 to $600,000 in only a year. A fifth of the staff had been laid off. Despite reductions in costs, Miriam's reserves had been exhausted in just three years. "We were trying to carve pieces off of our budget until in 2010, there was nothing left to shave off," said Miriam's executive director Tim Fretz (Small, 2012). In addition to the economic downturn, Miriam's House was adjusting to changes in the need for its services. Miriam's hospice model was becoming outdated, as medical advances were extending the lives of people with HIV and increasing the need for HIV treatment programs (Small, 2012). Given the environment, Miriam's House, like NSV, began looking for a partner.

The partnership began with NSV offering mental health and employment services at Miriam's House, which Miriam's would have been unable to provide with its strained resources (Tomassoni, 2011). But talk soon turned to the possibility of merger. As Stribling recalls, "Given the very strong mission-fit and positive chemistry between our two organizations, it occurred to me right away that we could make a successful merger that would strengthen our collective impact.... [We] quickly progressed to candidly proposing a merger—a 'partnership on steroids'" (FitzGerald, 2013).

NSV retained Peter Shields, an attorney experienced in corporate mergers, to manage the process. It began with an exchange of formal letters covering points such as real estate, programming, intellectual property, corporate structure, government contracts, and human resources. Both boards began considering the tough questions: What would happen to the executive director of Miriam's House? What about other staff of both organizations? What about the name of Miriam's House (FitzGerald, 2013)?

In September 2011, N Street Village and Miriam's House agreed to merge. Miriam's would continue to house homeless women in one of its facilities, but its board would be dissolved and its programs would become a part of N Street Village. The Miriam's name would be preserved, but as a program of NSV. Reflecting on the merger, Stribling stated, "This feels like a marriage" (Tomassoni, 2011). The process had required 10 months. As Shields explains, "In a for-profit merger, it's full speed ahead and get it done as soon as possible. This was the opposite. The driver was the mission, so it required sensitivity and attention" (Small, 2012).

How had success been achieved, when obstacles had derailed other proposed mergers in the nonprofit sector? Reflecting on the experience, Stribling cites three factors. First, the merger had positive endorsements from key constituents, including key funders, founders,

and donors. Major Washington foundations provided financial support for the merger. Stribling conducted "insider previews" for other donors and constituents throughout the process to keep them informed and prepare them for what might result. Second, both executive directors kept their staff members informed and planned social activities to build relationships and trust among them. As Stribling describes, "We did a lot of gathering, greeting, socializing, processing, and celebrating both during and after the process ... to try and honor and preserve and promote the positive culture and morale that both organizations enjoyed" (FitzGerald, 2013). And, third, the process was carefully managed, by Shields and by Tracy Cecil, an NSV senior staff member who was assigned as project director. Shields's involvement was critical, as Stribling explains, because "He was able to represent our board in the negotiations and also take some sensitive staff elements ... offline and into the board-to-board communication" (FitzGerald, 2013).

But the period following the merger also required continued sensitivity. One member of Miriam's former board who had financial expertise was added to the NSV board, and Tim Fretz moved from Miriam's staff to become operations manager at NSV. Sam Collins went on to serve as president of the Lutheran Volunteer Corps. NSV implemented combined staff training programs and clients adjusted to the change. As one client explained in a newspaper interview, she previously had lived at Miriam's House and was reluctant to go to another organization at a different location to receive services. Following the merger, she continued to live at Miriam's but also attended classes and groups at NSV, several blocks away. Despite her initial discomfort, she eventually reported, "It pretty much feels like a family" (Tomassoni, 2011).

Looking back on the merger process, Stribling offers advice to other organizations, frankly noting costs as well as benefits. She observes that while mergers offer the efficiencies of larger scale in the long run, there are high immediate investments that need to be made and hidden costs over the long run, both tangible and intangible. Those include, for example, needed investments in IT infrastructure and the greater commitment of effort required to maintain organizational culture in a larger organization (FitzGerald, 2013). The principal benefits relate to mission:

> By joining forces with Miriam's House, we were able not only to reinforce the financial position of both organizations, but we have been able to expand HIV services to hundreds of

women, AND we have opened the potential to add to our supportive housing inventory even further at more moderate cost than we could have otherwise. These are significant positive outcomes that will have a lasting impact for the people we exist to serve. (FitzGerald, 2013)

As the economy improved and the benefits of the merger came to be realized, N Street Village sought new ways to grow and increase its impact. But growth would require new strategies and new partnerships.

NSV "had exploited every inch" of space at its flagship property on N Street, which occupied an entire block (Neibauer, 2012). Expansion at that location had been foreclosed by changes in the neighborhood. Ironically, what had been an urban wasteland in the 1970s had become, by 2013, a remarkable example of urban gentrification, with the development of expensive new condos, restaurants, theaters, and clubs along a booming 14th Street (Shin, 2013). The women living at NSV were now residents of what had become an expensive neighborhood. Although its facility was worth millions, NSV could not sell it and relocate, since there were restrictions on the use of the building (Neibauer, 2012). Future growth would require distributing NSV's facilities and services to other parts of the city.

In 2008, the city's Human Services Department had become concerned about troubling trends. People who became homeless were remaining homeless for longer periods and were returning frequently to emergency and temporary shelters. The department initiated a plan that adopted the "Housing First model," which had been tried with success in other cities. The idea was to move homeless people into sustainable permanent housing *first* and *then* provide services to help them advance their lives, such as medical care and counseling. In addition, this approach called for a break from the previous model, which placed people in scattered housing units with city subsidies. The new program would place them in a common location, with the goal of building a sense of community and facilitating the provision of services. Stribling described the benefits of this approach, saying, "When there's a community, there's a sense of support you can't get elsewhere. [Adopting the Housing First model] is a direction we've been hoping the district would move in" (Driessen, 2012).

Consistent with the city's new strategy, in 2012, N Street Village opened its third residential site to provide supportive services for 31 of the city's most vulnerable homeless women. Located five blocks from NSV's main building, the new residence was named Erna's House, in honor of Erna Steinbruck, cofounder of N Street Village (N Street Village, n.d.-a). The building, once foreclosed by the U.S. Department of Housing and Urban Development, was purchased and renovated in 2011 by private developers and then was leased by the city's Department of Human Services for $750,000 a year. Operation of Erna's House would be the responsibility of NSV and would cost about $400,000 a year, with NSV covering about $100,000, and the city funding the balance (Neibauer, 2012).

NSV initiated a new round of strategic planning in 2014, focusing on strategies for continued growth. In 2016, the organization opened its fourth housing site, the Patricia Handy Place for Women, offering emergency housing and housing for women receiving on-site intensive medical care (N Street Village, n.d.-a) Using funds from its successful capital campaign, NSV also completed renovations to Miriam's House and added new units and amenities at that location (N Street Village, n.d.-b). Growth continued in 2017 with the opening of new programs at the Phyllis Wheatley YWCA, giving NSV a presence in three of the city's eight wards (N Street Village, n.d.-a).

Amid the dramatic gentrification of Washington, DC, during the first two decades of the 21st century, some of its most vulnerable citizens had been left behind. A rapidly decreasing supply of affordable housing and growing income disparities increased the number of such citizens and exacerbated their needs. Fifty-three percent of NSV clients were at least 50 years old. Seventy-five percent had chronic health problems, and 11 percent were living with HIV. Eighty-four percent had a history of trauma. Ninety-two percent had a history of mental illness, substance abuse, or both (N Street Village, 2014). There were more than 6,500 homeless people in Washington in 2012, about 24 percent of whom were women (Neibauer, 2012). N Street Village served 1,400 of them.

As Stribling (2014) explained,

> We have a lot of work to do … and it will take every community—every board/group/mission/organization AND our government partners—to make progress and to address deeply entrenched poverty and its related problems.… I always encourage us to remember and share the idea that 'we are more alike than we are different.' A few small turns of fate or circumstance could render us in one another's position. Whether we are motivated by our faith or a sense of justice or compassion, we should fulfill a social compact that ensures equity, dignity and opportunity for everyone.

Questions Related to Case 8.1

1. Which of the drivers of mergers discussed in this chapter were at work in the case of N Street Village and Miriam's House?

2. Which of the obstacles to merger discussed in this chapter existed in the case of NSV and Miriam's House and how were they overcome? Could the successful process used in this case be adopted by other organizations or were there unique conditions and circumstances that worked in favor of NSV and Miriam's House?

3. How does the evolution of the relationship between N Street Village and Miriam's House reflect the collaborative map developed by La Piana Consulting?

4. Do NSV's relationships with the city government seem to be collaborations or partnerships or is it principally a government contractor?

5. How would you define NSV's relationships with Unity Health Care, Mary's Center, Luther Place Memorial Church, and private real estate developers?

6. How might the perspective of N Street Village as a nonprofit organization be different from that of government agencies and for-profit real estate developers when considering partnerships?

QUESTIONS FOR DISCUSSION

1. In deciding whether to recognize the tax-exempt status of a new nonprofit, should the Internal Revenue Service consider whether or not it will duplicate the services of other, existing organizations in its community? Why or why not?

2. If you were a foundation funder, how would you balance the need for efficiency in the nonprofit sector with the desirability of encouraging innovative new approaches?

3. If you were a nonprofit CEO and were approached by another nonprofit CEO about the possibility of collaborating, what are some of the first questions you might have?

4. If you were a nonprofit CEO, what concerns might you have about collaborating with a local government agency?

5. As a nonprofit CEO, how would you balance the self-interests of your organization with opportunities to achieve greater impact through collaboration with others?

APPENDIX CASES

The following cases in the Appendix of this text include points related to the content of this chapter: Case 2 (Share Our Strength/No Kid Hungry); Case 4 (Girl Scouts of the United States of America).

SUGGESTIONS FOR FURTHER READING

Books

Boris, E., & Steuerle, C. E. (2017). *Nonprofits and government: Collaboration and conflict* (3rd ed.). Lanham, MD: Rowman & Littlefield and Urban Institute Press.

Crutchfield, L. R., & Grant, H. M. (2012). *Forces for good: The six practices of high-impact nonprofits* (Rev. ed.). San Francisco, CA: Jossey-Bass.

Forrer, J. J., Kee, J. E., & Boyer, E. (2014). *Governing cross-sector collaboration*. San Francisco, CA: Jossey-Bass.

McLaughlin, T. A. (2010). *Nonprofits mergers and alliances: A strategic planning guide*. New York, NY: Wiley.

Mendel, S. C., & Brudney, J. L. (2018). *Partnerships the nonprofit way: What matters, what doesn't* (Philanthropic and Nonprofit Studies Series). Bloomington: Indiana University Press.

Articles/Report

Abramson, A., Soskis, B., & Toepler, S. (2012). *Public-philanthropic partnerships in the U.S.: A literature review of recent experiences*. Arlington, VA: Council on Foundations.

Kania, J., & Kramer, M. (2011, Winter). Collective Impact. *Stanford Social Innovation Review, 9*(1). Retrieved from http://www.ssireview.org/articles/entry/collective_impact#comments

Kania, J., & Kramer, M. (2013, January 21). Embracing emergence: How collective impact addresses complexity. *Stanford Social Innovation Review*. Retrieved from

https://ssir.org/articles/entry/embracing_emergence_how_collective_impact_addresses_complexity

Taylor, A. (2017, May 17). Hacking nonprofit collaboration. *Stanford Social Innovation Review*. Retrieved from https://ssir.org/articles/entry/hacking_nonprofit_collaboration

Wolff, T. (2016, March 15). Ten places where collective impact gets it wrong. *Global Journal of Community Psychology Practice, 7*(1). Retrieved from http://www.gjcpp.org/en/resource.php?issue=21&resource=200.

Websites

The Bridgespan Group: http://www.bridgespan.org/

Foundation Center Nonprofit Collaboration Database: http://collaboration.foundationcenter.org/search/searchGenerator.php

Grantmakers for Effective Organizations: http://www.geofunders.org/

La Piana Consulting: http://www.lapiana.org/

StriveTogether: http://strivetogether.org/cradle-career-network

Venture Philanthropy Partners: http://venturephilanthropypartners.org/

Volunteers are a major component of the workforce of many nonprofits.

iStock/dolgachov

Chapter Outline

Managing Staff and Service Volunteers

Chapter 5 discussed how nonprofit chief executives provide leadership to their organizations. Some of the theories considered there also help inform how to lead the individuals who work in those organizations. This chapter takes a closer look at the management of what are called human resources—people—including both staff and volunteers. We will begin with an overview of human resources management in nonprofit organizations, and then look at some theories that help explain the motivations of staff and volunteers and specific practices based on those theories that experts recommend to ensure a productive workforce. This chapter combines a discussion of managing staff with the topic of managing service volunteers because, as explained further in the chapter, many of the same principles apply whether the nonprofit's workforce is composed of paid staff, volunteers, or is a combination of both. This is true because the foundations of human motivation are similar whether individuals are compensated for their work financially or only through nonfinancial rewards. It is useful to note that while management of staff and volunteers is an internal function, some principles of leadership apply.

It is important to distinguish between volunteers who serve as members of a nonprofit's governing board and volunteers who help provide its programs and services—for example, individuals who prepare food for the homeless or ill, tutor children, bring relief to the victims of disasters, or guide Boy Scout and Girl Scout troops and other youth organizations as unpaid leaders. The latter, usually termed service volunteers, are the focus of this chapter. They are to be contrasted with policy volunteers, that is, individuals who may serve on a board or council but may not be engaged in delivering services. In many organizations, service volunteers work alongside staff, perform similar functions, and require similar management approaches.

There may be overlap between policy and service volunteers. For example, it is not unusual for service volunteers to develop a broad understanding of the organization and eventually come to serve on its board. However, not all service volunteers will acquire that perspective and not all will be well suited to board service. Likewise, policy volunteers may bring special knowledge and expertise to their board roles but may

Learning Objectives

After reading this chapter, students should be able to:

1. Describe prominent theories of human motivation.

2. Identify basic principles of human resources management.

3. Summarize best practices for supervising staff members in the nonprofit sector.

4. Define various types of volunteers.

5. Summarize best practices for developing volunteer programs.

6. Explain trends in volunteerism.

7. Analyze cases, applying concepts from the chapter.

not possess the technical skills needed for the delivery of services. Having service volunteers on the governing board may bring advantages as well as disadvantages. Service volunteers may have in-depth knowledge of the organization's programs, the needs of clients, and what may be appropriate standards for evaluation. That knowledge can be highly important to the board. On the other hand, service volunteers on the board may be especially committed to a particular program and perhaps share the perspectives of staff members, alongside of whom they often work, and thus may not always have a broad view of the organization's overall strategies and directions. Reflecting these pros and cons, some organizations encourage or permit service volunteers to serve on the board, but others prohibit it (Brudney, 2016, p. 690).

Again, this chapter focuses on both staff and service volunteers. The discussion blends theory and the recommendations of practitioner-oriented authors, addressing questions such as the following: What does management theory and research tell us about human motivation, especially in the workplace? Are nonprofit staff members motivated in the same way as those who work in for-profit environments or government, or are there differences that need to be understood? Are there differences in the motivations of staff and volunteers? What practices should nonprofit managers use to organize and direct staff members and volunteers in ways consistent with their motivations and needs that also will lead to optimum performance?

Human Resources Management

The missions of most nonprofit organizations involve people, and people are the most important input in programs that serve the mission. Unlike businesses that produce *things*, most nonprofits provide services and are not capital intensive; that is, the costs of personnel are likely to be the major portion of their total expenses. Even when volunteers provide services, there is a cost associated with the management of volunteer programs. Thus, the systematic management of human resources is a critical function for all but the smallest of nonprofit organizations.

Human resources management (HRM) involves "the design of *formal systems* [italics added] ... to ensure the effective use of [individuals'] knowledge, skills, abilities, and other characteristics ... to accomplish organizational goals" (Pynes, 2013, p. 3). HRM involves "the recruitment, selection, training and development, compensation and benefits, retention, evaluation, and promotion of employees, and labor-management relationships within an organization" (Pynes, p. 3). These activities must be approached in a systematic way, as part of an integrated strategy for accomplishing the organization's goals (Watson & Abzug, 2016, p. 601). And, again, while HRM is usually discussed with regard to employees, well-managed volunteer programs employ many of the same principles and practices and volunteers are an important component of the workforce for many nonprofit organizations.

One essential aspect of a human resources management program is ensuring compliance with the law. Employment law applies to staff members, but some aspects also may relate to volunteers. Some laws apply to all organizations; organizations that receive government funds may face stricter requirements; and some, notably religious organizations, may be exempt from certain aspects of employment laws. There are a variety of federal, state, and local laws related to employment, including those regulating wages and hours, workplace safety, benefit programs, and many other areas (Watson & Abzug, 2016). Federal law prohibits discrimination on the basis of race, national origin, religion, sex, age, and disability. At the time of this writing, federal law does not explicitly prohibit discrimination on the basis of sexual orientation in private employment, although the Equal Employment Opportunity Commission (EEOC) considers discrimination based on sexual orientation or gender identity to be a form of sex discrimination under Title VII of the Civil Rights Act of 1964 (Watson & Abzug, p. 611). Federal legislation that would prohibit discrimination based on sexual orientation has been proposed in Congress, but has not passed as of this writing. However, about half of the states have laws prohibiting discrimination based on sexual orientation and some state and local laws also ban discrimination related to sexual identity (Nolo, 2017). Five general points must be kept in mind. First, discrimination law applies to how people are treated throughout their employment, not just during the hiring process. Second, even if discrimination is not intentional, it may occur if a neutral policy has **disparate impact** on persons in a protected class, and the policy is not job related or consistent with business necessity. Thus, an organization should not require certain credentials or characteristics that are unrelated to the duties to be performed, because that might have the effect—even if unintended—of creating disadvantages for certain groups (Watson & Abzug, pp. 606–607); for example, requiring that an individual be able to lift a certain weight might give an advantage to men over women, but it would be a discriminatory requirement if the job did not actually involve lifting such weight. Third, courts have extended the application of some laws beyond the specific wording of the legislation. For instance, while Title VII of the Civil Rights Act does not explicitly address sexual harassment, the courts have held that it is a form of discrimination based on gender (Watson & Abzug, pp. 608–609). Fourth, a nonprofit may be held accountable for the actions of vendors, clients, and contractors as well as staff members; for that reason, it is essential to have formal policies and mechanisms to systematically monitor legal compliance (Watson & Abzug, p. 604). And, finally, a responsible nonprofit assures that its treatment of all people is *fair* as well as legal.

A thorough discussion of employment law is beyond the scope of this text, but students will find suggested readings and websites at the end of this chapter that provide more information. It is important that organizations consult with legal counsel regarding specific legal issues and not rely on books or articles, including this text.

An Overview of Management Theories

Management theory is not static. Theories are advanced and sometimes gain wide acceptance for a period of years. As scholars test them through research, they may find that the theories do not provide adequate explanations. Some theories thus pass into the dustbin of academic history. But often some of their principles are taken forward and incorporated into new theories. Other theories, even though challenged by research, have an intuitive appeal for managers and take hold in the conventional wisdom, despite evidence of their shortcomings. If there were one accepted approach to management, perhaps there would be need for only one management book, but a survey of Amazon or any library will reveal that such is not the situation. In other words, management theory remains unsettled territory, although many theories, both old and new, offer at least some insights that may inform practice. This chapter discusses just a few theories relevant to the topic of staff and volunteer management. Students should recognize in advance that almost all of them have critics as well as adherents.

Thinking about the management of people has shifted since the earliest theories were proposed. For example, one influential management theorist of the early 20th century was Frederick W. Taylor, whose approach, developed in industrial settings, became known as **scientific management**. Taylor saw organizations as operating much like machines and emphasized procedures and systems rather than human motivations and relationships. Much of his research involved time-and-motion studies in factories, with the purpose of increasing efficiency—in other words, finding ways to have people operate more like machines.

There were early theorists who pursued an approach that differed from Taylor's, placing more emphasis on human psychology. Among them were Hugo Munsterberg and Mary Parker Follett (Denhardt, Denhardt, & Aristigueta, 2016, p. 9). Such thinkers were pioneers whose views were not fully accepted in the age of scientific management in which they wrote. But a series of experiments conducted in the 1920s at the Hawthorne plant of the Western Electric Company had a profound influence on thinking about management. Among other findings, the experiments suggested that the mere attention of supervisors had an influence on the performance of workers. When workers were being studied, productivity went up. When they were not, it went down, although everything else stayed the same. That suggested that social and psychological factors might be important in creating a more productive workforce. Although the **Hawthorne experiments** have been controversial right from the beginning, they provided "pathbreaking illustrations of the influence of social and psychological factors on work behavior" (Rainey, 2014, p. 27). Management theory continues to evolve, but it has not returned to the era of Taylor, in which humans were viewed as cogs in the industrial machine. The shift in attention from the rules and mechanics of the workplace to an emphasis on human motivations and attitudes was a lasting change in our understanding and perspective. It is reflected in most contemporary scholarship.

Understanding Human Motivations

Theories about human **motivation** are of practical importance. Every manager holds some theory about motivation, even if only implicitly. What a manager may believe about human nature will dictate how he or she interacts with people, seeks to motivate them, and addresses disappointments with their performance. Many people have known great bosses, who inspired loyalty and created a pleasant, productive working environment, and perhaps also screamer bosses, whose demands, rants, and insults created a dysfunctional workplace. Such differences may in fact reflect the psychology of the manager and his or her own needs, but they likely also reflect the manager's theory of how other people operate. It is thus important for a manager to hold some explicit theory of human motivation, rather than just an implicit homegrown theory, perhaps developed through his or her own life experiences.

Theories of human motivation can be divided into categories, as depicted in Table 9.1. While Table 9.1 is not exhaustive—that is, there are theories that do not neatly fit into any category and there are others that this brief summary excludes—many of the best-known theories are listed, along with the names of representative scholars whose research and writing have been influential. This text does not discuss all of these theories in detail, but at the end of this chapter, students will find suggested readings that provide more information about any that may be of particular interest.

Maslow's Hierarchy of Needs

One of the most influential of motivation theorists was Abraham Maslow, who developed his principal concepts in the 1940s and 1950s. Although it has been challenged by some scholars, Maslow's (1954) theory had an important influence on later thinking and has been the foundation for later work. For example, Burns's (1978) concept of transformational leadership, which we discussed in Chapter 5, draws substantially on Maslow's **hierarchy of needs**.

As the term hierarchy implies, Maslow's (1954) theory states that human needs progress from those at lower levels to those at higher levels as the lower-level needs are met. Human beings strive to meet their lower-level needs before addressing those in higher categories. In the lowest category—that is, at the bottom of the hierarchy—are basic physiological needs. Any student who has tried to study while hungry will readily recognize that it is difficult to focus on higher pursuits until more immediate needs are addressed. But once the basics such as food, drink, and shelter are met, people can turn their attention to meeting their higher-level needs. The next steps up the hierarchy are safety needs, social needs (also called love),

Table 9.1 Summary of Selected Motivation Theories

Category	Representative Scholar(s)	Summary
Need theories	Maslow (1954)	People behave in ways that satisfy their needs. Needs exist in a hierarchy: physiological, safety, love (social), esteem (ego), and self-actualization. People are motivated to meet higher-level needs once lower-level needs have been satisfied.
	McGregor (1960)	Describes managers' views of motivation. Theory X is the traditional view that people are lazy, lack ambition, etc. Theory Y is the view that people are capable, enjoy work, accept responsibility, and accept change. Managers' behavior depends on which theory they hold.
	Herzberg (1968)	Identifies separate factors that are satisfiers or dissatisfiers. Satisfiers are motivators. Managers should reduce or eliminate dissatisfiers and increase satisfiers.
	McClelland (1961)	Focuses on three needs: for achievement, for power, and for affiliation. Examines how managers' needs affect their behavior.
Expectancy theories	Vroom (1964)	Human motivation can be understood by the strength of a person's desire for an outcome (valence) and the person's expectation that a certain behavior will be related to that outcome (expectancy). Valence and expectancy determine motivation force.
Goal theories	Locke (2000)	Goal setting and the existence of goals motivate people.
Equity theories	Adams (1965)	People expect a fair relationship between effort and reward and change their behavior in response to perceived inequity.
Operant behavior	Skinner (1953)	Behavior that is positively reinforced (rewarded) is repeated. Behaviors that result in punishment are less likely to be repeated. Positive reinforcement could include praise or monetary rewards.
Participation	Likert (1967)	People are motivated through participation in goal setting and a democratic approach to determining rewards, methods, and evaluation.
Life stages	Erikson (1959)	Erikson identified needs that people have in different stages of their lives. Other theorists have discussed how the issues associated with certain life stages affect people at work and how organizations can provide appropriate support.
Integrative theories	Steel and Konig (2006)	Combine various perspectives into an overarching theory of motivation.
Emotions	Seo, Barrett, and Bartunek (2004)	Explain how emotions may cause people to behave in ways that are not considered rational.

self-esteem needs (also called ego), and, finally, self-actualization needs. Thus, once human beings have met their physiological needs, they may focus on safety. (A hungry person would take risks to obtain food or drink; in other words, those basic needs would outweigh the desire for safety.) Once individuals feel safe, they are then able to focus on meeting their needs for the camaraderie and affection of others and on meeting needs that satisfy their own egos and build their self-esteem. At the top of the hierarchy, self-actualization encompasses the need for self-fulfillment and achievement commensurate with one's ultimate capacity. People motivated at this level are the self-starters so often described as ideal candidates in job advertisements. They are in essence free to pursue their goals for fulfillment and achievement by having met lower level needs.

Another way to understand Maslow's (1954) hierarchy is to think about how people might descend to lower-level needs under certain adverse circumstances. For example, someone engaged in fulfilling his or her ego and self-actualization needs might retreat to address lower-level needs if faced with a threat to safety or nourishment. For example, a person in fear of losing his or her job may not be thinking much about taking classes to expand his or her skills; that person's attention probably will be focused on the essential need to do the job at hand and remain employed. The person also may not be thinking much about how to bring innovation to his or her job—he or she will probably stick with the basics. But someone who feels safe in his or her employment and life may be able to reach farther up the hierarchy to address higher-level needs, perhaps seeking greater personal and professional challenges or experimenting with new approaches to his or her work. This also explains how an individual's personal life may influence his or her performance at work. For example, if a man or woman is concerned about the safety of a child in day care, greater achievement at work is unlikely to be his or her highest priority. Maslow's (1954) theory helps us understand that human beings have their own psychological needs that they bring to the workplace from other aspects of their lives. They may be highly motivated to address whatever needs they have, regardless of what practices the manager may follow. That insight is an essential one for any realistic manager to grasp.

McGregor: Theory X and Theory Y

Another influential theorist, who wrote in the 1960s, was Douglas McGregor. McGregor (1960) is known for his definitions of **Theory X and Theory Y**. Theory X, which McGregor saw reflected in management practices in most industrial organizations, is based on the assumption that workers are lazy, resistant to change, and not concerned with the organization's needs. It is basically a negative view of human nature and might be used to justify an approach something like Taylor's scientific management. Someone who subscribes to Theory Y, on the other hand, views employees as capable of self-motivation and self-direction and sees his or her role as a manager as supporting the development of the people supervised.

McGregor's perspective places the responsibility for performance on managers as well as subordinates. If people are by nature capable and responsible, then a manager holding that theory of human behavior would likely give individuals more autonomy, decentralize responsibility, and seek to unleash human potential. If workers are not motivated, then the manager needs to examine ways to make the job more satisfying, so as to unleash the innate positive qualities of people. This is obviously a very different way of seeing the work environment from that reflected in Taylor's scientific management.

McClelland: Three Needs Theory

David McClelland, also writing in the 1960s, placed the focus even more on managers themselves. He explained that it is not only workers who have needs that affect their behavior in the workplace. Managers have their own psychological needs, too, which influence how they behave with regard to their subordinates. McClelland's (1961) theory is called the **three needs theory** because he identified three principal needs that people have: the need for achievement, the need for power over others, and the need for affiliation or good relationships with others. McClelland's theories stimulated a large body of follow-up research and the development of instruments to measure managers' needs. The standing of his theories today is mixed, with some still supporting them and others criticizing them harshly (Rainey, 2014, p. 275). But, like Maslow, McClelland helped us recognize that managers, like all human beings, do not come to the workplace as empty canisters; they come with their own psychological needs and may behave at work in a way that helps address them.

Myers and Briggs: Personality Types

Katharine Cook Briggs and her daughter Isabel Briggs Myers made an important contribution to management by developing a tool known as the **Myers-Briggs–type indicator**, which is widely used in the workplace today. Myers-Briggs and other similar instruments are used to reveal **personality style**, which "refers to the manner in which individuals gather and process information" (Denhardt et al., 2016, pp. 29–30). Based on the theories of the psychologist Carl Jung, personality tests like Myers-Briggs are used to provide individuals with insights about their own perspectives and preferences, which may help them understand their own behavior and that of others with whom they work. Perhaps the best-known distinction made by Myers-Briggs is that between introverts and extroverts, although it measures personality in many additional dimensions.

Herzberg: Motivators and Dissatisifers

Like most theories, those of Frederick Herzberg, first described in the late 1960s, have been challenged by other researchers. However, his findings are still widely cited. Herzberg claimed to identify two sets of factors that influence motivation. He called them **motivators** and **hygiene factors**, but they are also sometimes called **satisfiers** and **dissatisfiers**. Table 9.2 shows both sets of factors. The motivators also are called **intrinsic motivational factors**, because they relate to individuals' feelings and the nature of the job itself. The dissatisfiers relate to what are called **extrinsic motivational factors**, since they come from the environment and are external to the work itself (Lee & Wilkins, 2011; Leonard, 2013). Hygiene is a term we usually associate with health and, indeed, we might think of the hygiene factors as determining whether the work environment is healthy or not. According to Herzberg (1968), there is a big difference in how these two sets of factors affect people. Hygiene factors can lead to dissatisfaction, but they cannot be used in a positive way to motivate people. Only the motivators can do that. This implies that managers should design work to reduce any hygiene factors that are creating dissatisfaction and increase motivators related to the work experience.

To understand Herzberg's (1968) theory, students may find it useful to think about their own work or volunteer experience and what they find to be satisfying or intolerable in specific cases. Looking at the right-hand column of Table 9.2, dissatisfaction with a job can be caused by the frustrations that derive from company policy or administration—for example, the mindless bureaucracy reflected in Dilbert cartoons. Dissatisfaction may arise from poor interpersonal relationships with a supervisor or peer or from physical working conditions that do not provide safety and security. (Remember Maslow's needs hierarchy!) A tyrannical or incompetent boss, petty colleagues, or an unclean and unsafe work environment are reasons that might cause most people to go home discouraged and start looking for alternative employment. Students will note that compensation—that is, salary, benefits, and other financial rewards—appears on the list of potential dissatisfiers, but not as a motivator! Let's return to that interesting point in a moment.

Take a look at the left-hand side of Table 9.2, a list of Herzberg's (1968) motivators. People who participated in his studies described the factors that motivated them at work as including achievement and recognition, opportunities for advancement, opportunities for greater responsibility and personal growth, and the inherent rewards of certain types of work. For example, tutoring children might be an intrinsically rewarding activity, as opposed to, let's say, slaughtering pigs. If that work is also carried out in an environment that provides the other motivators, the job may prove very satisfying, unless some dissatisfiers from the right-hand column get in the way. If the dissatisfiers are present at significant levels, even rewarding work may not be enough to compensate for the aggravation, and people may become unmotivated and perhaps inclined to look for other places to spend their working hours.

What about money? It may seem counterintuitive to many people that salary appears in Herzberg's (1968) theory not as a motivator but rather as a potential dissatisfier. After all, do not many companies, and an increasing number of nonprofits, offer financial incentives to encourage higher performance? That practice suggests an underlying theory that people are motivated in a positive way by the opportunity to make a greater income. But then, how do we explain the fact that many nonprofit staff members—and, indeed, people in other sectors—work for less income than they could earn elsewhere? Or that volunteers work for no financial compensation at all? And, we might wonder, how many people would be inclined to leave a job they love for a job they hate only because it pays more money, assuming that their current pay is sufficient to meet their needs? Surely, if the wage is so low that it isn't livable, or if employees feel that they are not paid what their effort is worth, that may be a source of dissatisfaction. If the employee believes that others, within the organization or elsewhere, are being paid more for the same work, that sense of unfairness may be dissatisfying. If Herzberg (1968) is right, sufficient and fair may be enough to remove money as a cause of dissatisfaction. As long as those standards are met, more money may not produce greater motivation. According to Herzberg, motivation comes from the factors on the left-hand side of Table 9.2.

Table 9.2 Herzberg's Motivators (Satisfiers) and Hygiene Factors (Dissatisfiers)

Motivators (Satisfiers) (Related to the job and to motivation)	Hygiene Factors (Dissatisfiers) (Related to the environment)
Achievement	Company policies and administration
Recognition	Relations with supervisor
The work itself	Interpersonal relations with coworkers
Advancement	Working conditions
Growth	Compensation
Responsibility	Status and security

Source: Adapted from Herzberg (1968).

Motivations of Nonprofit Staff

It is important to understand that Herzberg's theory was not focused on nonprofit organizations. So it is useful to consider how Herzberg's concepts may apply in the nonprofit sector. Is motivation in the nonprofit sector somehow different than in the public sector or in the for-profit sector?

First, let's consider how nonprofit staff members compare to individuals working in government. A number of studies concerning **public service motivation** have established that employees working in government hold values that are distinguishable from those working in the private sector and some studies suggest that the motivations of nonprofit employees may be similar to those of individuals who work in government (Word & Carpenter, 2013). Others find that despite a similar commitment to public service, government and nonprofit employees also demonstrate some differences. For example, employees in the public sector may be motivated by good benefit programs, job security, and opportunities for advancement, while nonprofit employees may be motivated more by family-friendly environments and opportunities to take on more responsibility. Nonprofit employees are also more likely to have served as volunteers, perhaps providing a clue as to their motivations (Lee & Wilkins, 2011). Thus, some research suggests that in both government and the nonprofit sector, intrinsic motivational factors may be more important than extrinsic factors, like financial compensation (Lee & Wilkins, 2011; Leonard, 2013). A study by Shuyang Peng, Sanjay Pandey, and Sheela Pandey (2015) found that nonprofits have an advantage over public agencies in fostering congruence between individual and organizational values. And Young-joo Lee (2016) found that nonprofit staff appreciate a clear description of their responsibilities, but also the independence to exercise discretion in carrying out their work. This may reflect the fact that the hierarchy is often less clear in a nonprofit than it is in government. How do nonprofit staff compare to those who work in business? A number of studies find that nonprofit staff have stronger intrinsic motivation than those working in for-profits, more commitment to "mission, activism, and social growth" (Chen, 2014, p. 740). These findings suggest that even though nonprofit staff often are paid less than their counterparts in the for-profit world and volunteers are, by definition, unpaid in financial terms, many may find their work very rewarding if Herzberg's motivators are present. Since they do not expect to receive the same salaries that are paid in some for-profit companies, perhaps they are not necessarily dissatisfied by their nonprofit incomes so long as they are at least adequate and perceived as fair. This perspective has many implications for nonprofit management practice. If managers can design jobs and create working environments in a way that provides their staff and volunteers with opportunities for achievement, recognition, advancement, and growth, and if the nature of the work is inherently rewarding, staff and volunteers may be highly motivated even within the limits of nonprofits' financial constraints. It could even be argued that nonprofits have an advantage over for-profit companies in motivating their workforces. Their sometimes limited financial resources do not prevent them from eliminating most of the potential dissatisfiers or increasing most of the Herzberg (1968) motivators. In addition, many offer work that is inherently rewarding because it is tied to a social purpose and the improvement or enrichment of human lives, something that only some, but not all, for-profit companies can offer. If nonprofit managers keep their staff and volunteers focused on the nonprofit's mission, they may keep them highly motivated. (Remember transformational leadership, discussed in Chapter 5.) Nonprofits may even have an advantage over government agencies, which also provide public service, since nonprofits may have the flexibility to offer some lifestyle advantages that would be more difficult for government employers to provide.

However, the reality of motivation in the nonprofit sector may be somewhat more complex and nuanced than some studies suggest. Gazley (2017) argues that most nonprofit staff members are motivated by both money and mission. Chung-An Chen (2014) agrees and explains why some research may get it wrong on this point. Some findings are based on comparing nonprofit staff with their counterparts in the for-profit sector. However, when scholars look *just* at nonprofit employees without comparing them to people in business, they find that extrinsic rewards, including salary, are also quite important to them (p. 740). Chen argues that the research has "disproportionately emphasized" the importance of intrinsic over extrinsic factors in the nonprofit workplace and agrees that most people likely are motivated by both.

Jasmine McGinnis Johnson, Jaclyn Schede Piatak, and Eddy Ng (2017) report research suggesting that Generation Y (also called "millennials") may place a higher emphasis on financial compensation than did previous generations of nonprofit staff members. So, we cannot assume that nonprofit staff members do not care about their financial compensation. Indeed, financial incentives to reward performance have become more common in the nonprofit sector, especially for CEOs and fundraising professionals. Financial incentives for nonprofit employees are not illegal or unethical, provided they are properly defined—for example, compensating fundraisers with a commission based on amounts raised is almost universally considered inappropriate, while paying them a bonus for having increased their number of visits to prospective donors is generally within accepted practice.

But introducing such financial incentives may entail certain risks for nonprofit organizations. Gerhard Speckbacher (2013) notes three presumed advantages that incentive compensation provides: motivation for increased effort, signals that lead to self-selection of high-performing people to the workplace, and channeling employee attention to desired outcomes (p. 1007). But, he finds, incentive compensation also may have an impact on a nonprofit's relationship with its employees. Introducing explicit incentives (i.e., money) changes the relationship from social to contractual—in other words, it becomes a market relationship. "Trust and the feeling of obligation may disappear" (p. 1021). Moreover, it is difficult to mix social incentives with financial incentives; the entire relationship is likely to become based on the latter. And if such incentives are introduced for some staff members (e.g., fundraisers), it is likely that there will be "spillover effects" on other staff members of the organization (p. 1021), who may come to see their relationship with their employer more in market terms. Speckbacher's analysis suggests that the debate about incentive compensation may have significant implications that the nonprofit sector must carefully consider.

Perhaps the most realistic understanding of motivation in the nonprofit sector is that employees choose their jobs based on a mix of motivating factors, including both mission and money, both intrinsic and extrinsic considerations. But the balance of intrinsic and extrinsic rewards offered requires care and judgment and must be considered in the context of each organization. As Gazley (2015) advises, "Nonprofits should begin by understanding the intrinsic motivations of prospective employees [and also] communicate the extrinsic rewards of a position in terms of both monetary and non-monetary benefits" (p. 97).

Life Cycles and Generations

Another category of theories relates to the changing needs of people as they advance through the various stages of their lives. **Life-cycle theories** of motivation have critics but also have received some attention in the scholarly literature in recent decades (Denhardt et al., 2016, pp. 162–163). Some theorists argue that both the skills and needs of workers change over their lifetimes. For example, young people may have "fluid intellectual abilities" and excel at abstract thinking (p. 163). By middle age, these abilities may diminish somewhat, but middle-age individuals will bring the benefits of greater experience. Similarly, motivations may change as people age. Young workers may be looking for opportunities to learn and be promoted, while middle-age and older workers may value job security and salary more (p. 163). This could imply that managers need to provide younger staff and volunteers with experiences that utilize their skills and meet their needs, while providing a somewhat different experience to those who are older. But, as some critics of life-cycle theories point out, this could also lead to ageism in the workplace, and managers need to be sure that they are not making erroneous assumptions about the skills or interests of individuals based exclusively on their stage in life (p. 163).

Life-cycle differences are, of course, distinct from generational differences. All people will advance through a cycle from young to middle age to older, and their needs and priorities may evolve in similar patterns. But the time period in which an individual was born and the significant events that marked the emergence of a generational cohort also may create differences that managers need to understand. There are three generations that predominate among nonprofit staff and volunteers today. The values and worldviews of each generation have been shaped in part by the economic conditions that prevailed during their formative years and by critical historical events that have occurred within their lifetimes. The baby boomers (born between 1946 and the mid-1960s) were shaped by the pressures of the Cold War and events such as Watergate and the Vietnam War. Many members of Generation X (born between about 1965 and 1979) were the first to grow up in families with both parents employed outside the home and witnessed such powerful events as the Challenger disaster and the fall of the Berlin Wall. The **millennials** (born after 1980) came of age with the development of the Internet, and some were shaped by events that included the terrorist attacks of September 11, 2001. Because of the advance of worldwide communication and increased opportunities for travel, many millennials have developed a greater international awareness than previous generations held. Although generalizations about individuals based on their generation can be as insidious as those based on age, sex, or other characteristics, a number of scholars have found some commonalities among members of particular generations. For example, some argue that baby boomers are committed to institutions and organizations and are most likely to be motivated by praise, money, and position. Members of Generation X may be distrustful of large organizations and are motivated by independence and involvement. Millennials (also called Generation Y) hold more graduate degrees than previous generations, are more inclined to change jobs frequently, and are more likely to switch sectors in their careers than were members of previous generations (Johnson et al., 2017, pp. 309–310). As mentioned previously, millennials are also more interested in extrinsic rewards, such as salary (Johnson et al., p. 308).

Again, it is essential to recognize that, as with life-cycle stages, individual differences may outweigh generational patterns. But it also may be useful for managers to recognize that individuals who are of generations different from their own may be motivated in different ways and that it may be a mistake to assume that one's own values and worldview are fully shared by others.

Again, there are many additional theories of motivation that this chapter does not discuss in detail, some of which are reflected in Table 9.1 and discussed in suggested readings listed at the end of this chapter. Much recent work has been devoted to attempts to integrate earlier theories. Most theories offer some useful insights that may help guide managers and increase their understanding of staff and volunteers. But, as Hal Rainey (2014, p. 259) states, "the basic research and theory provide no conclusive science of motivation. Leaders have to draw on the ideas and apply the available techniques pragmatically, blending the experience and judgment with the insights the literature provides." This nuanced advice is consistent with the philosophy expressed throughout this text.

Applying Theories to Managing the Nonprofit Workforce

As noted at various points earlier in this book, the literature of nonprofit management includes both theory and the prescriptions of practitioner-oriented authors. This book attempts to integrate both perspectives. Now that we have reviewed some of the theoretical literature on human motivation, let's look at one attempt to translate that theory into specific recommended practices in managing the nonprofit workforce.

In the fourth edition of their book, *Managing Human Behavior in Public and Nonprofit Organizations,* Denhardt et al. (2016, pp. 172–174) review the motivation literature and offer nine suggested "ways of acting" for nonprofit and public sector managers, which they found to reflect commonalities of the various theoretical approaches. The following paragraphs discuss each of their recommendations and how they may relate to the various theories discussed earlier.

1. *Managers should be reflective and proactive about their own motivation.* McClelland (1961) and other theorists have suggested that the manager's own psychological needs and motivations affect how he or she interacts with and communicates with colleagues and subordinates. This is a point that is also reflected in McGregor's (1960) description of Theory X and Theory Y. The manager's values and worldview, perhaps shaped by his or her generational experience or stage of life, also may affect his or her behavior with regard to the people supervised. This would imply that self-knowledge and understanding are essential for any individual who aspires to be an effective manager of others.

2. *Managers should be aware that what motivates them is not necessarily what will motivate others.* This advice is supported by several theories and reflects the simple but important understanding that people are not all alike. As Maslow (1954) and other theorists suggest, they bring their own needs to the workplace, which may reflect circumstances in their personal lives, their cultural backgrounds, or other characteristics. Or they may have different preferred ways of communicating, perhaps reflecting their personality styles or comfort with various media. Again, generational and life-stage differences may be relevant.

3. *Managers should have realistic expectations about the extent to which they can influence the motivation of others.* Again, as Maslow (1954) and other theorists explain, people come to the workplace already motivated. They are motivated to meet whatever psychological needs they may already have. The manager may not be able to influence those motivations very much. It may be more productive to assign people to jobs that enable them to meet their existing needs or perhaps redesign jobs to make them a better fit with the natural inclinations of those who hold them. Of course, if individuals' needs and motivations simply do not align with the goals of the organization, it may be best to suggest that they find employment in a more suitable environment. Too much effort to change the individuals may prove frustrating and fruitless.

4. *Managers should participate in setting clear and challenging goals.* As Herzberg (1968) discovered, the opportunity for achievement is a motivator for most individuals. But achievement requires that there be clear goals by which it is defined. Otherwise, effort yields no emotional reward, or a situation may evolve in which individuals feel that even "enough" is not sufficient to please their supervisors. And, as Rensis Likert (1967) and others have proposed, participation in goal setting may itself be an important source of motivation. The manager thus should establish goals in a participative manner so that the staff member accepts them as his or her own, provide regular feedback on progress, and grant recognition when the goals are reached. As Christine Letts, William Ryan, and Allen Grossman (1999) observe, managers often face two challenges: getting the job done and keeping the staff satisfied. But they state, "Organizing jobs so employees can achieve and see results does both: It advances the organization's mission and motivates people in the process" (p. 108).

5. *Managers should think about the salience of various rewards.* Again, individuals are motivated differently. They have different values. And what they will find rewarding may be different in each case. A manager needs to listen, determine what each member of the staff finds important, and provide rewards consistent with that insight. Some may thrive on recognition—for example, being named "staff member of the week." Others may value the opportunity for flexible hours or to earn additional free time through outstanding performance. Some may need to have a clear understanding of the social impact of their efforts. And some may have financial needs that make salary a priority. As Denhardt and colleagues (2016) emphasize, and as the Hawthorne experiments suggested so many years ago, the interest and attention of the manager may itself be a reward that will reinforce high performance for some members of the staff. Or, as Denhardt and colleagues suggest, such attention may actually reinforce the undesirable behaviors of someone who is not performing well. And, as discussed previously, some staff may consider their financial compensation to be highly important.

6. *Managers should be honest with people about what rewards are possible and what rewards are not.* As **expectancy theory** (Vroom, 1964) describes, individuals may be motivated not only by the value of rewards but also by the probability that they can be obtained. A manager who is unrealistic in promising increased compensation, increased responsibility, community recognition, or some other reward for achievement of goals may buy some short-term motivation. But over time, such a manager will lose credibility and the power to influence the behavior of his or her staff.

7. *Managers should treat people equitably and fairly.* People in a workplace have a sense of what is equitable, in terms of effort, compensation, status, and other matters. As Herzberg's (1968) theory suggests, inequities in salary paid to individuals who perform similar work or put forth comparable effort may create more dissatisfaction than fair compensation that is modest in absolute terms. Similar points are made by the equity theorists (Adams, 1965). Of course, no person should be treated unfairly for reasons of his or her race, nationality, religion, sex, sexual orientation, gender identity, disability, political perspective, or other personal characteristics. To do so is morally wrong and generally illegal. And it is just poor management, likely to result in a dysfunctional, dissatisfied, and unproductive workforce that will not build a high-performing organization. Effective nonprofit organizations today go beyond the requirements of law and embrace diversity and inclusion as organizational values, seeking to draw the strength that comes from bringing together people of different perspectives, experiences, cultures, and backgrounds. In our complex society, any organization that does not incorporate such diversity will quickly lose touch with its community and constituency and, by excluding important talent, weaken its ability to serve its mission and achieve its goals.

8. *Managers should make the work satisfying and meaningful.* Motivation arises not only from the characteristics of people but also from the nature of the work they are given to perform. As Herzberg (1968) observed, some work is intrinsically motivating. But routine tasks may become monotonous and dissatisfying. Even interesting work may become less interesting if it is unchanging over time. Good managers provide their staff members with opportunities to grow personally and professionally, to take on new challenges, and to develop new skills in a variety of areas. This may be accomplished by rotating assignments or redesigning jobs, by providing training, and by offering opportunities for advancement from within the organization. Those who are employed in nonprofits are usually motivated by the impact of their work on the lives of clients. It is good practice to provide staff with as much exposure to clients as possible, enabling them to see firsthand the outcomes of their efforts.

9. *Managers should think about the life stages of the people they work with and offer appropriate support.* The life stage (or life-cycle) theories describe the needs and motivations of people in various periods. Such theories do have many critics, but they suggest that understanding the issues facing individuals in their personal lives may provide the manager with a useful perspective that is of benefit both to the individual and to the organization. It is also an approach that creates a humane environment consistent with the values of most nonprofit organizations. In addition, as discussed above, there may be differences among generations in what workplace culture or management style may be preferred and most effective. A manager needs to understand these differences and adjust the work experience in order to gain the maximum contribution from each individual.

Managing Volunteers

The discussion in the previous section of this chapter was focused primarily on the management of nonprofit staff members. Let's now shift our discussion to look at some principles that apply specifically to managing service volunteers. Effective management of volunteers is an important topic because volunteers are a major component of the workforce of many nonprofits. The Corporation for National and Community Service estimates that 63 million Americans engaged in volunteer service in 2015, providing almost 8 billion hours of service (Corporation for National and Community Service, n.d.-c). These data were little changed from the previous year. Some express concern about a possible long-term decline in the number of Americans who volunteer, which reached a high in 2003 (O'Neil, 2015b). However, others note that the decline has not been that significant in real numbers and that the data may reflect just some churn in volunteers, as some drop out and others are recruited (Brudney, 2016, p. 717).

The service of volunteers is of enormous economic importance to nonprofit organizations and to society. Independent Sector (2017b) estimates that each hour of volunteer time contributed to nonprofits in 2016 was worth $24.14; that is an average of what organizations would have needed to pay to obtain similar services from paid staff—not an inconsequential sum. It is important to note, however, that individuals cannot claim a tax deduction for the value of their volunteered time. A nonprofit organization can cite the value of volunteer services in its communications, to demonstrate wide community support or for purposes of recognizing volunteers like donors. However, there are limitations on how that value can be used on nonprofit financial statements. According to rules established by the Financial Accounting Standards Board (1993), the value of volunteer work can be used on financial statements, in grant proposals, and in other formal ways only if the volunteers are providing specialized services for which the nonprofit would otherwise have paid. That might include, for example, services of accountants, architects, doctors, and similar professionals.

As Michael O'Neill (2002) observes, "Nonprofits differ greatly with regard to the role of volunteers." Many nonprofits are small, all-volunteer efforts. Many nonprofits with paid staff also rely heavily on volunteers. Others, such as research institutes, universities, and private foundations, use few volunteers (p. 31). Recent decades have seen the increased professionalization of nonprofit management, with paid staff replacing volunteers in some organizations, especially the largest and most commercialized. Today, volunteers often work alongside paid staff, and **volunteer management** has itself become a specialty of professional nonprofit management.

Types of Volunteers

There are different types of volunteers, summarized in Table 9.3. The types are characterized by the pattern of their participation, the extent of their commitment, and their motivations. There is not a consensus about the definitions of the various types (Brudney, 2016, p. 708).

Sunney Shin and Brian Kleiner (2003) identify one type as what they call **spot volunteers**, whose participation is casual. For example, individuals may respond to a call for volunteers to help clean up a park or a hiking trail—it is a one-day commitment, and there is likely enough work to occupy as many people as show up. The effort may not need to be repeated again, at least for some period of time, and there is no special skill required to participate.

Other volunteers may participate more than once, but only for a short period of time or during a certain time of the year, for example, during the holiday season or in the summer. Some authors refer to them as **episodic volunteers**, although, again, there is not a universally accepted terminology. Some use the term episodic volunteer to describe both someone who volunteers just once (same as a spot volunteer) or who volunteers from time to time, that is, episodically (Brudney, 2016, p. 708).

Another type defined by Shin and Kleiner (2003) are known as **regular volunteers**, who make a commitment to the activity and gain a sense of gratification and accomplishment from the work. Such volunteer assignments may have the formality of regular paid jobs; there may be job descriptions, clear statements of responsibilities, and specific skills required to perform the work. Continuity may be important; for example, those who participate in tutoring programs need to be present in every session in order to develop relationships and gain the trust of the children. In other situations, dependability is essential; for example, volunteer fire departments or disaster relief organizations cannot rely on whoever may choose to show up on a given occasion.

An additional type of volunteer is one who is pressured (or perhaps just strongly encouraged) to engage in service. Robert Stebbins (2009) refers to this type as the marginal volunteer, but that term might have unfair negative connotations, so we refer to them simply as **encouraged or mandated volunteers** in this chapter. For example, a significant number of corporations encourage their employees to engage in community service activities, as a

Table 9.3	Types of Volunteers
Spot volunteers	Participate casually, usually on one occasion, for example, in a one-day effort to clean up the park
Episodic volunteers	May participate on only one occasion or on multiple occasions or for brief periods of time, for example, distributing food during the holiday season
Regular volunteers	Serve essentially as unpaid staff, performing duties specified in job descriptions and requiring specialized skills, for example, tutoring children one or two days per week on an ongoing basis or standing prepared to provide disaster-relief services to a community
Encouraged or mandated volunteers	Participate primarily because service is encouraged or required, often by an employer, educational program, or court, but may also find their volunteer activity to be rewarding
Virtual volunteers	Serve an organization from afar, usually via electronic technology

strategy both for gaining goodwill for the company and for building camaraderie among the workforce. Some employees may find this encouragement almost impossible to resist if they desire to gain advancement in their company. In other cases, someone may volunteer because they are asked to do so by friends, for example, in an activity such as a walk or run. They may enjoy the experience but participate primarily because of peer pressure; without a personal commitment to the organization, they may be unlikely to become regular volunteers. Many states require (or mandate) that high school students complete a volunteer experience as a graduation requirement. In addition, some professional education programs require that students complete an internship as a requirement of graduation. (Whether an intern is truly a "volunteer" and whether interns should be compensated is an issue with some legal considerations; National Council of Nonprofits, 2017a). And, of course, courts often assign first-time offenders of minor crimes to community service as a form of restitution. Although some may regard mandatory voluntarism, or even that performed under pressure, as an oxymoron, others speculate that the requirement of service for young people may be helpful in introducing them to the concept, perhaps beginning a commitment that they will continue throughout their lives. Of course, volunteers who are encouraged or even required to participate may also be motivated by other reasons and may find their service rewarding.

Virtual volunteers are relatively new on the scene, but their numbers are growing. These volunteers work from a distance using electronic technology, perhaps serving the nonprofit via e-mail, the Web, or postings on Twitter, Facebook, and other social media (Brudney, 2016, p. 707). The nonprofit website VolunteerMatch.org matches volunteers to organizations' needs and identifies numerous opportunities for virtual volunteers (volunteermatch. org). Jayne Cravens and Susan Ellis (2014) emphasize that principles of sound volunteer management, which we will discuss further later in this chapter, apply to virtual volunteers as well as those who serve on-site. Those principles encompass recruitment, supervision, and support. Special efforts are required to build and maintain a sense of community among virtual volunteers in order to retain their interest and commitment. That includes frequent communication, both online and through regular mail, and recognition of success (Cravens & Ellis, pp. 70–71).

In recent years, there has been growth in international volunteering, perhaps reflecting the increased international awareness created by global communications and the visibility of philanthropic organizations such as the Gates Foundation, which focuses on global problems. Volunteers, mostly from the United States and other western nations, travel to other parts of the world to work on conservation, educational, and humanitarian projects, usually for a brief period of time. In the vocabulary discussed above, they are generally spot or episodic volunteers, rather than a distinctive type.

Some international volunteer experiences fall under the rubric of **voluntourism**, also called volunteer vacations. Some are structured to place the primary emphasis on the volunteer project, with some period of vacation attached. Others are primarily vacations with work on a volunteer project incorporated for some portion of the trip. Individuals who participate in such programs often have mixed motives; some are undoubtedly motivated at least in part by altruism, but some may be seeking primarily an opportunity for adventure and self-development (Chen & Chen, 2011). Some authors have questioned the impact of such short-term projects and have questioned whether voluntourism primarily benefits the volunteers more than those it intends to help (Kahn, 2014).

Motivations of Volunteers

We need to consider the motivations of volunteers in two ways: first, in terms of what motivates people to become volunteers in the first place, and second, what factors motivate them to perform at a high level and continue in their volunteer roles.

Research provides us with insights on *who* volunteers. People who volunteer tend to have more diversity in their friendships, more education, and greater intensity of religious belief. They also are more likely to engage in religious activities, social networking, and social groups (Forbes & Zampelli, 2014). But *why* do people volunteer? Some may be motivated by the mission of the organization, the desire to advance a cause, or perhaps the desire to repay for some benefit that the individual received. These are altruistic reasons; that is, the individual's motivation for volunteering is based on the public good accomplished, not by any benefits that may accrue to the volunteer himself or herself. On the other hand, some people may volunteer because of benefits that they receive from doing so. This may include the intangible warm feeling of emotional satisfaction or more tangible benefits, such as gaining increased job skills, building an enhanced resume, or making social contacts. As Jeffrey Brudney (2016) observes, research on the motivations of volunteers has been "voluminous" and the basic conclusion it reaches is that motivations are "complex and multi-faceted" (p. 711). In other words, most volunteers may be motivated by a combination of reasons; as Femida Handy and Laurie Mook (2010) describe, they are "impure altruists." The fact that people may be motivated by a combination of altruism and personal needs does not diminish the value of their efforts or make them less admirable. However, it is essential for the nonprofit manager to understand these sometimes mixed and complex motivations in order to create an experience that will attract and retain the volunteer workforce.

A considerable body of research on volunteers suggests that the factors leading to their motivation and satisfaction are very similar to those for paid staff. For example, studies have found that volunteers are motivated by a desire to serve the mission, that volunteers who remain with the organization are those who experience positive relationships with other volunteers, that those who continue to serve are those who find the nature of the work itself rewarding, and that volunteers value opportunities to learn new skills through their voluntary service. Volunteers who have participated in studies assign importance to factors such as clearly defined responsibilities, a reasonable work schedule, and competent supervision, all consistent with the motivation theories we have previously discussed. Although not all experts agree (Brudney, 2016, p. 694), some research suggests that recommended practices for managing volunteers should include many points similar to those for the management of staff (McCurley, 2005). Some studies suggest that nonprofits desiring to maintain relationships with volunteers over the long term should avoid subjecting them to pressure, deadlines for completing work, or external controls; in other words, volunteers may highly value autonomy in completing their assignments (Oostlander, Güntert, van Schie, & Wehner, 2014).

Volunteer Program Practices

There is much information available on the design of volunteer programs and on the management of volunteers. The list of suggested readings at the end of this chapter provides a small sample of the many publications and websites that offer access to additional materials. Although there are varied opinions on many points, there is also much commonality among the experts on recommended practices in developing and managing an effective volunteer program. Most authors offer some or all of the following points (see, e.g., Brudney, 2016; McCurley & Lynch, 2006).

Assess the need for volunteers. Before an organization launches a program for the use of volunteers, it needs to determine why volunteers are needed and desired. If the need is for spot volunteers to complete an essentially simple, one-time project, that is obviously a different matter from establishing a program that will engage regular volunteers in delivering ongoing services to clients. Some may assume that regular volunteers offer a cost-effective way to provide services, but that may not always be the case. The costs related to recruiting, supporting, and managing volunteers—possibly requiring the appointment of additional paid staff—must be taken into consideration (Brudney, 2016, p. 691). Moreover, volunteers who are inadequately supported may well become dissatisfied, and high turnover could affect the quality of programs. Although regular volunteers are unpaid, they are not free, since they can only be effective in the context of an organized and managed effort.

Nonprofits may have reasons for desiring the involvement of volunteers that go beyond the economics of needed labor. The involvement of volunteers may increase connections with the community or clients, inject passion and energy into the organization's culture, and even open doors to new sources of funding (Brudney, 2016). These are all among the good reasons for maintaining a volunteer program, but again, the organization should be clear and explicit about what it expects to gain and clear eyed about the costs of making the program successful. Recruiting volunteers exclusively for the sake of community engagement or fundraising and without a clear understanding of how they will make substantive contributions toward achieving the organization's mission is likely to be a counterproductive approach.

One fundamental decision to be made is which jobs or functions may best be performed by volunteers and which require the full-time attention of paid staff. Lack of clarity on this question may lead to unrealistic expectations, tensions between staff and volunteers, or a mismatch of volunteers' skills to their responsibilities. Although writing for a scenario of financial retrenchment, Ellis (2010) offers a suggested approach that may be more broadly applicable. She recommends reviewing all jobs in the organization, both staff and volunteer, and considering the following questions:

- What is someone doing once a week or periodically rather than daily or on an inflexible schedule?

- What is someone doing that really does not require his/her specialized training? (For example, a lot of time is spent in making follow-up telephone calls, composing letters, etc. that may take someone away from direct service to clients.)

- What is someone doing that might be done more effectively by someone else with special training in that skill? (Ellis, p. 131)

Once tasks have been classified according to these questions, Ellis (2010) advises that those requiring daily attention, specialized training, and critical responsibilities be assigned to staff members. Periodic or less technical responsibilities may then be assigned to volunteers, along with any that require special talents or skills for which volunteers have been specifically enlisted (p. 131).

Determine the structure of the volunteer program. A successful volunteer program requires that the relative roles of volunteers and staff be clearly defined and that the responsibility for supervision of volunteers be explicit. Again, engaging spot volunteers for a one-time effort may not require that much thought be devoted to organization, but the regular involvement of volunteers raises questions of how they will be integrated within the operations of the organization.

One model takes a decentralized approach, with volunteers based in specific programs and supervised by the leaders of those programs, whether staff or other volunteers. This approach offers the advantage of being able to match volunteer interests and skills to specific activities. But it also may lead to uneven experiences and limit the organization's flexibility to reassign volunteers as needs change across its departments. An alternative model is a centralized program, with management of all volunteers assigned to a single department or office, perhaps led by a paid professional volunteer manager. This may facilitate training, evaluation, and coordination of effort across the organization. It also provides some protection against risk, since potential volunteers can be screened by the same criteria and a single manager can monitor their performance to assure both the quality of programs and the safety of volunteers and clients. But there also may be potential downsides to a centralized model if support for the volunteer program is not broadly present in all departments (Brudney, 2016).

The manner in which the volunteer program is organized should be consistent with the overall structure of the organization. Thus, a highly decentralized organization, in which many decisions are delegated to program directors or local offices, may best engage and manage volunteers in a decentralized manner. But an organization that is highly centralized in other aspects of its operation most likely will take a more centralized approach to volunteers. The size of the organization is an obvious consideration in selecting the organizational model, but the overall management culture also needs to be considered.

Develop volunteer job descriptions. If volunteers are to serve episodically (e.g., a group is going to the woods for one day to clean up trash and repair hiking trails), there may not be a need for much formality in defining volunteer jobs—a supervisor can just assign those who show up to the tasks that need to be done. But if the organization needs volunteers to play an ongoing role as a part of its workforce, then volunteer jobs need to be designed and defined with some precision in order to establish clear expectations and ensure that the volunteer's work is related to program needs. Having formal job descriptions also helps communicate to volunteers that they are accepting a significant responsibility and that their assignment involves doing real work that is central to the program of the nonprofit.

Job descriptions do not need to be complex or extensive but should carefully state the type of work, skills needed, and expectations of volunteers. For example, the job description for a volunteer at the Harry S. Truman Library in Independence, Missouri, shown in Box 9.1,

Box 9.1   Volunteer Job Description

Harry S. Truman Library & Museum

TITLE OF POSITION: ARCHIVES ASSISTANT

SUPERVISED BY: Archives Staff
PURPOSE OF JOB: Assist archives staff with basic archival functions such as processing, preservation, reference, etc. Objective is to assist in increasing availability of research material.

DUTIES MAY INCLUDE BUT ARE NOT LIMITED TO:

1. Photocopying and filing.

2. Maintain proper care and maintenance of all documents handled.

3. Create finding aids (indexes, catalogs, etc.).

4. Data entry.

5. Stamping of documents.

6. Prepare material for preservation work.

7. Attend orientation sessions and complete training readings.

8. Communicate regularly with assigned supervisor as to concerns, issues, or ideas arising from the current project.

9. Participate in reviews within archives of assignments prior to extension, reassignment, or completion.

10. Ensure the goals and policies of the archives and library are promoted and adhered to.

(Continued)

Box 9.1 (Continued)

COMMITMENT REQUIRED:
A minimum commitment of 4–5 hours per week for a 3-month period is required. Volunteer opportunities will be available Monday–Friday, 9:00 a.m.–4:30 p.m. There are no weekend or evening opportunities for this position.

QUALIFICATIONS NEEDED:

- Must be age 16 or older

- Basic computer skills and/or good handwriting helpful

- Flexible to changing situation

- Reliable, responsible

- Able to work independently as well as in a group environment

- Able to accept supervision

- Interest in history

- Ability to perform repetitive tasks and detail oriented

- Good organizational skills

TRAINING/ORIENTATION PROVIDED:
Since the duties performed by the Archives Assistants are varied, training and work assignments are both designed to meet the individual requirements of the task to be accomplished. Training is provided on-the-job by the Truman Library's archives staff.

Basic reading material on the Truman presidency and archives work is additionally provided.

LOCATION OF JOB:
The Harry S. Truman Library, Independence, Missouri

VOLUNTEER BENEFITS:
Knowledge about Harry S. Truman, the Library and Museum, and the educational aspects offered to visitors through a variety of programs/exhibits; discount prices in the museum gift shop; invitations to special events; volunteer appreciation programs; free parking; free subscription to *Whistle-Stop*, the quarterly newsletter of the Harry S. Truman Library Institute; free admission to the museum for you and your immediate family; work with original and unique historical documents.

Source: Harry S. Truman Library & Museum website (http://www.trumanlibrary.org/voluntee/archivjd.htm).

lists the specific tasks that the volunteer will perform and the qualifications required for the position, as well as the organization's commitment to provide training and compensation in the form of nonfinancial benefits.

Develop formal volunteer policies. Volunteers may be unpaid, but they are a part of the organization's workforce. Indeed, they often work alongside of paid staff in delivering services. There should be formal policies that spell out the expectations, rules, and standards by which volunteers will be evaluated and, if necessary, terminated. The policies should describe the relationship between volunteers and any paid staff by whom they are supervised or whom they may supervise. Organizations have personnel policies to govern their relationship with paid staff; not having such policies for volunteers might imply that they are not as essential as staff and may set the stage for misunderstandings, conflict between volunteers and staff members, or even legal problems.

Having formal volunteer policies is also an important element of risk management for the organization. This is especially important in settings where volunteers will have direct contact with clients or access to confidential client information, or in which clients are particularly vulnerable or potentially volatile. For example, Box 9.2 includes sample volunteer policies suggested by the Indiana Nonprofit Resource Network for health care organizations, which may present an especially sensitive environment. New volunteers should be given a copy of the policies and should sign a statement acknowledging that they have read them. In addition, most organizations should carry liability insurance, to protect both organizational assets and volunteers.

Box 9.2 Sample Organizational Volunteering Policy (Health Care)

This is a sample policy geared toward a hospital volunteer program. However, many of the aspects included in the policy are items that are considered best practice to have in any organization volunteering policy. In most areas, you may be able to replace the word *hospital* or *health care* with your organization's specialty: hospice, senior center, after-school program, etc.

PURPOSE

1. To establish the Director of Volunteer Services as responsible for recruitment, utilization, and supervision of volunteers throughout [the organization]

2. To provide [the organization's] customers the benefit of an organized and consistent volunteer program

3. To recruit, train, and retain community members for an effective hospital system volunteer program, thereby creating good public relations between [the organization] and the community it serves

4. To provide volunteers from all segments of the community a means of meeting the need to provide service to others

6. To provide community members 14 years of age and older an opportunity to become acquainted with the health care field and to encourage their interest in health careers as student volunteers, or special case volunteers

DEFINITIONS

Volunteer: Anyone who, without compensation or expectation of compensation beyond reimbursement, performs a task at the direction of and on behalf of [the organization]. A "volunteer" must be officially accepted and enrolled by [the organization] prior to performance of the task. Volunteers must be at least 14 years of age to be officially accepted and enrolled by [the organization's] Volunteer Services department.

(Continued)

Box 9.2 (Continued)

Special Case Volunteers: [The organization] also accepts as volunteers those participating in student intern projects, corporate volunteer programs, and other volunteer referral programs. In each of these cases, however, a special agreement must be in effect with the organization, school, or program from which the special case volunteers originate and must identify responsibility for management and care of the volunteers.

[The organization] does not accept volunteers who must complete community service hours related to a court order.

GENERAL INFORMATION

1. Volunteers will be encouraged, but not required, to become members of [the organization].

2. New volunteer opportunities shall be proposed to various hospital system departments. All qualified volunteers will have the opportunity to staff the service. The Director of Volunteer Services will work cooperatively with the designated staff person to implement the service. All new programs are the responsibility of the Director of Volunteer Services or his/her designee.

3. Volunteers will not replace paid employees but serve to supplement and enhance existing services to patients, their families, and hospital system programs.

4. Volunteer service will be an important, honored role at [the organization], including Hospice and the Community Health Center with every effort made to integrate and coordinate volunteer talents and needs with the hospital system's program.

5. Volunteer programs and activities will be monitored and evaluated on an ongoing basis by the Director of Volunteer Services or his/her designee in conjunction with other involved staff members.

PROCEDURE

1. Potential volunteers will complete an application and submit to the Director of Volunteer Services or his/her designee. Volunteers 18 years of age and older will complete and submit a Release of Information, which will be reviewed by the County Sheriff's Department for history. Volunteers assisting in secured hospital departments will also complete a criminal background application for the State of Indiana.

2. Reference checks will be completed on all volunteers.

3. Volunteers will be interviewed by the Director of Volunteer Services, his/her designee, and/or department manager to assure placement is in accordance with skills of the volunteer.

4. All volunteers will receive a TB test or a chest x-ray and a photo ID badge before volunteerism begins. Departmental training will be done by department staff or trained volunteer.

5. Volunteers are required to attend volunteer orientation session provided by Volunteer Services Department.

6. Hospital system managers wanting volunteer assistance will complete a volunteer service requisition and submit it to Volunteer Services. After the Director of Volunteer Services or his/her designee has selected a volunteer, the requesting department will be notified.

7. A record of individual hours of service by all volunteers will be maintained by the Volunteer Services Department.

8. The Director of Volunteer Services will maintain a ... database record and a personnel file on each volunteer, to include

   - Application
   - Background check(s)
   - Reference checks
   - Medical clearance (sick leaves)
   - Orientation record
   - Attendance at educational in-services
   - Evaluations

9. Volunteers will be honored each year for the hours they have volunteered in the previous year for [organization]. Activities to honor the [organization's] volunteers are held during National Volunteer Week.

Source: Indiana Nonprofit Resource Network (http://www.iuw.org/indiana-nonprofit-resource-network/resources/staff-volunteer/organizational-volunteering-policy.pdf). Indiana Nonprofit Resource Network (INRN) is a regionally based service delivered on behalf of Indiana United Ways. Used with permission.

Provide a sufficient budget and personnel to manage the volunteer program. Without adequate resources, such as books, computers, tools, transportation, supervision, or whatever their work may require, volunteers are no more likely than staff to be successful. Depending on the scope of the volunteer program, it may be important to have a full-time member of the paid staff to manage the organization's overall relationship with volunteers. This does not imply that volunteers necessarily report to the volunteer manager with regard to their specific assignments but that the manager maintains an overall view of volunteers' involvement and performance. It is also important that all members of the paid staff who work with volunteers, including perhaps program or unit directors, are provided with training on the special considerations in managing them.

Recruit and hire volunteers as if they were employees. Some organizations may be in such need of volunteers that they may be tempted to accept anyone who indicates an interest. This is what Stephen McCurley (2005, p. 595) calls warm body recruitment, the implication being that if the person is breathing and willing, they are signed on as a volunteer. But taking this approach may produce only a short-run gain and, indeed, it is likely to neither meet the organization's needs nor provide a satisfying experience for the volunteers.

In contrast to the warm-body approach, targeted recruitment of volunteers "is designed to attract fewer, select volunteers for jobs that require particular skills or interests or are appropriate for specific age or cultural groups" (McCurley, 2005, p. 595). A well-managed program is likely to attract, at least over time, sufficient interest to permit selectivity in the hiring of volunteers. A selective volunteer program requires that prospective volunteers complete an application and undergo an interview process. Background checks may also be required by law or be advisable in consideration of risk management.

Gaining the ability to be targeted and selective in choosing volunteers offers the organization at least two advantages: First, it can select people with the right skills to meet its needs and those who are likely to remain committed to their volunteer responsibilities. Second, the organization may be able to craft its volunteer program in order to include individuals from prospective donor companies, religious congregations, or other groups with which it wishes to establish closer relationships. A volunteer program thus can become not only a vehicle for delivering the organization's programs but also an instrument of its fundraising, communications, and community relations efforts. However, as stated previously, it is important not to permit the latter considerations to predominate. Engaging volunteers simply as a fundraising strategy but failing to provide them with a structured and meaningful experience is likely to lead to their frustration, and undermine, rather than enhance, their perception of and affiliation with the organization.

Provide orientation and training to volunteers. Volunteer orientation should include an introduction to the organization that covers not only practical operational matters but also a discussion of its mission, values, and culture. It should clarify the relationship between volunteers and paid staff and the expectations of each. Depending on the nature of the volunteer's work, training may include working with another, more experienced volunteer for a period or a more formal program designed to develop specific skills.

Set clear goals, evaluate performance, and recognize achievement. As discussed previously, people are motivated by clear goals, the explication of a clear path to their achievement, and recognition for having succeeded in reaching them. Since volunteers are not compensated financially, their achievement of goals and recognition may be their primary rewards. This suggests that volunteer job performance should be evaluated, which of course implies that volunteers could be terminated when appropriate as well, the same as paid staff. Some organizations may find that a difficult decision to reach because they are in need of volunteers and feel they cannot afford to let one go. Or perhaps the culture of the organization may not encompass individual performance standards, at least not for volunteers. It also can be problematic if volunteers are also donors—even board members, whose termination might bring additional consequences. However, such concerns should be balanced against the need to maintain the overall quality and reputation of the program, the importance of achieving quality in service delivery, and the negative consequences for the morale of both staff and other volunteers of retaining someone whose work or attitude does not make a positive contribution. Of course, evaluation should be a two-way street. Volunteers should be given opportunities to provide feedback on the quality of their experience, including the conditions, supervision, and resources with which they work.

In summary, many experts suggest that, in most respects, volunteers should be managed with many of the same practices that apply to paid staff. To be sure, volunteers are entitled to respect and gratitude. Their impact is much the same as that of donors of financial gifts, and they are a precious asset that nonprofits need to nurture and cultivate. However, for all these reasons, they also deserve a structured and professional approach that maintains high expectations and stays focused on achievement of the organization's mission and goals.

Volunteer Management as a Career Field

As mentioned before, volunteer management has become a distinct specialty in nonprofit management. In some organizations, the staff member responsible for volunteer engagement also has other responsibilities, so the focus on volunteers is part time (Ellis, 2010, p. 70). But full-time positions are increasing in number. Titles of such positions are varied, including volunteer manager or director of volunteers. However, Ellis (2010) argues that the most appropriate titles are something like "director of volunteer services," "manager of volunteer resources," or "volunteer program manager," since they address the management of programs and activities rather than individuals (p. 74). The distinction may be useful and conducive to maintaining positive relationships between staff and volunteers.

There is a multitude of training programs for volunteer program managers, including university-based and online courses as well as professional conferences and workshops. The Association of Leaders in Volunteer Engagement (ALIVE) is one organization that offers membership and various resources to professionals employed in the management of volunteer programs (http://volunteeralive.org). Similar professional organizations also exist in most states. The Council for Certification in Volunteer Administration offers professional credentials to volunteer management professionals (http://cvacert.org/cva-certification/).

The Future of Volunteerism

Scholars who have studied volunteerism in the United States have identified trends that offer opportunities for nonprofit organizations but that may also present challenges to nonprofit managers who rely on volunteers for delivery of important programs and services. The long-term trend in volunteering has been positive. One study, conducted by the Corporation for National and Community Service in 2006, examined rates of volunteer participation all the way back to 1974. While there were periods of decline, participation in volunteer activities had generally increased and reached an all-time high by 2005 (Corporation for National and Community Service, 2006). But participation in volunteering has been generally stagnant since 2005 and, as mentioned earlier, it declined in 2015 (Corporation for National and Community Service, n.d.-c). Some have speculated that the reason for this downturn may have been lingering effects of the economic recession of 2007–2009 or a lack of nonprofits' capacity to recruit and train volunteers. Some have called for more foundation funding to increase the ability of nonprofits to manage volunteer programs. Others argue that the data miss the growing numbers of virtual volunteers (Perry, 2014).

But some scholars have discerned deeper social changes. Based on a 2005 study, Walter Rehberg makes a distinction between "old volunteering" and "new volunteering." He argues that old volunteering was based on a connection to religious or political communities and was motivated by a sense of membership, altruism, and concern for the collective good. In new volunteering, "volunteers are not particularly loyal to organizations, tend to be choosy about what they do, and expect some personal benefit from their [volunteer experience]" (Rehberg, p. 109). According to Rehberg, this shift is more than a statistical trend; it reflects more profound social changes in which individuals are less inclined to find inspiration in commitment to a local community, traditional institution, or set ideology and are more inclined to see volunteering as a way to combine "self-directed or instrumental motives with a sense of compassion or duty" (p. 110). In other words, as discussed earlier in this chapter, volunteers may be motivated both by altruism and the personal benefits derived from their voluntary activities. But, as Rehberg suggests, the sense of connection and duty to communities and traditional institutions may be less than in the past. People may have become more concerned with personal growth and identity. If so, then the latter set of motives may continue to grow in importance.

Both demographic and social changes may have significant implications for how nonprofit organizations enlist and manage volunteers. First, in the years ahead, older people may be the most promising source of regular volunteers; that will require that volunteer managers understand and address their particular interests and needs. Second, with regard to volunteers of all ages and generations, the sense of duty and obligation may not be sufficient to compensate for a poor volunteer experience. This is not to suggest that altruism and the desire to help others will not continue to be an important motivation for volunteering; it is to suggest that volunteers may be unwilling to participate for long in an experience that is unrewarding and offers little opportunity for personal growth. Nonprofits will need to become even more mindful of principles discussed in this chapter, in order to assure that volunteer efforts are well defined, well managed, and meaningful to those who participate.

CHAPTER SUMMARY

Human resources management (HRM) involves formal systems and activities related to recruitment, selection, training and development, compensation and benefits, retention, evaluation, promotion, and labor–management relationships. One important aspect of human resources management is assuring compliance with the law. Some laws affect only employees, but others also apply to volunteers and contractors.

Early management theories were often developed in industrial settings and portrayed human beings as part of a production machine, whose performance could be increased by focusing on procedures and rules. Since at least the Hawthorne experiments of the 1920s, theorists have focused on human psychology and motivation, emphasizing the influence of human needs and feelings on behavior in the workplace. Theories are often advanced, gain wide acceptance, and are subsequently discredited through further research. But most offer some principles that are adopted in new approaches or that gain continued acceptance by practitioners.

One theory, advanced by Frederick Herzberg, suggests that there are two sets of factors present in the workplace. One set of factors, which includes rewarding work and opportunities for achievement, recognition, and advancement, serves to motivate workers. Another set of factors, related to the work environment and including supervision, working conditions, and compensation, may be dissatisfiers but are not in themselves motivating. Managers should try to reduce or eliminate dissatisfiers and increase motivators. These principles may apply to the motivation of volunteers as well as paid staff members. Other theories, including those of Maslow, McClelland, and Myers and Briggs, suggest that individuals bring their own personal needs and styles into the workplace. This may require that managers design jobs to reflect the existing motivations of their staff and volunteers. Some research suggests that employees in nonprofit organizations have unique motivations, including commitment to the mission, but other research suggests that extrinsic variables, including salary, also may be important to people who work in the nonprofit sector. Some nonprofits provide financial incentives to reward performance and some scholars warn that doing so may change employees' relationship with the organization from social to contractual. Nonprofits should understand the intrinsic motivations of prospective employees but also communicate about extrinsic rewards, including financial and nonmonetary benefits.

Based on motivation theory, some recommended practices for managers of paid staff include being reflective about their own needs and motivations, being aware that what motivates the manager may not necessarily be what will motivate others, holding realistic expectations about the extent to which a manager can influence the motivation of others, participating in setting clear and challenging goals, thinking about the salience of various rewards to individuals who have different needs, being honest with people about what rewards are possible and what rewards are not, treating people equitably and fairly, making the work satisfying and meaningful, and considering the implications of life stages and of personal life events for the individuals they manage.

Fostering workplace diversity, encompassing characteristics such as race, gender, nationality, religion, sexual orientation, and others, is not only the right thing to do but also is an essential element of sound management. Effective nonprofits embrace diversity as a strength, recognizing that combining individuals of different backgrounds, perspectives, values, and views adds to the organization's capacity for high performance.

Volunteers are the only workforce for some organizations and constitute an important component of the workforce for many others, including those that employ paid staff. Individuals may be motivated to volunteer by altruism and concern for others, by their own needs, or by some combination of factors. In the workplace, they are usually affected by many of the same principles of motivation as paid staff. Some recommended practices for managing volunteers include assessing the need for volunteers; determining the organizational structure for the management of volunteers; developing volunteer job descriptions; developing formal volunteer policies; providing a sufficient budget and personnel to manage the volunteer program; recruiting and hiring volunteers as if they were employees; providing orientation and training; and setting clear goals, evaluating performance, and recognizing achievement.

Following these practices may be especially important if volunteers provide regular service in the organization's programs, but it may be less essential with regard to episodic volunteers who just participate occasionally. The number of virtual volunteers, who work from a distance using the Internet, is growing. Experts suggest that principles of managing such volunteers are similar to those applied to volunteers who work on-site, including frequent communication and recognition of achievements. Volunteer program management has become an identified subspecialty of nonprofit management, and its practitioners have access to professional associations, publications, and training to improve their skills.

The number of volunteers has increased long term but has leveled off or even declined in recent years, for reasons that may be complex. Research indicates that younger volunteers have become more selective and may not be as strongly motivated by a traditional sense of duty, requiring that volunteer assignments are rewarding and provide opportunities for growth and learning. Nonprofits that hope to attract and retain them will need to ensure that volunteer programs are well organized, well managed, and provide meaningful experiences.

KEY TERMS AND CONCEPTS

CASES 9.1–9.4

9.1 Getta Grant

Getta Grant is director of development at a medium-sized nonprofit that provides a range of services to adolescents from disadvantaged urban communities. She reports to the executive director. The organization receives some government funding but is also reliant on foundations and individual donors. Getta's responsibilities include staying informed about foundation interests and giving patterns, and working with the organization's three program directors to identify foundations that may be prospects for support of their programs and projects. She drafts letters of inquiry and, where appropriate, meets with foundation officers and writes proposals. Getta has been with the organization for five years and was hired by the previous executive director, who always gave her "excellent" (the highest rating) on her annual performance reviews. The current executive director has been in her job less than a year. She inherited Getta from her predecessor. When she had just arrived, it was already time for Getta's annual evaluation. The new executive director read a couple of proposals that Getta had written, thought they were good, and continued her "excellent" rating without much further thought. Getta seemed pleased to have her high rating continued.

When Getta writes something, it is generally of high quality. But over the past year, the executive director has become unhappy with the amount of work Getta produces and with her inability to meet deadlines. Since her last review, Getta has produced only a handful of letters and two proposals. The executive director gave her positive feedback on that work, which was indeed good, thinking that would motivate her to work harder and faster. But Getta has continued to produce relatively few proposals, and in some cases, they have taken so long that she missed foundation deadlines. She is coming up soon for her second evaluation with the executive director, who is now quite frustrated with her performance.

The executive director met with Getta recently and explained that she is unhappy. She warned Getta that her next performance evaluation might not be so positive this year. Getta seemed shocked. "But you said my proposals are good," she protested, "and you gave me an 'excellent' rating last year!" Since that meeting, Getta has missed several of days of work, calling in sick or saying she was "working at home." And the executive director has seen almost no additional work.

9.2 Rita Writer

Rita Writer is a member of the communications and marketing staff at a large environmental nonprofit. She has various responsibilities, including writing press releases, articles for the quarterly magazine, copy for brochures that are produced for fundraising and other purposes, and material for the organization's website. Rita had previously worked as a marketing specialist in the alumni relations office of a local college and came with outstanding references. When she accepted her new job, she said she wanted to make the change so that she would have more opportunity to write, since her job in alumni relations also included responsibility for attending events and required considerable travel.

Rita now has been in her current job for about three months. She produces an adequate volume of writing, but it is consistently full of glaring errors. Her manager, the vice president for communications and marketing, sometimes sends the work back to Rita for revisions. But most times the vice president just edits the work himself, not wanting to confront Rita and thinking that it is faster for him to take on the task. He has not said anything to Rita, but he is becoming increasingly unhappy with her performance. He is concerned that firing her would make him unpopular among the other staff, so he is reluctant to do so. But he is wondering what he can do to increase Rita's contribution to the organization.

One of Rita's colleagues mentioned to the vice president that Rita spends a lot of time on the phone talking to people in chapter offices around the country. In addition, the organization sponsors a number of public events, including lectures on environmental issues that are followed by receptions. Although she is not required to do so, Rita attends many of them on her work time and always stays for the reception, mingling with the guests. One of her colleagues said sarcastically to the vice president, "Rita just seems to prefer socializing to doing her job."

9.3 Bob the Builder

Bob is a volunteer at an organization that provides services to older people in the community, enabling them to continue living in their own homes. Older clients are matched with volunteers, who agree to visit with them at least once a week to assist them with matters such as paying bills, performing light housework or yard work, and similar tasks. When their homes need modest upkeep or repairs, such as painting, volunteers with appropriate skills are assigned as a team to complete the job. The organization's director of volunteers recruits volunteers with needed skills, assigning them to clients and projects and ensuring quality in the work they perform.

Bob was a building contractor and has recently retired. He has been a long-time but occasional volunteer. His wife, Mary, is a member of the board of directors, and Bob and Mary have been regular contributors to the annual fundraising campaign. A few months ago, Bob approached the director of volunteers and said that he now will have more time and would like to do more work with the organization. Delighted at the offer, especially in light of his professional skills, the director assigned him to supervise several home repair project teams.

Recently, however, she became concerned when she heard from another volunteer that Bob was going way beyond the scope of the projects assigned. In one case, the project team was sent to do some painting for a homeowner, but Bob had performed some electrical wiring in the woman's house. In another case, he replaced some plumbing. The director became concerned about the risks in that type of work and the potential liability to the organization should something go wrong. In addition, she is now receiving complaints from other volunteers who have worked with Bob. One volunteer has told her that Bob treats other volunteers as if they were members of the crew of his former construction company. And he doesn't treat them well. He assigns them work and then criticizes them for not doing it fast enough or well enough. Some of the volunteers have said that they will not work with him again.

The director of volunteers met with the executive director and discussed her concerns about Bob. The executive director was somewhat dismissive, saying she thinks Bob is a great asset to the organization. "After all," she said, "He's a professional builder. We are fortunate to have someone with his skills involved." She then added, "Anyway, it's difficult to do anything about it with Mary serving on the board."

9.4 Myra the Volunteer Manager

Myra had been a volunteer for many years at a nonprofit that provides after-school enrichment programs for children from low-income neighborhoods. The organization has always had a professional executive director but no staff member serving as volunteer manager. But managing the volunteers directly became too time-consuming for the executive director, and she was able to place funds in the budget to create a volunteer manager position for the first time last year. Because Myra had been a longstanding volunteer, the executive director offered her the new position, thinking that her experience would enable her to build and manage the program. Myra accepted the assignment and has been in her position for about a year. She recruits volunteers, provides them with orientation and training, and supervises their work.

Until recently, the organization always had attracted well-qualified volunteers in the numbers it needed to sustain its programs. But over the past year, the turnover of volunteers has increased, and both the number and quality of individuals expressing an interest in serving has declined. The executive director met with Myra and expressed her concern. Myra became defensive. She said that she recruits volunteers the same way the organization always has, through churches and other organizations in the community and through word-of-mouth among friends. "People just don't seem to be as committed as they used to be," she complains. The executive director suggests, "How about trying to get the word out at the local university. I would think that some students would be interested in working with us. And maybe we should be more visible on Facebook and other social networking sites." "I tried the university," Myra responded, "I even put up flyers on some bulletin boards on the campus, but we didn't get any responses. And I don't think it is appropriate for us to be on those 'websites' where people put up pictures of their pets!" She added, "I guess young people just have so much else going on in their lives that they don't have time for our children."

The executive director observed, "But we have enlisted some younger volunteers and they don't stay with us for long. Why are we having such high turnover?" Myra again became defensive. "We can't just let people do things however they want. We have an established program, and there are established procedures and policies that volunteers need to follow. Some of the young people who come in just want to question everything. No matter what I tell them to do, they ask why and want to discuss new ideas with me. I don't have time for all of that. I just think people today are different from the folks who used to volunteer with us."

Questions Related to Cases 9.1–9.4

1. Which theories of motivation might be most relevant to the situations described?

2. What recommended practices for the management of staff or volunteers may not have been followed in each of these cases?

3. What psychological needs might each staff person or volunteer be trying to meet?

4. What does the manager's behavior in each case suggest about his or her psychological needs?

5. Are there principles of human motivation and behavior that the manager seems to not know or understand?

6. What new approaches or strategies might the manager consider to address the problem?

QUESTIONS FOR DISCUSSION

1. Think about your most rewarding (or unrewarding) experience as a volunteer or nonprofit staff member. Which of Herzberg's satisfiers and dissatisfiers were present in the environment?

2. Think about the best (or worst) supervisor you have had, either as a volunteer or a nonprofit staff member. What do you think were his or her predominant needs, as described by McClelland?

3. In your opinion, is human nature closer to McGregor's Theory X or Theory Y? Or somewhere in between?

4. Are the values and motivations of millennials really different from those of previous generations or do people become more alike as they proceed through various life stages?

APPENDIX CASES

The following cases in the Appendix of this text include points related to the content of this chapter: Case 2 (Share Our Strength/No Kid Hungry); Case 4 (The Girl Scouts of the United States of America).

SUGGESTIONS FOR FURTHER READING

Books/Book Chapter

Brudney, J. L. (2016). Designing and managing volunteer programs. In D. O. Renz & Associates (Eds.), *The Jossey-Bass handbook of nonprofit leadership and management* (4th ed., pp. 688–733. Hoboken, NJ: Jossey-Bass.

Denhardt, R. B., Denhardt, J. V., & Aristigueta, M. P. (2016). *Managing human behavior in public and nonprofit organizations* (4th ed.). Thousand Oaks, CA: Sage.

Kearney, R. C., & Coggburn, J. (Eds.). (2015). *Public human resource management: Problems and prospects* (6th ed.). Thousand Oaks, CA: CQ Press.

Word, J. K. A., & Sowa, J. E. (Eds.). (2017). *The nonprofit human resource management handbook: From theory to practice*. New York: Routledge.

Websites

Association of Leaders in Volunteer Engagement (ALIVE): http://www.volunteeralive.org/

Corporation for National and Community Service: http://www.nationalservice.gov/about/volunteering/index.asp

Energize: https://www.energizeinc.com/

Equal Employment Opportunity Commission: http://www.eeoc.gov/

Idealist: http://www.idealist.org/

Independent Sector: http://www.independentsector.org/

Points of Light Institute: http://www.pointsoflight.org/

Volunteers of America: http://www.voa.org/

Nonprofits must work to integrate their marketing and communications so that the message they craft is consistent across all channels and constituencies.

iStock/microgen

Chapter Outline

Marketing and Communications

In this chapter, we will consider the use of marketing principles by nonprofit organizations and the planning and management of communications programs. Although developed in the for-profit sector, marketing is widely applied by nonprofits for various purposes. Some organizations, for example in the fields of education, health care, and the arts, have products and services to sell and were among the early adopters of marketing in the nonprofit sector. This type of marketing is commercial marketing, whether undertaken by a for-profit or nonprofit, because its goal is to attract additional customers to programs and services (Andreasen & Kotler, 2008, p. 8). Other nonprofits engage in social marketing, which is intended to change human behavior and improve society, for example, to reduce smoking or obesity or increase the use of seat belts or condoms. Marketing principles are also applied in fundraising and in cause marketing (or cause-related marketing), which involves a partnership between a nonprofit and a corporation that is intended to increase sales of the for-profit's products with financial and other benefits going to the nonprofit organization or a cause. This chapter focuses on principles of marketing as applied in nonprofits' marketing of products and services related to their mission programs (commercial marketing) and in social marketing. We will explore nonprofit advocacy in Chapter 11, fundraising in Chapter 13, and marketing partnerships between nonprofits and corporations (a source of earned income to nonprofits) in Chapter 14. We will revisit some principles of marketing that are discussed in this chapter in those specific contexts.

Defining and Understanding Marketing

At their monthly meeting, members of the (fictional) Siwash College faculty were informed by the college's president that "we are enhancing our communication with prospective students in order to increase applications, especially from highly qualified students." The news was greeted with enthusiasm. "We really need to get the word out," said one

Learning Objectives

After reading this chapter, students should be able to:

1. Define marketing.

2. Explain how marketing differs from advertising, communications, and public relations.

3. Summarize the key principles of marketing.

4. Identify components of the marketing process.

5. Describe elements in the marketing mix.

6. Describe the process for developing a brand.

7. Define integrated marketing communication.

8. Summarize principles of crisis communication.

9. Identify opportunities and challenges regarding social media.

10. Analyze cases, applying concepts from the chapter.

professor. "We have excellent programs that nobody knows about." Another professor added, "Communication is a general problem here; some of our own colleagues don't know how strong many of our departments are. I'm pleased to hear that the administration will be doing something about it."

A month later, the college's vice president for communications presented a follow-up report to the faculty. In her comments, she said things a little differently:

> We are really investing significantly in our marketing and, in fact, we are bringing in a team of marketing consultants to help us position the college and differentiate our brand, and we will be hiring more recruiters on our own staff to target highly qualified students.

One professor immediately came to his feet, saying, "Wait a minute. Are you saying we are going to market the college like a brand of soda? We have a good reputation now and that will just tarnish it by making us look desperate." Another added,

> I agree. We attract students now because of the quality of our academic programs. If we want more and better students to apply, the money should be spent on academic resources, like the library, science labs, and computer technology. Those are the things that will attract the kind of students we want.

A third member of the faculty joined the conversation, saying,

> It concerns me that we are going for the hard sell. We don't need Madison Avenue types out representing us, exaggerating and misleading students into coming to Siwash. That wouldn't be fair to the students and could cause people to question our integrity.

While the concerns of the Siwash College faculty may not be completely unfounded, they may also reflect an incomplete understanding of marketing. Although marketing principles are widely applied in many nonprofit organizations, misunderstanding of the concept is still common, and some individuals have a viscerally negative reaction to the use of marketing's vocabulary in organizations that are based on values and driven by missions. In part, the comments and concerns of the Siwash College faculty may reflect the shadows of earlier approaches to marketing in the business sector that remain prominent in some people's understanding of the concept.

When marketing first came on the business scene around the beginning of the 20th century, it reflected a **product mind-set**. In other words, the prevailing view was "that to be an effective marketer, you simply had to 'build a better mousetrap,' and, in effect, customers would beat a pathway to your door" (Andreasen & Kotler, 2008, p. 37). That was essentially what Henry Ford did by inventing the Model T, and it may be the view of the Siwash faculty, who think it sufficient to improve the college's educational programs, assuming that prospective students will inevitably discover them and apply in greater numbers.

But the product mind-set became obsolete in business in about the mid-20th century. It became increasingly clear that simply making a better product would not provide assurance that customers would buy it. An increasingly competitive economic environment led to a new approach to marketing in the business world, one reflecting a **sales mind-set** (Andreasen & Kotler, 2008). The goal for a company or an organization with a sales mind-set is to *convince* customers that they should buy the company's product rather than buy nothing or buy what a competitor is offering. With the adoption of this marketing perspective by American business in the middle part of the 20th century, advertising became a major industry, and the hard sell became the preferred tactic of businesses trying to survive in a competitive environment.

For many people, marketing is still synonymous with sales, and like some members of the Siwash faculty, they see it as something possibly inconsistent with the values and the culture of the nonprofit sector.

Both the product and sales mind-sets lead an organization to begin the marketing process *inside* its own walls, with the goal it wishes to achieve—more sales of the product or service, resulting in more revenue for the organization. When the sales mind-set is predominant, messages are pushed out through advertising and other channels of communication with the hope that they will fall on receptive ears—the goal is to "change the … audiences to fit what the organization [has] to offer" (Andreasen & Kotler, 2008, p. 38). Both the product and the sales mind-sets still exist and are reflected in the practices of some for-profit and nonprofit organizations today (Andreasen & Kotler, 2008), but modern marketing reflects a **target-audience mind-set**. It is outside in, not inside out. As Alan Andreasen (2006) explains, "The key to marketing is to focus on our audiences and not ourselves" (p. 12).

Following this outside-in approach requires that

> the organization systematically study target audiences' needs, wants, perceptions, preferences, and satisfaction, using surveys, focus groups, and other means … [and that] *the organization … constantly act on this information to improve its offerings to meet its customers' needs better* [italics added]. (Andreasen & Kotler, 2008, p. 39)

Understood in this way, then, marketing seems not so contrary to nonprofit values, as the Siwash faculty may have initially believed. For nonprofits, marketing is focused on the needs of constituents or consumers; it is not about pushing something that those individuals do not want, nor does it require misrepresentation or exaggeration.

Unlike the sales model, which tries to persuade the customer that he or she wants what the organization has to offer, target-audience marketing implies that the organization develops its product to be responsive to what the *customer* needs and wants.[1] Of course, businesses do so readily. If consumers want larger cars, the automakers will produce them. If consumers shift their priorities to saving energy and preserving the environment, automakers will respond to that change by producing more fuel-efficient vehicles. If the product or service is well matched with what people really want, it will still be necessary to let potential customers know of its existence and the benefits it provides—there is still a need for advertising and communication—but there will be little need to persuade individuals or sell them on the desirability of purchasing it. The situation is, of course, more complicated if the goal of marketing requires the customer to sacrifice—for example, to quit smoking or change his or her dietary habits—but the purpose is nevertheless to improve individuals' situations, through better health or in some other aspect of life. In those instances, the sale requires communicating a value proposition in which members of the target audience see the benefit they will receive through the exchange.

Marketing Serves the Mission

Of course, even the more up-to-date, target-market mind-set may still give some pause to the faculty of Siwash College and to others who work in nonprofit organizations. How responsive should a nonprofit be to the expressed desires of its clients or customers? Should a college's curriculum be designed to encompass only what students say they wish to know, or should it reflect what the faculty believe to be the essential elements of a sound education? If a performing arts center is not attracting symphony audiences of sufficient size, should it abandon Beethoven in favor of rock concerts? If patients express displeasure about having their blood tested, should hospitals skip that procedure in order to gain more customer satisfaction? If church attendance is declining, should the pastor yield on fundamental principles? Should a museum abandon its mission to preserve antiquities and educate museum patrons in order to provide entertainment along the lines of Disney World? Stated at the extreme, all these ideas are obviously inappropriate, indeed ridiculous. A nonprofit organization cannot abandon its mission or act in a way that is contrary to its values merely to increase sales of its product or service. To do so would be inconsistent with the essence of its nonprofit character and status. Marketing must serve the mission and not become the driver of the nonprofit organization's program.

However, nonprofits cannot ignore the reality that they operate in a competitive environment, even if they do not compete directly against each other. A homeless shelter may not compete with another for clients, but two such organizations may compete for gifts from local corporations, foundations, and individuals. Organizations that advocate a cause or social goal may compete against others that advocate opposing positions; they compete in a marketplace of ideas, attitudes, and beliefs. Even those that may advocate relatively noncontroversial ideas like eating more vegetables and avoiding addictive drugs still compete against complacency and habit, and they compete for attention amid the distraction of all the other messages with which people are bombarded every day, what communication theory calls noise.

Of course, many nonprofits do offer products and services for a fee, and they may compete against one another as well as against for-profit companies and public organizations engaged in similar activities. For example, two colleges may compete for students, and two theaters may compete for audiences. Even without such direct competition, organizations face generic competition from alternative uses of individuals' time and money. People can only be in one place at a time. Attending the museum, especially if it charges an admission fee, competes with attending a theater performance, going to the movies, or staying home on the couch watching TV. The museum must offer something that will motivate people to spend their time, and perhaps their money, to visit the museum rather than engage in such alternative activities. Marketing is a strategy for competition, whether for resources, convictions, or customers, and thus marketing principles may prove useful for every nonprofit, regardless of its mission.

Marketing Means Action

Marketing and communications are terms often combined in the titles of individuals or offices—for example, the Director of Communications and Marketing or the Office of Marketing and Communications. The concepts are related but also distinguishable.

Communication, in the simplest of definitions, is the transmission or exchange of information. As a discipline, **communications** is more complex, encompassing an understanding of the principles by which information is transmitted and received—that is, "how messages are encoded, transmitted, screened, decoded, stored, retrieved, and acted on" (Gainer & Moyer, 2005, p. 303), as well as the various technologies employed, for example, print and electronic media. We will discuss more about communications theory later in this chapter. **Strategic communications**, as the term implies, is undertaken in the context of a master plan and in pursuit of specific organizational goals ("What is Strategic Communications?" 2011). But communications is not synonymous with marketing; it may be undertaken with multiple goals.

Marketing also is different from **public relations**. The Public Relations Society of America (PRSA), the professional association of individuals working in the field, defines public relations as "a strategic communication process that builds mutually beneficial relationships between organizations and their publics" (Public Relations Society of America, n.d.). Every organization has **internal publics**, including, for example, employees, volunteers, suppliers, customers, and neighbors, and **external publics**, including news media, educators, government officials, and others. One important component of public relations involves relationships with news media. As John Burnett (2007, p. 228) observes, communication channeled through news media places a third party between the organization and the intended recipients of the communication, sometimes complicating the task of evaluating the impact of the public relations program. The same complication arises with social media, in which the communications may be filtered by various individuals over whom the public relations professional has no control.

As Burnett (2007) notes, "the ultimate objective of [public relations] is to retain, as well as create, goodwill" (p. 226). It thus "deals with [an] intangible—creating a positive image of the organization" (p. 224). In other words, public relations is primarily concerned with advancing and protecting the reputation of the organization. It may help to establish the environment in which marketing occurs, but it is not the same function.

Marketing is a process that uses communication, but with a very specific purpose: to influence the behavior of someone else. Marketing focuses on exchanges. For example, you buy a ticket and hear the symphony in exchange for your payment. Or you change your behavior, say by eating fewer sweets, and realize the benefit of greater fitness in return. An exchange does not occur until the individual—a member of the target audience—takes action. As Andreasen and Kotler (2008) explain,

> Marketing's objectives are not *ultimately* either to educate or to change values or attitudes. It may seek to do so as a *means* of influencing behavior.... If someone has a final goal of imparting information or knowledge, that person is in the education profession, not marketing. Further, if someone has a final goal of changing attitudes or values, that person may be described as a propagandist or lobbyist, or perhaps an artist, but not a marketer. While marketing may use the tools of the educator or the propagandist, its critical distinguishing feature is that its ultimate goal is to influence behavior (either changing it or keeping it the same in the face of other pressures). (p. 36)

Marketing as a Process

Marketing is more than just blasting out compelling messages. It is a process. Consistent with our discussion above, it begins with defining the target audience and gaining understanding of its members' values, needs, and wants; it acknowledges the environment, including the presence of direct and generic competition; it focuses on defining an exchange, honing and delivering the message (communication); and it ends with action by members of the target audience. Communication (i.e., honing and delivering the message) is a part of the marketing process but does not encompass it or substitute for it. Again, the ultimate goal is not persuasion in and of itself, but rather *action* by members of the target audience. Evaluation of a marketing program thus must be based on measuring what actions have been taken. As Andreasen (2006) emphasizes, that requires thinking "beyond our far-off mission (like helping people overcome poverty, increasing consumer access to affordable health care, or strengthening schools) and zero[ing] in on specific audience actions that are tangible, achievable, and measureable" (p. 14).

The Marketing Mix

Marketing implies an interaction between the customer and the organization. As discussed earlier, it begins with research to identify the needs and wants of potential customers or clients, which informs the development of the products or services to be offered. A simple description of the marketing process that is often stated says, "Find a need and fill it." That implies a malleable marketer, one who will create almost any product or service for which there is a demand. This simple understanding of course may raise difficult issues for nonprofit organizations that are driven by the missions and values that are at the heart of their existence.

However, any organization hoping to exchange its services for payment cannot be oblivious to the desires of its potential consumers. A college with great programs but no students eventually will close, and one that does not introduce new programs to address emerging new fields and industries will not keep pace with others that are more innovative. It is necessary and appropriate that nonprofits sometimes push back against the market to preserve their core values in pursuit of their missions, but tailoring the product to address the target market is also essential to survival. Fortunately, there is a middle choice between rigidity and complete capitulation to the market: A nonprofit can change its marketing mix in response to information about what customers, clients, or donors need and want, while remaining faithful to its core purposes. By doing so, it can differentiate its product from that offered by others, **position** itself in a unique market niche, and gain a **competitive advantage** over others.

To illustrate the ideas of the **marketing mix**, **differentiation**, and **market niche**, let's start with a familiar example from the for-profit world—Starbucks. The campus on which this author works is in an urban setting; there are many places to buy coffee, including the student center, street vendors, and other restaurants and delis in the neighborhood. For many years, there was a large study room located in the front of the university library that was accessible through a door directly from the street—24 hours a day. It was rarely used at any time of the day or night. Then the university decided to lease the space to Starbucks, which converted it to one of its ubiquitous coffee shops. The Starbucks is always busy; indeed, students, faculty, and staff sometimes stand in lines extending out the door to pay a higher price for Starbucks coffee than they would need to pay for coffee at other nearby locations. And, in the space formerly occupied by an underused study room, students now spend time studying—at Starbucks! How has Starbucks differentiated itself from the other coffee sellers in the neighborhood? What is it that people receive in exchange for their money when they patronize Starbucks, and how is that different from what others are offering?

Obviously, it's the coffee, which is pretty good, but it's also the atmosphere of the store, the convenience of its location, the comfortable chairs and laid-back atmosphere—the fact that Starbucks lets you stay for a long time and offers wireless Internet access for those who wish to use their laptops or tablets. It's also the familiarity and instant recognition of the Starbucks logo, which lets you know exactly what to expect inside, and something that's just cool about buying coffee with complex-sounding names in sizes other than "small, medium, and large." In other words, there are more variables involved than just the core product, or service, that is being sold by any business. The four key variables—**product**, **place**, **promotion**, and **price**—are called the **four Ps of marketing**. Various combinations of these variables are called the marketing mix.

Product

The product, generally the good or service being offered, seems like the simplest variable to understand. In the nonprofit sector, it's education, health care, counseling, tutoring, food, or whatever programs the organization may operate. Products have both tangible and intangible qualities, like the consumption of Starbucks coffee. Education offers a clear example. There is little basis on which to conclude that an Ivy League education is always superior to that offered at other colleges and universities across the country, and indeed, other institutions may be stronger than any of the Ivy League schools in some fields. Why would a student be willing to pay more at an Ivy League university than perhaps at a local college or state university that may provide an equally good education? Because the prestige of holding an Ivy League degree is itself an intangible quality of the product. An Ivy League degree may instantly convey intellectual distinction because those universities are known to be selective in admissions. Membership in the alumni association of such a university may bring influential contacts and open important doors throughout life. Furthermore, it happens that most Ivy League campuses are also attractive ones that provide an intellectually stimulating environment outside as well as inside the classroom. In other words, the product is not just the education itself; it's also the experiences and intangible benefits that may go along with it.

Intangibles may also be a part of the product in health care. For example, a hospital that provides a pleasant, modern environment may be preferred to one with a rundown facility that nevertheless provides excellent medical treatment. If the doctors and the nurses are nice and take the time to explain medical conditions to their patients, they are offering a different product from another hospital that follows exactly the same medical protocols but in which the staff are more distant or abrupt. A nonprofit that provides services to homeless individuals without significant barriers—that is, helps anyone without preconditions to receiving service—is offering a different product than one that is more difficult to access, although both may offer food, counseling, and housing of basically the same quality.

Think back on the meeting of the Siwash College faculty earlier in this chapter. Their concern that the academic program be centered on educational values and not be shaped entirely to suit the expressed desires of high school students is understandable. But the college's product is not just its curriculum. The product also includes the quality of its facilities, the teaching skill of its professors, the closeness of relationships that professors form with their students, the quality of student activities offered, and many other aspects of the student experience that go beyond the classroom. These are qualities of the product that can be enhanced in response to student wants and needs without compromising the college's commitment to its educational mission or values.

Place

The location at which the product or service is available is an important variable in the marketing mix. A program operated in a location that is convenient for clients is a different product from the same program offered in a remote place beyond easy reach. A college located in a small rural town offers a different experience from one located in the suburbs of a big city, although it may offer an identical curriculum. A concert hall located on a bus line offers something different from one located in the distant suburbs accessible only by car. Some programs need to be taken to where the clients are. For example, many colleges offer off-campus courses for working adults and online courses for those who cannot (or prefer not to) attend classes on a campus. Symphony orchestras located in cities periodically bring their concerts to smaller towns in their regions. Major museums place exhibits on tour across the country. And hospitals send vans offering mammograms into neighborhoods in which many women do not have easy access to health care. The decision about place involves consideration of both the physical and the virtual worlds. An attractive and interactive website and a presence on Facebook, Twitter, and Instagram may be as much a part of the overall product as services provided in a physical location.

Promotion

In the minds of some, marketing may be virtually synonymous with promotion, which is the visible activity that everybody can see—the announcements, advertisements, brochures, tweets, and other efforts undertaken to gain visibility and notice for the organization's products. Marketing is not synonymous with promotion, but promotion is part of the marketing mix. Clients and customers cannot partake in products or services if they do not know of their existence or what they comprise. But to whom should the nonprofit's programs and services be promoted? A simple answer might be "to the public," but that would require a foolishly expensive effort, since most of the public is likely to have no interest in or need for the organization's offerings. The need to keep promotion cost-effective requires focusing communication on segments of the public most likely to respond—that is, on the target market. This **segmentation** is based on research and may employ sophisticated tools developed in the business sector and increasingly adopted by many nonprofits as well.

Market Segmentation

For an organization's promotion to be cost effective, it needs to identify its **target market/ target audience**. This is the initial step in thinking about a marketing program. The target market is a subset of the larger general population. Some of this may seem intuitive. For example, a college likely will focus its promotion of undergraduate programs on high school students and their parents. A symphony orchestra might limit its mailing of concert announcements to people who live in higher-income areas, who can afford the cost of the tickets. A medical clinic that provides screenings for HIV might target its communication to neighborhoods with low income or younger single people rather than areas with primarily families and older residents. But variables used for segmentation are often more sophisticated than these somewhat obvious examples suggest.

Objective measures include **demographic variables**, for example, age, gender, race or ethnicity, income, and geography, that is, where people may live, work, or travel. The examples described previously reflect simple segmentation along these lines. Markets also may be segmented according to behavioral measures—in other words, patterns of past behavior that divide people into identifiable groups. For example, people who have never attended the theater constitute a segment different from those who attend occasionally, which is, in turn, different from the group of people who are season ticket holders. A theater would design its strategy to communicate with these different segments of its market in different ways, perhaps offering varied prices or emphasizing unique aspects of the theatergoing experience to each.

Some of the most sophisticated methods of segmentation involve **psychographics**. Psychographic measures combine demographic data with knowledge about individuals' lifestyles, defined by their activities, interests, and opinions (AIOs; Andreasen & Kotler, 2008; Sargeant, 2005). Market researchers group individuals according to various lifestyles that are associated with certain behaviors, attitudes, or likes and dislikes. For example, we might assume that a young single person who lives with roommates, rides a motorcycle, and holds politically progressive views may have different tastes in music than a couple with two young children and an SUV who live in the suburbs and have moderate views or a retired couple with a politically conservative orientation who live in a condo and travel only by public transportation. Individuals' lifestyles often predict not only the type of music they prefer but also the political and social causes they may favor, the kinds of artistic events they may attend, and the types of nonprofits they may support. Their patterns of behavior can help identify them as part of the target market for a particular product or service.

For example, in one study undertaken in selected cities, Andreasen and Russell Belk were able to identify six lifestyle groups, which they labeled Passive Homebodies, Active Sports Enthusiasts, Inner-Directed Self-Sufficients, Active Homebodies, Culture Patrons, and Social Actives. People in the Culture Patron lifestyle were more likely than others to attend the theater or the symphony, while those in the Social Active lifestyle were more likely to attend only the symphony (Andreasen & Kotler, 2008, p. 148). That kind of insight would be useful to a performing arts center in selecting those segments to which it would promote specific performances, ensuring that marketing dollars are used most efficiently. In other words, segmentation enables the nonprofit to target its promotion like a rifle shot, rather than scattering it like buckshot at greater total expense and with the result that much of it is wasted on those who are unlikely to attend its programs or feel a need to use its services.

The smallest conceivable market segment is, of course, the individual, and the most sophisticated for-profit marketers have become adept at targeting their messages to one person at a time. Think, for example, about experience you may have had with Amazon.com. Amazon remembers what you purchased before and suggests new titles and other products that may be in line with your demonstrated interests—it segments based on your past behavior. Knowing your interests in reading and in music, it lets you know what products are being purchased by other people who are reading the same books or listening to the same music as you; this reflects the company's assumptions about your lifestyle. Facebook knows what you like and what your friends like. Your interests and preferences are also revealed through your use of Google searches and the websites that you visit. Online advertising then is targeted to match the profile you have provided of yourself through your past behavior, defining the characteristics of a very precise market segment that includes just you! Among nonprofits, segmentation at this level is increasingly applied in online fundraising.

Our discussion above has focused on identifying market segments for the commercial marketing of nonprofits' programs and services. Of course, in the case of social marketing, segmentation is equally important. Target audiences will include those who engage in behaviors that the marketing is intended to change, but there is still a need for differentiation. For example, if the goal is to prevent texting while driving, different strategies may be required to address adolescents, parents, businesspeople, and other segments.

Price

The price of a product or service is a straightforward concept for most people. It's what we pay to obtain what we want in the marketplace. Let's first consider how nonprofits that charge fees for their services might go about establishing those prices and then return to the idea of marketing as an exchange—an approach to thinking about price that may be a better fit than our usual understanding of the term for nonprofits engaged in social marketing.

Pricing can be an especially sensitive issue for nonprofit organizations. Some provide their services to clients without charge; others have missions suggesting that prices should be kept as low as possible to encourage participation.

There are essentially four methods for establishing the price at which a product or service will be offered. One approach is **cost-oriented pricing**, in which the price charged to the customer or client is set to cover what it costs the organization to produce or provide it. A popular method is to set prices to produce a break-even situation for the organization overall. This method may seem the most appropriate for a nonprofit organization, which does not have the purpose of maximizing its profits. But it is important to ensure that the price reflects the direct costs of providing the service as well as the overhead needed to run the organization (Gainer, 2016). Indeed, as we discussed in Chapter 7, earned income, including fees for service, may be a principal source of funds for capacity building, and a price set to break even might need to encompass the costs of such efforts.

Cost-oriented pricing is popular in the nonprofit sector for a variety of reasons. First, it is simple. Second, since costs are likely to be similar for different organizations, this method often will mean that different organizations charge about the same, eliminating competition based on price and perhaps reorienting competition to the quality of programs. Third, some people see it as socially fair: "Sellers do not take advantage of buyers when the demand becomes acute, yet sellers earn a fair return on their investment" (Andreasen & Kotler, 2008, p. 244).

Another way to establish prices is by using **competitive pricing** (Gainer, 2016, pp. 387–388). The nonprofit might look at its competitors, perhaps in order to charge a bit less or provide a somewhat better product than others are offering at the same price. As discussed before, even if a nonprofit does not compete directly with another, it must take generic competition into account in establishing its prices. For example, a theater needs to consider how its ticket price compares not only with that of other theaters, but also with the cost of going to the movies instead. The price and the product interact. What does the theater experience offer to justify spending the price of a ticket rather than just staying home and watching TV? Does the product need to be more than just a play? For example, can a higher ticket price be justified and obtained if the experience includes a backstage reception attended by the cast of the play?

A third way of establishing prices is **value-based pricing** (Andreasen & Kotler, 2008), which may also be described as **demand-based pricing** (Gainer, 2016, p. 386). This approach takes into consideration the perceived value of the product or service to the customer, which may not be closely related to the costs of production. Indeed, some consumers may equate higher price with quality, for example, in buying wine or automobiles. A $30 bottle of wine may not be demonstrably better than a $10 bottle of wine, and it likely did not require three times as many grapes to make it. But buyers who are not wine experts might prefer to pay more, believing that the price will equate to quality—or at least that their dinner guests will believe so. Is a Lexus a much better car than a Civic? Possibly it is, although both will go about the same speed and arrive at a destination with equal dependability. But there is some psychological value to the buyer in owning a car that comes with more prestige, based at least in part on its higher price. A controversial example of value-based pricing involves the tuition policies of many colleges and universities. Critics have charged that some higher education institutions have intentionally increased their tuition to create the image that they are elite, since that will be attractive to some students and their families.

Price Discrimination

Price discrimination sounds like something unethical, immoral, or even illegal, but it is an essential element of marketing strategy. It does not mean charging people different prices based on their race or ethnicity, sex, religion, or other personal characteristics. Rather, it means charging people different prices based on the market segment to which they belong, determined by objective variables.

Nonprofits may undertake price discrimination to cover the actual higher costs of serving a particular segment. For example, a college may charge more for on-campus courses than those offered off-campus or online, to cover the additional costs of providing library support and other services to students who come onto the campus. Price discrimination may also be used as a way to match the price to the perceived value of the experience. For example, concert halls charge more for seats close to the stage than for seats in the balcony, although the music may sound much the same from either location. A third reason to charge different prices might be to shift utilization. Theaters often charge less for matinees than for evening performances as a way to fill the hall at a time when it might otherwise be empty. Price discrimination also can help maximize a nonprofit's revenues by pricing the most desirable products or services at a high point that some may be willing and able to pay. An interesting example of that is provided by the Bolshoi Theater in Moscow.

One of the world's most renowned ballet companies, the Bolshoi was heavily subsidized by the government of the former USSR. But with the fall of communism, it faced two challenges. One was to pay its artists at competitive rates, since they were now free to perform elsewhere in the world for potentially higher compensation. The other challenge was to replace reduced government support with other sources of revenue.

Under the communist system, the Bolshoi's best seats always had been reserved for artists, high-ranking government officials, and other VIPs, but, in fact, they often had not been used by those people. Instead, the tickets were sold to scalpers, who became known as "pillar people" because they often waited for possible customers while lurking behind the pillars in the lobby. Because the seats for which they had tickets were desirable, the scalpers could sell them for a profit and had done so for many years. Facing a new need to generate revenue on the introduction of a market economy, and freed from the constraints of the previous system, the Bolshoi revised its pricing policies to capture the higher value of those better seats for itself and put the pillar people out of business. It introduced price discrimination, charging varied prices for seats depending on their perceived desirability. The result was an increase in its ticket revenue of 82 percent in the first month. At the same time, it lowered the prices for less desirable seats, making them more accessible for students and others without wealth (Klintsov & von Löhneysen, 2001, p. 6).

Defining the Exchange

In the examples mentioned above, the concept of price is what most of us would understand from the term; it's what a client or customer pays to receive a good or a service. Theaters charge for admission, colleges charge tuition, and hospitals charge for medical procedures, although some may be provided free for those who cannot pay. But what about nonprofits engaged in social marketing, with the goal of bringing about changed behavior believed to be of benefit to individuals who are part of the target market? How can we understand the concept of price in these situations?

Setting a price essentially means defining a benefit exchange (Andresen, 2006, p. 131). In a commercial transaction, you give something up (money) in exchange for a reward that you receive, whether an education, a concert, or medical care. Social marketing similarly requires that an individual pay some price in the form of changed behavior—for example, by refraining from texting while driving eating healthier foods, or going to the gym rather than napping. That change will only occur if the marketer can offer a reward that equals or exceeds the perceived sacrifice involved in making the change.

As Katya Andresen (2006) explains, the most effective rewards are those that are immediate, personal, reflective of audience values, better than competing rewards, and credible. Positive rewards are more effective than threats (p. 131). "The Truth" antismoking campaign offers a classic example of an effective strategy. For some teenagers, smoking is rewarding because it is a form of rebellion. An appeal to quit in order to avoid getting cancer years later may not be effective, because the reward of changed behavior is not sufficiently immediate. An appeal to quit because smoking annoys their parents may not be competitive with the reward of continuing to smoke because pleasing their parents is not as highly valued as rebellion. "The Truth" campaign took a different approach. It engaged teen spokespeople to encourage their peers to picket tobacco companies' headquarters, crank-call the companies, and speak out about their manipulation by the tobacco industry. This approach offered the reward of rebellion and was, of course, inconsistent with continuing to be a smoker (Andresen, p. 143). In other words, the price paid in giving up (or avoiding) one behavior was justified by a reward that *exceeded* the reward of the alternative. The reward was offered based on what was known about the inherent motivations of the target market.

Building the Brand

Remember that competition requires an organization, nonprofit or for-profit, to differentiate its products or services from those of others. One strategy for doing so is building a recognizable brand and a positive image for that brand. When we think about a brand, what most readily comes to mind are commercial products, such as soda, cars, or clothing, and names like Coke or Pepsi, Honda or Toyota, Nike or Under Armour, but nonprofits have brands as well.

Burnett (2007) and other authors define **brand** in a narrow sense as "a name, term, sign, symbol, design, or a combination of these that is intended to identify the goods and services of one seller or group of sellers and differentiate them from those of competitors" (p. 179). Thus, some brands may be names, some may be brand marks (or logos), and others may be trademarks—brand marks that have legal protection (p. 179). Many brands are instantly recognizable, for example, the Nike swoosh and Apple's apple. They do not even require a word for people to identify them with the companies and their products. Some nonprofit logos are equally well-known worldwide—for example, the Red Cross's red cross and WWF's (formerly the World Wildlife Fund's) panda. But some authors offer a more encompassing definition of brand. For example, according to Nathalie Kylander and Christopher Stone (2012), "A brand is more than a visual identity: the name, logo, and graphic design used by an organization. A brand is a psychological construct held in the minds of all those aware of the branded product, person, organization, or movement."

In other words, a name or logo is shorthand for a collection of perceived qualities of the organization or its products, known as **brand attributes**. A brand may evoke feelings, attitudes, memories, and other intangibles that we associate with the name or symbol. Coke may bring to mind a refreshing break on a summer day. Disney may evoke memories of a childhood trip with one's family. Depending on one's age, either Chevy or Honda may evoke a sense of confidence, quality, and durability. Greenpeace or Doctors Without Borders likely stimulate very different images—and feelings—from Harvard or MoMA (the Museum of Modern Art in New York City).

An individual's reaction to a brand may, of course, be quite different from that of others, depending upon his or her own values and perception of the values of the organization. A brand is a promise, and the term brand promise describes the expectations that you have about what you will receive when you buy a specific product or service. For example, as discussed previously, when you walk into Starbucks, you expect the coffee to be good and the atmosphere to be comfortable and welcoming; those are experiences that Starbucks has promised you by placing its logo over the door (Sargeant, 2005). When you make a gift to Doctors Without Borders, you expect it to be used effectively because such responsible behavior is an attribute of the organization's brand.

Establishing a strong and positive image for a brand brings many benefits to an organization. Examples are provided by responses to natural disasters, for example Hurricanes Harvey, Irma, and Maria in 2017. Horrified by the scenes unfolding on their television screens, many Americans went to their computers or used text messaging to make a gift to help those displaced by the disaster. They were most likely to go to organizations with known brands—for example, the Red Cross or the Salvation Army—both because their brands were familiar and because donors attributed to them the qualities of competence and trust. Of course, a brand image can be fragile, and if an organization fails to deliver on the implied promise of its brand, the negative effect can be both immediate and long lasting. For example, when a former employee posted a blog accusing the ride-sharing company Uber of having a sexist work environment, that set off a string of events that eventually led the CEO, Travis Kalanick, to step down from his role. Although the allegation did not directly affect Uber customers, it did affect their perceptions of the company. In following months, Uber's rival Lyft gained market share, which some observers attributed to the negative perceptions of Uber's brand (Cava, 2017). Similarly, when, in 2002, the CEO of the United Way of the National Capital Area was forced to resign amid allegations of his misuse of donor funds, United Way's national CEO highlighted the need to rebuild trust in the brand: "To a United Way—to a nonprofit—trust is everything. [The National Capital Chapter] need[s] to do everything that has to be done to address the issues, create aggressive long-term resolutions to them, do it transparently, do it quickly—and that's the way you build trust back" (Lipman & Williams, 2002, p. 30).

A positive brand image has value—monetary value, called **brand equity**. For example, if another company were to buy Nike, a part of the purchase price would reflect the value of the swoosh logo, which the buyer would expect to continue, stimulating sales and thereby increasing future revenue. When, in the 1990s, Nike was criticized for allegedly employing people in sweatshop conditions, the value of the brand, and thus the company, was at least temporarily suppressed. In 2017, Apple also responded quickly when it was reported that the company was slowing down older devices to compensate for the diminishing capacity of their aging batteries. Eager to prevent the controversy from tarnishing the company's brand, Apple apologized and reduced the price of new batteries (Kelly, 2017). A company that finds its brand degraded can be expected to undertake aggressive action, not necessarily to change its products or services but to resuscitate the value of its brand. Although nonprofit organizations are not bought or sold like corporations, their brands also have value. Its brand value is among the assets that a nonprofit brings to the table when it negotiates a partnership with a for-profit company, which will be discussed further in Chapter 12.

While the value of brand is often considered in terms of its appeal to external audiences, some authors emphasize its broader importance. Laidler-Kylander and Stenzel (2014) see a shift in thinking about brand, which they explain:

> This shift involves a change in the perception of the role of the brand, away from a fundraising and PR tool to a critical strategic asset focused on mission implementation. Instead of thinking of the brand as a logo and tagline, the new paradigm understands brand as the embodiment of the organization's mission and values.

In this broader conception, brand not only affects the external image of the nonprofit but also helps to define its mission, building internal cohesion, clarifying its position on the causes it addresses, and determining the types of partnerships it may seek to establish (Laidler-Kylander & Stenzel, 2014).

How does an organization build its brand? In her book *Brandraising*, Sarah Durham (2010) provides a model, depicted in Figure 10.1, which is in some aspects reminiscent of McKinsey's capacity-building model that we saw in Chapter 7.

The process begins at the top of the pyramid, at the organizational level, with decisions about fundamental purposes of the organization, including its vision, mission, values, and objectives (which some would call "goals"). These are concepts that will be familiar to students from our earlier discussion on strategic planning. Next, the organization must identify its audiences, which Dunham (2010) places in three categories: fundraising audiences (i.e., donors and prospects), program audiences (i.e., clients, patrons, members), and advocacy audiences (i.e., community leaders, media, policymakers, and other influential people). As discussed above, the organization must decide how it will be positioned in order to differentiate itself from others—in other words, as Durham explains, it must determine "the single idea [it] hopes[s] to own in the minds of [its] target audience" (p. 59). An organization's personality is defined by the attributes it hopes will become attached to its brand. Only after these steps have been addressed does the brandraising process move down to the next level of the pyramid, the identity level.

The identity level involves the organization's visual identity—the logo, color palette, typography, imagery, and use of graphics (Durham, 2010, p. 73). In addition, it encompasses the message platform, also called the written brand. The message platform includes such elements as the organization's name; taglines; mission, vision, and values statements written

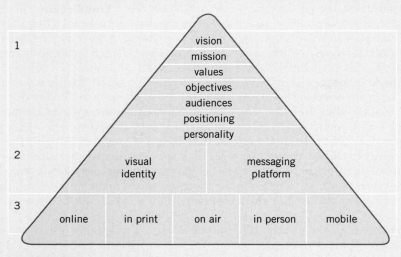

Figure 10.1   Brandraising Model

1

vision
mission
values
objectives
audiences
positioning
personality

2

visual
identity

messaging
platform

3

online | in print | on air | in person | mobile

1. ORGANIZATIONAL LEVEL: Includes the core elements that direct all aspects of the organization's work

2. IDENTITY LEVEL: What most people think of as *branding*—specifically, the visual identity and messaging platform

3. EXPERIENTIAL LEVEL: The channels and tools through which audiences connect with the organization

Source: Durham, S. (2010). *Brandraising.* San Francisco, CA: Jossey-Bass, p. 30.

for external presentation; key messages (ideas that the organization will weave throughout its statements in order to establish its position in the minds of its audiences); boilerplate copy (an "about us" of sorts) that will be used in various publications and media; an elevator pitch (brief statement of the organization's positioning); and a recommended lexicon (Durham, p. 89). Embedding the lexicon in the culture of the organization can help to communicate values. For example, referring to "children experiencing poverty" may be less degrading than "children at risk." Finally, in Durham's model, the brandraising process moves to the experiential level, where audiences are matched with communications media and a communications strategy is developed.

Integrated Marketing Communication (IMC)

Building a positive and consistent brand image requires that an organization integrate its marketing and communication efforts—in other words, that it ensures "that all the communications [it] generates represent a coherent whole" (Sargeant, 2005, p. 140). This is known as **integrated marketing communication (IMC)**.

An integrated approach requires that the messages and the values that they reflect permeate every aspect of the organization's work. If, for example, the organization desires to create an image of itself as "caring," its logo might include fuzzy small animals. However, its staff also must treat clients in a caring manner, answer the phone in a responsive tone, and create an internal culture consistent with the external image the organization seeks to build. As Adrian Sargeant (2005) expresses it, the organization needs to "live the brand" in everything it does (p. 140). The brand and its image are unlikely to settle too far from the reality of what the organization actually does or what it really is.

In an integrated approach, communications with various constituencies and stakeholders, both internally and externally, must be coordinated and consistent. As illustrated in Figure 10.2, internal audiences may include staff, board members, volunteers, and perhaps regional chapters or offices of a national or international organization. External audiences may include clients or customers; partners (such as sponsors, donors, and other organizations that are collaborators); other nonprofits (both competitors and otherwise); and various publics, such as government, the media, and professional or industry associations of which the nonprofit may be a member. There is also a need to achieve integration—that is, consistent messages—across communication channels. That includes printed materials, online presence, and personal (one-on-one) communication.

The need for integration is perhaps greater in a nonprofit organization than in any other type. This reality is rooted in the essential nature of nonprofits. As mentioned before, the constituencies of a nonprofit are often overlapping and interlaced. Remember the idea of open systems from back in Chapter 3? Staff members talk to clients and to volunteers, who may also be donors, who may communicate the staff's attitudes to their family, friends, and neighbors in the broader community. Although the organization may have high-quality publications and may skillfully manage its communications with the news media, these are unlikely to outweigh the word-of-mouth information and impressions communicated by those who have firsthand knowledge about the organization. The growth of social media has made it more challenging for every organization to maintain consistent messaging. In effect, it has made nonprofits, and most organizations, even more open systems than they were before. Anybody with a Twitter or Facebook account now can join the conversation and react to the organization's messages in ways it cannot control. We will return to discussing the impact of social media later in this chapter.

The *source* of information is a critical variable in its credibility. People are more inclined to believe what they hear from other individuals than what they read in the newspaper or hear on television. This is especially the case if the individual who provides the information is someone close to them, whom they trust, or close to the organization and thus presumed to know the real truth. This is one of the reasons why members of nonprofit boards, who are generally respected citizens in their communities, are so important as advocates for the organization's goals.

The sources of information people find to be most credible are family members, closely followed by friends and associates. This may include verbal communication or postings that known people may make through social networks such as Facebook. Professionals like clergy, doctors, and counselors rank right after friends as credible sources of information. Newspapers, direct mail, and the Internet come next. Although positive publicity from a mass media source is often highly prized by organizations that wish to improve their image, the mass media, including radio and TV, have the least credibility as sources of information (Bonk, Tynes, Griggs, & Sparks, 2008). The most credible medium of communication is word of mouth. One research study, reported in 2006, found that 53 percent of Americans were inclined to accept the credibility of what they were told by friends and family and that 51 percent are likely to pass along the information they received by word of mouth to others (Hall, 2006). Positive coverage in the news media is thus unlikely to outweigh the comments of an unhappy staff member to a client or of a disgruntled volunteer to his or her neighbor. Consistency of message—and of behavior—is thus essential to establishing and maintaining the organization's positive brand image.

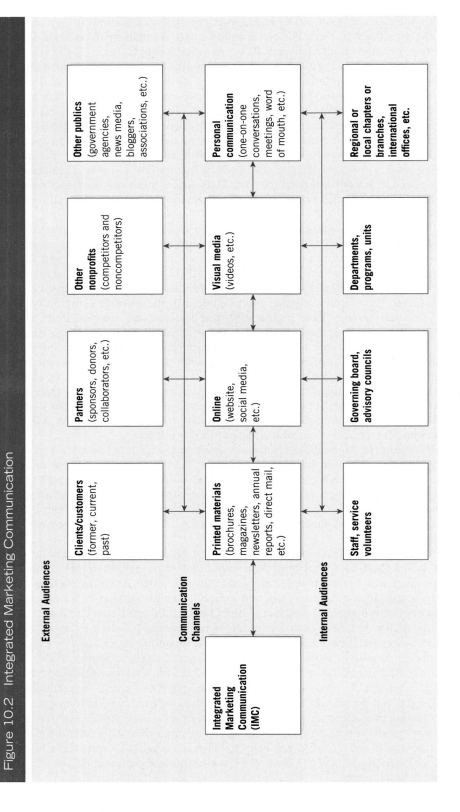

Figure 10.2 Integrated Marketing Communication

External Audiences

| Clients/customers (former, current, past) | Partners (sponsors, donors, collaborators, etc.) | Other nonprofits (competitors and noncompetitors) | Other publics (government agencies, news media, bloggers, associations, etc.) |

Communication Channels

Integrated Marketing Communication (IMC)

| Printed materials (brochures, magazines, newsletters, annual reports, direct mail, etc.) | Online (website, social media, etc.) | Visual media (videos, etc.) | Personal communication (one-on-one conversations, meetings, word of mouth, etc.) |

Internal Audiences

| Staff, service volunteers | Governing board, advisory councils | Departments, programs, units | Regional or local chapters or branches, international offices, etc. |

Crafting an Effective Message

What makes an effective message? Andresen (2006) offers a convenient acronym to remember the essential elements: CRAM. Effective messages are those that establish a Connection, promise a Reward, inspire Action, and stick in Memory (p. 163). Communicating a message requires tailoring it to both one-way communication and two-way communication, and brevity is essential. A slogan or tag line represents shorthand for the message in one-way communication, such as advertising (p. 172). For example, "Share the power of a wish" is a clear call to action from the Make-A-Wish Foundation. The Nature Conservancy summarizes its mission and its programs in just four words: "Protecting nature. Preserving life" (www.nature.org). The central message also needs to be communicated in conversation—in two-way communication, and brevity is again essential. The story must be capable of summary in the course of an elevator ride, called an elevator pitch. Clarity, brevity, and consistency are the essential elements of effective communication.

It is important to bear in mind a reality that has been established in communications theory: The way a message is received has as much to do with the predilections of the receiver as with the intentions of the sender. The receiver will interpret the message in the context of his or her own values, culture, and preformed attitudes about the organization. And established views may be difficult to change. For example, if a woman who has been a loyal donor to the local Humane Society hears rumors that animals are being mistreated, she may respond in one of four ways: (1) She may practice denial—persuade herself that the rumors just can't be true; (2) she may search for disconfirmation of the rumors, perhaps calling the director of the shelter hoping that he or she will tell her they are not correct; (3) she may minimize the problem, rationalizing that perhaps there have been a few cases of mistreatment, but that surely they are not part of a consistent pattern and the stories have just been exaggerated by people who, for some reason, have it in for the Humane Society; or (4) she may accept the rumors as true and change her beliefs, discontinuing her financial support (Andreasen & Kotler, 2008). Human beings tend to resist changing their beliefs, whether positive or negative; thus, a minimum goal of communication is to communicate messages that reinforce the positive attitudes that your friends may hold, positively affect those of individuals who have been previously indifferent, and do nothing to further strengthen the negative attitudes of those who may already hold them. Just as for an individual, a tarnished reputation for an organization may be difficult to repair.

Crisis Communications

In 2010, BP's oil well in the Gulf of Mexico exploded, leading to the worst environmental disaster in history. In the early days of the crisis, BP's management provided little information, minimized the problem, and blamed the contractor that operated the well. The low point was a comment from the company's CEO some days into the crisis, when he said, "There's no one who wants this thing over more than I do. You know, I'd like my life back." Some people viewed the comment as somewhat insensitive in light of the devastating impact of the crisis on the lives and livelihoods of people living in the Gulf region. BP's response was called "a textbook example of how not to do crisis management" (Shogren, 2011). The crisis also affected The Nature Conservancy (TNC), which was criticized for the financial support it had received from BP. TNC responded by posting a blog on its website, explaining its relationship with BP. The blog elicited many comments, to which TNC staff responded. The conservancy's CEO and director of external affairs also participated in an online discussion, responding to questions from many critics (Wallace, 2010b). The incident demonstrated alternative approaches to communicating with an organization's various publics in the face of a crisis or controversy.

A crisis is "a significant threat to operations that can have negative consequences if not properly handled" (Coombs, 2011). The crisis may involve public safety, financial loss, or a loss of reputation (Coombs, 2011). As mentioned previously in our discussion of brands, for a nonprofit organization, a loss of reputation or trust can be especially devastating.

There is, of course, a distinction between crisis management and crisis communications, with the former encompassing all actions taken to address the situation and the latter, as the term implies, related to how the organization communicates information about the situation to its various constituents. As discussed in Chapter 7, nonprofits should maintain a risk management plan, to minimize the potential for a crisis occurring in the first place and to define the process for responding to such an event if and when it occurs. Depending on the nature of the crisis, the overall response likely will involve various individuals and departments, including, for example, public relations, legal, security, finance, human resources, and others (Coombs, 2011). Our focus in this chapter is on the communications response, that is, **crisis communications**.

The literature on crisis management and crisis communications is extensive. Much of it consists of principles or rules prescribed by public relations practitioners based on cases, but theories also have been developed. One of the best-known theories is W. Timothy Coombs's (2007) situational crisis communication theory (SCCT). Coombs's theory states that how much of a threat a crisis may present to an organization's reputation depends on three variables: the extent to which it is responsible for the crisis, rather than a victim itself; its crisis history; and its reputation prior to the crisis (Sisco, 2012). Managers can identify the appropriate strategies for responding to a crisis by considering these three variables. Research studies testing this theory and others have involved corporations, but some suggest that similar principles of crisis communications can be applied in nonprofit organizations (Sisco, 2012).

Organizations facing a crisis are advised to respond quickly, accurately, and consistently (Coombs, 2011). Failure to speak out quickly may leave an information vacuum, which the news media or others (for example, bloggers) may try to fill, possibly with information that is not accurate. In addition, by responding quickly, even if it does not have much information to provide, the organization positions itself as a resource and thus takes control of the story, rather than permitting it to be driven by others (Coombs, 2011). It is essential that information provided by the organization be accurate, even if it is limited, since later inconsistencies will diminish credibility. Maintaining consistency does not necessarily require that the organization have only one spokesperson, but "spokespersons should be briefed on the same information and the key points the organization is trying to convey in [its] messages" (Coombs, 2011). If people have been harmed by the crisis, then the organization's spokespersons should express sympathy and concern for the victims. Research suggests that reputational harm is reduced when such feelings are voiced, rather than expressions that may seem indifferent or self-focused, such as the statement by the BP executive mentioned in the earlier example (Coombs, 2011).

Much of the advice that experts offer on crisis communications relates to working with the news media. Communicating through the news media may be an effective way of reaching a large number of people quickly and is especially appropriate to get the message out if there is some threat to public safety (Coombs, 2011). But microsites, intranets, systems to send alerts to mobile phones, and social media have added communications channels that also can be used to provide a quick response. Some of these channels enable an organization to bypass the news media and engage in direct communication with constituents and the public, as exemplified by the example of The Nature Conservancy during the Gulf oil crisis. That can be advantageous, since it enables the organization to control its message and tell its side of the story without filtering or interpretation by the news media. But such media also empower others over whom the organization has no control, including bloggers and individuals who post online comments, not all of whom may be totally accurate or respectful. The growth of online media thus has changed the rules, not only for crisis communications but for all communications programs. Let's take a closer look at the implications in the next section of this chapter.

Social Media

Many nonprofit organizations have maintained websites and sent e-mail newsletters since the late 1990s or early 2000s. In many ways, static websites are merely brochures on a screen. That is, their content is produced and controlled by the organization. With the exception of registering to make a gift or receive additional information, the viewer of the site had limited ability to interact. But development of **Web 2.0** in the 2000s introduced a revolution in communication that has significantly changed how nonprofits interact with their constituencies for the purposes of transmitting information, building communities, advocating for action, and raising funds (Lovejoy & Saxton, 2012). Chapter 11 provides further discussion of social media in nonprofit advocacy and Chapter 13 discuses online fundraising in greater detail.

From Gatekeepers to Connectors

Although many people use the terms **social media** and **social networks** interchangeably, it is often useful to understand the distinction. As Daniel Nations defines the term, "Social media are web-based communication tools that enable people to interact with each other by both sharing and consuming information (Nations, 2017). Social networks are built on social media, but as the term "network" suggests, they are communities of people who intentionally come together to form a community. As Nation (2017) further explains, "Media refers to the information you're actually sharing—whether it's a link to an article, a video, an animated GIF, a PDF document, a simple status update or anything else. Networking, on the other hand, has to do with who your audience is and the relationships you have with them. Your network can include people like friends, relatives, colleagues, anyone from your past, current customers, mentors and even complete strangers."

Nonprofit organizations use social media to communicate and to build communities. Sites and apps such as Facebook, Twitter, Snapchat, Instagram, LinkedIn, YouTube, and others have enabled users to create their own content and engage in dialogue. The organization's clients, donors, and volunteers—even its critics—have the ability to interact and to add their own comments and viewpoints to the well-considered messages originated by the organization itself. As Ruth McCambridge (2016, p. 6) describes this reality, "No longer can we just blast out a message and expect it to have impact as is—emerging substantively unchanged from the scrum of interactions among those who receive it, pass it along, argue back with it in sometimes very public ways, or support or shame you for it." Members, donors, and other groups also can connect with the nonprofit, making themselves a part of its community, engaging in an ongoing dialogue.

Previously, communications theory and practice, including many of the principles discussed above in this chapter, were based on the notion that organizations could determine their own messages, ensure consistency in their expression, and thereby shape their own brands. Today, anybody can begin or join a discussion about a nonprofit organization and have a powerful impact on the brand. This has increased transparency and enabled individuals to become reporters—or citizen journalists—who can draw attention to an organization in a positive or negative light. In this environment, nonprofits are no longer "gatekeepers" that control the flow of information about the causes that concern them. Rather they have become connectors of "people to information and networks, and of networks to networks" (McCambridge, 2016, p. 9).

Social Media Planning

Social media is no longer just an adjunct to other communication strategies; in many cases, it may be central to achievement of the organization's mission. There needs to be a well-considered plan for social media, that follows a logic model culminating in achievement of strategic outcomes (Guo & Saxton, 2016, p. 10). In other words, as Guo and Saxton (2016) explain, "It is not enough to simply *be* on social media; instead, the organization needs to think strategically about what it wants to achieve through its presence" (p. 12). Figure 10.3 portrays a logic model, similar to those we discussed in Chapter 6, that could serve as a basis for planning. It begins with inputs (the resources the organization devotes to online media) and social media activities (connections and messages). These activities lead to immediate outcomes, which Guo and Saxton (2016) define as **social media capital**, meaning media-based social capital. Social media capital leads to intermediate outcomes in the form of "cultural, financial, human, intellectual, or reputational capital" and, ultimately, strategic outcomes that relate to the mission (Guo & Saxton, 2016, p. 12).

Operational Questions

One operational question to be addressed is the appropriate level and allocation of resources to electronic communication. Although the cost of establishing an online presence, for example a Facebook page, may be minimal, there is a continuing cost to maintaining it. Indeed, as interaction increases, so too may the need for resources devoted to online communication, possibly requiring a trade-off with resources dedicated to traditional communication programs. This reality requires that organizations identify their goals for online media and tools to evaluate its impact on their performance. As discussed in Chapter 6, measuring outputs may be relatively easy, but determining the impact on outcomes related to mission and goals requires development of a logic model. As Christine Durand and Kristen Cici (2011) write,

Figure 10.3 Logic Model for Achieving Strategic Outcomes From Social-Media Use

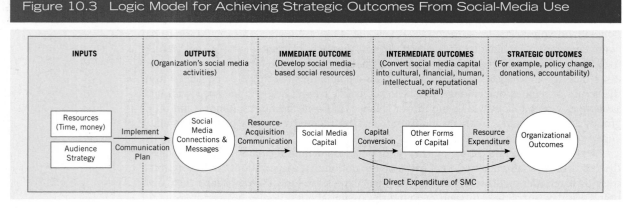

Source: Guo, C., and Saxton, G. D. (2016, Winter). Social media capital for nonprofits: How to accumulate it, convert it, spend it. *Nonprofit Quarterly, 23*(4), 12.

Counting the number of fans, followers, visits, or likes is the norm. Knowing that you have 1,378 followers on Twitter is great, but what does that actually mean? Nonprofits need to ask themselves: "Why are we using social media?" The answer probably isn't to have a thousand likes on Facebook.... What does it mean to have a thousand likes? Is that translating into more volunteers, more donations, more education about your mission or your issues?

Another operational question, especially relevant in larger organizations, is whether the online presence should be managed centrally by social media staff or be dispersed throughout the organization. Allison Fine (2011) makes the case that having "social media plans or departments to live separate and distinct from the rest of an organization is a mistake." Rather, she recommends, social media tools should be "integrated into every department and every function of the organization." If various staff members may be active in social media, then there is a need for a social media policy that defines standards regarding appropriate messages to be conveyed. There is also a need for ongoing training of staff throughout the organization. For example, the National Wildlife Federation has trained staff members to use Twitter, "to share their work with the world, using their own voice, using their own identities" (Fine, 2011).

The technologies of online media likely will continue to evolve, requiring continuing analysis and learning. But maintaining an active presence online has become an essential component of communications and marketing for nonprofit organizations and is certain to grow in importance in the years ahead. Fortunately, a substantial number of books, articles, training programs, and consultancies exist to guide organizations in addressing key issues in developing their online media strategy. Some resources are listed as suggested reading at the end of this chapter.

Evaluating Marketing and Communication

As in other aspects of nonprofit management, the important question about any marketing or communication plan is a simple one: Does it work? In other words, what impact does adoption of a marketing approach have on the performance of a nonprofit organization? By now, readers who have progressed through this book from the beginning will recognize the issues associated with the question—the complexity of defining what constitutes nonprofit organizational performance and how to measure it once defined.

It is, of course, relatively easy to establish the link between marketing and performance in a for-profit company. Indeed, most research on the link between marketing and performance has been focused on the business sector, and a number of studies have identified a relationship between market orientation and financial outcomes, such as return on investment (Gainer & Moyer, 2005; Shoham, Ruvio, Vigoda-Gadot, & Schwabsky, 2006). Similar methods may be suitable to studying marketing by nonprofits that also provide services in a competitive environment, such as health care. For many nonprofits, however, assessing the benefits of marketing and communication efforts also requires measuring the effects on donors, clients, and the advancement of causes or ideas, outcomes that may be less easily quantified.

The findings of several studies suggest that nonprofit organizations that hold a market orientation, perhaps better defined as a social orientation, do attain greater financial support and client satisfaction than those that do not (Gainer & Moyer, 2005). In an exploratory study published in 2012, Helisse Levine and Anne Zahradnik (2012) looked specifically at nonprofits' use of online media and focused on financial impact. They tracked nonprofits' website content over time and compared it with financial indicators for those organizations at corresponding points in time. They found a "positive relationship between higher market orientation via online media presence and improved financial viability" (p. 26). Their article reporting on the study also provided a tool for nonprofits to use in assessing their online media. As the authors acknowledge, an expansion of the research would be useful to determine how the findings may apply to various types of nonprofits and to explore the cause-and-effect question—whether financially viable nonprofits maintain a more active online presence or whether having a robust online presence indeed produces financial benefits. In addition, there is a need for additional research that goes beyond financial indicators to further explore the impact of online media in advancing nonprofit missions.

CHAPTER SUMMARY

Marketing, communications, and public relations are related fields, but also have specific definitions that distinguish them. Communications is the transmission or exchange of information; public relations is "a strategic communication process that builds mutually beneficial relationships between organizations and their publics" (Public Relations Society of America, n.d.). Marketing is a process distinguished by its objective: to influence the behavior of someone else. Marketing focuses on exchanges.

Marketing principles have been widely adopted in the nonprofit sector. Some nonprofits engage in commercial marketing to attract customers to the goods and services that they provide. Others use social marketing to change behavior in order to benefit people and society. Some remain concerned that commercial marketing may not be appropriate to nonprofit values and cultures. This may reflect, in part, an understanding of marketing that is a throwback to earlier mind-sets about the concept, especially the idea that marketing is equivalent to sales.

Contemporary marketing follows a customer mind-set that requires that "the organization systematically study customers' needs, wants, perceptions, preferences, and satisfaction ... and act on this information to improve its offerings to meet its customers' needs better" (Andreasen & Kotler, 2008, p. 39). This implies that the organization's programs and services need to be adapted to meet identified customer desires; but this should not be taken as a reason for a nonprofit to abandon its mission or central values. Rather, marketing should be used as a tool for pursuing the mission and achieving mission-related goals.

The marketing mix includes four variables (recall the four Ps of marketing): product, place, price, and promotion. Organizations can adjust the marketing mix to differentiate themselves from others and position themselves in a unique market niche, gaining an advantage over other organizations or alternative activities with which they may compete. Nonprofits may compete directly with other organizations, nonprofit or for-profit, but they also face generic competition from all alternative uses for individuals' time and money.

Products have tangible and intangible qualities; for example, the latter include the prestige associated with a degree from a well-known university or the environment in which coffee is consumed. Place, or location, determines access to a program or service and is a critical variable in the marketing mix. Some products and services need to be taken to where the customers are—for example, vans that provide mobile medical care. Prices for products and services may be set to provide a break-even result for the nonprofit, to compete with what others are charging, or to reflect the perceived value of the product or service to the customer. Sophisticated marketers practice price discrimination, charging different prices to different segments of their target market. Price discrimination may be intended to match differences in product value, for example, seats closer to or farther from the theater stage; to shift utilization from peak to nonpeak periods; or to maximize revenue by charging the highest prices that some consumers are willing to pay.

Brand is commonly defined as "a name, term, design, symbol, or any other feature that identifies one seller's good or service as distinct from those of other sellers" (Burnett, 2007, p. 179), but some offer a broader definition that includes intangible perceptions as a part of a brand. Individuals attribute qualities to a brand, and organizations work to establish a positive brand image, which may help attract both clients and donors. A positive brand has a monetary value, called brand equity, which may form the basis of some partnerships between nonprofits and for-profit companies. Building an organization's brand requires initiatives at the organizational level, the identity level, and the experiential level (Durham, 2010).

Communications and marketing must be integrated; that is, their goals must permeate all aspects of the organization with consistent messages being delivered to various constituencies. This approach is known as integrated marketing communication, or IMC. It is especially important in nonprofits because their borders are porous, and members of various constituencies, including staff, volunteers, and donors, may communicate with each other. Individuals attribute greater credibility to information they receive through word of mouth than to what they read or see in the public media, especially if the source is someone close to them or with inside knowledge of the organization. This requires that messages delivered both internally and externally be consistent.

Nonprofit organizations should have a plan for risk management that includes both prevention of crises and preparation for communicating, should a crisis occur. Principles of crisis communications include the need to respond quickly, accurately, and consistently, and with expressions of empathy and concern for any individuals who may have suffered as a result of whatever incident occurred.

The development of social media that permit users to create content and join conversations regarding an organization, requires new communications strategies and presents nonprofit organizations with critical decisions about the resources and staffing needed to adapt. It is essential to develop a plan that reflects a logic model leading from the investment of resources in electronic communication to the achievement of the organization's strategic outcomes. Some have adopted social media policies to guide the way in which volunteers and staff members communicate about the organization and provide training to staff members on the use of online media.

Research suggests that nonprofits that adopt a market orientation or a societal orientation do achieve greater financial support and client satisfaction. Research also has found a relationship between an organization's online presence and financial viability.

NOTE

1. If a product or service is provided for a fee, then the relevant variable is what the customer *wants,* not what he or she may need. For example, a person may need more exercise, and his or her doctor may even recommend it. That person should join a health club. But unless the person also *wants* more exercise, personal need is irrelevant from a marketing perspective because he or she will not be willing to spend money on health club dues.

KEY TERMS AND CONCEPTS

brand 286
brand attributes 286
brand equity 287
communication 278
communications 278
competitive advantage 280
competitive pricing 284

cost-oriented pricing 283
crisis communications 292
demand-based pricing 284
demographic variables 282
differentiation 280
external publics 278
four Ps of marketing 280

integrated marketing communication (IMC) 288
internal publics 278
marketing 279
marketing mix 280
market niche 280
place 280

CASE 10.1 Rebranding 4-H

In the late 19th century, more than half of all Americans lived on farms. New farming techniques, based on science, were being developed through university research, but older generations of farmers were slow to adopt them (Joslyn, 2017). Some thought that the only way to achieve implementation of new methods might be to educate young people, who would eventually take over their family farms. In 1902, A. B. Graham started an after-school program for farm kids in Ohio (4-H, n.d.-a). The Cooperative Extension System was established within the U.S. Department of Agriculture in 1914 and Graham's clubs eventually became nationalized as the nonprofit organization known as 4-H, meaning "head, heart, hands, and health" (Stein, 2016). The goals were to advance new farming technology by educating young people and to provide opportunities for growth for rural kids. By 2016, 4-H had become the largest youth development organization in the United States, serving six million young people through a network of 110 public universities and 3,000 local agricultural extension offices across the country (National 4-H Council, 2016). Although less well-known as an organization by many Americans, 4-H was engaging more young people than the Boy Scouts and Girl Scouts combined (Joslyn, 2017).

By 2016, the world had changed since the founding of 4-H and the organization needed to adapt in order to continue its impact and growth. More than 80 percent of Americans were living in urban areas (Joslyn, 2017). Less than one half of American kids ages 8 to 18 were engaged in any youth-development organization at all (Joslyn, 2017). More than one half of 4-H members were white, at a time when African American and Hispanic communities were growing, especially in urban areas (Shapiro, 2016). Even in some rural areas, many young people were of Hispanic backgrounds and most were not involved in 4-H (Joslyn, 2017). Many of 4-H's 25 million alumni said they had lost their connection to the organization (Stein, 2016).

The organization's programs had evolved with the changing times, but its brand had not kept pace. Originally established to advance scientific techniques in agriculture, by the 2000s 4-H programs were emphasizing science, technology, engineering, and mathematics (STEM), including a popular robotics curriculum (Joslyn, 2017). But its plan to increase participation to 10 million young people by 2025 was hampered by perceptions; it was still seen by many people as being all about "cows and plows" (Stein, 2016).

Changing the brand would require reemphasizing the mission of youth empowerment and the relevance of 4-H programs to developing skills for addressing diverse issues in today's society, not just agriculture (Wood, 2016). It would also require moving beyond agricultural regions and into cities as well as attracting a more diverse membership. "We want to ensure that our program has a welcome mat in every community," 4-H's national CEO explained. "We know if we don't get them ready for leadership, we may have a huge leadership void affecting every industry and sector in the future" (Shapiro, 2016).

Working with an advertising agency that provided pro bono services, the national 4-H office launched a rebranding campaign, focusing on three program areas: STEM, healthy living, and civic engagement (Stein, 2016). A plan was developed for advertising to promote the new themes on TV, radio, and the Internet (Stein, 2016). The messages were developed in consultation with young people and 4-H alumni. Advertising was targeted on Generation X and millennial mothers who were former 4-H members and who had children in the 6 to 18 age range (Stein, 2016). Alumni were another target. Most had grown up in rural areas but now lived in urban communities. The marketing would try to remind them of 4-H's roots while also informing them about its contemporary focus (Tadena, 2016).

A First-Generation 4-H Families Initiative was launched in Midwestern states to engage Hispanic kids (Joslyn, 2017). A survey of young people had revealed a desire to develop leadership skills and confidence. In response, 4-H launched its "Grow True Leaders" campaign, with a rally in Washington, DC, that featured prominent alumni (National 4-H Council, 2016). New online resources were developed to provide kids with the ability to give a "shout out" to examples of strong leadership and to share their own stories (4-H, n.d.-b).

Writing about the 4-H brand makeover, Heather Joslyn (2017) identifies five lessons that she offers as points of advice:

- Be willing to rethink everything about how you operate.

- Double down on popular programs.

- Tell your story. And give the participants the tools to tell their stories.

- Invite alumni to stay involved.

- Listen to your staff, your affiliates, and the people you serve.

Andrew Bosworth, a 4-H alumnus who went on to become an executive at Facebook, also offers advice on building a brand in the era of social media. It is just no longer possible for an organization to control its brand as it might have done in the past. Today, Bosworth says, "you really have to empower your community to own your brand, to be its ambassadors. And that means giving up some control you used to assert" (Joslyn, 2017).

Questions Related to Case 10.1

1. Which principles from this chapter are illustrated by the case of 4-H?

2. Think back on (or read again) the discussion of strategic planning in Chapter 7. What strengths, weaknesses, opportunities, and threats do you think 4-H might have identified, leading to the changes discussed in this case?

3. Can you think of other nonprofit organizations with brands that may not accurately reflect their programs today, perhaps some with which you have been involved or have read about? In broad terms, how do you think their messages might be revised in order to change perceptions? Can new messages solve their problems or will that also require new programs?

CASE 10.2 Susan G. Komen Foundation

In 2012, the Susan G. Komen Foundation, one of the nation's leading breast cancer research organizations, announced that it was discontinuing funding to Planned Parenthood, one of the nation's largest providers and advocates in the field of reproductive health care. Komen had provided funds to Planned Parenthood to support breast cancer screenings. The announcement that it would no longer fund Planned Parenthood created a national controversy that eventually led Komen to reverse its decision. The reaction, much of it expressed on social media, reflected the nation's divided views regarding abortion, but it also provided a case study of nonprofit communication strategies and the power of social media.

Planned Parenthood responded quickly to Komen's announcement, immediately posting information on its Facebook page and on Twitter, attracting more than 1,000 comments during its first 24 hours online. In contrast, Komen waited two days to mention the controversy on its Facebook page and then offered a less-than-detailed explanation: "Grant-making decisions are not about politics—our priority is and always will be the women we serve" (Panepento, 2012). By that time, Planned Parenthood's posting had received more than 2,000 comments, and the extensive online discussion had captured the attention of traditional news media. The story came to dominate national news, with Planned Parenthood largely framing the dialogue.

In subsequent days, Komen's founder and CEO, Nancy Brinker, responded in more detail. But she offered inconsistent explanations for the termination of funding to Planned Parenthood. At first, she stated that Komen's policy prohibited funding for organizations that were under investigation. Some noted that while a

Congressional committee was investigating the question of whether Planned Parenthood had used federal funds to provide abortions, there was no criminal investigation of the organization underway. Brinker then explained that Planned Parenthood did not conduct breast cancer screenings directly, but rather referred women to other providers, offering that as a reason for defunding by Komen (Condon, 2012). In another interview, Brinker suggested that the reasons for ending support were related to Komen's "new standards of criteria for how we can measure our results and effectiveness in communities," but she did not explain how Planned Parenthood had failed to meet those standards (NBC News, 2012).

Within three days of its announcement that it would cease funding Planned Parenthood, Komen reversed its position and offered an apology. Komen's board chair and other officials resigned. Contributions to Komen declined by 22 percent in the year following the controversy, while gifts to Planned Parenthood increased ("Komen Gifts Plunged," 2014). In 2014, Komen's CEO, Judith Salerno, said that the organization had "moved past" the controversy ("Komen Has 'Moved Past,'" 2014). Contributions continued to decline, to $201 million in 2015, but then increased to $211 million in 2016, suggesting that perhaps Komen was indeed rebounding (Leslie, 2017). Meanwhile, a new phrase to describe the potential impact of social media criticism on a nonprofit had entered the vocabulary: "getting Komened" (Peregrine, 2012).

Although differing political and social views were one explanation of the controversy, some authors who analyzed the events objectively viewed it as a case study in crisis management and communications, drawing lessons for nonprofit organizations generally. Some cited Komen's delayed and inconsistent responses as critical mistakes. As one author wrote, "YouTube, Facebook, and mass e-mail contributed mightily to the uproar by quickly informing and galvanizing hundreds of thousands of concerned individuals. Cyberspace proved to be a tenuous place, even for the dedicated. The need for charities to be media savvy was never more evident, never more on display" (Grunfeld & Lash, 2012).

Questions Related to Case 10.2

1. Is the case of Planned Parenthood and the Susan G. Komen Foundation primarily related to the concepts of marketing, communications, or public relations? Explain.

2. How does Coombs's situational crisis communication theory (SCCT) apply to the case of Planned Parenthood and the Susan G. Komen Foundation?

3. Leaving aside your personal views on the issues that were involved, how do you think the controversy between the Susan G. Komen Foundation and Planned Parenthood may have affected the brand of each organization?

QUESTIONS FOR DISCUSSION

1. Following these questions is a list of some well-known nonprofit organizations and a list of attributes. Look at each nonprofit and identify up to three attributes that you would use to describe your impression of the organization. Don't think too long; just write down the first three words that come to mind when you read the organization's name. (If you've never heard of the organization, just leave it blank.) When you are done, consider these questions:

2. How do your results compare with those of your classmates?

3. What do the results suggest about attributes of the brand in each case?

4. Why do you think each organization has the image that it does, either positive or negative?

American Red Cross	___,___,___	(a)	innovative
Boy Scouts of America	___,___,___	(b)	well-managed
The Nature Conservancy	___,___,___	(c)	caring
Greenpeace	___,___,___	(d)	poorly-managed
Girl Scouts of the United States of America	___,___,___	(e)	unresponsive
Teach for America	___,___,___	(f)	dependable
National Geographic Society	___,___,___	(g)	high quality
City Year	___,___,___	(h)	patriotic
United Way of America	___,___,___	(i)	responsive
Boys and Girls Clubs	___,___,___	(j)	untrustworthy
Doctors Without Borders	___,___,___	(k)	cold-hearted
Habitat for Humanity	___,___,___	(l)	friendly
Children's Defense Fund	___,___,___	(m)	radical
Boston Symphony Orchestra	___,___,___	(n)	exciting
Yale University	___,___,___	(o)	prestigious
YMCA	___,___,___	(p)	traditional

APPENDIX CASES

The following cases in the Appendix of this text include points related to the content of this chapter: Case 1 (New York City Opera); Case 2 (Share Our Strength/No Kid Hungry); Case 3 (The Y); Case 4 (The Girl Scouts of the United States of America).

SUGGESTIONS FOR FURTHER READING

Books/Journals

Coombs, W. T. (2014). *Ongoing crisis communication: Planning, managing, and responding* (4th ed.). Thousand Oaks, CA: Sage.

Durham, S. (2010). *Brandraising: How nonprofits raise visibility and money through smart communications*. San Francisco, CA: Jossey-Bass.

International Journal of Nonprofit and Voluntary Sector Marketing. Hoboken, NJ: Wiley. (Available at http://onlinelibrary.wiley.com/journal/10.1002/(ISSN)1479-103X)

Kim, C. M. (2016). *Social media campaigns: Strategies for public relations and marketing*. New York: Routledge.

Websites

American Marketing Association: http://www.marketingpower.com

Network for Good: http://www.networkforgood.org

Public Relations Society of America: http://www.prsa.org

Nonprofit organizations have played an essential role in shaping our country by bringing issues to the public's attention, influencing attitudes, and lobbying for new laws.

Library of Congress

Chapter Outline

Advocacy and Lobbying

Within the lifetime of many people alive today, African American children were taught in schools segregated by law. Women could legally be denied jobs, barred from entire professions, and paid less than men simply because of their gender. Lesbian and gay people were regularly fired from their jobs if their sexual orientation became known. People with physical disabilities were unable to access many public buildings, limiting their opportunities for employment and life experiences. Companies dumped raw sewage and industrial wastes into rivers with impunity. Highways were lined with ugly billboards and trash thrown from cars by un-seat-belted motorists. People could smoke in offices and other public places, and driving while drunk often was punishable by no more than a minor fine, even if it resulted in the death of another person. There remain many injustices, threats to the environment, diseases to be cured, and other problems to be solved, but over decades, public attitudes have changed and new laws have been enacted to correct many of the intolerable situations mentioned above.

As explained in Box 11.1, social issues often follow a life cycle. In the beginning, there may be inattention to the problem, although it exists. Some event may cause the problem to be discovered by individuals and the news media. Advocates, usually including nonprofit organizations, then drive the issue to higher visibility and courses of possible action are identified and evaluated. Initial interventions may include efforts by government and social marketing by nonprofits, as discussed in Chapter 10. Progress may be uneven as time goes by, but the problem ultimately is either resolved or found to be intractable. It may drop off the public's radar until some new event causes it to gain attention again (Andreasen, 2006).

In most instances, nonprofit organizations have played an essential role by bringing the issue to the public's attention, influencing attitudes and building support for change, and lobbying for new laws. Indeed, nonprofits have been at the forefront of every important social change in the United States from the beginning of the nation. They have been the principal advocates for people who are disadvantaged or disenfranchised and for causes that initially concern only a minority of people.

Learning Objectives

After reading this chapter, students should be able to:

1. Describe the life cycle of a social change issue.

2. Define advocacy, lobbying, organizing, civic engagement, and political activity.

3. Summarize federal law related to nonprofit lobbying.

4. Describe the points that need to be considered when implementing an advocacy program.

5. Explain current policy issues related to nonprofit advocacy, lobbying, and political activity.

6. Analyze cases, applying concepts from the chapter.

Box 11.1   Stages in the Life Cycle of a Social Change Issue

Stage 1: Inattention to the problem	The social problem exists, as evidenced by concrete data or dramatic anecdotes, but it has not yet become anyone's concern.
Stage 2: Discovery of the problem	The problem comes to the attention of individuals or groups (including the media) who think it needs to be addressed. At this stage, initial baseline analyses or measurements will be undertaken. Nuances of the problem will begin to emerge—for example, learning who is most affected by the problem.
Stage 3: Climbing the agenda	Activists, advocacy groups, individual politicians, investigative reporters, and nonfiction writers raise the volume on the issue. They marshal even more evidence, produce real victims, and potentially raise the guilt level of those not affected. At this stage, funders and potential interveners begin to find the issue sufficiently important for attention and possible action.
Stage 4: Outlining the choices	Analysts and advocates look at the data and consider how the problem might be addressed. Evidence about causal linkages will be important, as will scenarios for possible intervention.
Stage 5: Choosing courses of action	This is where debate takes place over the benefits and costs that action and inaction will have on society, victims, and those who have to take action (e.g., donate money, pass laws) if there is to be a solution. Attention will be paid to the efficacy of various solutions. Opposing forces emerge and solidify their positions.
Stage 6: Launching initial interventions	Foundations or government agencies put money into programs. Organizations mount pioneering efforts and test alternative strategies and tactics. These will involve both downstream and upstream interventions, in which social marketing can play a major role.
Stage 7: Reassessing and redirecting efforts	With most difficult changes, progress is slow, and there are periods of acceleration, deceleration, progression, and regression. At some point, key figures will feel that it is time to take stock of where the problem stands. The outcome may be a reorientation and resurgence of interventions—or it may not.
Stage 8: Achieving success, failure, or neglect	After a number of years, the problem will have found some major solutions or will have proven basically intractable and, in the absence of dramatic progress or new data, will "drop off the radar screen." The latter may also be the result of new competition from the latest social problem that captures the public's imagination and drives the "old" problem into the "dustbin of history" (Cohen, 2000, cited by Andreasen, 2006).

Source: Andreasen, A. R. (2006). *Social marketing in the 21st century.* Thousand Oaks, CA: Sage, p. 42.

Nonprofits often have identified and given visibility to emerging issues and problems that ultimately became the focus of national attention and action.

Nonprofits may be found on every side of any issue, and they reflect all shades of opinion. There are organizations that advocate pro-life positions and others that are pro-choice. There are nonprofits that work to advance religious values and others that strive to protect the separation of church and state. There are those whose mission is to promote sound government and those who seek to limit government's size and power. There are nonprofits that work toward economic growth and others with a mission to preserve and protect the environment, historic structures, animals, and communities from the effects of commercial development. The public interest that is served by such diversity is the preservation of an uninhibited marketplace of ideas, allowing the free exchange of information and discussion that is believed to lead ultimately to sound public policy. Nonprofit advocacy and lobbying is thus a fundamental pillar of a democratic society.

Despite the important role of nonprofit advocacy, various authors observe that indeed most nonprofits do not engage in a significant amount of advocacy or lobbying. For example, a survey by BoardSource found that less than one third of nonprofits had policies related to advocacy and that less than one half of boards were well-informed about policy or active in advocacy activities (BoardSource, 2017). There are various reasons why many nonprofits do not engage in advocacy. One obvious reason is that many lack the staff or resources, especially given the many demands of managing core service programs. Not surprisingly, larger national nonprofits are more likely to be directly involved in advocacy and lobbying than are smaller, local organizations, and such activity is more common among organizations in fields that are significantly regulated, such as health care (Child & Grønbjerg, 2007). Although small nonprofits might not conduct much lobbying on their own, they may belong to an association or coalition that represents their interests and issues at the state or national level. Such coalitions exist to serve specific groups of nonprofits, for example, higher education institutions, health care providers, and organizations concerned with homelessness.

Concern about alienating government or foundation funders may be a barrier for some, and nonprofits that are dependent on gifts from individuals also may be reluctant to take a position on issues that affect the organization but on which their donors hold different opinions. For example, in the debate about tax reform legislation in 2017, some analysts were concerned that an increase in the exemption from the federal estate tax might lead to fewer charitable bequests. Nonprofits that actively opposed this change were advocating against the financial interests of some of their own donors, presenting obvious potential tension. But a common conclusion about why nonprofits do not lobby more is that many nonprofit executives are simply unclear about what the law allows. They may decide to err on the side of caution by keeping their distance from the legislative process.

Basic Distinctions

Before we go further into this topic, let's clarify five basic concepts and terms: **advocacy**, **lobbying**, **organizing**, **civic engagement**, and **political campaign activity**.

- *Advocacy* includes action taken in support of a cause or an idea. As Robert Pekkanen and Steven Smith (2014) observe, advocacy may encompass a wide range of activities, "from organizing a massive demonstration to encouraging board members to write letters to the editor of the local paper (p. 1). And it may occur at the local, state, federal, or international level (p. 1). Advocacy is a basic right of every individual and organization in the United States and may be practiced without limit; it is an exercise of free speech protected by the U.S. Constitution.

- *Lobbying* is action taken to support or oppose specific legislation at the national, state, or local level. This could include, for example, contacting a member of Congress, a state legislator, or a city councilperson to request his or her sponsorship or vote in favor of or against a specific bill. It does not include contacting members of the executive branch, unless that individual is in a position to influence legislation.

- *Organizing* includes identifying people you think will share your positions and enlisting them to be a part of your base of support, which may enhance the effectiveness of your advocacy and lobbying (Avner, 2016).

- *Civic engagement* includes nonpartisan organizing efforts that "inform people about issues" and help them become involved in the electoral process (Avner, 2016, p. 399).

- *Political campaign activity* is action taken in support of or in opposition to specific candidates for office, including the publication or distribution of statements or printed materials. It does not include, however, conducting nonpartisan activities such as get-out-the-vote efforts or sponsoring a candidate debate or forum (Halloran, 2013). That would be civic engagement. But the line sometimes has seemed fuzzy, and there have been some controversial cases in recent years surrounding the involvement of nonprofits in political campaigns. There also have been proposals to change the law to expand what is permissible for charitable nonprofits. This debate is discussed further later in this chapter.

There is sometimes understandable confusion between what is advocacy and what is lobbying. Indeed, the former encompasses the latter. For example, the marches, protests, and sit-ins of the Civil Rights movement were advocacy for equal rights, but they were not lobbying since they were not actions undertaken with the purpose of supporting or opposing any specific item of legislation. Once the Civil Rights Act of 1964 was up for consideration in Congress, many individuals and organizations contacted their elected representatives to urge a favorable vote. That activity was lobbying. The law defines lobbying quite precisely, including the identification of specific activities it does and does not include.

Overview of Lobbying Law

The law on lobbying is complex and may change from time to time. The following discussion thus simplifies some concepts and definitions and it should not be relied upon as legal advice. Students should check various Web resources to see if there have been changes since this chapter was written and, of course, nonprofit organizations always should consult legal counsel about what activities are permissible in this area.

Our discussion throughout the text has emphasized the charitable nonprofits, tax-exempt under Section 501(c)(3) of the Internal Revenue Code, and the social welfare or advocacy organizations that are tax exempt under Section 501(c)(4). Students will recall from Chapter 2 that there also are other types of tax-exempt organizations that fall under other sections of the tax code. They include, for example, labor unions, exempt under Section 501(c)(5); business associations, exempt under Section 501(c)(6); and political action committees (called PACs), most of which are classified under Section 527. These various types of organizations are subject to differing requirements with regard to their activities.

Charitable nonprofits, exempt under Section 501(c)(3), must comply with legal restrictions on their lobbying activity, which are discussed in more detail soon. Social welfare organizations, exempt under Section 501(c)(4) are permitted to engage in lobbying essentially without limit, so long as it is consistent with their purpose of advancing social welfare. They are also permitted to engage in political activities, including the endorsement of candidates, so long as doing so is not their primary purpose. But they are not allowed to contribute directly to a candidate's campaign (Schadler, 2015). As discussed in Chapter 2, some 501(c)(3) organizations work with related 501(c)(4) organizations. The 501(c)3 offers programs that address the charitable mission and the 501(c)4 engages in advocacy that often includes lobbying. The relationship between the Sierra Club and the Sierra Club Foundation was presented as an example in that earlier discussion.

The 501(c)(5) and 501(c)(6) organizations are treated similarly to 501(c)(4) organizations under lobbying laws. Political action committees, mostly exempt under Section 527, are permitted to engage in partisan political activity—indeed, it is their primary purpose—but

Table 11.1　Summary of Allowable Activities

	Tax Exempt	Deductible Gifts	Engage in Lobbying	Engage in Partisan Political Activity
501(c)3 Public Charities	Yes (with some exceptions)	Yes (up to 60% of donor's income, annually, for cash gifts)	Yes, but limited, using either "no substantial part" test or 501(h) expenditure limits	No
501(c)3 Private Foundations	Yes (pay excise tax on investment earnings)	Yes (up to 30% of donor's income, annually, for cash gifts)	No, and may not make grants earmarked for lobbying	No
501(c)4 Social Welfare Organizations (also 501(c)5 and 501(c)6 organizations)	Yes	No	Yes (without limit)	Yes, but cannot contribute directly to campaign and political activity cannot be the organization's "primary purpose." Not required to disclose donors to the public.
527 organizations (political action committees)	Yes	No	Limited (insubstantial) lobbying permitted. May be subject to tax if not furthering political purposes.	Yes, but expenditures are subject to state and federal limitations on campaign contributions. Must disclose donors to the public.

Sources: Based on Independent Sector (2016b, 2016c); Schadler (2015); Stelter (2017).

face some limitations on their lobbying. Table 11.1 summarizes permissible activities and limitations that apply to various types of tax-exempt organizations, but our discussion in this chapter focuses on charitable nonprofits and social welfare organizations.

The reason that charitable nonprofits face restrictions on lobbying is related to the tax deductibility of gifts, which is viewed as a form of public subsidy given to the organization. Donors to 501(c)(4) organizations do not receive the benefit of such deductions; the trade-off is the ability of those organizations to engage in unlimited lobbying. In other words, the foregone tax revenue attributable to the deduction of gifts to charitable nonprofits is regarded as public money. The purpose of the subsidy is to support an organization's charitable activities, and the law requires that its resources be used to pursue those purposes as its primary activity. Any lobbying it conducts must be limited. But what is the limit?

Prior to 1976, the answer was unclear. Nonprofits were instructed that their lobbying needed to be "insubstantial" in relationship to overall activities. What is the meaning of insubstantial? The Internal Revenue Service (IRS) never defined it precisely and looked at each situation on a case-by-case basis. One of the problems was that the **substantial part test**, which determined whether lobbying was a "substantial part" of an organization's activities, looked not only at how much a nonprofit spent on lobbying activity, but also at how much time and effort was devoted to the activity. Some courts held that nonprofits were safe if they spent less than 5 percent on lobbying, but other courts said such an arbitrary standard was not appropriate. Thus, like a child whose parents just say, "Don't wander too far," many nonprofits were unsure exactly how far they could safely go, that is, how much lobbying the IRS might find to be a substantial part of their activities. Some were inhibited from engaging in lobbying at all for fear of losing their tax-exempt status by crossing the fuzzy line.

In 1976, Congress passed Public Law 94-455 (the 1976 Lobby Law), which sought to clarify the situation. Since then, nonprofits have two options, as follows.

Option I: Substantial Part Test

The first option is to continue to be covered by the substantial part test, essentially the same imprecise standard that applied before 1976. This may be a reasonable option for an organization that does not engage in lobbying or that does very little. If it is careful to differentiate lobbying from advocacy, it may find that it spends too little time or money on actual lobbying to be concerned about it. This might be the simplest approach for the majority of nonprofit organizations.

Option II: 501(h) Expenditure Test

The second option, provided by the 1976 Lobby Law and subsequent IRS regulations, is for the nonprofit to file Form 5768 with the IRS, electing to be covered by the specific expenditure guidelines under **Section 501(h)** of the Internal Revenue Code. Selecting this option offers a number of advantages. First, the limits do not consider the amount of time or effort devoted to lobbying—they are based entirely on how much the organization spends on lobbying activity, as a percentage of its total budget.[1] The standard is thus exact, and an organization can easily determine whether it is within or is approaching the limit. Second, it means that lobbying that does not involve expenditure is not limited at all. For example, if a volunteer calls on a congressperson or a local legislator, that effort does not count unless the organization spends money to support it. If the organization reimburses the volunteer for his or her cab ride to the meeting, that expense would need to be included in its lobbying expense, but the volunteer's time would not. The **501(h) option** also presents fewer risks for nonprofits and their staff than does the substantial part test. Nonprofits that exceed the spending limits will not lose their tax exemption unless they exceed them by at least 150 percent averaged over a four-year period. Moreover, there are no penalties imposed on individual managers of an organization that exceeds the limit (National Council of Nonprofits, 2017b).

The spending limits are stated as a percentage of the nonprofit's total expenditures (on exempt activities), on a sliding scale depending on the size of the organization. Table 11.2 summarizes the expenditure limits on lobbying for nonprofits of various sizes. Keep in mind that for organizations that selected the 501(h) option, lobbying activity does not count against the limit if it does not involve the expenditure of money by the nonprofit. The limit is thus not that restrictive in terms of the amount of activity it allows.

There is an important distinction between the limit for direct lobbying and for grassroots lobbying. **Direct lobbying** includes any communication the organization has "to influence

Table 11.2   Limits on Lobbying Expenditures for Charitable Nonprofits

If the amount of exempt purpose expenditures is:	Lobbying nontaxable amount is:
≤ $500,000	20% of the exempt purpose expenditures
>$500,00 but ≤ $1,000,000	$100,000 plus 15% of the excess of exempt purpose expenditures over $500,000
> $1,000,000 but ≤ $1,500,000	$175,000 plus 10% of the excess of exempt purpose expenditures over $1,000,000
>$1,500,000 but ≤ $17,000,000	$225,000 plus 5% of the exempt purpose expenditures over $1,500,000
>$17,000,000	$1,000,000

Source: Internal Revenue Service (2017b).

a legislative body through communication with a member or employee of a legislative body, or with a government official who participates in formulating legislation" (Internal Revenue Service, 2017a). This would include, for example, a nonprofit organization calling or visiting a congressperson, or a member of his or her staff. It does not usually include communication with officials of the executive branch of government or communication that just provides information without expressing an opinion for or against specific legislation.

Grassroots lobbying "refers to attempts to influence legislation by attempting to affect the opinion of the public with respect to the legislation and encouraging the audience to take action with respect to the legislation" (Internal Revenue Service, 2017a). This would include sending out letters or e-mails, urging people to "call your Senator." But, if the communication does not include a call to action, that is, does not ask people to *do* something to support or oppose the legislation, then it is not lobbying. The "public" means the general public, which includes any individuals who are not members of the organization. But "members" is broadly defined. It includes donors to the organization as well as those who may be members in the formal sense of someone who pays dues in order to belong. Thus, if a nonprofit sends an e-mail to its donors urging them to contact their elected representatives to support or oppose a bill, that expenditure comes under the limit for direct lobbying. But if it takes out an ad online or in the newspaper or hands out flyers on the corner urging members of the general public to do the same, that is grassroots lobbying. Again, if the communication does not specifically ask individuals to take action, it does not count as lobbying at all.

The distinction between direct and grassroots lobbying is important because different spending limits apply. An organization may devote only one fourth of its total lobbying expense to grassroots lobbying. As shown in Table 11.2, there is an overall cap of $1 million. So, for example, if a nonprofit spent the maximum of $1 million on all of its lobbying, only $250,000 of that could be spent on grassroots efforts. The remaining $750,000 could be spent on direct lobbying (Internal Revenue Service, 2017b).

There are various types of activities that do not count as lobbying and are thus not subject to the spending limit. For example, if the legislature asks the nonprofit for advice on a bill, responding to that request does not count. **Self-defense activity** also does not count as lobbying. For instance, if the city council is about to pass an ordinance that would adversely affect the nonprofit, it may contact council members to oppose the legislation without having any expense involved count against its lobbying limit. Policy research organizations, such as the Brookings Institution or the American Enterprise Institute, may prepare reports that are nonpartisan and objective, and they will not count as lobbying efforts even if they recommend a specific course of action. In sum, the 1976 Lobby Law is quite generous in permitting nonprofit organizations to engage in lobbying. This is especially true if the distinction between what is lobbying and what is advocacy is carefully maintained, since expenditures on the latter do not count against the limits at all.

Charitable nonprofits must report their lobbying expenses on Form 990. In addition, organizations that employ professional lobbyists and spend more than $12,500 on lobbying during a quarter at the federal level must meet the requirements of the Lobbying Disclosure Act. This requires that they register and report their lobbying expenditures to Congress on a quarterly basis (Independent Sector, 2016b).

The rules discussed so far apply to nonprofits that are public charities. Private foundations face stricter limitations. They may not endorse or oppose legislation in communications with legislators or the general public if the communication includes a call to action. However, like public charities, they may provide technical advice to a legislature if asked to do so, provide nonpartisan analyses and studies, and lobby in self-defense. Like public charities, foundations are barred from participating in political campaigns. They can support nonpartisan activities such as candidate forums and get-out-the-vote drives, but they face strict regulation of their participation in voter registration drives (Independent Sector, 2016c). What if a private foundation makes grants to a nonprofit that comes under the more generous rules applied to public charities? Well, to start with, in general, the foundation would not be permitted to designate a grant to support lobbying. That would be just an obvious end-run around the restrictions on its activity. But if the foundation provides unrestricted operating support to a public charity, there is nothing to prevent that organization from spending the money on lobbying activity. If a foundation makes a grant to support a nonprofit's program that has lobbying as one component of it, the lobbying is acceptable, but it must be paid for using funds from some other source, not with the foundation's grant funds. In addition, the grant amount may not exceed the budgeted non-lobbying expenses of the program (Independent Sector, 2016c).

In addition to the basic provisions we have discussed in this chapter, nonprofits also must comply with various laws related to lobbying practice, which include restrictions on the participation of elected officials in charity events and on the way in which lobbyists can interact with legislators and their staff. In January of 2007, the 100th Congress amended House Rule 25, called the **gift rule**, placing stricter limits on what gifts or privately supported travel members of the House of Representatives can accept from lobbyists. However, the law is always in a state of flux, and students with an interest in more details should check contemporary sources. The website of Independent Sector (www.independentsector.org) provides timely updates on recent legislation and policy actions and should be consulted for the latest information. Other websites listed as resources at the end of this chapter also track and report on recent changes in law with regard to lobbying, campaign finance, and other relevant activities. And, of course, nonprofits should consult their legal counsel and not rely on publications, including this text.

Political Campaign Activity

As discussed earlier, charitable nonprofits—including public charities and private foundations—are prohibited from engaging in campaigns and from endorsing candidates, either implicitly or explicitly. They may not coordinate their activities with those of a candidate or a campaign, contribute money or time to working for a candidate, or contribute the use of their facilities for a candidate or campaign (Halloran, 2013). But some types of nonprofit face fewer restrictions on such activity, and the rules were changed by a Supreme Court decision in 2010.

The Supreme Court's decision in the case of **Citizens United v. FEC** was focused on corporations. Previous law prohibited corporate contributions in support of political candidates. Corporations still cannot make monetary or in-kind contributions directly to candidates for federal office or coordinate their communication with candidates' campaigns. However, after Citizen's United, they now can make independent expenditures from their general treasury to expressly support or oppose candidates for the U.S. House, Senate, and president. This ruling also affected certain nonprofits, including the social welfare organizations, which are exempt under Section 501(c)(4), and organizations exempt under Sections 501(c)(5) and 501(c)(6), which include labor unions and business associations. They now can engage in political activities, so long as political activities are not their primary purpose. But, to emphasize, the 2010 Supreme Court ruling did not change the law for charitable nonprofits, which continued to be prohibited from supporting or opposing candidates or making expenditures on communications that may suggest who is the "better" candidate (Halloran, 2013).

There have been some controversial cases that highlighted the fine—and sometimes blurry—line between what is permissible advocacy and what is illegal involvement in electoral politics by charitable nonprofits. In an attempt to clear up the confusion, in June of 2007 the IRS released a Revenue Ruling (2007-41) to clarify the criteria by which it would determine what is and is not illegal campaign involvement. The ruling included 21 hypothetical examples of activity and a discussion of why each does or does not constitute a violation of the law. But the topic remains a subject of debate.

As mentioned earlier in this text, the prohibition on political activity by charitable nonprofits is included in an amendment to the Internal Revenue Code that was proposed by then-Senator Lyndon B. Johnson in 1954 and is commonly called the **Johnson Amendment**. It prohibits political activity by churches and religious organizations as well as other 501(c)3 organizations. The amendment became controversial during the 2016 presidential campaign and in May 2017, president Donald J. Trump issued an executive order that directed the IRS to exercise "discretion" in enforcing the Johnson Amendment. This executive order did not repeal the law and experts advised nonprofits not to change their practices unless Congress made changes to the law itself (Shell, 2017). Legislation was considered by Congress in late 2017 that would have repealed the Johnson Amendment but it was not passed (O'Neil, 2017). Further efforts to change the law may arise in the future and students should consult the Web for the current status of this issue.

Implementing an Advocacy Program

Now that we have explored basic concepts and reviewed the law governing nonprofit advocacy, let's turn our attention to the practice of advocacy and lobbying. There is an extensive practitioner literature on lobbying. Various authors have developed manuals that offer guidance specifically to nonprofit organizations and take into consideration the unique requirements that apply to them. Some are listed as suggested additional reading at the end of this chapter. In addition, websites listed in this chapter provide practical suggestions and guides, as well as links to other resources. Since the law changes from time to time, the websites are usually the best sources of legal information. However, the techniques or tactics of lobbying are more consistent over time, and even some relatively dated but classic sources provide guidance that is still sound.

Various sources that advise nonprofits on developing an advocacy and lobbying effort offer many common points, including the following:

- *Determine the reason for lobbying and how it advances the nonprofit's mission.*
  For a social welfare organization that exists for the purpose of influencing public policy, the connection to the mission is obvious. A charitable nonprofit will need to consider how lobbying may advance its programs or the welfare of the constituents it serves and make strategic decisions about the emphasis to be given to lobbying in relationship to its service programs.

- *Understand the legislative process.* To lobby effectively, the organization needs to understand how legislation is considered at the local, state, or national level— wherever its lobbying efforts will be focused. This includes knowledge of which committees play important roles and the stages in the process at which a lobbyist's intervention may be most helpful or persuasive.

- *Stay focused on long-term goals.* Change may not occur immediately and the advocacy effort must be sustained, adapting tactics as conditions change over time (Independent Sector, 2012).

- *Consider the motivations of public officials.* It is important to form relationships with public officials, come to understand their perspectives, and understand the pressures they face. That can help determine the most effective activity to motivate the official around a particular issue (Independent Sector, 2012).

- *Identify the sources of funds to be used for lobbying.* As discussed above, there are restrictions on the use of government or foundation funds, but unrestricted revenues from gifts, grants, or earned income may be used to fund a lobbying effort.

- *Undertake research to develop an understanding of the public policy issues related to the organization's mission and to obtain data needed to make the case with legislators.* Such information is available from, among others, policy research organizations, national charitable organizations with established public policy programs, and coalitions concerned with issues in particular areas. Approaching a legislator with facts is not only important to persuasion but may indeed be providing a real service to the legislator, whose time and staff may not be sufficient to undertake the depth of research that an interested nonprofit may offer.

- *Develop an infrastructure to support the lobbying program.* For an ongoing effort, this may require hiring staff or working with a professional lobbying firm, but smaller efforts may be managed by an existing staff member as a part-time assignment. An information system may be needed to track the progress of legislation and calls or visits with legislators. Managing a lobbying program has many of the same requirements as fundraising management since it involves developing and maintaining relationships, and undertaking contacts, in a systematic manner.

- *Inventory existing relationships and identify decision makers.* A nonprofit may have many existing relationships in its community, through staff, members of the board, or other friends who may in turn know key decision makers in the relevant legislature. They may be effective ambassadors who can be armed with information to deliver the nonprofit's messages to those decision makers, or they may help open the door to communications and visits by the nonprofit's CEO.

- *Use a strategic mix of tactics.* Direct lobbying with legislators may be the centerpiece of a lobbying program, but such efforts are more effective if they are used in conjunction with grassroots lobbying to influence and mobilize the community's opinions and with a media relations program to gain wider visibility for the issues. The latter might include developing relationships with reporters who may have an interest in writing articles about the issue as well as paid advertising, op-eds, and letters to the editor written by the nonprofit's CEO or volunteers. Walks, runs, marches, and demonstrations also are available tactics for drawing attention to a cause (Hessenius, 2007).

- *Form a coalition.* Forming a coalition with other organizations may be an important part of the strategy and "the broadest possible array of stakeholders [may help] to show that it is more than the 'usual suspects' that are affiliated [with the cause]" (Libby, 2012, p. 104). It is common to form coalitions around specific, short-term issues. The coalition may be disbanded when the goal has been achieved and new coalitions then can be created for the next issue (Independent Sector, 2012).

The tools used for lobbying vary depending on whether the effort is grassroots or direct lobbying. Grassroots lobbying engages many of the principles and techniques of marketing that were discussed in Chapter 10. Direct lobbying also may use those tools as well as personal visits with legislators and their staff members. Both approaches use various communications vehicles, including letters, phone calls, faxes, petitions, e-mails, and social media. The Internet offers great advantages to nonprofits in developing coalitions and constituencies as well as for contacting legislators. However, because e-mails are so easy to send and thus can arrive in volume, some legislative staff have come to ignore them or to prevail on organizations to cease such efforts. Ironically, because e-mail has become so common and voluminous, the old technology of regular mail sometimes may be more effective. A letter, especially if written by a constituent of the legislator, signifies that the individual cares enough to have taken the time to write, rather than tap out a quick e-mail or text message. Letters from clients of a nonprofit also may have an impact on the legislator and even gain the attention of the news media. However, form letters that make it obvious they have been solicited by the nonprofit or a professional lobbyist have less credibility than those that appear to genuinely express the views of an individual (Hessenius, 2007). As in fundraising, there is no tool more powerful than the personal visit by an individual or group of individuals to a legislator or a member of his or her staff who is in a position to influence what information and data the legislator receives.

Using Social Media

Social media have become increasingly important for nonprofit advocacy. Consider the impact of one example:

> In March 2012, Invisible Children, a San Diego-based nonprofit advocacy organization dedicated to bringing awareness to the activities of indicted Uganda war criminal Joseph Kony, started an Internet video campaign called *Kony 2012*. The goal was to make Kony internationally known in order that he be arrested by year's end. Within three days, the *Kony 2012* video quickly became one of the greatest viral successes in the short history of social media, drawing millions of viewers on YouTube. Within three weeks, it spurred action on Capitol Hill: Over a third of U.S. senators introduced a bipartisan resolution condemning Kony and his troops for "unconscionable crimes against humanity." (Guo & Saxton, 2014)

Facebook, Twitter, and other social networking sites have provided nonprofits with an important mechanism for educating and engaging people who share their interests (Held, 2014). Illustrating the growing importance of the Internet as a tool for advocacy, Change.org, an online platform enabling individuals to start and sign petitions related to issues, had 100 million users in 196 countries in 2017 (www.change.org/about). As David Yarnold (2016), president of the National Audubon Society, writes, "Today grant makers want to see the nonprofits they support produce 'transformational change' and 'measurable outcomes' and 'reflect a new America.' This requires reaching people where they are most comfortable—on their phones, tablets, and laptops."

Chad Guo and Gregory Saxton (2014) studied nonprofits' use of Twitter for advocacy and describe three stages: reaching out, keeping the flame alive, and stepping up to action. The first stage includes sending out information; it is communication more than advocacy. Hashtags are introduced to serve as bookmarks under which information can be organized. The primary goal in this stage is to make connections and build a following. In the second stage, the goal is to deepen ties with the organization's community. More communications are targeted to the organization's own online community and more are interactive, sparking a dialog. In the third stage, online communication becomes a "mobilization practice," calling on individuals to take action. Hashtags are still important, but many tweets provide links to additional information, for example, concerning public events (Guo & Saxton, 2014).

As Guo and Saxton (2014) conclude, the increasing use of social media in nonprofit advocacy raises important questions about the future: "If more advocacy work moves online, and it involves primarily coalition building, calls to action, and public education—as we found [in our research]—what will the implications be for the sector as a whole? What will it mean if administrative lobbying and expert testimony, among other tactics, are less common?"

Continuing Issues and Concerns

For nonprofits that are social welfare organizations, advocacy and lobbying are common and permissible activities—it is the reason that many exist. Some charitable nonprofits also engage in substantial advocacy, and lobbying up to the legal limits, but others remain cautious. In *Forces for Good,* Leslie Crutchfield and Heather Grant (2012) urge nonprofits that provide programs to expand their advocacy activity. The authors identify 12 organizations that have high impact, that is, that are "catalytic agents of change" (p. 18). One defining characteristic is their involvement in advocacy and lobbying as well as program delivery. Some began by offering programs and later expanded into advocacy roles. Others went the other way, having begun as advocacy organizations and later added direct service programs. "And," the authors state, "the more they advocate *and* serve, the greater the impact they achieve" (p. 38).

One consequence of shifting a nonprofit's activities from direct service to advocacy may be that it becomes more challenging to measure impact. As Pekkanen and Smith (2014) observe, this is true for three principal reasons. First, the definition of what constitutes advocacy is blurry and it may involve different levels of effort: "dashing off a quick letter is one thing, but spending hours or days crafting a thoughtful and substantive epistle is a substantially different endeavor" (p. 1). Second, causality is difficult to determine; a new public policy may be approved, but it may not be possible to attribute that to the efforts of nonprofits overall or one nonprofit in particular. And, third, "advocacy is fungible" (p. 2). A nonprofit may delegate advocacy to a separate, related organization or to a trade association, or to a chapter or national headquarters (Pekkanen & Smith, 2014). Thus, a shift toward advocacy may make it more difficult for some organizations to measure their results at a time when the importance of such measurement is being emphasized.

In addition to complicating the measurement of impact, nonprofit advocacy and lobbying may involve some ambiguity and potential risk. Roger Colinvaux (2016) argues that current public policy regarding nonprofit lobbying does not work well. He observes that relatively few nonprofits elect the expenditure test, described earlier in this chapter. The reason, he argues, is that smaller organizations may not fully understand the law and the larger organizations may find the overall limit of $1 million, as well as the more restrictive limit on grassroots lobbying, to be too low (Colinvaux, p. 211). The definition of "no substantial part" remains vague, causing charitable nonprofits to "operate in a state of caution and concern" (p. 211). On the other hand, the IRS has limited resources for enforcement. Some speculate that some organizations may exploit the ambiguity, a situation that Colinvaus argues "leads to an erosion of the rule of law" (p. 209).

Some proposals that have been advanced to repeal the Johnson Amendment are limited to the activity of religious organizations, but some would permit all nonprofits to engage in political campaigns (McCambridge, 2017). Such proposals have been opposed by most national organizations representing the nonprofit sector and such advocacy likely prevented repeal in 2017 (McCambridge, 2017). However, Colinvaux (2016) notes pros and cons regarding possible changes. If the prohibition on political activity is lifted, that could cause charitable nonprofits to become vehicles for deductible political contributions and bring "the taint of politics" to organizations and the sector (p. 210). On the other hand, some people think that the prohibition is an unreasonable restraint on free speech, difficult to enforce, and may cause some organizations to "compromise mission, especially those that are faith based" (p. 210). Questions about nonprofit advocacy, lobbying, and political activity are likely to remain a matter of discussion and debate in future years.

CHAPTER SUMMARY

Advocacy by nonprofits has played an important role in the most significant social changes throughout U.S. history, including the Civil Rights movement, the expansion of women's rights, and environmental protections. Issues often move through stages of public awareness and action, and nonprofits play an important role in that process (see Box 11.1). Nonprofits may advocate on any side of any issue, and their advocacy and lobbying is thus a fundamental pillar of a democratic society. However, various studies have found that some nonprofits are hesitant to engage in advocacy and lobbying for various reasons, including lack of staff and resources, concern about alienating private or government funders, and misunderstanding of what the law permits them to do without jeopardizing their nonprofit status.

Advocacy includes communication undertaken in support of a cause or an idea. It may include, for example, providing education, distributing information, or holding events to dramatize an issue or the effects of a problem on people or a community. Advocacy is a basic right of every individual and organization in the United States and may be practiced without limit—it is an exercise of free speech protected by the U.S. Constitution. Lobbying goes beyond advocacy—it is action taken to support or oppose specific legislation at the national, state, or local level. Advocacy is the larger concept, which encompasses lobbying.

Some nonprofits—for example, 501(c)(4) social welfare organizations—are permitted to lobby without limitation but are not eligible to receive tax-deductible gifts. Because they can receive such gifts, which are a form of public subsidy, charitable nonprofits exempt under Section 501(c)(3) face limitations on their lobbying activity. There are two standards under which a charitable nonprofit can determine the amount of permissible lobbying. The substantial part test was the standard that existed prior to the 1976 Lobby Law, and organizations can still choose to be subject to it. However, "substantial part" applies to both time and expenditures, and it is not precisely defined.

The other option is to elect the expenditure test provided under Section 501(h) of the Internal Revenue Code. That section establishes a specific percentage of total qualified expenditures that nonprofits of various sizes can spend on lobbying, with an overall cap of $1 million. This option also distinguishes between direct and grassroots lobbying. A lower limit applies to grassroots activities that attempt to influence the public's attitudes and that include a call to action in support of or in opposition to specific legislation. It also identifies specific activities—for example, self-defense—that do not count as lobbying. The expenditure test does not consider activities of volunteers or other efforts that do not involve expenditures. It is thus relatively generous in the amount of lobbying that it permits nonprofits to undertake.

Private foundations are not permitted to lobby or to make grants to other nonprofits designated for support of lobbying. Foundation grants to public charities that provide unrestricted operating support may be used for lobbying by the charity within its allowable limit.

Charitable nonprofits may not participate in political campaigns or endorse candidates. The 2010 Supreme Court decision in the case of *Citizens United v. FEC* changed the law to permit corporations and nonprofits exempt under sections 501(c)(4), 501(c)(5), and 501(c)(6) to endorse candidates, subject to the requirement that political activity not be the organization's primary purpose, but the prohibition on campaign activity by charitable nonprofits remained, as the trade-off for the tax deductibility of gifts made to them. The section of the Internal Revenue Code that prohibits political activity by charitable nonprofits is called the Johnson Amendment. There were efforts to repeal this restriction in 2017, but the legislation did not pass the Congress at that time. This may remain a topic of continuing debate.

There are many guides to the practice of lobbying. Most practitioner guides emphasize linking the activity to the nonprofit's mission, understanding the legislative process, identifying sources of permissible funds to support lobbying, developing an infrastructure of staff and systems to support the lobbying effort, conducting research to identify public policy issues and gathering facts needed to make the organization's case, conducting an inventory of friends and identifying their relationships with key legislators, and developing a strategic mix of tactics to be employed. Some tools include letters, e-mails, media coverage, events, and personal visits with legislators and their staff members. Nonprofits are making increased use of social media and social networks to share information, deepen relationships with their online communities, and issue calls to action.

It can be challenging to measure the results of nonprofit advocacy, since it is not always possible to establish causation between such activity and changes in public policy. Some call for a greater role for nonprofits in advocacy and electoral politics, but such activity may increase risks. Nonprofits should remain informed as to the latest legal requirements and students should consult online and other sources to learn what changes may have been enacted since this chapter was written.

NOTE

1. Specifically, this means its expenditures on exempt activity, which excludes fundraising and certain administrative expenses.

KEY TERMS AND CONCEPTS

advocacy 305
Citizens United v. FEC 310
civic engagement 305
direct lobbying 308
501(h) option 308

gift rule 310
grassroots lobbying 309
Johnson Amendment 311
lobbying 305
organizing 305

political campaign activity 305
Section 501(h) 308
self-defense activity 309
substantial part test 307

CASE 11.1 Mothers Against Drunk Driving (MADD)

As MADD executive director Chuck Hurley describes it, "Before the 1980s, drunk driving was how people got home. It was normal behavior." In May of that year, Candy Lightner's 13-year-old daughter was killed by a hit-and-run driver while walking to a church carnival. As her mother was soon to learn, drunk driving was just not on society's radar as an issue. Although 60 percent of automobile deaths were alcohol related, drunk driving was a low priority for law enforcement and the courts. Congress had spent $35 million on Alcohol Safety Action Programs, with little effect. After her daughter's death, Candy Lightner established Mothers Against Drunk Driving (MADD), determined to change society's attitude and behavior as well as the law.

She found other victims' families through classified ads and mailings, learned about California laws and lobbied the governor for new legislation, made speeches, and raised money. In October of 1980, MADD held a news conference on Capitol Hill that captured the nation's attention. Other mothers began establishing chapters in their hometowns and the organization grew rapidly, with 100 chapters in place by 1982.

Mothers shared their grief and the stories of their loved ones who had been killed or injured by drunk driving, putting human faces on the issue. MADD lobbied in state legislatures and at the federal level. President Ronald Reagan established a Presidential Commission on Drunk Driving, and Congress passed legislation denying federal highway funds to states that did not pass strict drunk-driving laws. A national law establishing a uniform drinking age was passed in 1984.

During the 1990s, MADD continued to grow and attracted many corporate partners. It also expanded its efforts to prevent alcohol abuse by young people, including programs in schools and two National Youth Summits to Prevent Underage Drinking. MADD also continued to advocate for stricter laws, for example, to reduce the allowable percentage of blood alcohol in drivers. By the 2000s, MADD was known to 97 percent of the public, thousands of laws had been passed, tens of thousands of lives had been saved, and the term designated driver had become part of the American lexicon. The public's attitude toward drunk driving, once signified by a "wink and a nod," had changed to recognize such behavior as socially unacceptable, reckless, and criminal. In 2016, MADD expanded its mission beyond drunk driving: "The mission of Mothers Against Drunk Driving is to end drunk driving, help fight drugged driving, support the victims of these violent crimes and prevent underage drinking."

Source: Summarized from Mothers Against Drunk Driving website (www.madd.org).

Questions Related to Case 11.1

1. Are MADD's activities advocacy or lobbying or both? If both, which activities fit each definition?

2. How does the case of MADD reflect the stages described in Box 11.1?

3. Think back on (or re-read) the discussion of marketing in Chapter 10. Which principles from that chapter seem most relevant to the case of MADD?

CASE 11.2 Housing First

In the early 1990s, most programs that were working to alleviate homelessness in American cities followed a similar model. Homeless men and women could visit shelters, but could not obtain permanent housing until they proved themselves "housing ready." That required abstaining from drugs and alcohol and undergoing treatment for mental illness (Greenwood, Stefanic, & Tsemberis, 2013). Some preferred to live on the streets rather than experience conditions in the shelters, which were not necessarily conducive to making the changes that were expected. Many would go through an "institutional cycle" of hospitals, shelters, and jails and end up chronically homeless (Greenwood et al., p. 648).

In 1992, Sam Tsemberis, a psychologist working in New York, decided the prevailing model had things backward. The way to eliminate homelessness was to place people in homes. Tsemberis's thinking was based on Maslow's hierarchy of needs. If an individual's need for shelter and security could be met, that person then could focus on addressing other problems. If someone could be placed in housing first, they would be in a more stable situation in which to receive the services needed to overcome their illnesses, return to school, find employment, and rebuild their lives (Culhane, 2016). The only requirement for housing would be that the individual agree to let a team, led by a peer mentor, check on them once a week (Greenwood et al., 2013). Most experts were skeptical about the idea, but Tsemberis decided to test it. The nonprofit he founded to do so was Pathways to Housing and his new approach became known as Housing First (McCoy, 2015).

Since 1992, Housing First has been adopted in cities across the United States and in other countries, with dramatic results. By 2015, Utah reported that it had nearly eliminated chronic homelessness using the Housing First model. Phoenix and New Orleans reported eliminating homelessness among veterans (McCoy, 2015). The U.S. government has adopted Housing First as official policy and the Department of Veterans Affairs reported that the model has achieved a sharp decline in homeless veterans across the country (Culhane, 2016). As described by Philip Mangano, a national expert on homelessness, Housing First "has moved us from managing to ending; from enabling to engaging; from funding to investing; from inputs to outcome; beyond programs to consumer; from shelter and street to home" (Greenwood et al., 2013, p. 650).

How did Housing First go from a radical idea to the national standard, despite initial and persistent resistance? One reason was a strategy that used research to evaluate programs and then used data as the foundation of advocacy designed "to persuade key champions and stakeholders of the model's efficacy" (Greenwood et al., 2013, p. 650).

Tsemberis incorporated research into his program from the outset, beginning with a four-year longitudinal study that compared Housing First to traditional programs on five variables that would be of particular interest to various stakeholders, including consumers (clients), clinicians, housing providers, funders, and policy makers. Studies followed rigorous methodology and the results were published in academic journals, helping to gain credibility. The results proved that Housing First reduced homelessness and at lower cost than traditional approaches (Greenwood et al., 2013).

Local nonprofits providing services to homeless people were frustrated with their traditional programs. Seeing the results of Housing First, they began to test it in their own communities. Tsemberis's organization provided research assistance to those using the model. There was still resistance in many communities, which local champions addressed by initiating small-scale efforts and continuing to publicize the research that proved success. These local nonprofit leaders became champions who helped persuade others at the state and national levels. The new approach gained the attention of the U.S. Interagency Council on Homelessness (USICH), a federal agency charged with coordinating the government's approach to homelessness across Cabinet-level agencies (https://www.usich.gov/about-usich). USICH was impressed by the proven results of Housing First and became a critical ally (Greenwood et al., 2013, p. 653). The tipping point came with a $35-million grant from USICH to support a Collaborative Initiative to End Homelessness, bringing together the U.S. Departments of Health and Human Services, Housing and Urban Development, and Veterans Affairs. Of the 11 organizations funded, nine adopted the Housing First model. Two dozen other cities that had not received grant funds moved forward to implement the model with their own funds. More than 250 cities developed 10-year plans to eliminate homelessness, using the same approach. Within the span of 20 years, Housing First had become the "gold standard of homelessness intervention in the United States" (Greenwood et al., p. 658).

What was the key to success in overcoming skepticism and resistance, and making Housing First the gold standard? Most important was the use of social science research that has "impact validity" (Massey & Barreras, 2013). This includes framing the research questions strategically, shaped by local understandings of the issue, and with a plan for disseminating the findings to allies and champions who can use the data to influence the opinions of the public and government officials (Greenwood et al., 2013). The "powerful concoction of research and consumer-driven, evidence-based practice, combined with a strong dose of advocacy" may provide a lesson to others attempting to bring about change in addressing other challenging social problems (Greenwood et al., p. 660).

Questions Related to Case 11.2

1. How was the goal of advocacy in the case of Housing First different from that of MADD, as discussed in Case 11.1?

2. How does the case of Housing First reflect the stages described in Box 11.1?

3. Think back on (or re-read) the discussion of marketing in Chapter 10. Which principles from that chapter seem most relevant to the case of Housing First?

Case 11.3   National Audubon Society

Outraged by the killing of birds, Harriet Hemenway and Mina Hall, founded the Massachusetts Audubon Society in 1896. Organizations were established in other states and worked cooperatively to advance protections for birds, including creation of the first National Wildlife Refuge in the United States in 1901. The National Audubon Society was founded in 1905 and today works to pursue its mission to protect birds and their habitats "today and tomorrow, throughout the Americas, using science, advocacy, education, and on-the-ground conservation" (National Audubon Society, n.d.-a). Audubon is a 501(c)3 charitable nonprofit that received over $115 million in revenue and spent $594,000 on lobbying in 2015 (National Audubon Society, 2015).

In addition to offering educational programs and managing on-the-ground conservation efforts, Audubon advocates at both the state and national levels on issues related to bird conservation, ecosystem restoration, and clean air and water (National Audubon Society, n.d.-b). This includes both direct lobbying and grassroots efforts to mobilize its network of Audubon Activists, working through 462 chapters, 23 state offices, and 13 international partner organizations across the Americas (Yarnold, 2016). Audubon influences policy by convening stakeholders surrounding issues and by mobilizing activists through communication outreach and chapter-based training (National Audubon Society, n.d.-b).

In 2010, Audubon initiated a major effort to expand its communication programs using technology. It expanded its communication and technology staff at the national level from just 3 in 2010 to 20 professionals by 2016. It developed new data-visualization software and mapping technology for use by all of its chapters. It began investing in paid Google and Facebook ads and increased online giving by 64 percent from 2014 to 2015 alone. Media visibility was enhanced and online Audubon material gained over two billion page views in 2014 (Yarnold, 2016).

The National Audubon Society also makes extensive use of technology in its advocacy efforts. Its website identifies pending legislation and regulation that might threaten birds and enables individuals to register their support or opposition. A "Fast Action" sign-up option makes it possible to take a position with a single click (National Audubon Society, n.d.-b). The organization has over 800,000 e-mail addresses for use in mobilizing action. Fundraising e-mails drive donors to the website and their opens and clicks guide future communication with them, especially during advocacy campaigns. Data mining enables Audubon to know more about its donors and to track their participation in hands-on activities, such as crowdsourced bird counts. That makes it possible to target future communication, for advocacy and other efforts (Yarnold, 2016).

Like many conservation organizations, Audubon has not had a very diverse membership in the past. Its members had been predominantly "older, usually white, and female" (Yarnold, 2016). Initiatives to expand its reach in recent years have included development of a Spanish-language website and field guide to North American birds, helping to reach new audiences both in the United States and other countries in the Americas (Yarnold, 2016). New mobile apps were developed to capture a younger audience (Yarnold, 2016). And in 2015, it announced a new initiative to expand diversity and inclusion, both among its workforce and constituency. As the organization's statement explains "Our business and conservation strategies are enriched and made stronger by the contribution of the experiences, perspectives, and values of diverse individuals and communities. Protecting and conserving nature and the environment transcends political, cultural and social boundaries, and so must Audubon in order to expand our network's reach and engage more people in protecting birds and habitat" (National Audubon Society, 2015).

Questions Related to Case 11.3

1. How does the National Audubon's enhanced advocacy initiatives reflect the principles of effective advocacy discussed in this chapter?

2. Thinking back on the discussion of marketing and communications in Chapter 10, how would you describe Audubon's brand?

3. What is National Audubon's market niche in environmental advocacy and what competitive advantages might it enjoy over other organizations in that field?

QUESTIONS FOR DISCUSSION

1. Should the law be changed to permit charitable nonprofits to endorse or oppose political candidates and provide financial support to political campaigns? Why or why not?

2. Do you think that nonprofits that receive government funds may feel inhibited from lobbying? If so, do you think such concerns are realistic or not?

APPENDIX CASE

The following case in the Appendix of this text includes points related to the content of this chapter: Case 2 (Share Our Strength/No Kid Hungry).

SUGGESTIONS FOR FURTHER READING

Books

Boris, E., & Steuerle, C. E. (Eds.). (2017). *Nonprofits and government: Collaboration and conflict* (3rd ed.). Lanham, MD: Rowman & Littlefield/Urban Institute Press.

Gardner, A., & Brindis, C. (2017). *Advocacy and policy change evaluation: Theory and practice*. Stanford, CA: Stanford University Press.

Libby, P. (2012). *The lobbying strategy handbook*. Thousand Oaks, CA: Sage.

Padgett, D., Henwood, B., & Tsemberis, S. (2016). *Housing First*. New York: Oxford University Press.

Pekkanen, R. J., Smith, S. R., & Tsujinaka, Y. (Eds.). (2014). *Nonprofits and advocacy: Engaging community and government in an era of retrenchment*. Baltimore, MD: Johns Hopkins University Press.

Articles

Fyall, R., & McGuire, M. (2015, December). Advocating for policy change in nonprofit coalitions. *Nonprofit and Voluntary Sector Quarterly, 44*(6), 1274–1291.

Guo, C., & Saxton, G. D. (2014, February). Tweeting social change: How social media are changing nonprofit advocacy. *Nonprofit and Voluntary Sector Quarterly, 43*(1), 57–79.

Handy, F., Brudney, J. L., & Meijs, L. C. P. M. (Eds.). (2014). Symposium: Nonprofit advocacy and engagement in public policy making. *Nonprofit and Voluntary Sector Quarterly, 43*(1), 5–120.

Websites

Alliance for Justice: http://www.afj.org/

Center for Effective Government: http://www.foreffectivegov.org/

Independent Sector: http://www.independentsector.org/

Internal Revenue Service: http://www.irs.gov/

National Council of Nonprofits: https://www.councilofnonprofits.org/

Urban Institute: http://www.urban.org/

Obtaining and Managing Resources

The principal financial challenge for most nonprofit organizations is to generate sufficient and reliable revenue to meet short-term operating costs and long-term capital needs.

iStock/echoevg

Chapter Outline

Financial Management

As emphasized before, nonprofit organizations do not measure their success exclusively or primarily by their financial results but rather by outcomes related to their missions or by a double bottom line that considers both financial and program results. That being the case, however, it is the reality that many boards and CEOs pay particular attention to their organizations' financial condition. Without adequate and well-managed resources, achievement of the mission is jeopardized, and the very survival of the organization may be threatened.

It is realistic to acknowledge that an organization may be of only mediocre effectiveness and still continue to survive for a long time without facing a crisis. On the other hand, budget deficits or the erosion of financial assets are likely to gain the focused attention of the board and CEO and require immediate action. Many nonprofit board members are drawn from the business community and may be more familiar, or more comfortable, with financial concepts than with the professional fields of the organization's staff, so they often focus their attention on the budget and financial statements. In addition, conservation of the nonprofit's assets is an essential part of the board's fiduciary responsibility, and any signs of trouble are likely to be addressed urgently. Few events can so quickly place a nonprofit CEO's tenure in jeopardy as an operating deficit, financial mismanagement, or a bad audit report. In sum, financial skills are necessary, even if not sufficient, for effective nonprofit management. This chapter considers some basic concepts in nonprofit financial management and accounting. The following chapters in this section discuss three principal sources of nonprofit revenue in more detail: philanthropic gifts, earned income, and government grants and contracts.

Some readers may have familiarity with the vocabulary of financial management, accounting, and financial statements. If so, they are encouraged to read this chapter for a refresher and perhaps a perspective on how concepts familiar to them from the business sector apply to nonprofit organizations. Others may not have studied finance or accounting at all before, but a background is not presumed here, so they should not be concerned about approaching this topic. Some financial and accounting concepts are greatly simplified in the discussion in this chapter, to accommodate those who may be encountering

Learning Objectives

After reading this chapter, students should be able to:

1. Define key terms and concepts in nonprofit financial management.

2. Explain financial statements developed by nonprofit organizations and the role of audits.

3. Summarize key financial ratios used in financial management of nonprofit organizations.

4. Explain principles of managing endowment funds.

5. Describe concepts related to developing and managing nonprofit budgets.

6. Identify circumstances that pose financial risks to nonprofit organizations.

7. Analyze cases, applying concepts from the chapter.

the topic for the first time. For that reason, this chapter should not be regarded as an authoritative technical guide to organizations for maintaining or reporting their financial data. Let's get started by defining some essential terms and concepts.

Definitions of Key Concepts

It is important to clarify the differences among the concepts of bookkeeping, accounting, and financial management. **Bookkeeping** refers to the methods and systems by which financial transactions are recorded. This chapter does not discuss nonprofit bookkeeping, but various manuals and other materials are readily available on this subject. **Accounting** encompasses the rules by which financial transactions are classified and reported. This chapter does not provide a detailed guide to nonprofit accounting but introduces some basic principles and concepts. Other readings suggested at the end of the chapter will be helpful for those who may wish to have a deeper understanding of accounting.

There are two types of accounting. **Financial accounting** "deals with the financial information published for use by parties outside the organization." **Managerial accounting** "deals with information that is useful to an organization's managers," but is not required to be made available to others (Anthony & Young, 2005, p. 466). For example, a banker considering a loan to a nonprofit would need to see financial accounting statements but might not be concerned about how much it costs per client to run each of the organization's programs, which is managerial accounting data. The latter, however, might be important information for a CEO to have when planning budget allocations.

Financial management is a broader concept than accounting. It relies on accounting statements for data, but it "focuses on the *meaning* of those figures" (Anthony & Young, 2005, p. 487). Financial management usually involves the analysis of various financial ratios that may provide indicators of trends and the organization's financial health. Thus, the key in bookkeeping is accuracy; in accounting, consistency and following the rules; and in financial management, making judgments and establishing policies to guide the organization's financial life.

The principal financial challenge for most nonprofit organizations is to generate sufficient and reliable revenue to meet their short-term operating costs and long-term capital needs. Sound financial management includes maintaining an appropriate balance among sources of revenue. In determining the ideal mix, managers consider their sustainability over time, the compatibility of funding sources with mission, and the extent to which some types of funding may be able to catalyze funds from other sources (Kearns, Bell, Deem, & McShane, 2014).

In offering a unified theory of nonprofit finance, Dennis Young (2007) suggests that the sources realistically available to a given organization will reflect the benefits it provides through its programs and services. For example, an organization that provides private goods can likely rely on earned income, since the individuals who benefit will be willing to pay. Those that produce public goods may be able to justify support from government. Nonprofits that provide programs that benefit some group—that is, more than an individual but less than the public (similar to Lohmann's concept of common goods, discussed in Chapter 3)—may attract gifts or dues payments from those who share an interest in their work. A nonprofit also may generate revenue by providing what Young (2007) calls trade benefits—for example, the value it provides to a partnership with another nonprofit or a corporation. Other organizations will have endowment funds, usually provided through gifts from individuals, which produce annual investment income to supplement funds available through other sources.

A well-managed organization will strive to achieve diverse revenue sources, both to minimize risk and to maximize its autonomy, that is, to avoid a follow-the-money approach in which its programs evolve in response to trends in government or foundation grants or the interests of major individual donors. Identifying an ideal and realistic income mix is thus one of the principal financial decisions for any organization. Young (2007) proposes the following approach:

- Start with a service portfolio that addresses mission.

- Analyze the nature of benefits conferred by these services.

- Seek income support from alternative sources in proportion with the mix of benefits. Justify resource solicitations as a quid pro quo for benefits provided. Avoid a tin cup mentality, that is, the feeling that you are begging for support.

- Make adjustments to the income portfolio to reflect feasibility factors, which may inhibit or enhance the collection of each sought form of income.

- Make adjustments to the income portfolio to reflect opportunities and problems associated with interactions among alternative income streams.

- Make adjustments to the income portfolio to ensure fiscal integrity and maximum mission impact. This may require adjustments in the service mix, particularly the balance between profitable and loss-making activity.

- Make adjustments to the income portfolio to account for risk. This may require adding additional income streams such as investment income from endowments, further diversifying the overall income mix so that it is less concentrated on a few sources, and cultivating more deeply certain income sources that show promise of stabilization through the building of trust. (p. 370)

Understanding Nonprofit Finances

Organizational finance may be unfamiliar to some individuals, but most of us have at least some understanding of how we manage our own assets and accounts. Thus, let's begin by looking at the types of funds that nonprofits manage and how they are like—or unlike—an individual's personal finances (Table 12.1). It will be necessary to oversimplify some ideas initially, but a number of more complex points will be introduced later on in our discussion.

A nonprofit's operating funds are much like those we manage in our checking accounts. In general, payments received are intended to be spent to pay current bills. Expenses may

Table 12.1   Nonprofit Organization and Individual Funds

Nonprofit Funds	Personal Funds
Endowment (permanent or pure)	Not comparable
Endowment (quasi or board designated)	Retirement funds
Other board-designated funds (earmarked for a specific purpose, for example, a new building)	Probably kept in a savings account
Operating reserves	Savings account
Operating funds—with donor restrictions	Checking account (e.g., birthday gift)
Operating funds—without donor restrictions	Checking account (e.g., salary)

be limited to what is available from income and may be governed by a budget, although both individuals and organizations also have the ability to borrow funds to meet current obligations, with obvious risks in both cases. Operating income—that is, the funds that flow into your checking account or the nonprofit's operating accounts—may be unrestricted or restricted. Fees that nonprofits receive for services provided to customers or clients, gifts from donors who do not designate a specific use, and revenue from earned-income activities are usually **unrestricted**, which means they may be used to meet any expense, including, for example, the salaries of staff, rent and utility bills, or capacity-building activities. An individual's salary is generally unrestricted income, too; that is, nobody tells you how to spend the money.

But suppose your grandmother gives you money for your birthday, directing that you use it to buy a new overcoat for the winter. You might deposit her gift in your checking account, but you would need to somehow keep that money separate, at least in your mind, because it has been restricted to a specific use. Nonprofits also receive payments that are designated for particular purposes and likewise need to ensure that they are spent accordingly. Your responsibility to follow your grandmother's direction may be only a moral obligation, while nonprofits are legally required to adhere to the purposes attached to **donor-restricted funds**. (Of course, both you and the nonprofit may also have the concern that a donor, or grandmother, could decide not to give again if the money is not properly applied.)

A nonprofit's operating funds that are donor-restricted might represent, for example, an advance payment on a grant or contract to cover some service that it has not yet performed. The organization has not yet incurred the expenses that the payment was intended to cover, and the money must be set aside until it has. The funds are restricted until such a time that the work has been completed and the revenue actually earned. Or the organization may have received a gift that is to be used for the purchase of a new item of equipment. The money is restricted until the item is purchased; it cannot be used for something else, just as you cannot use the money from your grandmother for a new iPhone. Donors may have made gifts to create endowment funds, which are intended to be invested in perpetuity. The nonprofit is obligated to follow that restriction. (We will discuss endowment funds in more detail soon.)

Most of us count on our weekly or monthly income to cover our expenses but recognize that something could go wrong. An unexpected car repair bill could arise that was not in the budget. Summer jobs may turn out to be in short supply this year, eliminating some of the additional income you had anticipated earning toward fall semester expenses. Knowing these risks, we might accumulate some money in a savings account, something we can turn to for the proverbial "rainy day." Organizations also establish rainy day funds, or **operating reserves**, to be available under similar circumstances. The existence of such reserves, often equivalent to six months or one year of the operating budget, is one hallmark of a soundly managed organization. Like your personal savings, operating reserves are generally invested in very secure, short-term instruments such as bank certificates of deposit or money market funds. As with your personal savings, there may be the hope that reserves will not need to be touched, but it is important that they be preserved and kept liquid in case they are needed.

Nonprofit boards may designate funds that the organization holds for some special purpose. For example, maybe the board sets aside money that it plans to use eventually to acquire a new building. These funds are not quite the same as reserves because they are not intended to meet something unforeseen. Rather, they are being put aside for something specific that is planned. As an individual, this might mean savings toward a new car or a new house; you could tap these funds if you needed to do so, but the reason would need to be fairly dire. You might keep such funds in your checking account, keeping track of them separately using some personal finance software or at least in your mind. But, more likely, you would keep them in a savings account, maybe a separate account that you would open for this purpose.

The analogy between individual and organizational funds breaks down a little when we talk about endowment, for one reason in particular—individuals are mortal, but organizations and institutions are not necessarily so! Many endowments are funds that are not intended to be spent—ever. The investment income that they generate may be expended for current operating expenses, but the principal is often preserved **in perpetuity**. No individual has a need for funds of such a permanent nature.

There are two basic categories of endowment funds: **board-designated endowment** (also called quasi endowment) and **permanent endowment** (also called pure endowment). Board-designated endowment includes, as the term suggests, money that the organization's board has decided to invest as an endowment. For example, maybe the organization has run an operating surplus for a while and has accumulated more operating reserves than it really needs. The money is not earning much interest in the safe bank account where it is being kept, and it seems unlikely that the organization will need to draw on its reserves, at least not all of them, for the foreseeable future. The board decides that some of that excess should be invested and preserved over the long term to provide additional income to support or enhance the organization's programs in future years. Its purpose might be to build up an independent source of annual income as a way to diversify revenue sources, enable the organization to sustain and enhance its programs, and gain more independence from traditional funding sources. Because its time horizon is long, and it does not foresee needing to tap the principal, the board likely would invest those funds in stocks, bonds, real estate, and other classes of assets, willing to ride out short-term fluctuations in order to gain greater investment returns over the long haul.

Since it was the board's decision to place funds into board-designated or **quasi endowment**, the board has the authority to withdraw the money from that type of endowment if it determines that to be necessary or desirable. That clearly is not a decision that the board is going to make lightly. These funds are intended to be investments for the long term. Just as you would not be quick to cash out your IRA (individual retirement account) to pay for lunch, or even to buy a new car, a board's decision to take funds out of board-designated endowment is not one that it would make except to meet some special need, for example, to build a badly needed new facility or some similar purpose that represents a major and long-lasting improvement. Since these funds are relatively inaccessible, the board's designation of them must be disclosed in a nonprofit's financial statements, in order to provide a full and fair picture of its financial situation. We will return to that point later.

With permanent or **pure endowment**, the board has limited or no flexibility. These are funds given by donors who specified that the principal be retained and be invested in perpetuity, meaning forever. They are donor-restricted funds. Donors may also have designated that annual income generated through the investment of endowment principal be used for certain purposes, for example, to provide scholarships to students or to maintain a chair for a violinist in the symphony orchestra. Under most circumstances, the board does not have the legal authority to invade the original principal of the gift or to use the income for purposes not consistent with the donor's direction without first obtaining the donor's approval or, with strong justification, permission from a court of law.[1]

In looking at your personal finances, the closest thing that you may have to endowment funds are the resources you or your employer have placed into retirement accounts, perhaps a 401(k), a 403(b), or an individual retirement account (IRA). These assets are not intended to be spent today or anytime soon and, indeed, the law may place significant barriers to your gaining access to the money now. They are like board-designated or quasi endowment; you might be able to withdraw the funds, but that is not your intention or plan, except under highly unusual circumstances. Obviously, there is a big difference between your retirement funds and a nonprofit's permanent endowment, since you probably intend to spend your retirement funds eventually to support yourself once you reach a more advanced age and end your career. A nonprofit's permanent endowment is intended *never* to be spent. Unfortunately, there is nothing comparable to "in perpetuity" for an individual.

In addition to financial assets, organizations—and individuals—have physical assets. Like an individual or a family, nonprofits own buildings, vehicles, equipment, and other things. (Physical assets are not depicted in Table 12.1.) Physical assets are quite different from money. For one thing, they are generally illiquid, meaning that they are not easy to sell. It is also often difficult to know exactly how much they are worth. For these reasons, they do not serve the same purpose as operating funds or reserves. They also are not the same as endowment because they generally do not generate income that might be used to meet current expenses. It could be possible, of course, to sell the car or the house if needed to pay bills, but that would reflect a relatively dire and undesirable situation for an individual or an organization.

Before looking at nonprofit financial statements, let's consider how two additional principles of accounting may be understood in terms of both an organization's and an individual's finances: the distinction between the **cash basis of accounting** and the **accrual basis of accounting** and the concept of **cash flow**. Using the cash basis, financial transactions are recorded only when money changes hands. This is the way most of us handle our checking accounts; we add to the balance when we make a deposit and subtract when we withdraw funds. But using a cash basis can provide a misleading picture of one's actual financial situation; for example, it ignores the purchases that have been placed on a credit card. The amount of those purchases may not yet have hit your checking account, but they should be subtracted from its balance—at least in your mind—to gain an accurate sense of where you stand. The credit card is an *account payable* (meaning the charges are owed but not yet paid). On the other hand, let's say you have sold something on eBay and are awaiting the payment to clear your PayPal account. The money is not reflected in your account balance, but you can plan your expenses in anticipation of receiving it, since it is on the way. It is an *account receivable,* and it needs to be taken into account in assessing your current position.

A nonprofit organization faces similar situations. For example, it may have sent bills to clients for services that it has provided, or it may have pledges from donors that have not yet been received. Those are **accounts receivable** and need to be taken into consideration along with the cash it has in the bank, since they represent money that it has earned or is entitled to receive. Alternatively, a nonprofit may receive payment on a grant or contract for services that it is going to provide in the future. It has received the cash, but it hasn't yet earned it, and it has future expenses to which it is obligated as a result of the terms of the grant or contract. It cannot look at that cash as money available to pay for salaries, rent, or the electric bill. The cash basis of accounting thus presents some drawbacks. As John Zietlow, Jo Ann Hankin, and Alan Seidner (2007) explain,

> In cash basis accounting, revenues are recorded when cash comes in and expenses are recorded when cash is expended. The problem is that revenues and expenditures are not properly matched during the year. This mismatch becomes serious whenever your organization has [a] significant dollar amount of payables, receivables, inventories, or depreciable assets. (p. 171)

Accounting on an accrual basis takes into account the money that a nonprofit has earned and is entitled to receive, as well as obligations for expenditures that it has not yet incurred. It thus presents a much more accurate portrayal of the nonprofit's actual situation than cash basis accounting and, indeed, is mandated for external financial reporting.

But the accrual basis of accounting also may lead to a misleading picture. For example, suppose your friend has a wealthy aunt who has promised to leave her entire large estate to him when she dies. He may think of himself as wealthy already; he has mentally recorded his inheritance as a receivable. But every time you are out together, he needs to borrow money from you to pay for dinner. He is thinking on an accrual basis, but unfortunately, he does not have sufficient cash flow right now to meet his living needs. A nonprofit organization could be in the same situation. For example, it may have landed some lucrative contracts, but it has not yet received payment. Using the accrual basis of accounting, the anticipated payment shows up as an asset in its financial reports. But it may not have cash on hand in the bank to meet this month's rent or payroll. For these reasons, organizations—and individuals—also need to track cash flow. We will see more about how they do so in the next section of this chapter.

Nonprofit Financial Statements

Again, accounting is about following the rules. For nonprofit organizations, rules are established by the **Financial Accounting Standards Board (FASB)**—often pronounced as "Faz-bee"—which defines **generally accepted accounting principles (GAAP)**. The rules changed in 2016, when FASB issued a new format to be followed in preparing nonprofit financial statements. FASB's **Accounting Standards Update (ASU) 2016-14**, *Not-for-Profit Entities (Topic 958): Presentation of Financial Statements of Not-for-Profit Entities* requires nonprofits to adopt the new format for years after 2017 (Lang, Eisig, Klumpp, & Ricciardella, 2017, p. vii). The changes reflect the first phase of a longer review by FASB, which may produce additional changes in standards for nonprofit accounting and financial reporting. Students may wish to check the FASB website, listed at the end of this chapter, for any further updates that may have occurred after the writing of this chapter.

FASB's purpose in issuing the new update was to "improve the overall understandability, comparability, and usefulness of nonprofit financial statements" and "to require enhanced disclosures" that make it possible to better assess an organization's liquidity (Lang et. al., 2017, p. 3). The hypothetical examples of financial statements provided in this chapter reflect the new formats required by ASU 2016-14. Some of the disclosures that nonprofits are required to provide under ASU 2016-14 are discussed later in the chapter.

Tables 12.2, 12.3, 12.4, and 12.5, respectively, provide examples of four financial statements that nonprofit organizations prepare: (1) statement of financial position (sometimes called the balance sheet), (2) statement of activities (sometimes called the income statement), (3) statement of cash flows, and (4) statement of functional expenses. The statements are for a hypothetical charitable nonprofit, which is just called "United States Charity." It is engaged in research and the dissemination of research findings. For purposes of space and simplicity, the hypothetical examples shown in this chapter do not include the Notes to the Financial Statements, but the notes are an integral part of an organization's overall financial statements and include important details as well as required disclosures.

The financial statements included here are hypothetical, but the statements of many actual organizations are available on their websites and from other sources, such as Guidestar (www.guidestar.org). Nonprofits' annual reports also commonly include the audited financial statements. Anyone wishing to have a complete understanding of an organization's financial position should read the full report, including the auditor's comments and the notes. Let's look at just a few key points in the financial statements of United States Charity that relate to some of the principles we discussed above.

Statement of Financial Position

The **statement of financial position** (sometimes called the balance sheet) provides a snapshot of the organization at a point in time, usually the end of a fiscal year. It summarizes its assets, that is, "the items that the organization possesses, with which it carries out its programs and service," and its liabilities, including the "amounts of borrowed money, or debt, that the organization has used to finance some of those assets" (Zietlow et al., 2007, p. 172). To put it in personal terms again, your personal assets may include your bank accounts, the book value of your car, and the market value of your house. They need to be offset by your liabilities, for example, the balances on your car loan, mortgage, and credit cards. The difference is equal to your personal net worth. In a for-profit company, the difference is called equity; it represents the value of the owners' interest in the firm. For a nonprofit, there is no ownership interest, so the difference between assets and liabilities is simply defined as net assets. The way balance sheets are constructed, assets always equal the sum of liabilities and net assets; if these totals do not agree, there is something wrong with the numbers.

United States Charity's balance sheet reflects some of the accounting principles discussed before (see Table 12.2). For example, notice that net assets (down toward the bottom of the statement) are divided into those that are restricted by donor requirements ("with donor restrictions") and those that are unrestricted ("without donor restrictions"). Some donors have indicated that their contributions are intended to be used for specific activities or there may be time-related restrictions on use of the funds. A breakdown of these restrictions must be provided in Notes to the Financial Statements, which are not shown in this simplified example. Assets without donor restrictions may represent gifts from donors who did not specify a use or assets that the organization has generated in some other way. The distinction is important, since it affects the organization's liquidity, a concept we will come back to soon.

Under "assets," United States Charity's balance sheet shows an item called "grants and contributions receivable." That reflects the accrual basis of accounting; these are gifts and grants that have been promised but not yet received. The total shown for contributions receivable usually includes an adjustment for what are called doubtful accounts, which means gifts and grants that may end up not being paid for some reason. That amount is estimated based on past experience. United States Charity does not show any doubtful accounts, since it expects full payment of all gifts and grants that have been committed.

Under "liabilities" on United States Charity's statement of financial position, we see another example of the accrual basis of accounting, **accounts payable** and accrued expenses, which represent commitments that the organization has made, but which have not yet been paid. For example, the organization has signed a lease and is obligated to pay rent under that contract for some period of time. Such obligations are liabilities that must be shown on the balance sheet.

Statement of Activities

Now, let's go to Table 12.3, United States Charity's **statement of activities**. The balance sheet, or statement of financial position (shown in Table 12.2), is a snapshot of the organization's finances taken at a point in time, either the end of the calendar year or the end of the organization's fiscal year if that is different. The statement of activities shown in Table 12.3 is more like a video that shows the flow of revenues and expenses of the organization, and the resulting changes in net assets, over a period of time, generally a year. Accordingly, some nonprofit organizations call this the "statement of revenues, expenses, and changes in net assets." For a business, this statement would be the same as its "profit and loss," or "P&L" statement (Zietlow et al., 2007, p. 179).

Revenues are divided between the categories of "without donor restrictions" and "with donor restrictions." There are different permissible formats for doing this. Table 12.3 uses what is called the "layered format" (Lang, et. al., 2017, p. 135). In the year depicted in Table 12.3, United States Charity reported revenue of $4,884,049 without donor restrictions, about half from grants and contributions. Notice that one revenue item, also comprising about half, is identified as "net assets released from restrictions due to expiration of time

Table 12.2   United States Charity—Statement of Financial Position

December 31, 20XX	
Assets	
Cash and cash equivalents	$765,827
Grants and contributions receivable	1,750,679
Prepaid expenses	20,178
Fixed assets, net of depreciation and amortization	163,102
Investments	25,000
Deposits	30,379
Total assets	**$2,755,165**
Liabilities and Net Assets	
Accounts payable and accrued expenses	$606,228
Capital lease payable	131,620
Deferred rent liability	10,220
Total liabilities	**$748,068**
Commitments and Contingencies **Net assets**	
Without donor restrictions	257,097
With donor restrictions	1,750,000
Total net assets	**2,007,097**
Total liabilities and net assets	**$2,755,165**

Source: Adapted from Lang, A. S., Eisig, W. D., Klumpp, L., & Ricciardella, T. (2017). *How to read nonprofit financial statements: A practical guide.* Hoboken, NJ: Wiley, p. 134.
Notes: 1. Notes to the Financial Statements are an integral part of financial statements, but are excluded in this simplified, hypothetical example.
2. Most nonprofit financial statements show data for two years. For simplicity, this hypothetical example just shows one year.
3. Shaded lines indicate the basic totals that must be presented.

restrictions." Look farther down in the statement of activities. The same amount is shown as a negative amount—($2,302,360)—under the heading "Change in Net Assets With Donor Restrictions." How do funds go from the *with* donor restrictions category to the *without* donor restrictions category?

First, if a donor provides no direction on the use of a gift, then it always is "without donor restriction" and is shown that way in this year's financial statements. Suppose the donor does designate the gift for a particular activity and that activity is completed this year. The gift also would be reported under "without donor restrictions" at the end of the year, since completing the activity removed the restriction and the money was spent. What if the

Table 12.3 United States Charity—Statement of Activities

Year ended December 31, 20XX	
Changes in Net Assets Without Donor Restrictions	
Revenue and support	
Grants and contributions	$2,560,000
Investment return, net	21,548
Other income	141
Net assets released from restrictions due to expiration of time restrictions	2,302,360
Total revenue and support	4,884,049
Expenses	
Program services	
Information dissemination	2,866,720
Research	274,569
Total program services	3,141,289
Supporting services	
General and administrative	1,102,369
Fundraising	683,469
Total supporting services	1,785,838
Total expenses	4,927,127
Change in net assets without donor restrictions	(43,078)
Change in Net Assets With Donor Restrictions	
Grants and contributions	1,750,000
Net assets released from time restrictions	(2,302,360)
Change in net assets with donor restrictions	(552,360)
Change in net assets	(595,438)
Net assets, beginning of year	2,602,535
Net assets, end of year	$2,007,097

Source: Adapted from Lang, A. S., Eisig, W. D., Klumpp, L., & Ricciardella, T. (2017). *How to read nonprofit financial statements: A practical guide*. Hoboken, NJ: Wiley, p. 135.
Notes: 1. Notes to Financial Statements are an integral part of financial statements, but are excluded in this simplified, hypothetical example.
2. Most nonprofit financial statements show data for two years. For simplicity, this hypothetical example just shows one year.

activity for which the gift was restricted has not yet been completed? Or the donor said the money could not be spent until after some period of time has passed? Then the gift is reported as an asset "with restriction" this year. When the required activity has been completed or the time period has passed, perhaps next year, then "net assets with donor restrictions" are reclassified to "net assets without donor restrictions" and are reported in the statement of activities as "net assets released from restriction" (Lang et al., p. 138). In other words, the change in the status of funds shows up as a decrease in the restricted category and an increase in the unrestricted category (Lang et al., p. 138). To use the simple example from earlier in this chapter, the money your grandmother gave you for a new coat is donor restricted, so you have put it in a separate pot, at least in your thinking. Once you have ordered the coat from Amazon and charged it to your credit card, you now may spend your grandmother's money to make a payment on your credit card balance, or for some other purpose. It has gone from restricted to unrestricted because you have purchased the coat.

Statement of Cash Flows

Table 12.4 shows United States Charity's cash flows for the year to which the statement applies. As discussed previously, the statement of activities does not give the whole picture of an organization's financial situation because of the accrual basis of accounting it reflects. (Remember your friend who never had any cash but thought himself wealthy because of his anticipation of future funds from his aunt.) For that reason, FASB requires that nonprofits also produce a **statement of cash flows** to show inflows and outflows over the year, enabling us to see how the cash amount changed from one year to the next. There are two methods of presenting cash flow, direct and indirect. Table 12.4 uses the direct method, but this chapter does not go into detail about these two methods.

Look again at United States Charity's statement of financial position in Table 12.2 and the first line under "assets" as of December 31—it shows cash and cash equivalents totaling $765,827. Now look at the line near the bottom of the statement of cash flows in Table 12.4— the line labeled "cash and cash equivalents, end of year"—it's the same number, $765,827. What the statement of cash flows does is walk us through exactly how the cash changed from the beginning to the end of the year, resulting in that final number.

Cash flow may occur through operating activities, investing activities, or financing activities and the statement of cash flows breaks it down into those three categories. Think again about your own checking account. Cash might flow in from your paycheck. You may have sold your car, a physical asset, and placed the proceeds in the same account. Or you may have borrowed money and then deposited the amount of the loan directly into your checking account. All those transactions comprise your cash flow, but again, tracking just the flow of cash into and out of your checking account would not provide a complete picture of your financial position; that requires looking at the cash flow in relationship to the other financial statements we have discussed.

Statement of Functional Expenses

The last financial statement we will consider is shown in Table 12.5—the **statement of functional expenses**. This statement shows how every category of expense was allocated among the uses of program services, general and administrative activities, and fundraising. FASB requires that nonprofit organizations provide a report on expenses by nature and function, but gives three options for how to do so. The information can be provided in the statement of activities (using a format different from the example in Table 12.3), in the Notes to Financial Statements, or in a separate financial statement. In this hypothetical example, United States Charity provides the information in a separate financial statement.

Table 12.4 United States Charity—Statement of Cash Flows

Year ended December 31, 20XX	
Cash flows from operating activities	
Cash received from grantors and contributors	$2,559,321
Cash collected on promises to give	999,321
Cash paid to employees	(1,821,262)
Cash paid to providers	(2,989,321)
Interest and dividends received	21,548
Other receipts	141
Interest paid	(781)
Net cash (used in) provided by operating activities	(1,231,033)
Cash flows from investing activities	
Purchase of investment	(35,000)
Purchase of fixed assets	(13,373)
Net cash used in investing activities	(48,373)
Cash flows from financing activities	
Payments on capital lease	(2,531)
Net cash used in financing activities	(2,531)
(Decrease) Increase in cash and cash equivalents	(1,281,937)
Cash and cash equivalents, beginning of year	2,047,764
Cash and cash equivalents, end of year	$765,827
Supplemental cash flow information:	
Noncash financing activities:	
Leased property under capital lease	$134,151

Source: Adapted from Lang, A. S., Eisig, W. D., Klumpp, L., & Ricciardella, T. (2017). *How to read nonprofit financial statements: A practical guide.* Hoboken, NJ: Wiley, p. 136.
Notes: 1. Notes to the Financial Statements are an integral part of financial statements, but are excluded in this simplified, hypothetical example.
2. Most nonprofit financial statements show data for two years. For simplicity, this hypothetical example just shows one year.
3. This statement uses the direct method of presentation, an option under ASU 2016-14.

Some expenses are obviously related to program services, administration, or fundraising. For example, the salary of a gift officer or the costs of a fundraising solicitation might be clearly identifiable as fundraising expense. Other expenses may not be that simple. Notice the next-to-last line in this statement, called "allocation of shared expenses." Some expenses that the organization incurs may not be directly related to any one function. For example, suppose

Table 12.5 United States Charity—Statement of Functional Expenses

Year ended December 31, 20XX

	Program Services			Supporting Services			Total
	Information Dissemination	Research	Total Program Services	General and Administrative	Fundraising	Total Supporting Services	Total Expenses
Consulting fees	$2,084,998	–	$2,084,998	$68,898	$291,525	$360,423	$2,445,421
Professional fees	$3,372	235,264	238,636	448,248	–	448,248	686,884
Salaries and benefits	430,029	24,175	454,204	400,316	272,387	672,703	1,126,907
Communications and public relations	136,749	–	136,749	–	–	–	136,749
Travel	62,090	1,752	63,842	10,604	71,538	82,142	145,984
Occupancy	–	–	–	233,920	–	233,920	233,920
Office supplies and small equipment	669	–	669	14,743	1,573	16,316	16,985
Telecommunications and Web hosting	5,483	–	5,483	37,954	1,698	39,652	45,135
Meetings	20,523	–	20,523	741	1,033	1,774	22,297
Miscellaneous	18,197	–	18,197	17,392	12,883	30,275	48,472
Insurance	–	–	–	2,225	–	2,225	2,225
Depreciation and amortization	–	–	–	13,036	–	13,036	13,036
Equipment rental and maintenance	–	–	–	2,031	300	2,331	2,331
Interest expense	–	–	–	781	–	781	781
Allocation of shared expenses	104,610	13,378	117,988	(148,520)	30,532	(117,988)	–
Total expenses	$2,866,720	$274,569	$3,141,289	$1,102,369	$683,469	$1,785,838	$4,927,127

Source: Adapted from Lang, A. S., Eisig, W. D., Klumpp, L., & Ricciardella, T. (2017). *How to read nonprofit financial statements: A practical guide.* Hoboken, NJ: Wiley, p. 147.

Notes: 1. Notes to the Financial Statements are an integral part of financial statements, but are excluded in this simplified, hypothetical example.

2. Most nonprofit financial statements show data for two years. For simplicity, this hypothetical example just shows one year.

3. Nonprofits must present the required analysis of functional expenses by function and nature in one location. This information may be presented in a separate basic financial statement, the statement of activities, or the notes. This hypothetical example reflects the choice to present as a separate basic financial statement.

someone is paid to serve as the executive director's assistant but also manages fundraising part of the time. Her salary and benefits need to be allocated, partly to "administration" and partly to "fundraising." This most likely would be done based on the portion of her time she spends on each activity. Obviously, this can sometimes be difficult to track exactly. For example, if the staff member is meeting with a board member who is also a donor and discusses both the organization's budget and the individual's gift, is that administration, fundraising, or both and in what proportions? Other expenses, such as rent and utilities, usually would be allocated among the various functions based on the square footage of space occupied by people engaged in those activities (Lang et al., p. 140). For example, if 90 percent of the organization's building is used for programs and 10 percent for administrative offices, the costs of rent and utilities would be split 90/10 between those functions. Under FASB's ASU 2016-14 update, nonprofits are required to disclose the methods they use to make such allocations (Lang et al., p. 7). The next-to-last line of the statement of functional expenses shows how some expenditures have been allocated to give an accurate total for each of the various functions. It is from these totals that some charity watchdogs, certain donors, and others calculate the ratios that some use to evaluate the efficiency of an organization's management and fundraising efforts.

One expense item shown in the statement of functional expenses needs some additional explanation—depreciation. The concept of depreciation, and the way it is handled in financial accounting, is sometimes difficult for individuals to relate to their personal financial life. Perhaps the most familiar experience that most of us have with depreciation is the decline in the book value of our cars. Your new car may lose much of its value as soon as it is driven off the dealer's lot, and it will continue to decline in value every year that you own it. If you keep it long enough, it will continue to decline until it is ready for the junkyard and is worth next to zero. You may not feel that decline as an expense as it occurs, since it is not coming out of your pocket or checking account each day, but clearly your personal net worth is less when the car is old than when the car was new. Thus, the car's depreciation is a real expense in terms of its effect on your total net worth, even though it may not affect your cash flow.

Let's say a nonprofit organization owns physical assets, including cars, buildings, and equipment. Those assets have a value, and that value is reflected on its balance sheet. But they are assets that will be used up or wear out over some period of time, so their value declines with every passing month or year. That decline must be accounted for as an expense, even though it does not involve an actual outlay of money. It is a change in the organization's assets.

Although depreciation is an accounting item rather than a cash outlay, some organizations fund depreciation, that is, they set aside money for future maintenance or replacement of their capital assets. This is not a cash expenditure in the given year because the funds are, in effect, placed in a savings account to be used when needed at a later time; they remain an asset of the organization. Failure to fund depreciation can present a problem for a nonprofit when its facilities or other capital assets do become inadequate. Deferred maintenance can make the financial picture look brighter than it really is, a fact that becomes clear when the organization is faced with the need for a major expense, say for a new roof on a building that it owns or replacement of a vehicle, without having put funds aside to cover it (Mattocks, 2008, p. 91).

Required Disclosures and Notes to Financial Statements

FASB's 2016 update (ASU 2016-14) requires some changes in nonprofit accounting, including the manner in which gifts toward capital purposes are recorded and a change in the calculation of the return from investments (Lang et al., 2017, p. 9). The details of those requirements are beyond the scope of the discussion in this chapter. Other requirements of FASB's revised standards do not affect nonprofit accounting, but rather the format in which data are presented; some of those requirements were mentioned in the previous section. Other requirements involve the disclosure of information that may or may not be provided in the basic financial statements, details that someone would need to know in order to accurately assess the financial condition of the organization. Some of those disclosures may be included in the Notes to Financial Statements. Again, while our simplified example in this chapter does not include notes, they are integral to an organization's financial reporting. Disclosure requirements include the following (Lang et al., pp. 5–10):

- Details on assets subject to donor restrictions. This includes restrictions based on time and purpose. For example, funds designated to be held in perpetuity are not available for the organization to spend and thus must be shown.

- Details on assets that are subject to board designation. These would include board-designated endowment funds and funds that the board may have set aside for specific projects, such as a new building.

- Details on underwater endowment funds. These are endowment funds that are currently valued at less than the original gift.

- Details related to the organization's liquidity, a concept that is discussed in more detail in a later section of this chapter.

Again, this chapter provides an introduction to nonprofit financial accounting and reporting, but many details are beyond the scope of this text. Students with an interest in this topic are encouraged to consult other texts and, indeed, to consider taking courses in accounting and financial management.

Audits

Many nonprofit organizations have their financial statements audited by independent, outside accountants and some are required to do so. The **audit** is undertaken by an accounting firm that employs professional certified public accountants (CPAs) who have no relationship to the organization. An audit may not be necessary for a very small organization, but those who receive funding from state government or the federal government are generally required to have an independent audit. In addition, some states require nonprofits to submit a copy of audited financial statements as part of registering for fundraising solicitation in the state. Some foundations also may request audited financial statements and if the organization applies for a loan, it is likely that the bank will require such documentation (National Council of Nonprofits, n.d.-b).

Even if an organization is not required to undertake an independent audit, it may be highly desirable to do so in order to provide transparency to donors and reassure charity watchdogs that the organization is conducting its financial affairs consistent with best practices. The governing board may desire an independent audit as an important tool in exercising its fiduciary responsibility. Many boards have an **audit committee** that selects and works with the independent auditor and takes responsibility for assuring that any recommendations from the auditor regarding changes in accounting practice or financial controls are indeed implemented by management. The audit committee of the governing board also sometimes serves as the organization's ombudsperson for the nonprofit, receiving any complaints about financial practices and enforcing the organization's whistleblower policy (National Council of Nonprofits, n.d.-b).

Audited financial statements include an auditor's report, or letter, which expresses the auditor's opinion. An **unmodified (clean) audit** provides assurance that the organization has compiled its statements in accordance with GAAP and that they fairly present its financial position. It is important to understand that the auditor's letter does not include the auditor's assessment of the organization's overall financial condition, just the auditor's opinion that the statements reflect the real situation (Lang et al., 2017, p. 31). A **modified (auditor's) opinion** suggests some issue, perhaps a variation from GAAP about which the auditor has concern. An **adverse (auditor's) opinion** indicates a more serious problem, for example, a departure from accounting standards that makes it impossible to fairly assess the organization's financial position. Such an opinion is obviously a serious issue that would require strong action by the organization's management and board (Lang et al., p. 35).

Most auditor letters follow a similar format and use standard language. Some may include a paragraph labeled "Emphasis of a Matter" or "Other Matter" that calls attention to some specific point. This does not necessarily mean that the audit is not clean; it may just be noting some point, for example, a change in format from previous years' statements (Lang et al., p. 33).

Using Financial Ratios

Now that we have examined some basic accounting principles and looked at the financial statements that nonprofits produce, what do we make of the data? How can we interpret the financial data and use it to make decisions about the financial management of the organization?

The concept of financial ratios was introduced back in Chapter 6, which discussed some ratios that external observers use to evaluate the performance of nonprofit organizations. Readers may recall from that chapter that a 2004 study (Fremont-Smith & Cordes, 2004) looked at 10 charity watchdog organizations that use financial ratios and found a variety of measures being applied, including variations of the following:

- The ratio of program expenses to contributed income

- The ratio of fundraising expenditures and private support received—that is, the cost of raising a dollar

- The percentage of total expenses (or income received from contributions) spent on charitable programs or activities

- The percentage of total expenses spent on fundraising and administration (overhead)

- Accumulated cash and asset reserves in relation to the operating budget

Most of these ratios measure an organization's efficiency rather than its effectiveness. They might be of interest to the organization's board and management, but taken alone, they may not provide an appropriate way to rate or rank nonprofits. Indeed, some argue that a misplaced emphasis on efficiency has prevented many nonprofits from building capacity and achieving impact (Pallotta, 2010).

There are a number of ratios that can be calculated from the data provided on an organization's financial statements or similar data obtained from the Form 990. The ratios that are most commonly tracked by managers are those that measure **profitability**, **liquidity**, **asset management**, and **long-term solvency** (Anthony & Young, 2005, p. 488). This chapter does not go into detail on the calculation of ratios but rather will focus on explaining the concepts that they are intended to measure and their significance to assessing the financial health of a nonprofit organization.

Although the term profitability may seem out of place in the nonprofit setting, it is just describing the change in net assets on the statement of activities; in other words, it considers whether the organization had an operating surplus, broke even, or operated at a loss. Liquidity relates to the organization's use of cash.

Remember from the earlier discussion the example of the friend who thinks himself wealthy because he anticipates an inheritance but who lacks the cash to pay for dinner. To avoid being in a similar bind, an organization needs to manage its cash flows effectively in order to be possessed of sufficient cash at the right times to meet its obligations as they come due. As mentioned previously, FASB requires that the notes to financial statements include details that make it possible to assess the organization's liquidity. An analysis of cash management would address areas such as accounts receivable, accounts payable, and inventory maintained. For example, if clients are slow to pay bills for service, the organization will need to keep more cash on hand to pay its own bills as they come due. If the collection process could be made more efficient, it would need to maintain less of a cash balance and that money then could be put to work in other productive ways. Vendors need to be paid on time, but effective management of the process could reduce the amount of unproductive cash needing to be kept on hand. To use another example from personal financial life, there may not be a need to keep money sitting in your checking account on the 15th of the month if the rent is not due until the 1st and you know you will be receiving a paycheck in the meantime. Tracking when revenues come in and when bill payments are due is a way to stretch dollars further and gain more leverage from your personal cash flow.

Another issue for organizations is management of inventories. If too much money is tied up in inventories, it may leave too little liquidity to meet cash obligations as they arise. For example, if a food program spends all its cash to fill up its freezers with a six-month supply of food, then it may be in a bind to pay its staff or other expenses. Developing a more efficient system for food purchases that could reduce the amount of inventory kept in the freezer could provide for more liquidity to meet other obligations or to be put toward more effective purposes.

Management of fixed assets requires looking at how efficiently they are being used; for example, how much revenue is being generated through the use of buildings and equipment? The condition of assets needs to be tracked and adequate funds earmarked for replacement or repairs. That is a way to avoid unexpected expenses for which there may not be funds readily at hand from current revenue.

Assessing long-term solvency, that is, evaluating whether the organization is financially strong or in jeopardy, requires looking at the liabilities shown in the statement of financial position as well as the revenue and expenses shown on the statement of activities. One big issue is the amount of debt, specifically the relationship between assets and liabilities. Borrowing funds may be a good thing; it provides the organization with a way to leverage its assets and support a larger program of services than it could just with current revenue. Debt also increases risk and requires careful management of cash flow to ensure that debt payments can be made when due (Anthony & Young, 2005).

Ron Mattocks (2008) describes a "zone of insolvency," a "period of … financial distress during which prudent people could at least foresee the possibility of insolvency" (p. 87). Insolvency means a situation in which the organization can no longer continue in business and may need to either declare bankruptcy or close down (see the case of Hull House at the end of this chapter). This condition can be detected by monitoring indicators and ratios that may sound an alarm bell. Most boards will be alert to the alarm, since the law imposes especially demanding requirements on the governing board in such a situation (Mattocks, 2008). What are the alarms that may signify the **zone of insolvency**? Liabilities exceeding assets is one, although that may occur temporarily without too much concern, for example, if the organization has recently borrowed money to expand its programs and anticipates increased revenue soon. One warning sign is inadequate cash flow, especially if it is inadequate in comparison to the organization's debt. Another test is whether the organization would be able to pay all of its creditors should it cease operations tomorrow; if not, then it may be in financially unhealthy territory (Mattocks, 2008).

Which are the most important financial ratios to watch and manage? Zietlow et al. (2007) make the case that for most nonprofit organizations, liquidity—"the ability of the organization to augment its future cash flows" (p. 23)—is the biggest potential problem. Many nonprofits depend on contributions, but giving may fluctuate from year to year. An unforeseen event, such as the loss of a key donor or grantor, can leave a nonprofit in a cash crunch, stretched to meet its own obligations. Some pledges, which are reflected on the financial statements as assets, may in fact not be paid, and estimates of how much may be uncollectible may not be based on reliable information. If the organization depends on earned income, it faces business risks; if a college's enrollment turns down, a concert attracts fewer than expected attendees, or a blizzard reduces attendance at a major fundraising event, revenue may turn out to be much different from what the budget anticipated.

Nonprofits that rely on contracts may face similar problems; for example, costs may exceed what was projected and exceed the revenue that the contract provides. Some clients may be slow to pay. The only options might then include obtaining short-term financing from banks or other lenders, making emergency appeals to donors, tapping into reserves or even quasi endowment, delaying payments to vendors, and reducing costs by cutting staff or their compensation. Zietlow and colleagues (2007) argue that such problems are "endemic to the nonprofit sector [and that liquidity] is one of the most important yet least studied areas in the management of nonprofits" (p. 23). Zietlow et al. criticize the charity watchdogs, such as the BBB Wise Giving Alliance and others, who set a maximum that organizations should keep in reserves. The view of the charity raters is that excess funds held in reserve should instead be used to support current programs and services. But Zietlow and colleagues argue, "[While] these policy guidelines may be appropriate for commercial nonprofits, [they] will severely limit the management style of small donative ... organizations" (p. 24).

Managing Endowment Funds

As noted previously, most nonprofit organizations do not have significant endowments; most are held by large institutions such as colleges and universities, health care institutions, museums, and major arts centers. The largest is the endowment of Harvard University, which was valued at almost $36 billion in 2016. Other institutions with substantial endowments in 2016 included the Metropolitan Museum of Art ($3 billion), the Smithsonian Institution ($1.4 billion), Harlem Children's Zone ($404 million), Save the Children ($125 million), and the American Cancer Society ($114 million; "How Nonprofit Endowments Performed," 2017).

Of course, the stock market decline in 2008 and early 2009 hit many nonprofit endowments hard. Many nonprofits were forced to make adjustments in their operating budgets to reflect the lower income available from endowment, and others postponed new projects or programs. But remember our discussion in the early part of this chapter; unlike individuals, many organizations and institutions intend to exist forever. They make adjustments to accommodate to economic cycles but also expect to recover their endowments as the economy turns around in years ahead. Indeed, by the fall of 2012, U.S. stock markets had almost doubled from the bottom reached in March of 2009, and, by 2018, market indexes had reached historic highs. Of course, the future is not predictable.

As discussed earlier, some endowment funds may be created by the nonprofit's board from internal resources, perhaps from operating surpluses accumulated over several years. Although board-designated endowment could be expended at the board's discretion, it is intended for long-term use and would generally be managed according to the same policies applied to permanent endowment created through donor-restricted gifts. Because of this long-term investment horizon, board-designated endowment may not be readily accessed to meet current needs, especially if the financial markets were to undergo a downturn. It is for that reason that FASB requires details about such funds to be disclosed in financial statements. Term endowments, which are established for a period of years, after which the funds may be spent, might be invested and managed differently, depending on the date of their anticipated termination. The discussion of endowment management here applies to funds that the organization intends, or must, hold for investment in perpetuity, using only the annual income earned from investments to support its operating needs.

There are two key concepts related to the management of endowment funds. One is the **total return** approach to investing endowment assets, and the other is the **spending limit** that determines how much will be available from endowment for expenditure each year. In earlier decades, a large portion of endowment assets was invested in relatively secure, interest-paying instruments, such as bonds and bank certificates of deposit. The drawbacks of this approach became evident in the high-inflation economy of the 1970s, since the fixed amount of interest income became increasingly inadequate to support the activities for which the endowment was intended. Over the long term, investments in stocks produce higher overall returns and keep pace with inflation, but stocks often pay dividends that provide less current income than bonds. Institutions found a way around this dilemma by adopting the total return approach to investing endowments, combined with a spending limit to determine how much can be used each year.

The approach includes investing in a portfolio that includes stocks, cash, bonds, real estate, and other classes of assets, providing for the long-term growth of the principal. The investment strategy is to maximize total return—that is, the total of interest, dividends, and appreciation in the value of stocks and other assets—consistent with a level of risk that the organization's board has determined to be acceptable. Each year, some percentage of the total market value of the endowment is withdrawn from the endowment fund and transferred to operating funds for expenditure that year. Any additional investment returns are left in the principal, enabling it to grow over time. The amount withdrawn and spent is determined by the spending limit (or payout rate) established by the board. It can be varied from year to year as economic conditions change. The goal is to provide enough payout each year to meet the needs of current programs, while also allowing the value of the endowment principal to grow to keep pace with inflation and provide more income to sustain programs in future years. The latter is not only important to maintain the benefit of the endowment to the organization; it is also essential in order to keep faith with the intention of a donor who wished to support some activity in perpetuity. This approach is similar to the way that some individuals might handle withdrawals from their retirement funds when they retire. Of course, their goal is not to sustain the principal in perpetuity, but to assure that it lasts as long as they do.

Let's take a look at an example in Table 12.6 to see how this approach might work over a period of five years. It is important to emphasize that Table 12.6 shows a greatly simplified example and that most organizations do not spend a percentage of the market value of their endowments based on its value at the end of a given year. For example, many calculate a multiyear average of the endowment's market value, and the spending policy is then applied to that average. That is a way to ensure that the amount available for spending each year does not fluctuate wildly with changes in the value of stocks and other assets—using the average will smooth out the ups and downs. Many foundations also use a similar methodology, which accounts for why their grant making may be affected only a few years after a significant downturn or upturn in the financial markets. Some endowments are managed using more complicated approaches, but a detailed discussion of those is beyond the scope of this discussion. Again, in order to simplify our discussion here, Table 12.6 does not reflect the averaging approach; it just assumes that the nonprofit has a spending policy that permits

Table 12.6 Hypothetical Endowment Fund

Year Following Gift	Tuition ($)	Total Return 10% ($)	Spendable 5% ($)	Reinvest 5% ($)	Endowment Principal ($)
					$500,000 gift made and invested
1	25,000	50,000	25,000	25,000	525,000
2	26,250	52,500	26,250	26,250	551,250
3	27,563	55,125	27,563	27,563	578,813
4	28,941	57,881	28,941	28,941	607,754
5	30,388	60,775	30,388	30,388	638,142

spending the following year equivalent to a fixed percentage of the endowment fund's value at the end of the previous year.

In looking at Table 12.6, assume a donor has made a gift of $500,000 for the purpose of endowing full-tuition scholarships to students in perpetuity. Tuition is now $25,000, but the assumption in this example is that it will increase by an average of 5 percent each year. Assume also that the original gift is invested in a portfolio of securities that will earn an average of 10 percent each year, in some combination of interest, dividends, and appreciation. Both the rate of tuition increase and the investment return would be high in terms of actual experience, but the round numbers simplify our example.

Based on the assumptions, in the first year, the $500,000 endowment earns $50,000. The college could spend $50,000 to award two full-tuition scholarships that year. The problem with that approach would start to become obvious in the second year. The endowment would still be just $500,000; it would again earn $50,000, which would no longer be enough for two full-tuition scholarships at the higher tuition rate. Instead, if the college awards one $25,000 scholarship the first year (equivalent to the 5 percent payout rate that the board has established), and reinvests the additional $25,000 back into the endowment, the principal of the endowment now becomes $525,000. If it follows that practice every year—spend 5 percent and reinvest 5 percent—look what happens as we go down the table to Year 5. Because the endowment principal has increased, the 5 percent available for spending also has increased sufficiently to cover the ever-higher cost of tuition.

Following this approach and continuing out forever into the future, if all the assumptions hold, there will always be sufficient income from this endowment to provide a "full-tuition scholarship," which was the intention of the donor. Now, if the market has a bad year, it may not earn 10 percent, but in some years it may do *better* than 10 percent, averaging out over the long haul. Tuition may increase more than expected, or less. The board can adjust the spending limit as well as the investment portfolio to accommodate these trends as they emerge. Properly executed, this approach enables the organization to count on ever-increasing income from its endowment and to keep faith *in real terms* with the intention of its endowment donors.

Endowment management is governed by state law. A model act, called the **Uniform Prudent Management of Institutional Funds Act (UPMIFA)**, was introduced in 2006 and has been adopted by most states. It requires that in making investment decisions, boards act "in good faith and with the care an ordinarily prudent person in a like position would exercise under similar circumstances" (National Association of College and University

Business Officers; NACUBO, n.d.). The law thus provides flexibility but places responsibility on boards for preserving the purchasing power of endowment funds and assuring that the intent of endowment donors is carried out to the extent possible.

If financial markets decline soon after a donor has made a gift to create an endowment fund, it is possible that the value of the fund will be lower than the original gift. That is called an **underwater endowment**. UPMIFA gives boards the discretion to decide whether or not to spend from an endowment fund in such a position, but the donor of the fund also may have an opinion that the organization is inclined to respect. Knowing something about these funds is essential to a full understanding of an organization's financial situation. It is for that reason that FASB requires the details on underwater endowments to be provided in the Notes to Financial Statements.

Developing and Managing the Budget

A nonprofit organization's financial statements are important documents to individuals both inside and outside the organization. On a month-to-month or day-to-day basis, for most people working in the organization, the budget and reports related to the budget are the guides to action. A full discussion of budgeting is beyond the scope of this text, but this section will summarize some important principles and concepts.

Most nonprofit organizations have three separate budgets: an **operating budget**, a **capital budget**, and a **cash budget**. As the terms suggest, the first tracks all revenues and expenditures; the second concerns the purchase or disposal of long-term physical assets, such as buildings and equipment; and the third tracks the flow of cash during the year, whether related to operating or capital activities. Some organizations also may have grant or contract budgets, related to specific funded programs (Corporation for National and Community Service, n.d.-b). As David Maddox (1999) observes, "Most people think of the operating budget when they think of a budget (if they do at all)" (p. 60). Our discussion in this section focuses generally on principles that relate to developing and managing the operating budget, although some are relevant to the others as well.

A budget is a political as well as financial document. Some say that the budget reveals an organization's "real strategy," despite what may be written in the strategic plan or other documents (Maddox, 1999, p. 12), because the budget is a tangible expression of what the organization's real priorities are. It reflects not only considered plans but also the push and pull of political forces within the leadership of the organization. Readers may recall the idea of nonprofit leaders' political frame, an idea described by Robert Herman (2016) and discussed in Chapter 5. Managers may be guided by a strategic plan, but various departments, programs, or purposes are in competition for the organization's limited resources, and the outcome of that competition may be important in determining where funds are actually allocated.

Budgets invariably create incentives and disincentives that will affect the behavior of managers and staff. For example, some organizations have a use-it-or-lose-it approach to annual budgets. If a department has not expended its budgeted funds by the end of the fiscal year, the remaining funds do not carry over to be available to the department the following year. The organization's top budget managers may be counting on unexpended funds in some department budgets to cover overspending by others or as a reserve of sorts to cover unanticipated expenses of the general organization. But savvy managers often work to ensure that no unspent money remains, rushing to place orders for supplies and new computers before the fiscal year ends. The use-it-or-lose-it policy thus may turn out to create a perverse incentive that results in needless spending.

The way in which budgets are structured, whether on an organizational or center basis, also affects incentives. For example, a university may develop a budget that treats tuition from all students as revenue to the institution as a whole. Individual colleges, schools, and programs then are given an expense budget on which they need to operate, and the dean or director of each is responsible for not exceeding the budgeted amount. Each individual unit thus is viewed as a **cost center**, and its manager may have little incentive beyond controlling costs. Or the university may budget on a center basis, that is, the university regards each unit as a **profit center**. In this model, the school or college keeps the revenue it generates, from which it meets its own direct costs and makes some contribution to cover general institutional costs and services provided to the unit by the overall organization, for example, its share of expenses related to utilities and information systems technology. This approach may create considerable incentive for unit heads to be entrepreneurial and undertake new efforts to increase revenue. However, the trade-off may be that the central administration has less control and a reduced ability to reallocate funds across units, either to address institutional priorities or to cross-subsidize less-profitable programs through the surpluses of others.

Another consideration is whether budgets are developed incrementally or allow for redistribution. A common and simple way to develop next year's budget is just to add some percentage to last year's budget or to the amounts actually expended. If the allocation is based on funds expended, then it will, of course, exacerbate the tendency of units to make sure they spend all of last year's budgeted amount before the year ends. If they do not, they take, in effect, a double hit: They lose the unexpended funds at the end of the year and also receive a reduced allocation for the year that follows. Other budgeting systems allow for considerable redistribution from one year to the next. One benefit of having a strategic plan with specific goals and objectives is that it can serve to justify such redistribution over time in order for the organization or department to pursue strategic priorities. If the plan has been developed in a participative process, with buy-in from all parts of the organization, it may help mitigate the inevitable political pressures that come to bear on annual budgeting.

Another process, perhaps at the extreme of the redistribution spectrum, is the zero-based approach. All programs and departments start at zero at the beginning of each year's budget process and need to justify their budgets from the ground up. This approach does require careful thinking about the justification for various expenditures, but it also has a number of disadvantages, including the amount of time and effort required to prepare justifications and the potential for management competition and negative staff morale (McMillan, 2003).

A fundamental idea in budgeting is to recognize the difference between controllable and uncontrollable expenses and to hold managers accountable accordingly. Individual departments or programs may be credited with or charged with revenues and expenditures attributable to them, but a manager can only be held responsible for line items under his or her control. For example, a manager may be able to control salaries, travel, and the use of outside consultants, but he or she may not be able to control, at the department or program level, items such as fringe benefits, rent, heat, or electricity. Monthly budget reports typically show—for each line item—the amount budgeted for the year, the amount and percentage of the annual budget for that item expended year-to-date, and a comparison with the amount spent the previous year to the same date. Such reports enable managers to note significant variations from the budget and make mid-year corrections as needed.

Bowman (2016, pp. 571–573) offers best practices for developing nonprofit budgets, including the following points:

- The budget should be prepared before the next fiscal year begins.

- The operating budget should be separate from the capital budget.

- An operating budget must be balanced without borrowing, whereas borrowing is an acceptable method for financing a capital budget.

- The line items in the operating budget should correspond to the accounting system's chart of accounts.

- An operating budget should not include restricted income, unless restrictions are expected to be satisfied during the fiscal year that the budget is in effect.

- An operating budget should include no more than a small amount of non-recurring income.

- An operating budget for a new year should be based on the current year's estimated income and spending—not the current year's budget.

- A narrative is an integral part of a budget.

Actual nonprofit budgets are difficult to find in public sources, such as on the Web, because they are not public documents. There are, however, a variety of online resources available that do provide templates and other guides to budget development.

Financial Policies and Controls

As discussed in Chapter 7, recent years have seen an increased emphasis on managing risk. As a part of the overall risk management discussed in that earlier chapter, well-managed organizations establish specific policies and controls with regard to the management of finances.

The organization may have **prescriptive policies** and **restrictive policies**. Prescriptive policies state what must be done, whereas restrictive policies limit or place boundaries on the actions that may be taken under certain circumstances. Zietlow and colleagues (2007) agree with John Carver (2006), whose views were discussed in Chapter 4, that "the prescriptive approach to policy is doomed to failure" (Zietlow et al., p. 145). It is just impossible to predict all future circumstances, it is undesirable to unduly limit the flexibility of managers, and enforcement is difficult with the prescriptive approach. For example, society can make laws that prohibit people from driving too fast, driving after consuming alcohol, or driving without seat belts. But a law that required "safe driving" would be unenforceable because it encompasses too wide a range of possible behaviors. Zietlow and colleagues identify three basic categories of financial policies that nonprofit organizations should have: accountability and regulatory compliance policies, financial and financial management policies, and data integrity policies. **Accountability and regulatory compliance policies** encompass matters such as filing Form 990, avoiding conflicts of interest, and meeting other requirements of behavior or disclosure required by law. Some of these topics were discussed in Chapter 7 of this text. Other policies are primarily focused on financial management.

Financial and financial management policies are established by the governing board. They may identify allowable ranges for specific financial indicators or ratios, for example, liquidity, debt, or assets held in the endowment fund. They may also encompass procedures for purchasing, risk management, internal financial controls, fundraising, and other areas of activity. The third category, data integrity policies, involves privacy, confidentiality, records retention, the separation of duties, data backup, and other such concerns (Zietlow et al., 2007, pp. 146–154).

Internal controls have increasingly become a focus of attention in the wake of several scandals of malfeasance by nonprofit executives, and some nonprofits have adopted internal control policies similar to those required of public corporations by Sarbanes-Oxley. By one widely accepted definition, an internal control is

> a *process*, [italics added] affected by an entity's board of directors, management and other personnel that provides reasonable assurance regarding the achievement of objectives with regard to the effectiveness and efficiency of operation, reliability of financial reporting, and compliance with applicable law and regulation. (Coe, 2011, p. 31)

As Charles Coe (2011) explains, the first step is to create a "control environment" (p. 34). This includes adopting codes of conduct and conflict of interest policies; implementing professional management of staff (for example, job descriptions, background checks, annual performance evaluations, and other recommended practices); maintaining an independent board and providing information to the board; a management style that includes communication with staff and fiscal conservatism; and an organizational structure that assures the flow of information. Coe recommends then establishing controls in five principal risk areas: staffing, accounting, information management, travel, and physical assets. Management and the board then need to create a robust information/communication system and regularly monitor the effectiveness of the control system through audits, financial reports, and internal control and compliance reports (Coe, pp. 35–40).

One fundamental principle of internal control requires that duties of individuals be separated so that no one person handles an entire transaction from beginning to end. For example, it is common to have policies that require that the person who enters donor gifts is different from the person who deposits the funds; that the person who reconciles the checking account monthly is different from the person who signs the checks; and that payments to vendors be made only with an invoice approved by someone other than the person who sends the payment.

As Zietlow and colleagues (2007) observe, "Depending on the nature of your organization and the specific policy, internal or external noncompliance can range from fraud to poor business management, from felony to raised eyebrows" (p. 138). Ensuring that such policies are in place and followed is a fundamental aspect of responsibility for nonprofit managers and boards. As discussed previously, an independent audit conducted by an external accounting firm may highlight any deficiencies and help the board assure that the appropriate controls are in place.

CHAPTER SUMMARY

Financial management goes to the heart of the board's fiduciary responsibility, and any problems involving budgets or assets are likely to demand immediate attention from the board and the nonprofit CEO. Bookkeeping involves the entry of financial transactions on the organization's records, and accounting encompasses the rules by which transactions are categorized and reported. Financial management is a broader concept. It includes developing diverse sources of revenue and requires making judgments based on data in financial statements, relationships among that data, and financial management policies of the organization.

Although the terminology of nonprofit accounting is precise and can be unclear to those without a financial background, the basic concepts have analogs in the personal finances of individuals. For example, operating funds are similar to a personal checking account and operating reserves are like savings. A nonprofit may have board-designated endowment, which is intended for investment over the long run, but the board can withdraw the funds if it has a compelling reason. Permanent endowment must be invested in perpetuity because donors have placed that requirement on their endowment gifts. The nonprofit can withdraw the principal from such an endowment only with agreement of the donor or a court. Individuals do not have a component of their personal finances that can be compared with permanent endowment, since they are mortal and do not hold funds in perpetuity.

There are two basic methods of accounting, the cash basis and the accrual basis. Very small organizations that do not have accounts receivable or payable may use the cash method, but most use the accrual method, which is required for audited financial reports. In accrual basis accounting, revenues and expenses are recorded as they are earned or as obligations are incurred, not necessarily when the cash is received or paid out. Thus, reports based on the accrual method may provide a better picture of the organization's real financial picture than ones based on cash. However, it is also necessary to look at cash flows to get a complete sense of the organization's financial position.

Nonprofit accounting standards are established by the Financial Accounting Standards Board (FASB), which defines generally accepted accounting principles (GAAP). In 2016, FASB issued an Accounting Standards Update (ASU 2016-14), which dictates a new format for nonprofit financial statements and requires certain disclosures that must be included in the Notes to Financial Statements.

There are four financial statements that many nonprofits produce for external purposes. The statement of financial position (or balance sheet) provides a snapshot of the organization's assets, liabilities, and net assets at a point in time, usually the end of its fiscal year. Net assets are equivalent to equity in a company or an individual's net worth.

The statement of activities shows revenues, expenditures, and changes in net assets over a period of time, usually a fiscal year. In a business, this would be the profit-and-loss statement. Revenues include receivables, for example, pledges from donors that have not yet been paid. Expenses must be allocated among programs and supporting services, including general management and fundraising.

The statement of cash flows reveals cash transactions from operations, financing, or investing activities and the changes in cash balances over the period of the report, generally one year. Depreciation of the value of physical assets is an expense that is shown in financial statements, even though it may not involve an actual outlay of cash by the organization.

The statement of functional expenses, which may be provided as a separate statement or in another place permitted by FASB, breaks out expenses among the categories of programs, administrative and general, and fundraising. Some expenses must be allocated among these purposes and nonprofits are required to disclose the methods that they use to make such allocations.

Notes are an integral part of financial statements and often provide important details, including disclosures and details required by FASB.

Some states require some nonprofit organizations to have annual audits conducted by independent outside accountants. Audits also are generally required of organizations that receive government grants or contracts and some states require audited financial statements. Many nonprofit organizations undertake audits by independent, outside accountants even if not required by law, in order to assure transparency and best practice and to enable the governing board to meet its fiduciary responsibilities. An unmodified (clean) audit means that the organization is following GAAP and that its financial statements accurately portray its financial position, but it is not an endorsement that implies the organization is financially strong.

Financial ratios provide an important tool of financial management, although they are not a sufficient basis on which to rate nonprofit organizational performance. Some say that an overemphasis on such ratios has limited nonprofits' growth and impact. Commonly used ratios include those related to profitability, liquidity, asset management, and long-term solvency. According to some experts, liquidity is an endemic problem for nonprofit organizations. Cash management strategies may include speeding up the receipt of payments, managing the timing of expenses, reducing inventories, and obtaining a line of credit to cover temporary cash needs. Analytical models are available to determine the appropriate target for liquidity. If key ratios are not within acceptable limits, an organization may be flirting with bankruptcy, that is, it has entered the zone of insolvency. This condition places increased responsibilities on governing boards.

The largest endowment funds are held by major institutions, such as universities, but in recent years, many types of nonprofits have worked to establish or build endowments. Most endowments are invested under the total return concept. The board of the organization sets a spending limit, which is a percentage of the endowment's market value each year (or, commonly, of an average over a period of months or years). That amount is spent to support programs, and any additional investment gain is reinvested in the principal of the endowment. The payout may come from interest, dividends, or the appreciation in value of equities. That approach enables the principal and the income to grow over the years to match the higher future costs of activities that the endowment is intended to support.

Most nonprofits have three budgets: an operating budget, a capital budget, and a cash budget. Some may also have grant or contract budgets related to specific funded programs. The operating budget usually commands the most attention. The budget is a political document that reflects not only plans but also the competition for resources within the organization. How budgets are constructed creates important incentives and disincentives that affect managers' behavior. One important consideration is whether budgets are maintained on an organizational or center basis and whether departments and programs are treated as cost centers or profit centers. Some budgeting methods simply add a percentage increment to previous years' budgeted or expended amounts, while others provide greater opportunity for the redistribution of funds across programs or units. Some expenses, such as salaries, are controllable. Others, such as fringe benefits, are less so. Unit managers should be accountable for expenses that are within their control. Experts offer best practices to guide nonprofit in developing budgets.

Risk management has gained more attention in the nonprofit sector in recent years (see Chapter 7). Some risks are primarily financial. Internal controls are established to prevent financial fraud or abuse. They should be applied within an environment of control and include processes related to risk areas. One essential principal is that financial transactions involve more than one person. Audits and other compliance reports can be used to monitor the effectiveness of the control system. Ensuring that appropriate policies and controls are in place is a fundamental aspect of the governing board's responsibility.

KEY TERMS AND CONCEPTS

accountability and regulatory compliance policies 345
accounting 324
Accounting Standards Update (ASU) 2016-14 329
accounts payable 330
accounts receivable 328
accrual basis of accounting 328
adverse (auditor's) opinion 338
asset management 338
audit 337
audit committee 337
board-designated endowment 327
bookkeeping 324
capital budget 343
cash basis of accounting 328
cash budget 343
cash flow 328
cost center 344

donor-restricted funds 326
financial accounting 324
Financial Accounting Standards Board (FASB) 329
financial management 324
generally accepted accounting principles (GAAP) 329
in perpetuity 327
internal controls 345
liquidity 338
long-term solvency 338
managerial accounting 324
modified (auditor's) opinion 338
operating budget 343
operating reserves 326
permanent endowment 327
prescriptive policies 345
profitability 338
profit center 344

pure endowment 327
quasi endowment 327
restrictive policies 345
spending limit 341
statement of activities 330
statement of cash flows 333
statement of financial position 329
statement of functional expenses 333
total return 341
underwater endowment 343
Uniform Prudent Management of Institutional Funds Act (UPMIFA) 342
unmodified (clean) audit 337
unrestricted 326
zone of insolvency 339

CASE 12.1 Hull House

Hull House was founded in Chicago in 1889 by Jane Addams and Ellen Gates Starr, with the purpose of serving Chicago's immigrants and helping the city's poorest citizens improve their lives. Hull House was the flagship of what became known as the "settlement house movement," including nearly 500 facilities by 1920. Hull House pioneered and established a model for many nonprofits founded in following years. In 1931, Addams received the Nobel Peace Prize for her work (Wade, 2005; West, 2012b). Hull House and other settlement houses provided residential facilities and a range of social services. In addition, Addams and house residents became advocates who worked for many social reforms of the early 20th century, including public recreational facilities, child labor laws, juvenile courts, and women's suffrage. By the 21st century, the Hull House Association had become a federation of neighborhood centers and programs, covering job training, homeless services, foster care, child care, domestic violence, and small business development, and serving 60,000 people a year in various locations throughout Chicago. In 2012, after 120 years, it was forced to close and dismiss its 300 staff members. Many of its programs were taken over by another nonprofit, Metropolitan Family Services (Wade, 2005; West, 2012b).

In its early years, Hull House was supported primarily by private funds raised by Addams. That pattern began to change in the 1960s, when the Great Society programs of president Lyndon Johnson expanded funding for social programs, much of it channeled through nonprofit organizations (West, 2012b). By 2012, Hull House depended on government funds for 85 percent of its budget (West, 2012b). With the economy entering recession in the late 2000s, the demand for services greatly increased, while government support did not keep pace.

The financial decline of Hull House had been evident by 2010, when it entered the zone of insolvency (Flynn & Tian, 2015). Revenue had declined from $41 million in 2001 to $23 million by 2010. Its government contractors often paid late and Hull House was borrowing every year to support its operations, based on those receivables. It also had accumulated substantial unfunded pension obligations. Its debt ratio (total liabilities divided by total assets) had reached four times the accepted industry standard (Flynn & Tian, 2015). As Flynn and Tian describe, "This irresponsible

cycle could not last forever and it contributed to organizational death."

There was disagreement about the causes of Hull House's demise. The board chair blamed the economic climate, although as noted previously, Hull House had financial problems even before the recession began in 2007 (Moyers, 2012). "We should have narrowed our focus even more," the board chair acknowledged (West, 2012b). The chair also claimed that the staff had sugarcoated the situation, providing financial statements that were late and failed to reveal the seriousness of the situation, although a former chief executive disagreed with that assessment (Moyers, 2012; West, 2012b). The former CEO was critical of the decision to close and criticized the board for "not understanding the idea of 'living on the edge'" (Moyers, 2012).

"Hull House is not an isolated situation," observed Irv Katz, president of National Human Services Assembly. "I have witnessed a couple of national groups that should have merged, but out of stubbornness or arrogance, allowed themselves to go too far down the tube rather than look for a partner" (West, 2012b). The former chief executive of Hull House said that he had suggested two potential partners to the board but that the board rejected them (West, 2012b). The board chair observed that by the time mergers were explored, Hull House had accumulated too much debt to be of interest to potential partners (West, 2012b).

Efforts to save Hull House in its later days included consideration of increased fundraising, with the goal of diversifying revenue sources and reducing dependence on government. This proved to be impractical, since the board did not include members who could provide major support personally or who were connected to sources of wealth and Hull House had little other capacity for philanthropic fundraising. Ian Bautista, president of United Neighborhood Centers of America, cited Hull House's situation as a widespread problem. In his view, many organizations that were once reliant on gifts, including United Way, have become too reliant on government funds and have "lost a lot of the connections and ability [to successfully raise private funds]" (West, 2012a).

Who was to blame for the death of Hull House? Flynn and Tian (2015) blame the board for not meeting its responsibility of care. "The financial woes at Hull House ran deep," they write, "but with strong, active governance, these problems could have been identified and rectified before organizational death." Rick Moyers, a former foundation officer and governance expert, blamed both the board and management for the failure, writing that "Hull House is a sobering case study of governance failure in which neither the board nor the staff seems to have recognized the crisis while there was still time to turn things around" (Moyers, 2012).

Questions Related to Case 12.1

1. Which principles of financial management discussed in this chapter are most relevant to the case of Hull House?

2. Was the closure of Hull House inevitable? If not, what actions might have been taken, and at what point, to prevent its demise?

3. Consider the obstacles to merger that were discussed in Chapter 8. Which of those were present in the case of Hull House?

4. Think back on (or reread) key principles regarding board responsibilities (Chapter 4) and executive leadership (Chapter 5). How does the case of Hull House relate to each of those principles?

CASE 12.2 Corcoran Gallery of Art and Corcoran School of the Arts and Design

The Corcoran Gallery of Art was established by Washington, DC, businessman William Wilson Corcoran, an early collector of contemporary American art. The gallery was opened in 1874 in a building that Corcoran had constructed and was moved to another new building, near the White House, in 1897, built to house an expanded collection and the recently established Corcoran School of Art.

Although it was a nonprofit institution, during the early 20th century, the Corcoran served as the nation's unofficial national art gallery. Even after establishment of the federally subsidized National Gallery of Art in 1937, it continued to enjoy the support of many wealthy Washingtonians. In 1989, the Corcoran was engulfed in controversy, when the director cancelled an exhibit of works by photographer Robert Mapplethorpe in the face of political controversy about its content. Demonstrators gathered outside the gallery to protest the decision. Some artists and donors expressed disappointment. Some Corcoran directors resigned and the gallery's reputation was badly damaged (Mullins, 2012).

David Levy joined the Corcoran as the new director in 1991, determined to turn the situation around. By 1995, many friends and donors had been reassured and fundraising had doubled, but the gallery still barely broke even. Maintaining its aging building was costly and it had difficulty attracting paid attendance in light of the free galleries of the Smithsonian just blocks away. Levy's idea was to build a dramatic new wing, designed by architect Frank Gehry, which would become an attraction in itself. The board agreed to spend millions on the plan and a fundraising campaign was launched, securing pledges for about half the cost. Then things fell apart. New security established in Washington in the wake of the terrorist attacks of September 11, 2001, made it difficult to access the gallery, and attendance declined. The crash of technology stocks that same year left some major donors unable to fulfill their pledges. The project was cancelled and, in 2005, Levy resigned (Mullins, 2012).

Fallout from the failed campaign was substantial. Some donors who had given were angry that their gifts had been spent but nothing had been accomplished. Others said they were insulted because the Corcoran never contacted them to offer an explanation. Outreach to former donors was not maintained and some who were called told the gallery never to contact them again. By 2008, the operating deficit had reached $2.6 million. The stock market decline of 2008 reduced the endowment by one third. Some board members refused to help with fundraising, saying they had been embarrassed by the fiasco over the Gehry building. By 2012, financial crisis loomed and the board was desperate for a solution (Mullins, 2012).

The financial challenges existed on two fronts. The operating budget deficit had increased to $7 million a year (Montgomery, 2012a) and the historic building required $130 million in repairs (Mullins, 2012). The board began to explore the possibility of moving to a new location, possibly even outside of the city. Upon learning this, employees and art students protested and wrote letters to the newspaper. Their anger was especially focused on the board chair and the president, whom the board had appointed and who was a businessman rather than a professional arts administrator. Trust with donors and the community was further eroded (Mullins, 2012).

One donor told the *Washington Post* that he was not even receiving solicitations from the Corcoran. Another reported, "I haven't gotten a phone call from the Corcoran in five years." "Years ago," one major philanthropist said, "we went to the Corcoran Ball (the gallery's principal annual fundraising event), "but we were never asked back that I know of." A former Corcoran trustee observed, "We never had the fundraising machine that I have experienced with other arts institutions, and I think we haven't had the fundraising base." The Corcoran's board chair tried to explain: "If you're going to go to serious people and serious foundations for serious amounts of money, seven-digit figures, you have to ... show how in the bigger picture the viability question is answered" (Montgomery, 2013a).

In 2010, the Corcoran sold one building it owned in Washington for $6.5 million and, in 2013, it received two large bequests, but these windfalls were not enough to resolve its financial problems. Also in 2013, it sold a 17th-century rug from its collection for $34 million, but it was not clear that the funds could be used to address the institution's financial problems, since museum ethics require that proceeds from a sale be used to purchase additional items for the collection, not to pay other bills (Capps & Montgomery, 2014). Other proposals to address the Corcoran's problems also encountered ethical concerns (Montgomery, 2013a).

In December 2012, the Corcoran board announced that it had abandoned the possibility of moving, but "mystery still [surrounded] exactly how the Corcoran

[would] chart a course forward" (Montgomery, 2012b). Months later, in April 2013, the Corcoran's interim director and president announced a new "Strategic Framework for a New Corcoran" that would include an agreement with the University of Maryland to explore a possible partnership. In February 2014, it was announced that the discussion with Maryland had not produced a workable partnership and that the Corcoran had reached agreements with two other institutions. The Corcoran's art collection would be given to the National Gallery of Art, which would keep some pieces for its own collection and give some to other galleries. The National Gallery also would maintain a small exhibit in the Corcoran's existing building. That building and the Corcoran School of the Arts and Design would become part of the George Washington University, which had its main campus nearby. The Corcoran would continue to exist as a legal entity, without any substantial assets and would continue to monitor the progress of its new partners (McGlone, 2016). Because the Corcoran was a nonprofit corporation, the changes required approval from the court, which was granted in August 2014 (Montgomery & Judkis, 2014). "There is no way to continue the Corcoran as we knew it or as we know it," its acting president stated. "That's going to be the kernel of pain for some people" (Montgomery, 2014).

The Corcoran School was integrated into the George Washington University's Columbian College of Arts and Sciences and some existing departments of the college were consolidated under the Corcoran umbrella. The university gained ownership of the historic Corcoran gallery building and, in 2016, began substantial renovations. A noted arts leader, Sanjit Sethi, was appointed as the director of the Corcoran as a component of the university. By 2016, only about one third of the former Corcoran faculty continued to be employed (McGlone, 2016). Two years after the court decision, some of the Corcoran's art collection had yet to find a permanent home. Some who had fought for the survival of the independent Corcoran were still disappointed and critical, both of the former board's actions and the court's decision (McGlone, 2016). Looking back, the former interim director of the Corcoran viewed the change as having been unavoidable. "I know what [the Corcoran] board went through," she said. "It was an excruciating decision. I think they made the only call they could" (McGlone, 2016).

QUESTIONS FOR DISCUSSION

1. Some people argue that nonprofit organizations should not have endowments at all. One of their arguments goes something like this: Putting money aside in endowment means depriving today's generation of the use of those resources so as to benefit future generations, who will receive services supported by income from the endowment. There are many people in great need of services today. Why are tomorrow's needy more deserving than today's? The funds should be spent now to meet current needs. Let future generations of donors support the needs of people in the future. Since the economy is growing, giving will increase over time, and there should be enough philanthropy to meet those future needs. It is thus especially unjust to provide for the future at the expense of people alive today, who live in less affluent times. Do you agree? Why or why not? What arguments would you make on the other side of this issue? Would your views be different with regard to different types of nonprofits, for example, homeless shelters, universities, museums, or environmental organizations?

2. Look up the Form 990 of a nonprofit organization that interests you. (It is likely available on GuideStar at www.guidestar.org.) Go through the financial data and develop your own analysis of the organization's finances. Questions you might think about include the following: Does it appear to have diversified sources of revenue? How vulnerable or unpredictable are these sources likely to be? What were its major categories of expenses for the year shown? What unforeseen expenses could arise? What kinds of assets does it hold? Does it have debt? What produced its cash flow for the year shown? Does it have endowment or other donor-restricted assets?

3. The following items were reported in the news media. In each case, what types of controls that might have prevented the incident were possibly either not in place or did not work?

- A former financial officer at a New York–based nonprofit that supports research into genetic illnesses was arrested ... on suspicion of embezzling more than $1.8 million from the organization ... [The individual] served for more than eight years as controller of the [foundation], exercising primary responsibility for paying the charity's bills and delivering grant funds for medical studies. A federal criminal complaint ... alleges [that the individual] disguised transfers to bank accounts she controlled as grant payments in the foundation's accounting software. ("Ex-Official at Medical Charity Accused," 2014)

- Eighteen months after ... one of the largest natural history museums in the country, shocked [its home] city by revealing that it was in a financial crisis, one of its top executives appears to be the only one to face criminal charges in the museum's near collapse. [The chief financial officer], who left his job ... after [the] problems became public, was charged by [the city's] district attorney with using money from the endowment to cover operating expenses as the museum sank into a financial crisis, and lying about his actions in board meetings to hold onto his job, according to criminal charges filed this month. He did not profit personally from his actions, according to the complaint. (Gose, 2006, p. 17)

- The ... former board president of a ... mental-health nonprofit was charged ... with siphoning hundreds of thousands of dollars from the organization.... Prosecutors allege that ... [the former board member] charged the organization exorbitant rents to lease buildings she owned and cut checks to employees for work that was not done so the money could be returned to her. ("Politically Prominent Philadelphian Accused," 2016)

APPENDIX CASES

The following cases in the Appendix of this text include points related to the content of this chapter: Case 1 (New York City Opera); Case 2 (Share Our Strength/No Kid Hungry); Case 4 (The Girls Scouts of the United States of America).

SUGGESTIONS FOR FURTHER READING

Books

Bowman, W. (2011). *Finance fundamentals for nonprofits: Building capacity and sustainability*. Hoboken, NJ: Wiley.

Lang, A. S., Eisig, W. D., Klumpp, L., & Ricciardella, T. (2017). *How to read nonprofit financial statements: A practical guide*. Hoboken, NJ: Wiley.

Weikart, L. A., Chen, G. G., & Sermier, E. (2012). *Budgeting & financial management for nonprofit organizations: Using money to drive mission success*. Thousand Oaks, CA: Sage.

Newsletter

Financial Accounting Standards Board. (2016, August). *Not-for-profit entities (Topic 958): Presentation of financial statements of not-for-profit entities* (FASB Accounting Standards Update No. 2016-14). Norwalk, CT: Author. Available at https://asc.fasb.org/imageRoot/56/92564756.pdf

Websites

Commonfund: http://www.commonfund.org/Pages/default.aspx

Financial Accounting Standards Board: http://www.fasb.org/

Nonprofit Finance Fund: http://www.nonprofitfinancefund.org/

Nonprofit Risk Management Center: http://www.nonprofitrisk.org/

Hundreds of billions of dollars are given each year to nonprofit organizations by foundations, corporations, and individuals.

iStock/donald_gruener

Chapter Outline

Fundraising is synonymous with nonprofit organizations in the minds of many people. They may associate it with the flood of solicitation letters that fill their mailboxes around the holiday season, some enclosing address labels, bookmarks, or other items from a charitable organization. Others may think of the charity golf tournament, tennis tournament, or some other event in which they participate. Some, perhaps, may think about the annual phone call they receive from a student at their college or university, or a former classmate, asking for a gift to the institution's annual fund. Increasingly, they may think about fundraising appeals that they have received through e-mail or an effort that one of their friends may have organized on a social networking site, directing them to a giving platform where they can make their gift using a credit card or other form of electronic payment. Indeed, charitable or philanthropic giving is an important source of revenue for many nonprofits, although just how important varies considerably among subsectors.

For example, gifts provide a small portion of total revenues for health services organizations, which receive most of their revenue from government or private payments for services provided. In contrast, most religious organizations and some human services organizations almost entirely depend on giving. Educational institutions are in the middle—gifts are important, but so are government grants and payments for services provided (tuition). However, even for institutions with substantial revenue from other sources, such as hospitals and universities, private gifts sometimes have an impact disproportionate to their share of total revenues, because they address organizational priorities rather than supporting specific programs or services. For example, unrestricted giving may help support core operations or capacity building, new facilities may require a combination of fundraising and borrowing, and new initiatives that do not yet attract paying customers or grants may be financed through discretionary dollars available to the CEO from endowment income or private gifts.

Although philanthropy in some form is common around the world, organized fundraising and philanthropy on a massive scale is still primarily an American phenomenon—and massive

Learning Objectives

After reading this chapter, students should be able to:

1. Define key terms and concepts related to fundraising and philanthropy.

2. Summarize the primary motivations of corporate, foundation, and individual donors.

3. Explain the fundraising process.

4. Identify the advantages and disadvantages of various solicitation methods.

5. Explain common planned giving vehicles and the types of donors to which each may be most attractive.

6. Describe the characteristics of campaigns.

7. Define key terms and concepts related to management of fundraising programs.

8. Identify ethical issues related to fundraising.

9. Analyze cases, applying concepts from the chapter.

it is. In 2016, an estimated $390 billion was given to nonprofit organizations by foundations, corporations, and individuals. When philanthropy is mentioned, some people think about corporate giving or perhaps the large national foundations, such as the Gates Foundation or the Ford Foundation. The reality is that living individuals are overwhelmingly the largest sources of giving, accounting for 72 percent of the total in 2016. The largest portion of giving by individuals is directed to religion, which accounts for almost one third of the total each year; however, even when religious giving is excluded, individuals still account for much more than either corporations or foundations in their impact on U.S. philanthropy. In 2016, corporations and foundations accounted for about 5 percent and 15 percent, respectively, of total philanthropy (Lilly Family School of Philanthropy at Indiana University, 2017).

An important and growing component of philanthropy is bequests—that is, gifts made by individuals through their wills or other estate-planning vehicles. Bequests accounted for 8 percent of total giving in 2016. With the aging of the population and the growing wealth of older people, giving through bequests is expected to grow substantially in the coming decades (Lilly Family School of Philanthropy at Indiana University, 2017).

Where does the money go? Next to religion, the largest recipient of philanthropy is education, accounting for 15 percent in 2016, followed by human services (12 percent). Giving to create or enlarge foundations accounts for another 10 percent of the total, followed by gifts to health (18 percent), and public-society benefit organizations (8 percent). The latter include organizations such as United Way and Jewish federations, among others. Although they are important causes for many people, the environment and animals and the arts, culture, and humanities receive relatively small shares of the philanthropic pie, together accounting for 8 percent of total giving in 2016.

Definitions and Distinctions

When Hurricane Katrina hit the Gulf Coast in 2005, the response was immediate and overwhelming, totaling more than $3.3 billion in gifts to organizations providing relief and support for rebuilding (Lipman, 2006). When Hurricane Sandy devastated sections of the U.S. East Coast in 2012, Americans again responded generously. In 2017, donors responded to the destruction of Hurricanes Harvey, Irma, and Maria as well as destructive wildfires in California. In these instances, millions of donors responded quickly to meet urgent human needs, many of them with relatively modest gifts. In contrast, in 2016 Phil Knight, the founder of Nike, and his wife, Penny, gave $500 million to the University of Oregon, Phil Knight's alma mater, to establish a new institute for scientific research (K. Strauss, 2017). These examples demonstrate the scale and impact of giving in the United States; they also illustrate two different approaches to giving—one focused on immediate needs and the other taking a more long-term, strategic perspective.

In Chapter 2, this text made a distinction between charity and philanthropy as two types of voluntary giving. **Charity** includes gifts to meet immediate human needs, for example, to provide food to those who are starving or shelter to those dislocated as a result of natural disaster. It is often impulsive and always driven by human compassion. **Philanthropy** is giving to strengthen the infrastructure of society, that is, to develop institutions that serve human needs or enhance human development over the long run. The objects of philanthropy often include hospitals, universities, museums, and arts organizations—institutions with missions that are perpetually relevant across generations, but which do not have the same urgency as immediate human suffering. Some philanthropic gifts go to create or expand foundations, such as the Bill & Melinda Gates Foundation, most of which are established to last forever or a very long time, tackling long-term problems and issues. Philanthropic gifts are made carefully and thoughtfully, often as the culmination of a long-standing relationship with an institution or cause. Emotion plays an important role in the decision to make philanthropic gifts—certainly for individual donors, but many also reflect a highly rational analysis that makes giving a form of investing in society and its important institutions. In practice, many people use the terms charity and philanthropy as if they were synonymous or use philanthropy as the broader concept, encompassing all voluntary giving. But the distinction is important, and it is useful for nonprofit organizations to be mindful of how their donors may think about their giving in these different ways.

The past 15 years have seen the rise of new concepts of giving, including **venture philanthropy**, **strategic philanthropy**, **catalytic philanthropy**, and **outcome-oriented philanthropy**. Each has a somewhat different definition—and various authors define them differently—but the common element is encompassed by the latter term. Outcome-oriented philanthropy refers to philanthropy in which "donors seek to achieve clearly defined goals; where they and [the organizations they support] pursue evidence-based strategies for achieving those goals; and where both parties monitor progress toward outcomes and assess their success in achieving them" (Brest, 2012). These are styles of philanthropy that emphasize the impact of gifts, and donors who follow these styles usually intend to bring about change to address social problems—for example, poverty and unemployment. These approaches may fall somewhere between charity and philanthropy as those terms have been defined above. Unlike charity, this type of giving is not intended to alleviate immediate human needs, for example, displacement by a natural disaster. Rather, like philanthropy, it is long term in its perspective and is intended to build organizations that can effectively address social needs. However, gifts from outcome-oriented philanthropists are generally not intended to sustain traditional institutions, such as universities and hospitals, but rather to build the capacity of nonprofit organizations that work for social change and improvement of educational and economic opportunity.

Before proceeding further, it is important also to clarify some other common terms that have somewhat different meanings but are sometimes used interchangeably in everyday conversation. **Fundraising** is an activity undertaken with the goal of eliciting charitable or philanthropic giving. Fundraising is related to philanthropy as teaching is to learning; that is, one is intended to accomplish the other, with no guarantee of success because the response lies within the power of the respondent to determine. In the simplest understanding, fundraising means "asking for a gift," although, as we will soon discuss, it is really a process in which asking for, or **soliciting**, a gift is but one step.

Many organizations have what is known as a development office. Staff who work in that office may be called development officers and have titles such as director of development. If asked what they do, they are likely to respond that they are engaged in fundraising. The two terms, fundraising and development, represent somewhat different concepts, although the difference is not always maintained in common usage. **Development** is a term that originated in the 1920s at Northwestern University (Worth, 1993, p. 6). The university had completed a fundraising **campaign** to build a new campus. When the campaign was completed, the university's leaders determined that fundraising should be an ongoing, organized effort to continually improve and develop the institution, rather than a sporadic activity undertaken now and then to meet a specific need. The university created a new department to manage this ongoing effort and called it the office of "development," meaning "institutional development." Although fundraising and development became interchangeable over time, the latter is properly understood as a more comprehensive approach to the long-term growth of an organization or institution. As I explain in an earlier work,

Fund raising[1] is but one aspect of a complex process involving the institution, its hopes and goals, and the aspirations of its benefactors. Fund raising is episodic; development is continuous. Fund raising is focused on a particular objective or set of goals; development is a generic and long-term commitment to the financial and physical growth of the institution. Successful fund raising requires a specific set of interpersonal and communication skills; development requires a broader understanding of the institution and its mission as well as patience, judgment, and sensitivity in building relationships over the long haul. A "fund raiser" is an individual skillful in soliciting gifts; a "development officer" may be a fund raiser, but he or she is also a strategist and manager of the entire development process. (Worth, 1993, pp. 7–8)

By the mid-1970s, however, the terms fundraising and development had become so interchangeable in use that when the Council for Advancement and Support of Education (CASE) was established in 1974 it adopted the new term **institutional advancement** to describe the activities performed by its members. Institutional advancement, or just **advancement**, encompasses not only fundraising or development but also the related activities of communications, marketing, and other programs for constituent relations. In other words, institutional advancement has a meaning similar to the original concept of development—a long-term and broad-based program to build an organization or institution. In the decades since CASE's founding, "advancement" has been widely adopted by colleges and universities and also has gained currency in nonprofit organizations more broadly. Ironically, it also has come to be used synonymously with fundraising by many people. It is not uncommon to meet people who work in the "advancement office," whose titles include "development" and, if asked what they do will respond, "fundraising."

Motivations for Giving

The question of what motivates donors is of obvious practical interest to nonprofit managers in determining which of their needs may be met through philanthropy and in designing their fundraising programs. Donor motivation is also a topic that has generated a substantial body of research. Let's look at motivation from the perspective of the three principal sources of giving—corporations, foundations, and individuals. Although they are the largest source of gifts, we discuss individuals last because their motivation is the most complex.

Understanding Corporate Philanthropy

Corporations make philanthropic gifts both directly and through foundations that some have established as separate nonprofit entities. Using a foundation offers advantages over direct giving by the corporation, including the ability to add resources to the foundation in highly profitable years and then sustain a relatively even level of giving in years when the business may not be as profitable. Corporations make cash gifts and also gifts of products, known as **gifts-in-kind**. Corporations also support nonprofits through a variety of partnerships, which, as the term implies, offer benefits to both the nonprofit and the business. These partnerships are sometimes complex and represent a growing component of nonprofit revenue. Although they provide financial benefit to many nonprofit organizations, they are not "philanthropy," since the company expects a financial return as well as a benefit to the nonprofit partner. Some types of nonprofit–corporate partnerships are discussed in Chapter 14 because the revenue they produce is earned income to the nonprofit.

Corporate philanthropy is a relatively recent phenomenon. Indeed, prior to the case of *A. P. Smith Mfg. Co. v. Barlow* in 1953, the courts imposed restrictions on corporate giving that did not directly benefit the interests of shareholders or employees of the firm. This landmark case opened the door to the concept of **enlightened self-interest**, that is, the idea that companies could make gifts that might not have a direct or immediate benefit to the bottom line, but that would generally help maintain a healthy society in which to do business.

Corporate giving generally increased during the decades of the 1960s, 1970s, and 1980s, and its purposes often reflected the interests and affiliations of the senior executives and directors of the company. However, during the 1980s and with increasing momentum in the 1990s and 2000s, corporate giving became professionalized. Many companies created committees to make decisions about where to direct the corporation's giving or created separate foundations to undertake philanthropy in the company's name.

Since the mid-1980s, corporate giving has increasingly reflected an approach known as strategic philanthropy—that is, giving according to a plan that relates the corporation's philanthropy to its overall strategic and business goals. Giving is viewed as an investment and is subject to evaluation based on how much return it produces—the extent to which it enhances the corporation's competitiveness. For example, a corporation might target its giving in communities where it plans to develop new facilities or to specific groups of people who are likely to be customers of its products. The various nonprofit–corporate partnerships, discussed in Chapter 14, have evolved from the strategic philanthropy approach. Today, the line between corporate philanthropy and marketing has become blurred, as has the line between fundraising and negotiating business relationships. Indeed, in 2004, the **Association of Fundraising Professionals** (AFP) thought it necessary to amend its code of professional ethics, which had long required that fundraisers not accept compensation based on a percentage of gifts, to include a similar prohibition with regard to the solicitation of corporate partnership arrangements (Hall, 2005).

To understand the motivation for corporate giving, a nonprofit needs to understand the company's business plans and goals on which its program of philanthropy is likely to be based. This is not to imply that corporations give in a way that is detrimental to the interests of nonprofits or society or that their motivations should be viewed as insidious. Many companies have principles of social responsibility to which they faithfully adhere and which include giving. Nevertheless, the realities do suggest that nonprofits begin their search for corporate dollars not in terms of their own needs but rather with a view to how there can be a mutual benefit to the nonprofit's welfare and the interests of the corporation from which it seeks support.

Foundation Giving

It is not difficult to understand the motivations for giving by foundations. Very simply, that is what they exist to do; indeed, it is what they are *required* to do as a condition of their tax-exempt status. Foundations are required to expend a minimum of an amount equivalent to 5 percent of the value of their invested assets each year. Those expenditures can be for grants or for operating expenses of the foundation, although there are some limitations on the operating expenses that can be counted within the 5 percent.

Foundations are created by corporations, individuals, or families and their activities generally reflect the interests of the founders. **Family foundations** are a type of independent foundation in which the board is dominated by members of the donors' family. They often evolve as they grow, expanding their boards beyond family members, employing professional staff, and developing formal programs and guidelines that make explicit their interests and priorities. Many foundations have geographic and other restrictions on their giving and have well-defined areas of interest and grant programs through which they provide support. Many provide guidelines on their websites that identify their priorities and any limitations on their grant making. It is fruitless for an organization to approach a foundation for support if it does not operate programs related to the organization's activities or has policies and priorities that exclude the organization from consideration. Because foundations are rational donors, obtaining foundation support often requires preparation of a written proposal. The art of

Box 13.1 Components of a Typical Proposal

- Executive summary

- Statement of need

- Project description

- Methods

- Staffing/Administration

- Evaluation

- Sustainability

- Budget

- Organizational information

- Conclusion

- Appendices and supporting materials

Source: Adapted from Grantspace: A service of the Foundation Center (http://grantspace.org/training/self-paced-elearning/proposal-writing-short-course#components).

doing so is often called grant writing, although the seeker is indeed writing a proposal, not a grant—the grant is made by the foundation, and if the grant is "written," the writing would be done by a foundation official. Proposal writing thus is a more accurate description of what a nonprofit organization or a member of its staff does. This text does not go into detail on the techniques of proposal writing, but many good guides are available, and organizations such as AFP and the Foundation Center offer training on the topic. Box 13.1 provides an outline of a typical foundation proposal, although each should be tailored to the guidelines and requirements of the specific foundation to which the proposal is being directed.

Other types of foundations include operating foundations that support their own programs and generally do not make grants to other organizations. In addition, as discussed earlier in this book, some public charities use the term foundation in their names, although they both raise money and distribute it, usually to a single organization or a defined community. Operating foundations usually are not good fundraising prospects for other nonprofits, nor are most foundations that are public charities, although some community foundations have discretionary funds that may be available to nonprofit organizations in their areas.

Motivations of Individual Donors

The motivations of individual donors are more complex and less calculated than those of corporations or foundations. They involve such fundamental matters as emotions, values, and psychological needs.

Individual donors have been the focus of a substantial number of research studies. In a 2011 review, René Bekkers and Pamala Wiepking provide a comprehensive overview of the academic research on the topic to that time. Most studies have examined characteristics that distinguish donors from non-donors and have identified statistical relationships between giving and certain characteristics, for example, age, gender, income level, and geographic location. They explain *who* gives, but not *why*. Fewer have explored the more complex question of donor motivation.

Traditionally, the literature has been divided between those who attribute giving to altruism—those who say that individuals are driven by their nature to help others and improve the human condition—and those who say that individuals give to obtain some benefit for themselves, perhaps recognition, social position or control, or just warm feelings. One important influence on individual donors is social relationships. While theories about social influences on giving apply to traditional fundraising strategies, they also can be observed at work in more contemporary strategies. Think about peer-to-peer fundraising that occurs on social media. The desire to be part of a group and to demonstrate support for a friend's efforts motivates others to give, perhaps even to causes that are not a priority for them personally (Worth, 2016). Paton (2007) argues that there may be a continuum of motivation from pure altruism to pure self-interest, as depicted in Figure 13.1.

A 1994 study by Russ Prince and Karen File identified seven motivational types that some fundraising practitioners find to be intuitively attractive. According to these authors, the largest group of donors (26 percent) is made up of "communitarians," motivated by the belief that giving makes good sense in terms of a better community for their businesses and lives. Another 21 percent are the "devout," who give because of their religious beliefs. The third-largest group is the 15 percent that Prince and File call "investors." These are donors who are particularly concerned with the tax and estate benefits of giving and will be interested to know exactly what result will be accomplished with their support. "Socialites," 10.8 percent of donors, give because it provides opportunities for social interactions; they are often people who will attend charity events. The "altruists," the selfless donors who may give without any desire for recognition, comprise another 9 percent. "Repayers," who give based on gratitude for benefits they have received, make up 10.2 percent. The final category, the "dynasts," are people who give because it is a family tradition; they constitute another 8 percent of donors (Prince & File, pp. 14–16). Different types of donors gravitate toward various nonprofit subsectors; for example, the devout tend to support religion, the socialites give to arts organizations, and repayers often direct their support to universities and hospitals that may have influenced their own or their family members' lives.

In the early 2000s, Paul Schervish and John Havens of the Social Welfare Research Institute at Boston College studied social-psychological factors influencing the giving of wealthy individuals and identified several "dispositions" or "inclinations" that motivate individuals to engage in significant philanthropy. These inclinations include hyperagency, the ability to make history and affect the conditions under which people live; identification, the unity of self-regard and regard for others; and consideration of income and estate tax benefits. The authors deemphasize the impact of tax incentives, arguing that their data suggest that as wealth increases, individuals gain a preference for leaving their estates to charity rather than to heirs. They speculate that removal of estate taxes thus would result in more money becoming available for bequests to nonprofit organizations (Schervish & Havens, 2001).

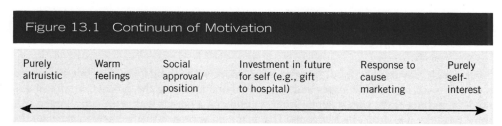

Figure 13.1 Continuum of Motivation

| Purely altruistic | Warm feelings | Social approval/ position | Investment in future for self (e.g., gift to hospital) | Response to cause marketing | Purely self-interest |

Source: Based on Paton, R. (2007). Fundraising as marketing: Half a truth is better than nothing. In J. Mordaunt & R. Paton (Eds.), *Thoughtful fundraising: Concepts, issues, and perspectives* (pp. 29–37). New York, NY: Routledge.

The influence of tax incentives on giving is controversial. In self-reports by donors, the importance of the charitable deduction is often minimized. Research sometimes tells a different story. Based on a meta-analysis of studies over 40 years, John Peloza and Piers Steel (2005) acknowledge a lack of consensus, but conclude that "changes in tax deductibility indeed appear to have a marked effect on charitable giving" (p. 269). Some studies addressing this topic may be flawed because they ask people to say what they would do under certain hypothetical circumstances rather than analyzing data reflecting actual past behavior.

The mathematics of giving and taxes suggests that tax rates may influence the amount that individuals are able to give, regardless of what their desire to give might be. For example, assume that an individual in a 35 percent income tax bracket makes a gift of $1,000 that is tax deductible. Because of the deduction, the donor's income is reduced by $1,000, which reduces his or her income tax bill by $350 below what it would otherwise have been (35 percent of $1,000). That makes the out-of-pocket or actual cost of the $1,000 gift $650, since there is a tax savings of $350. Now, assume that the donor's tax rate has been reduced to 10 percent. The $1,000 gift now saves $100 in taxes, making its **out-of-pocket cost** $900. Although it may seem counterintuitive, a lower tax rate increases the cost of a gift. Depending on donors' overall financial position, this could have the effect of making it more difficult for them to give as much as they otherwise might have been able to, regardless of how highly motivated they might be to give.

The question of how tax policy affects charitable giving became particularly relevant following passage of the Tax Cuts and Jobs Act of 2017, applying to federal income taxes for 2018 and subsequent years. This law increased the amount of the standard deduction, resulting in fewer people who would itemize their deductions at all, including charitable gifts. In addition, the law reduced tax rates. As the hypothetical example demonstrates, this would have the effect of actually increasing the out-of-pocket cost of gifts for some taxpayers. The 2017 act also increased the number of estates that would be exempt from the federal estate tax. While some scholars argue that this will make more money available for charitable bequests, others argue that it may provide less incentive to make a bequest, since it raises the cost of giving (Carrns, 2017).

The preponderance of research suggests that the motivations of most individual donors are mixed, including some combination of altruism and self-interest, and that tax policies have an impact on the amount that individuals are able to give, whether during their lifetimes or through their estates on their death. Both topics are likely to remain controversial and the focus of future research.

With the increasing diversity of the American population, a number of studies in recent years have examined the particular giving traditions and patterns of various groups, including women, African Americans, Hispanics/Latinos, and members of the LGBTQ community. The topic is of increasing interest to many nonprofits, as greater wealth is being accumulated by women and members of minority groups. Students will find additional reading on this topic suggested at the end of this chapter.

The Fundraising Process

Some people may think of fundraising as synonymous with asking for money, but it is indeed a process with identifiable stages and steps. Without following the process, fundraising is random and not really very different from standing on a corner with a tin cup, hoping that some passerby will drop in a few coins. That is not an approach that is likely to generate the substantial and continuing support needed to sustain an organization.

The fundraising process is depicted in Figure 13.2 and includes six basic steps. Once an organization has (1) identified its priorities for financial support and developed a case to

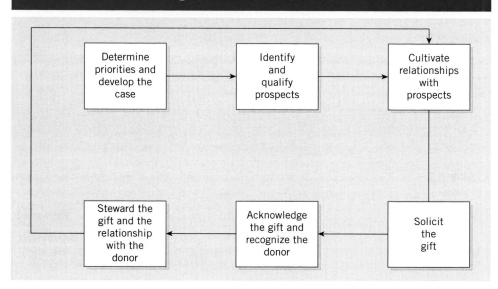

Figure 13.2 Fundraising Process

justify its goals, it must (2) identify the prospects most likely to give. (3) A process of cultivation develops a relationship between the organization and the prospect and, at the appropriate point in the relationship, (4) the prospect is asked (solicited) for a gift. (5) The gift is acknowledged and the donor is recognized. (6) The organization then works to properly steward the gift, keeping the donor engaged and informed of what it has accomplished with the support provided. The process is usually described as a cycle because effective fundraising programs seek to develop a base of donors who continue to give on a regular basis. **Stewardship** is really part of the process of continued cultivation of donors who may provide additional, and it is hoped increased, support in the future. Let's walk through each step in the process in greater detail.

Identifying Priorities and Developing the Case

Fundraising without a purpose is unlikely to elicit support. As Thomas Broce (1986) writes in his classic book, "Donors give gifts to meet objectives, not simply to give money away" (p. 19). This reality requires that an organization base its fundraising on identified priority needs related to achievement of its mission and rooted in a plan for its future growth and improvement. Strategic planning is often the first step in setting the organization's vision and goals for the future, which then can be translated into specific fundraising objectives with a rationale for why the support will enhance its ability to achieve its social mission.

The organization must develop a case for support, or a rationale for giving, that goes beyond its own needs and links its goals to broader social and human purposes. An organization's leaders may be convinced of its worthiness and the importance of its financial needs, but in a competitive philanthropic marketplace, they must make the case for how support for its purposes will bring a greater benefit than a gift to another organization or cause. To illustrate this point, Box 13.2 presents summaries of two arguments, or cases, for the support of the (fictional) Siwash College. Case #1 is based entirely on what its faculty and students perceive to be important to them and on the institution's self-interest. The needs may be real, but this statement is unlikely to inspire many donors to sacrifice in order to address them. In contrast, Case #2 explains Siwash's need for philanthropy in relation

Siwash College Case #1

Our classrooms are crowded, and we have inadequate office space for the faculty. Colleges are competing for the best students with offers of scholarship support. The college's enrollment has increased in the past decade, but we now have fallen behind our competitors in the quality of our facilities and the amount of financial aid that we can provide. We are losing many of the best students to other institutions. For this reason, we are seeking $10 million in funds for new campus construction and scholarships that we will offer to the students from our region who have the highest SAT (Scholastic Aptitude Test) scores.

Siwash College Case #2

The United States always has been a nation of economic opportunity. Today, as we face great challenges from global economic competition, the talents of too many young men and women are undeveloped because they lack the financial means to attend college. College tuition has risen dramatically, and financial aid has not kept pace. This is unjust and threatens America's future economic prosperity. Educational opportunity always has been fundamental to the mission and values of Siwash College. The board of trustees has established a plan to maintain our tradition by expanding enrollment and providing additional scholarship support for young men and women of our region. To that end, we seek $10 million in support to expand our facilities and increase scholarship support to promising and worthy students.

to social justice and economic prosperity, helping place its needs in a broader context and appealing to the values and emotions of potential donors.

The **case for support** should provide the reason the organization seeks support, derived from its mission and values—it is the answer to the questions, "Why should I give to this organization?" and "Why is this cause more important than others that also ask for my support?" It is often expressed in a **case statement**, a document that may include a comprehensive discussion of the organization's fundraising objectives and the justification for each. Case statements may be developed to provide a resource within the organization, an **internal case statement**, or as a printed or electronic document for use in communicating with donor prospects, an **external case statement**. It is also common to produce a video, which expresses the case statement in a visual format. It is important not to confuse the product known as the case statement with the *idea* of the case. An organization that rushes to produce a glossy brochure or website without careful thought about the essence of its case is unlikely to successfully address the motivations of donors, whether corporations, foundations, or individuals.

Identifying and Qualifying Prospects

Just as an individual seeking a marriage partner likely would not do well by texting people at random or by proposing to strangers on the street, an organization seeking gift support needs to focus on prospects who offer a better-than-average chance of giving. Otherwise, its time and fundraising resources will be allocated inefficiently and ineffectively. The **identification of prospects** begins by limiting the search to those who have the financial ability or capacity to give. Obviously, an individual or company in bankruptcy or a foundation that has already allocated all its resources would not be worthy of further attention. They might have a keen interest in the nonprofit, but their financial inability would preclude considering them as prospects. However, making a list of successful companies and wealthy individuals still does not provide likely prospects for a particular nonprofit; it would be a large list and include many who are remote or already deeply committed to other causes. It would be like making a list of marriage prospects that included every single person in the world; they might have the ability to consider marriage, but it would still be a fruitless task to send proposals to all of them. The list would need to be culled by some additional criteria. For example, it might help to limit the search to people with whom the marriage seeker already has some connection— maybe schoolmates, individuals who attend the same church, or friends of friends. And, being single does not automatically imply a desire to be married, so it would be wise to limit the list of prospects to those who may have indicated some interest in getting married. (It is instructive to observe that online dating sites do provide tools for screening a large pool of people in order to identify those with the ability and desire to marry and who have some interests in common with the searcher—the matching is not random.)

Like marriage prospects, the most likely prospects for charitable gifts will be those who have not only the ability to give but also some linkage to and interest in the organization or the area of activity in which it is engaged (Seiler, 2016, p. 32). A **prospect** is described as "qualified" only when both financial capacity and potential interest have been determined. Identifying individuals, foundations, and corporations who are prospects is a task often performed by professionals engaged in **prospect research**, a specialty increasingly in demand by nonprofit organizations with sophisticated fundraising programs. Prospect researchers have a variety of tools and techniques, including a growing array of electronic databases, to help narrow the list to those with the greatest likelihood of making a gift to their organizations. Financial ability may be easily determined for foundations, on which information is readily available in published sources. Corporations may be somewhat less easily assessed, but some indication of ability to give may be assumed from revenue and profits. Individuals present more of a challenge. Although public information can help determine levels of income and wealth—for example, real estate values—some wealth will be less visible.

Linkage to the organization may occur in a variety of ways. Volunteers, graduates, and former patients or their families have obvious connections to the organizations that have served them. Other types of nonprofits may need to build their network of prospects in a pattern similar to concentric circles, beginning with those who are already part of the organization's inner circle of friends and donors, then moving outward to less-connected members of the community. The organization's governing board is its principal link to the outside world and, absent an easily identifiable constituency of potential donors with direct linkage, board members' efforts in identifying and engaging prospects among their own business and social contacts may be important.

Interest may be relatively easy to determine for a foundation, if it provides a clear statement of its priorities. Some corporations that have formal giving programs offer similar clarity about their interests, while in other cases, interest may be presumed because the company's business activities bear a close relationship to the work of the nonprofit. For example, a home builder or a mortgage lender may have an interest in the issues of homelessness and affordable housing; similarly, companies that manufacture products for use by women are often among the most prominent contributors to nonprofits that address women's issues or diseases. For individual prospects, interest may be revealed by past gifts to the organization or perhaps gifts to another organization addressing similar issues or needs, but often an individual's interest can be determined with confidence only through personal contact and discussion.

Cultivating Prospects

To invoke again the metaphor of courtship, most people would not consider proposing marriage on the first date. The odds of such a proposal gaining a positive response are increased if some time and effort have been devoted to cultivating a relationship, perhaps involving smaller steps such as having dinner and going to the movies. A nonprofit cultivating a prospective donor likewise will increase the chances of gaining support if it devotes some time and attention to cultivating a relationship before moving to solicit a gift. The larger the amount of the gift to be solicited, the greater the investment that will need to be made in cultivating the relationship in advance of asking.

In fundraising for small gifts, solicitation may not require significant **cultivation**. For example, very little cultivation precedes broad-based solicitations by mail, phone, or the Internet. However, fundraising for a major gift involves developing and executing a series of planned initiatives expected to move an individual toward a closer relationship with the organization, leading to support. Major-gift fundraisers manage and track such activity through what are known as moves management systems.

Soliciting the Gift

Nonprofit fundraisers have an array of techniques available for soliciting gifts, and a full discussion is beyond the scope of this chapter. Box 13.3 provides a summary of some commonly used methods and the advantages and disadvantages of each. In general, the more personal the contact, the more effective it is. Personal solicitations and mail or e-mail that include a message tailored to the individual being asked are more effective than communications that are very impersonal, such as broad-based mailings. On the other hand, direct mail remains a popular method of soliciting gifts, especially from older donors, and provides something tangible—a letter and/or a brochure—that an individual may retain and reread sometime after its receipt. This may even be an advantage over e-mail, which many people skim and delete.

The selection of methods employed by a nonprofit depends on several considerations. First, the method used must be appropriate to the level and type of support that the organization needs. Soliciting by direct mail, by phone, or through e-mail may be appropriate to secure a large number of relatively small gifts on a recurring basis to support the current operating budget. Major gifts to address capital or endowment needs will require personal contact and time for a full discussion of the organization's plans and the purpose that will be achieved through the gift. If the gift being requested is for the organization's endowment, the personal contact with the prospective donor may need to be prolonged, in order to fully explore the individual's desires about his or her legacy to society beyond his or her lifetime. The use of social media and crowdfunding may be effective in raising funds for one-time projects that generate excitement, but may not lead to the ongoing support on which many organizations rely. Most gifts made in response to a challenge from friends or celebrities are likely to be relatively modest, not major gifts.

A second, related consideration would be the costs and benefits of the method selected. Personal solicitation, by fundraising staff or volunteers, is generally more effective than solicitation by phone, mail, or e-mail, but it may also require a substantial commitment of time by the CEO, a development officer, and perhaps a volunteer; it may also involve costs for travel. Personal visits are to be reserved for the most promising prospects for the largest gifts. Personalized letters are generally more effective than impersonal, "Dear Friend" letters, but they also require more labor or more sophisticated technology to produce. The expected better returns always need to be balanced against the costs of a particular method. Third, an organization needs to consider what resources are available to it at particular points in its organizational life cycle. For example, a nonprofit that has little visibility, no clear donor constituency, and a fundraising program that is just beginning, may find special events to be a useful method for engaging new people, increasing its visibility in the community, and raising some funds. Fundraising or benefit events are not an especially effective way of raising money, and the costs of producing them may in fact consume much or all of the gross

Box 13.3 Common Solicitation Methods: Advantages and Disadvantages

Method	Advantages	Disadvantages
Personal solicitation	• Focused attention of prospect • Includes nonverbal cues • Builds relationship	• Expensive • Low volume
Direct mail	• Inexpensive • Creates a visual image • Long life (may be kept and read again later) • Can communicate complex message	• Easily ignored, lost in clutter • Requires donor initiative to make gift • Limited ability to personalize
Telemarketing	• Two-way communication • Can negotiate gift • Can tailor message to individual • Immediate gift (credit/debit card)	• More expensive than mail • Barriers (caller ID, mobile phones) • Intrusive
Events	• Visibility/involvement • May provide first contact with potential new donors	• Not usually cost-effective (hidden costs) • Sometimes the event makes no connection to the cause
E-mail	• Inexpensive • Can personalize/segment message • Interactive/relationship building • Immediate gift	• E-mail list maintenance • Barriers (e.g., spam filters, overload)
Crowdfunding	• Inexpensive • Generates interest • Mobilizes networks	• More useful for one-time projects rather than ongoing support • Requires exciting cause that will go viral
Text	• Inexpensive • Immediate response	• Limited content • Intrusive • Barriers to follow up with donor

revenues. However, if they can be used as a strategy for developing a new group of interested friends who may later be solicited for gifts through more effective methods, including mail, phone, and personal contact, then they may play a useful role in a comprehensive fundraising strategy.

Fourth, the nonprofit organization should adopt the solicitation method that is most likely to reach its target audience. For example, direct mail is effective with older donors, who have time to read letters, may be uncomfortable with providing credit card information on the telephone or over the Internet, and may not use other forms of electronic payment, such as PayPal. Events or the Internet may be a better way if the organization is hoping to reach younger donors, who may not respond to direct mail.

Again, the organization's position in its life cycle is important to consider and will determine the type of philanthropy that can be attracted. For example, a young organization, perhaps with a somewhat uncertain future, would be unlikely to attract significant bequests for its endowment. Many people would question whether it would use such gifts effectively or whether it provides a lasting purpose for their philanthropy. However, a well-established nonprofit that continues to raise funds through events and e-mail and does not solicit larger gifts is not maximizing its long-term revenue potential. In other words, the methods used to raise funds, and the purpose for which they are raised, must match the realities of an organization's financial needs and philanthropic market—or, as architects say, form should follow function.

E-mail, Portals, Social Media, and Social Networking

Direct mail remains a primary source of gifts and of new donors, but giving online is growing at a rapid pace, having increased by 7.9 percent in 2016 alone (Blackbaud Institute for Philanthropic Impact, 2016, p. 4). The most common method of online solicitation is e-mail. The purpose of the e-mail is to drive donors to the organization's donation page. This page may be maintained by the organization itself or it may be operated by an outside vendor, such as Network for Good (www.networkforgood.org), which provides back-office support for processing online gifts. Soliciting gifts through e-mail follows many principles that are similar to those for direct mail. It starts with list development and requires continuing attention to list maintenance. As in direct mail, e-mail lists can be segmented to deliver personalized messages and costs can be very low. However, as with all methods, there are disadvantages, as well, including the use of spam filters and the ease with which prospective donors can delete a message from their crowded in-box without opening it. Many organizations make effective use of e-mail to stay in touch with current and past donors and even to discuss or negotiate the terms of a major gift, but such gifts will generally require some other form of contact, usually in person (Network for Good, 2014).

A growing number of nonprofit organizations are using social media as a tool for communicating, building a constituency, and advocating a cause (as discussed in Chapter 11). Some are also benefitting from fundraising events organized through social networks and the capabilities of social media platforms are expanding, suggesting that they are likely to become more important tools for fundraising in the future. Social networks are especially useful in peer-to-peer fundraising, in which friends invite friends to participate in such activities as walks and runs. As Julie Dixon and Denise Keyes (2013) emphasize, social networks enable individuals to become advocates, or "cause champions" for organizations and causes, bringing value beyond their own giving. Again, fundraising through social media is likely to grow as the capabilities of those platforms continue to evolve.

Crowdfunding sites have received increasing attention. They include sites such as Kickstarter (www.kickstarter.com), which enables individuals to support creative projects, and Donors Choose (donorschoose.org), through which individuals can support specific needs of classroom teachers. Other well-known sites include CauseVox (www.causevox.com),

Fundly (fundly.com), Razoo (www.razoo.com), and indiegogo (www.indiegogo.com). All have unique features. These sites have proven effective in raising funds for projects, but may be less useful for developing ongoing support. For example, a campaign on indiegogo in 2012 raised almost $1.4 million to build a museum in honor of electricity pioneer Nikola Tesla (Bray, 2013, p. 104). In 2015, the Smithsonian Institution launched a crowdfunding campaign to preserve the space suit worn by Neil Armstrong on the moon. It reached its goal of $500,000 within five days and extended the campaign to raise an additional $200,000 to preserve the suit worn by Alan Shepard, the first American in space (McGlone, 2017).

In order to be successful, a crowdfunding appeal needs to go viral. That may only occur if it is something especially exciting or urgent. If the organization intends to raise the funds from its established constituency, then other strategies may be more effective in reaching them. According to Ilona Bray (2013, pp. 104–105), crowdfunding may be an effective strategy only under specific circumstances, including the following:

- [The organization] has a particular, tangible goal in mind, such as a new piece of equipment; a trip to a project site; medical care for an individual; production of a film; or a time-delineated concept around which to fundraise, such as a matching grant.

- [The organization] can confidently predict that the goal is sufficiently exciting, moving, or fun that [its] existing supporters and social media contacts will tell their friends about it and they, despite knowing little to nothing about [the] organization, will be moved to pitch in.

- [The organization] has the skills to present the idea in an attractive way, preferably complete with photos, graphics, and videos.

Some nonprofits also have used text messaging as a method for soliciting and receiving gifts. For example, texting was a significant component of giving to the Red Cross following the earthquake in Haiti in 2010. Readers interested in knowing more about this method may wish to review the standards for mobile giving developed by the Mobile Giving Foundation, which is sponsored by several telecommunications providers (http://www.mobilegiving.org/about/).

The technology of fundraising is in transition. It seems likely that an increasing proportion of dollars will come through online and mobile giving in the years ahead, but the traditional methods of direct mail and phone calls remain important; indeed, these methods remain the backbone of fundraising for many organizations. The continuing effectiveness of direct mail, along with the growing importance of online giving, suggests that nonprofit organizations need to pursue a multichannel strategy, combining new technologies with traditional methods. For some, the costs of doing so may be daunting, but there may be little choice except to invest in growing new technologies while also maintaining traditional programs in order to meet current fundraising goals. Remember, however, it is essential that the use of the various channels be integrated and consistent in the messages that are delivered.

Acknowledging and Recognizing Donors

Well-managed development offices acknowledge gifts promptly, and most tailor the acknowledgment to the level of the gift or status of the donor. For example, donors of gifts above a certain level may receive a letter, e-mail, or phone call from the CEO. Others may receive a letter or e-mail from the director of development. Small gifts may be acknowledged only with a preprinted paper or online receipt. Nonprofits are required by law to provide and donors are required to have a formal receipt in order to deduct cash gifts of $250 or more from their taxes. Additional rules apply to the substantiation of the value of gifts-in-kind.

Recognition of donors may include listing their names in an annual report or on the website, including them in special recognition societies according to the level of the gift, and displaying their names on plaques or wall displays. Larger gifts may be recognized through the naming of facilities or endowment funds. While some donors may request anonymity, most appreciate tasteful and appropriate recognition, which itself becomes a part of the process of cultivation for the next gift.

Stewarding the Gift and the Relationship

The stewardship of past donors is an activity that has received more attention in most development offices in recent years. Experience suggests that past donors are the best prospects for future gifts, and it is therefore important to continue building their relationship with the organization after a gift has been made.

The concept of stewardship can have two meanings. The most common usage encompasses the activities that the organization undertakes to keep the donor informed and engaged. These may include sending reports about the impact of the gift and developing events to strengthen donors' involvement and knowledge about the organization's activities. Stewardship is essentially the cultivation of current and past donors with an eye toward future support. The second meaning of stewardship is more substantive, relating to the organization's responsibility to manage the gift according to the donor's intention, that is, to keep faith with the donor. This is especially important with gifts made to endowment, which are invested in perpetuity to produce income supporting current programs. Many organizations have developed regular written reports to endowment donors, informing them of the fund's financial performance as well as the activities undertaken with the income it produces. Some have developed websites where donors can receive updated information on the impact of their gifts; for example, they can read the biographies of students who are receiving scholarships that the donors have funded. Recent legal cases involving claims by donors or their heirs that gifts are not being used as originally intended have caused nonprofit organizations to exercise greater care in documenting the mutual understandings of the donor and the organization in formal, written gift agreements.

Although the previous discussion has mostly involved individual donors, it is important to note that the fundraising process is essentially the same even if the donor is a corporation or a foundation. Corporate and foundation philanthropy may be more professionalized and giving decisions may be made more objectively than they are by individuals, but it is still essential to identify likely prospects based on what is called **linkage, ability, interest (LAI)**; to cultivate the prospect's interest; to solicit the gift in the appropriate manner at the appropriate time; to acknowledge the gift and recognize the donor; and to steward the gift and the relationship with the donor for the long run.

Corporate and foundation giving patterns may change over time as their strategies are redefined. They are less likely than individuals to develop an emotional connection to an organization and become regular, long-term donors. Indeed, while the individuals working in a corporation or a foundation may have personal feelings about the organizations it supports, the corporation or foundation itself is not a living thing capable of such relationships. Corporations and foundations thus support an organization so long as its activities are consistent with their goals—there is inevitably a quid pro quo element to their giving—and many limit their support to specific programs or activities and do not provide unrestricted gifts that can be used to meet general operating expenses, undertake capacity building, or address other organizational goals. Second, corporations and foundations are not mortal. Unlike individuals, they do not consider their giving over the course of an expected lifetime; they do not write wills or plan for the disposition of their estates. Understanding the giving behavior of individuals requires analysis of how they view their philanthropy at various points in their lives and how they develop giving relationships with favored nonprofits over time. Working with corporate and foundation donors requires many of the same principles as working with individuals, but it is also essential to understand the differences discussed here.

Individual Donor Life Cycles

The **fundraising pyramid** is a classic depiction of how individuals are believed to develop their giving relationship with an organization. It is a standard element of fundraising training and has been a part of fundraising theory for many decades. Depicted in Figure 13.3, the pyramid is broader at the base and narrows as the level of gift increases going toward the top, because a smaller number of donors will ascend to each successively higher level. The organization's constituency, that is, its database of prospects, contains the largest number and is thus the widest part of the pyramid. Some, but not all, prospects will provide annual gifts to support current operating needs. Of those who do become regular annual donors, some, but not all, may respond to special needs of the organization by making a **major gift**. The definition of a major gift will vary among organizations, depending on the overall levels of support they receive, but such gifts typically are at least five figures or more and are often pledged to be paid over a period of three to five years. Major gifts often come from the individual's assets rather than current income, and many are paid using securities, real estate, or other marketable assets. Some, but only a few, of those who make major gifts will eventually make a principal gift to the organization. Like major gifts, principal gifts are defined by their size—they are large major gifts. Although definitions vary among organizations and institutions, it is common for gifts of $1 million or more to be identified as principal gifts. In large fundraising programs, relationships with prospects for such gifts are managed by a dedicated principal gifts staff member or team.

David Dunlop, a thoughtful fundraising practitioner with Cornell University for many decades, defined many of the terms used in major gifts fundraising. He identifies three types of gifts that people make, and they generally correspond with the annual, major, and principal gifts depicted in the fundraising pyramid. In Dunlop's (1993) terminology, **regular gifts** are the ones that people make on a recurring basis, usually to support the annual fund. Dunlop's **special gifts** are those that individual donors make to meet some nonrecurring need of the organization, for example, a capital project or perhaps a campaign to increase the organization's endowment assets. They are stretch gifts, meaning that giving them requires some real sacrifice on the part of the donor. Some individuals who make regular gifts and

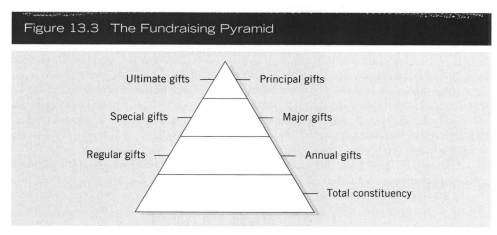

Figure 13.3 The Fundraising Pyramid

- Ultimate gifts — Principal gifts
- Special gifts — Major gifts
- Regular gifts — Annual gifts
- Total constituency

Note: The terms *regular*, *special*, and *ultimate gifts* were introduced by Dunlop (1993).

periodically stretch to make special gifts will develop a lifelong relationship with a nonprofit organization, making it the beneficiary of their **ultimate gift**. In Dunlop's definition, an ultimate gift is not necessarily the individual's last gift, but rather "the largest gift that the person is ultimately capable of making" (p. 98). Some individuals make their ultimate or largest gift while living; others make their ultimate gift in the form of a bequest or other charitable provision that takes effect on their death. It is not unusual for ultimate gifts to be made to endowments, usually to large nonprofits such as universities and museums or to establish or enhance a foundation created by the donor.

Although the fundraising pyramid has been used for a long time to show how individual donors develop their relationships with favored organizations and as an analytical tool to describe the outlines of an organization's donor constituency, some question whether its principles still apply. Many donors today are entrepreneurial donors, and many of them are relatively young individuals who have made their fortunes as business entrepreneurs. They tend to approach giving like investing, preferring to fund organizations that are engaged in cutting-edge approaches rather than traditional programs. They wish to be actively involved in an organization rather than be a passive donor. They may select organizations based on their demonstrated performance rather than on the basis of traditional loyalties. Their first gift may indeed be a major gift if it supports a program of particular interest to them and one that is consistent with their own social values.

To the extent that there is a new generation of philanthropists whose behavior is markedly different from that of previous donors, the traditional fundraising pyramid may have less validity. However, many of the new donors are also relatively young people; what has changed is that wealth is now held by individuals at earlier ages than in the past. Whether their giving behavior will become more traditional as they age is a question to which there is yet no answer. It is also possible that individuals will engage in both traditional and strategic philanthropy, following the patterns suggested by the pyramid for some of their giving but engaging in more investment-like giving as well.

Another criticism of the fundraising pyramid is that it describes a situation most applicable to large nonprofit institutions, such as universities, and that it is less relevant for smaller nonprofits. Colleges and universities have natural lifelong relationships with their graduates, and most have sufficient financial stability that they can patiently nurture relationships leading to ultimate gifts. For many nonprofits in urgent need of increased support to balance current budgets, the distant promise of an ultimate gift may seem unworthy of too much time and effort today. However, as Dunlop (1993) emphasizes, most organizations have at least a few close friends and donors with whom they should be cultivating long-term relationships with the hope that they will eventually produce the level of giving that can be transformative.

Planned Giving

A rapidly growing component of philanthropy includes gifts that are made in connection with individuals' financial or estate planning, known as planned gifts. Many major gifts today do involve the use of sophisticated financial instruments, and **planned giving** has become a major subfield within the fundraising profession. Experienced planned giving officers, or gift planners, are highly sought after by all types of nonprofit organizations. The aging of the U.S. population and the increasing wealth held by older people suggests that this form of giving will grow in importance in coming decades.

As shown in Table 13.1, there are three basic types of planned gifts: **outright planned gifts**, **expectancies**, and **deferred gifts**. Some outright gifts are planned gifts because they involve complex assets, such as stocks or real estate, and may require the assistance of financial experts to complete. An expectancy is a promise that a donor makes to provide a gift to the organization at some future time, generally at death, through a bequest, life insurance, or a retirement plan. Deferred gifts are gifts that the donor makes now, but which are not available

Table 13.1 Common Planned Giving Vehicles

Name	Description	Most Attractive to...
OUTRIGHT GIFTS		
Gift of appreciated property	Individual gives an asset, for example, stock or real estate, which has a value greater than what was paid to acquire it (cost basis).	Individuals who wish to receive an income tax deduction for the full value of the asset and avoid paying a capital gains tax on its sale.
Donor-advised fund	An individual irrevocably transfers assets to a fund, maintained by a community foundation or other charitable entity. The donor (or other designated individual/s) retains the right to recommend recipients of gifts to be made from the fund but cannot direct or require the distributions.	Individuals who wish to earn an immediate income tax deduction for their gifts to the donor-advised fund but to have the funds paid to one or more nonprofit organizations in the future. This may be the case with individuals who have a year in which they receive unusually high income, for example, upon sale of an asset or a business.
Lead trust	An individual places assets in a trust, which is managed by a trustee. The trustee pays income earned by investments of the trust to a nonprofit organization for a specified period of years. At the end of that period, the trust ends and the assets are returned to the donor, the donor's heirs, or to other named beneficiaries.	Individuals who own income-producing assets, do not need the income they produce, and wish to make gifts to a nonprofit organization. There are also potential estate tax savings if the assets are ultimately returned to the donor's heirs.
EXPECTANCIES (TESTAMENTARY GIFTS)		
Bequest	A statement in an individual's will or revocable trust that designates a specific asset, amount, or percentage of the estate to be paid as a gift to a nonprofit organization upon the individual's death.	Individuals who wish to retain control of their assets during their lifetimes and who seek a simple method of making a charitable gift at death.
Retirement plan or IRA	An individual names a nonprofit organization as the beneficiary of assets remaining in a retirement plan or IRA at the individual's death. Alternatively, an individual can directly transfer funds from a retirement fund to a charity.	Individuals who wish to retain access to their retirement funds while living and who seek a simple method of making a charitable gift at death or individuals who wish to make a gift without having to claim the retirement fund withdrawal as income.
Life insurance	A nonprofit organization is named as the owner and beneficiary of a life insurance policy that will pay a benefit to the organization upon the individual's death.	Individuals who can afford premium payments but wish to make a larger gift at death than their assets may permit.

(Continued)

Table 13.1 (Continued)

Name	Description	Most Attractive to...
DEFERRED GIFTS		
Charitable gift annuity	A contract between an individual and a nonprofit organization in which the organization agrees to pay a fixed lifetime income to the individual (or to another designated individual/s) in exchange for the gift. The income payments are secured by the full faith and credit of the organization. Some charitable gift annuities are immediate (the income starts as soon as the gift is made) and others are deferred (the income begins at some designated future date). There are other variations.	Individuals who wish to receive an immediate income tax deduction (for a portion of the gift) and receive a relatively secure but fixed lifetime income. A fixed income may be more attractive to older donors, who are less concerned with the effects of inflation over their remaining lives.
Charitable remainder trust	An individual gives assets to a trust. The trustee manages the trust and pays income to the individual (or to one or more other designated individual/s) for life. Upon the death of the last surviving income recipient, the trustee pays the trust's principal to a designated nonprofit organization. There are two basic types. Charitable remainder annuity trusts pay a fixed income. Charitable remainder unitrusts pay a variable income that is a fixed percentage of the trust's assets each year. Income payments would cease if the trust's assets became depleted. There are other variations.	Individuals who own appreciated assets and wish to avoid or defer capital gains taxes that would be payable if the assets were sold outside of the trust. Individuals who seek an immediate income tax deduction (for a portion of the gift.) The unitrust may be attractive to individuals who want the possibility of increasing income payments over their lifetimes and are willing to accept the risk of an income that may vary from year to year.
Life estate	An individual gives his or her personal residence to a nonprofit organization, retaining the right to continue living there for his or her lifetime.	Individuals who desire to use their homes as an asset to make a gift but also desire to continue living there.

Source: Worth (2016, pp. 218–219).

to the organization until some future time, generally after the death of the donor or some other individual (Regenovich, 2016, pp. 269–281). Table 13.1 provides a brief summary of vehicles available for planned gifts; this chapter discusses only a few of the most common.

One of the simplest forms of a planned gift is a **bequest**, which is merely a statement in an individual's will or living trust dictating that on his or her death, some amount or portion of his or her estate is to be given to a charitable organization. Other planned gifts, for example, those using **charitable remainder trusts** and **charitable gift annuities**, are arrangements that provide for the donor or another beneficiary to receive lifetime income, with the charitable organization not gaining full use of the donated assets until after the death of the donor or the last income recipient. Such gifts provide a tax deduction for some portion of the gift, but not for the full amount, since the donor has a retained life income interest attributable to the non-charitable portion of the payment. In addition to qualifying for income tax deductions, donors may avoid or defer capital gains taxes on appreciated assets used to make a planned gift and, since the donated assets are removed from the donor's estate, there may be an estate tax saving, as well. As in our earlier example, these tax benefits reduce the out-of-pocket cost of the gift, which can make the rate of income received by the donor an attractive feature.

Other planned giving vehicles include lead trusts and life estates. A donor may place an asset in a **lead trust** for a period of years, with the income being paid to the nonprofit organization. At the termination of the trust, the asset is returned to the donor or the donor's heirs. A donor who gives his or her personal residence to a nonprofit organization may retain the right to continue living in the property for the balance of his or her life, an arrangement that is known as a **life estate**. **Donor-advised funds**, maintained by community foundations and other managers of charitable funds, permit individuals to make a gift and earn a tax deduction currently, while reserving the right to make future recommendations on how the funds are to be distributed. It is important to recognize, however, that the donor does not have the right to direct gifts and can only make recommendations to the trustee of the fund.

Planned giving could be affected by changes in the federal estate tax enacted by the Tax Cuts and Jobs Act of 2017. Assets that a donor gives during life or at death are removed from the individual's estate, and thus, there is a tax saving, similar to the saving produced by the income tax deduction for gifts, as discussed above. However, the 2017 law significantly increased the amount of an estate that is exempt from the federal estate tax and all but wealthy individuals will never have to consider it in their financial or charitable planning. Some states do have inheritance taxes, which also may be part of the calculus for some donors. The law regarding donor-advised funds is a topic of recurring debate and future changes could affect the attractiveness of these vehicles to some donors. Students are encouraged to check with websites such as Independent Sector (www.independentsector.org) or AFP (www.afpnet.org) for up-to-date information on the law.

Planned giving is a complex topic, and a full discussion is beyond the scope of this text, but additional reading is recommended at the end of this chapter for those who wish to pursue a more in-depth understanding. The **National Association of Charitable Gift Planners** (https://charitablegiftplanners.org) is a professional organization of individuals who work in the planned giving field and offers important education and materials. There are also websites that provide cases, resources, and tools for planned giving professionals and some are listed at the conclusion of this chapter.

Campaigns

Fundraising campaigns have been a part of the nonprofit landscape since the early years of the 20th century, when the campaign method was developed by fundraisers for the YMCA. The model was later adopted by higher education institutions and subsequently by most other nonprofit organizations. Historically, campaigns were known as capital campaigns and were usually undertaken specifically to construct new physical facilities. Over the past three decades, however, many campaigns have become comprehensive, including within their goals not only funds for facilities but also endowment, operating funds, and support for programs. At any given time in most communities today, there will be highly publicized campaigns underway by multiple organizations, seeking funds for all these purposes. The dollar goals are often substantial and to be achieved typically in five to eight years.

What distinguishes a campaign from just ordinary fundraising? First, a campaign is intensive, ranking among the highest priorities of the organization and usually commanding a significant amount of time and energy from the CEO, board members, fundraising staff, and others. This intensity is created by two essential characteristics of a campaign—an announced dollar goal and a deadline. A campaign has defined objectives, that is, specific purposes for which the funds are being raised that are spelled out in campaign literature. The solicitation of gifts to a campaign follows the principle of sequential fundraising, in which prospects are solicited in a planned sequence beginning with those closest to the organization and the most promising prospects, proceeding later to those who are less related or who are deemed to have less financial potential. This process helps raise the sights of prospective donors by offering the example of those who have already made impressive financial commitments. Finally, solicitations in a campaign request a specific amount that has been deemed realistic for the particular donor. Donors are rated according to their capacity to give and are solicited, in the appropriate order, for a gift at that level. Without meeting these essential conditions, a fundraising effort is not really a campaign. Thus, fundraising that aims to raise "as much as possible" or "as soon as possible" is, by definition, not a campaign, because it does not proceed against a specific goal that it intends to reach within a defined period of time. Solicitations that ask people to give as much as they can represent a collection, but not a campaign, which seeks specific gifts from donors deemed capable of making them (Worth, 2017b).

Campaigns proceed in phases, as depicted in Figure 13.4. They are rooted in the organization's strategic planning, which defines goals and directions and financial needs. Planning for a campaign itself is a process that may encompass months or years and includes the identification of prospects, enlistment of volunteer leaders, and the hiring of fundraising staff. In order to maximize the solicitation of significant early gifts, and their impact on the sights of donors in later phases, a campaign is not announced to the public until a significant portion of its total goal has been raised. These early gifts comprise the campaign's **nucleus fund** and are secured during what is known as the campaign's quiet period or **quiet phase** (sometimes called the silent phase). A formal **kickoff** of the campaign usually includes announcement of the overall goal, celebration of the amount already raised toward it as part of the nucleus fund, and recognition of nucleus fund donors. The kickoff is intended to establish momentum, generate good feelings, demonstrate that the campaign is likely to be successful, and inspire prospects who have not yet given to set their sights in relationship to what the nucleus fund donors already have done.

Following the kickoff, the campaign is in its public phase. Efforts to bring visibility to the campaign and its goals often become a significant component of the organization's communication efforts for the duration of the campaign. Planning for today's campaigns

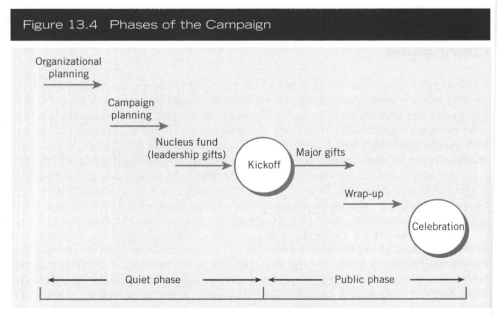

Figure 13.4 Phases of the Campaign

Source: Worth (2017b, p. 24).

includes marketing and communication goals that are nearly as important to the organization as the financial goals addressed by the campaign. They have become tools for positioning organizations and, indeed, some campaign goals, especially in higher education, are often set at least in part to make a statement about the institution's relative rank and prestige, rather than reflecting exclusively its considered financial needs.

An important tool in planning and managing a campaign is the **gift chart (gift standards chart)**, although the format might more accurately be called a table and some authors use that term. An example, based on a campaign goal of $250 million, is provided in Table 13.2. The chart reflects the **proportionate giving** necessary to achieve the campaign's overall goal, starting with a lead gift that is at least 10 percent of the goal, and then doubling the number of gifts needed at each successively lower dollar level. The ratios used to construct the table have been developed through experience in many campaigns over the past century and often reflect the pattern of giving to a campaign when studied retrospectively. In recent years, however, many campaigns have diverged from these historic patterns, with an increasingly large percentage of the total coming from a decreasing number of very large gifts at the top of the chart—in other words, from fewer major donors but larger gifts. That change reflects the increasing concentration of wealth in the United States and other economic and demographic changes. Table 13.2 depicts traditional ratios and would need to be adapted to the specific circumstances of a planned campaign.

The gift-range chart is useful in projecting how many gifts will be needed to obtain a specified goal. Using the industry standard, that about 3 to 5 prospects are required to produce every closed gift, it also provides a way to assess if the organization has developed a donor constituency sufficient to support a proposed campaign goal. It may also be useful in demonstrating to the early donors, often including board members, why their gifts need to be exceptional, in order to meet the requirements at the upper ranges of the chart and set the standard for others who ultimately will be asked to support the campaign.

Table 13.2 Traditional Gift Range Chart for Campaign With Goal of $250 Million

Gift Range (in $)	Number of Gifts Required	Number of Prospects Required	Total of Gifts in This Range (in $)	Cumulative Total (in $)	Cumulative Percentage of Goal
25,000,000	1	4	25,000,000	25,000,000	10
10,000,000	3	12	30,000,000	55,000,000	22
5,000,000	6	24	30,000,000	85,000,000	34
2,500,000	12	48	30,000,000	115,000,000	46
1,000,000	27	108	27,000,000	142,000,000	57
500,000	52	208	26,000,000	168,000,000	68
250,000	100	400	25,000,000	193,000,000	77
100,000	180	720	18,000,000	211,000,000	84
50,000	300	1,200	15,000,000	226,000,000	90
25,000	560	2,240	14,000,000	240,000,000	96
Less than 25,000	Many	Many	10,000,000	250,000,000	100
Totals	1,241+	4,964+	250,000,000	—	—

Managing Fundraising Programs

Fundraising programs today are sophisticated undertakings, even at modestly sized nonprofit organizations. In larger institutions, the staff of a development office may include dozens or even hundreds of professionals in various specialties, including annual giving, corporate and foundation relations, major gifts, and **advancement services**.

Advancement Services

Advancement services (or development services) has emerged as an important subspecialty in the field, encompassing all the back-office operations such as gift recording and acknowledgment, prospect research, and information systems management. Most nonprofit organizations use one of the commercially available software packages that are comprehensive in their capabilities to maintain donor information and gift records as well as track cultivation and solicitation activity and evaluate the productivity and effectiveness of specific initiatives of fundraising staff.

As mentioned earlier, the growing availability of information on the Web has revolutionized the field of prospect research. Databases of corporate and foundation giving programs enable researchers to identify promising prospects quickly. The giving capacity of individual prospects can be evaluated using a number of sophisticated electronic screening tools that will also identify known relationships of prospects, for example, to members of the organization's board. However, the costs of such screening can be high for many small nonprofits, and there is still much insight and information to be obtained through the more traditional method of having prospects screened by peers. Individuals in the same business community, the same church, or in the same graduating class may have a good sense of the financial capability and interests of their peers and are often willing to rate their capacity in a setting that provides confidentiality.

Prospect Management

In sophisticated fundraising programs, relationships with donors and prospects are not developed casually or randomly. Contacts are planned, scheduled, and tracked, a process known as **prospect management**. The member of the development office staff responsible for moving a relationship forward is known as the prospect manager. A strategy is developed for each major prospect, and **contact reports** entered into the fundraising information system document every interaction and make it possible for a fundraising manager to monitor the movement of prospects through the fundraising cycle.

In large organizations, especially those with multiple units and decentralized fundraising, policies requiring prior clearance of contacts with donors are essential. For example, this situation is common in universities, where alumni may hold degrees from more than one school and be viewed as prospects for giving to all of them. It is also common in some national nonprofits that have local chapters engaged in fundraising from donors in their local areas. Multiple contacts by different units of the organization may be irritating to donors and create the impression that the organization is poorly managed or inept. In addition, there is always the risk of a preemptive smaller gift that disrupts a careful plan that might have led to a more significant commitment.

Fundraising Efficiency and Effectiveness

The costs of fundraising are a topic that receives considerable discussion and that has been the focus of various studies. As discussed in Chapter 6, some charity watchdog organizations have established guidelines suggesting that fundraising costs should not exceed about one third of the total funds contributed. The Supreme Court has held that government may not set a maximum level of fundraising expenditure because doing so would be an abridgement of free speech rights under the U.S. Constitution, but the public availability of Form 990 and other financial information has made organizations sensitive to the appearance of high costs in the eyes of their donors as well as the watchdog raters.

Some people say that setting limits on fundraising costs is unfair to organizations that are new or controversial and, therefore, must expend more effort and more money in order to meet their needs for gift support. In addition, it can sometimes be difficult to determine the true total costs of fundraising by an organization. As explained in Chapter 12, some portion of the time and effort of a CEO may be devoted to cultivating and soliciting gifts, but it is not always easy to identify that portion exactly, since some activities may involve donors but may also have other purposes. Accounting rules describe how the cost of activities such as mailings and materials are to be allocated between fundraising and mission-related purposes, but some nonprofits may not be clear about exactly how such costs should be apportioned.

Historically, the ratio most commonly used to evaluate the efficiency of fundraising was **cost-per-dollar-raised (cost to raise a dollar)**. The ratio is produced by dividing the amount of expenditure on fundraising by the total gifts received—it is a cost–benefit ratio stated in dollar terms. For example, if an organization spends $50,000 on fundraising and receives $500,000 in gifts as a result, its cost would be 10-cents-per-dollar-raised. If the same expenditure brought in $1,000,000, its relative cost would be half as much, just five-cents-per-dollar-raised. However, many now argue, this ratio is an inappropriate measure for at least two reasons. First, it is a negative way of looking at fundraising—as an expense rather than as an investment. For example, if an organization spends as much as 50 cents to raise a dollar, which would be considered a relatively high cost, that would still represent a 100 percent return on its original investment. There are few investments in which it is possible to double one's money, and a 100 percent return would be considered very good performance by a manager of an investment portfolio.

The second related objection is that cost-per-dollar-raised measures fundraising efficiency, but it says nothing about fundraising effectiveness. For example, if one organization spends $50,000 to raise $500,000, its cost is just 10-cents-per-dollar and its net revenue is $450,000. Suppose another organization spends twice as much, $100,000, and its efforts result in gifts totaling $600,000. Its relative cost is much higher than the first organization— almost 17-cents-per-dollar. Its fundraising is less efficient, but its net revenue of $500,000 is higher than that of the first organization and its fundraising is thus more effective. For these reasons, many organizations today consider the **return on investment (ROI)** in fundraising and look at what is spent in relation to what is raised over a time frame of years.

Attention to the costs—and results—of fundraising is commanding more attention by nonprofit managers as well as charity watchdogs and donors. Despite the argument that fundraising costs and returns should be viewed on a long-term basis, it is also the reality that organizations spending a high percentage of gift revenue on fundraising activities may be subject to criticism. The negative impact of controversy may more than offset whatever financial gains their fundraising plan anticipates.

Staff Performance and Accountability

An important question, especially in larger development offices with staff members who are specialized in the area of major gift fundraising, is how to evaluate the performance of individual fundraising professionals.

Perhaps the simplest measure would be the amount of money each staff member raises, but that approach creates a number of issues. First, most major gifts do not result from the efforts of a single individual. As we have discussed, a donor's relationship with an organization may develop over a long period of time, perhaps exceeding the tenure of any single member of the staff. There are many key players in building such relationships, including perhaps the CEO and volunteers, as well as members of the board. It is often not easy to identify exactly who is responsible for the receipt of a major gift; indeed, the individual who solicits the gift may have played a relatively minor role.

A second problem with using dollars raised to evaluate the performance of a development staff member is that it might create incentives that would lead to inappropriate behavior. That is not to suggest that the fundraiser would necessarily engage in unethical or immoral behavior with regard to a donor, but it is possible that a development staff member who knows he or she will be evaluated on the basis of gifts secured will, even if unconsciously, short-circuit the process in a way that is disadvantageous to the organization. For example, a fundraiser with such an incentive might direct his or her efforts toward soliciting gifts from prospects who are known to be ready to give, rather than cultivation of prospects who may not be ready yet but whose long-term capacity to give is much higher. The staff person might neglect stewardship of past donors who are still making payments on long-term pledges and who have a high likelihood of giving again, while pursuing new donors to hit some dollar target on which his or her own performance will be evaluated. Of course, there could be instances in which a development staff member under pressure to maximize gift revenue misleads a donor or exaggerates the benefits of a gift under a reward system that values only gifts completed. For these reasons, some organizations evaluate the performance of fundraising staff primarily on the activity they undertake, for example, the number of visits made and the number of proposals submitted. Others use formulas that combine credit for such activity with the value of gifts closed.

Again, while it is an issue mostly in larger fundraising operations, the best method for evaluating and rewarding professional staff is a topic of perennial discussion and debate. Some development staff are paid incentive-based compensation, including bonuses, which may reward activity (e.g., the number of donor visits completed) exceeding some predefined objectives. Such programs need to be carefully designed to ensure that the fundraising staff is not being paid a commission—that is, a percentage of the gifts they raise. Basing staff compensation on a percentage of gifts raised is unethical behavior, explicitly prohibited by the ethical codes of the Association of Fundraising Professionals and other professional organizations in the field. The practice would not only raise concerns about the possibility of incentivizing inappropriate or unproductive behavior by fundraisers; it also goes to the heart of the philanthropic relationship and the assumption of trust and mutual commitment to a cause that donors assume to be present when they discuss a gift with the organization's representative.

Ethics and Professional Standards

The question of compensation for fundraising staff is just one area of potential ethical challenge always present in the complex relationships among organizations, their donors, and the individuals who solicit funds on the organization's behalf. Most ethical questions that arise in fundraising can be placed into one of five principal categories (Worth, 2016, p. 397).

First, some issues involve the behavior of the staff person who is interacting with the donor. They would include making misleading or dishonest representations, for example, exaggerating the organization's effectiveness, lying about how the gift will be used, or making unreasonable or unrealistic promises to the donor about recognition or the financial benefits of giving. It is also unethical for a nonprofit staff member who is managing a relationship with a donor to attempt to use that relationship for his or her personal benefit or gain or to engage in behavior toward the donor that would be morally repugnant, for example, sexual harassment.

A second category of ethical issues that may confront nonprofit organizations relates to the donor rather than the staff member. For example, what if the organization has reason to believe that the donated funds were illegally obtained? Should a nonprofit accept gifts from a company that makes products it knows to be harmful? What about the question of accepting a gift from a donor who has been convicted of a white-collar crime or who simply has an unsavory reputation that might reflect badly on the organization, were the gift to receive publicity? There have been a number of examples of such dilemmas posed by gifts from businesspeople who were later involved in corporate corruption scandals, after a building or program had been named to recognize a past gift. Should the organization remove the name? By whose judgment should such decisions be made and what are the limits of the organization's responsibility—and right—to investigate and judge the character of donors who may offer them support?

A third, and sometimes less obvious, ethical question is presented by restricted gifts: Under what circumstances should an organization refuse to accept a gift that may require it to undertake new programs and perhaps incur additional expenses that it had not anticipated? What if the new program is not entirely consistent with the organization's mission or would require a redefinition of its mission? For example, if an organization concerned with young children were offered a gift to begin a new program to help prevent high school students from dropping out, it would need to consider whether expanding its mission in that way would jeopardize its focus on its primary mission. It also would need to consider what additional costs the new efforts might create in the future and whether such expansion might endanger the organization's overall health and other sources of support. It might not be an easy decision to make if the offered gift were very substantial and, especially, if the donor were an important local businessperson or even a member of the organization's board. The risk to the relationship in turning down the gift would need to be weighed against the potential risk to the organization if it were accepted with the conditions that accompany it.

Another subcategory of questions arises with gifts that come with conditions that might give the donor inappropriate control. For example, most colleges will accept scholarship gifts that require recipients to be enrolled in certain academic programs; that raises few problems unless, for example, the college thinks it unlikely it will be able to recruit many students meeting the conditions. But there are limits to how much influence a donor can be allowed to have in the process of selecting specific scholarship recipients. Allowing a donor to select the recipient of scholarships would not only present an ethical concern; it also would invalidate the tax deductibility of the donor's gift, making it legally a gift to the scholarship recipient *individually* rather than to the college, university, or school.

A fourth category of ethical concern that has increased with the growing sophistication of prospect research involves maintaining appropriate safeguards to protect the privacy of donors and prospects. The development offices of many organizations may possess information obtained from public sources about individuals' financial wealth and income, real estate holdings, and even family situations. It is legal to obtain such data. However, some would argue that when it is assembled to create a donor profile, its wide distribution might be an inappropriate invasion of privacy. In addition, development office files may include information gained from reports written by staff members who have visited the donor over the years or heard secondhand from others who know the donor. Maintaining such information in the files of the fundraising office runs the risk that the donor, and the organization, could be embarrassed if it were inappropriately or inadvertently disclosed to another person.

Fifth, an organization that accepts a gift designated by the donor for a specific purpose undertakes a responsibility to honor that restriction. If the gift is not used as directed, that is an ethical violation and may even give the donor the right to undertake legal action.

The Association of Fundraising Professionals "Code of Ethical Principles" and "Principles of Professional Practice" cover many of the major issues that nonprofits and members of their staff may encounter in raising philanthropic funds. But possible situations are so varied that no code can substitute for continuing ethical awareness and the application of good judgment by nonprofit managers who value the interests of their organizations and their missions above all else (see Box 13.4).

Box 13.4 AFP Code of Ethical Principles and Standards

(Ethical principles adopted in 1964; amended in October 2014)

The Association of Fundraising Professionals believes that ethical behavior fosters the development and growth of fundraising professionals and the fundraising profession and enhances philanthropy and volunteerism. AFP members recognize their responsibility to ethically generate or support ethical generation of philanthropic support. Violation of the standards may subject the member to disciplinary sanctions as provided in the AFP Ethics Enforcement Procedures. AFP members, both individual and business, agree to abide (and ensure, to the best of their ability, that all members of their staff abide) by the AFP standards.

PUBLIC TRUST, TRANSPARENCY & CONFLICTS OF INTEREST

Members shall:

1. not engage in activities that harm the members' organizations, clients or profession or knowingly bring the profession into disrepute.

2. not engage in activities that conflict with their fiduciary, ethical and legal obligations to their organizations, clients or profession.

3. effectively disclose all potential and actual conflicts of interest; such disclosure does not preclude or imply ethical impropriety.

4. not exploit any relationship with a donor, prospect, volunteer, client or employee for the benefit of the members or the members' organizations.

5. comply with all applicable local, state, provincial and federal civil and criminal laws.

6. recognize their individual boundaries of professional competence.

7. present and supply products and/or services honestly and without misrepresentation.

8. establish the nature and purpose of any contractual relationship at the outset and be responsive and available to parties before, during and after any sale of materials and/or services.

9. never knowingly infringe the intellectual property rights of other parties.

10. protect the confidentiality of all privileged information relating to the provider/client relationships.

11. never disparage competitors untruthfully.

SOLICITATION & STEWARDSHIP OF PHILANTHROPIC FUNDS

Members shall:

12. ensure that all solicitation and communication materials are accurate and correctly reflect their organization's mission and use of solicited funds.

13. ensure that donors receive informed, accurate and ethical advice about the value and tax implications of contributions.

14. ensure that contributions are used in accordance with donors' intentions.

15. ensure proper stewardship of all revenue sources, including timely reports on the use and management of such funds.

16. obtain explicit consent by donors before altering the conditions of financial transactions.

TREATMENT OF CONFIDENTIAL & PROPRIETARY INFORMATION

Members shall:

17. not disclose privileged or confidential information to unauthorized parties.

18. adhere to the principle that all donor and prospect information created by, or on behalf of, an organization or a client is the property of that organization or client.

19. give donors and clients the opportunity to have their names removed from lists that are sold to, rented to or exchanged with other organizations.

20. when stating fundraising results, use accurate and consistent accounting methods that conform to the relevant guidelines adopted by the appropriate authority.

COMPENSATION, BONUSES & FINDER'S FEES

Members shall:

21. not accept compensation or enter into a contract that is based on a percentage of contributions; nor shall members accept finder's fees or contingent fees.

22. be permitted to accept performance-based compensation, such as bonuses, only if such bonuses are in accord with prevailing practices within the members' own organizations and are not based on a percentage of contributions.

23. neither offer nor accept payments or special considerations for the purpose of influencing the selection of products or services.

24. not pay finder's fees, commissions or percentage compensation based on contributions.

25. meet the legal requirements for the disbursement of funds if they receive funds on behalf of a donor or client.

Source: Used with permission of the Association of Fundraising Professionals (http://www.afpnet.org/Ethics/Enforcement Detail.cfm?ItemNumber=3261).

CHAPTER SUMMARY

Gifts are a significant component of revenue for many nonprofit organizations, although patterns vary widely among subsectors. Gifts comprise a small percentage of revenue for health care institutions, which derive most of their revenue from fees for service. At the other end of the spectrum, gifts are almost the only source of income for religious congregations and some arts and human services nonprofits. Organized fundraising is rapidly becoming more common across the world, but it is still most highly developed in the United States. The term fundraising is often used synonymously with the terms development or advancement, but the latter two terms

are properly understood to encompass a more comprehensive approach to institution building that includes other external relations functions.

It is important to distinguish between charity, that is, giving to address current human needs, and philanthropy, which seeks to establish or strengthen institutions that address society's needs on a long-term basis. Charity is sometimes impulsive and is emotionally driven; philanthropy is often more thoughtful and deliberate.

The motivation to give is quite different among corporations, foundations, and individual donors. Corporate philanthropy generally seeks to advance the corporation's business interests while also accomplishing some social benefit. Corporate support of nonprofits encompasses philanthropy and also various partnerships, which will be discussed in the next chapter. Foundations exist to make gifts and are required by law to do so. There are various types of foundations, some of which may be prospects for support of nonprofit organizations and others that operate their own programs and generally do not provide grants to others.

Most individual donors are likely to be less rational in their giving than are corporations or foundations. A considerable body of research exists on the motivations of individual donors. Findings generally suggest that individuals are motivated by altruism, a desire to pay back for benefits that they have received, desires for social advancement and recognition, as well as other reasons. The influence of tax incentives on giving by individuals is a subject of debate among economists and other experts but most evidence suggests it does affect the amount that some people are able to give.

Fundraising is a process that begins with the organization identifying its own priorities. It then develops a case for support and progresses to identify prospects who have linkage, interest, and the ability to give. The organization then cultivates relationships with those prospects, solicits the gift, and proceeds to acknowledge and recognize the donor. Stewardship is required to maintain and strengthen the relationship and gain continued support from past donors. Development of the case, or the rationale for why the organization deserves support, is a critical step. A strong case is larger than the organization—it starts with the social needs that the organization's programs address and then becomes more specific in describing how funds will enhance the organization's ability to address those broader needs.

The solicitation of gifts may use various media, including mail, phone, personal meeting, and—increasingly—electronic communication, such as the Internet, e-mail, texting, and social media. Each of these approaches offers advantages and disadvantages. The fundraising pyramid depicts how many donors evolve in their giving relationship with an organization, beginning as regular annual donors and possibly advancing to become major donors and eventually donors of ultimate gifts. Organizations often build their fundraising programs in accordance with the pyramid, beginning with solicitations for annual gifts

and then developing major gift and planned gift programs as their constituency is ready.

Planned giving is a growing area of fundraising and philanthropy. There are three basic types of planned gifts—outright planned gifts, expectancies, and deferred gifts. Each offers various advantages to the donor, and the vehicle selected will reflect the individual's financial and estate considerations. Campaigns are intensive fundraising efforts that seek to raise a given amount by a specified deadline for specific purposes or campaign objectives. Campaigns proceed in phases, and it is important that the model be followed to ensure success in achieving the goal. The gift-range chart depicts the pattern of giving necessary to achieve a dollar goal and is a useful tool in planning and managing a campaign.

Advancement services, encompassing the back-office operations of fundraising, has become an important subspecialty of the field. This area includes prospect research, gift accounting, and the maintenance of fundraising information systems and records.

Questions about the efficiency and effectiveness of fundraising are often discussed and debated. Evaluating the ratio of fundraising cost to dollars raised may be disadvantageous to younger, smaller organizations and does not reveal the effectiveness of a fundraising program in maximizing net revenue. The return on investment in fundraising is a more appropriate measure of effectiveness, but some still emphasize the ratio of costs to revenue and prefer to see fundraising expenditures at a minimum. Fundraising costs that are high may attract the attention of the media, donors, and government officials and result in negative publicity. Discussion also surrounds the compensation of fundraising staff, some of whom receive financial incentives for performance. Compensation based on a percentage of gifts secured is considered unethical in the field.

Fundraising often raises ethical issues, including, among others, those related to the behavior of fundraisers themselves, the reputation of the donor or the source of that individual's wealth, the impact of restricted gifts on the mission of the organization, concerns about donor privacy and the use of information resulting from prospect research, and the organization's faithfulness in following donor intent. AFP and other organizations have established ethics codes that are widely followed by practitioners.

NOTE

1. Students may notice that the term that describes the activity seeking gifts is written in various styles, including "fund raising," "fund-raising," and "fundraising." This depends on the particular style the author is following and to some extent on the time period of the writing, since the use of the single word "fundraising" has become more widely adopted in recent years. This text uses "fundraising" except where quoting another work that uses a different style.

KEY TERMS AND CONCEPTS

advancement 358
advancement services 378
Association of Fundraising
  Professionals 359
bequest 374
campaign 357
case for support 364
case statement 364
catalytic philanthropy 357
charitable gift annuities 374
charitable remainder trusts 374
charity 356
contact reports 378
cost-per-dollar-raised (cost to raise a
  dollar) 379
crowdfunding 368
cultivation 366
deferred gifts 372
development 357

donor-advised funds 375
enlightened self-interest 358
expectancies 372
external case statement 364
family foundations 359
fundraising 357
fundraising pyramid 371
gift chart (gift standards chart) 377
gifts-in-kind 358
identification of prospects 364
institutional advancement 358
internal case statement 364
kickoff 376
lead trust 375
life estate 375
linkage, ability, interest (LAI) 370
major gift 371
National Association of Charitable
  Gift Planners 375

nucleus fund 376
outcome-oriented philanthropy 357
out-of-pocket cost 362
outright planned gifts 372
philanthropy 356
planned giving 372
proportionate giving 377
prospect 365
prospect management 378
prospect research 365
quiet phase 376
regular gifts 371
return on investment (ROI) 379
soliciting 357
special gifts 371
stewardship 363
strategic philanthropy 357
ultimate gift 372
venture philanthropy 357

CASE 13.1a–g Fundraising Ethics

Case 13.1a

A generous gift is offered to your organization by a donor whose company was involved in the mortgage crisis of the late 2000s. His gift would be recognized through naming of a major wing on the new building that the gift would help to fund. Although he was not personally accused of legal wrongdoing, members of your governing board express concern that identifying his name with the organization could harm its image and reputation. One board member also raises the possibility that the donor might become involved in questionable business practices in the future and suggests that you negotiate a gift agreement that specifically permits the organization to remove the donor's name from the facility should he ever be criminally indicted or otherwise become an embarrassment to the organization. Do you accept the gift? How do you approach the donor about the proposed terms of the gift agreement?

Case 13.1b

A donor wants to give an art collection to the art gallery at which you are employed. Her requirement is that the gallery be set up just like her home and that she be able to use it for private events on request. She also requires that this arrangement be maintained in future years. Do you accept? What are the ethical issues and what are some possible legal concerns?

Case 13.1c

You are a gift officer who has a private conversation, with a donor. That donor tells you that another donor, whom you also know, is seriously ill and that the family has financial problems, despite appearances. With whom do you share that information, if at all? Do you record the information in a database or include it in your written report of the visit?

Case 13.1d

A donor is considering a major gift to create a "center on competitiveness" at your institution, a public policy think tank. You know that he is a strong proponent of tariff protection for U.S. companies. A leading proponent of free trade is about to be appointed as a senior fellow in your research center. You know this, but it has not yet been publicly announced. Do you tell the donor about the impending appointment or just stay quiet?

Case 13.1e

A donor you had cultivated on behalf of your nonprofit employer dies. In her will, she leaves you a watch you had once admired as a personal gift. (Assume that your employer does not have a formal policy prohibiting this.) Do you accept it? Why or why not? What if she leaves you $5,000? What if it's $5 million? Does the amount make a difference?

Case 13.1f

A donor pledges $1 million payable over five years to name a room in a new building. Another donor pledges $1 million to name the identical room next door but says he can only pay it over 10 years. Do you accept the second gift and name the room? If so, are you obligated to tell the first donor about the difference in terms? If you think you are not, then how would you handle questions from the first donor were he or she to learn of the arrangements through a conversation with the second donor?

Case 13.1g

An older donor says that she wants to change her will, leaving everything to your organization. This will cut out her daughter from whom she is estranged. The daughter, whom you know personally, is disabled. Do you encourage the donor? Do you tell the daughter what is going on? Do you tell anyone else or just let this woman make her own decision? What if you personally have doubts about the donor's mental ability to make financial decisions?

Questions Related to Cases 13.1a–g

1. In the cases above, do the ethical issues involve the behavior or ethics of the fundraiser; conditions placed on the gift or the impact of the gift on the organization's mission and resources; characteristics or personal reputation of the donor; concerns about privacy; issues of the donor's intent; or something else?

2. How would you handle the issues raised by each case?

QUESTIONS FOR DISCUSSION

1. Do you think that people give primarily for altruistic reasons or in order to receive benefits for themselves, including warm feelings, recognition, and social approval? Might the motivations differ among various types of gifts and various organizations? Explain your answer and provide examples.

2. Some people argue that donors should receive a more generous tax deduction for gifts to organizations that serve the poor, such as homeless shelters, than they receive for gifts to institutions that primarily serve the affluent, such as symphony orchestras. Do you agree or disagree? Why?

3. If a friend asks you to sponsor his or her participation in a charity event, such as a run or walk, do you usually give a positive response or not? Why? Would your response be different if that friend asked you to do something similar again the next month? Why?

APPENDIX CASES

The following cases in the Appendix of this text include points related to the content of this chapter: Case 1 (New York City Opera); Case 2 (Share Our Strength/No Kid Hungry); Case 3 (The Y); Case 4 (The Girls Scouts of the United States of America).

SUGGESTIONS FOR FURTHER READING

Books

Herzog, P. S., & Price, H. E. (2016). *American generosity: Who gives and why*. New York, NY: Oxford University Press.

Salamon, L. (Ed.). (2014). *The new frontiers of philanthropy*. New York, NY: Oxford University Press.

Worth, M. J. (2016). *Fundraising: Principles and practice*. Thousand Oaks, CA: Sage.

Worth. M. J. (2017). *Leading the campaign* (2nd ed.). Lanham, MD: Rowman & Littlefield.

Zunz, O. (2014). *Philanthropy in America: A history* (Rev. ed.). Princeton, NJ: Princeton University Press.

Articles

Bekkers, R., & Wiepking, P. (2011, October). A literature review of empirical studies of philanthropy: Eight mechanisms that drive charitable giving. *Nonprofit and Voluntary Sector Quarterly, 40*(5), 924–973.

Mesch, D. J., Brown, M. S., Moore, Z. I., & Hayat, A. D. (2011, November). Gender differences in charitable giving. *International Journal of Nonprofit and Voluntary Sector Marketing, 16*, 342–355.

Websites

Association for Healthcare Philanthropy: http://www.ahp.org/

Association of Fundraising Professionals: http://www.afpnet.org/

Council for Advancement and Support of Education: http://www.case.org/

Foundation Center: http://foundationcenter.org/

Lilly Family School of Philanthropy at Indiana University: http://www.philanthropy.iupui.edu

National Association of Charitable Gift Planners: https://charitablegiftplanners.org/

Network for Good: http:www.networkforgood.org/

Planned Giving Design Center: http://www.pgdc.com

Many nonprofits have found that starting a business has forced the entire organization to become more focused and to sharpen its goals and management skills in all aspects of its work, thereby improving their balance sheets as well as their effectiveness in achieving their charitable missions.

iStock/ijeab

Chapter Outline

Social Enterprise and Earned Income

This chapter discusses efforts by nonprofit organizations to increase and diversify their sources of revenue through relationships with business corporations and through their own business activities. Such activities generate what is called earned income, that is, revenue that comes from payments for goods and services that the nonprofit has provided, rather than contributed income (gifts). Some authors call the activity that generates earned income social enterprise, but as we will discuss soon, others make a distinction between earned income and social enterprise. Some writers also use the terms social enterprise and social entrepreneurship interchangeably, but in this book, we define social entrepreneurship as related to social innovation, which may or may not involve earned income or social enterprise. That distinction is discussed in more detail in Chapter 16, which is focused on social entrepreneurship.

As mentioned earlier in this book, most revenue to the nonprofit sector overall is earned income. This is especially true in education and health care, in which payments made by students and patients, respectively, are by far the largest sources of revenue. Many organizations also receive a significant portion of their revenue from government, but most government funds are not gifts or grants. They are payment for services that the nonprofit has provided and for which the government is paying on behalf of the clients served. Obvious examples include government reimbursements paid to health care institutions under the Medicare and Medicaid programs and scholarship funds paid to a college or university to be applied to a student's tuition bill. Both are earned income to the recipient organizations, since they pay for services the organization provided to specific patients or students, respectively. Government grants and contracts are discussed in Chapter 15.

Defining Social Enterprise and Earned Income

What is the difference between earned income and social enterprise? The answer is not a simple one and it's easy to

Learning Objectives

After reading this chapter, students should be able to:

1. Define key terms and concepts related to social enterprise and nonprofit earned income.

2. Explain questions that nonprofits should consider in evaluating earned-income opportunities.

3. Describe common types of partnerships between nonprofit organizations and business firms.

4. Explain the process for identifying and developing nonprofit earned-income ventures.

5. Evaluate the potential risks and rewards of earned-income strategies.

6. Analyze cases, applying concepts from the chapter.

become confused. One reason is that some authors use "social enterprise" to describe an *organization*, while others use it to describe an *activity*. The Social Enterprise Alliance defines a **social enterprise** as an organization that "address[es] a basic unmet need or solve[s] a social problem through a market-driven approach," meaning essentially that most or all of its revenue comes from fees for goods and services rather than gifts or grants (Social Enterprise Alliance, 2017). Other authors say that if a nonprofit undertakes an initiative to generate earned income it is engaging in "social enterprise," using the term to describe that activity rather than the organization itself (Ridley-Duff & Bull, 2016).

Some authors make a distinction between **earned income** and social enterprise depending on whether the income-generating activities are related or unrelated to the organization's mission. They use "earned income" to mean revenue from the sale of goods and services that are directly related to the organization's mission but use "social enterprise" to describe activities that are not related to the mission. (Lyons, Townsend, Sullivan, & Drago, 2010, p. 5). Thomas S. Lyons and his coauthors challenge the usefulness of this distinction, arguing that earned income and social enterprise are essentially the same thing for most organizations. As they explain,

> There is considerable confusion among both experts and the general public as to what "social enterprise" actually is. At the heart of this puzzlement is a repeated attempt on the part of some to draw a distinction between "social enterprise" and "earned income." These individuals claim that it is possible to generate earned income without engaging in social enterprise. To them, social enterprise is about nonprofit organizations generating revenue that has nothing to do with mission … [but] there is no useful distinction to be drawn between earned income activities and social enterprise. (Lyons et al., 2010, p. 5)

Others agree that relatedness to the mission should not be the critical test, but still argue that earned income and social enterprise are two different things. For example, Kim Alter (n.d.) argues that many organizations generate some form of earned income through activities that are integrated into their ongoing programs, whether related to the mission or not, but those activities can be considered a social enterprise only when they are established as a distinct business. As she explains,

> Though subtle, and subject to debate, the defining characteristic is that an income-generating activity becomes a social enterprise when it is operated as a business. The following characteristics apply: The activity was established strategically to create social and/or economic value for the organization. It has a long-term vision and is managed as a going concern. Growth and revenue targets are set for the activity in a business or operational plan. Qualified staff with business or industry experience manage the activity or provide oversight, as opposed to nonprofit program staff. (Alter, n.d.)

Alter (n.d.) provides two interesting examples to illustrate the distinction she draws. The National Zoo, in Washington, DC, sold elephant waste to the public for use as fertilizer in their gardens, calling it "Zoo Doo." This activity generated some additional revenue, which was useful, but it was not a significant portion of revenue for the zoo overall. It is more a marketing and public relations strategy that catches attention and may cause people to think about visiting the zoo. The activity generates earned income, which is not directly related to the zoo's mission, but in Alter's definition, it is not social enterprise. On the other hand, zookeepers in Thailand have turned elephant waste into a lucrative business that provides significant support for the zoo's operations. As Alter describes, "The Thais transform the animal excrement into high-quality handmade paper which is sold in stationary stores, nature shops, and used in premium paper products in domestic and export markets. The enterprise employs several people who process the organic pulp to produce handmade paper." In her definition, that is a social enterprise because it is operated as a business and has achieved some scale.

This chapter discusses earned-income strategies that nonprofits pursue, that is, strategies for generating revenue from market-based activities. Those strategies encompass commercial relationships between nonprofits and corporations, which this chapter simply calls corporate partnerships. Such relationships generate earned income—the revenue is not philanthropy—since there is an exchange between the nonprofit and the corporation. They involve a quid pro quo that makes the revenue something other than a gift. This chapter also discusses **nonprofit business ventures**, but avoids the debate about whether these initiatives are consistent with one of the definitions of social enterprise. Readers are encouraged to think about the various definitions of social enterprise and how they may or may not apply to the examples that are discussed. Figure 14.1 depicts the array of earned-income strategies that we will explore.

Why Earned Income?

Why would a nonprofit want to pursue earned income? Why has interest in this area increased? Primarily because there is increased competition for revenue, resulting from some of the

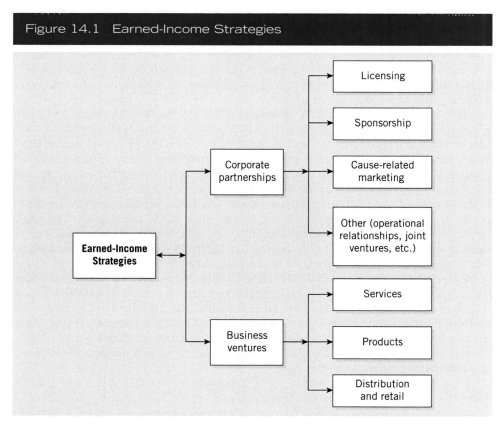

Figure 14.1   Earned-Income Strategies

Source: Adapted from Community Wealth Ventures (now Community Wealth Partners; 2001, p. 7). Used with permission.

changes of the past two decades that were discussed in Chapter 3 of this book. Government funding for social programs generally has declined or has shifted to a voucher approach that has given potential clients choices about where to obtain services, introducing competition into the nonprofit marketplace. Government increasingly has outsourced the provision of services based on competitive contracts, forcing nonprofits to go head-to-head with each other as well as with for-profit firms. Concern about government funding increased after the passage of federal tax cuts in late 2017, which were anticipated to create larger budget deficits and pressure to reduce expenditures on social programs in future years.

Philanthropic giving has increased over the long term with the growth of the general economy but has remained relatively constant as a percentage of gross domestic product, while the number of nonprofits has continued to grow in real terms. This has increased the need disproportionately more than the revenue that comes from giving. In addition, nonprofits have sought to diversify their sources of revenue, in order to protect themselves from the vicissitudes of shifting political priorities that affect government support and the economic cycles that determine charitable giving. (Think back on the discussion of resource dependence in Chapter 3.)

But it's not all about money. Many nonprofits have found that pursuing earned income also helps them advance their missions—for example, organizations that offer recovery and job-training programs provide catering and food service or maintenance services, and retail stores employ their clients as well as generate income to support their core programs. Others have found that operating a business has forced the entire organization to become more focused and to sharpen its goals and management skills in all aspects of its work. Partnerships with corporations offer not only the opportunity for new revenue but also the increased visibility that may come from the company's promotion of the partnership, benefiting the nonprofit's efforts to raise traditional charitable support. Such relationships also have given nonprofits access to new volunteers and to the management skills and resources of corporate partners. In sum, many nonprofits have found that pursuing earned-income strategies can improve their balance sheets as well as their effectiveness in achieving their charitable missions.

Jane Wei-Skillern, James Austin, Herman Leonard, and Howard Stevenson (2007) offer a way to think about earned income in terms of how important it is to the organization and how closely it is related to the mission. As depicted in Figure 14.2, if earned income is not closely related to the mission and generates a small portion of total revenue (the bottom, left quadrant), it may be considered "disposable." It provides a little extra, but it is not critical, like the sale of elephant waste by the National Zoo mentioned earlier. If an activity is related to the mission but does not generate much money (the upper left quadrant), that could be called "supplemental"—it helps, but it also is not critical to the organization. This might be the case, for example, if clients are charged a modest, token fee to attend some type of training seminar. In the bottom right quadrant of Figure 14.2 are earned-income activities that are an important source of revenue to the organization but that are not directly related to the mission; they might be called "sustaining," because the nonprofit is very dependent on them. For some organizations, some commercial partnerships with corporations might fall into this category. And, finally, some earned income that is closely related to the mission and provides a major portion of the nonprofit's revenue could be called "integral." This would be the case for a number of commercialized nonprofits that derive the largest portion of their revenue from the sales of goods and services that are central to their missions, for example, in education, health care, and other fields.

Of course, earned-income activities offer downside risks as well as potential benefits. Earned income is not a panacea for the nonprofit sector, nor is it a realistic expectation for every organization. Indeed, some critics view the commercialization of nonprofits with deep concern. Some suggest that establishing for-profits, using emerging legal forms that were discussed in Chapter 3, offers a more promising approach to addressing social problems than

Figure 14.2 Earned Income and the Organization

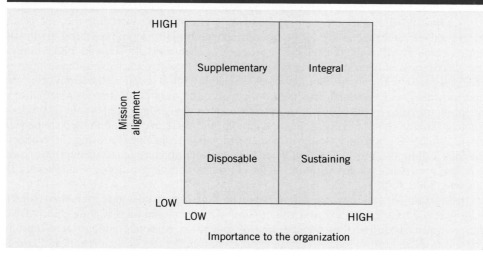

Source: Wei-Skillern, J., Austin, J. E., Leonard, H., & Stevenson, H. (2007). *Entrepreneurship in the social sector.* Thousand Oaks, CA: Sage, p. 140.

can be achieved with the nonprofit form. This perspective is controversial (Starr, 2012b). Some issues will be discussed more fully toward the end of this chapter.

Partnerships With Business

Let's begin our discussion of earned-income strategies with the top half of Figure 14.1—the various types of relationships nonprofits may establish with corporate partners. First, we need to be clear what we are talking about when we refer to nonprofit–corporate partnerships. The term partnership is sometimes used rather loosely. For example, nonprofit donor lists may include the names of "corporate partners," but they are really corporate *donors,* since the company has not received much in return for its payment beyond its inclusion on the list. A true partnership is not a one-directional transaction; rather, it is a relationship that advances the goals of *both* parties, an arrangement in which both sides receive specific benefits related to their goals.

If a corporation gives money to a nonprofit based on altruism or a general sense of corporate responsibility without receiving any specific benefit beyond perhaps the modest recognition given to all donors, that is an example of corporate philanthropy but not a partnership. The revenue in this instance is not earned income; it is **contributed income**. The corporate partnerships discussed in this chapter produce earned income because the nonprofit is not receiving a gift, but rather is earning the revenue through its participation in the relationship.

Not all partnerships between nonprofit organizations and corporations represent earned-income strategies. For example, the Environmental Defense Fund (EDF) works with corporate partners to implement innovations that have a positive environmental impact but also bring benefits to the corporation, such as reduced costs. EDF does not accept gifts or grants from its corporate partners, in order to maintain its credibility and independence, although it does accept gifts from some corporations with which it is not programmatically involved. It also limits the total of such contributions to no more than 3 percent of its annual operating budget. However, the partnerships we are discussing in this chapter are those that do provide a financial benefit to both the nonprofit organization and the corporate partner and are undertaken at least in part for that purpose (Environmental Defense Fund, 2017).

Chapter 13 discussed the history of corporate philanthropy, including the emergence of strategic philanthropy in the 1980s. Strategic philanthropy is an approach that aligns the corporation's giving with its competitive strategy as a business. In strategic philanthropy, the effectiveness of corporate giving is measured by its impact on achieving the company's business goals, ultimately the bottom line of profitability. But it is still philanthropy since the company does not receive an immediate quid pro quo. One example of strategic philanthropy might be provided by gifts-in-kind. A software company might give a nonprofit its product for free. That is surely of benefit to the nonprofit and there may be no immediate benefit to the company. It also may result in people becoming accustomed to using the product, perhaps leading them to stick with it when they consider purchasing software for their own business or personal use in the future, so the gift serves a strategic purpose (Galaskiewicz & Colman, 2006, p. 190).

Corporate philanthropy remains an important force. Companies gave more than $18.45 billion in 2015, including cash and gifts-in-kind of company products (Giving USA, 2016). But commercial partnerships are the area of growth in corporate support of nonprofit organizations and causes today. The watershed event came in 1983, when American Express supported renovation of the Statue of Liberty by offering to contribute a penny to the campaign each time a consumer used his or her American Express credit card. Use of American Express cards increased by 28 percent during the campaign. Other companies noticed and nonprofit–corporate partnerships took off (Wall, 1984, pp. 1, 29). By 2008, Reynold Levy, a former president of the AT&T Foundation, observed the shift and pronounced that "the age of pure corporate philanthropy is drawing to a close" (Levy, 2008, p. 66), although as mentioned previously, corporate philanthropy still remains important today.

The discussion in this chapter encompasses a few of the most common nonprofit–corporate relationships—licensing agreements, sponsorships, cause-related marketing, and operational relationships. Let's run through brief descriptions of each and look at some examples.

Licensing

If students buy T-shirts or coffee mugs with the name and logo of their college on it, they probably do not think that the college manufactured the item, but they may not know by what arrangement the school's logo is displayed. It is likely to be an example of a licensing agreement between the college and the manufacturer of the shirt or mug.

A **licensing agreement** is a contract that permits a for-profit company to use the nonprofit's name or logo on its products in return for a royalty payment to the nonprofit. The benefit to the nonprofit is the revenue it gains from the royalty and the increased visibility of its name. For the company, having the nonprofit's logo on its products will presumably attract purchases from individuals who are affiliated with the nonprofit or who prefer the product to others because of the perceived benefit to the nonprofit cause. But there is also something subtler at work. By using the nonprofit's name or logo on its product, the company gains some of the attributes of the nonprofit's brand; that is, the company may come to be seen as more "caring," more "green," or more concerned about specific groups of people by virtue of its association with the positive qualities that people attribute to its nonprofit partner. In effect, when it enters a licensing agreement, a nonprofit leverages some of its brand equity into a stream of income in the form of royalties from the corporation.

Most licensing agreements bring few risks. For example, there is probably little that can go wrong by having a college's logo on a sweatshirt. But some licensing is more controversial, especially agreements that place nonprofit logos on products that relate to food, health, or the environment. The concern is that the presence of the logo implies the nonprofit's endorsement of the product; that is, the appearance of the name implies that the nonprofit is certifying the product's benefits, which may or may not be the case. In the American Heart Association's food certification program, for example, the products have been screened and found to comply with the association's nutrition requirements (American Heart Association, 2017). However, in other instances, the appearance of the logo may mean only that the company has provided a royalty payment to the nonprofit. It does not ensure that the nonprofit has investigated the product or guarantees its consistency with the organization's values. This could be easy for consumers to misunderstand. One historic licensing fiasco occurred in 1997, when the American Medical Association (AMA) licensed its name to be used on home medical products manufactured by Sunbeam Corporation. The endorsement implied that the AMA had established the effectiveness of the products, but it had not done so. There was public criticism and an outcry by doctors, who are the association's members. The AMA was forced to end the relationship with Sunbeam, paying the company almost $10 million in a lawsuit settlement. Not surprisingly, some AMA employees also lost their jobs (Sagawa & Segal, 2000).

Sponsorships

In a licensing agreement, a corporation pays for use of a nonprofit's name or logo on its products. In a **sponsorship**, the company pays for the use of *its* name or logo in connection with the nonprofit's products or events. We are all familiar with corporate sponsorships; they would be hard to miss. They are represented by the corporate logos on the scoreboards in many university stadiums and arenas, on the T-shirts worn by participants in many charitable events.

It is important to note that some authors (e.g., Galaskiewicz & Colman, 2006) define sponsorship as a form of strategic philanthropy, rather than a commercial partnership. For one thing, unlike licensing agreements and cause-related marketing (which we will discuss in a following section) sponsorships do not tie the nonprofit's revenues directly to the company's products. In addition, sponsorship is not the same as advertising. Advertising communicates more information and describes the virtues of the company's products—it is intended to increase sales of those products. Sponsorship is limited to exposure of the company's name or logo and, perhaps, a brief mention like those that precede programs on public television. It is intended to enhance the company's overall visibility and image. In this chapter, as in much other writing about the topic, sponsorships are included as a type of commercial relationship rather than philanthropy because they do involve an exchange: the nonprofit receives a payment in exchange for permitting the corporation to associate its name with the nonprofit's cause, in a specific format and location that is negotiated as a condition of the payment, and in a manner that is more visible than just the company's name on a donor list. It is, in effect, a method for the nonprofit to leverage its brand or cause in order to create a stream of income.

Corporations sponsor events such as charity walks, runs, and rides, or athletic competitions. Some also sponsor organizations, entitling the companies to visibility and recognition across a broad range of programs, products, and communications. Others sponsor facilities, such as athletic arenas and concert halls, which may be named for the corporation. The facility may be named in perpetuity to recognize a corporate gift, but many are named only for the term of a sponsorship contract under which the company makes annual payments to the organization or institution operating the facility. Again, sponsorship does not include detailed descriptions of the company's products, and the payment to the nonprofit is tied to opportunities for visibility and exposure, not directly to sales.

Like licensing of a nonprofit's own name and logo, corporate sponsorships offer nonprofits the benefits of added revenue and increased visibility through the company's promotion of the relationship. Since they do not imply as strongly the nonprofit's endorsement of the company's products, the risk to the nonprofit's reputation may be somewhat less. But there are still reasons for caution. One consideration, of course, is the consistency of the corporation and its products with the mission and values of the nonprofit organization. It would be unlikely for an athletic event to accept sponsorship from a tobacco company or an organization serving children to be visibly associated with a company that sells alcohol. But some cases are closer calls, and it is wise to review sponsorship opportunities against a predetermined list of criteria reflecting the judgment of the organization's board.

Cause Marketing

Some writers use the term **cause marketing** (or **cause-related marketing**) broadly to encompass virtually all relationships in which a nonprofit's and a corporation's identities are combined, including licensing and sponsorships. This text uses the term in a more specific way to mean an arrangement under which the company contributes either a fixed amount for each sale of a product or a specified percentage of its sales of a product to the nonprofit, usually in connection with a short-term promotion. Cause marketing is different from social marketing, which we discussed in Chapter 10. The purpose of social marketing is to influence behavior in order to bring a benefit to the individual or society. Social marketing has no direct impact on revenue of the nonprofit, although it may create greater visibility for the cause and possibly bring additional gifts to the organization promoting it. The purpose of cause marketing is to sell more of the corporate partner's products, with a financial benefit to the nonprofit. There may be, of course, the additional benefit of visibility, which can increase awareness of the cause it advances, with an indirect impact on social behavior.

Unlike sponsorships and licensing arrangements, the nonprofit's revenue from a cause-marketing relationship usually is transaction based; that is, it is directly related to the volume or amount of sales of the company's products. Let's look at a few examples:

- Yoplait promised to give 10 cents to Susan G. Komen, Bright Pink, or Living Beyond Breast Cancer (based on the customer's choice) for every pink yogurt lid mailed in between October 1, 2014, and March 31, 2015, up to a maximum of $350,000 in total (https://blog.generalmills.com/2014/10/a-new-way-to-help-women-battling-breast-cancer/).

- From March 27 to April 23, 2017, Church's Fried Chicken sold a coupon book, providing discounts on future purchases, for the price of $1. All of the proceeds from sales of the book went to nonprofit Share Our Strength for the No Kid Hungry campaign (https://www.prnewswire.com/news-releases/churchs-chicken-renews--expands-partnership-with-no-kid-hungry-300428462.html).

- Avon sells a reusable water bottle, called Hello Green Tomorrow. In the United States, 100 percent of the net proceeds from the sale of such bottles goes to WWF (formerly World Wildlife Fund) and other conservation organizations for the restoration of critically endangered forests (https://www.worldwildlife.org/partnerships/avon-products).

Again, cause marketing ties the nonprofit's income directly to the number or amount of total sales made by the corporate partner and thus represents a true partnership in which the interests of both parties are aligned. The corporation may find the relationship beneficial both as a strategy for increasing sales and as a way to improve its image and attract a new customer base, perhaps among the members of a specific market segment. In a number of studies, consumers have indicated that they would be more inclined to buy products when they know that the sale benefits a charitable organization. For example, a 2017 study conducted by Cone Communications, a company that works with businesses on nonprofit partnerships, found that 87 percent of consumers would buy a company's products because it supports a cause they care about (Cone Communications, 2017). Of course, such studies may be subject to positivity bias; in other words, people are inclined to give the "right" answer to questions about what their hypothetical behavior might be, and that does not ensure that they will actually behave in that manner.

For the nonprofit, the marketing relationship may generate not only additional revenue but also increased visibility. Promotions of the relationship often feature the logos of both the nonprofit and the corporate partner, and a comprehensive campaign may include advertising, in-store displays, and exposure in other media.

Cause-marketing relationships are governed by a contract between the nonprofit and the corporate partner. Among other matters, the contract usually spells out how much is to be paid (e.g., a fixed amount per sale or a percentage); the length of time for which the promotion will be in effect; the maximum sum (if any) that the corporate partner will give; and rights of approval that each partner retains with regard to ad copy, use of its logo, and related concerns. One important question is whether and how the terms of the contract will be clearly disclosed to consumers. Promotions that include statements such as "a portion of your purchase will be given to charity" are inadequate, since they do not disclose what portion, whether the promotion covers only certain dates, or whether the total contribution by the company is capped at some maximum amount, as many are. In sum, such a statement does not assure an individual consumer that his or her own purchase will result in a payment to the nonprofit.

Standard 19 of the Better Business Bureau (BBB) Wise Giving Alliance Standards of Excellence addresses these potential issues, requiring that nonprofit organizations clearly disclose how the charity benefits from the sale of products or services and the terms and conditions of its agreement with the corporate partner. It reads as follows:

> Cause Marketing Disclosures - Clearly disclose how the charity benefits from the sale of products or services (i.e., cause-related marketing) that state or imply that a charity will benefit from a consumer sale or transaction. Such promotions should disclose, at the point of solicitation: a) the actual or anticipated portion of the purchase price that will benefit the charity (e.g., 5 cents will be contributed to abc charity for every xyz company product sold), b) the duration of the campaign (e.g., the month of October), and c) any maximum or guaranteed minimum contribution amount (e.g., up to a maximum of $200,000). (Better Business Bureau Wise Giving Alliance, n.d.)

Standard 19 applies to the conduct of the nonprofit organization. It requires that when a nonprofit enters a cause-related marketing contract, the contract it negotiates with the corporation should include the disclosure requirements as a provision binding on both parties. In addition, laws in 22 states (as of 2017) require registration by commercial co-venturers, including nonprofits and corporations that are engaged in cause marketing. Some require specific provisions in the contract between the nonprofit and the corporation as well as registration with a state agency (Copilevitz & Canter, 2017).

Other Variations

While the traditional definition of cause-related marketing is transaction based and based on the sale of the company's products, as explained in the previous section and addressed in Standard 19, a number of variations have emerged. While some of these are not tied directly to transactions, many authors include them in a broad definition of cause marketing, since the company's goal is to increase product sales. Some common variations are identified by Cone Communications (2010), a public relations and marketing firm.

The Proud Supporter Method. The company makes a gift to a cause or nonprofit organization, and the gift is not tied to sales of a product or action by the consumer. This is similar to traditional philanthropy, except that the company's role as a "proud supporter" is mentioned on its product displays, with the expectation that consumers will be encouraged to buy them.

Donation With Label or Coupon Redemption. The company makes a gift when the consumer submits, online or in a store, a code or label that comes with the product. The gift is not triggered by the sale itself but by this additional action by the consumer.

Donation With Consumer Action. This method does not require a purchase. The company promises to make a gift when the consumer takes some action, for example, hosts an event. It is not directly tied to the sale of the product but may help to identify the product with the cause.

Dual-Incentive Method. With this method, the company asks the consumer to make a gift and offers an incentive to do so, for example, a discount coupon. It is "dual" because it both creates an incentive to make a gift and also to buy the product, with a discount. It helps to build consumer loyalty.

Consumer Pledge Drives. This is similar to the dual-incentive approach. The company encourages consumers to pledge a gift to a social issue or nonprofit partner, sometimes offering a corporate match. One variation occurs when a customer at the supermarket checkout is asked if he or she wishes to make a gift, or round up the total of the bill, to support a nonprofit cause. Of course, in these programs, the individual is not recognized individually as the donor.

Buy One, Give One (BOGO) Method. With the buy one, give one (BOGO) approach, the company promises to give a product, or some equivalent, when a consumer purchases its product. For example, the shoe company Tom's promises to give a pair of shoes to a child in need for every pair of shoes that consumers purchase.

Consumer-Directed Donation. This is a variation of crowdfunding, which is discussed in more detail elsewhere in this text. The company permits consumers to vote on the organizations or causes that will receive a company gift. It is not tied directly to sales but may drive traffic to the company's website and help to develop interactive relationships between the corporation and consumers.

Volunteerism Rally. This type of promotion encourages consumers to volunteer in support of a social cause. Consumers are rewarded for their volunteerism with complimentary goods or services. It is not tied directly to the sale of a product but may help to generate consumer loyalty and drive traffic to the company's website.

All of these arrangements have advantages and disadvantages, from the perspective of the corporation and the nonprofit, including the extent to which they directly affect sales or simply provide a longer-term benefit through an enhanced relationship between the company and its customers (Cone Communications, 2010).

Integrated Relationships

Many nonprofit relationships with corporations are now comprehensive and integrated. They may include sponsorship, cause marketing, corporate philanthropy, employee volunteering, and additional interactions. Some are also long-term relationships that result in a close identification of the corporate brand with the nonprofit organization or cause. Another trend has been the development of products branded with a cause. For example, Product Red is a brand licensed by the Global Fund to Fight AIDS, Tuberculosis, and Malaria to a variety of corporate partners (https://red.org/our-partners/). Pink products, intended to raise awareness of breast cancer and provide support for breast cancer research, also have become ubiquitous. Such programs have attracted critics, who express concern about a lack of transparency regarding the use of funds generated. Some fear that consumers will believe the problem has been sufficiently addressed through their shopping habits and will divert their attention and charitable giving elsewhere (Raymond, 2009).

Operational Relationships

The relationships we have been considering so far all involve the blending of nonprofit and corporate identities in some manner. The nonprofit's principal contribution to the partnership is its name, recognition, and reputation, for which the corporation is willing to pay in order to enhance its own visibility, image, and sales. Such relationships are largely an exchange of intangibles. But some nonprofit–corporate relationships bring the nonprofit into the heart of the company's business operations by "acting as a supplier, improving training or recruitment services, offering benefits for employees, or serving as a test site for new products" (Sagawa & Segal, 2000, p. 23). For example, Pioneer Human Services in Seattle provides rehabilitation and employment services for individuals who are ex-offenders or in recovery from alcohol or drug addiction. Pioneer has a long-standing relationship with Boeing, under which it manufactures parts for Boeing aircraft (Pioneer Human Services, 2017). Goodwill Industries International, Inc., through its independent local chapters, provides training for individuals who are disadvantaged or have disabilities. The nonprofit has contracts with businesses to provide temporary workers in document management, assembly, mailing, custodial work, grounds keeping, and other fields (www.goodwill.org). Both Pioneer and Goodwill would meet some definitions of a social enterprise discussed previously.

As discussed in Chapter 8, such relationships are not collaborations and usually do not meet the strict definition of a partnership, although that term is sometimes used to describe them. Operational relationships between nonprofits and corporations are business relationships, but a corporation may be motivated to undertake them in part by social responsibility as well as business interests.

As in the Pioneer and Goodwill examples, a number of operational relationships involve nonprofits that provide employment or training programs. The nonprofits provide services and resources that corporations need for their business operations, but they also provide opportunities for companies to achieve a social benefit with resources that are outside their philanthropic or marketing budgets. By directing some portion of their payroll or purchasing dollars to a nonprofit serving people with needs, companies gain a kind of double impact: They advance a social purpose while also meeting their own core operational needs.

Joint ventures are another type of operational relationship between nonprofits and for-profit companies. As the term suggests, they are new initiatives undertaken jointly by the two entities. A joint venture may involve a specific activity or the creation of a new entity jointly owned by the two partners. Joint ventures between nonprofit hospitals and for-profit health care companies have been especially common, reflecting the high capital needs of such institutions. Entering a joint venture with a for-profit company can provide a nonprofit access to capital that it might find otherwise impossible to raise and access to management and technical skills that it does not possess. But there are risks, including possible distraction from the nonprofit's mission, potential financial losses, damage to the nonprofit's image and reputation through actions of the for-profit partner or the joint venture, and a multitude of legal hurdles. The Internal Revenue Service (IRS) requires that the joint venture serve a charitable purpose and that the nonprofit be free to act exclusively to pursue its own purposes without benefit to the for-profit co-venturers (National Council of Nonprofits, n.d.-a). The law regarding joint ventures is complex and beyond the scope of this text.

Putting Partnerships Together

Successful partnerships have a logic to them, and a nonprofit seeking a corporate sponsor needs to think in terms of the company's interests and goals. For example, it makes sense for The Home Depot to help nonprofit KaBOOM! build playgrounds. It sells building materials, its employees know something about construction, and it has stores in many locations and an interest in maintaining good relationships with the communities from which it attracts both employees and customers. The Home Depot also supports the American Red Cross with disaster relief, which also makes sense, since recovery from a disaster often includes repairing buildings. These relationships are good fits. It is understandable that Church's Fried Chicken works with the No Kid Hungry campaign, since it is in the business of providing food. It is logical that Yoplait would support the fight against breast cancer, since many of its customers are women. These relationships make sense; the nonprofits and causes that are supported are important to individuals who are part of the company's target market, and there is an obvious relationship between what the company does, where it does it, and the work of the nonprofit partner. But it would not be logical, or even appropriate, for a tobacco company or a brewer to partner with an organization serving children, nor would it make obvious sense for a company that manufactures entertainment products to be a partner with a nonprofit concerned with homelessness. For a nonprofit seeking a corporate partner, it therefore is essential to identify potential partners who are a logical fit and to be prepared with a rationale that makes the connection between the company's interests and goals and the mission and programs of the organization.

Successful partnerships are not automatic. Shirley Sagawa and Eli Segal (2000) identify five obstacles that can get in the way. First, nonprofits and corporations often speak a "different language" (p. 181). They use different jargon with nuances that may complicate communication across sector lines. Second, they may have different cultures; for example, corporations may be accustomed to top–down decision making, while nonprofits need to build consensus before acting. Third, the different status of the two partners may be an issue; after all, the corporation has the money the nonprofit needs, and it may expect greater deference than the nonprofit anticipates providing (p. 180). Fourth, the two parties may hold different worldviews. Nonprofit leaders may be skeptical about business motives, and business people may not hold nonprofit management in high regard. Fifth and finally, the two organizations have different bottom lines; the nonprofit is mission driven while the corporation, whatever the level of social consciousness it may hold, exists to generate profit and wealth for its owners. To identify and avoid such potential hazards, nonprofits are advised to enter partnerships with an understanding of themselves and their own needs, to seek out potential corporate partners consistent with their values, to engage in discussion and with due diligence to explore the possibility of a relationship, and to test it with small steps before expanding it to a wider engagement (Sagawa & Segal, p. 181).

Partnerships have become attractive to corporations, some of which eagerly seek relationships with nonprofits that provide a good fit with their strategic goals. Some engage for-profit marketing firms to identify organizations and negotiate the partnership agreement. This suggests the need for careful judgment on the part of organizations that are approached, to ensure that potential partnerships offer both the promise of financial reward and an appropriate fit with the organization's mission, values, and image.

Nonprofit Business Ventures

Let's now shift our attention to the bottom half of Figure 14.1 and consider some strategies and tools available to nonprofit organizations that wish to explore the idea of starting their own revenue-generating business ventures. Again, some of these initiatives might be identified as social enterprises under some definitions of that term offered by some authors—depending on their scale, relationship to the mission, and the extent to which they are operated separately from the nonprofit organization.

As Figure 14.1 depicts, nonprofits engage in three principal business activities: services, manufacturing, and distribution or retail. Some are very familiar and have been around for a long time. For example, many of us have shopped in retail stores operated by Goodwill or the Salvation Army. Most museums and hospitals operate gift shops and restaurants. Colleges and universities also have bookstores and restaurants, and some have created or acquired for-profit subsidiaries engaged in research or online education. But the range and variety of nonprofit businesses across the country is reflected in many examples of creative and unusual enterprises as well. Some examples will help us get the picture.

- Triangle Residential Options for Substance Abusers (TROSA), located in North Carolina, helps recovering drug and alcohol abusers change their addictive behaviors. Residents receive food, clothing, and therapy for free for two years but are required to work in one of TROSA's seven businesses, engaged in moving, brick masonry, catering, commercial and residential painting, lawn maintenance, picture framing, or retail sales (www.trosainc.org).

- Mobile School is a Belgian organization that develops mobile street carts that provide educational materials and games to street children in 21 countries. It also trains street workers, people who do outreach to children who are on the streets and provide them with educational activities (www.mobileschool.org/en/about-us). Since street children are unable to pay for the services, Mobile School's founder, Arnoud Raskin, started a consulting firm, Streetwize. Board members of Mobile School are shareholders of Streetwize, which produces revenue to sustain Mobile School's programs (Battilana et al., 2012).

- First Book, headquartered in Washington, DC, is a nonprofit that promotes children's literacy by giving children from low-income families the opportunity to read and own their first new books. First Book Marketplace, its business venture, sells new, high-quality children's books at low cost to organizations serving disadvantaged children. It acquires large quantities of books at deep discounts from its publishing partners and sells them to organizations at prices lower than they could obtain on their own. First Book Marketplace makes a small profit, which it uses to support First Book's core literacy programs (www.firstbook.org/first-book-story/innovation-in-publishing/marketplace).

Identifying Business Opportunities

How does a nonprofit organization that wishes to establish a business enterprise get started? It will not surprise students who have read previous chapters on strategic planning and marketing that the first steps involve looking both outward to the marketplace and inward to the organization itself. Planning for a successful business enterprise requires that the organization know itself as well as the environment surrounding it.

There are three fundamental questions that the organization needs to answer to narrow down its search for business ideas. First, does the organization possess marketable assets?

In other words, is there anything it *has,* anything it *does,* or anything it *knows* that others may find valuable and worth paying for (Mosher-Williams, 2018)? Are there assets that might be leveraged to provide a source of revenue? Second, is there a market opportunity waiting to be seized? Is there some unmet need that consumers would be willing to pay to have met? Answering this question may require use of some of the tools we have discussed earlier, including market research and portfolio analysis, as well as some imagination. The third fundamental question relates to the capacity of the organization to undertake a new enterprise. Does it have the staffing, the skills, the access to financial resources, and a culture that will support entrepreneurial activity? It makes no sense to stretch an already struggling staff to explore something that is just beyond the organization's capacity to even consider. In other words, organizations need to be realistic (Community Wealth Ventures, 2001, p. 6).

Figure 14.3 illustrates some types of assets that a nonprofit might possess and that could have value in the marketplace. Some assets may seem obvious—for example, space. Many museums rent their attractive spaces for special events, and some have opened restaurants. Underutilized space might be leased to a commercial retailer, like Starbucks on a university campus, or perhaps unused offices could be rented for use by other nonprofits. But relationships and access to a constituency may be assets that can be leveraged, too. In the example mentioned previously, First Book leveraged its relationships with networks of other nonprofits, assets that made it possible to negotiate favorable financial arrangements with for-profit suppliers whose access to those markets was not as well established.

Feasibility Analysis and Business Planning

Having identified some assets that might be leveraged into business ventures, a nonprofit may proceed to analyze the feasibility of a selected set of ideas. A **feasibility analysis** uses many of the tools we have described previously in this text; it looks both to the market and to the organization's own capacities (Community Wealth Ventures, now Community Wealth Partners, 2004). The external variables that need to be considered include

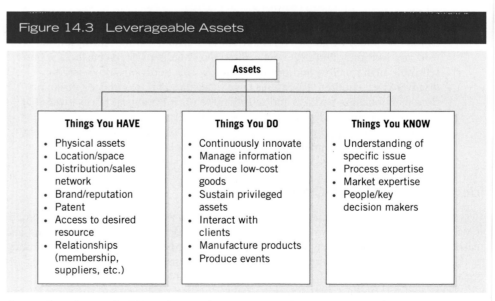

Figure 14.3 Leverageable Assets

Source: From Community Wealth Ventures (now Community Wealth Partners; 2001, p. 14).

- the overall size of the market for the product or service that the nonprofit plans to provide;

- the outlook for the industry in which it will be engaged—for example, whether it is expanding or contracting;

- competitive factors, including the study of others offering the same or competing goods and services, as well as generic competition for the same consumer dollars;

- the ease of entry—that is, how much investment will be required to break in; for example, starting a coffee shop may be relatively easy to do, but setting up a factory to manufacture complicated electronics would be a more daunting challenge; and

- profitability—whether this is a business in which it is possible to make money or whether it is, like many restaurants and retail stores, an enterprise that is likely to have a very small profit margin, if any at all.

Looking at itself, the organization needs to ask whether

- the venture fits with its mission;

- the organization possesses the skills and expertise, or capacity, to undertake it;

- its facilities and other material resources are adequate to the challenge; and

- it is prepared to undertake and manage the risk associated with the new activity.

Of the few business opportunities studied in detail, one may be selected for development of a full **business plan**. Some nonprofits develop business plans to guide the overall operation of the organization. Such plans encompass strategy and may be an alternative to traditional strategic planning, discussed in Chapter 7. This might be the approach taken by an organization that defines itself as a social enterprise, for which the business model is integral to the overall strategy. More commonly, business plans are developed with regard to a specific initiative, an earned-income business venture, rather than the organization as a whole. Developing such a plan is a time-consuming endeavor, and it would not be practical to make such an investment of effort unless the feasibility analysis has produced an encouraging result. A business plan is a detailed, comprehensive document that encompasses elements of strategic, marketing, business, and operational plans. It is an essential tool both internally, to guide development of the business, and externally, as a sales document for enlisting donors or investors.

Business plans may follow somewhat different formats, but most include the same essential components. Box 14.1 provides a typical outline for a business plan and its major sections. Most plans begin with an executive summary that gives a thorough but succinct overview of the major points made in the following sections of the plan. A potential investor or donor should be able to read the executive summary and have a basic understanding of what the venture entails. Another section of the plan describes the nature of the business and the products or services it intends to offer, provides an overview of the industry in which it plans to operate, and summarizes the strategic plan. A section on management and organization includes the organizational structure and the backgrounds of key staff and board members.

If the venture is created as a distinct business, meeting the definition of a social enterprise offered by Alter (n.d.), there is still a decision to be made about how it will relate to the nonprofit organization itself. The business could be established as a department of the organization, as a subsidiary or affiliate of the organization, or as a discrete organization (Helm, 2016, p. 344). If the business is established as a separate legal entity, then there is a

1. Executive summary

2. Description of the business

3. Management, organizational structure, key personnel

4. Market analysis and marketing plan

5. Description of products and services

6. Operational plan

7. Financial assumptions

8. Detailed financial plan

9. Uncertainties and risks

10. Plan for growth or exit

decision to be made about the legal form. It could be a nonprofit or it could be incorporated as a benefit corporation, a low-profit limited liability company, or in another of the forms that were discussed in Chapter 3. All these alternatives have pros and cons, and there are advantages and disadvantages to each approach. Students interested in reading more about the options and their pros and cons will find additional reading suggested at the end of this chapter.

A business plan needs to include a detailed market analysis. What data have been identified, perhaps during the feasibility study process, to ensure that there is a demand for the products or services to be offered? Who are the competitors, and what will be the competitive advantage of the proposed new venture? The four Ps of marketing, which readers will remember from Chapter 10, need to be addressed in this section of the business plan.

The products and services should be described in detail. If the business is a retail store, exactly where will the store be located, how will it be designed, and what types of goods will it carry? If the business involves manufacturing or distribution, what technologies will be used? How will customer satisfaction be measured, and how will the quality of the product be controlled?

To set the stage for the financial plan, a section is devoted to summarizing the assumptions on which financial projections are based. These may include, for example, assumptions about the economy, about demographics, or about growth in a particular market or industry. Careful business plans will include a **sensitivity analysis** that shows how projected results will vary if the assumptions are wrong by some percentage. For example, if sales are 10 percent less than forecast or inflation is two points higher than expected, how will the changes in those assumptions affect the venture's bottom line?

The financial section of the plan shows pro forma income statements, pro forma cash flows, and pro forma balance sheets, usually projected for the first three years. Putting this section of the business plan together is essentially like writing the entries of income and revenue, by date, in your checkbook—hypothetically looking out into the future. As a result of this exercise, the business planner should be able to project a point at which the business reaches a break-even position and then, hopefully, begins to earn a profit.

Although some business plan outlines may arrange sections in a different order, closing sections usually discuss potential risks and the precautions that the business is taking to protect against them. For example, risk management may include carrying sufficient insurance or operating the business venture as a subsidiary organization so as to protect the parent from liabilities it may incur. An exit strategy may be one aspect of risk management; in other words, if the business is not viable and needs to shut down, how will that be accomplished in an orderly way while minimizing risks and losses?

The previous paragraphs have provided a very brief discussion of business plans, but it is a large topic. Students will find many books devoted to the subject, and software packages are available to guide the writing of such a plan. Other sources listed at the end of this chapter provide useful information and materials.

Earned-Income Strategies: Issues and Decisions

Readers will recall from Chapter 2 of this book that the growth of earned income—what some call the "commercial transformation of the nonprofit sector" (Weisbrod, 1988)—has elicited debate. Some have reacted negatively to specific cases that they found to be inappropriate, while others have expressed more generic concerns about the threat that commercialization may pose to the nonprofit sector and society.

Sorting Out the Issues

Let's look at three cases, each of which created a swirl of controversy, and try to sort out the issues that they raised. In 2006, the Smithsonian Institution and Showtime Networks created a joint venture, Smithsonian Networks, to produce documentaries using the museum's archives and artifacts. The agreement provided Showtime with semi-exclusive rights to some museum resources. Although an investigation by the Government Accountability Office (GAO) found that the arrangement did not hamper researchers' access to the museum's materials, there was an outcry of criticism from curators, historians, and the documentary filmmaking community (Trescott, 2006). Critics raised objections not only to the terms of the arrangement itself, but also to the fact that as a business contract, some of its provisions would be kept confidential. The *Washington Post* editors weighed in:

> The Smithsonian argues that the filmmakers in question make money out of their work: Why can't the Smithsonian do so, too? Of course it can ... but it must be under different rules from a purely private body. As a quasi-public institution that receives taxpayers' money, the Smithsonian is obligated to reveal the details of its business deals to the public. It is also obligated not to make deals that restrict public access. Charging larger fees when its collections are to be used for commercial purposes may be acceptable; writing complex, secret rules about who can use them and who cannot is clearly wrong. ("The Nation's Attic," 2006, p. A16)

In 2004, the Museum of Fine Arts, Boston, agreed to lend 21 Monet masterworks to the Bellagio Casino in Las Vegas. The Bellagio paid the museum a fee of $1 million for its use of the pieces from the museum's collection (Edgers, 2004). Critics, including art historians, raised pointed questions: "Is the MFA's art available to the highest bidder?" "Should priceless works of art be displayed in the vicinity of slot machines and ... blackjack tables?" (p. A1).

In 2012, The Nature Conservancy entered a partnership with a marketing firm, the Gilt Group, to promote the annual swimsuit issue of *Sports Illustrated*. The Nature Conservancy received payments for products sold in connection with the promotion, including proceeds of a reception at which members could meet the models for a $1,000 ticket price that benefitted the conservancy's "beaches and oceans conservation work." Some staff members of the Conservancy expressed great concern about the appropriateness of this relationship (Flandez, 2012).

All three cases raise legitimate, but somewhat different, issues. For example, the Smithsonian case raises the question of whether collections, or information, or performances, or other products or services owned or produced by nonprofit organizations should be available only to individuals or companies who can pay for them, or whether an institution's nonprofit status, especially if the institution also receives public funds, requires it to serve a broader public interest. If the latter, what is the appropriate balance between that interest and the nonprofit's inescapable need for revenue? How can a nonprofit organization engaged in a contractual relationship with a for-profit entity meet its own responsibilities for transparency and disclosure while respecting the need of its partner to protect business secrets?

But some criticisms also reflect entrenched traditions and perspectives. Some may find it inherently offensive to see Monets in a casino, or a Starbucks on a university campus, or a corporate logo on the entrance to a music hall. Some may find the annual swimsuit issue of *Sports Illustrated* to be inherently offensive and the involvement of a respected nonprofit in its promotion to be inappropriate. However, unless the corporate interest affects what is shown, what is taught, what is played, or what issues the nonprofit organization pursues, such concerns may be more a matter of personal values than a threat to the organization's mission.

The issues are often separable, and it is those that relate to the mission that require the most thoughtful and careful consideration. However, perceptions (or what some people call "optics") also matter, especially if they might erode confidence in the nonprofit, cause people to think that it has acted in a manner inconsistent with its values, or create the impression that it no longer needs other sources of support, such as philanthropic giving. David O. Renz (2016) writes that "The oft-uttered admonition to 'run [a nonprofit] like a business' is a half-truth, valid except when it's not" (p. 739). He notes that "businesses ultimately have the option of ignoring or shortchanging some values or expectations in favor of others," since their obligation is to maximize benefits to their shareholders. But, "nonprofit leaders and managers ... must recognize *and accommodate* a much larger array of stakeholders' competing values and perspectives as they determine what their organizations should do [and] how they should do it" (p. 739). As attractive as they may be financially, partnerships that compromise the organization's mission require particular scrutiny. But even those that are consistent with, or even advance, the mission must be evaluated in terms of how the organization's stakeholders—donors, clients, volunteers, staff members, and others—may perceive them. For a values-based organization, such considerations are of tangible importance. Good business judgment requires that they be taken into consideration.

Another issue that some have raised is the need for better evaluation of the benefits to nonprofits from partnerships with corporations. For example, Alan Andreasen (2009) cites a study of a partnership between Toyota and the Sierra Club in which the benefits to both sides were monetized, that is, assigned a value in dollars. The total value of the partnership was calculated to be $12 million, but 83 percent of that value went to Toyota and only 17 percent went to the Sierra Club. As Andreasen notes, there is a need to improve the metrics by which partnerships are evaluated so that nonprofits can use the data in negotiating equitable relationships with their corporate partners (p. 184).

Evaluating Opportunities Against Mission

Leaving aside for the moment the view of those who do not favor the involvement of nonprofits in commercial activities at all, opinions on the appropriate relationship of the activity to the mission fall at two poles. Some argue that nonprofits should consider only ventures that are aligned with their missions and should not undertake activities intended solely to produce additional revenue. In other words, some say nonprofits should confine their businesses to the top half of Figure 14.2. As Hochberg (2002, p. 35) explains, "those who hold this view would consider it suitable for a nonprofit group that trains its clients in culinary skills to start a restaurant business to provide a quality work experience for its graduates, but would look askance at an environmental organization that opened a restaurant."

Others take a different view, arguing that nonprofits should look almost exclusively at whether a business venture is financially profitable. Since the profits are plowed back to support mission-related programs, maximizing revenue from the business ultimately helps deliver more and better services to clients, thus serving the mission. In addition, some say, even successful business ventures that are not related to the mission may create a halo effect that brings other benefits to the nonprofit, including greater visibility and the ability to attract and retain capable staff (Hochberg, 2002). But the question may involve more shades of gray than these two positions encompass.

The economist Dennis Young (2006) provides a useful framework for decision making, which is illustrated by Table 14.1. Young's model helps in thinking through the risks and rewards of possible partnerships or business ventures. As the table suggests, a profitable opportunity is worth exploring if it also supports the mission or if its impact on the mission is neutral. The former would seem to offer the best of all possible worlds. In the latter case, nothing really is lost, and additional revenue may be gained. However, an activity that could be profitable but that threatens the mission surely would require the most exacting of scrutiny. If it offered the possibility of a huge gain in revenue that would make it possible to greatly expand mission-related programs, with considerable benefit to the organization's clients, then a nonprofit might consider it, making adjustments to manage the mission risk.

What about a partnership or business venture that would just break even financially? If it enhances the mission, then it makes sense to explore it. It may be an opportunity to expand mission programs and services, totally supported by new revenue. If the new venture would just break even while having no impact on the mission, it might seem to be nothing more than a potential distraction that has little to offer. It would best be avoided unless it could be tweaked in some way to either produce more profit or better serve the mission. A break-even business that threatens the mission offers nothing, except for those who may be feeling masochistic. Undertaking a business that loses money while either having no impact on the mission or actually threatening it may appeal only to nonprofit managers who are, indeed, professionally suicidal. Unless such possibilities can be redesigned to overcome their shortcomings, they are most certainly best avoided.

Finally, there is the possibility of a partnership or business venture that actually generates a financial loss but contributes in some way to advancing the mission. A nonprofit might consider engaging in that activity, but it would need to be evaluated very carefully. The benefits and costs of the proposed venture would need to be weighed against those of alternative activities that might serve the mission equally or better, at the same or a lower cost.

Table 14.1	Evaluating Earned-Income Opportunities		
	Mission Enhancing	**Mission Neutral**	**Mission Threatening**
Profitable	undertake (fine-tune)	undertake (fine-tune)	scrutinize (adjust)
Break-even	undertake (fine-tune)	avoid (or redesign)	avoid (or redesign)
Loss creating	consider (adjust)	avoid (or redesign)	avoid (or redesign)

Source: Young (2006).

A Continuing Debate

There is a continuing debate regarding **commercialization** in the nonprofit sector and the relative value of earned income and philanthropy as sources of nonprofit revenue. For example, an article in the *Harvard Business Review* (Foster & Bradach, 2005) argued against encouraging nonprofits to pursue "the holy grail of earned income," saying that "sending social service agencies down that path jeopardizes those who benefit from their programs— and it harms society itself, which depends for its well-being on a vibrant and mission-driven nonprofit sector" (p. 100). Just months before, the economist Burton Weisbrod (2004) had argued in the *Stanford Social Innovation Review* that Congress should discourage nonprofits from undertaking business ventures and instead should increase the tax incentives to donors for philanthropy. Angela Eikenberry and Jodie Kluver (2004), in the *Public Administration Review,* made the case that,

> though marketization may be beneficial for the short-term survival needs of nonprofit organizations, it may have negative long-term consequences. Marketization may harm democracy and citizenship because of its impact on nonprofit organizations' ability to create and maintain a strong civil society. (p. 132)

Others argue that earned income is preferable to nonprofits' dependence on philanthropy and government support and that shifting to an earned-income model makes an organization more sustainable and effective. Thomas Lyons and colleagues (2010) write that "philanthropy, alone, is not sustainable." And Carrie Rich, cofounder of the Global Good Fund, argues that moving toward reliance on earned income makes an organization more nimble and adaptable, attracts talented people to the staff, opens doors to corporate partnerships, and permits the organization's "growth and impact [to] become accelerated and exponential" (Rich, 2014). But such authors sometimes minimize the fact that running a business can be no less demanding of effort and attention than traditional fundraising or grantsmanship and that sustainability of a business enterprise itself is far from guaranteed. In addition, there are examples of nonprofit organizations that have developed a base of donors that has sustained them well for many years.

But some critics of earned-income initiatives may be extreme in their alarms. For one, their writing sometimes implies that the nonprofit sector is synonymous with social service agencies, not acknowledging that many nonprofits, including colleges, schools, performing arts groups, health care institutions, and many others, long have generated earned income as a major portion of their revenue without apparent abandonment of their missions or the loss of philanthropic support. Nor do the critics always acknowledge that as many as 90 percent of nonprofit business ventures conducted by nonprofits that do provide human and social services are "directly or closely related to their missions" (Hochberg & Wise, 2005, p. 50). These include Girl Scout cookie sales and Goodwill and Salvation Army thrift shops, which have long been significant components of their respective organizations' revenue without inflicting apparent harm.

Some critics also do not sufficiently acknowledge the substantial dependence of many nonprofits on government support and the implications of changed policies that have forced them into competitive situations. Nonprofits' responses are sometimes portrayed as capitulation to the market rather than accommodation to the realities that public policy has thrust on them. It is reasonable to ask if their clients and society would be better served were the nonprofits forced from existence by rigid adherence to traditional methods of revenue generation. Increased incentives to philanthropy do not offer a realistic alternative to meeting nonprofits' financial needs, for a variety of reasons that go beyond the scope of this discussion. And, it must be acknowledged, even small nonprofits are increasingly dependent on major gifts from a relatively small number of donors, a situation that presents no less of a threat to their autonomy than their partnerships with the for-profit sector.

As noted at previous points in this text, this author recommends a balanced perspective. Earned income offers one way for nonprofits to obtain revenue and to diversify sources, managing the risks inherent in reliance on philanthropy and government alone. It will be a more appropriate and useful strategy for some organizations than for others. Some may rely entirely on earned income, but for most it is one component of a diversified funding base, together with philanthropy, government funds, and earned income from core mission programs. Indeed, some nonprofit organizations that long have been reliant on earned income are increasing their efforts to obtain philanthropic support, with the goal of creating a more balanced revenue profile.

Opportunities for earned income always need to be evaluated against their impact on achievement of the mission (as shown in Table 14.1). Those that threaten it generally should be avoided. Others may serve both financial and mission goals. Some may provide income to advance the mission from activities that bear no relationship to it but also do it no harm. Leaving aside the tax implications of unrelated business income, which we discussed earlier in this text, that is really no different in its ultimate effect from investing endowment funds in the stock of companies and using the dividends to support charitable purposes, a practice in which many nonprofits engage without receiving much complaint.

It is ultimately the responsibility of the nonprofit's board to establish, after thoughtful reflection and discussion, policies and guidelines, rooted in the organization's mission and values, against which such decisions will be made. Those policies should take into consideration mission-related, financial, and public relations risks; they need to be in place before the organization enters into new partnerships or ventures, and not put together as a response once the editorialists are at the door.

CHAPTER SUMMARY

Although nonprofits in some sectors have long derived a major portion of their revenue from earned income, that is, fees for goods and services they provide, there has been an increased emphasis on such activities in recent decades. Terminology varies in the literature of the field. This book adopts the term earned-income strategies to encompass a variety of partnerships between nonprofits and corporations as well as business ventures undertaken by nonprofit organizations themselves. Some of the latter activities are called social enterprise by some authors. That term is used in various ways by different people and authors apply various criteria to differentiate earned income from social enterprise. Nonprofits engage in such activities to increase and diversify sources of revenue and to advance their missions and gain other benefits. Some writers say that the pursuit of earned income is the same as being a social entrepreneur. But social entrepreneurship is

defined differently by other authors, including in this text, and it is considered as a separate topic in Chapter 16 of this book.

This chapter discussed four types of relationships between nonprofits and corporations that are among the most common. Licensing agreements permit a company to use a nonprofit name or logo on its products in exchange for a royalty paid to the nonprofit. Sponsorships are arrangements by which a corporation contributes to support an event, facility, or organization in exchange for the prominent association of its name or logo. It is not the same as advertising because it does not include descriptions or depictions of the company's products. Cause-related marketing (or just cause marketing) refers to partnerships in which a nonprofit is paid a fixed amount per sale or a percentage of total sales of a company's product, usually in connection with a short-term promotion. This type of relationship became popular following a very successful arrangement in 1983 whereby American Express made a payment to the Statue of Liberty campaign each time its credit card was used. There are many variations of cause marketing that have merged in recent years and not all of them are transaction based. Some nonprofit–corporate partnerships have been criticized. Partnerships that are inconsistent with the nonprofit's mission raise the most serious concerns. Those that may be perceived as inappropriate by the organization's stakeholders also require careful evaluation.

Some nonprofits have operational relationships with companies, often as suppliers or sources of workers. Others have entered joint ventures with corporations; that is, they have become partners in the ownership and operation of a business. Successful nonprofit–corporate partnerships are built on commonality of values and interests. There is usually a logical connection between the company's products or target markets and the mission and programs of the nonprofit.

Some nonprofits have launched their own business ventures; most provide services, manufacture products, or are in the fields of retail or distribution. Nonprofits begin to identify business opportunities by inventorying their assets—things they have, things they do, or things they know. Assets may be tangible, such as space, or may include relationships with particular constituencies, knowledge of specific cultures, or the organization's reputation and brand. Once it has identified assets that might be used to produce earned income, the organization analyzes the feasibility of using a select few of them. The feasibility analysis looks both inside the organization, to ensure that it has the capacity to undertake the venture, and outside, to gain knowledge of market demand and competitors.

Some nonprofits develop a business plan to guide the overall organization, but others only do so with regard to a specific business venture. Development of a full business plan is an intensive and time-consuming effort and likely will be undertaken only for the most promising of business opportunities that have been identified.

Nonprofits' efforts to increase earned income have generated controversy. Some critics raise legitimate issues about the impact of commercialization on nonprofits' commitment to mission. Others reflect traditional views of what are appropriate activities and revenue sources for nonprofit organizations. Dennis Young (see Table 14.1) offers a framework for evaluating nonprofit enterprise opportunities that may be profitable, break-even, or money losing, each in terms of whether it advances the mission, is mission neutral, or mission threatening. Ventures that threaten the mission usually should be avoided.

Some see commercialization of the nonprofit sector as desirable, and others see it as a threat to democracy and civil society. This book advocates a balanced perspective, in which nonprofit–corporate partnerships and nonprofit business ventures offer one way to increase and diversify revenues. A well-managed nonprofit seeks a balanced portfolio of revenue streams, from earned income, philanthropy, and possibly government sources. Nonprofit boards have a responsibility to develop policies and guidelines to ensure that partnerships and earned-income activities are consistent with their organizations' mission and values and that financial and reputational risks also are weighed.

KEY TERMS AND CONCEPTS

business plan 403
cause marketing 396
cause-related marketing 396
commercialization 408
contributed income 393

earned income 390
feasibility analysis 402
joint ventures 399
licensing agreement 394
nonprofit business ventures 391

sensitivity analysis 404
social enterprise 390
sponsorship 395

CASE 14.1 Minnesota Public Radio

In 1969, William Kling, then age 26, was managing a radio station at St. John's Abbey and University in Minnesota. He hired a young man named Garrison Keillor to host a classical music program in the morning. Kling then moved to Minneapolis–St. Paul to start a radio network, Minnesota Public Radio (MPR), taking Keillor with him. Keillor introduced a show he called *Prairie Home Companion*, which by 1978 had developed a cult following. In 1981, Keillor offered his listeners a free poster and over 50,000 requests came in. Offers of T-shirts and other products soon followed and sales were highly successful (Gallagher, 2001). At the same time, the Reagan administration was encouraging public broadcasting to become less reliant on federal funds and to begin seeking more earned income (Gallagher, 2001). MPR soon created Rivertown Trading Company as a wholly owned subsidiary to handle the growing sales of *Prairie Home Companion* items, which reached $200 million by 1998. For a time, Rivertown remained a nonprofit, fully owned by MPR (Phills & Chang, 2005).

But the organizational structure continued to evolve and become more complex, and the issue of unrelated business income became a concern for MPR. Faced with the risk that the IRS could challenge its nonprofit status because of its growing commercial revenues, in 1987, a reorganization was undertaken. Minnesota Communications Group (later renamed American Public Media Group) became the parent organization and was a nonprofit. It owned both the nonprofit MPR and a for-profit company called Greenspring, which encompassed Rivertown Trading and other for-profit enterprises established by MPR. The for-profit businesses produced dividends and royalties that supported MPR (Miller, 1998). MPR continued to grow, building a regional network that rivaled the larger National Public Radio. William Kling continued to serve as CEO of both nonprofit MPR and for-profit Greenspring, and other senior officers also held dual roles with both organizations. These relationships eventually became controversial.

Kling described MPR's earned-income initiatives as "social purpose capitalism" and was recognized with numerous awards. But some charged that his aggressive tactics were all about money and also questioned the level of his compensation. He was paid by both MPR and Greenspring; for example, in 1998 he received $69,200 from MPR and an additional $429,155 from Greenspring, which some at that time thought to be too much for a nonprofit executive (Miller, 1998). Others defended Kling's compensation as reasonable considering the scope of the enterprises he managed and pointed to the fact that other nonprofit executives in the state were paid even more (Phills & Chang, 2005, p. 69). A different issue arose in 1995 when executives of American Public Media asked MPR employees to volunteer to help prepare Rivertown holiday orders for shipping. Some said this was improper use of nonprofit resources to benefit a for-profit company. Kling defended the activity, noting that all Rivertown profits went back to benefit nonprofit MPR. The attorney general of Minnesota investigated the case and ultimately agreed with Kling, but the controversy further highlighted some of the complexity in the relationship between a nonprofit and a highly successful related for-profit business (Phills & Chang, p. 68).

Controversy emerged again in 1998 when Greenspring agreed to sell Rivertown Trading to the department store chain Dayton Hudson for $120 million. A total of $90 million went to MPR's endowment. Kling described the transaction as "converting an operating asset to an endowment asset," which would provide more security to MPR in case Rivertown's profits declined (Phills & Chang, 2005, p. 70). Kling and other senior executives also had worked out arrangements that provided them with personal bonuses when Rivertown was sold. Kling received $2.6 million (Abelson, 1998). Some said the case was an example of personal enrichment accomplished through the use of public funds that had, in part, supported development of MPR's popular programs, on which Rivertown's sales were based (Abelson, 1998). The Minnesota attorney general again determined that Kling and the other executives had done nothing wrong. As Kling described the situation, "We have very nice, diversified revenues. We've earned about $275 million from for-profit activities for the benefit of the nonprofit. If you have that kind of boost, it is an extra advantage" (Hall, 2007).

MPR continued to expand and prosper after the sale of Rivertown. In 2010, Kling announced that he would retire in 2011, to be succeeded by Jon McTaggart, who had been the chief operating officer (Kerr, 2011). In announcing his retirement, he also presented an ambitious expansion plan that would extend MPR's presence in 100 cities nationwide (Brauer, 2010). In 2013, American Public Media, MPR's parent, sold Greenspring to another media company ("APM selling Greenspring," 2013). In 2017, the board of Minnesota Public Radio decided to name its headquarters and broadcast facilities the Kling Public Media Center in honor of his achievements (Minnesota Public Radio, 2017).

Questions Related to Case 14.1

1. Was Rivertown Trading a social enterprise under the various definitions summarized at the beginning of this chapter?

2. Which of the principal issues discussed in this chapter are reflected in the case of Minnesota Public Radio?

3. What does the case suggest about the best ways to structure the relationship between a nonprofit and its earned-income venture?

4. Do you think MPR's commercial activities were consistent with its mission?

5. Did MPR's commercial activities under Bill Kling create appearances that might have been inconsistent with the values of its stakeholders?

CASE 14.2 Aspire CoffeeWorks

In 2007, James Kales was appointed as the CEO of Aspire of Illinois, a nonprofit located in the suburbs of Chicago that assists people who have developmental disabilities. Aspire offers programs that include therapy, group homes, clinics, and preparation for employment. Although he had previously served as the CEO of a Big Brothers Big Sisters affiliate, he knew he would face larger challenges at Aspire, with a much larger budget and 10 times the staff of his previous employer. Although Aspire had been in existence for 50 years, it was facing stagnant government funding, which accounted for 90 percent of its revenue. Kales would need to find new and more diverse sources of financial support (Glenn, 2007).

Meanwhile, the economy was about to sink into a major recession that would make philanthropic fundraising more difficult. Kales started to think about earned income as a possible source of increased revenue and perhaps also a strategy to create jobs for people with disabilities. With a grant from the UPS Foundation, he and his staff started exploring possibilities. In a meeting one morning, they were all drinking coffee and the idea hit: How about coffee? They began researching the coffee market, studying both low-priced and upscale coffee brands, analyzing trends in coffee price, and looking for a niche that Aspire might be able to fill (Frechette, 2011).

Just a few years earlier, Tony Dreyfuss had launched a new business in Chicago. He had worked at a coffee shop while a graduate student and had learned the business, working his way up to a management position. In 2003, with his father as a partner, he established Metropolis Coffee Company. The company operates a café, roasts coffee in small batches to fit customers' preferences, and sells coffee retail to grocery stores. The company features coffee that is hand-roasted, organic, and purchased according to fair-trade principles (Metropolis Coffee Company, 2018). His market research led James Kales to discover Metropolis and he called Tony Dreyfuss to propose a partnership. Dreyfuss's response was positive. "Where have you guys been?" he asked, adding "We've been looking for an opportunity like this!" After some further discussion, Aspire CoffeeWorks was launched in 2009 (Frechette, 2011).

Aspire CoffeeWorks is not a separate company; it is a partnership of Aspire and Metropolis that generates profits that go entirely to support Aspire's program serving people with disabilities (Aspire CoffeeWorks, n.d.). The coffee is produced by Metropolis under the Aspire brand. Aspire-branded coffee is sold in stores like Whole Foods at a modestly higher price than the Metropolis-branded coffee, providing additional revenue to Aspire and also a choice for socially conscious consumers who wish to provide support for people with disabilities (Frechette, 2011).

Aspire clients work side by side with Metropolis staff, grinding the coffee, weighing it, packing it, calculating inventory, and shipping it (Frechette, 2011). But there is more to Aspire's strategy than providing these jobs; it also advances the goal of bringing people with disabilities out of a sheltered work environment into the real world, where they learn to develop skills that they may be able to take to other employers. Aspire provides additional training as a part of the CoffeeWorks program and, indeed, some Aspire workers have been hired in full-time jobs with Metropolis (Frechette, 2011).

Aspire has continued to develop partnerships with businesses, including Groupon and Office Max, which sells Aspire coffee for use in commercial settings. Aspire advises other nonprofits to see companies not just as donors, but as potential business partners, and emphasizes the importance of approaching potential partners with a proposal that brings benefits to their bottom lines as well as serving the nonprofit's cause (Ronquillo, n.d.).

Questions Related To Case 14.2

1. Is Aspire CoffeeWorks a social enterprise under the various definitions summarized at the beginning of this chapter?

2. What was the asset that Aspire of Illinois leveraged to create a source of earned income from Aspire CoffeeWorks? Was that asset something it had, something it did, something it knew, or some combination of these?

3. How important is it that Aspire CoffeeWorks helps to advance Aspire's mission? Would it have made sense to undertake if it only provided a source of revenue not directly related to the mission?

4. Why do you think Metropolis was interested in the partnership with Aspire? What does it stand to gain?

5. What might be some risks of the partnership to Aspire and to Metropolis?

QUESTIONS FOR DISCUSSION

1. Some well-known nonprofit–corporate partnerships are listed below. In each case, what do you think is the logic behind the relationship; in other words, why does this relationship make sense? What may be the principal benefits that each party receives as a result of the partnership? Do you see any possible issues or problems related to each of these relationships?

   - Neutrogena sells sunscreen with the American Cancer Society logo.

   - The Sierra Club endorsed a new line of environmentally friendly cleaning products from Clorox, called "Green Works," in exchange for a fee (Jensen, 2008).

   - Microsoft created technology centers at Boys & Girls Club of America locations.

   - Christmas in April is a nonprofit that renovates homes for the elderly and disabled. The Home Depot has provided the organization with training for its volunteers, assistance from The Home Depot employees, and lines of credit for merchandise at its stores, as well as cash gifts.

   - In 2010, Susan G. Komen for the Cure, a nonprofit organization that works to fight breast cancer through research, community health outreach, and advocacy, and restaurant chain KFC (formerly Kentucky Fried Chicken) initiated a promotion called "Buckets for the Cure." KFC agreed to give Komen 50 cents for every special pink bucket of chicken purchased … from April 5, 2010, through May 9, 2010 (Huget, 2010).

2. Some well-attended exhibits at art museums have included collections of automobiles, motorcycles, and photographs of rock stars. Are these appropriate subjects for exhibition in a nonprofit art museum? Why or why not? Do they put the museum's mission at risk—in the short term or long term? Why or why not?

3. The Cystic Fibrosis Foundation invested $150 million in a small biotechnology company to support development of new drugs to treat the deadly lung disease with which the foundation is concerned. In 2014, the foundation announced that it would receive $3.3 billion from selling the right to royalties related to the new drugs that were developed, an amount 20 times its annual budget. Some people said the investment helped produce needed new drugs and also fund future research. They said it should be a model for other disease-fighting nonprofits. Other people noted that use of one new drug would cost a patient $300,000 per year and said that the foundation should have done more to push for lower prices. Critics argued that charities should support academic research but that it is a conflict of interest for an organization like the Cystic Fibrosis Foundation to invest in research by a company when it stands to gain financially. What is your opinion (Pollack, 2014)?

APPENDIX CASES

The following cases in the Appendix of this text include points related to the content of this chapter: Case 1 (New York City Opera); Case 2 (Share Our Strength/No Kid Hungry); Case 3 (The Y); Case 4 (The Girls Scouts of the United States of America).

SUGGESTIONS FOR FURTHER READING

Books

Lane, M. J. (2015). *Mission-driven venture: Business solutions to the world's most vexing problems*. Hoboken, NJ: Wiley.

La Piana, D., Gowdy, H., Olmstead, R., & Copen, B. (2012). *The nonprofit business plan: A leader's guide*. Nashville, TN: Turner Publishing.

Reiser, D. B., & Dean, S. A. (2017). *Social enterprise law: Trust, public benefit and capital markets*. New York, NY: Oxford University Press.

Ridley-Duff, R., & Bull, M. (2016). *Understanding social enterprise: Theory and practice* (2nd ed.). London: Sage.

Articles

Maier, F., Meyer, M., & Steinbereithner, M. (2014, December 12). Nonprofit organizations becoming business-like: A systematic review. *Nonprofit and Voluntary Sector Quarterly*, 45(1), 64–86.

Osberg, S. R., & Martin, R. L. (2015, May). Two keys to sustainable social enterprise. *Harvard Business Review*. Retrieved from https://hbr.org/2015/05/two-keys-to-sustainable-social-enterprise

Websites

Duke University Center for the Advancement of Social Entrepreneurship: http://www.caseatduke.org/

Social Enterprise Alliance: https://socialenterprise.us/

Government support is a significant component of revenue for the nonprofit sector.

iStock/DenisTangneyJr

Chapter Outline

Nonprofits interact with government in various ways, and the relationship is often complex. Theorists have identified three basic models of how nonprofits relate to government: as supplementary to government, as complementary to government, and as adversaries of government. In the supplementary model, nonprofits provide public goods to fill gaps left by government programs and services, as discussed in Chapter 3. In this case, nonprofits use private resources to provide goods and services to address public purposes to which government has not fully responded, possibly for various reasons, and their efforts thus supplement those of government. In the complementary model, nonprofits work with government. Nonprofits use government funds, perhaps combined with private funds, to provide goods and services that the government desires but may not be able to fully provide as effectively or efficiently itself. Third, sometimes the relationship between nonprofits and government is adversarial. Nonprofits may oppose current government policy and advocate for change. Going in the other direction, government monitors and regulates nonprofit activities. This is adversarial in the sense that if a nonprofit violates the law or regulations, the government may impose penalties or sanctions (Young & Casey, 2017, pp. 39–40).

In the taxonomy of these three possible nonprofit–government relationships, this chapter is focused on the complementary model. It discusses various ways in which nonprofits may seek, receive, and manage public funds to support their programs. Chapter 11 discussed the role of nonprofits in advocacy and lobbying; government regulation of nonprofit activity has been discussed at various points in preceding chapters in this book.

Government funds comprise a significant portion of revenue for the nonprofit sector. In 2013, almost one third of nonprofit revenue came from public sources, including 8 percent from grants and 24.5 percent in the form of payments for goods and services (McKeever, 2015). And these data understate the overall impact of government because they do not include such benefits as tax exemption, the tax deductibility of charitable gifts for some donors, and nonprofits' access to tax-exempt bonds as a source of capital, loan guarantees, and

Learning Objectives

After reading this chapter, students should be able to:

1. Define grants, contracts, and fees.

2. Describe the differences between grants and contracts.

3. Describe the differences among various types of government contracts.

4. Identify the benefits and risks for a nonprofit organization in receiving government support.

5. Identify principal sources of information on the availability of government grants and contracts.

6. Analyze cases, applying concepts from the chapter.

a variety of other indirect subsidies that government provides to the nonprofit sector (Smith, 2017).

The impact of public funds varies significantly among the charitable subsectors. For example, the largest portion of government funds is received by hospitals and other nonprofit health care institutions in the form of reimbursements under Medicare and Medicaid. And government payments represent the largest source of revenue for human service organizations. In contrast, public funds are a relatively small portion of revenue for arts and cultural organizations and environmental nonprofits (Smith, 2017, p. 103).

Changes in Sources and Patterns of Support

There have been significant changes in government funding of nonprofit activity over the past 35 years. Government funding to nonprofits increased substantially in the 1960s, with the introduction of Medicare and Medicaid, community actions agencies, community mental health centers, neighborhood health centers, and child protection agencies. Major federal student aid programs, the National Endowment for the Arts, and the National Endowment for the Humanities also were created in that decade. In the 1970s, new programs emphasized drug and alcohol treatment programs, battered women's shelters, rape crisis programs, and emergency shelters for runaway youth. In the 1980s, new federal funding addressed the emerging issues of AIDS, homelessness, and hunger.

As discussed previously in this text, during the Reagan administration in the 1980s, direct federal spending on social services and programs was curtailed. This was accomplished in part by devolving responsibility to states and converting federal funding into **block grants**, which permit states the flexibility to allocate the money to meet local needs. Many states also expanded their spending, either by using their own funds or finding new ways to tap federal programs, for example, by redefining some human needs as medical conditions in order to qualify for coverage under Medicaid (Smith, 2017, p. 105). Medicaid became an even more important source of revenue for some nonprofits after passage of the Affordable Care Act (ACA) in 2010 (Smith, 2017, p. 107). The Tax Cuts and Jobs Act of 2017 made some changes that affected implementation of the ACA and some continued to argue for its repeal. The outcome of the continuing debate about health care could, of course, have significant implications for some nonprofit organizations and institutions.

Since about the 1990s, the management of government grants has become more focused on accountability and performance. **Pay-for-success contracts** have become more common, tying government's payments to the achievement of outcomes for programs and clients. **Social impact bonds** are a type of pay-for-success concept that has gained wide attention in the United States as well as other countries. In this approach, private investors lend money to a nonprofit to carry out its programs. Independent third-party evaluators determine if the intended outcomes have been achieved. If they have, the government pays back the investors with interest, but if the outcomes are not achieved it is the investors who absorb the loss. Such arrangements can be quite complex, accounting for why the use of social impact bonds so far has been limited (Smith, 2017, p. 110).

When government funding is mentioned, some people may think primarily of the federal government. But the reality is more complex. Some well-known programs, for example the Supplemental Nutrition Assistance Program (SNAP), which some people call "food stamps," is state administered, although entirely funded by the federal government. Others, such as Medicaid and Temporary Assistance for Needy Families (TANF) are state administered and funded through a mix of federal and state funds. In some states, counties and municipalities act as agents for the state in administering programs and some local governments also provide funds directly to nonprofit organizations. Many nonprofits work with multiple government funders at various levels simultaneously. For example, a 2009 study of human service nonprofits found that 75 percent had more than one government grant or contract and 50 percent received funding from all three levels of government (Boris, de Leon, Roeger, & Nikolova, 2010). While the publicly available Form 990 reports revenue nonprofits receive from government, the form does not break that revenue out into federal, state, and local government sources. In addition, the way that funds are distributed among various levels of government is complex. For that reason, the 990 data alone do not make it possible to identify how much of nonprofit's revenue has been passed through from the federal level and how much represents direct state or local funds (Bowman & Fremont-Smith, 2006). As sources of government resources have become more diverse and funding mechanisms more complex, nonprofits have been required to develop a sophisticated understanding of multiple application and reporting processes and to adapt their thinking to deal with more varied and less predictable funding streams (Smith, 2016).

Grants, Contracts, and Fees

To refresh our understanding of distinctions that were discussed in Chapter 8, the terms cross-sector collaboration and public–private partnership are widely used, sometimes loosely, to describe any activity in which both government and a private entity are involved. But a grant or contract awarded by government to a nonprofit is not a partnership. A partnership is a principal–principal relationship, in which the parties share risks and rewards. For example, a local government and a private real estate developer might reach an agreement for the developer to construct a public building on government land in exchange for the right to include apartments and retail space that the developer would lease in the commercial market. But when nonprofits are merely government contractors, that is more like a principal–agent relationship in which the power lies primarily with the funder (Gazley & Brudney, 2007). This chapter is concerned with government grants and contracts received by nonprofit organizations rather than the cross-sector collaborations and partnerships discussed in Chapter 8.

Government funds may reach a nonprofit's accounts in three primary ways, including through grants (or grants-in-aid) made directly to the organization; as payments under contracts, requiring the nonprofit to provide specific goods or services to the government or its citizens; and indirectly through vouchers or voucher-like benefits that are awarded to individuals and which they may expend to pay fees for service at providers of their choosing. The latter is the case, for example, with Medicare, student aid grants, and some social programs, such as child care and job training. In this instance, nonprofits do not secure public funds by applying to the government; rather, they often must compete for clients, with other nonprofit providers as well as for-profit firms. Such cross-sector competition is common in certain subsectors, for example health care, nursing homes, child care, and, increasingly, education.

Although individuals possessed of **voucher-like benefits** may choose where to use them, all organizations or companies must meet government requirements in order to be eligible to serve clients whose fees are paid with public funds. For example, in 2011, the U.S. Department of Education implemented requirements on colleges and universities known as the gainful employment rule. Under this requirement and based on the loan repayment rates and debt loads of graduates, some institutions could be deemed ineligible to enroll students using federal aid. The purpose was to prevent disreputable educational institutions or companies from enrolling unqualified students, in order to receive tuition paid with grants or federally guaranteed loans and then failing to provide them with the skills necessary to obtain employment, leaving them with high debt that they might be unable to repay. The regulation was especially controversial with for-profit schools but also held implications for nonprofit educational institutions (Nelson, 2012). In 2017, the U.S. secretary of education suspended some rules related to gainful employment and announced formation of a committee to rewrite the regulations (V. Strauss, 2017).

Grants and contracts are two mechanisms through which nonprofits may receive government funds directly. Although there are similarities, grants and contracts are different in the restrictions and accountability requirements placed on the recipient. A **grant** is an award of money made by the government with the hope that a public purpose will be achieved, but the services are not provided to the government. A grant may be paid up front or in regular installments. The recipient organization generally has some flexibility in the use of a grant and the required reporting is usually less detailed than for a contract. The recipient of the grant is, of course, obligated to spend the money for the designated purpose and must provide evidence that the funds were properly applied. But failure to achieve a result, despite diligent effort, is likely to result only in the inability to secure future grants rather than nonpayment or punitive actions. Grants are often short term, covering perhaps one project, for example, a research study, purchase of equipment, or development of a new program or facility.

A **contract** is a legal agreement, in which the recipient of the payments is obligated to provide specific goods or services to the government and often to achieve defined results. Failure to provide the goods or services described in the contract would be more than a disappointment; it would be a breach of contract possibly involving legal remedies and penalties. Thus, when government makes a grant to a nonprofit, it is in a sense a donor, meaning that the government is expecting that the funds will have a positive impact, but is unlikely to become involved in implementation of the program or project. But when government contracts with a nonprofit to provide goods or services, it is more a customer of the nonprofit and may refuse to pay or take its business elsewhere if its performance requirements are not met.

The government decides up front whether its purposes will be best served through a grant or a contract. The Federal Grant and Cooperative Act of 1977 provides standardized questions that are used to make this determination. The questions relate to whether the government is the direct beneficiary of the activity or whether the project is serving the organization's own purposes, whether the government has determined the specifications for the project or is just providing financial support to a project designed by the organization, and whether the government has identified the needs or is just supporting the project because it is generally complementary to the mission of the agency involved (Pettijohn, 2013). It is important for potential contractors to understand that federal government contracts are subject to the Federal Acquisition Regulation (FAR), issued by the Office of Management and Budget (OMB) and by the Competition in Contracting Act (Pettijohn, 2013). But grants are not covered by these laws. Federal agencies thus have more discretion in selecting recipients of grants than they do in awarding contracts, but for the nonprofit organization, this flexibility cuts two ways. If an organization thinks that it has been treated unfairly in the award of a federal contract, it can appeal to the Government Accountability Office (GAO). But the nonprofit does not have the same right to appeal if it does not receive a grant (Pettijohn, 2013, p. 6).

If the government decides to undertake a contract, there are various types. As summarized in Box 15.1, these types vary according to the circumstances under which the contract is awarded, the extent of government oversight, and the risks to the contractor (Pettijohn, 2013). The nature of the contract is something that a nonprofit manager needs to clearly understand in order to weigh the potential benefits and risks involved.

Under a **firm-fixed price contract**, the amount the nonprofit will be paid to perform the specified services is set, although some contracts may provide for adjustments. This means that the organization is responsible for the costs of providing the services the government

Box 15.1 Types of Government Contracts

Type	Use	Government Oversight	Risk to Contractor
Firm-fixed price	To acquire commercial items or other goods that have a definite function; when the specifications have little uncertainty	Minimum. Contractors must act efficiently and effectively to ensure costs do not exceed the price of the contract.	Maximum. Government pays negotiated cost regardless of the actual cost incurred by the contractor.
Cost reimbursement	When there is too much uncertainty in the function or specification of the good or service being procured for a firm-fixed price contract	Maximum. Government closely monitors expenses to ensure costs submitted for reimbursement are authorized.	Minimum. Contractor does not bear the full responsibility for all costs.
Incentive	When government wants to motivate the contractor to perform tasks that are hard to define and specify, and when government wants to discourage contractor inefficiency and waste	Moderate	Moderate
Indefinite delivery	When exact times and/or exact quantities are uncertain at the time the contract is awarded	Moderate	Moderate
Time and materials and labor hour	Time and materials contracts are used only when no other contractor is appropriate. Labor-hour contracts are used when the government is supplying the materials and the contractor is supplying the labor.	Maximum. There is no incentive for contractors to control costs so government will monitor contractors for quality and cost controls.	Minimum. Contractors are reimbursed costs associated with time and materials (if a time and materials contract) consumed for the service.
Letter	When government needs work to begin immediately but a final contract has not been negotiated; used until a final contract is complete	Maximum. Government closely monitors expenses to ensure costs submitted for reimbursement are authorized.	Minimum. Contractors are reimbursed authorized costs until a final contract is complete.

Source: Pettijohn, S. L. (2013). *Federal government contracts and grants for nonprofits* (Brief 01). Washington, DC: Urban Institute (https://www.urban.org/sites/default/files/publication/23671/412832-Federal-Government-Contracts-and-Grants-for-Nonprofits.PDF).

specifies and could either earn a profit or have a loss. This type of arrangement "maximize[s] the financial risk" to the organization (Pettijohn, 2013, p. 2).

A contract that is awarded on a **cost-reimbursement basis** is less risky for the nonprofit. The contract begins with an estimate of the costs of the services to be provided and may have a cap on total costs that cannot be exceeded unless the government approves. But there is some flexibility and the organization is protected against having a loss so long as the costs incurred are appropriate. Of course, this flexibility comes with a tradeoff. The government will want much more detail on costs than it would under a firm-fixed price contract (Pettijohn, 2013, p. 3).

Time and materials contracts are a hybrid of the firm-fixed price and cost-reimbursement models. The government reimburses the nonprofit for labor on an hourly basis and covers the cost of materials used in providing its services. A variation is the **labor-hour contract**, under which the government pays the contractor for labor but provides its own materials (Pettijohn, 2013, p. 4).

Incentive contracts are similar to the pay-for-success contracts discussed previously. The government's payments are contingent on the achievement of certain targets. "The government uses [such contracts] to motivate activities of the contractor that are hard to define and specify [and] to discourage inefficiency and waste" (Pettijohn, 2013, p. 3).

Indefinite-delivery contracts are awarded when the government is not sure exactly how much it may want in goods and services or exactly when. A minimum and maximum are specified and the government places orders as needed. There is the risk to the nonprofit that it will gear up to provide the product, but the government will end up only ordering the minimum (Pettijohn, 2013, p. 3).

The government sometimes might use a **letter** as a temporary agreement with a contractor, on a temporary basis until a formal contract is negotiated (Pettijohn, 2013, p. 4).

Government Support: Opportunities and Challenges

Nonprofit organizations and government have a shared interest in working together, and both reap benefits. Many nonprofits would find it difficult or impossible to replace government funds with philanthropy or earned income, at least in the short run, and government would find it difficult or impossible to provide services directly if nonprofit organizations did not exist. From the perspective of government, contracting with nonprofits offers the potential to reduce costs, increase efficiency, and enhance choice for those who receive services.

A study published in 2012 found that nonprofits may have competitive advantages over for-profits in securing government contracts (Witesman & Fernandez, 2012). Public officials perceive that the public-interest purposes of nonprofits more closely align with the purposes of government than do the financial incentives of for-profits and therefore hold a greater trust in the former. Nonprofits may have closer relationships with local officials and their communities than do for-profit firms. They may be less costly than for-profits, and their dependence on government contracts may make them more eager to be flexible and responsive to government officials (Witesman & Fernandez, p. 5). Understanding that for-profits primarily serve the interests of their owners (shareholders), public officials may be concerned that they will reduce costs contrary to the government's desire to maximize the benefit of services provided and that they will use any discretion in the contract to enhance profit rather than the impact of programs (Witesman & Fernandez, p. 4).

However, the priorities of nonprofits and government may not be perfectly aligned. Some nonprofits will be interested in a particular constituency rather than the broad public interests served by government and the fact that some organizations manage multiple contracts may provide an incentive to try and shift from one activity to another. And, of course, from the perspective of government officials awarding contracts, the ideological or political perspective of some nonprofits may be a cause for concern (Witesman & Fernandez, 2012, p. 4). Nevertheless, scholars Eva Witesman and Sergio Fernandez conclude that government officials do trust nonprofits more, monitor them less than they do for-profits, and award them contracts for longer periods, especially when the nature of services includes task uncertainty (p. 1). However, competition for government contracts, the increase in performance-based contracts, and other trends may give some competitive advantages to larger nonprofits and for-profit firms (Smith, 2016).

Despite the attractions and benefits of working with government, according to Elizabeth Boris, Erwin de Leon, Katie Roeger, and Melina Nikolova (2010), nonprofit organizations that receive public funds also may face some challenging realities, which include the following:

- Some government grants require nonprofits to obtain matching funds from other sources to cover a portion of the program costs. This may mean that some of the organization's fundraising capacity or earned income may be diverted from other purposes.

- Government funds are often inadequate to fully cover the organization's indirect costs, that is, the nonprofit's general administrative expenses (e.g., rent, fundraising, etc.) or even the costs of the supported program. Government agencies are often inconsistent in defining administrative costs, making them difficult to allocate between funded programs and general management. This reality confronts nonprofit managers with difficult choices. As Smith (2016, p. 545) explains, "Underfunded contracts put nonprofit managers in a delicate position: relinquish the contract, with its implications for staff layoffs and shrinkage of the agency, or continue the contract, albeit at an underfunded level."

- Government contracts and grants may involve uncertainty. For example, awarding of a contract may be delayed, forcing the nonprofit to identify other sources of funding in order to maintain ongoing services, without assurance that the government ultimately will pay at all. Other times, even when the contract has been awarded, the receipt of payments may be delayed. In a 2010 study, according to Boris et al., this was found to be more of a problem with state and local governments than with the federal government and may have reflected the serious financial pressures facing those entities that year.

- In some cases, the terms of contracts can be changed unilaterally by the government agency after they have been approved.

- The costs of administering the grant or contract itself, including the development of proposals, recordkeeping, and reporting, are seldom covered by the award.

- Contracts are increasingly performance based, meaning that payment and renewal are contingent on meeting outcome goals. The pay-for-success movement and funding innovations such as social-impact bonds raise the risk that a contract will be terminated or that payment will be less than the nonprofit anticipated (Smith, 2017, p. 110).

A follow-up study undertaken in 2012 confirmed that many of these problems continued for nonprofits in many states (Pettijohn & Boris, 2013). In addition, studies conducted by the federal Government Accountability Office have found that these realities are not the exception, but rather are common, especially with regard to nonprofits that provide human services (Boris et al., 2010). In light of these problems, scholars at the Urban Institute have offered the following recommendations to government and nonprofits on how to improve their relationships: Government should standardize and simplify applications, financial reporting formats, and outcome reporting requirements across agencies with input from nonprofits; implement prompt payment processing standards; create feedback mechanisms to learn how practices are working; collect and report data on contracting practices and assess their impact on nonprofits; and work with nonprofits to agree on mutually beneficial accountability processes. Nonprofit organizations should help create feedback mechanisms regarding contracting processes; participate in efforts to simplify and standardize; encourage foundations and other private funders to accept the standard formats and standards in their reporting requirements; build the capacity to obtain and manage government contracts, including the ability to track staff time and allocate its costs and the capability to track outcomes; and educate the public about the importance of government grants and contracts in providing community services (Boris et al., p. 23).

The current realities of government funding discussed above favor larger organizations over smaller ones, since larger nonprofits have the diversified revenues, endowments, and philanthropic giving to offset shortfalls or delays in government payments and a scale of administrative operations that can absorb the complex record keeping and reporting (Smith, 2017). The administrative requirements of managing public funds have driven increased investment in information systems and professional managers, resources that larger organizations can more easily obtain. These considerations also have played a role in some nonprofit mergers and may force smaller organizations to collaborate with others, in ways discussed in Chapter 8, in order to gain necessary scale. Performance-based contracts have increased competition among nonprofits as well as competition between nonprofits and for-profits. That may have implications for the culture of nonprofit organizations and the sector. For example, some researchers have found that where government contracts are a substantial portion of a nonprofit's revenue, the power of the CEO may be enhanced and the role of the board diminished, with implications for governance (Smith, 2016, p. 549). Finally, becoming primarily or exclusively a government contractor reduces a nonprofit organization's autonomy and may lead to mission drift. As Jeremy Hall (2010, p. 5) describes, "The great paradox of grant seeking is that those organizations … with the least resources (i.e., the greatest need) find grant funding to be very appealing, often valuing production of something over doing nothing and thus allowing grantor priorities to overwhelm local values and priorities. This is a significant burden to bear."

None of this discussion is intended to imply that nonprofit organizations should always avoid accepting government funds, but rather that managers must be prepared for the various contingencies that doing so may create and clearly understand the risks as well as the potential benefits. It is also important to recognize the impact that public funding may have on nonprofit organizations and on the nonprofit sector overall. Faced with the uncertainties and complexities of public funding, the fact that many grants and contracts do not cover full costs, and a desire to preserve autonomy and focus on mission, many nonprofit executives have intensified efforts to diversify revenues by increasing philanthropic support and earned income, as discussed in Chapters 13 and 14.

Seeking Government Support

The pursuit of support from government (or foundations) is commonly called grant writing (e.g., the NIH website at grants.nih.gov/grants/grant_tips.htm), but that is not an accurate term. More correctly, the process of pursuing a grant is **grant seeking** and the specific activity of preparing a proposal is **proposal writing**. Grant seeking is a broader process than proposal writing, since it includes the identification and investigation of funding opportunities as well as planning and preparation that precedes the preparation of an application or proposal. This is analogous to the discussion in Chapter 13 about fundraising as something that encompasses more than the act of soliciting a gift.

Identifying Grant Opportunities

The first step in pursuing government support is to identify available programs. In some instances, this task may be relatively easy, since the funding agency may issue a **request for proposals (RFP)**. The RFP invites applications and generally is quite specific about the purposes and terms of the grants or contract that will be awarded. The RFP also usually defines the specific format and content for a proposal and the process for submitting it; nevertheless, the organization may be well advised to seek further information and insight through communication with officials in the agency before preparing the written proposal (Hall, 2010, p. 53).

Unless an RFP has been issued, nonprofits can identify grant opportunities through their own research. This is similar to engaging in prospect research with regard to philanthropic fundraising as discussed in Chapter 13. For grants at the federal level, one resource is the **Catalog of Federal Domestic Assistance (CFDA)**, which provides an exhaustive list of programs and is available online at www.cfda.gov. The CFDA lists all programs that have been authorized; the availability of funding that has been appropriated can be found in the *Federal Register* (https://www.federalregister.gov/), the federal government's daily newspaper, where Notices of Funding Availability (NOFAs) are published. Another essential federal resource is Grants.gov (https://www.grants.gov/), a centralized resource that provides access to over 1,000 grant programs of the federal government and through which proposals may be prepared and submitted. The websites of individual federal agencies also include descriptions of grant opportunities. There is no comprehensive source of grant opportunities at the state or local levels, and a search usually requires reviewing the documents or websites of relevant agencies (Hall, 2010, p. 57). There are also a variety of additional government and commercial databases and guides that can be useful tools in the search for grant programs, a full catalog of which is beyond the scope of this chapter.

Evaluating Grant Opportunities

In Chapter 13, we discussed the fact that not every individual, corporation, or foundation is a prospective donor to every organization. Similarly, not every government grant program is a realistic opportunity for a given nonprofit organization. Hall (2010) suggests six criteria by which organizations should evaluate grant opportunities and decide which may be appropriate to pursue: eligibility, conditions, matching funds required, **allowable costs**, program purpose, and the funding amount (p. 33).

Eligibility to receive a grant under a government program may be defined by four variables: the type of organization, the activities that the organization wishes to undertake, geographic location, and characteristics of the organization or a geographic area. For example, some research grants offered by National Institutes of Health and the National Science Foundation can only be awarded to universities or research institutes, so it would be a wasted effort for any other type of nonprofit to apply. Grant programs also may require, prohibit, or limit the expenditure of funds on certain activities, for example, construction, outreach, or research. It would be useless to consider such a program if it simply does not include the activities for which the organization seeks support. Some grant programs may be limited to certain geographic areas (e.g., rural or urban) or to areas or organizations with certain characteristics, for example, communities with high rates of poverty or organizations with demonstrable experience in treating certain diseases (Hall, 2010, pp. 33–39). If an organization is not eligible for a grant from a particular agency or program, that is an obvious reason to look elsewhere. But even if the nonprofit and its activities are eligible for a grant, a careful review of grant conditions may screen out some programs from consideration. For example, if the grant would impose administrative burdens that the organization cannot support or require matching funds that it cannot obtain, it would be inadvisable to pursue it.

Grant awards usually define what specific costs may be covered by the grant and which may not. For example, some may permit grant funds to be used for equipment or salaries—or not. A nonprofit must consider what expenditures it wishes to cover through grant support and alternative sources of support to meet expenses that are excluded. However, as Hall (2010, pp. 46–47) points out, some dollars may be **fungible**. That means that if a grant covers some expense that the organization is currently incurring, that may free up other money to be spent for things that the grant cannot directly support. For example, the CEO may contribute a portion of his or her time toward the grant-funded project, and thus a portion of the CEO's compensation may be eligible for reimbursement under the grant. In that circumstance, it is both ethical and legal to reallocate that portion of the CEO's compensation, which would have been paid in any event from other revenues, to accomplishing something that the grant itself cannot support, for example, a facility renovation, purchase of equipment, or the salary of a position unrelated to the grant (Hall, pp. 46–47).

It is important to understand the purpose of the grant program and consider whether that purpose is consistent with the organization's mission and values. For example, if a grant program's purpose is to advance medical approaches to addiction treatment and the organization's values favor a faith-based approach to the same end, there might not be a good fit. And, finally, the range of grants available under certain programs may exclude them from consideration by a nonprofit organization with an identified need. It may make no sense to apply under a program that makes average grants of $10,000 if the need is to fund a program requiring $100,000 per year or to apply under a program that awards multimillion-dollar grants when the nonprofit is small and does not have the capacity to manage activities at that scale (Hall, 2010, p. 48).

Preparing and Submitting an Application or Proposal

There are extensive resources available on proposal writing and on the management of contract and grant funds, including books, manuals, and websites. The management of grants is often complex and involves technical elements, such as performance management systems, cost allocation, and procedures for purchasing. This book does not include a detailed discussion of these specific topics, but suggested readings listed at the end of this chapter may be useful for students who wish greater depth. Chapter 13 provides a basic outline of a proposal in the section discussing foundation support. But proposals submitted for government grant programs are often more complex than those required by private funders, especially in their requirements for detailed budgets and timelines. Again, many RFPs or program guidelines will include specific guidelines on the format and content of proposals and often will differ, so no one template is applicable.

Preparing to submit a grant proposal does not begin with the drafting of a document. There is a need for advance planning and discussion of important questions. For example, in some cases the chances of obtaining a grant may be enhanced if a nonprofit works collaboratively with other nonprofit partners. Some grant programs are designed to encourage collaboration. Collaboration may be necessary to support the infrastructure needed to manage programs at a larger scale and provide the administrative support needed for grant management. Collaboration also may enable organizations to share the risk of new programs and the uncertainties that come with accepting public funds, as discussed earlier in this chapter. But, of course, as discussed in Chapter 8, collaboration involves additional considerations, including the organization's autonomy and the potential for disagreement, even conflict. There are pros and cons and larger questions that an organization needs to consider before adopting this approach for the purpose of securing a grant (Hall, 2010).

Whether an organization decides to proceed in collaboration with others or alone, it is often important to secure broad support for the proposal. Government officials at any level of government are ultimately accountable to elected officials, who are in turn accountable to their constituents. Most will be reluctant to award funding to an organization that is viewed as risky or disconnected from its community. In preparing to apply for a grant or contract award, some nonprofits solicit letters of endorsement from community leaders, create an advisory board or council to signify community engagement, or engage "symbolic partners" (Hall, 2010, p. 83), that is, community organizations that have an interest in the program for which the grant is sought but who will not actively participate in its activities.

Before developing a proposal, or even before beginning the grant-seeking process, a nonprofit organization may need to address fundamental questions with regard to the possibility of government support. In the terminology of Richard Chait, William Ryan, and Barbara Taylor (2005), discussed in Chapter 4 of this text, some questions may be fiduciary in nature. For example, will the resources and attention devoted to the funded program distract from other important activities? Do we have sufficient resources to accept the potential risks of becoming a government contractor? Will our organizational culture permit us to accept the accountability that comes with public funds? Others are similar to generative questions of Chait et al. (2005). For example, is our purpose in seeking the grant primarily financial, that is, to bolster our revenues, or to enhance our impact? And, most fundamentally, will the purpose, terms, and conditions of the grant be consistent with our organization's mission and values?

Nonprofits in the Policy Arena

Although some nonprofit managers may be focused on the mechanics of grant seeking and grant management, nonprofits hoping to secure and continue government funding cannot ignore the public policy process or the importance of maintaining relationships with individuals in government. As Steven Smith (2016, p. 553) observes, the political process can have a significant impact not only on the availability of funds, but also on the regulations, terms, rules, and procedures under which contracts and grants are awarded. To be successful as recipients of government funds, nonprofits need to maintain ongoing engagement with their communities, constituencies, and public agencies and officials. This would include, for example, agency and program directors, state legislators, city councilpersons, and school boards through which their programs may be funded or administered. As in any type of fundraising, relationships do matter, and the insights and understandings that may be obtained through personal contacts and conversations are as useful as the information that may be conveyed in documents. Larger organizations may find that they are able to effectively advocate on their own behalf, while smaller organizations may find it more effective to participate as members of an association representing the interests of multiple nonprofits (Smith, pp. 554–555). But with government funding representing a significant component of nonprofit revenue, neither nonprofit organizations nor the sector can stand totally apart from the larger policy arena.

CHAPTER SUMMARY

Government support is a significant component of revenue for the nonprofit sector, especially for organizations in certain subsectors, including health care, education, and human services. There has been change over the past 30 years in the patterns and mechanisms through which government funds are delivered, with many federal programs devolved to states and by states to local governments. Many nonprofits receive support from all three levels of government and need to have an understanding of complex policies and procedures.

Public funds may be awarded to nonprofit organizations directly as grants, which may permit some flexibility to the recipient, or funds may be paid under contracts, in exchange for the delivery of specific goods and services and with defined performance requirements. The distinction between a grant and a contract are defined in federal law and the government applies specific questions in deciding which route to follow to address a particular need or project. Some government benefits are provided to individuals in the form of vouchers or as voucher-like benefits; the funds come to the nonprofit organization in the form of payments for services delivered to the individual. The government nevertheless will impose requirements on nonprofit or for-profit organizations that serve clients receiving public support. There are various types of contracts that will be used by the federal government, depending on the circumstances under which the award is made. The types involve varying levels of government oversight and risk for the contractor. The trend toward pay-for-success contracts has increased the need for management of government-funded programs.

Nonprofits benefit from public funding, which they may not be able to obtain at comparable levels from other sources. Government benefits from the impact of services provided by nonprofits, which it may not be able to provide effectively or efficiently on its own. Nonprofits may have a competitive advantage over for-profit firms in competing for government contracts, since they may be viewed by government officials as more worthy of trust. However, the receipt of government support may present challenges to nonprofits, and some research has found that these challenges are common. They may include matching requirements, delayed payments, complex administration and reporting,

changed conditions, and performance requirements that may lead to termination of support. Government funding also may affect the culture and the distribution of power within a nonprofit organization. Nonprofits that seek and accept public funds need to prepare to address any such challenges that may occur.

The administrative requirements that come with public funds favor larger over smaller organizations and encourage collaborations or mergers among organizations, intended to gain the scale and depth of management capacity that is needed. Experts have offered recommendations to government and nonprofits on how to improve their relationships, including the simplification and standardization of processes and requirements and increased nonprofit capacity to manage contracts and grants.

Grant opportunities may be identified through various resources, including the Catalog of Federal Domestic Assistance (CFDA), the *Federal Register*, the website Grant.gov, or through individual agencies of the federal, state, and local governments. Nonprofits should evaluate grant opportunities and decide which may be appropriate to pursue based on six criteria: eligibility, conditions, match requirements, allowable costs, program purpose, and the funding amount.

The process of pursuing government support is correctly called grant seeking. A part of that process usually involves proposal writing. Proposal writing and grant management are not topics covered in detail in this text, but many resources are available—as books, on websites, and in other media. Writing a proposal is not the first step in grant seeking. Rather, nonprofit organizations need to engage in planning, address the advantages and disadvantages of collaboration with other organizations, consider ways of developing and demonstrating broad community support, and address fundamental questions regarding the purpose of seeking grant support and the consistency of grants or contracts with the organization's mission and values.

Given the importance of government support, nonprofits should remain engaged with the policy process. Larger organizations may be able to do this alone, but many organizations will need to work through associations with other nonprofits.

KEY TERMS AND CONCEPTS

allowable costs 425
block grants 418
Catalog of Federal Domestic
    Assistance (CFDA) 425
contract 420
cost-reimbursement basis 422
Federal Register 425

firm-fixed price contract 420
fungible 426
grant 420
grant seeking 424
incentive contracts 422
indefinite-delivery contract 422
labor-hour contract 422

letter 422
pay-for-success contracts 418
proposal writing 424
request for proposals (RFP) 425
social impact bonds 418
time and materials contracts 422
voucher-like benefits 419

CASE 15.1 SEED Foundation

Founded in 1997 in Washington, DC, by social entrepreneurs Rajiv Vinnakota and Eric Adler, the SEED Foundation operates urban, college-preparatory, public boarding schools in Washington, DC, Maryland, and Miami, with plans for further expansion. SEED schools serve young people from low-income backgrounds with a rigorous academic program, provided in a 24-hour nurturing environment. SEED's program is comprehensive, including life skills, health and medical, and social components. As of 2017, 90 percent of SEED students who entered the ninth grade graduated from high school, and 94 percent of graduates were accepted in college (SEED Foundation, 2017a, 2017b). SEED has gained national attention. In 2009, president Barack Obama visited the Washington, DC, SEED school to sign the Edward M. Kennedy Serve America Act. In 2010, SEED was featured on CBS's *60 Minutes* and in the documentary film *Waiting for Superman* (SEED Foundation, 2017a).

SEED's funding model is a mix of private and government funds. The costs of developing a school's facilities and its start-up costs are provided by philanthropists. Once opened, the school's operating costs are mostly covered by public funds. But the patterns and mechanisms of public funding vary, depending on the environment in each state. In opening the Washington, DC, school in 1998, SEED lobbied the U.S. Congress and the District of Columbia City Council to amend the education budget to fund a boarding school and then obtained a charter from the District of Columbia Public Charter School Board. Charter schools are public schools, but they are given more autonomy than traditional public schools, in exchange for their agreement to produce specific results, as identified in their charters. Charter schools receive payment on a

per-pupil basis, generally equivalent to the per-pupil expenditure for traditional public schools (Pham, 2015). The Washington SEED school receives operating funds equivalent to other charter schools, but special legislation was needed in order to add extra payments to cover the boarding component (Bruce, 2010).

SEED's approach in Maryland was somewhat different than it was in Washington, DC. Rather than operating as a charter school, SEED's Maryland program is funded under an act of the Maryland legislature, passed and signed by the governor in 2006 (Maryland State Department of Education, 2017). Students come from all parts of the state of Maryland; the state provides the school with a payment equivalent to 85 percent of the per-pupil amount that would have been spent if the student had remained in his or her home school district, plus additional payments for transportation and school administration (McCausland, 2008).

In early 2012, SEED obtained approval for a charter school from the Miami-Dade public school board in Florida. The SEED School of Miami opened in 2014 on the campus of Florida Memorial University with 60 sixth graders (SEED Foundation, 2017a). The funding model was complex. First, it required a change in state law to allow public funding of boarding schools. Now that it is operating, the school receives an allocation on a per-student basis from Miami-Dade schools, under a charter contract between the school district and SEED. The Florida Department of Education adds to the funds provided by the local school district, under a separate contract it holds with SEED (Smiley, 2014).

In 2013, SEED explored opening a school in Cincinnati, Ohio, but the project was abandoned when a foundation decided not to proceed with funding, concerned about the future of state appropriations to sustain the school's operation (Poiner, 2015). The SEED Foundation continues to explore possible opportunities for additional schools (SEED Foundation, 2017a).

In 2015, the founders of SEED, Rajiv Vinnakota and Eric Adler, left their positions as staff leaders. Lesley Poole, a longtime member of the executive staff was appointed as CEO (SEED Foundation, 2017a).

Questions Related to Case 15.1

1. Based on the information provided in the case of the SEED Foundation, are public funds contractual payments, grants, voucher-like benefits, or some combination?

2. Do the SEED schools meet the definition of a public–private partnership, as discussed in Chapter 8? Why or why not?

3. If you were a private donor considering a gift to build a SEED school, how concerned would you be about the future of government support needed to sustain its operations? Would the specific model (e.g., funding as a charter school or through a special annual appropriation) affect your thinking?

QUESTIONS FOR DISCUSSION

1. If you were a government official, would you prefer to contract with a small community-based nonprofit organization or with a for-profit company that might have greater resources? What could be the advantages and disadvantages of each?

2. If you were a nonprofit CEO, how would you summarize the advantages and disadvantages of

the three primary sources of nonprofit revenue: philanthropy, earned income, and government?

3. What do you think explains the persistent problems that nonprofits face in receiving government support, as discussed in this chapter?

APPENDIX CASE

The following case in the Appendix of this text includes points related to the content of this chapter: Case 2 (Share Our Strength/No Kid Hungry).

SUGGESTIONS FOR FURTHER READING

Books

Boris, E. T., & Steuerle, C. E. (Eds.). (2017). *Nonprofit and government: Collaboration and conflict* (3rd ed.). Lanham, MD: Rowman & Littlefield/Urban Institute Press.

O'Neal-McElrath, T. (2013). *Winning grants step by step* (4th ed.). San Francisco, CA: Jossey-Bass.

Articles

Knutsen, W. L. (2017, August). Retaining the benefits of government–nonprofit contracting relationship: Opposites attract or clash? *VOLUNTAS: International Journal of Voluntary and Nonprofit Organizations, 28*(4), 1373–1398.

Lu, J. (2016, Summer). The philanthropic consequences of government grants to nonprofit organizations: A meta analysis. *Nonprofit Management & Leadership, 26*(4), 381–400.

Websites

Catalog of Federal Domestic Assistance: https://www.cfda.gov/

Grants.gov: http://www.grants.gov

Special Topics

Social entrepreneurship has gained increased interest as a strategy for solving social problems and creating a positive impact on society, the economy, and the environment.

iStock/subman

Chapter Outline

Social Entrepreneurship and Innovation

Reflecting on the explosion of new nonprofit and nongovernmental organizations in recent decades, Peter Goldmark, former president of the Rockefeller Foundation, observes,

> Nobody could make that [growth] happen at the same time. You have restless people seeking to deal with problems that were not being successfully coped with by existing institutions. They escaped the old formats and were driven to invent new forms of organizations. (Bornstein, 2007, p. 4)

What Goldmark is describing is the work of social entrepreneurs. This chapter discusses social entrepreneurship and provides examples in the United States and globally. Chapter 14 discussed how the term social enterprise is used differently by various writers. The same is true of social entrepreneurship—different people mean somewhat different things when the term is used. That requires that we begin with some definitions.

Defining and Understanding Social Entrepreneurship

What is an entrepreneur? The term is generally identified with business, and many people probably first think about prominent figures in business, for example, Henry Ford, Bill Gates, or Estée Lauder, who founded new companies. Or perhaps they may think about a small businessperson who sets up a store or a stand and operates independently. Or they might just say that a young person who mows lawns and shovels snow for neighbors is "entrepreneurial," when what they really mean is that he or she is hardworking and ambitious. Indeed, entrepreneurs are almost always hardworking, ambitious, and independent people, and most create new enterprises, but the term has more precise definitions. Moreover, the role of entrepreneurship in the economy and society has been a subject of scholarship for centuries.

Learning Objectives

After reading this chapter, students should be able to:

1. Define social entrepreneurship.

2. Explain the role of entrepreneurs in society and the economy.

3. Summarize theories that explain entrepreneurship.

4. Describe characteristics of high-impact nonprofit organizations.

5. Identify characteristics that hinder or enhance innovation in existing organizations.

6. Analyze cases, applying principles from the chapter.

One of the first to study the role of **entrepreneurship** in the economy was the 19th-century French economist Jean-Baptiste Say; indeed, the word **entrepreneur** comes from the French verb *entreprendre,* meaning "to undertake" (A. Brooks, 2009, p. 2). Say described an entrepreneur as someone who "shifts economic resources out of an area of lower and into an area of higher productivity and greater yield" (Martin & Osberg, 2007, p. 31). In other words, an entrepreneur is someone who creates value by improving efficiency and effectiveness in the use of society's limited resources.

A century later, an Austrian economist, Joseph Schumpeter, introduced what has become the best-known understanding of an entrepreneur—someone who identifies an opportunity; creates a venture to pursue it; and ultimately upsets the status quo and makes previous products, services, and approaches obsolete. This can be seen, for example, in how the personal computer eliminated the typewriter and the Internet challenged the survival of traditional newspapers. Companies and organizations adhering to old ways decline and disappear, while new companies and industries grow to replace them, a process that Schumpeter calls **creative destruction** (Martin & Osberg, 2007, p. 31). The process is similar to a forest fire—nature's way of clearing out old and dying trees and making way for new growth. It may be ugly and disruptive, but it ultimately leads to a healthier and more vibrant forest. Entrepreneurs thus are central to competition in free market economies and play an essential role in economic progress; without them, we would live in a stagnant world without economic growth or rising prosperity.

So, we now understand what an entrepreneur is in the context of the economy, but what is a social entrepreneur? Like many other concepts discussed in this text, it has no universally accepted definition. For some, a **social entrepreneur** is someone who uses business concepts and methods in pursuing a social purpose. Some think of a social entrepreneur as someone who starts a new organization. Others use the term almost synonymously with leadership. But the literature reflects two principal schools of thought about social entrepreneurship that offer more specific definitions. J. Gregory Dees (Dees & Anderson, 2006) calls them the social enterprise school and the social innovation school.

Social Enterprise School

Those in the **social enterprise school** think about social entrepreneurship as the creation of earned-income ventures by nonprofits, like those we discussed in Chapter 14, or for-profit companies that serve a social purpose. For example, Jerr Boschee and Jim McClurg (2003) state simply, "A social entrepreneur is any person, in any sector, who uses earned income strategies to pursue a social objective." Those who come from the social enterprise school emphasize the importance of nonprofits freeing themselves from reliance on government and philanthropic support and achieving sustainability through revenue-producing business activities. They propose market-based solutions to social problems and often emphasize the blurring of the sectors, advancing the idea of the double bottom line, which we have discussed previously in this text, or even a triple bottom line, which considers environmental impact as well as financial and social value. For example, Steve Case, former chair of America Online, reflects this point of view when he says,

> Too many people act as if the private sector and the social sector should operate on different axes, where one is all about making money and the other is all about serving society. A better approach is to integrate these missions, with businesses that are "not-only-for-profit" and social service groups with their own earned income. (Dees & Anderson, 2006, p. 44)

Social Innovation School

On the other hand, those who belong to the **social innovation school** offer a broader definition of social entrepreneurship. In their view, social entrepreneurs play a role in society similar to that of the business entrepreneur in the economy, as described by Say and Schumpeter. They are "distinguished from other leaders in the citizen sector [nonprofit sector] by their long-term focus on creating wide-scale change at the systemic level" (Leviner, Crutchfield, & Wells, 2006). In this view, the social entrepreneur is an innovator; a change agent; a disrupter; someone who identifies an opportunity, undertakes direct action to pursue it, and produces change that improves the condition of people and society. This may include the application of business principles and the pursuit of earned income, but not necessarily. The emphasis is on innovation and transformational approaches to combining resources in order to achieve social outcomes, not on the sources of funds applied to doing so. Thus, social entrepreneurs might access traditional philanthropy or government funds as well as earned income—whatever is needed and available—in order to implement their innovative ideas.

As Dees and Anderson (2006) explain this perspective,

> social entrepreneurship is not about generating earned income or even about incremental innovation in the social sector. It is about innovations that have the potential for major societal *impact* [italics added] by, for instance, addressing the root causes of a social problem, reducing particular social needs, and preventing undesirable outcomes. (p. 46)

Thus, in this view of social entrepreneurship, one defining characteristic is impact or systemic change. In other words, not all founders may be social entrepreneurs and not all social entrepreneurs need to be founders. For example, someone who establishes a new nonprofit that increases or extends services offered in a community may make a great contribution but might not be considered a social entrepreneur if the person uses established models and methods that are not innovative and do not drive fundamental change (Martin & Osberg, 2007). Moreover, entrepreneurs may not be founders of new organizations at all; they may be individuals who lead innovation and change within an established company or nonprofit. Indeed, some companies and nonprofits include individuals whose title is **intrapreneur** and whose job is to drive creativity and innovation within the organization. In this broader conception of the term, social entrepreneurs may be identified working in nonprofits, businesses, or government.

There are points of intersection among academic and practitioner authors from both perspectives and, indeed, Dees and Anderson (2006) suggest that academic study of the field should focus on a blend of the schools, that is, on what Dees calls "enterprising social innovation" by entrepreneurs "who carry out innovations that blend methods from the worlds of business and philanthropy to create social value that is sustainable and has the potential for long-term impact" (p. 50). Again, *impact* is a key term in this blended definition.

This text adopts the social innovation conception of social entrepreneurship for the discussion in this chapter, but the use of business methods and market mechanisms do characterize many of the innovative approaches that we will discuss. As Sally Osberg and Roger Martin (2015) observe, social entrepreneurship is "a way to identify and bring about potentially transformative social change." As they also note, "sometimes [it] may even spawn a profitable business." However, before we leave this discussion of definitions and move on to other points, it is useful to note one interesting finding of a study by the Duke Center for the Advancement of Social Entrepreneurship (2008). Many social entrepreneurs who were surveyed do not identify themselves with the term at all and some think that "the seemingly endless definitional disputes are 'getting in the way' of [actually] doing the work" (p. 4).

History of Social Entrepreneurship as a Field

Examples of what we today call social entrepreneurs can be found throughout history. For example, David Bornstein (2007) includes as an example St. Francis of Assisi, founder of the Franciscan Order, who "built multiple organizations that advanced pattern changes in his field" (p. 3). Others might include important historical figures such as Clara Barton, founder of the Red Cross, and Robert Baden-Powell, founder of the Boy Scouts movement, and others. Antecedents of social entrepreneurship as a defined field include the "scientific charity" movement in the United Kingdom in the late 19th century and the emergence of "professionalized philanthropy" in the United States in the early 20th century. But use of the term social entrepreneurship has become common only since about the 1980s (Fritz, 2016).

Some writers cite the work of Bill Drayton, founder of Ashoka, as having been particularly influential in establishing social entrepreneurship as a field. Drayton was a U.S. Environmental Protection Agency official in 1978 when he became interested in the potential of social entrepreneurs to bring about social change. He founded Ashoka: Innovators for the Public, taking the name from the Sanskrit word meaning "active absence of sorrow" (Bornstein, 2007, p. 15). He and his colleague set out on a global search to identify the most promising social entrepreneurs and to raise funds with which to support their efforts. Ashoka Fellows are selected through a rigorous process, which includes evaluation of their proposed work as well of their personal qualities (Bornstein, 2007, p. 125).

The first Ashoka Fellow, Gloria de Souza, was selected in 1981. De Souza was an elementary schoolteacher in Bombay who had developed new educational methods and was convinced that their application could revolutionize education in India. With a four-year living stipend from Ashoka, totaling $10,000, she dedicated herself full-time to advancing her ideas. In 1982, she founded an organization called Parisar Asha and began building a team to implement her ideas. By the end of the 1980s, she had proven her methods and they were formally adopted by the Indian government as part of its national curriculum for Grades 1 through 3 (Bornstein, 2007, pp. 17–20). By 2017, Ashoka was supporting fellows in more than 90 counties (Ashoka, n.d.-a), providing them with funding, professional assistance, contacts with companies, and other types of support.

Ashoka was a pioneer, but soon other organizations adopted some of its concepts and methods. In 1987, the private equity firm General Atlantic founded Echoing Green, which follows a venture philanthropy approach to providing start-up funding and other support to social entrepreneurs in the United States and across the globe. The first entrepreneur supported by Echoing Green was Diana Propper de Callejon, who created an economic base and livelihood for residents of the Amazon region, as an alternative to deforestation (Echoing Green, n.d.-a). By 2017, Echoing Green had supported more than 700 social entrepreneurs and counted among its fellows the founders of such well-known organizations as Teach For America, City Year, College Summit, Citizen Schools, One Acre Fund, and SKS Microfinance (Echoing Green, n.d.-a).

Interest in social entrepreneurship exploded in the 1990s and the years since, generating numerous books, articles, journals, and conferences and academic programs dedicated to its study, including the Center for the Advancement of Social Entrepreneurship at Duke University, the Center for Social Innovation at the Stanford University Graduate School of

Business, and similar entities at other colleges and universities. As discussed in Chapter 1 of this text, courses in social entrepreneurship have become common in business schools and in nonprofit management programs in schools of public policy and public administration. As mentioned in that earlier chapter, there is continuing discussion and debate about the relationship between these two educational approaches and how they may evolve in the years ahead (Mirabella & Young, 2012).

Theories of Social Entrepreneurship

Scholars in various disciplines have studied entrepreneurship, usually in the business sector, and have developed theories to explain it. Theories of entrepreneurship are analogous to the theories of leadership that we discussed in Chapter 5 in that some of the theories emphasize the characteristics or traits of individuals who become entrepreneurs. Other theories emphasize behaviors, things that entrepreneurs (and social entrepreneurs in particular) do. Still others stress the environment in which entrepreneurship occurs and take a situational approach, arguing that entrepreneurship occurs when an individual with the right characteristics coincides with circumstances in the environment that are conducive to entrepreneurial activity. And, of course, there is some debate about whether entrepreneurs are born or made, that is, whether some innate qualities are essential or whether training can make it possible for almost anyone to become an entrepreneur.

Scholars have identified demographic characteristics of entrepreneurs, finding, for example, that such activity is more likely among immigrants, first-born children, and individuals who have suffered some trauma earlier in their lives. They also often undertake entrepreneurial endeavors around milestone ages, that is, turning 30, 40, or 50 (A. Brooks, 2009, p. 12). Other research has focused on the psychological characteristics of entrepreneurs, finding that they exhibit innovativeness, an achievement orientation, independence, a sense of control over their destiny, low risk aversion, a tolerance for ambiguity, and—in the case of social entrepreneurs—a high community awareness and social concern (A. Brooks, pp. 12–13). Some have studied the motivations of entrepreneurs. For entrepreneurs in business, making money is usually the principal motivation, whereas social entrepreneurs are motivated mostly by a desire to create social change. But entrepreneurs in both sectors may also share some common motivations, what Schumpeter described as the "desire to found a private dynasty, the will to conquer in a competitive battle, and the joy of creating" (Bornstein, 2007, p. 24). Many writers describe entrepreneurs in heroic terms; for example, Roger Martin and Sally Osberg (2007) include "courage" and "fortitude" among the characteristics that they exhibit (p. 33).

Other writers emphasize the behaviors in which social entrepreneurs engage, although some also imply certain traits or characteristics. For example, Dees, Jed Emerson, and Peter Economy (2001) write that social entrepreneurs behave in the following ways:

- *Adopting a mission to create and sustain social value.* For social entrepreneurs, the mission of social improvement is critical, and it takes priority over generating profits. Instead of going for the quick fix, social entrepreneurs look for ways to create lasting improvements.

- *Recognizing and relentlessly pursuing new opportunities to serve that mission.* Where others see problems, entrepreneurs see opportunities! Social entrepreneurs have a vision of how to achieve their goals, and they are determined to make their vision work.

- *Engaging in a process of continuous innovation, adaptation, and learning.* Social entrepreneurs look for innovative ways to ensure that their ventures create social value and obtain needed resources and funding as long as they are creating value.

- *Acting boldly without being limited to resources currently in hand.* Social entrepreneurs are skilled at doing more with less and attracting resources from others. They explore all resource options, from pure philanthropy to the commercial methods of the business sector, but they are not bound by norms or traditions.

- *Exhibiting a heightened sense of accountability to the constituencies served and for the outcomes created.* Social entrepreneurs take steps to ensure that they are creating value. They seek to provide real social improvements to their beneficiaries and the communities, as well as an attractive social and/or financial return to their investors. (p. 5)

Other theorists emphasize the environment or context in which entrepreneurship occurs. Some argue that entrepreneurial behavior is stimulated when there is some perturbation, that is, when "people are displaced from their regular business routines by political, cultural, or economic factors" (A. Brooks, 2009, p. 9). Thus, for example, the seeds of new business ventures may be planted in economic recessions, when people lose their jobs and pursue new ventures as an alternative. The later decades of the 20th century and the first decade of the 21st saw significant changes in the world, including the fall of repressive governments around the world, increasing levels of education, the advancement of women in most regions, increased communication and awareness of global conditions, and a shift in attitudes that favored private or government action to solve social problems. These changes were often disruptive and provided new opportunities for business and social entrepreneurship across the globe (Bornstein, 2007).

Students will recall from Chapter 5 that some scholars have proposed models that integrate various approaches to leadership theory. (See Dym and Hutson's alignment map in Table 5.3.) Similarly, Arthur Brooks (2009) describes a kind of "perfect storm" for entrepreneurship, where external conditions and the internal characteristics of individuals converge to provide the opportunity for the entrepreneurial process to unfold. According to Arthur Brooks (2009), entrepreneurship is possible when social, economic, and political conditions are conducive. But even in an environment favorable to entrepreneurship, there must be individuals with the right characteristics and the right education and experience in order for the entrepreneurial process to begin. In other words, change may occur when the right person is in the right place at the right time with the right skills.

Jane Wei-Skillern, James Austin, Herman Leonard, and Howard Stevenson (2007) describe a similar model of entrepreneurship, involving the fit among four variables: the People, the Context, the Deal, and the Opportunity. In business, the "deal" refers to the "bargain that defines who in a venture gives what and who gets what and when those deliveries and receipts will take place" (p. 11). In the case of social entrepreneurship, "the deal" translates to the **social value proposition** (pp. 21–22). Similar to Arthur Brooks, Wei-Skillern et al. (2007) emphasize that "because these [four components] are interdependent and situationally determined, the entrepreneur must manage the fit among them and adapt continuously to new circumstances over time" (p. 10).

Social Entrepreneurship Across Fields and Around the World

Now that we have defined social entrepreneurship and considered some theories that explain it, let's look at a few examples of social entrepreneurs at work. Ashoka categorizes the work of its fellows into eight topic areas: Children and Youth, Environment and Sustainability, Health and Fitness, Civic Engagement, Human Rights and Equality, Peace and Harmonious Relations, Development and Prosperity, and Business and Social Enterprise. A few selected examples based on the work of Ashoka Fellows illustrate a wide array of innovation across these fields.

Betsy Krebs. Betsy Krebs was a legal advocate for foster care children in New York. She observed the difficult challenges they faced and the poor life outcomes that many experienced. Determined to improve the situation, she created the Youth Advocacy Center, with support from the court system and others. The center was based on Krebs' recognition "that young people who are able to identify their own needs, speak up for themselves, and assert control of their lives while in the system are far more likely to succeed in life when they are beyond it." Krebs was not just an advocate for youth; she became "an advocate for youth self-advocacy." The center developed an innovation program model, called the Getting Beyond the System® (GBS) seminar. As Krebs describes, the program includes "a semester-long seminar in a campus setting that teaches young people ages 17 and up how to set goals and how to get information about how to reach those goals from leading professionals in the community" (Ashoka, n.d.-b).

Richard Seshie. Most Ghanaians live in rural areas, where many are isolated without access to markets or other resources. One of the biggest challenges is the "first mile," that is, the distance over which goods need to be moved to reach established transportation channels. Richard Seshie had an idea. If motorbikes and drivers could be strategically positioned in an organized network, they could transport farmers' products to markets and deliver supplies in return, increasing financial returns to the farmers and providing employment for the drivers. By 2013, he had completed a successful pilot project and was preparing to take his idea to scale across Ghana (Ashoka, n.d.-c).

Sumaira Abdulali. In Mumbai, India, as in many urbanizing areas, noise is a major problem, causing hearing loss and other health issues. Working through the Awaaz Foundation, Sumaira Abdulali works to increase public awareness of noise pollution as a public health problem and to monitor and report noise problems. She developed a system for tracking the locations of excessive noise and engaged volunteers to help encourage government and businesses to take steps to reduce the risks (Ashoka, n.d.-d).

Mohammad Alhabsyi. In 2003, an outbreak of malaria killed 267 people in South Halmahera, Indonesia. Mohammad Alhabsyi, a physician, realized that the top–down approach to preventing and treating malaria followed by the government just was not working. Malaria prevention needed to involve everyone and be centered at the local level. He founded the Malaria Center, which organized communities to identify and prevent outbreaks. Village Malaria Committees take the lead and provide a channel of communication to the government when further support is needed. He also initiated a curriculum to educate children on the causes of malaria and promote immunization. He established treatment centers, gaining support for them from government at various levels, and set up Internet cafés, which generated revenue to support the centers while also increasing Internet access in the villages (Ashoka, n.d.-e).

Lauren Diaz Arias. In 2013, nearly 11,000 people were sentenced to prison in Costa Rica, many of them for relatively minor offenses. Rather than rehabilitating inmates, the prisons were continuing a cycle of crime; many of those sentenced were recidivists, meaning that they had been in prison before. Lauren Diaz Arias founded Fundacion Nueva Oportunidad, which began operations in 2013, aiming to "empower inmates, decrease recidivism and develop a more empathic society that understands and reintegrates ex-convicts, keeping them away from crime" (Ashoka, n.d.-f). Fundacion Nueva Oportunidad works with prison staff as well as inmates who have committed minor crimes and are nearing the end of their sentences, to help them develop a plan for a business that will provide self-employment upon release. Seven inmates completed the program in the first year, and Diaz developed plans to expand the program to serve 200 prisoners eventually, while also advocating for changes in public policy that would support their integration back into society (Ashoka, n.d.-f).

The examples above illustrate some points expressed earlier in this chapter. All of the cases involve innovative ideas for addressing social problems. Some involve earned income, but others do not; some rely on philanthropy, government support, or both. Some use business methods, but others achieve results primarily by building communities and engaging volunteers. As the examples also demonstrate, social entrepreneurship extends beyond the United States to all parts of the world. Indeed, some people argue that social entrepreneurship that incorporates business approaches is even more important in parts of the world outside the United States and Western Europe, where traditional philanthropy may be less a part of cultures and where governments may be less prepared to address social problems. In such circumstances, social entrepreneurship may provide a more realistic strategy than philanthropic fundraising or government social programs based on Western models. For example, Muhammad Yunus (2007), founder of **microfinance** pioneer Grameen Bank, makes the case that business, government, and the nonprofit sector as we know it are not able to meet the challenges and advocates for creating **social businesses** as an alternative strategy.

Yunus (2007) argues that "Unfettered markets in their current form are not meant to solve social problems and instead may actually exacerbate poverty, disease, pollution, corruption, crime, and inequality" (p. 5). Nor, says Yunus, can government be the solution. Government provides public goods such as national defense, central banking, public schools, and public health services, and sets the rules by which markets work. But governments in developing nations are too often slow and bureaucratic, prone to corruption, and controlled by vested interests that resist change (p. 9). Yunus also questions whether nonprofits alone can solve the problem of poverty. Echoing Bill Shore and others who advocate more reliance on nonprofit earned income, he considers the voluntary giving that supports nonprofits to be a form of "trickle-down economics"; in other words, nonprofits receive only the economic surplus that affluent people voluntarily give and do not have a sustainable revenue model of their own. Yunus agrees that corporate social responsibility may be a good thing, but is doubtful that social goals can ever trump the drive for profit, since corporate directors have an obligation to shareholders to maximize financial returns. Nor does he believe that hybrid organizations can overcome the ultimate pressure to favor profit over social impact. Multinational institutions dedicated to poverty alleviation, such as the World Bank, have focused on the development of infrastructure (e.g., roads, dams, and airports) in the belief that such projects will stimulate economic development, but Yunus sees two problems. First, this approach is also a form of "trickle down," and the poor are not actors. "The poor can be actors themselves," he writes. "The poor can be self-employed entrepreneurs and create jobs for others" (p. 12).

Although he generally adopts the social innovation definition of social entrepreneurship, Yunus (2007) advocates the creation of social businesses, of which he identifies two types. The first type operate as businesses, but with a positive social impact; that is consistent with the idea of social enterprises as many people use the term. The second type are owned by individuals who are poor, helping them to achieve personal economic independence.

Building High-Impact Nonprofits

If social impact is a defining characteristic of social entrepreneurship, what do we know about organizations that achieve it? What makes them different from others?

In research that was reported in an influential 2008 book, revised and updated in 2012, Leslie Crutchfield and Heather McLeod Grant (2012) describe characteristics of nonprofit organizations that they identify as representing "a new cadre of entrepreneurial nonprofits [that have] created extraordinary levels of social impact" (p. 13). They argue that entrepreneurial nonprofits will define the future:

> If the 1980s and early 1990s were all about replicating programs and the [2000s were] about building effective organizations, we believe the next leap is to see nonprofits as *catalytic agents of change.* We must begin to study and understand nonprofits not merely as organizations housed within four walls, but as catalysts that work within, and change, entire systems. The most effective of these groups employ a strategy of leverage, using government, business, the public, and other nonprofits as *forces for good,* helping them deliver even greater social change than they could possibly achieve alone. (p. 18)

Crutchfield and Grant (2012) examined hundreds of nonprofits using two criteria: (1) Did the organization achieve substantial and sustained results at the national level? (2) Did the organization have an impact on an entire system? After extensive research, the authors identified 12 organizations—in various subsectors—that they determined to be exemplary (although not an exhaustive list of organizations that might meet their criteria). The 12 organizations—some of which have already been mentioned in this text—are listed in Table 16.1.

According to Crutchfield and Grant (2012), these entrepreneurial nonprofits shatter "myths" of "perceived wisdom in the field [of nonprofit management]" (p. 30). Many are not perfectly managed and do not have low overhead. Many do not have prominent brand names. Not all are based on a breakthrough new idea. Not all have textbook mission statements or large budgets. Moreover, many do not rate highly on conventional metrics. Rather, the authors identified six practices common to all 12 organizations:

1. *Advocate and serve.* Some began by offering programs, and others began as advocacy organizations, but over time, all evolved to include both types of activity.

2. *Make markets work.* Some have corporate partnerships or earned income, while others rely primarily on philanthropy, but all have used market forces and use private sector methods in their work.

Table 16.1 High-Impact Nonprofits Identified by Crutchfield and Grant (2012)

- Center on Budget and Policy Priorities
- City Year
- Environmental Defense Fund
- Exploratorium
- Feeding America (formerly America's Second Harvest)
- Habitat for Humanity
- The Heritage Foundation
- National Council of La Raza
- Self-Help
- Share Our Strength
- Teach for America
- YouthBuild USA

3. *Inspire evangelists.* All have created committed advocates on their behalf.

4. *Nurture nonprofit networks.* All form partnerships with other nonprofits as well as government.

5. *Master the art of adaptation.* All are capable of adjusting their strategies to environmental changes.

6. *Share leadership.* The CEOs of these organizations empower others and delegate authority within their organizations.

If impact is measured in terms of transformational change, the organization Community Wealth Partners offers useful resources. The organization was originally named Community Wealth Ventures, founded as a for-profit subsidiary of nonprofit Share Our Strength. Community Wealth Ventures initially focused its work on helping nonprofits launch earned-income business ventures. It later shifted its focus to helping organizations achieve **social transformation** and changed its name to Community Wealth Partners (CWP), reflecting that evolution.

Community Wealth Partners engages in partnerships and offers consulting services to help organizations gain greater impact on social problems. CWP also offers a variety of useful resources, including its Social Transformation Lifecycle, a tool for organizations seeking to advance transformational change. The lifecycle is depicted in Figure 16.1 and provides a checklist of questions to be considered as an organization plans its work.

Sustaining Innovation

Again, social entrepreneurship is not synonymous with founding new organizations and social innovation may occur in various settings, including established organizations. As James Phills, Kriss Deiglmeier, and Dale Miller (2008) point out, "Innovation can emerge in places and from people outside the scope of social entrepreneurship and social enterprise. In particular, large, established nonprofits, businesses, even governments are producing social innovations." But what determines the capacity for innovation and what can organizations do to enhance it?

There is an extensive research literature on innovation, but most of it relates to businesses rather than nonprofit organizations. In a study funded by the Rockefeller Foundation and discussed in a 2012 report, Christian Seelos and Johanna Mair surveyed the literature on innovation in nonprofits and offered a model of organizational capacity for continuous innovation (OCCI), which leaders may apply to analyzing their own organizations (Seelos & Mair, 2012a). The authors emphasize that innovation should be thought about as a *process* rather than just an outcome. In other words, innovations don't just happen; there are steps through which new ideas are generated, analyzed, tested, and eventually formalized as ongoing new programs (pp. 8–9). What are the factors that either hinder or promote innovation? Seelos and Mair (2012a) identify some factors that involve the organization's relationships with the outside world and others that are related to internal realities. An organization's capacity for innovation may be hindered or enhanced by its relationships with funders, competitors, collaborators, customers, and communities. But internal factors are important, too, including creativity, strategy, structure, culture, leadership, vision, and mission (p. 11). Warren Nilsson and Tana Paddock (2014) also studied innovative organizations and, like Seelos and Mair, they emphasize the importance of both external relationships and internal factors, writing "The organizations that we worked with ... have in common one apparently simple practice: They pay a great deal of attention to the inner experiences of the people who work in them. The key to changing the world may have less to do with understanding

Figure 16.1   Social Transformation Lifecycle

Community Wealth Partners

A Share Our Strength Organization

dream forward

Social Transformation Lifecycle

A tool to help you ask the powerful questions necessary for gauging and advancing your progress toward transformational change.

At Community Wealth Partners we are focused on one powerful question: Why do some social change efforts achieve transformational results while others only make incremental progress? Drawing on lessons from our client work and in-depth research on efforts that have tackled social problems at the magnitude they exist, we've identified four broad stages along which transformational efforts generally evolve.

Acknowledging that all such efforts are unique and none progress in a linear fashion, we would encourage you to ask the following questions:

❶ Into which stage(s) does your effort seem to fit?

❷ Around which questions have you established clear answers?

❸ What questions are holding you back?

❹ What questions do you need to address before progressing to the next stage?

	STAGE 1: Framing the Effort	STAGE 2: Proving the Solution(s)	STAGE 3: Reaching Dramatic Improvement	STAGE 4: Reinvigorating the Effort
BOLD GOAL & STRATEGY	What is our bold goal? What is our role in achieving this goal?	What is our approach to realizing our bold goal?	How will we scale our approach to reach our bold goal?	How do we need to change our approach, if at all, to realize our bold goal?
SHARED LEADERSHIP	Who are the founding leaders of this effort? How do we organize ourselves to be most effective?	What does it mean to lead? How will this leadership structure be sustained over time?	What changes, if any, do we need to make to the leadership structure as we scale?	How must our leadership structure adapt to sustain the effort needed to realize our bold goal?
STAKEHOLDER ENGAGEMENT	Who should be engaged? (key influencers, shared leaders, early adopters, people affected)	How do we engage early adopters?	What key stakeholders are necessary to achieve scale? How do we convert the "maybes"?	How do we sustain interest? Are there stakeholders critical to realizing our bold goal who we have failed to engage so far?
ENVIRONMENTAL CONTEXT	What is the micro and macro context?	How will certain environmental factors affect our effort? What factors might help propel the effort forward?	What new micro or macro factors must we consider as we scale? Do we have an opportunity to influence the environment?	How has the micro and macro context changed? What are the implications?
DISCIPLINED EXECUTION	Where do we start? What early wins should we target?	What actions do we need to take to prove the concept? Can we get closer to our goal by narrowing our focus?	What actions must we take to scale? What must we stop doing in order to scale?	What new actions must we take to realize our bold goal?
FINANCIAL SUSTAINABILITY	How do we envision financially supporting the work in the long term?	How will our efforts be financially sustained?	How do we maintain financial sustainability as we scale?	How will we adapt our funding/revenue streams to reflect internal and external changes?
ADVOCACY/ PUBLIC POLICY	What is the regulatory or legislative environment surrounding this issue?	What are the short-term opportunities to influence policy and systems?	What is the long-term systems change necessary to make dramatic improvement?	How do we achieve the long-term systems change given the current political and cultural environment?
COMMUNICATION	What messages and channels will help build awareness among key stakeholders?	What messages and channels will build engagement, inspire action and contribute to behavior change?	How do we create contagious ideas and equip others to "own" the message(s) and the solution(s)?	How should we adapt our communication strategy, messages and actions?
CONTINUOUS IMPROVEMENT & LEARNING	What does success look like?	How do we know if our approach is working? What changes need to be made if we're not achieving the desired result?	How do we know if our approach continues to work as we scale? What changes need to be made if we're not achieving the desired results?	How close are we to our bold goal and what do we need to learn to get closer?
CULTURE (VALUES, NORMS, BEHAVIORS)	How do we establish an intentional culture across the effort? (roles, ground rules, expectations, decision-making)	How do we ensure that we are living what we believe?	How do we maintain our culture as we grow?	How must we adapt our culture to the new context?

Source: Adapted from Community Wealth Partners (2013; http://communitywealth.com/wp-content/uploads/2016/12/Community-Wealth-Partners-Social-Transformation-Lifecycle.pdf).

far-flung stakeholders than with understanding the person who sits at the desk right next to us" (p. 48).

So, exactly what should nonprofits do to increase their capacity for innovation? There is no shortage of practical advice, most directed at organizational leaders. The following provide a sampling of common points:

- Create a culture of innovation, which starts with the leader (Hoque, 2014).
- Align innovation systems with organizational strategy (Emmons, Hanna, & Thompson, 2012).
- Listen and stay open, both to internal and external sources of possible new ideas (Hoque, 2014).
- Engage in collaboration, since partners bring new perspectives and ideas (Hoque, 2014).
- Maintain a flat organizational structure, facilitating communication and a quick approval process for new initiatives (Hoque, 2014).
- Define jobs around innovation (Emmons et al., 2012).
- Build a culture that embraces failure (Hoque, 2014).

But despite the abundance of advice offered in the literature, Seelos and Mair (2012a) do not endorse easy formulas and, like Crutchfield and Grant, they challenge some established wisdom. First, they emphasize, social innovation may not even be necessary for an organization to create social value. Maintaining effective programs over time, with incremental improvements, may be sufficient and, indeed, bring less risk. Second, while the literature offers many recommendations, there is no unified theory of how to build an innovative organization; there is no one right way. As Seelos and Mair (2012b) explain:

> Easy recipes in "three steps to better innovation," often at the core of popular innovation books, are not justified, no matter how tempting they may be or how plausible they may sound … Innovation is a complex process and depends on the unique constellation of many organizational factors…. Serious engagement with existing organizational theories and knowledge requires that we deal with innovation in all of its complexity, and case by case.

Seelos and Mair's conclusion is thus consistent with the observation offered elsewhere in this book with regard to other topics. Nonprofit managers need to maintain a balanced perspective, avoid one-right-way prescriptions, and select strategies and methods that are best adapted to their particular organizations and circumstances.

The Future of Social Entrepreneurship

Social entrepreneurship has become a subject that is not only of worldwide interest to philanthropists and nonprofit leaders; in recent years, it also has been adopted as a key strategy of the U.S. government to promote social goals both at home and around the world. The Edward M. Kennedy Serve America Act, signed by president Barack Obama in 2009, created a federally funded Social Innovation Fund to provide grants to funding intermediaries in local communities, which would in turn use them to "identify high-performing nonprofit organizations working in low-income communities that have innovative solutions with evidence of compelling results" (Corporation for National and Community Service, n.d.-a).

The grants required matching with private funds, and many were accompanied by technical assistance to help nonprofits increase their impact. Similarly, the European Commission embraced social innovation and established programs to provide both funding and support for such efforts (European Commission, 2014).

But, amid growing interest, some observers offer a somewhat critical assessment regarding the impact of social entrepreneurs. Some views reflect political perspectives, especially regarding the efficacy of government and markets. Public administration scholar Paul Light (2011) writes that "At best, social entrepreneurship creates the fantasy that solving intractable problems is only one mad scientist away; at worst, it reinforces the budget-cutter's illusion that anything old cannot be worth saving." Light acknowledges the importance of the social entrepreneur as "inventor, steward, explorer, and advocate," but he argues that the greatest breakthroughs in social programs have come through collaborative efforts rather than the work of a single individual. He suggests that the term social entrepreneurship be replaced with the more traditional concept of public service (Light, 2011).

Free market economies are likely to continue to be a dominant model and the creation or funding of larger government social programs appears unlikely in the near term in most countries around the world. At the same time, the commitment of world leaders to improving global living conditions remains substantial. In this environment, social entrepreneurship is likely to continue as a growing movement. It is likely to complement rather than supplant more traditional approaches, such as philanthropy, charity, and government action. Entrepreneurship in business represents one component of overall activity, not the entire business sector. Likewise, social entrepreneurship is an important component of activity in the nonprofit sector as well as business and government. But it is not an alternative to nonprofit management. At the same time, the thinking of social entrepreneurs likely will continue to impact the management of more traditional nonprofit organizations, by further increasing the emphasis on measuring performance and on developing innovative solutions to persistent social ills.

CHAPTER SUMMARY

Social entrepreneurship has gained increased interest as a strategy for solving social problems. Some (called the social enterprise school) define it as synonymous with social enterprise, that is, with the pursuit of earned income. But others (the social innovation school) use the term to describe a broader concept. In the broader definition, social entrepreneurs are innovators and change agents, who may pursue earned income or other sources of revenue to implement their new ideas. Their role in the nonprofit sector is similar to that of entrepreneurs in business, described by Say and Schumpeter many years ago. They are disruptive forces that bring about the introduction of new models, which eventually create systemic change. Many social entrepreneurs found new organizations, but they also may act within established organizations, including nonprofits, businesses, and government.

Social entrepreneurs have existed throughout history, but social entrepreneurship as a field has gained attention primarily since the 1990s and was defined in part by organizations like Ashoka and Echoing Green, which provide funding and other support to social entrepreneurs around the world.

Theories that explain entrepreneurship are analogous to the leadership theories discussed earlier in this text. Some theories describe the traits or characteristics of entrepreneurs; others identify entrepreneurial behaviors; and others emphasize the interaction of individual characteristics and skills with an environment conducive to such activity, which is a situational approach.

Social entrepreneurs are active in various fields and around the world. Some people say that using business methods to address social problems, which many social entrepreneurs do, is especially important in many parts of the world where traditions of philanthropy are not well established. Yunus (2007) observes the shortcomings of government, business, and traditional nonprofits and recommends the creation of social businesses, both to have social impact and to help the poor become independent.

Most definitions of social entrepreneurship emphasize impact, and a widely noted study identified characteristics of high-impact nonprofits that are "forces for good." Such organizations advocate and serve, make markets work, inspire evangelists, nurture nonprofit networks, master the art of adaptation, and share leadership. Social transformation may advance in stages and tools are available to assist organizations that work to advance it. Innovation does not always require starting new organizations. Existing organizations can build cultures, systems, and practices that lead to continuous innovation, although incremental improvements also are useful and carry less risk. Many authors offer recommendations on how to build innovative organizations, but the research is complex and there are no one-right-way formulas. Nonprofit leaders should adapt strategies that are appropriate to their particular organizations.

Despite some critics who believe that collaborative efforts are more effective than the actions of a lone individual, social entrepreneurship is likely to continue growing. Its emphasis on innovation will influence even the management of traditional organizations.

KEY TERMS AND CONCEPTS

creative destruction 436
entrepreneur 436
entrepreneurship 436
intrapreneur 437

microfinance 442
social businesses 442
social enterprise school 436
social entrepreneur 436

social innovation school 437
social transformation 444
social value proposition 440

CASE 16.1 KaBOOM!

Darrell Hammond and his eight brothers and sisters grew up in a group home outside Chicago, supported by members of Moose International. In the early 1990s, while a student at Northwestern University, he volunteered to help build a playground in a Chicago neighborhood. Observing the impact the playground had on the community, he was inspired to pursue a nonprofit career. He joined City Year in 1994 and worked organizing service projects in Chicago, an experience that gave him insight into the needs of low-income neighborhoods. He developed the view that building communities requires common spaces and that projects should involve local residents, rather than be delivered from "on high." The project itself could strengthen community ties, provide a healthy experience for neighborhood residents, and give the neighborhood a sense of ownership over its environment. He remembered the impact of the playground he had built and turned his attention to Anacostia, one of the poorest neighborhoods in Washington, DC.

Hammond approached The Home Depot, which agreed to provide materials and volunteers to build a playground near a public housing community. Other companies contributed funds, and community members raised money through events such as car washes and bake sales. The day the Anacostia playground was built, over 500 volunteers participated, including The Home Depot employees and neighbors. Following the success of the Anacostia project, in 1996, Hammond and his friend Dawn Hutchison set out to replicate the model in cities across the country. They founded KaBOOM!, with the mission to "inspire individuals, organizations, and businesses to join together to build much-needed safe and accessible playgrounds" (Sagawa & Segal, 2000, p. 33).

By 1996, The Home Depot remained a partner, and other corporate partners had signed on, including

Kimberly-Clark. In 1997, vice president Al Gore and General Colin Powell helped KaBOOM! launch the "Let Us Play" campaign to build 38 additional playgrounds. By 1999, KaBOOM! was building 50 new playgrounds a year. By 2003, the organization turned its attention to the needs of older children and began building parks for skateboards and BMX bikes (KaBOOM!, 2017).

Over time, Hammond perfected the model, developing a step-by-step process for playground construction, including the roles of volunteers and neighbors. In 2004, in order to accelerate growth, KaBOOM! refined its model to empower communities with less oversight. Training programs were increased, and tools and resources were placed online. The Home Depot announced a $25-million partnership to build or refurbish 1,000 playgrounds in 1,000 days (see KaBOOM! website, kaboom.org). One of the hallmarks of KaBOOM! has been its focus on measuring performance. In 2002, a system was developed to consistently report progress on selected performance metrics—the report came to be known as the "KaBOOM! Formula" (Wei-Skillern et al., 2007, p. 382).

In 2011, KaBOOM! began to undertake research on children's play and expanded its advocacy efforts to inform local policy and practice on the topic (KaBOOM!, n.d.). In 2016, KaBOOM! built 152 playgrounds, engaging 30,000 volunteers, and benefitting 830,000 children (KaBOOM!, 2016). But it also pursued a broader mission, working in partnerships with cities and communities to expand opportunities for children's play. Such efforts included mobilizing communities in response to crisis in challenged areas such as Flint, Michigan, and Baltimore, Maryland. KaBOOM! also honored 257 communities that expanded access to play areas with designation as a Playful City USA. And with philanthropic partners, KaBOOM! made grants of $1 million toward innovation in play spaces and the development of play areas in unconventional locations, such as bus stops and vacant lots (KaBOOM!, 2016).

Questions Related to Case 16.1: KaBOOM!

1. How does Darrell Hammond exhibit the characteristics of a social entrepreneur?

2. How does KaBOOM! illustrate characteristics of high-impact nonprofits as identified by Crutchfield and Grant?

3. How does KaBOOM! illustrate the Social Transformation Lifecycle proposed by Community Wealth Partners?

CASE 16.2 Harlem Children's Zone

Geoffrey Canada, who served as president and CEO of Harlem Children's Zone (HCZ) from 1990 to 2014, is one of the country's best-known social entrepreneurs. The *New York Times Magazine* called HCZ "one of the most ambitious social experiments of our time," and *U.S. News & World Report* named Canada one of America's "best leaders" in 2005. HCZ and Canada have been featured in numerous media stories, a book (Tough, 2008), and the documentary film *Waiting for Superman*, which focused the nation's attention on school-reform programs in 2010. When Canada arrived at HCZ (then called Rheedlen), he observed that a number of programs seemed to be doing some good for some children but that his efforts were largely spent in obtaining continuing funding for each program, without much demand from the funders that the programs demonstrate outcomes. And he needed to think about how the programs related to one another. Then he had an insight. What if he started with the outcomes he wanted to achieve and then designed comprehensive and integrated programs to achieve them, supporting children from "cradle to college" (Hernandez, 2005) and driving all efforts by measures of results (Tough, 2008, pp. 1–8)?

At first, he put in place integrated programs that encompassed parenting classes for parents of young children, prekindergarten programs, and after-school tutoring for children in public schools. Becoming discouraged with public schools, he later established a charter school, Promise Academy, with support from the New York school system as well as private donors (Tough, 2008, pp. 1–8). Continuing to take a comprehensive approach that would transform lives as well as education, new programs included initiatives to educate families about asthma, obesity, and other health problems. Under a 10-year business plan, HCZ became a leader in tracking results and revising programs to achieve the best outcomes. HCZ programs run on two tracks, supporting students who attend its charter schools as well as children who attend public schools or who live in the neighborhood and attend school elsewhere (Harlem Children's Zone, 2014).

HCZ's growth since 1990 has increased its impact. In 1997, the program served a 24-block area. By 2007, it had expanded to 100 blocks (Harlem Children's Zone, 2017). In 2016, HCZ served more than 12,000 children and 96 percent were accepted in college (Harlem Children's Zone, 2016). Beyond its impact

in New York City, HCZ's comprehensive approach to transforming neighborhoods became a model for other cities as well.

Measurement of results is at the heart of HCZ's model, and its website includes data on performance under each of its programs. But its approach also has been part of a larger policy debate about the best ways to improve education and fight poverty. A study by Roland Fryer and Will Dobbie, reported in 2009, found that HCZ schools produced "enormous gains" in students' test scores, prompting one author to call the program "the Harlem miracle" (D. Brooks, 2009). Some critics have focused on the expense of the programs (about $16,000 per student a year) and cite a drop-off in scores in 2010 to question its usefulness as a national model (Otterman, 2010).

In 2014, Geoffrey Canada stepped down as the CEO of HCZ, but remained as president of the board. The chief operating officer, Anne Williams-Isom, became the CEO in a planned transition.

Questions Related to Case 16.2: Harlem Children's Zone

1. Is Geoffrey Canada a social entrepreneur?

2. How does HCZ illustrate characteristics of high-impact nonprofits as identified by Crutchfield and Grant?

3. How does Harlem Children's Zone illustrate the Social Transformation Lifecycle proposed by Community Wealth Partners?

QUESTIONS FOR DISCUSSION

1. Are social entrepreneurs born or made? In other words, can individuals be educated or trained in a way that will result in entrepreneurial behavior?

2. Which of the two schools of thought, or definitions of social entrepreneurship, do you find most satisfactory? Explain.

3. In 2014, Malala Yousafzai, a Pakistani activist who achieved fame as an advocate for the rights of girls, was awarded the Nobel Peace Prize. Is Malala a social entrepreneur? Why or why not?

4. Go back and read the case of Aspire CoffeeWorks in Chapter 14. Is James Kales a social entrepreneur? Why or why not?

5. Scholar Paul Light argues that the greatest breakthroughs in social programs have come through collaborative efforts rather than the work of a single individual. He suggests that the term social entrepreneurship be replaced with the more traditional concept of public service. How would you evaluate this argument?

APPENDIX CASE

The following case in the Appendix of this text includes points related to the content of this chapter: Case 2 (Share Our Strength/No Kid Hungry).

SUGGESTIONS FOR FURTHER READING

Books/Journal

Bornstein, D., & Davis, S. (2010). *Social entrepreneurship: What everyone needs to know*. New York, NY: Oxford University Press.

Gaudiani, C., & Burnett, D. G. (2011). *Daughters of the declaration: How women social entrepreneurs built the American dream*. New York, NY: PublicAffairs.

Guo, C., & Bielefeld, W. (2014). *Social entrepreneurship: An evidence-based approach*. San Francisco, CA: Jossey-Bass.

Liedtka, J., Salzman, R., & Azer, D. (2017). *Design thinking for the greater good: Innovation in the social sector*. New York, NY: Columbia University Press.

Martin, R. L., & Osberg, S. (2015). *Getting beyond better: How social entrepreneurship works*. Boston, MA: Harvard Business School Publishing.

Stanford Social Innovation Review (journal)

Websites

Ashoka Foundation: http://www.ashoka.org/

Duke Center for the Advancement of Social Entrepreneurship: http://www.caseatduke.org/

Echoing Green: http://www.echoinggreen.org/

Unlike a century ago, when most people lived in rural areas or small communities and had little awareness of events in other parts of the world, we now live in a globalized society. The pace of globalization appears to be accelerating, and technological, economic, political, and cultural changes have created a world in which the greatest threats and the most promising opportunities require cooperation among nations and people from all parts of the world.

iStock/BrianAJackson

Chapter Outline

Governing and Managing International and Global Organizations

A century ago, an increasing number of people were becoming employed in industrial settings, including factories and mines, but most people still lived and worked on farms or in small communities. Travel was expensive, and communication was slow. The Wright brothers' first flight had just occurred in 1903, and the majority of American homes would not have electricity until 1930. Television, the Internet, and space travel were still decades in the future.

Events in other parts of the world had little impact on most Americans' lives and, indeed, seldom intruded on their thinking, which was focused on the communities in which they lived and worked. Circumstances were similar in other parts of the world, where people experienced life in their own countries but had limited awareness or contact with people elsewhere. Philanthropy in the United States included giving to one's church and an occasional campaign to build a new firehouse, hospital, or school. The greatest threats to human health included common diseases for which there were yet no cures; the life expectancy for Americans at birth was less than 50 years (Shrestha, 2006). Over the past 100 years, the pace and magnitude of change have been staggering. Today, the greatest threats facing humanity, including disease, terrorism, climate change, and natural disasters, are ones that cannot be confined within national boundaries nor isolated by the oceans that separate the continents. Instant communications and frequent travel transmit ideas, images, news, even diseases, as rapidly as people a century ago could cross the town squares of their small communities. At the same time, the greatest opportunities for technological and economic advancement lie in cooperative efforts that engage people, and minds, across the globe. Philanthropy, once primarily an American phenomenon, now flows in significant amounts all around the world and a gift requires only the click of a computer mouse or a touch to a tablet's screen to complete. While the nonprofit sector in the United States remains the largest and philanthropy on a large scale remains predominantly American, similar organizations are increasing in number and importance in many nations and on a global basis. Many of these are turning to fundraising in the American style.

Learning Objectives

After reading this chapter, students should be able to:

1. Define various types of international organizations.

2. Summarize trends in international philanthropy and fundraising.

3. Describe various models for governing international and global organizations.

4. Identify unique considerations in managing international organizations.

5. Analyze cases, applying principles from the chapter.

Why has the world become smaller? And why have nonprofit organizations come to play an important role on the world stage? The answer lies in advances in communication technology as well as changes in political, cultural, and economic realities. One reason is the end of the Cold War and more open societies in some parts of the globe. This change removed political barriers to economic interaction and to nonprofit organizations, which had often been viewed as threats by repressive governments. The establishment of free-trade areas and organizations in the 1990s, including the World Trade Organization (WTO), the European Union (EU), and the North American Free Trade Agreement (NAFTA), led to greater economic integration across national boundaries (Thomas, 2002), a reality that became controversial in the 2016 election in the United States and in the decision by British voters to leave the European Union.

The movement toward devolution of government services and outsourcing to the private sector that has occurred in the United States has also been seen in other nations, which have sought to lower tax rates in order to encourage economic and business growth. As in the United States, private organizations have been called on to replace services previously provided through government programs and to seek financial support from the private sector, leading to the growth of fundraising as a worldwide profession. This new philosophy also has been reflected in the management of international aid programs, with governments preferring to deliver assistance through private organizations rather than directly (Anheier & Themudo, 2005).

Among the most powerful forces for change has been technology. The development of the Internet, the World Wide Web, satellite communications, and social media has made global communication instantaneous. It has driven international economic competition in a "flat" world, in which national borders prevent no barrier to entry into the mainstream of business life (Friedman, 2006). It has become a force in political struggles around the world and is used by groups of all ideologies. And it has been raising the awareness of people in developed nations about the needs of others on the planet, stimulating unprecedented global responses to humanitarian needs.

Globalization presents all societies with significant challenges. Those who will live their lives—and manage nonprofit organizations—in the balance of the 21st century will need to understand, accept, and be prepared to work with different mind-sets and different skills than have ever been required before.

In this chapter, we will consider some basic definitions and concepts related to international and global organizations and some of the unique considerations in governing, managing, and fundraising in the international arena.

Definitions and Scope of International Organizations

As in the United States, the terminology used to discuss organizations across the world is sometimes inconsistent and confusing. The term international organization is used as an umbrella term that encompasses two types—international institutions and international nongovernmental organizations. International institutions include, for example, the United Nations, the World Bank, and the International Monetary Fund, which have governments as members and are controlled by agreements among those governments (Missoni, 2014a). There are also **transnational hybrid organizations (THOs)**, such as the International Committee of the Red Cross, which have government members but also an independent status of their own (Missoni, 2014c). Our focus in this chapter is on the type of international organization usually called a nongovernmental organization or NGO.

The term nonprofit organization is not widely used in the international environment, although there are organizations in many countries that fit the definitions of nonprofit that were considered in Chapter 2. Although the term has different meanings in different parts of the world, what we call nonprofits in the United States are elsewhere most commonly referred to as **nongovernmental organizations (NGOs)**. The term nongovernmental organization has its origins in the United Nations system, and, indeed, the United Nations (UN) has formal consultative relationships with many such organizations engaged in economic development activity (United Nations, n.d.). Unlike international institutions, NGOs are chartered under the law of one nation and are not recognized under international law (Bongiovanni, Missoni, & Alesani, 2014).

There are different types and classifications of NGOs, some analogous to those in the United States that we discussed in Chapter 2. They include **public interest NGOs (PINGOs)**, which provide a public benefit, and **business interest NGOs (BINGOs)**, which are similar to trade and professional associations in the United States and advance the agenda of business industries or sectors (Missoni, 2014b). Some NGOs operate within one country and engage in activities similar to those of U.S. nonprofits, but they vary widely in the legal frameworks within which they exist, the sources of their funding, and especially their relationships with government. Some organizations are indeed operated by government and are known as **government-operated nongovernmental organizations (GONGOs)**. There is no concept quite like the U.S. nonprofit sector in most parts of the world. In the international context, some scholars refer to the collection of organizations that reside between government and the private sector as the "civil society sector" (Salamon, Sokolowski, & Associates, 2004, p. 11).

The best-known NGOs are the **international nongovernmental organizations (INGOs)**. These are organizations whose activities are not confined to a single country. They "make significant operating expenditures across national borders and do not identify themselves as domestic actors [within one nation]" (Anheier & Themudo, 2005, p. 102). In addition, they are sometimes said to be transnational because, as the term implies, they "organize … in pursuit of goals and purposes that transcend the boundaries of national territories and state jurisdictions" (Boli, 2006, p. 333). Until recent decades, most INGOs were based in the United States or Western Europe, but they are now more diffused around the world (Anheier & Themudo, 2005). INGOs include the large brand-name organizations that most people know, including, for example, the Red Cross, Oxfam, Friends of the Earth, Greenpeace, Amnesty International, CARE International, and Save the Children.

Bonnie Koenig (2004) describes a continuum along which some nonprofits have evolved. They start as local organizations with local interests. Then they begin to develop an international awareness, perhaps including international topics in their conferences and published materials. They may then move along to develop some international programs, possibly hosting conferences attended by people from around the world or publishing materials in various languages. At this point along the continuum, they have started to become **international organizations**. At a later point in their evolution, such organizations may begin to admit international members, open offices or form chapters in other countries, and enter alliances or partnerships with organizations in other nations. Finally, some ultimately may evolve into **global organizations** "with members, programs, or operations in many different regions around the world and having a multinational board of directors or other decision-making group" (Koenig, p. 5). Some INGOs were created as global organizations from the beginning. For example, CIVICUS, an international alliance that works to strengthen civil society around the world, was founded in 1993 with a multinational board—it was global from the beginning, both in its purposes and its governance (Koenig, 2004).

It is important to clarify the distinction between organizations that are international and those that are global, especially since the terms are sometimes used interchangeably.

An international organization is somewhere along Koenig's continuum: It may have some programs in other countries, but it is governed within and maintains a focus on its home country. A global organization is one that has activities throughout the world and probably has a governance structure that places decision making in the hands of individuals from multiple countries. Today, most American national nonprofits are at least international. Many of the large brand-name INGOs are global organizations.

INGOs have grown in number, especially within recent decades. *The Yearbook of International Organizations,* published by the Union of International Associations, identifies more than 69,000 organizations in its 2017 edition (Union of International Associations, 2017). The INGOs are often large and visible, but it is a more complex challenge to track NGOs within various countries around the world. There is no single source of comprehensive data, although research interest has increased in recent years. One of the most ambitious efforts, begun in 1991, is the Johns Hopkins Comparative Nonprofit Sector Project, a collaborative investigation led by Lester Salamon at Johns Hopkins University. The project began with teams of local researchers in 13 countries. Now working in 45 countries, the project has developed extensive comparative data on civil society organizations, philanthropy, and voluntarism and has produced numerous books and papers, and the Johns Hopkins **Global Civil Society Index**. The index makes it possible to access more than 300 research products, including many focused on global civil society and others related to the U.S. nonprofit sector (ccss.jhu.edu).

Like nonprofits in the United States, NGOs in other nations engage in a variety of activities. According to the Johns Hopkins project research, the largest number provide services, including education and social services. Another significant percentage are engaged in what Salamon and Sokolowski (2004) call expressive functions, including arts, culture, recreation, and professional associations. Others are **advocacy organizations** that bring social and human problems to public attention and work for change—for example, to protect human rights, preserve the environment, and other goals.

The World Bank divides INGOs into two basic types: advocacy INGOs and **operational NGOs**. Advocacy INGOs are organizations that promote a cause or issue on a multinational basis. In the World Bank's definition, operational INGOs are those whose primary purpose is to design and implement economic development projects. However, the mission of other INGOs that also operate programs, for example, the Red Cross, is to provide immediate and short-term relief from human suffering, rather than support economic or infrastructure development over the long run. The latter distinction is analogous to the differences between charity and philanthropy that we discussed earlier in this book.

Many development INGOs, working in partnership with the UN and the World Bank, are focused on accomplishment of economic development goals. The **UN Millennium Development Goals**, adopted by world leaders in 2000, included specific targets for the reduction of poverty, disease, illiteracy, environmental degradation, and discrimination against women to be achieved by 2015. Some of the goals were accomplished by that deadline, but other work remained. In 2015, the UN announced 17 Sustainable Development Goals for 2030, which envision an even larger role for nonprofits (O'Neil, 2015a). Most efforts in pursuit of UN development goals are funded by governments, although philanthropy has played an increasing role.

International Philanthropy and Fundraising

Recall from our discussion in Chapter 2 that nonprofit organizations in the United States have varied patterns of revenue. Some organizations are highly dependent on philanthropy, while others may be more reliant on government support or earned income. The revenue strategies of international NGOs are similarly diverse (Stroup, 2012). For example, CARE USA relies mostly on grants from the U.S. government and receives only 17 percent of its revenue from American individual donors. In contrast, Oxfam in Great Britain receives most of its revenue from private gifts and Médecins Sans Frontières (MSF; Doctors Without Borders in the United States), based in France, receives only private support—about half from French donors and half from other parts of the world, including the United States (Stroup, p. 81). This reflects in part the sources of support that are available in their home countries as well as differences in the causes that the organizations address. Individual donors may be drawn to giving to MSF in disasters and emergencies, but perhaps not to the long-term programs of CARE, for which government support is more appropriate. But there are also issues related to resource dependence. (Remember the discussion back in Chapter 3 of this book.) For example, some are critical of CARE's reliance on government, charging that it limits the organization's independence. MSF's sections hold different views on whether to accept government funds, for reason of similar concern (Stroup, p. 86). MSF is limited in its ability to raise funds in France, where individual giving in not substantial, and relies on its U.S. section for about of a third of its revenue (Stroup, p. 87).

International Giving

Global poverty and health have become the focus of a growing number of substantial gifts and priorities for foundation grant programs. U.S.-based donors are the largest source of international giving; for example, the largest U.S. foundation, the Bill and Melinda Gates Foundation, is primarily concerned with global health and global economic development. Gates gave more than $3.4 billion in those areas in 2016 alone (Bill & Melinda Gates Foundation, 2016). Other developed nations have given more as their economies have expanded in recent years (Hudson Institute, 2017).

Developing reliable data on international philanthropy faces significant challenges of methodology as well as definition; the totals reported by various researchers differ widely and are likely understated (Hudson Institute, 2017). For example, as measured by the Lilly Family School of Philanthropy at Indiana University (2017) and reported by the Giving USA Foundation, American philanthropy directed to international programs and purposes totaled $22 billion in 2016. But the data do not include funds spent on international activities by U.S.-based nonprofits in fields such as education, health care, arts and culture, youth development, and religion, which are reported in other categories; they do not capture all foundation and corporate giving; and they do not include gifts that individuals made to organizations based in other countries that are not chartered in the United States. Unless the recipient organization is registered in the United States, the donor cannot claim a tax deduction for the gift. Some organizations headquartered abroad establish U.S.-based nonprofits, often called a foundation or "friends of" in order to qualify to receive deductible gifts from U.S. citizens. Gifts to those organizations could be captured in the Giving USA totals, but gifts that Americans make directly to organizations abroad could not be, since the estimates are based on tax data. Giving USA data also do not include the substantial payments made by private individuals, including recent immigrants to the United States, who send funds directly to their home countries to support either families or projects. Such payments are called **remittances** rather than gifts. By one estimate, such payments totaled over $580 billion in 2014, most of it originating from the United States (Hudson Institute, 2017, p. 24).

Global Fundraising

At the same time that international giving from the United States and other developed countries has increased, NGOs in many parts of the world have been required to pursue new sources of revenue. For example, governments in many nations have reduced funding for higher education institutions, forcing them to institute or increase tuition charges and to look to U.S.-style fundraising for their future growth. Nonprofits in other fields, facing limited resources and growing needs, also have adopted and adapted many of the techniques of organized fundraising that were discussed in Chapter 13.

Fundraising and philanthropy face obstacles in many nations. First, philanthropy requires the presence of surplus income or wealth, which does not exist within many nations. It is illogical to assume that a country in which most individuals are desperately poor will be able to generate a level of giving that can sustain the growth of local organizations sufficient to have an impact on the country's overwhelming problems, and the competition for international giving is difficult for small organizations without internationally recognized brand names.

Second, while most religions and cultures include expectations of altruistic behavior beyond one's family, not all cultures support organized fundraising or voluntarism on the U.S. model (Wagner, 2004). For example, in some cultures, it would be deemed inappropriate to ask another for funds to support an organization on whose board the solicitor served. For another example, in Japan there historically has been no tradition of charitable bequests, with estates going only to families. Only 10 percent of individuals make a will, and inheritance is distributed among family members according to the law (Cagney & Ross, 2013, p. 57). There are legal obstacles in some nations, which have inhibited the growth of independent nongovernmental organizations. For instance, until recently, China required organizations to work through a dual registration and management system, which made it difficult to become registered. Organizations were required to obtain a government agency to sponsor them and then also a second government agency to monitor and audit them (Cagney & Ross, 2013, p. 25).

Even the desirability of philanthropy is a subject of debate in many nations. Some people are concerned about the potential for philanthropy to undermine the responsibility of the state to meet social needs. Others view philanthropy as extending control by wealthy elites, and some governments view NGOs as threats to their authority. For example, anti-NGO legislation was passed or proposed in 2013 in Russia, Ethiopia, and Rwanda and some prodemocracy organizations were shut down after the Arab Spring uprisings in Egypt (Cagney & Ross, 2013, pp. 4–6). In addition to cultural barriers, few national tax systems include benefits for giving as generous as those available to donors in the United States, although some have increased incentives in recent years (Cagney & Ross, 2013). As discussed previously, incentives in the United States may have become less attractive as a result of the Tax Cuts and Jobs Act of 2017.

There are also technical obstacles to the implementation of U.S.-style fundraising techniques; for example, telephone and mail systems may not support sophisticated telemarketing or direct-mail solicitation, and some countries have low rates of connectivity to the Internet. However, the Internet also has greatly increased the ability of NGOs to reach potential donors on a global basis at minimal cost and has enabled donors in developed countries to learn about needs abroad and make gifts to support their needs. For example, GlobalGiving, a 501(c)(3) U.S. nonprofit, operates a website through which donors can make gifts to support specific projects listed by organizations throughout the world. Projects can be selected by country, theme (e.g., children, women, the environment), and other criteria. By 2017, almost 604,000 donors had provided gifts totaling nearly $268 million to more than 15,000 projects (GlobalGiving, 2017).

Despite obstacles, fundraising has grown in nations around the world. Some have adopted U.S.-style methods and strategies, including direct mail, phone solicitation, and campaigns, but others have developed methods more suited to their unique traditions and environments. A comprehensive overview is beyond the scope of this chapter, but a few selected highlights provide a rich tasting of the varied methods in use:

- Argentina has a poor postal system but high levels of online giving (Cagney & Ross, 2013, p. 4).

- Ethiopia has mounted some of the largest mass participation events (Cagney & Ross, 2013, p. 4).

- In Japan, most individual donors use giving boxes or respond to face-to-face solicitations on the street (Uo, 2013, p. 50).

- Although Latin America is a diverse region encompassing diverse cultures, historically, fundraising from individuals has surrounded events, including galas and sporting events (Galafassi, 2013, p. 68).

- Western Europe also is a diverse region, each with different traditions. In some, many of the fundraising methods developed in the United States also are common; for example, direct mail is used in continental Europe. Raffles are popular in the United Kingdom, and individuals in Spain and Italy can make gifts via their tax returns (Carnie, 2013, pp. 98–99).

- In Australia and New Zealand, fundraisers use a method known as the two-step. Street canvassers collect information from individuals that is then used for a follow-up contact by phone, Internet, or mail (Triner, 2013, p. 147).

- A technique used in India is, in essence, the opposite of the two-step. Called telefacing, it involves a phone call that sets up an appointment for a face-to-face solicitation (Menon & Tiwari, 2013, p. 283).

- In Kenya, fundraising follows the tradition of Harambee, which means "all pull together." Harmabee events include small and large events and are often advertised on social media (Muchilwa, 2013, p. 193).

There have been examples of successful U.S.-style campaigns in other countries, especially in higher education. For example, the University of Oxford announced a £1.25 billion campaign in 2008, with £575 million already having been committed, and in 2013 increased its goal to £3 billion (University of Oxford, 2017).

Fundraising as a professional field has emerged in the United States primarily over the past 50 years and more recently internationally. Professional associations, like the Association of Fundraising Professionals (AFP) in the United States, have developed in a number of countries, and some have relationships with AFP and the Fund Raising School, part of the Lilly Family School of Philanthropy at Indiana University. The Mexican Center for Philanthropy (Centro Mexicano para la Filatropía) was founded in 1988 and provides fundraising courses, conducts research, and fosters voluntary service. The Council for Advancement and Support of Education (CASE) opened a London office in 1994, a Singapore office in 2007, and a Latin American office in 2011 (Council for Advancement and Support of Education, n.d.). In 2014, CASE appointed as its president a fundraising professional whose primary experience had been in the United Kingdom and Australia, rather than an American college or university (Council for Advancement and Support of Education, 2014).

International Nonprofit Governance and Management

Managing an international or global organization combines the complexities of nonprofit management that have been discussed throughout this book with the additional challenges of working across legal systems, languages, cultures, and geographic distances.

Just as there has been a revolution in nonprofit management in the United States in recent decades, as discussed in Chapter 1 of this book, management is becoming more important for international and global organizations. Daniele Alesani and Eduardo Missoni (2014) argue that "a management approach [to international organizations] only recently started surfacing" and that the development of management practices is still developing (p. 1). A full discussion of international NGO management could easily follow the same sequence of chapters as that of this book and identify unique considerations of international management related to virtually every topic—governance, leadership, accountability, staff and volunteer management, fundraising, communications and marketing, and so forth. Many of the pressures facing nonprofit organizations in the United States—including growing needs for services amid declining government support, call for strengthened governance and accountability, and the need to balance commitment to mission with competition for resources—are all present in the international environment. Thus, with globalization, "international managers [both in business and NGOs] face an external environment more complex, more dynamic, more uncertain, and more competitive than ever before" (Thomas, 2002, p. 10). Space does not permit a full discussion of all these topics in this chapter, but the following sections consider briefly some of the issues related to managing across cultures, governance of international and global organizations, and models for organizational structure in the global environment.

Managing Across Cultures

NGO managers must accommodate national and regional differences in legal systems, political environments, and culture. Among the three, David Thomas (2002) argues, culture is uniquely important for three reasons. First, "the economic, legal, and political characteristics of a country are a manifestation of a nation's culture." Second, while the legal and political characteristics of nations are explicit and observable, culture is often invisible, especially to those who have grown up in different environments. "The influence of culture is difficult to detect and managers therefore often overlook it" (p. 19). Finally, the practice of management often focuses on interpersonal relationships—with staff, volunteers, donors, and others— and it is in such interactions that cultural differences may be most manifest. It affects such ordinary events as how individuals greet each other, how directions are communicated, and other everyday interactions. It involves both language and customs regarding physical space, body language, and other subtle differences. An understanding of culture and its implications is essential to any manager expecting to work in the international environment, which, as discussed above, likely includes most nonprofit managers of the future. There is an extensive theoretical literature on culture and its implications for international management, but a full discussion is beyond the scope of this chapter.

Governing International and Global Organizations

In addition to the generic issues of nonprofit governance and organization that have been discussed earlier in this text, working across different legal and political systems, cultures, languages, and physical distances presents unique challenges. For example, as a U.S.-based nonprofit begins to internationalize and seek board members from other countries, it will be adding members who may not fully understand the fiduciary responsibilities of governing boards under U.S. law or the expectations of board members in American nonprofits, which may be quite different from those in their home countries. This suggests the importance of additional orientation and training for international members of such boards (Koenig, 2004).

As the organization moves along the continuum described earlier in this chapter, evolving from an international to a global organization, its governance structure will need to reflect its evolving nature. Table 17.1 summarizes three common governance models and the advantages and disadvantages of each.

Table 17.1 Common Models for International Governance

Structure	Advantage/s	Disadvantage/s
Provide a seat for a representative from each region served by the organization	Ensures geographical representation	Board may become large as the organization expands Does not ensure that representatives will primarily serve the interests of the entire organization
Provide for a specific number of members or percentage of the board to be international, without specifying regions	Ensures some international representation Limits the size of the board Does not imply that international members represent regional interests	May not ensure representation of all regions served by the organization
Open elections, with a nominating committee mindful of the need for geographic diversity	Limits size of the board Makes it possible to craft the board based on skills rather than geographic origins Focuses the board on the organization as an integrated global entity rather than on regional interests	Relies on the membership or a nominating committee to achieve a diverse board and does not ensure it

Source: Based on Koenig (2004, pp. 101–102).

As Table 17.1 shows, one way to achieve international representation is to adopt bylaws that provide for a seat on the governing board for individuals representing each of the regions served by the organization. This might be an approach taken by an organization that is internationalizing: For example, a European seat might be created when it opens a European chapter of affiliates with a Europe-based partner, then a seat for a Latin American representative might be created as its programs expand into that region, and so forth. But as the organization continues to expand around the world, two problems may arise. First, the regional representatives may see their role as advocating for the interests of the region they represent, rather than focusing on the overall welfare of the entire organization. The board could become a forum in which regional representatives vie for favorable treatment of their regions, with a diminishing portion of the board focused on building an integrated organization. Second, as programs expand and seats for a larger number of regional representatives are added, the board may become unmanageably large.

In the second model, an internationalizing organization might decide to add some number of international members to its board, for example, identifying 3 seats on an 11-person board to be held by individuals from other countries but without specifying particular regions to be represented (Koenig, 2004). This approach keeps the board at a manageable size and does provide for an international perspective. In addition, since the international members are elected or appointed at-large, they may not be as inclined to view their role as advocating for regional interests. However, as the organization's programs expand around the world, this approach does not ensure that the perspectives and views of all its constituencies will be represented at the board table.

The third approach is one that Koenig (2004) describes as the "most common" in organizations that have adopted "a greater global mindset throughout the organization … because it puts a premium on an integrated organization" (p. 102). In this model, board members are enlisted from around the world, based on the organization's needs for various skills, perspectives, and experiences. The board membership can thus be crafted to meet the organization's leadership needs at various times, much as a well-governed board limited to one country might identify its members. In this approach, the organization's needs would be paramount, and the board's goal would be to enlist the best members from wherever they may be around the world. Gaining representation of various regions would also be a consideration, of course, but the nominating committee and the board would not be constrained by such requirements in selecting people who bring desired qualities. The downside of this approach is that it does not ensure that the perspectives of all regions will be reflected on the board.

Structuring International NGOs

Some issues related to the organizational structure of nonprofits in the United States, including relationships between national offices and chapters and the trade-offs between centralized and decentralized management, were discussed earlier in this book. Such issues and challenges become exacerbated as the organization expands internationally.

As mentioned previously, some NGOs have come into existence as global organizations; the example offered was CIVICUS, an international alliance that works to strengthen civil society around the world, founded in 1993 with a multinational board. Others have evolved from local to international organizations by establishing chapters or clubs abroad, maintaining a close relationship with headquarters. For example, Make-A-Wish International was founded in 1993 and is headquartered in Phoenix, Arizona. It now has 39 affiliates serving children in 50 countries around the world (Make-A-Wish, 2017).

An alternative is to maintain relatively autonomous national organizations that are affiliated with but do not receive direction from a headquarters. One example is Sister Cities International (SCI), which facilitates educational and other exchanges to promote cultural understanding, social development, and economic growth. SCI is a U.S. national organization that certifies relationships between U.S. cities and others abroad, which maintain their own independent organizations (Koenig, 2004, p. 99).

Some organizations have evolved a hybrid model, combining chapters linked to headquarters and affiliations with independent organizations abroad that share similar purposes. When AFP began to expand internationally, there were already some existing organizations in other countries. In nations where no such organization existed, new AFP chapters were established with a close relationship to headquarters in the United States. However, wishing to preserve its good relationships with existing organizations and not be viewed as a competitor, AFP chose to develop strategic alliances with them. The first three alliances were formed in 2002 and 2003 with the Institute of Fundraising in the United Kingdom, the Fundraising Institute of Australia, and the Fundraising Institute of New Zealand. Members of these national organizations can elect to join AFP and vice versa. Linked through the Web, members of both partners can access each other's members, databases, publications, and other information resources (Koenig, 2004, p. 101).

As in national nonprofits within the United States, achieving the proper balance between centralized control and local autonomy in an international organization requires careful calibration. Historically, many NGOs had centralized structures that were pushed out to chapters as they were established, but as growth extends into more geographically remote regions and diverse national and cultural settings, there is a trend toward greater autonomy for regional chapters or affiliates. The challenge is to determine what policies and what functions need to be retained centrally in order to maintain ethical standards, quality of programs, and adherence to a common mission, and which decisions can be left to local organizations. For example, Oxfam International is a confederation of national groups that was created in its present form in the mid-1990s. At the international level, the groups work together in advocacy, program harmonization, and emergency response. Local affiliates are responsible for allocating resources and managing their own programs (Koenig, 2004).

Regarding the balance between centralization and decentralization, Koenig (2004) offers three pragmatic standards:

- The more parts of the world in which an organization has interactions or activities, the more it will want to determine which practices need to be standardized among its local entities or partners and which can vary or be locally determined.

- The larger an organization's international presence is, the more flexible it should be in looking at options for its operations.

- Organizations that want to grow internationally and develop sustainable structures must be willing to review their progress in relation to their organizational goals and make modifications as needed. (p. 126)

It is ironic that in a period of time when increasing calls for accountability may suggest tighter centralized controls and when concern about image and control of the message also would dictate more uniform standards, the realities of communications technology and internationalization pull in the opposite direction. Access to the Internet provides local organizations with control over messages seen around the world, and the need to adapt to widely diverse laws, cultures, and economic realities increases the benefits of a decentralized approach.

Questions about centralization and decentralization are, of course, familiar ones even in national nonprofits within the United States. Working across legal, cultural, and language differences and considerable geographic distances makes them even more complex and delicate in the international environment, placing a premium on communication, flexibility, and a tolerance for ambiguity. In the nonprofit world, as in business, "conventional organizational forms are giving way to networks of less hierarchical relationships and cooperative strategic alliances with other [organizations]" (Thomas, 2002, p. 5). Managing such enterprises is likely to be a challenging task for control freaks or those who do not possess or acquire communication skills, trust in others, and sophisticated cultural understanding. For nonprofit managers of the 21st century, developing such skills and qualities is essential to effective leadership.

CHAPTER SUMMARY

Unlike a century ago, when most people lived in rural areas or small communities and had little awareness of events in other parts of the world, we now live in a globalized society. Technological, economic, political, and cultural changes have created a world in which the greatest threats and the most promising opportunities require cooperation among nations and people from all parts of the world. Nonprofit organizations are playing an increasing role in global affairs and in efforts to address such problems as poverty and health. Those who will manage nonprofit organizations in the balance of the 21st century need to understand, accept, and be prepared to work with a different perspective and different skills than have ever been required before.

As within the nonprofit sector in the United States, the terminology used to discuss organizations across the world is inconsistent and can be confusing. In most parts of the world, such organizations are known as nongovernmental organizations (NGOs) rather than nonprofits. NGOs that work within a single nation vary widely in the legal frameworks within which they exist, the sources of their funding, and especially their relationships with government. The best-known NGOs are the international nongovernmental organizations (or INGOs). They are organizations that have activities not confined to a single country and that usually reflect a global approach to governance. Some organizations have been global since the beginning, while others were national nonprofits that became **internationalized** by opening chapters abroad or forming alliances with organizations abroad that pursue similar missions or causes.

The number of INGOs has increased exponentially in recent decades. Although there is no single source of comprehensive data on NGOs around the world, one of the most ambitious research efforts was the Johns Hopkins Comparative Nonprofit Sector Project, which developed the *International Classification of Nonprofit Organizations* and a Global Civil Society Index.

NGOs in other nations engage in a variety of activities, including educational and social services, arts, culture, recreation, and professional activities. Others are advocacy organizations that bring social and human problems to public attention and work for change. The World Bank divides INGOs into two basic types: operational NGOs and advocacy INGOs. Operational NGOs of interest to the bank are those engaged in economic development. However, other NGOs are limited to providing temporary relief, for example, to victims of disasters or wars.

International philanthropy, especially that flowing from the United States and Western Europe to the rest of the world, has grown rapidly in recent years. Some of the largest U.S. foundations, including the Gates Foundation, have been focused on global health and poverty and on achievement of the UN's Millennium Development Goals, which were to have been accomplished by 2015, and the Sustainable Development Goals, established in 2015 for achievement by 2030.

Fundraising and philanthropy of the type known in the United States face obstacles in many countries, including culture, tax laws, and technical issues. However, NGOs are adopting and adapting U.S.-style fundraising, and there have been some notable successes as a culture of philanthropy is developing around the world. Some countries have developed fundraising methods that are unique and reflect their particular environments. Fundraising is emerging as a worldwide profession, through efforts by the Association of Fundraising Professionals, the Lilly Family School of Philanthropy at Indiana University, the Council for Advancement and Support of Education, and professional associations that have been established in other nations.

Managing an international or global organization combines the complexities of nonprofit management that have been discussed throughout this book with the additional challenges of working across legal systems, languages, cultures, and geographic distances. Culture may be the most important variable, since the economic, legal, and political characteristics of a country reflect its culture; culture is invisible and may be overlooked by managers; and much of managers' work involves personal interactions with people, in which cultural differences may be highly relevant.

As organizations evolve from local or national to international and global in scope, they need to adapt their governance structures to accommodate board members from various parts of the world. There are various models for doing so, each of which offers advantages and disadvantages. Another question that arises as a nonprofit begins to operate in various regions is how centralized or decentralized its policies and operations should be, that is, which matters need to be determined by headquarters and which can be left to local groups. The trend appears to be toward greater decentralization, and that presents challenges in terms of accountability and communication of an integrated message.

Managing nonprofit organizations or NGOs in the international environment requires skills in communication, flexibility, and a tolerance for ambiguity. Managers of the 21st century need to possess or develop these qualities in order to be effective leaders.

KEY TERMS AND CONCEPTS

advocacy organizations 456
business interest NGOs
  (BINGOs) 455
Global Civil Society Index 456
global organizations 455
government-operated
  nongovernmental organizations
  (GONGOs) 455

International Classification of
  Nonprofit Organizations 464
international nongovernmental
  organizations (INGOs) 455
internationalized 463
international organizations 455
nongovernmental organizations
  (NGOs) 455

operational NGOs 456
public interest NGOs (PINGOs) 455
remittances 457
transnational hybrid organizations
  (THOs) 454
UN Millennium Development
  Goals 456

Médecins Sans Frontières (MSF), known as Doctors Without Borders in the United States and some other countries, was founded in France in 1971 by doctors and journalists. Its purpose is to provide assistance to victims of natural or man-made disasters, epidemics, neglect, malnutrition, or armed conflict. MSF is independent of government and religious organizations and receives 89 percent of its funding from over three million private donors worldwide.

Observing strict principles of neutrality and impartiality, MSF provides medical care and other services, bears witness, and speaks out to bring the public's attention to humanitarian crises. For example, in 1985, MSF spoke out about the forced displacement of people by the Ethiopian government and, in 2004, called for international attention to the crisis in Darfur. MSF was forced to leave Afghanistan in 2004 when it was perceived by the Taliban to be an instrument of the West, and five of its staff members were killed. The organization was prominent among relief organizations that responded to the earthquake in Haiti in 2010 and the Ebola outbreak in West Africa in 2014 and 2015.

MSF's principles of independence and impartiality are outlined in its charter and other core documents. Its dual role of providing services and also speaking out against inhumane conditions and actions inevitably creates difficult and sometimes controversial situations. For example, how can an organization speak out and also remain neutral, or be perceived as neutral, by both sides in a conflict? Two MSF officials explain the complexity of the distinction that is required (Tanguy & Terry, 1999):

> If neutrality is defined as remaining silent, even when confronted with grave breaches of fundamental humanitarian principles, MSF is not neutral. However, as long as neutrality is defined, as "not taking sides with warring parties," MSF upholds a spirit of neutrality throughout its operations.

MSF views itself as a "movement" rather than an international organization (Fox, 2014, p. 2). It is made up of 24 country associations, also called "sections," located around the world. The U.S. section, MSF-USA (known in English as Doctors Without Borders or DWB), was founded in New York in 1990 to raise funds and to advocate regarding humanitarian concerns within the United Nations and the U.S. government. Decisions regarding implementation of MSF's principles are made by the five operational centers that have considerable autonomy. There have been occasions when disagreement arose among the various sections. For example, in 1999, MSF Greece was excluded from the movement over disagreement regarding how the principles of impartiality and independence should be applied in Kosovo. In 2005, the Greece association rejoined the international movement after an agreement was reached (Médecins Sans Frontières, 2005).

MSF's governance structure balances local autonomy with the need for coordination. Each national association is responsible to a board of directors elected by its own members. The 24 associations, as well as individuals and the international president, are members of MSF International. Representatives meet at the annual MSF International General Assembly (IGA), where they set broad policies to govern the entire movement and elect members of the international board (Médecins Sans Frontières, 2017). The international board was created as part of a governance reform in 2011 and represented an effort to gain greater coherence and accountability across the movement, while preserving decentralized operations (Médecins Sans Frontières, 2011). The need for more coordination was judged necessary in order to increase the organization's effectiveness in handling complex global challenges and to facilitate the creation of additional sections around the world, but some people expressed concern about MSF becoming "more formally structured, hierarchically ordered, and bureaucratic" (Fox, 2014, p. 5). In her study of MSF's culture, Renée Fox (2014) found that within MSF such institutional thickening is regarded as antithetical to the value that it places on egalitarianism, participatory democracy, consensual decision making, the spontaneous exchange of ideas, and effervescence—qualities that MSF associates with its conception of itself as a movement, rather than a formal institution that is "just an organization" (p. 5).

In 2016, MSF provided almost 10 million outpatient consultations and treated more than 671,000 admitted patients, among many other services. Almost one third of its services were provided to individuals in war zones in the Middle East, Africa, and South Asia and to refugees moving to escape intolerable situations (Médecins Sans Frontières, 2016). The organization was awarded the Nobel Peace Prize in 1999.

CASE 17.2 Haitian Earthquake Relief and Recovery

On January 12, 2010, a 7.0 earthquake struck Haiti, leveling thousands of homes, cutting off electricity and telephone service, killing thousands, and leaving thousands more homeless and destitute in what had already been the poorest country in the Western Hemisphere (Romero & Lacey, 2010).

The philanthropic response to the catastrophe was immediate. Within 24 hours of the earthquake, people began responding with online gifts. Within three days, the Red Cross had received more than $1 million on its website and by phone and another $1 million in $10 gifts sent through text messages. Within a few months, gifts made by text totaled $50 million, compared with just $1 million given by text in all previous times. Social media played a significant role. Within days of the disaster, Oxfam received more than $800,000 in gifts, including $10,000 through Facebook. Haiti quickly became a trending topic on Twitter, and users began posting advice on which organizations to support, warning against some and recommending others (Preston, 2010).

Celebrities mobilized for Haitian relief. Actor Sean Penn created a new organization dedicated to helping Haiti, and many performers began opening their concerts with appeals for gifts to Penn's and other Haiti-related nonprofits. A telethon hosted by actor George Clooney and many other celebrities raised over $57 million through phone, text, and the Web, and iTunes contributed the proceeds of sales of the concert ("Haiti Telethon Haul," 2010). Former president Bill Clinton visited Haiti and announced a new initiative of the Clinton Foundation. He joined with former president George W. Bush in creating the Clinton Bush Haiti Fund for Haitian relief and rebuilding, which raised over $36 million from U.S. citizens and businesses (H. Cooper,

2010). President Barack Obama gave $200,000 of his Nobel Peace Prize money to Haitian relief. In addition to the initial outpouring, assistance continued to flow to Haiti for years following the disaster, totaling $13.5 billion by 2016 (Simmons, 2016).

Following the earthquake, progress on the ground was slow. It was not possible for organizations to quickly and effectively spend the funds that were given. The biggest problem was the extensive devastation, inaccessible roads, and the fact that the earthquake had occurred near Haiti's capital city, incapacitating many government agencies. But observers also cited other issues. There was an overall lack of coordination among the various agencies responding to the disaster and no centralized leadership that could give direction to the efforts (Fiscale & Missoni, 2014). One NGO executive described "a swarm of well-meaning but in some cases inexperienced aid organizations and individuals" who came to Haiti, claiming that "their money [was] disproportionately spent … on isolated, random activities [and] could have been better used by groups already working in Haiti" (Letson, 2010). Some NGOs were criticized for not working more closely with local organizations and grassroots leaders. The international community did not fully appreciate the existing capacity of local organizations and institutions and often shut them out of decision making (Fiscale & Missoni, 2014). Some community meetings were held in English, rather than Creole, the language spoken by most Haitians. Local realities also hampered efforts to rebuild. For example, many Haitian schools are run by individuals, rather than the government, and some were not willing to have a school rebuilt on their land (Preston & Wallace, 2011).

A year after the earthquake, conditions remained difficult. The dialogue began to shift from immediate disaster relief to longer-term economic development in Haiti, and debates about the best way to accomplish it continued. The U.S. State Department's representative for Haiti explained the importance of making rebuilding "a Haitian-led effort, not a donor-led effort" (McCambridge, 2012). Another report noted the challenges of tracking progress, given the multiple agencies and organizations that were involved: "Given the explosion of international actors, achieving standardization on reporting will be a challenge, and even more so in large, complex emergencies. In future disasters, it will be important to dedicate and deploy staff charged exclusively with the collection, standardization, and compilation of data" (Weisenfeld, n.d.).

In 2015, five years after the earthquake, Haiti had received about 80 percent of the international financial aid that had been promised. Some parts of the capital city, Port-au-Prince, had recovered. But 80,000 Haitians still lived in 170 tent cities in its suburbs (Voice of America, 2015).

Some criticized the Red Cross in particular for the slow pace of recovery (Elliott & Sullivan, 2015). The Red Cross responded, noting challenges presented by the environment in Haiti and explaining various strategies that it had successfully pursued to the benefit of millions of Haitians, often partnering with other organizations ("American Red Cross Responds," 2015). As one example, Sean Penn acknowledged support that his organization had received from the Red Cross (Penn, 2015). Even critics acknowledged that the task of rebuilding in Haiti was complicated by endemic problems, including the lack of clear title to much land, making it impossible to build houses on it (Elliott & Sullivan, 2015). Some also noted the fact that the Haitian government had lost one third of its workforce the day of the earthquake, making it difficult for NGOs to work with the government as a partner (Beaubien, 2015).

In October, 2016, Haiti was stricken by disaster once again. Hurricane Matthew, a category 4 storm, killed 600 people and displaced another 175,000 (Thomas, 2017). The areas impacted were primarily rural and relief efforts again were met with challenges, some similar to those that arose following the earthquake in 2010. The philanthropic response was muted compared with the earthquake six years earlier, which some attributed to "donor fatigue" and perhaps disappointment with the results of recovery efforts following the earthquake (Thomas, 2017, p. 14). One report, published by Refugees, International, focused on the need to increase the capacity of Haitians and their government: "In the absence of a more unified, strategic, long-term approach to building the resilience of the Haitian people among and between the Haitian government, development, and humanitarian agencies, it is likely that the country's tragic pattern of 'one step forward, two steps back' will continue" (Thomas, 2017, p. 17).

Questions Related to Case 17.2

1. Did the philanthropic response to the Haiti earthquake in 2010 provide lessons that may apply to nonprofit organizations in non-disaster fundraising, or was it a unique situation?

2. How are some of the challenges of international management discussed in this chapter reflected in the case of Haitian earthquake relief and recovery?

3. What outcomes would you define and try to measure to determine whether aid efforts in Haiti have been effective? What obstacles do you think might exist in tracking progress?

4. What do you think might account for the reduced level of philanthropic response to Hurricane Matthew in 2016, compared with the earthquake six years earlier? Was it most likely because of donor fatigue, disappointment with the results of efforts following the earthquake, or some other reason?

QUESTIONS FOR DISCUSSION

1. Thinking back on the discussion in Chapter 13 about the importance of developing a case for philanthropic support, how do you think an organization's case might need to be tailored to cultural differences? In other words, do you think people around the world are motivated by similar values and emotions? Why or why not?

2. If you had the financial capacity to be a significant philanthropist, would you focus your giving on reducing world poverty or on addressing social problems in your own country? Explain your answer.

3. Should governments be the principal sources of assistance for economic development and poverty reduction, or should philanthropy play the leading role? What are the advantages and disadvantages of each type of action? What should be the relationship between private and government efforts? Explain.

SUGGESTIONS FOR FURTHER READING

Books

Battersby, P., & Roy, R. K. (Eds.). (2017). *International development: A global perspective on theory and practice*. London, UK: Sage.

Cagney, P., & Ross, B. (2013). *Global fundraising: How the world is changing the rules of philanthropy*. Hoboken, NJ: Wiley.

Missoni, E., & Alesani, D. (Eds.). (2014). *Management of international institutions and NGOs: Frameworks, practices, and challenges*. New York, NY: Routledge.

Rosenfield, P. L. (2014). *A world of giving: Carnegie Corporation of New York—A century of international philanthropy*. New York, NY: Carnegie Corporation.

Websites

Global Giving: http://www.globalgiving.org/

InterAction (American Council for Voluntary International Action): http://www.interaction.org/

International Society for Third-Sector Research (ISTR): http://www.istr.org/

Johns Hopkins Center for Civil Society Studies: http://ccss.jhu.edu/

Union of International Associations: http://www.uia.be/

Conclusion

Readers who have persisted through this entire text hopefully will have learned many things. Even those who may have had some prior experience working in a nonprofit organization may have found some new theory, some new concept, or some new data that added to their existing body of knowledge or understanding. Those for whom this book has been an initiation into the subject will have learned even more. But some may be wondering, "So exactly what have I learned?" "What *is* the right way to manage a nonprofit organization?" "Is there a future for nonprofit management as a distinct profession? And, if so, what qualities, skills, and perspectives are needed to pursue a career in the field during the decades ahead?"

This book has no simple answers to offer. The nonprofit sector is so diverse that no specific approach can be equally effective in all organizations. Some of the skills needed to manage a university may be quite different from those required to manage an international nongovernmental organization or a community-based nonprofit serving low-income citizens of one particular city. Indeed, when I began writing the first edition of this textbook, some friends advised me that the diversity of the nonprofit sector would render the task of writing a broadly useful book about nonprofit management far too challenging. Rather, they suggested, there should be a series of books on nonprofit management, each focused on a particular type of organization, such as universities, hospitals, arts institutions, human services organizations, and others. Of course, many such specialized books already exist; indeed, there are academic programs of study that focus on each of those areas. But the wide acceptance of the first four editions of this book demonstrated that there are commonalities that run across the management of nonprofit organizations and institutions and thus some basic principles on which individuals seeking to lead such organizations should be well informed. This fifth edition has attempted to address shortcomings in the first four and to provide a balanced perspective that may be of benefit to students and future nonprofit executives in all types of organizations.

The rationale for this book lies with the management commonalities we have discussed. These include the need to balance mission and money—to measure success by a double bottom line—and the need to manage relationships with multiple constituents who may hold competing or conflicting views of what the organization should be and do, and who are both free and motivated to express them. There is also a political dimension to the job of a nonprofit leader. Thus, two constants of nonprofit management would be a highly nuanced leadership ability and—even for the commercialized and hybrid nonprofits—the deep underlying commitment to a mission that differentiates good leaders of nonprofits from good leaders in organizations guided by the pursuit of wealth or constrained by the limits of political feasibility.

It remains true that such wide variation among organizations and the rapid pace with which the sector is changing suggest that there can be no one right way to manage a nonprofit that students can learn today and then apply throughout their careers. Rather, as it has been said at various points in the book, successful management in this sector and in this period of history requires an approach that is pragmatic, eclectic, and flexible. Successful managers select the tools and approaches that best fit the circumstances and needs of their organizations, ever mindful of the overriding and immutable centrality of the mission. That may suggest the application of commercial methods or the exercise of charismatic leadership to inspire philanthropy. It may call for a strategic management approach or for creating an entrepreneurial culture. Indeed, it may call for founding a new organization or leading a transformational process that brings systemic change. It may require seeking government funds or working to develop earned income or philanthropy to diversify support and preserve greater autonomy. It may require considering new corporate forms, going beyond the traditional nonprofit legal structure. Or it may require doing all these things—and others—at the same time.

While contemporary concerns such as accountability and compliance, effectiveness and performance, capacity and strategic management, social enterprise and earned income, and collaborations and mergers are all important, it is also essential not to become too committed to the management fads or buzzwords of the day. Of course, no manager can ignore current legal, social, and financial pressures; deny the realities of competition; or pretend that organizations can be managed as they may have been at some earlier time. Rather, students and future nonprofit managers need to maintain both openness to new ideas and a healthy skepticism about those that are offered as one-right-way prescriptions.

In his conclusion to the 2005 edition of the *Jossey-Bass Handbook of Nonprofit Leadership and Management,* its editor, Robert Herman, asks the question of whether nonprofit management as a distinct profession will continue to exist in the future. He concludes that it will, because the nonprofit sector will continue to exist. Herman (2005) bases this optimistic prediction on the supply-side theories about "the motives and desires of those who actually take the time and effort to create and sustain an organization" (p. 733). More than a decade later, his prediction continues to be correct. The nonprofit sector continues to exist and, indeed, it has continued to expand.

But Herman's (2005) tone is one of cautious optimism rather than conviction. He emphasizes commercialism as a threat that could turn nonprofits into nothing more than businesses and government contractors, requiring nothing distinctive from their managers and causing some to question whether they should continue to exist in nonprofit form at all (pp. 733–734). Indeed, the increase in organizations adopting new legal forms, the emergence of the Fourth Sector, impact investing and performance-based contracting— discussed earlier in this text—could portend that Herman's caution was prescient and that nonprofit organizations as we traditionally have defined them may become less a part of the mix. At the time of this writing, there are serious concerns about the impact of federal budget changes on funding for social programs as well as on charitable giving, posing threats to the funding models of many nonprofit organizations. Perhaps social needs and problems will increasingly be addressed by for-profit social enterprises that are integral to the market economy. It is, as Yogi Berra is reported to have said, difficult to make predictions, especially about the future. But my view is that the nonprofit sector is likely to survive and thrive in the decades ahead, providing unprecedented opportunities for professional managers, volunteer leaders, and philanthropists alike.

Commercialism in the nonprofit sector is not new. It has existed in education and the arts for decades, yet most institutions in those fields continue to exhibit cultures and qualities that affirm their nonprofit identities. Of course, many authors who express concern about commercialism are primarily focused on the human and social service organizations, which constitute the largest number of organizations in the sector. Critical observers worry that some of those organizations have become almost exclusively government contractors or that philanthropists have come to see their support of them as a form of investment requiring a measurable return, transplanting the culture of capital markets into the nonprofit arena. Such concerns are not without foundation, but they may sometimes overshadow more promising developments and trends.

Concerns that there are too many nonprofit organizations are often expressed. Some believe, and not without any foundation, that limited resources, duplication of management infrastructure, and inefficiencies should be addressed by consolidation within the nonprofit sector. Calls for such change likely will continue, and increasing collaboration, even mergers, may be driven by even tighter financial conditions in future years. However, nonprofit organizations are also differentiated, including many whose mission statements may make them sound alike. Just as there is a place for McDonalds and Burger King, as well as Five

Guys—because their burgers are all a little different—many nonprofits represent a particular theory of change or philosophy of action, and many reflect the emotional commitment of donors and volunteers to their unique characteristics and cultures. Some who see too many nonprofits may be undervaluing the hold of such distinctions on the hearts of those who staff and support many organizations—and that undeniably drive the creation of new organizations every year. Indeed, one of the joys of teaching nonprofit management at a university is the opportunity to interact with students who are not only aspiring social entrepreneurs, savvy in the methods of the marketplace but also driven by compassion, conscience, and commitment to a social mission. Some will create new organizations or try; some will succeed and others fail. Others will bring change to existing organizations and increase their impact. There is no reason to believe that the numbers of such individuals will diminish; indeed, their numbers may be growing in response to increasing awareness of the social, economic, and environmental problems that will occupy future generations of people worldwide. The energy of young people—and the sustained commitment of older people, who may find that their life priorities turn increasingly toward a broader engagement with society—will continue to add new nonprofit organizations to the mix and to drive renewal of existing ones, redefining the sector over and over again.

Even those philanthropists who emphasize measurable results and think like investors are not primarily interested in a financial bottom line. To be sure, many expect and demand that their resources be used efficiently and effectively, but in all cases, their involvement is driven by a passion for a cause, not by the desire to make a profit. Genuine philanthropists are motivated by emotion, however rational their methods. It is still true, as Seymour (1966) wrote in his classic book on fundraising, that "the heart has to prompt the mind to go where logic points the way" (p. 29). Some social entrepreneurs and contemporary philanthropists may apply the tools and techniques of business to their endeavors, but their motivations still relate to the social missions of the organizations they support.

It is certain that nonprofit managers of the future will need to be able to implement business judgments and methods in their work. Skills in marketing, financial management, strategic planning, and other business techniques will become ever more essential, and students are strongly encouraged to pursue knowledge in these and other areas far beyond the brief introduction that this book provides. Nonprofit managers of the future will need to accept and master new organizational forms and new methods with an open mind and a willingness to adapt to changing principles, values, and norms. But also essential will be the ability to envision and to inspire, as well as the qualities of effective leadership that can only derive from deep personal commitment. In his widely viewed TED Talk in 2013, Dan Pallotta describes philanthropy as "the market for love" and notes that it is hard to place a price on that. It is important to remember that nonprofits serve expressive as well as instrumental purposes. In addition to whatever positive results they may produce, they also provide a vehicle for individuals to work together toward unselfish goals. Nonprofit management is likely to remain a distinct field because the nonprofit sector is likely to remain distinctive. It reflects the noble impulses and humane instincts that are the best elements of human nature and that cannot be fulfilled or expressed as fully anywhere else.

Appendix: Cases for Discussion

Appendix Case 1: New York City Opera

Relevant chapters:
Chapter 4 (Nonprofit Governing Boards); Chapter 5 (Executive Leadership); Chapter 7 (Developing Strategy, Building Capacity, and Managing Risk); Chapter 10 (Marketing and Communications); Chapter 12 (Financial Management); Chapter 13 (Philanthropic Fundraising); Chapter 14 (Social Enterprise and Earned Income)

"Throughout its history as The People's Opera, the New York City Opera (NYC Opera) has made opera accessible and affordable. And now NYC Opera needs help to produce its upcoming season," read the funding appeal (New York City Opera, 2013). This seemingly commonplace request for donations did not take the form of an e-mail to longtime patrons or a glossy brochure mailed to established donors. Instead, in September 2013, the NYC Opera—one of the city's premier cultural institutions—took the unprecedented step of attempting to fund its upcoming season by turning to Kickstarter, a crowdfunding website used by amateur musicians, artists, theater troupes, filmmakers, inventors, and others to collect small donations from the public to fund their projects.

The fundraising strategy was a failure. The NYC Opera needed to raise $7 million to fund its upcoming season, $1 million of which it hoped to raise via Kickstarter. The organization brought in only $300,000 from about 2,100 Kickstarter donors, in addition to $1.5 million in other funds (New York City Opera, 2013). After this last-ditch attempt fell far short of the mark, on October 3, 2013, NYC Opera filed for Chapter 11 bankruptcy protection (Cooper, 2013b).

How could one of New York City's most lauded and beloved cultural assets have reached such an unfortunate situation? Was it the result of the fundraising challenges in an economy that was still recovering from the financial crisis of 2008? Were demographic changes to blame, with younger New Yorkers perhaps having less interest in opera than previous generations? Or could the organization's collapse have been the result of poor decisions made by its management and board of directors? Was it a combination of these reasons? And could anything be done to bring the NYC Opera back from the brink of extinction?

Background and History

NYC Opera was established in 1943 with the assistance of New York City Mayor Fiorello La Guardia, who deemed it "The People's Opera." In keeping with this characterization, the organization's mission was "to inspire audiences with innovative and theatrically compelling opera, to nurture the work of promising American artists, and to build new audiences through affordable ticket prices and extensive outreach and education programs" (Guidestar, n.d.).

The scope of NYC Opera's activities was consistent with this mission. For example, it presented a variety of operas each season and performed a wide range of distinguished compositions. At its peak, each season NYC Opera presented 12 to 16 different operas and gave 130 performances (Associated Press, 2013). Its repertoire encompassed 275 works spanning from Baroque compositions to modern-day operas, including 29 world premieres and 61 American or New York premieres. NYC Opera also remained true to its mission by attracting and promoting high-caliber artists. It launched the international careers of 3,000 singers, including for example, noted artists Reneé Fleming, José Carreras, Beverly Sills, Plácido Domingo, and Frederica von Stade. The organization also sought to bring diversity to the world of opera, which it achieved by giving the first starring opera role to an African American singer, giving the first regular opera contract to an African American singer, and premiering the first opera written by an African American composer (National Public Radio, 2013).

NYC Opera further achieved its mission by making opera more accessible to New Yorkers. For example, in 1983 it was the first U.S. opera company to use supertitles. That means it projected onto a screen the text of the opera in English, allowing audiences to more easily follow the plot. Today this is a standard feature of operatic performances. NYC Opera also strove to keep its performances affordable, with ticket prices beginning at a relatively low $25 in its 2013 season (Iaboni, 2013). Additionally, NYC Opera sought to cultivate future opera audiences through its in-school NYC Opera Education program, which introduced thousands of public school students in the New York metropolitan area to opera each year and took them behind the scenes of opera productions (New York City Opera, 2013).

The NYC Opera had years of great success. For example, during the 1980s, it was led by Beverly Sills, an international opera star who got her start with NYC Opera. During her tenure from 1979 to 1989, her tireless fundraising and prodigious promotion of the organization led to an increase in its budget from $9 million to $26 million, and turned a $3 million deficit into a $3 million surplus. According to Kevin Russell, who served as NYC Opera's director of special events under Sills, "She knew who had money and knew who would give it. And she had no problem asking anybody for it" (Godfrey & Schneiderman, 2013). But when Sills left her position, "she also left behind a daunting problem: NYC Opera's fundraising success had been mostly dependent on her. Sills was the very face of American opera; many donors who gave to the New York City Opera were giving money to *her*" (Cohn, 2012).

By the 2000s, NYC Opera faced a series of crises that culminated in its bankruptcy. It began running large deficits in 2003, and its funding was hit hard by the 2008 financial crisis. The organization offered no performances in its 2008–2009 season and thus earned no ticket revenue, due to the renovation of its performance venue, the New York State Theater (now named the David H. Koch Theater) at Lincoln Center. Also in 2008 and 2009, NYC Opera invaded its endowment to cover operating expenses and pay down debt. In 2011, in an effort to trim fixed costs, NYC Opera moved out of Lincoln Center yet did not secure a permanent performance venue, resulting in the loss of a major component of the organization's identity. Throughout the decade, NYC Opera responded to financial difficulties by reducing its performance schedule, such that it gave just 16 performances of four different operas in 2012, compared with 115 performances of 17 different operas a decade prior (Cooper, 2013b).

Years of Crisis and Decline

While a key player in the cultural life of New York City, NYC Opera was unable to raise funds adequate to carry it into its 71st year. The organization experienced financial instability throughout much of its history, but this instability was especially pronounced in the final decade before its bankruptcy (Cooper & Pogrebin, 2013). The elements of NYC Opera's decline include an unstable funding model heavily dependent upon grants and gifts, multiple invasions of the organization's endowment, and a series of strategic decisions that may have exacerbated the problems.

Unsustainable Revenue Model

A key contributing factor to NYC Opera's closure was its unsustainable revenue model, particularly in the years leading up to its bankruptcy filing. NYC Opera began running dangerously high deficits beginning in 2003 (Cooper & Pogrebin, 2013). Its accumulated deficit in 2012 reached $44 million (Cooper, 2013b). NYC Opera's revenue model lacked diversification, relying significantly on gifts and grants. Until its 2000–2001 season, the organization had operated as a "50/50" company; that is, it derived its revenue equally from contributed income (gifts and grants) and from earned income (ticket sales; Cohn, 2012). However, this changed after the September 11 terrorist attacks, which resulted in a decline in performing arts attendance throughout New York City. For NYC Opera, this decline was permanent (Cohn, 2012). Consequently, ticket sales contributed less and less to the organization's bottom line, while gifts and grants became increasingly important.

And although New York's mayor and the city's commissioner of cultural affairs served as ex-officio members of the NYC Opera board and sent representatives to its meetings (Stewart, 2013), the organization reported only $153,000 in government grants in 2011.

As a point of comparison with other New York City organizations, in 2011 the Metropolitan Opera had program service revenue roughly equal to its contribution and grant revenue (at about $141 million and $137 million, respectively; Guidestar, 2011). Likewise, in 2010 the New York Philharmonic had program revenue of roughly $28 million and contribution and grant revenue of nearly $35 million (Guidestar, 2010).

The growing reliance on philanthropy, rather than earned income, may have reflected NYC Opera's commitment to its mission as the "People's Opera" and its reluctance to increase ticket prices. Keeping prices so low may have been a strategic error. However, given the relatively high demand elasticity of luxury goods, such as opera tickets, it is also possible that doubling or tripling ticket prices would have lowered revenue even further. In other words, any additional money earned from higher ticket prices might have been more than offset by fewer tickets being sold.

In addition, NYC Opera curtailed its performance schedule precipitously in an effort to rein in costs. That action reduced costs, but it also reduced revenue. Severely reducing the number of performances may have had the effect of sending NYC Opera into a downward spiral, wherein fewer performances led to fewer tickets sold, thereby further reducing revenues and necessitating even fewer performances. It also may have reduced the donor base, as it made NYC Opera less effective in achieving its mission and weakened its organizational identity. When coupled with large deficits, insufficient diversification of revenue sources eventually made the organization's financial situation untenable.

Endowment Invasions

In the face of financial pressures, the NYC Opera board repeatedly drew upon the organization's endowment to cover routine expenses and pay down debt, a practice known as "endowment invasion" (Godfrey & Schneiderman, 2013). NYC Opera gained approval from the courts and the New York attorney general to withdraw about $24 million from its endowment, $17.5 million in 2008 and $6.6 million in 2009. In 2001, its endowment stood at $51.6 million; by June 2013, it totaled just $5.2 million. The reduction reflects investment losses as well as the endowment invasions (Stewart, 2013).

The principal of most endowments is not intended to be spent, but rather to ensure the existence of the institution in perpetuity, especially during financially tumultuous times. Indeed, the Lila Acheson and DeWitt Wallace Fund for Lincoln Center, the source of most of NYC Opera's endowment, mandated the funds be maintained "in perpetuity as an endowment fund" (Stewart, 2013). However, the income the endowment generates *can* be used to cover current operating expenses. By depleting the principal of its endowment, NYC Opera also reduced the future income that it would receive from endowment earnings. Its endowment once returned $3 million annually in investment income to the organization, but after the $24 million in withdrawals, that amount dwindled to under $200,000—less than the revenue NYC Opera earned from a thrift store it managed in Manhattan (Cooper, 2013a).

The endowment invasions made it possible for NYC Opera to cover immediate funding shortfalls, but those decisions undermined the organization's ability to meet future funding needs. According to Manuela Hoelterhoff, a well-known opera critic and executive editor of the arts and culture section of Bloomberg News, drawing down its endowment "was a suicidal thing to do" (Stewart, 2013).

Another financial decision made by the board was to switch the endowment's investments from stocks to cash in response to the 2008 financial crisis. While this was intended to shield the organization's endowment from the stock market selloff during that period NYC Opera failed to switch back to stocks as the market recovered in 2009. Consequently, it realized a $9.5 million investment loss in fiscal 2008 (which ended in June 2009), at a time that coincided with the decision to raid its endowment. It was reported that the board did not have an investment committee to oversee investment of the endowment (Stewart, 2013).

Critical Leadership Decisions

In its last several years before entering bankruptcy, the NYC Opera board made a series of key decisions. These included the 2007 hiring of Gerard Mortier as general manager and artistic director, essentially the CEO; the decision to offer no performances during the 2008–2009 season due to the renovation of its performance venue; the 2009 appointment of George Steel as CEO; and NYC Opera's 2011 move out of its newly renovated performance space at Lincoln Center without first securing a new permanent venue.

Susan Baker became chair of the NYC Opera board in 2004. In 2007, general manager Paul Kellogg announced his departure. Baker was reported by some to be a hands-on board chair, frequently in the company's offices and involved in management decisions. Some said that Kellogg retreated in the face of Baker's forceful presence, which created confusion on the part of staff about who was really in charge (Cohn, 2012).

Belgian opera maestro Gerard Mortier was hired to replace Paul Kellogg as general manager and artistic director. Mortier, who was concluding his tenure at the Paris Opera, had made his name with elaborate, iconoclastic productions, and the board thought he could inject new energy and vitality into NYC Opera. He effectively ended NYC Opera's ongoing search for a more suitable performance venue by pushing for the renovation of its longtime concert hall, New York State Theater at Lincoln Center, although some said that it was both too large and too close to the Metropolitan Opera, which was also housed at Lincoln Center. The renovation helped improve the hall's acoustics, but it did not address the fact that the venue was too large to allow for smaller scale, more intimate performances that donors and audiences desired. Additionally, some said that it prevented NYC Opera from clarifying its identity by physically distancing itself from its rival, the Metropolitan Opera (Pogrebin, 2009).

Renovating New York State Theater led to the cancellation of NYC Opera's 2008–2009 season, as the musicians had nowhere to perform. This inflicted an additional financial wound. For calendar year 2008, NYC Opera had program revenue of only $922,000 (from the New York City Opera 2009 Form 990). In short, the "missing season caused a loss in revenue and momentum from which the company ... never recovered" (Cohn, 2012). Mortier stepped down in late 2008 upon his discovery that the $60 million budget he had requested from the board—an amount he felt necessary to achieve his artistic vision—would not be granted. Indeed, he would receive only $36 million (Cohn, 2012). His departure introduced additional uncertainty into an organization contending with severe financial challenges, a cancelled performance season, and the renovation of its performance hall. In addition to creating a leadership vacuum, Mortier's resignation compounded NYC Opera's financial difficulties by making it impossible for the board to capitalize on his name recognition among donors to raise additional funds (Pogrebin, 2009).

Some board members and others thought that Mortier's appointment had been a mistake. His experience had been in Europe, where the arts receive generous government support. Some people said that his unfamiliarity with fundraising in the private sector was a shortcoming in the NYC Opera's environment and in view of its financial problems. Additionally, some said, Mortier's artistic vision proved too large for NYC Opera's financial capabilities, as evidenced by his request for a $60 million budget that the board was simply unable to provide (Godfrey & Schneiderman, 2013).

Following Mortier's departure, the NYC Opera board appointed George Steel to become NYC Opera's general manager and artistic director. Steel had for 11 years served as executive director of Columbia University's Miller Theater, a small musical theater that he reinvigorated with innovative performances of both contemporary and early music. Aside from a few months as head of the Dallas Opera, the position he held at the time of his appointment to NYC Opera, he had no experience running an opera company. For these reasons, some observers were surprised by his being named to the post (Cohn, 2012).

Steel's tenure was defined by two moves he made in an attempt to shore up the organization's finances. The first of these was the curtailing of NYC Opera's season; it gave just 16 performances in 2012. The second was the controversial decision in 2011 to move NYC Opera out of its longtime home at Lincoln Center—which had just been renovated—without first securing a new permanent performance venue.

While the move helped to save the fixed costs of renting and operating an enormous venue, it relegated the NYC Opera to a nomadic troupe that performed at various locations scattered throughout Manhattan and Brooklyn. Julius Rudel, general director and principal conductor of NYC Opera from 1957 to 1979, argued that the organization's Lincoln Center home conferred upon it a high degree of respectability and prestige and helped it attract top-shelf talent. In arguing against the 2011 move, he wrote that "Lincoln Center solidified the company's place not as New York's *second* opera company, but as New York's *other* opera company" (Rudel, 2011). The move out of Lincoln Center was seen as a highly visible symbol of NYC Opera's grave financial situation. Steel's decision was sharply criticized by the musicians' unions, which picketed his press conference announcing the decision. Former opera company members also spoke out and a *New York Times* op-ed criticized the move (Cohn, 2012). The decision also alienated donors, and further compounded NYC Opera's fiscal woes (Cooper & Pogrebin, 2013).

The New York City Opera was not the only arts organization facing challenges during the years of its decline and eventual bankruptcy. Organizations in New York City and across the country have had to contend with audiences' changing tastes and with a difficult fundraising environment due to the economy. These factors were especially pertinent to NYC Opera; the organization suffered from the 2008 financial crisis, and opera had traditionally struggled to attract the younger audiences whose patronage was becoming increasingly important to performing arts nonprofits. But some saw other factors at work in the case of the NYC Opera. One reviewer described the events as "an epic saga of economic hardship, mismanagement, and just plain bad luck" (Cohn, 2012). Others criticized the board. John Godfrey and Jason Schneiderman (2013) reflect the views of some critics, arguing that "Amongst the board's chief roles are to appoint the CEOs and to have fiduciary responsibility toward the company's donors," adding that "the board of the New York City Opera appears to have failed at both."

The opera *Anna Nicole* is based on the life of Anna Nicole Smith, who gained notoriety for her marriage to her wealthy and much-older husband, J. Howard Marshall II, and for the bitter dispute between Marshall's family and Smith regarding her inheritance from his estate.

Anna Nicole was NYC Opera's final performance before slipping into bankruptcy and closing down. There is a scene in which the star's elderly husband collapses of what appears to be a heart attack. But he quickly rises and delivers the line "I'm not dead yet." When "Not Dead Yet" was sung by tenor Robert Brubaker in NYC Opera's final performance in 2013, the irony could not have been fully appreciated by the audience that night (Maloney, 2013). Some people were still determined to revive the historic organization.

Bidding for Rebirth

When an organization files for bankruptcy, the court is responsible for dividing up whatever assets may remain and settling claims by its creditors. The court invites bids for the remaining assets in order to try and recover some value for the creditors. In 2014, a group known as NYCO Renaissance, led by former NYC Opera board member and investor Roy Niederhoffer, bid for the remaining assets and the name of NYC Opera, intending to bring it back to life. The opera's board requested that the court approve the offer, although some creditors pressured the court to approve a rival, higher offer for the opera's assets that also had been presented (Cooper, 2015). While awaiting the court's decision, NYCO Renaissance moved forward with plans to relaunch NYC Opera with a benefit performance at the Rose Theater in Lincoln Center, honoring the memory of Julius Rudel, the opera's former director (Cooper, 2014). Held in March 2015, the benefit raised $800,000 (Tommasini, 2015).

Some questioned whether NYC Opera could be revived in a changed environment. They argued that other organizations had come to play the role that had for many years belonged exclusively to NYC Opera (Milnes, 2015). Smaller opera companies, including the Gotham Chamber Opera and Loft Opera, were selling out shows and receiving favorable reviews (Milnes, 2015). Moreover, New York's major opera company, the Metropolitan Opera, also had evolved.

During the years of NYC Opera's decline, the Metropolitan Opera faced some of the same external realities of a struggling economy and changing audience preferences. Of course, the Metropolitan Opera had greater resources than the NYC Opera, which enabled it to better weather challenging economic conditions. However, in recent years, the Metropolitan Opera also brought opera to new audiences through various innovative endeavors. Since 2006, the year Peter Gelb became the organization's general manager, it set fundraising records, nearly doubling the number of new annual productions, brought younger audiences to its performances, started a 24-hour channel on Sirius XM radio, and created an iPad app (Brown, 2013). Additionally, the Metropolitan Opera made its performances available to audiences across the country and around the world through its "Live in HD" program, which broadcasts opera performances in high definition to movie theaters. As of 2012, it reached 1,700 theaters in 54 countries and had begun to turn a profit. In short, Gelb "[had] guided the opera company into the digital age and … put an art form long associated with aristocratic privilege on a more populist footing" (Brown, 2013). Some argued that these initiatives had indeed made the Metropolitan the people's opera.

In 2016, the bankruptcy court approved the plan submitted by NYCO Renaissance and NYC Opera announced a new season. Its long-term survival was still uncertain and it would face a challenge to "woo back audiences and skeptical donors, and navigate a cultural landscape that [had] changed dramatically since the heyday of the old company" (Cooper, 2016). In December 2016, the new NYC Opera presented Leonard Bernstein's *Candide*. The operetta ends with "Make Our Garden Grow," the lyrics of which celebrate the optimistic view that hard work can create a better future, consistent with the determination of the new NYC Opera to work its way back to stability and recognition (Cooper, 2016):

> We're neither pure, nor wise, nor good
> We'll do the best we know.
> We'll build our house and chop our wood
> And make our garden grow …
> (https://www.stlyrics.com/lyrics/candide/finalemakeourgardengrow.htm)

Note: This case was written by Michael McCarthy, a graduate student at the George Washington University in fall 2013. It has been substantially adapted and expanded by the textbook author, including sections related to events after 2013.

CASE 1: QUESTIONS FOR DISCUSSION

1. How do decisions made by the NYC Opera board relate to the responsibilities of nonprofit governing boards discussed in Chapter 4?

2. Did NYC Opera exhibit symptoms of syndrome during some periods of its history, even when led by executives who were not literally the founder?

3. What are some strategies that NYC Opera might have pursued to broaden its sources of revenue beyond gifts and grants in order to have avoided bankruptcy in 2013?

4. Did the NYC Opera appear to have a strategy, as defined in Chapter 7, during its years of decline? If so, how would you summarize it? If not, what strategy might you have recommended during that period?

5. What principles of financial management, discussed in Chapter 14, might have made a difference to NYC Opera during its approach to bankruptcy?

6. Which principles of marketing discussed in Chapter 10 are most relevant to the case of New York City Opera?

7. What do the efforts to revive New York City Opera after its bankruptcy suggest about its brand? In what ways is its brand different from that of other operas?

8. Some people say that younger donors are not as interested in contributing to traditional arts institutions, such as opera companies and symphony orchestras? Do you think that is correct? If so, is it due to generational differences or a failure of communication and marketing by such institutions?

Appendix Case 2: Share Our Strength/ No Kid Hungry

Relevant chapters:

Chapter 7 (Developing *Strategy, Building Capacity, and Managing Risk*); Chapter 8 (*Collaborations, Partnerships, and Mergers*); Chapter 9 (*Managing Staff and Service Volunteers*); Chapter 10 (*Marketing and Communications*); Chapter 11 (*Advocacy and Lobbying*); Chapter 12 (*Financial Management*); Chapter 13 (*Philanthropic Fundraising*); Chapter 14 (*Social Enterprise and Earned Income*); Chapter 15 (*Government Grants and Contracts*); Chapter 16 (*Social Entrepreneurship and Innovation*)

Bill Shore grew up in a working-class neighborhood of Pittsburgh, where his father instilled in him a concern for the plight of people who were facing challenges in their lives. Motivated by those values and by the social activism of the 1960s, he had gravitated toward politics and by 1984 held a staff position in the first presidential campaign of Senator Gary Hart. Following the senator's withdrawal from the race and a brief vacation, Shore was on his way back to work in the senator's office when he saw a headline in the *Washington Post*: "200,000 to Die this Summer in Ethiopia." The threat of imminent famine that would claim so many lives caused Shore to reflect on his own life's work. As Shore recalls,

> I sat thinking about what the famine meant, what it would be like for the ravaged families who lived there. For the first time since my involvement in the presidential campaign, I really felt something about world events; I made an emotional connection to something beyond the usual calculations of how they could be turned to political advantage. It just seemed that since I felt so strongly about it, I ought to pay attention to that impulse. ("More Than Food," 1998)

Later that year, working in the basement of a row house in Washington's Georgetown neighborhood, Shore and his sister Debbie acted on the impulse by founding a new nonprofit organization, using a $2,000 cash advance on a credit card ("Q&A," 2015). Believing that "everyone has a strength to share in the global fight against hunger and poverty," they named the new organization Share Our Strength (Share Our Strength, 2017).

Creating Community Wealth

By 1986, the Shores were again working for Senator Hart while running Share Our Strength (SOS) on the side. Their fundraising for SOS consisted primarily of mailings to chefs and restaurant owners, whom they thought might have a particular interest in food. The results from this traditional method were modest. Then, while working for Hart in Denver, the Shores persuaded local chefs to participate in a special event to benefit their young organization. The chefs would offer a sampling of gourmet dishes to guests, with the ticket fees going to benefit SOS. The event raised $10,000, and the Shores calculated that the chefs had given far more in the form of gifts-in-kind and their own time and effort than they ever would have given in cash in response to direct-mail solicitations. This success provided an important insight: "[N]onprofits needed to move away from seeking charitable contributions and toward building *strategic partnerships* with companies" (Crutchfield & Grant, 2012, p. 91).

Despite numerous historical antecedents, the term "social enterprise" was not as widely used in 1984 as it is today, but Shore became convinced that organizations working for social change needed to pursue a new model. He argued that too many nonprofits were dependent on traditional sources of revenue, primarily philanthropy, and were struggling to achieve impact. Too many nonprofit CEOs were distracted from building programs by the constant need to engage in fundraising. Traditional revenue sources were insufficient to bring successful programs to a scale that they could achieve lasting change or assure the sustainability of even successful organizations. Wealth was being created at a historic rate in the business sector, but "nonprofit organizations [had] been left behind" (Shore, 1999, p. 212). Most were "wed to practices that rely on redistributing wealth, rather than committed to the entrepreneurial activities that create wealth" (p. 212). SOS would join other pioneering nonprofits taking a different approach: "creating *community wealth* through business enterprise, cause-related marketing partnerships, and licensing—directing profits back into the community [italics added]" (p. 143).

Partnering With Business

For its first 20 years, Share Our Strength operated primarily as a funding intermediary that raised funds and made grants to other nonprofits providing direct services, including food banks and other emergency food assistance programs (Crutchfield & Grant, 2012). The funds were raised by mobilizing the food and restaurant industry through sponsored events.

Based on the Shores' experience in Denver, Taste of the Nation was launched in 1988. The event brought together dozens of chefs and charged diners an entry fee to sample the fare of participating restaurants. The first event, held simultaneously in several cities, raised nearly $250,000 in one day. Over just the next two years, Taste of the Nation expanded to 18 American cities (Crutchfield & Grant, 2012). The events were mutually beneficial to all participants, providing funds for SOS; helping chefs and restaurateurs to get publicity and to visibly associate with SOS's cause; and providing corporate sponsors, such as Anheuser-Busch, opportunities to develop relationships with participating chefs and restaurants.

In 1993, a partnership between Share Our Strength and American Express achieved breakthrough success and became a widely studied example (Crutchfield & Grant, 2012). Share Our Strength already had established relationships with restaurants through Taste of the Nation and other programs. The Charge Against Hunger campaign leveraged those relationships to provide another source of revenue for SOS and a marketing benefit for its corporate partner. Consumers were encouraged to dine out at participating restaurants to help fight hunger. American Express donated three cents from every transaction during October, November, and December from 1993 to 1996 (Nelson, Kanso, & Levitt, 2007). Over the four-year period, Charge Against Hunger raised $21 million for Share Our Strength, as well as increasing awareness of hunger issues and raising the profile of American Express, which was working to improve its image within the restaurant industry (Nelson et al., 2007). The campaign was lauded as a model for future cause-marketing endeavors. Other corporation-sponsored events were developed, including the Great American Bake Sale, Restaurants for Relief, and A Tasteful Pursuit. Although not all events succeeded, SOS became a "cause-marketing machine" (Crutchfield & Grant, 2012).

Community Wealth Ventures

By 1998, SOS had attracted wide attention for its fundraising success and other nonprofits were calling for advice on how they could create successful commercial partnerships with businesses and start their own revenue-generating enterprises. SOS decided to leverage that visibility by establishing its own for-profit subsidiary, to provide consulting services to other nonprofits desiring to establish cause-marketing partnerships and earned-income ventures. The new consulting firm, Community Wealth Ventures (CWV), would generate profits to help support SOS.

Community Wealth Ventures refined and expanded Shore's concept of community wealth and developed materials for nonprofits to use in planning commercial partnerships and earned-income ventures (including some content that was included in Chapter 14 of this text). Community Wealth Ventures returned $1 million in profits to SOS in its first eight years and successfully partnered with hundreds of organizations, including high-profile clients such as City Year, KaBOOM!, and the Campaign for Tobacco-Free Kids.

In 2013, Community Wealth Ventures changed its name to Community Wealth Partners, reflecting a shift in emphasis from commercial partnerships and earned-income ventures to a broader relationship with nonprofit clients, related to achieving social change. This refocus was consistent with new directions adopted by its parent, SOS, which are discussed in the next section of this case (Celep, 2013).

Refocusing for Greater Impact

By most measures, Share Our Strength's first 20 years in operation were a success. By 2004, it had raised more than $200 million for thousands of hunger and poverty organizations, received positive media attention, and had created a widely emulated model for successful cause-marketing initiatives with major corporate sponsors. But it had become clear to Shore that SOS's activity as a grant maker was not achieving the broader impact that was needed. As Shore observed, "we made grants to thousands of organizations around the United States, all of which were doing an impressive job of feeding hungry people, but few of which were focused on ending hunger … much of the focus, internally and externally, was on the entrepreneurial ways it [SOS] generated funds (through innovations in cause-related marketing) rather than on how it [SOS] used the funds to advance its mission" (Shore, Hammond, & Celep, 2013).

Indeed, despite the efforts of Share Our Strength and public programs such as the Supplemental Nutrition Assistance Program (SNAP), hunger in America persisted. As Shore explained, "It was … unsatisfying that we could not quantify our impact. Was the funding we provided equal to 1 percent of what was needed, or was it 50 percent? When was our job done? Without a specific measure of success it was impossible to know" (Shore et al., 2013). Additionally, after years of growth, SOS's fundraising totals were flat (Blum, 2012b).

Shore knew that a new approach was essential. The only way to maximize impact was to markedly change how the organization was approaching the hunger problem. SOS needed to develop a vision of what success would look like, develop a scalable model that would permanently change the system, and define what its impact would be. Perhaps most important, SOS would need to leverage its strong existing assets to challenge the root of the hunger problem in new, significant ways (Shore, 2013). Shore recognized that SOS would need to "go big or go home" (Blum, 2012b). He concluded that the answer would lie in shifting activities from broad anti-hunger issues to a specific problem and with a specific achievable goal: end childhood hunger in America (Shore et al., 2013).

The problem of childhood hunger is widespread. Nearly half of the 47 million people receiving support through the SNAP program (sometimes referred to as "food stamps") are children. One in five American children do not consistently receive the nutritious food they need. All American children are eligible for school breakfasts, but only 11 million were receiving them in 2015 ("Q&A," 2015). The effects of childhood hunger are profound. A study conducted by the consulting firm Deloitte (Augustine-Thottungal, Kern, Key, & Sherman, 2013) found hungry children under age three suffer from cognitive impairment that limits their future educational and economic success. In addition, hungry children are 31 percent more likely to be hospitalized and are 3.4 times more likely to be overweight or obese (Augustine-Thottungal et al., 2013). A lack of nutritious food leads kids to higher levels of anxiety and aggressive behavior, and hungry teens are more likely to be suspended from school and suffer from difficulty in interpersonal relationships (Share Our Strength, 2011).

To achieve its new goal, SOS would launch a new nationwide campaign: No Kid Hungry (NKH). Its strategy would shift from funding programs that provided food to connecting kids in need with existing programs that provide food but remained underutilized, such as the School Breakfast Program (SBP) and the Summer Meals programs. It also would launch the Cooking Matters program to provide low-income families with food skills to stretch their food budgets, use nutrition information to make healthier food choices, and cook affordable meals (Augustine-Thottungal et al., 2013). But No Kid Hungry would become more than just a slogan, a campaign, or a collection of programs—it would become the rebranded face of Share Our Strength.

No Kid Hungry

No Kid Hungry would focus on initiatives state-by-state and on building cross-sector collaborations in order to achieve scale, consistent with the concept of collective impact (Shore et al., 2013). The campaign operated under the premise that American children are not hungry because of a lack of available food in society or a lack of nutrition programs intended to provide this food to children. Rather, kids lack access to these programs ("Q&A," 2015). So, instead of focusing on providing food, Share Our Strength would become an organization that served as a connector—connecting children to federal nutrition programs; connecting state agencies, nonprofits, and donors in order to achieve state-level solutions; and connecting federal food dollars with states. SOS's role would be to provide the coordination and resources each community needed to remove the roadblocks that were keeping children from participating in food and nutrition programs (Shore et al., 2013).

Share Our Strength developed a network of state- and city-based No Kid Hungry campaigns to achieve these purposes ("Q&A," 2015). The campaign was addressed to both children and parents through a number of new and existing programs, in order to increase the number of kids who were eating three nutritious meals a day.

Implementing No Kid Hungry

The new strategy would require additional investments and entail some risks. As Shore explains, "The challenge is: Are you willing to do less program and less service in the short term if that frees up money to allow you to make the investments you need to do even more program and service in the long term" (Blum, 2012b)? SOS spent $300,000 to develop the new brand identity (Blum, 2012a), introducing a new name, tagline, and logo. As illustrated in Figure 1, No Kid Hungry became SOS's primary consumer-facing brand, with the original name of the organization reduced to the equivalent of a tagline (Shore et al., 2013).

With its new strategy, Share Our Strength needed to build its internal capacity, and it grew quickly, hiring nearly 100 additional employees and increasing its operating budget from $6 million in 2009 to $14 million in 2013. The new staff members included individuals with strengths in advocacy, marketing, accounting, public policy, and program management (Blum, 2012a). This change was not easy for existing staff, some of whom had to train for new roles, change their working style, or even transition out of the organization

Figure 1   No Kid Hungry Branding

Source: No Kid Hungry (http://www.nokidhungry.org).

(Shore et al., 2013). The growth included the hiring of a chief strategy officer, who was responsible for removing established silos among Share Our Strength's fundraising, administration, and program initiatives in order to leverage all of the organization's assets together. The staff was reorganized to create cross-departmental teams, leading to a more integrated way of thinking about the deployment of assets to support the NKH campaign. An organization-wide dashboard was introduced to track performance metrics and all staff were provided with access so that they could celebrate successes and learn from failures (Case Foundation, n.d.). The focus on capacity was also reflected in changes to SOS's board of directors, which began to include more individuals with diverse business and political experience (Blum, 2012a).

The strategic shift posed several challenges for internal communications. Share Our Strength's leaders knew it was vital that each employee could explain the organization's new goal and inspire others to join the cause, so staff spent several weeks on efforts to ensure message cohesion (Shore et al., 2013). In some cases, new employees hired to implement the new direction brought work styles and experiences that were different from those of the existing SOS team, which led to some initial tensions. For example, new political campaign operatives were accustomed to operating in fast-paced, urgent environments, while some existing staff had been accustomed to working at a more deliberate pace (Shore et al., 2013). These styles needed to be reconciled before moving forward. Share Our Strength's leadership understood that it was important to build national awareness around childhood hunger, both to inspire the public and increase political support for food programs. Though its new branding helped, SOS would need to reframe the discussion around hunger, both to show that it was a solvable problem and to build a bigger network of support. Instead of talking about hunger on its own, SOS sought to connect it with other problems that resonated in communities across the nation, presenting childhood hunger as an education issue, a health issue, and an economic issue.

In some cases, SOS's new strategy caused discomfort and misalignment with existing nonprofit partners. As Shore explains, "Some of our nonprofit partners were nervous about being held accountable for ending childhood hunger" (Shore et al., 2013). Some corporate partners also failed to make the transition to the new approach and discontinued their support (Shore et al., 2013).

Expanding School Breakfasts

Working with the consulting firm Deloitte, SOS began to identify the barriers to receiving school breakfasts. One problem they discovered was that this meal was typically served in the school cafeteria before the first morning bell rang (Augustine-Thottungal et al., 2013). With variable bus schedules and busy parents, students often missed the school's breakfast. Additionally, research found that the notion of school breakfast holds a stigma—the idea that "poor kids" must go to the cafeteria to get an extra meal; therefore, some hungry children would avoid going. SOS's solution was to take breakfast out of the cafeteria and make it part of the school day so that more children would have the chance to participate. The organization created a model for students to eat together in the classroom after the bell rang (Augustine-Thottungal et al., 2013).

In order to make this delivery model effective, SOS needed to capitalize on one of its own strengths—the ability to build partnerships. Instead of just relying on corporate partners as it had in the past, the No Kid Hungry campaign would require SOS to reach into its networks to achieve a multisector approach—using private money to collaborate with governments and local nonprofits to unlock the government funds that were available but untapped (Blum, 2012a).

In the school breakfast program's pilot state of Maryland, Share Our Strength reached out to then-governor Martin O'Malley, who, in 2008, declared that his state would be the first to end childhood hunger (Share Our Strength Center for Best Practices, n.d.). O'Malley brought together school superintendents from throughout the state to urge them to adopt breakfasts in the classroom, as well as increasing funding for Maryland Meals for Achievement, a state-run program that connects high-need schools with resources to provide free and reduced-price meals for students. Additionally, Share Our Strength recruited a core advisory group, made up of state offices and corporate and nonprofit partners, such as Kellogg, Kaiser Permanente, the Walmart Foundation, Maryland Hunger Solutions, and faith-based and food-focused organizations (Share Our Strength Center for Best Practices, n.d.). These collaborations helped provide funding, food resources for meals, school access, and awareness. Following the Maryland pilot, the No Kid Hungry School Breakfast Program was expanded to a number of states, where the campaign often works with small community nonprofits and state legislatures to advance its efforts (Shore et al., 2013).

Team No Kid Hungry

Although Bill Shore had a background in politics, lobbying and advocacy were not a major emphasis for SOS during its first 20 years. With the introduction of No Kid Hungry, advocacy efforts became a central part of SOS's strategy. Share Our Strength has sought to influence food-based legislation, including reauthorization of the Child Nutrition Act, which provides funding for School Breakfast, National School Lunch, Child and Adult Care Food, Summer Food Service, and the Fresh Fruit and Vegetable programs. It also has lobbied for funding of SNAP and the U.S. Department of Agriculture's Special Supplemental Nutrition Program for Women, Infants, and Children (WIC). Advocacy activities have included visits to Capitol Hill by SOS leaders, prominent celebrities, and children affected by hunger. SOS also has arranged multiple advocacy days and flooded congressional offices with meetings, calls, and e-mails (Share Our Strength, n.d.).

As it had in Maryland, Share Our Strength met with governors to unlock state and local funding on anti-hunger initiatives (Crutchfield & Grant, 2012). With the support of elected officials, other states increased aid for school breakfasts in thousands of schools. After-school snacks and summer meals also became a target area for SOS's state advocacy (Shore et al., 2013).

SOS also used its new strategy to create a nationwide grassroots advocacy campaign to mobilize individuals to take action in their own states. Its Team No Kid Hungry initiative enlists volunteers to speak out for childhood hunger issues by attending town hall meetings, e-mailing and calling legislators, and recruiting additional members through social media efforts. Team No Kid Hungry has sent hundreds of thousands of letters and e-mails, and made calls to advocate in support of the goal to end childhood hunger in America, including more than 40,000 pieces of correspondence in 2013 alone (Share Our Strength, 2014). No Kid Hungry's social media presence was expanded and by 2017 the organization had over 184,000 Facebook followers (https://www.facebook.com/nokidhungry).

Growth and Impact

Though it had already been a leader in fundraising efforts, No Kid Hungry provided SOS with a new platform for support from diverse audiences, including additional corporate sponsors, government, and individual donors. Following the launch of the No Kid Hungry campaign, revenues increasing from $13 million in 2008 to nearly $55 million in 2016 (Share Our Strength, n.d.). In 2016, 43 percent of revenues came from corporations, 20 percent from foundations, 20 percent from individual giving and events, 10 percent from investments, and 7 percent from government grants. The organization reported that 69 percent of revenue was spent on programs, 24 percent on fundraising, and 7 percent on management and general expenses (Share Our Strength, n.d.).

Some fundraising programs that previously had floundered achieved new success after the introduction of the No Kid Hungry campaign. For example, in 1996, Share Our Strength had partnered with chain restaurants to launch a program called Dine Across America, in which the restaurants would donate a portion of their proceeds. Dine Across America's goal was to raise $1 million in 1996, but instead it produced only $250,000. In view of this disappointment, SOS had abandoned the program. But the idea was resurrected as Dine Out for No Kid Hungry (Crutchfield & Grant, 2012). The new weeklong, annual event is sponsored by well-known industry names, such as Arby's, Denny's, and Grimaldi's Pizzeria (Share Our Strength, 2017).

By 2016, SOS reported that No Kid Hungry had "helped to achieve" a total of 500 million meals served and a 20 percent reduction in the "number of kids at risk of hunger in the United States. In addition to other achievements, the organization reported 40,000 new summer meal sites to serve children when school is out, 464,000 families taught about healthy meals through the Cooking Matters program, and three million more kids eating school breakfast since the beginning of the No Kids Hungry campaign (Share Our Strength, n.d.).

Lessons Learned

What lessons can be drawn from Share Our Strength's evolution and growth following introduction of the No Kid Hungry campaign? Cofounder and CEO Bill Shore attributes its success to the clear goal the campaign has set. "Holding ourselves accountable to a specific outcome that was bold but believable inspired our stakeholders and gave them confidence that we merited their investment" (Shore et al., 2013). A study by the Case Foundation also identifies the importance of "making a big bet," which for Share Our Strength involved "[setting] a goal to end childhood hunger in the United States, not just reduce it" (Case Foundation, n.d.). But it also was essential to maintain a "delicate balance of boldness and believability." In other words, it was necessary to demonstrate that the goal could be within reach and provide evidence that strategies put in place could be effective in achieving it.

Establishing that credibility required "[proving] the concept first and then [going to] scale" (Case Foundation, n.d.). That was accomplished by testing methods and models in two pilot states, Maryland and Arkansas, before expanding to a national effort. That required concentrating resources in target programs, despite the sensitive fact that funds were raised in other states and communities as well (Case Foundation, n.d.).

As the Case Foundation observes, addressing major problems like childhood hunger "takes more than a village" (Case Foundation, n.d.). It requires building diverse networks, which was central to the No Kid Hungry campaign. That included bringing together public officials, school leaders, corporations, parents, and other stakeholders and connecting childhood hunger to other national social problems, such as education and health care.

Continuing Challenges

The No Kid Hungry campaign has shifted the way SOS looks, how it conducts business, and the strategies it employs to end childhood hunger. It has been a success by many measures. However, key questions and challenges remain. Some critics charge that SOS is feeding hungry children on a daily basis but still not getting to the underlying problem of hunger in America (Shore et al., 2013). Shore acknowledges that getting to the root causes of hunger and poverty is essential, but argues that school breakfasts and lunches are a bridge toward the goal, since these nutrition programs enable children to become self-sufficient and remove barriers to learning (Shore et al., 2013).

Other questions apply to the future of SOS itself. For example, No Kid Hungry was always intended to be a *campaign*, not the new name of the organization. But has the No Kid Hungry brand effectively replaced the brand of Share Our Strength? If Share Our Strength succeeds in achieving its goal, that is, if childhood hunger is eventually eliminated, then the rationale for No Kid Hungry will cease to exist and the organization will need to redefine its mission. SOS could become a victim of its own success. If it decides to change its focus in future years, will it ever be able to reestablish its original brand?

SOS receives a significant portion of revenue from corporate marketing partnerships (Blum, 2012a). The No Kid Hungry rebrand became a more recognizable, and therefore attractive, prospect to corporate sponsors, which has caused SOS's revenues to surge. But, with 43 percent of revenue coming from corporations in 2016 (Share Our Strength, n.d.), could resource dependence prove to be a vulnerability should corporate priorities shift or a new recession affect companies' ability to provide sponsorship support? What if government priorities were to shift and funding for food programs was substantially increased—or reduced? How would that impact the No Kid Hungry campaign? Or, again, what if childhood hunger someday ceases to be a national problem? The latter would appear to be a possibility, but not an imminent likelihood.

By 2015, the rate of U.S. food hardship had declined to 16 percent, from 19 percent in 2013, as the economy continued to recover from the Great Recession (Food Research and Action Center, 2016). But the percentage was barely below what it had been prior to that economic catastrophe and millions of American families, including children, still faced insecurity about their access to food (Food Research and Action Center, 2016). As the Food Research and Action Center observed, hunger often is an invisible problem:

> In America's communities, hunger often is hidden by individuals or families that do not want to share with their neighbors the fact that they are struggling economically. Sometimes hunger hides behind doors of nice houses with mortgages in default, or the heat turned off, or all of the income going to housing costs, leaving little or none for food. Sometimes it hides behind the stoic faces of parents or grandparents who

skip meals to protect their children or grandchildren from hunger. It goes unseen by those not looking for it. (Food Research and Action Center, 2016)

NOTE: This case was written by Gretchen Wieland, a graduate student in the Trachtenberg School of Public Policy and Public Administration at the George Washington University in spring, 2015. It has been substantially adapted and updated by the textbook author, including new material, recent data, and events since 2015.

CASE 2: QUESTIONS FOR DISCUSSION

1. Leslie Crutchfield and Heather McLeod Grant (2012) write:

   > If the 1980s and 1990s were all about replicating programs and the [decade of the 2000s] was all about building effective organizations, we believe the next leap is to see nonprofits as catalytic agents of change. We must begin to study and understand nonprofits not merely as organizations housed within four walls, but as catalysts that work within, and change, entire systems. (p. 16)

   Does Share Our Strength illustrate this point? If so, explain how.

2. What principles of marketing discussed in Chapter 10 are illustrated in the case of Share Our Strength?

3. The No Kid Hungry campaign has achieved wide brand awareness. If that campaign were to come to a conclusion, what steps would Share Our Strength need to take to reassert its organizational brand?

4. Is Bill Shore a social entrepreneur? If so, which definitions of that term seem to apply most closely?

5. Many factors affect the prevalence of hunger, including general economic conditions, the commitment of state officials, and political support for government food programs. In light of these various factors, how should Share Our Strength try to evaluate its own impact on the problem?

6. What changes in internal culture may have been required when Share Our Strength shifted its strategy from funding other nonprofits that provided food toward advocacy to increase funding for government food programs?

7. Go back to Chapter 14 and review the discussion regarding nonprofit earned-income strategies. What assets did Share Our Strength leverage in creating partnerships with corporations and other businesses?

8. Go back to Chapter 6 of this text. How do the various terms related to the outcomes model related to SOS and how it reports the impact of No Kid Hungry?

9. If Share Our Strength desired to diversify its revenues in order to reduce its dependence on events and corporate sponsors, which fundraising strategies and methods discussed in Chapter 13 do you think might hold promise? Explain.

Appendix Case 3: The Y

Relevant chapters:

Chapter 1 (Nonprofit Management as a Profession and a Field of Study); Chapter 3 (Theories of the Nonprofit Sector and Nonprofit Organizations); Chapter 6 (Ensuring Accountability and Measuring Performance); Chapter 7 (Developing Strategy, Building Capacity, and Managing Risk); Chapter 10 (Marketing and Communications); Chapter 13 (Philanthropic Fundraising); Chapter 14 (Social Enterprise and Earned Income)

The Young Men's Christian Association (YMCA) was founded in London in 1844 by George Williams. During that period of history, young men were migrating in large numbers from rural parts of England to the cities and Williams was concerned about the "bleak landscape of tenement housing and dangerous influences" that they faced in the urban environment. The YMCA would engage young men in Bible study and prayer, in order to provide an "escape from the hazards of life on the streets" (YMCA of the USA, n.d.). Several years later, Thomas Valentine Sullivan, a retired sea captain, became concerned about the welfare of sailors and merchant seamen in Boston and founded the first YMCA in the United States, adopting the English model (YMCA of the USA, n.d.).

The early YMCAs in the United States were not open to African Americans. Anthony Brown, a freed slave, founded the first Y for African American men in Washington, DC, in 1853 (YMCA of the USA, n.d.). African American YMCAs became common meeting places during the Civil Rights movement in the 1960s. A national YMCA resolution in 1946 had banned segregation, but some local Ys continued to exclude African Americans. Stronger action to ban discrimination was taken by the national organization in 1967. Remaining segregated Ys were subsequently closed, although some local Ys continued to serve predominantly African American communities ("A Brief History of the YMCA," 2010).

The YMCA is a federation of independent local associations. The YMCA of the USA, headquartered in Chicago, is a national resource office serving affiliated local associations across the country. In 2016, that included 2,700 Ys in the United States, serving 22 million members (Tugend, 2016). The Y's mission is "to put Christian principles into practice through programs that build healthy spirit, mind, and body for all" (YMCA of the USA, 2014).

From Evangelism to General Service

In its early years, the YMCA was an interdenominational Protestant organization, with an evangelical purpose. YMCA workers distributed religious materials and worked actively to convert young men to Christianity (Miller & Fielding, 1995). But this focus presented some challenges. For one, local YMCA associations had considerable autonomy and held various viewpoints on the appropriate balance of evangelism and service programs. Second, the emphasis on religious conversion did not necessarily hold the interest of young men, limiting membership and thus revenue (Miller & Fielding, 1995). And, third, reliance on philanthropy placed the Y's revenue in jeopardy in economic downturns, when it was especially difficult to compete with churches for members and gifts. The YMCA began new programs that would generate earned income, while also remaining consistent with its mission (Minkoff & Powell, 2006).

Among the new programs were lectures and educational programs. For example, the first known course on English as a second language was offered by the YMCA in Cincinnati, Ohio, in 1856 to serve German immigrants (YMCA of the USA, n.d.). In the 1860s, beginning in Chicago, the YMCA began to build residential dormitories for men. Its inventory totaled 100,000 rooms by 1940, making it larger than any hotel chain at the time (YMCA of the USA, n.d.).

Development of residential facilities was given impetus by the growth of railroads in the late 19th century. Beginning in Cleveland, Ohio, in 1872, the YMCA initiated programs to serve railroad workers, who were often young men away from their homes. "Railroad YMCAs" were established at major points along rail lines, and the Y's transportation department worked directly with the railroad companies, which provided 40 percent of the financial support for these facilities and their programs. "The railroad Ys provided practical things, such as clean beds, good meals, and hot showers, but also addressed the educational, spiritual, and recreational needs of the workers with Bible study, instructional courses on a variety of subjects, organized sports, and other activities" ("History of Transportation Department," 2005). The need for the railroad Ys diminished with changes in the railroad industry, and the Y's transportation department was disbanded in 1989 ("History of Transportation Department," 2005).

YMCA dormitories came to include gymnasiums. That feature attracted new members and also was consistent with the philosophy of serving the whole person, including physical and other dimensions. Physical activities became an increasing emphasis, perhaps driven in part by the boards of local YMCAs, which included businessmen with an interest in that area (Miller & Fielding, 1995). In 1881, a YMCA staff member in Boston coined the term "body building" and developed exercise classes that presaged today's fitness movement (YMCA of the USA, n.d.).

Despite its roots as a religious institution, the YMCA evolved toward becoming a nonprofit that provided services. Once dependent on gifts, earned income became the primary source of revenue for some YMCAs—in other words, they became commercialized. Fees for service diminished the need for gifts and also required that the Y become more responsive to the "demands of its clientele," that is, more like a secular business organization (Minkoff & Powell, 2006, p. 590).

Positioning for Growth

In the 20th century, the increased reliance on earned income led the Y's leaders to identify new target markets for growth. The focus of programs extended beyond men to families. Although the Y had been founded to serve young urban workingmen, it began to reach out to a more affluent clientele. Starting as early as the 1920s, some Ys offered a more expensive and exclusive "second tier" of membership, called Business Men's Clubs or Men's Health Services, which featured such amenities as private lockers and steam rooms. With the migration of middle-class families to the suburbs during the 1950s and 1960s, more branches were built in suburban areas and the Y's membership became increasingly affluent. By the 1970s, even some urban Ys were building state-of-the-art new facilities to attract downtown business professionals during the working day (Stern, 2011).

Y membership continued to grow as a result of the national fitness boom that began in the 1970s. But so did the number of commercial health clubs, which presented direct competition to the Ys. In 1968, there were only 350 commercial gyms in the United States. That number grew to over 2,000 by 1976 and to more than 15,000 by 2000 (Stern, 2011). There was internal debate among Y officials about whether to emulate the features and practices of new competitors. Some were concerned about the possible impact of a more commercial image on fundraising. However, the Ys responded to the challenge from for-profit gyms by continuing to upgrade their own facilities.

By the 1980s, the Y's competition with for-profit gyms had become controversial. Some began to question whether the Y was truly a nonprofit and whether it should remain tax exempt (Stern, 2011). The executive director of the International Health, Racquet, and Sportsclub Association (IHRSA), which represented the for-profit gyms, wrote in 2000 that the industry's main enemy was "a rogue charity that is often ... no charity at all" (Stern, 2011, p. 1). The debate came to include fundamental questions about the very definition and purpose of a nonprofit organization.

Defining Nonprofit

In the view of the commercial health club industry, the YMCA presented unfair competition because of the benefits conferred by its nonprofit status. The IHRSA argued that tax exemptions represented a subsidy to the Y that lowered its operating costs. Some of that subsidy was passed along to members in the form of lower prices that the for-profit clubs could not match. At the same time, the industry argued, the Y was serving a middle-class clientele that did not need subsidies and that represented the same target market that for-profit clubs were pursuing (Miller & Fielding, 1995). Moreover, the commercial clubs argued, the Y's expansion into new competitive markets was relatively easy, given its brand recognition, ability to receive charitable gifts toward capital projects, and the requirement that its profits be reinvested in the organization rather than distributed to stakeholders, consistent with the non-distribution constraint that faces all nonprofits (Miller & Fielding, 1995).

Criticisms of the Ys went to the very justification for nonprofit organizations' tax exempt status. Some said that the purpose of nonprofits is to "provide goods and services that the for-profit sector is not interested in providing ... hence, the need for government subsidies if the product is to be provided at all" (Miller & Fielding, 1995, p. 89). In other words, they cited market failure as a justification for the nonprofit sector (Hansmann, 1987; Weisbrod, 1975, 1988). Defining a public good narrowly as "[providing] food, shelter, and/or clothing ... for those incapable of providing for themselves or their children," critics argued that the commercialized Ys did not meet the test, since most of their members were middle- and upper-class people, who could well afford the dues of a for-profit health club (Miller & Fielding, p. 90).

Y leaders met with the IHRSA and agreed not to market their associations as purely health or athletic facilities, but rather as human service agencies. But they also maintained that "proposals to restrict nonprofits to serving the poor exclusively ... are unacceptable" (Stern, 2011, p. 9). Nevertheless, some continued to argue that the YMCA should pay unrelated business income tax (UBIT) on *all* of its revenue derived from activities that compete with the private sector and that the Internal Revenue Service (IRS) standard of exempting commercial revenue that is "substantially related" to the charitable mission should be repealed (Miller & Fielding, 1995, p. 95). In essence, this could have subjected *all* of the Y's earned income to taxation.

Challenges to its tax-exempt status "posed an existential threat to the Y" (Stern, 2011, p. 12). But in the view of some observers, the challenges also strengthened the Y as a national organization, by forcing it to "respond and rethink its practices, its mission, and its presentation of itself as a community organization and presence in American society" (Stern, p. 1).

Rebranding and Focusing on Mission

By the 2000s, the Y was facing increasing challenges. The challenges went beyond the criticisms of the for-profit health club industry. Membership and fundraising were stagnant and the Y had acquired a "stodgy image" (Daniels, 2014a). Y leaders began exploring new strategies for refocusing and expanding their mission, improving the Y's image, and generating new strategies for revenue and growth (Daniels, 2014a).

The transformation began with a 10-year planning cycle initiated in 2007. Strategic plans developed by the YMCA of the USA, the national organization, established broad goals and directions to serve as guidelines for local associations in developing their own plans. Within the 10-year cycle, the first of a series of three-year plans was developed to cover the period of 2007–2010. Titled "Mission Impact," the plan focused on strengthening the capacity of the national office. The second three-year plan (2011–2013) was titled "Advancing Our Cause." It focused on increasing visibility and enhancing the capacity of local associations, following the rollout of a new branding program in 2010.

The Y's image was a common element in many of the challenges it faced. As Amber Stephenson (2013) describes the situation, "The general public, stakeholders, and organization influencers perceived the YMCA as a fitness facility that offered *some other programs* [italics added]." This did not accurately reflect the wide-ranging impact of Y programs in communities. Changing public perceptions would be necessary to attract more membership and more philanthropic support and to expand the Y's impact (Daniels, 2014a).

The rebranding included a new logo and slogan. Instead of YMCA, the new official name would be what many people had always called the organization—the Y. The national organization would be known as Y-USA. This new name would be used in conjunction with a new slogan: "The Y. So much more" (Daniels, 2014a). The intended message was that "The Y isn't just a place to work out; it's a force for change" (Daniels, 2014a).[1]

The Y's transformation would require more than rebranding; it would include a refocusing and expansion of its mission and a plan for growth (Daniels, 2014a). Given its federated structure, development of the Y's 2014–2017 strategic plan required a participative process, which began in 2012. Engagement in various aspects of the process included 1,701 individuals and 459 local YMCAs. This was necessary to achieve buy-in from the local associations and greater consistency in the Y's image and programs. Many of the ideas included in the plan came from local Y leaders (Daniels, 2014a). As the head of the Y-USA explained it, the re-engineering came from the national organization listening to the voices of the affiliates, not by using "carrots and sticks" (Daniel, 2014a). But local Ys would be required to align their branding and programs with national priorities and to cooperate in some activities, including fundraising, with changes to be phased in over five years (Daniels, 2014a).

The strategic plan for 2014–2017 defined desired outcomes for the entire Y movement in three program areas: youth development, healthy living, and social responsibility (YMCA of the USA, 2014). Youth development initiatives include summer camps for children, which the Y has offered for many years. The Y also provides leadership-training courses and other educational programs for young people. Healthy living programs include exercise and cooking classes, designed to prevent chronic diseases. The Y also is encouraging communities to develop farmer's markets, build pathways that people can use for exercise, and take other actions to promote good health. And the Y created a Community Health Living Index to rate communities on such variables as bike paths, produce stands, and the number of fast-food restaurants. Under the rubric of social responsibility, the Y advocates for food banks and operates programs that provide after-school meals, adult literacy training, and preparation for high-school equivalency (GED) testing ("3 Causes," 2014). The plan for achieving the stated outcomes in all three program areas included three "strategic imperatives"—elevate membership and improve program efficacy, build organizational capacity, and generate the

---

1. The Y's style guidelines state that "The Y" is to be used to refer to the collective organization and "The YMCA of (Location)" is to be used in referring to a local association.

awareness and financial resources needed to sustain the Y cause (YMCA of the USA, 2014). Specific objectives and related metrics were identified for each strategic imperative, to be achieved by 2017 (YMCA of the USA, 2014).

Just as the need for diversified revenue had influenced the Y's evolution from evangelism to general services in its early years, new strategies implemented since 2007 were related to revenue needs as well as mission. One strategy was to increase fundraising through a more coordinated effort. The decentralized structure of the Y and autonomy of local associations had sometimes resulted in disjointed fundraising initiatives. For example, before 2015, Ys in Massachusetts conducted their annual giving solicitations according to their own calendars, at various times. Beginning in 2015, Ys were to be grouped together within states or regions and would run their annual programs simultaneously. They also would work together in planning their annual campaigns and share data regarding their fundraising costs and results. The national office would increase its support of local fundraising, distributing a "Red Book" of tips and ideas (Daniels, 2014a).

New programs also held the potential for new sources of earned income. For example, the diabetes prevention program, implemented in 2005, would have an impact on community health, but objectives also included increasing Y membership among participants in the program by 30 percent. And the Y advocated new federal legislation that would provide reimbursement for its service to pre-diabetes clients under Medicare and Medicaid (Daniels, 2014b; YMCA of the USA, 2014).

As Daniels observed at the time, "The story of the Y's transformation is still unfolding … [and] it holds lessons about how both rewarding and tough it can be to remake a large and traditional nonprofit organization" (Daniels, 2014b). But the Y had transformed itself before, from an evangelical organization established to protect young men from the dangers of urban life to a nonprofit serving 10,000 communities, both urban and rural, with a range of programs for young people and families. It had evolved from an organization mostly dependent on philanthropy to one with substantial earned income—a hybrid organization. And it had helped shape American culture. The Y "launched the first basketball teams and group swim lessons … popularized exercise classes and created the oldest summer camp still in operation" (Weeks, 2015). With a new strategic plan and a new brand, the Y in 2014 was ready for another new era in its long history. In 2016, about one third of the Y's revenue came from membership dues and the balance from program fees, government, and gifts (Tugend, 2016). With continuing competition, increasing philanthropic support was a priority. In January 2016, the Y launched the first advertising campaign in its history, including a series of television spots that portrayed the stories of people in challenged communities and highlighted the tag line, "When communities are forgotten, the Y remembers" (Tugend, 2016). The Y's CEO, Kevin Washington explained, "Lots of people know and like the Y. But they see it as a gym and swim place. We're also a charity, and that is the missing ingredient. We want people to realize we're deserving of their charitable donations" (Tugend, 2016).

CEO Washington was frank about the remaining challenge of gaining buy-in to a common vision among the independent YMCAs across the country. As he observed, some will ask, "What's in it for my association" ("CEO Perspective," 2017). He explained his strategy for building consensus: "One of the things that will be helpful is having champions. I know I'm not going to have all 900 or so Y leaders as champions, but I do need to find those 15 or 20 who are heavily influential and willing to champion this work, because when they reflect the key messages, that can bring along so many other associations" ("CEO Perspective," 2017). Despite the challenges, Washington was optimistic that the Y's transformation would be successful. As he explained, "Innovation and impact are in the Y's DNA" (Weeks, 2015).

CASE 3: QUESTIONS FOR DISCUSSION

1. Is access to a health club a public good, a private good, or a common good? How about access to programs that provide education about health and fitness?

2. Should a nonprofit that competes with a for-profit business be taxed just to level the playing field, even if its earned income is related to its mission?

3. How are models of organizational life cycles, discussed in Chapter 7 of this text, reflected in the history of the Y?

4. As discussed in Chapter 1 of this text, Robert Herman (2016) observes that nonprofit management uniquely requires the ability to integrate mission, the acquisition of resources, and strategy. How are those points reflected in the case of the Y?

5. How does resource dependence theory relate to the case of the Y?

6. How does the process followed in developing the Y's 2014–1017 strategic plan compare with the process followed by Brian Gallagher at United Way, discussed in Case 5.2? How is it similar and how is it different? How would you explain any similarities or differences?

7. How is Kotter's model for change, discussed in Chapter 5, related to the case of the Y?

8. What might have been some variables identified in the Y's SWOT analysis that are reflected in its strategic plan?

9. How does the Y's plan to implement a more coordinated approach to fundraising relate to trends discussed in Chapter 13?

Appendix Case 4: The Girl Scouts of the United States of America

Relevant chapters:

Chapter 4 (Nonprofit Governing Boards); Chapter 5 (Executive Leadership); Chapter 6 (Ensuring Accountability and Measuring Performance); Chapter 7 (Developing Strategy, Building Capacity, and Managing Risk); Chapter 8 (Collaborations, Partnerships, and Mergers); Chapter 9 (Managing Staff and Service Volunteers); Chapter 10 (Marketing and Communications); Chapter 12 (Financial Management); Chapter 13 (Philanthropic Fundraising); Chapter 14 (Social Enterprise and Earned Income)

In the first decade of the 20th century, English war hero Robert Baden-Powell founded a new organization to help boys "develop self-reliance, confidence and personal and leadership skills" (Cloninger, 2011, p. 30). It would emphasize outdoor activities, such as camping and tracking, and would be called the Boy Scouts. In that period, girls were not expected to engage in strenuous physical activities or to become leaders, but some were attracted by the activities of the new organization that Baden-Powell had founded. Some actually tried to join, using their initials instead of their full names (Cloninger, p. 30). Baden-Powell and the boys objected, so girls were excluded (Cloninger, p. 8). In 1910, Baden-Powell's wife and sister founded another organization to accommodate them, naming it Girl Guides in England (Cloninger, p. 8).

Juliette Gordon Low, an American from Savannah, Georgia, who was visiting England, happened to be seated next to Baden-Powell at a luncheon. She was inspired by his work and eventually returned to Savannah with a copy of Baden-Powell's *Scouting Manual* as her guide. At a time before women had the right to vote in the United States, Low was looking for a way to help girls to grow and discover their own potential, much like the Boy Scouts and Girl Guides were doing for boys and girls in England. In 1912, she founded the first troop of the Girl Scouts of the United States of America in her hometown, with just 18 girls (Girl Scouts of the USA, n.d.). Girl Scouting grew throughout the 20th century, both in the United States and around the world. Within four years of its founding, the organization had 7,000 members and four years later that number had increased to 70,000. When Low died in 1927, there were 200,000 Girl Scouts in the United States (Cloninger, 2011, p. 32).

Girl Scout programs and activities evolved in response to historical events and a changing American society in the 20th century. During the Great Depression, Girl Scouts collected clothing and food. During World War II, they assisted the war effort by serving as bicycle couriers, collecting scrap metal, growing Victory Gardens, and other efforts (Girl Scouts of the USA, n.d.). Reflecting changes in American society in the latter half of the century, the Girl Scouts desegregated its troops in the 1950s, and elected the first African American National Girl Scout president in 1975 (Chatel, 2015). In the 1980s, the growing number of mothers working outside the home had created a need for programs serving younger girls. The Girl Scouts responded by introducing a new program for girls in kindergarten, called the Daisy Scouts (Murray, 2016). Women gained the right to vote in 1920. Within less than a century, by 2016, Girl Scout alumni included 15 of the 20 women serving as U.S. Senators and more than one half of 88 women members of the U.S. House of Representatives (Girl Scouts of the USA, n.d.; Murray, 2016).

Despite its distinguished history, by 2004 the Girl Scouts of the United States of America was in trouble. Membership totaled 3.8 million, but it was experiencing alarming decline (Murray, 2016). When Kathy Cloninger arrived as CEO that year, she quickly determined that the survival of the 90-year-old organization was at risk. "The more I studied Juliette's

[Juliette Gordon Low] message and the history of the Girl Scouts," she wrote, "the more I saw that the Girl Scout movement had drifted, over the decades, from adventure to complacency, and from shaking up the status quo to riding along with it" (Cloninger, 2011, p. 96). Cloninger recognized that incremental changes would not be sufficient. The Girl Scouts needed transformation.

The Need for Transformation

The Girl Scouts were facing challenges on multiple fronts. The organization had developed an image as "musty and uncool" among prospective members (LaBarre, 2006). Social trends, including more mothers having careers, were making it more difficult to attract volunteers. Changing demographics meant that more girls were growing up in families that did not have a tradition with the Girl Scouts. A greater range of available activities for girls was presenting increased competition for their time, attention, and participation. Delivery of the organization's programs was fragmented and the quality of the experience being provided to girls and volunteers was uneven across the country. Regional variations in programming reflected the organization's structure as a federation, which also made accomplishing transformational change a complicated challenge.

The Federated Structure

Local Girl Scout councils are independent 501(c)3 organizations. The national office, based in New York, provides service to the local councils, and overall policy and direction are established by a national council of about 2,000 elected delegates. But local councils retain a high degree of autonomy.

As Sarah Murray (2016) observes, the federated structure offers some advantages. It permits local programs to reflect the cultures and needs of their particular areas and local independence attracts committed volunteers. The downsides include uneven quality and inefficiencies arising from the duplication of some functions. The federated model also had created a decentralized culture within the Girl Scouts organization. When Cloninger arrived, the relationship between the national office and local councils had sometimes been uneasy, with some councils resistant to centralized direction or control.

Population trends were creating sharp disparities at the local level. There were 312 councils across the country. Sixty were on the brink of failure. The largest 20 percent were serving 50 percent of the membership and the smallest 20 percent were serving just 5 percent of the members (LaBarre, 2006, p. 49). Small councils were finding it difficult to fund programs or attract talented executives. Larger councils with relatively abundant resources were mired in bureaucracy (Murray, 2016).

Competition and Brand

Changes in society had provided girls with new options for their time and attention, competing with what the Girl Scouts had to offer. That included the attraction of new communication technology, such as social networks, the expansion of sports programs for girls, and the opening of opportunities for education and careers that had not been available to previous generations of women. As Cloninger (2011) observes, "The image of girls in a Girl Scout troop learning to tie knots or go camping seems dowdy to girls who have many flashier and wider-reaching options for how to spend their free time" (p. 88).

Fragmented Programming

In the decentralized model, some councils were able to fund innovative programs and others were struggling to serve their dwindling memberships with inadequate resources. Some councils were primarily serving girls in rural areas, while others were serving girls in urban communities, with different backgrounds and interests. Some troops were introducing girls to science and robotics, while others were focused on arts and crafts (Cloninger, 2011, p. 84). No one could say what the Girl Scout experience actually included with any consistency.

Funding Model

Sales of Girl Scout cookies began in 1917 and came to provide an important source of revenue. In 2004, the Girl Scouts' revenue was derived mostly from earned income, including cookie sales, member dues, and the sale of merchandise, such as uniforms. The cookie program, perhaps one of the best-known activities of the Girl Scouts, was generating about $800 million in annual revenue and also served the mission by providing girls with leadership opportunities (Murray, 2016). As Cloninger (2011) assessed the situation, the dependency on earned income also posed significant financial risks. There was a need to diversify funding, but there were significant challenges. Historically, programs that addressed girls were not a high priority for philanthropy and the Girl Scouts found it difficult to address the demands of contemporary funders for measurable impact. As Cloninger explains, "We could tell donors that we served girls in every zip code in the country ... [but] platitudes and ethereal concepts such as 'Well, you'll be helping girls' don't open the vault" (p. 87).

Mission

It was perhaps most significant that the Girl Scout's mission statement did not provide a unifying vision.

As shown in Box 1, the mission statement had changed over the decades, reflecting the advancement of girls and women in society. But, in 2004, the statement no longer seemed consistent with Low's original purpose of "breaking boundaries ... and instilling

---

Box 1 Selected Girl Scout Mission Statements

1912. To train girls to take their rightful places in life, first as good women, then as good citizens, wives, and mothers.

1924. The purpose of this organization is to help girls to realize the ideals of womanhood as a preparation for their responsibilities in the home and service to the community.

1957. We in Girl Scouting dedicate ourselves to the purpose of inspiring girls with the highest ideals of character, conduct, patriotism, and service that they may become happy and resourceful citizens.

2007. Girl Scouting builds girls of courage, confidence, and character who make the world a better place.

Source: Cloninger (2011, pp. 95–99).

confidence in girls so they could be change agents in their world" (Cloninger, 2011, p. 94). Moreover, as Cloninger described the situation, "No one was able—in a unified voice—to say what Girl Scouting does for girls, what our purpose is, and what the mission is" (Murray, 2016).

A Process for Change

Cloninger knew that transformational change would not be easy and accomplishing it would require an inclusive process. She created a strategy group of 26 executives from the Girl Scout network. The group's first task was to identify 15 desired outcomes that could be used to evaluate the impact of the Girl Scout experience on the development of girls (Murray, 2016). The group also identified the strategic issues facing the organization and began work on developing a new mission statement, resulting in the new statement adopted in 2007, as shown in Box 1.

After the strategy group had addressed the big picture issues, Cloninger (2011) created six "gap teams" to focus on how to implement change in key areas: brand, culture, funding, organizational structure and governance, programming, and volunteerism (Murray, 2016). What Cloninger called "the elephant in the room" (p. 103) was the need for changes in organizational structure and governance. The gap team that was focused on that issue ultimately recommended not just downsizing, but a massive reduction in the number of councils. This would require "agonizing decisions ... about who must merge with whom.... Council traditions would be cast aside and identities lost" (Cloninger, p. 105). And, perhaps, the most sensitive issue was the need to "describe what a 'high capacity' council should look like and what its infrastructure should be" (p. 105).

The gap team considered various options, including the possibility of merging all chapters into a single national organization. It decided to retain the federated structure, but to redraw the boundaries and consolidate many councils in order to align those that would remain with the profile of a high-capacity council (Cloninger, 2011, p. 105). The question then became "how to get there" (p. 106). Cloninger sought input from councils across the country and engaged a team of demographers to develop data that could guide decisions on council boundaries. In March 2006, the CEOs and board chairs of the 312 Girl Scout councils met to hear the demographers' report, which included revealing a new map of how the fewer number of councils would be defined across the country. Cloninger describes the scene:

> The two demographers we'd hired—who looked poignantly small and human as they stood onstage beside a covered easel and addressed more than 600 Girl Scout council leaders—told of the reasoning that had gone into their map of new councils.... There was a breathtaking silence as every council CEO and board chair took a first instant to see what it meant not just for the organization, but for them personally. Slowly someone started to clap. Then the room erupted in a standing ovation. (pp. 107–108)

The plan was accepted and the restructuring process began. By 2010, the number of local councils had been reduced from 315 to 122. The Girl Scouts were preparing to launch a $1-billion fundraising campaign and celebrate the organization's 100th anniversary with a major event on the National Mall in Washington, DC, in 2012 (Murray, 2016). Cloninger retired as CEO in 2011 and was succeeded by Anna Maria Chávez, who would be responsible for continuing to implement the new plan.

Implementing the Plan

Chávez began her new job in the continuing aftermath of the serious economic recession that began in 2007. In addition to financial pressures, there were still remaining issues related to the restructuring that Cloninger had begun. Work remained to make Girl Scout programs consistent with the new organizational model and revised mission.

Relationships With Councils

Relationships between the national office and some local councils remained strained. Chávez worked to redefine them, attempting to shift from a top–down model to a more collaborative approach and develop a culture in which the councils were viewed as customers to be served by the national office. She commissioned surveys, appointed a new chief customer officer at national headquarters, and refined national services to better address local needs (Murray, 2016).

Introducing New Programs

New programs were introduced to reflect the new mission and the changing interests of girls. New badges were introduced in fields such as financial literacy and business. In 2011, new "Journeys" were designed to supplement the traditional system of badges, promoting leadership in three areas of activity (Murray, 2016). A new initiative was launched in 2017, under Chávez's successor as CEO, intended to close the gender gap in science, technology, engineering, and mathematics ("Girl Scouts Launches," 2017).

Updating Technology

The fragmented technology platform posed another challenge. When Chávez took charge, every chapter had its own website. The organization ran on 10 IT platforms and 100 e-mail systems (Murray, 2016). Chávez hired a chief technology officer, who developed a shared Web platform and a social media strategy. The streamlined system made it more efficient to engage volunteers and provide volunteer training. Introduced in 2014 and enhanced in 2015, a Digital Cookie Platform made it possible for girls to sell cookies and manage orders online (Murray, 2016).

Improved information systems also made it possible for the Girl Scouts to introduce more sophisticated fundraising, in an effort to diversify revenues and reduce dependence on earned income, including cookie sales. New systems also were implemented to collect data that could be presented to donors to demonstrate the impact of their gifts. A $1-billion campaign was announced in 2012, with $100 million to be raised by the national office and a total of $900 million by local councils (Hall & Perry, 2013).

Continuing Challenges

Despite its significant restructuring, reforms, and program innovation, by 2013 the Girl Scouts still faced significant challenges. The Great Recession had taken a financial toll on all nonprofit organizations. Some local councils were finding it difficult to meet their fundraising goals (Hall & Perry, 2013). Downsizing the number of councils and staff had entailed significant financial costs. That included severance payments and a significant number of people added to the pension plan, leaving the organization saddled with $347 million in liabilities (Hall & Perry, 2013; Murray, 2016). Proposals to sell summer camps and other issues had exacerbated tensions between the national office and local chapters, even gaining the attention of Congress. Some council leaders had become critical of Chávez's leadership at the national level ("Dissension and Fiscal Troubles," 2013). Although the rate of decline had slowed, membership was still falling in 2015 (Murray, 2016).

In 2016, Anna Maria Chávez resigned as CEO and was replaced by national board member Sylvia Acevedo on an interim basis. Following a search, Ms. Acevedo was selected as the permanent CEO later in 2017 (Girl Scouts of the USA, 2017). But she would not face a tranquil time.

Girls and Boys

As mentioned previously, the origin of the Boy Scouts was in England, with founder Robert Baden-Powell. The American version began with Chicago businessman William Boyce, who adopted Baden-Powell's model and incorporated the Boy Scouts of America in 1910, two years before Juliette Gordon Low founded the Girl Scouts of the United States of America ("Boy Scouts Movement Begins," 2017). Like the Girl Scouts of the United States of America, the Boy Scouts of America faced the challenges of a changing society and economy in the early decades of the 21st century.

By 2017, membership in the Boy Scouts was also in decline, and so were financial assets. The organization had faced multiple lawsuits alleging sexual abuse or inappropriate behavior by volunteer leaders and staff, which reportedly cost the organization millions of dollars (Cauterucci, 2017). The Boy Scouts also had faced controversy and pressure over its refusal to admit gay and transgendered members or engage gay volunteer leaders or staff. Decisions to modify those policies, announced in 2013 and 2015, were met with strong objections from some faith-based organizations that sponsored local scouting units. Some said that they would end their involvement with the Boy Scouts altogether (Boorstein, 2015). In 2018, the Church of Jesus Christ of Latter-day Saints (the Mormon Church) announced that it would sever all ties with the Boy Scouts. Mormon boys had comprised nearly 20 percent of the Boy Scouts' membership. The church did not identify any specific policies of the Boy Scouts as the reason for the change (Schmidt, 2018).

Girls had been admitted to Boy Scout programs for older youth—Exploring and Venturing—since 1971. But in October 2017, the Boy Scouts of America announced that girls would be admitted to additional programs. Younger girls would be able to join the Cub Scouts in 2018, although the smallest units (called "dens") could be segregated by gender. Beginning in 2019, girls would be eligible to pursue the rank of Eagle Scout, comparable to the Gold Award in Girl Scouts (Breuninger, 2017). The decision prompted spirited debate and questions about its implications for the future of the Girl Scouts of the United States of America. In 2018, the Boy Scouts announced that the name of its *program* serving youth ages 11 to 17 would be changed to "Scouts BSA," dropping the word "boy." However, the name of the organization itself would remain the Boy Scouts of America. (Boy Scouts of America, 2018).

The Boy Scouts explained its decision in terms of meeting the needs of families. As Michael Surbaugh, the chief scout executive, explained,

> Families today are busier and more diverse than ever. Most are dual-earners and there are more single-parent households than ever before, making convenient programs that serve the whole family more appealing. Additionally, many groups currently

underserved by Scouting, including the Hispanic and Asian communities, prefer to participate in activities as a family. Recent surveys of parents not involved with Scouting showed high interest in getting their daughters signed up for programs like Cub Scouts and Boy Scouts, with 90 percent expressing interest in a program like Cub Scouts and 87 percent expressing interest in a program like Boy Scouts. (Boy Scouts of America, 2017a)

Some heralded the decision as opening more opportunities for girls, but others voiced negative responses (Boorstein, 2015). Having received word of the Boy Scouts impending decision even before its announcement, the Girl Scouts national president, Kathy Hopinkah Hannan, called it "reckless." She suggested that instead of recruiting girls, a better target market for the Boy Scouts might be the large percentage of boys who were not involved in Scouting (Cauterucci, 2017). Heated controversy arose surrounding the question of whether the Boy Scouts had conferred with the Girl Scouts about their planning or whether the change had come as a surprise (Godfrey, 2017).

In the face of the new competition, the Girl Scout organization moved to reinforce its brand and emphasize its unique capabilities. "We believe strongly in the importance of the all-girl, girl-led and girl-friendly environment that Girl Scouts provides," said the organization's chief customer officer, "[the GSUSA is] the best girl leadership organization in the world" (Crary, 2017). Another spokesperson for the Girl Scouts, said "We're seeing this as potentially a truth-in-advertising issue.... They're saying they're opening the doors up to girls, isn't it fabulous, but there's a blur. Are they keeping girls' needs top of mind? We've been doing this for over 100 years and, frankly, are the experts in the category" (Pasquarelli, 2017).

The Girl Scouts launched a new marketing campaign, "G.I.R.L. Agenda Powered by Girl Scouts," launched at a major event with celebrity participants (G.I.R.L. stands for "go-getter, innovator, risk-taker, leader"). The organization stepped up its social media presence, joining the #MeToo campaign and speaking out against sexual abuse and harassment of girls and women. In 2017, as mentioned previously, 23 new badges were introduced in fields such as cybersecurity and space science, and new partnerships were announced with NASA and the SETI Institute, with the goal of engaging 2.5 million girls in STEM programs by 2025. A $70-million fundraising initiative was launched to support these new efforts ("Girl Scouts Launches," 2017).

In some European nations, the Boy Scout and Girl Scout organizations have merged and in others they have maintained a close relationship (Hosking, 2017). Could a merger of the two organizations in the United States be on the horizon? The response from one Girl Scout executive ruled it out: "A merger would not benefit girls" (Mazzola, 2017). Would the Girl Scouts answer the Boy Scouts' challenge by opening their own programs to boys? According to a spokesperson from the national office, that also was not under consideration: "We're been an all-girls organization since inception—that is what we do best.... We owe it to the girls to continue delivering a one-of-a-kind exceptional journey for them" (Pasquarelli, 2017).

Note: Students may find it interesting to search the Web for articles that describe events related to this case that may have occurred since publication of this text.

CASE 4: QUESTIONS FOR DISCUSSION

1. Suppose you had a member of the gap team considering reforms to the Girl Scouts' structure and governance during Kathy Cloninger's administration. How would you have evaluated the pros and cons of eliminating the federated structure and consolidating into a single national organization, rather than keeping the existing structure and downsizing? Might a different approach have avoided issues that subsequently arose or would it have exacerbated them?

2. Considering the various fundraising strategies and techniques discussed in this textbook, what suggestions would you offer to the Girl Scouts of the United States of America in attempting to diversify its revenue beyond earned income?

3. How did Kathy Cloninger's approach reflect the models of change discussed in Chapter 5 of this text?

4. Did Kathy Cloninger meet the definition of a social entrepreneur, discussed in Chapter 16? Why or why not?

5. The mission statement of the Girl Scouts says "Girl Scouting builds girls of courage, confidence, and character who make the world a better place." What might be some approaches to defining and measuring outcomes against that statement?

6. How do the marketing concepts of product, place, promotion, market segmentation, and price, discussed in Chapter 10, apply to the Boy Scouts of America and to Girl Scouts of the United States of America today?

7. How would you describe the brands of the Girl Scouts and Boy Scouts? How might each of them need to modify their brand in light of the new competition between them?

8. Chapter 8 of this text discussed drivers and obstacles related to mergers. How do those points apply to the restructuring of the Girl Scouts under CEO Kathy Cloninger?

9. Which of the drivers and obstacles to merger discussed in Chapter 8 might apply to the Boys Scouts of America and the Girl Scouts of the United States of America?

References

Abelson, R. (1998, March 27). At Minnesota Public Radio, a deal way above average. *New York Times.* Retrieved from http://www.nytimes.com/1998/03/27/business/at-minnesota-public-radio-a-deal-way-above-average.html

Adams, J. S. (1965). Inequity in social exchange. In L. Berkowitz (Ed.), *Advances in experimental psychology* (Vol. 2, pp. 267–299). New York, NY: Academic Press.

Adelman, K. (2005, September 1). *Interview with president of the National Trust for Historic Preservation, Richard Moe: Bricks tell a story.* Retrieved from https://www.washingtonian.com/2005/09/01/interview-with-president-of-the-national-trust-for-historic-preservation-richard-moe/

Adizes, I. (1999). *Managing corporate lifecycles: How organizations grow, age, and die.* Paramus, NJ: Prentice Hall.

Aldrich, H. E. (1999). *Organizations evolving.* Thousand Oaks, CA: Sage.

Alesani, D., & Missoni, E. (2014). Introduction. In E. Missoni & D. Alesani (Eds.), *Management of international institutions and NGOs* (pp. 1–10). New York, NY: Routledge.

Allison, M., & Kaye, J. (2015). *Strategic planning for nonprofit organizations: A practical guide for dynamic times* (3rd ed.). Hoboken, NJ: Wiley.

ALS Association. (2017). [Home page]. Retrieved from http://www.alsa.org/fight-als/ice-bucket-challenge.html?referrer=https://www.google.com/

Alter, S. K. (n.d.). *Social enterprise typology.* Retrieved from http://www.4lenses.org/setypology

American Cancer Society. (2017). *ACS mission statement.* Retrieved from http://www.cancer.org/aboutus/whoweare/acsmissionstatements

American Heart Association. (2017). *Heart-Check Food Certification Program*

nutrition requirements.* Retrieved from http://www.heart.org/HEARTORG/GettingHealthy/NutritionCenter/HeartSmartShopping/Heart-Check-Mark-Nutritional-Guidelines_UCM_300914_Article.jsp

American Red Cross responds to latest ProPublica and NPR coverage [Statement by the American Red Cross]. (2015, June 3). Retrieved from http://www.redcross.org/news/press-release/American-Red-Cross-Responds-to-Recent-ProPublica-Report-on-Haiti

Anderson, N., & Svrluga, S. (2015, March 3). Sweet Briar College to close because of financial challenges. *Washington Post.* Retrieved from https://www.washingtonpost.com/news/grade-point/wp/2015/03/03/sweet-briar-college-to-close-because-of-financial-challenges/?utm_term=.5e3fc31636eb

Andreasen, A. R. (2006). *Social marketing in the 21st century.* Thousand Oaks, CA: Sage.

Andreasen, A. R. (2009). Cross-sector marketing alliances: Partnerships, sponsorships, and cause-related marketing. In J. Cordes & E. Steuerle (Eds.), *Nonprofits and business* (pp. 155–191). Washington, DC: Urban Institute.

Andreasen, A. R., & Kotler, P. (2008). *Strategic marketing for nonprofit organizations* (7th ed.). Upper Saddle River, NJ: Prentice Hall.

Andresen, K. (2006). *Robin Hood marketing: Stealing corporate savvy to sell just causes.* San Francisco, CA: Jossey-Bass.

Anheier, H. K. (2014). *Nonprofit organizations: Theory, management, policy* (2nd ed.). New York, NY: Routledge.

Anheier, H. K., & Themudo, N. (2005). The internationalization of the nonprofit sector. In R. D. Herman & Associates (Eds.), *The Jossey-Bass handbook of nonprofit leadership and management* (2nd ed., pp. 102–127). San Francisco, CA: Jossey-Bass.

Anthony, R. N., & Young, D. W. (2005). Financial accounting and financial management. In R. D. Herman & Associates (Eds.), *The Jossey-Bass handbook of nonprofit leadership and management* (2nd ed., pp. 466–512). San Francisco, CA: Jossey-Bass.

APM selling Greenspring Media Group. (2013, July 29). *MPR News.* Retrieved from https://www.mprnews.org/story/2013/07/29/business/apm-selling-greenspring-media-group

Arnsberger, P., Ludlum, M., Riley, M., & Stanton, M. (2011). A history of the tax-exempt sector: An SOI perspective. In J. S. Ott & L. A. Dicke (Eds.), *The nature of the nonprofit sector* (2nd ed., pp. 125–150). Boulder, CO: Westview.

Aschbrenner, J. (2017, April 21). United Way's new U.S. president wants to reverse revenue dip. *Des Moines Register.* Retrieved from https://www.desmoinesregister.com/story/money/business/biz-buzz/2017/04/21/new-united-way-head-mary-sellers/305675001/

Ashoka. (n.d.-a). *About Ashoka.* Retrieved from http://www.ashoka.org/en/about-ashoka

Ashoka. (n.d.-b). *Betsy Krebs on how foster kids can get out of the system.* Retrieved from https://www.ashoka.org/en/node/3580

Ashoka. (n.d.-c). *Profile of Richard Seshie.* Retrieved from https://www.ashoka.org/en/fellow/richard-seshie

Ashoka. (n.d.-d). *Profile of Sumaira Abdulali.* Retrieved from https://www.ashoka.org/en/fellow/sumaira-abdulali

Ashoka. (n.d.-e). *Profile of Mohammad Alhabsyi.* Retrieved from https://www.ashoka.org/en/fellow/mohammad-alhabsyi

Ashoka. (n.d.-f). *Profile of Lauren Diaz Arias.* Retrieved from https://www.ashoka.org/en/fellow/lauren-diaz-arias

Aspire CoffeeWorks. (n.d.). *About us.* Retrieved from https://www.aspirecoffeeworks.com/learn/company/

Associated Press. (2013, October). *New York City Opera to shut down after failing to meet $7m funding goal.* Retrieved from http://www.theguardian.com/world/2013/oct/01/new-york-opera-files-bankruptcy

Augustine-Thottungal, R., Kern, J., Key, J., & Sherman, B. (2013). *Ending childhood hunger: A social impact analysis.* Retrieved from https://www.nokidhungry.org/pdfs/school-breakfast-white-paper.pdf

Avner, M. (2016). Advocacy, lobbying, and social change. In D. O. Renz & Associates (Eds.), *The Jossey-Bass handbook of nonprofit leadership and management* (4th ed., pp. 396–426). Hoboken, NJ: Jossey-Bass.

Baird, R. (2015, December 18). *The Chan-Zuckerberg initiative may be more important than Facebook* [Web log post]. Retrieved from https://techcrunch.com/2015/12/18/the-chan-zuckerberg-initiative-may-be-more-important-than-facebook/

Baruch, Y., & Ramalho, N. (2006, March). Communalities and distinctions in the measurement of organizational performance and effectiveness across for-profit and nonprofit sectors. *Nonprofit and Voluntary Sector Quarterly, 35*(1), 39–61.

Bass, B. M. (1985). *Leadership and performance beyond expectations.* New York, NY: Free Press.

Bass, B. M., & Avolio, B. J. (Eds.). (1994). *Improving organizational effectiveness through transformational leadership.* Thousand Oaks, CA: Sage.

Battilana, J., Lee, M., Walker, J., & Dorsey, C. (2012, Summer). In search of the hybrid ideal. *Stanford Social Innovation Review.* Retrieved from http://www.ssireview.org/articles/entry/in_search_of_the_hybrid_ideal

Beaubien, J. (2015, June 5). Behind the story: What made NPR look into Red Cross efforts in Haiti? *NPR.* Retrieved from http://www.npr.org/sections/goatsandsoda/2015/06/05/412071811/behind-the-story-what-made-npr-look-into-red-cross-efforts-in-haiti

Bekkers, R., & Wiepking, P. (2011, October). A literature review of empirical studies of philanthropy: Eight mechanisms that drive charitable giving. *Nonprofit and Voluntary Sector Quarterly, 40*(5), 924–973.

Bell, J., Masaoka, J., & Zimmerman, S. (2010). *Nonprofit sustainability: Making strategic decisions for financial viability.* San Francisco, CA: Jossey-Bass.

Benefit Corporation Information Center. (n.d.). *Benefit corporations & certified B corps.* Retrieved from http://www.benefitcorp.net/what-makes-benefit-corp-different/benefit-corp-vs-certified-b-corp

Bennis, W. G., & Nanus, B. (1985). *Leaders: The strategy for taking charge.* New York, NY: Harper & Row.

Berger, P. L., & Neuhaus, J. (1977). *To empower people: The role of mediating structures in public policy.* Washington, DC: American Enterprise Institute for Public Policy Research.

Berk, C. B. (2016, June 30). Hershey board unanimously rejects preliminary offer from Mondelez. *CNBC.* Retrieved from https://www.cnbc.com/2016/06/30/hershey-shares-pop-7-on-report-of-mondelez-takeover-bid.html

Berkshire, J. C. (2011, October 2). Mergers are just one way charities find to team up and battle a tough economy. *Chronicle of Philanthropy.* Retrieved from http://philanthropy.com/article/CollaborationsMergers-Get/129197/

Berman, H. (2010). Meeting community needs. *Inquiry, 47*(3), 186–198. Retrieved from http://www.jstor.org/stable/23035569

Better Business Bureau Wise Giving Alliance. (n.d.). *How we accredit charities.* Retrieved from http://www.give.org/for-charities/How-We-Accredit-Charities/

Bibb, E., Fishberg, M., Harold, J., & Layburn, E. (n.d.). *The Blended Value glossary.* Retrieved from http://www.blendedvalue.org/wp-content/uploads/2004/02/pdf-blendedvalue-glossary.pdf

Biemiller, L. (2017, September 15). To compete, Sweet Briar plans an ambitious overhaul. *Chronicle of Philanthropy, 64*(3), A24–A25.

Bill & Melinda Gates Foundation. (2016). *Annual report 2016.* Retrieved from https://www.gatesfoundation.org/Who-We-Are/Resources-and-Media/Annual-Reports/Annual-Report-2016

Bixler, M. (2005, April 16). Habitat founder forms rival group. *Atlanta Journal-Constitution,* A1.

B Lab. (2017). [Website]. Retrieved from https://www.bcorporation.net/

Blackbaud Institute for Philanthropic Impact. (2016). *Blackbaud charitable giving report.* Charleston, SC: Author.

Blackwood, A. S., Dietz, N., & Pollack, T. (2014). *The state of nonprofit governance.* Washington, DC: Urban Institute.

Blake, R. R., & Mouton, J. S. (1985). *The managerial grid III: A new look at the classic that has boosted productivity and profits for thousands of corporations worldwide.* Houston, TX: Gulf Publishing.

Blended Value. (n.d.). *Welcome to Blended Value.* Retrieved from http://www.blendedvalue.org/wp-content/uploads/2004/02/pdf-bv-map.pdf%20/

Block, S. R. (2001). A history of the discipline. In J. S. Ott (Ed.), *The nature of the nonprofit sector* (pp. 97–111). Boulder, CO: Westview.

Block, S. R., & Rosenberg, S. (2002). Toward an understanding of founder's syndrome: An assessment of power and privilege among founders of nonprofit organizations. *Nonprofit Management & Leadership, 12*(4), 353–368.

Blum, D. E. (2012a, December 2). Bigger staff and bolder goals turn around a quiet hunger-fighting charity. *Chronicle of Philanthropy.* Retrieved from http://philanthropy.com/article/Bold-Goals-Turn-Around-a-Quiet/135988/

Blum, D. E. (2012b, December 2). Go big or go home: Tips from Share Our Strength. *Chronicle of Philanthropy*. Retrieved from http://philanthropy.com/article/Go-Big-or-Go-Home-and/135990/

BoardSource. (2010). *The handbook of nonprofit governance*. San Francisco, CA: Jossey-Bass.

BoardSource. (2017). *Leading with intent: A national index of nonprofit board practices*. Washington, DC: Author.

BoardSource. (2018). *12 principles of governance that power exceptional boards*. Washington, DC: Author.

Boli, J. (2006). International nongovernmental organizations. In W. W. Powell & R. Steinberg (Eds.), *The non-profit sector: A research handbook* (2nd ed., pp. 333–354). New Haven, CT: Yale University Press.

Bolman, L. G., & Deal, T. E. (2003). *Reframing organizations: Artistry, choice, and organizations* (3rd ed.). San Francisco, CA: Jossey-Bass.

Bongiovanni, I., Missoni, E., & Alesani, D. (2014). Governance models and reforms. In E. Missoni & D. Alesani (Eds.), *Management of international institutions and NGOs: Frameworks, practices and challenges* (pp. 215–238). New York, NY: Routledge.

Bonk, K., Tynes, E., Griggs, H., & Sparks, P. (2008). *Strategic communications for nonprofits* (2nd ed.). San Francisco, CA: Jossey-Bass.

Boorstein, M. (2015, July 27). Boy Scouts of America votes to end controversial ban on openly-gay scout leaders. *Washington Post*. Retrieved from https://www.washingtonpost.com/news/acts-of-faith/wp/2015/07/26/the-boy-scouts-are-slated-to-lift-ban-on-openly-gay-adult-leaders/?utm_term=.88989ab396bf

Boris, E. T., de Leon, E., Roeger, K. L., & Nikolova, M. (2010). *Human service nonprofits and government collaboration: Findings from the 2010 national survey of nonprofit government contracting and grants*. Washington, DC: Urban Institute.

Retrieved from http://www.urban.org/uploadedpdf/412228-nonprofit-government-contracting.pdf

Bornstein, D. (2007). *How to change the world: Social entrepreneurs and the power of new ideas*. New York, NY: Oxford University Press.

Bornstein, D. (2011, March 7). Coming together to give schools a boost. *New York Times*. Retrieved from http://opinionator.blogs.nytimes.com/2011/03/07/coming-together-to-give-schools-a-boost/

Boschee, J., & McClurg, J. (2003). *Towards a better understanding of social entrepreneurship: Some important distinctions*. Retrieved from https://www.law.berkeley.edu/php-programs/courses/fileDL.php?fID=7289

Boston Consulting Group. (2011, October 3). *Brian Gallagher on uniting United Way: An interview with the president and CEO*. Retrieved from https://www.bcgperspectives.com/content/videos/leadership_transformation_brian_gallagher_uniting_united_way/

Bowman, W. (2016). Tools and techniques of nonprofit financial management. In In D. O. Renz & Associates (Eds.), *The Jossey-Bass handbook of nonprofit leadership and management* (4th ed., pp. 564–594). Hoboken, NJ: Jossey-Bass.

Bowman, W., & Fremont-Smith, M. R. (2006). Nonprofits and state and local governments. In E. T. Boris & C. T. Steuerle (Eds.), *Nonprofits and government: Collaboration and conflict* (pp. 181–218). Washington, DC: Urban Institute.

Boy Scouts movement begins. (2017). *History Channel*. Retrieved from http://www.history.com/this-day-in-history/boy-scouts-movement-begins

Boy Scouts of America. (2017a, October 11). *The BSA expands programs to welcome girls from Cub Scouts to highest rank of Eagle Scout* [Press release]. Retrieved from https://www.scoutingnewsroom.org/press-releases/bsa-expands-programs-welcome-girls-cub-scouts-highest-rank-eagle-scout/

Boy Scouts of America. (2017b). *Mission & vision*. Retrieved from http://www.scouting.org/scoutsource/Media/mission.aspx

Boy Scouts of America. (2018, May 3). BSA's organization name not changing, and other facts to know and share. *Scoutingwire*. Retrieved from https://scoutingwire.org/the-boy-scouts-of-america-organization-name-is-not-changing-and-other-facts-to-set-the-record-straight/

Bradshaw, P. (2009, Fall). A contingency approach to nonprofit governance. *Nonprofit Management & Leadership*, 20(1), 60–81.

Brauer, D. (2010, October 12). More details on Bill Kling's $100 million, 100-journalists-per-city public-media plan. *Minnesota Post*. Retrieved from https://www.minnpost.com/braublog/2010/10/more-details-bill-klings-100-million-100-journalists-city-public-media-plan

Bray, I. (2013). *Effective fundraising for nonprofits: Real-world strategies that work* (4th ed.). Berkeley, CA: Nolo.

Breen, M. (2016). Mark Zuckerberg's 'initiative' adds new wrinkle to tech philanthropy. *NBC News*. Retrieved from http://www.nbcnews.com/tech/tech-news/mark-zuckerbergs-initiative-adds-new-wrinkle-tech-philanthropy-n473066

Brest, P. (2012, Spring). A decade of outcome-oriented philanthropy. *Stanford Social Innovation Review*, 10(2), 42–47.

Breuninger, K. (2017, October 11). Girls can now join Boy Scouts and earn Eagle Scout rank. *CNBC*. Retrieved from https://www.cnbc.com/2017/10/11/girls-can-now-join-boy-scouts-and-earn-eagle-scout-rank.html

Brian Gallagher, president/CEO, United Way of America [Interview]. (2007, August 15). *Philanthropy News Digest*. Retrieved from https://philanthropynewsdigest.org/newsmakers/brian-gallagher-president-ceo-united-way-of-america

Bridgespan Group. (n.d.). *Case study: Cincinnati, Covington, and Newport.* Retrieved from https://www.bridgespan. org/bridgespan/Images/articles/needle-moving-community-collaboratives/profiles/community-collaboratives-case-study-cinncinnati.pdf

A brief history of the YMCA and African American communities. (2010). Minneapolis, MN: University of Minnesota Libraries, Kautz Family YMCA Archives. Retrieved from https://www.lib. umn.edu/ymca/guide-afam-history

Brinkerhoff, D. W., & Brinkerhoff, J. M. (2011). Public–private partnerships: Perspectives on purposes, publicness, and good governance. *Public Administration and Development, 31*(1), 2–14.

Broce, T. E. (1986). *Fund raising: The guide to raising money from private sources* (2nd ed.). Norman: University of Oklahoma Press.

Brooks, A. C. (2009). *Social entrepreneurship: A modern approach to social value creation.* Upper Saddle River, NJ: Prentice Hall.

Brooks, D. (2009, May 7). The Harlem miracle [Op-ed]. *New York Times.* Retrieved from http://www.nytimes. com/2009/05/08/opinion/08brooks.html

Brothers, J., & Sherman, A. (2012). *Building nonprofit capacity: A guide to managing change through organizational lifecycles.* San Francisco, CA: Jossey-Bass.

Brown, C. (2013, March 21). The epic ups and downs of Peter Gelb. *New York Times Magazine.* Retrieved from http://www.nytimes.com/2013/03/24/magazine/the-epic-ups-and-downs-of-peter-gelb.html

Bruce, M. (2010, June 9). Taking a chance; public boarding school reaps great success. *ABC News.* Retrieved from http://abcnews.go.com/US/article/public-boarding-school-reaps-great-success/story?id=10828451

Brudney, J. L. (2016). Designing and managing volunteer programs. In D. O. Renz & Associates (Eds.), *The Jossey-Bass handbook of nonprofit leadership and management* (4th ed., pp. 688–733). Hoboken, NJ: Jossey-Bass.

Bryman, A. (1992). *Charisma and leadership in organizations.* London, UK: Sage.

Bryson, J. M. (2016). Strategic planning and the strategy change cycle. In D. O. Renz & Associates (Eds.), *The Jossey-Bass handbook of nonprofit leadership and management* (pp. 240–273). Hoboken, NJ: Wiley.

Burnett, J. J. (2007). *Nonprofit marketing: Best practices.* Hoboken, NJ: Wiley.

Burns, J. M. (1978). *Leadership.* New York, NY: HarperCollins.

Cagney, P., & Ross, B. (2013). *Global fundraising: How the world is changing the rules of philanthropy.* Hoboken, NJ: Wiley.

Caligiuri, P. (2012, August 14). When Unilever bought Ben & Jerry's: A story of CEO adaptability. *Fastcompany.* Retrieved from http://www.fastcompany.com/3000398/when-unilever-bought-ben-jerrys-story-ceo-adaptability

Cantrell-Bruce, T., & Blankenberger, B. (2015, Summer). Seeing clearly: Measuring skill sets that address the "blurred boundaries" of nonprofit management education. *Journal of Public Affairs Education, 21*(3), 367–380.

Capps, K., & Montgomery, D. (2014, April 25). The great divide. *Washington City Paper.* Retrieved from http://www.washingtoncitypaper.com/articles/45699/the-great-divide-22-questions-for-the-corcoran/

Carlson, M., & Donohoe, M. (2003). *The executive director's survival guide: Thriving as a nonprofit leader.* San Francisco, CA: Jossey-Bass.

Carnegie, A. (1889, June). Wealth. *North American Review, 148*(391), 653–665.

Carnie, C. (2013). Western Europe. In P. Cagney & B. Ross, *Global fundraising: How the world is changing the rules of philanthropy* (pp. 89–107). Hoboken, NJ: Wiley.

Carrns, A. (2017, December 15). Charities' fear under tax bill: Less money to help the needy. *New York Times.* Retrieved from https://www.nytimes.com/2017/12/15/business/charities-tax-bill.html

Carson, E. (2012a, August 31). Rethinking collective impact [Web log comment]. *Huffington Post.* Retrieved from http://www.huffingtonpost.com/emmett-d-carson/rethinking-collective-imp_b_1847839.html

Carson, E. (2012b, September 5). Rethinking collective impact: Part two [Web log comment]. *Huffington Post.* Retrieved from http://www.huffingtonpost.com/emmett-d-carson/collective-impact-_b_1847972.html

Carver, J. (1990). *Boards that make a difference: A new design for leadership in nonprofit and public organizations.* San Francisco, CA: Jossey-Bass.

Carver, J. (1997). *Boards that make a difference: A new design for leadership in nonprofit and public organizations* (2nd ed.). San Francisco, CA: Jossey-Bass.

Carver, J. (2006). *Boards that make a difference: A new design for leadership in nonprofit and public organizations* (3rd ed.). San Francisco, CA: Jossey-Bass.

Case Foundation. (n.d.). *Share Our Strength: A be fearless case study.* Washington, DC: Author. Retrieved from https://casefoundation.org/befearless/

Cash, S. (2002, April). Smithsonian $35m gift. *Art in America, 90*(4), 33.

Cauterucci, C. (2017, October 11). Warring camps. *Slate.* Retrieved from http://www.slate.com/articles/double_x/doublex/2017/10/why_there_s_never_been_more_bitter_rancor_between_the_girl_scouts_and_the.html

Cava, M. d. (2017, June 13). Uber has lost market share to Lyft during crisis. *USA Today.* Retrieved from https://www.usatoday.com/story/tech/news/2017/06/13/uber-market-share-customer-image-hit-string-scandals/102795024/

Celep, A. (2013, April 23). *We are Community Wealth Partners: Here's why*. Retrieved from http://communitywealth.com/why-community-wealth-partners/

Cellini, S. R., & Kee, J. E. (2010). Cost-effectiveness and cost-benefit analysis. In J. S. Wholey, H. P. Hatry, & K. E. Newcomer (Eds.), *Handbook of practical program evaluation* (3rd ed., pp. 493–530). San Francisco, CA: Jossey-Bass.

CEO perspective: YMCA of the USA's Kevin Washington on evolving a national network. (2017, April 21). *Bridgespan Group*. Retrieved from https://www.bridgespan.org/insights/library/organizational-effectiveness/ceo-perspective-kevin-washington-y-usa

Chait, R. P., Holland, T. P. & Taylor, B. E. (1996). *Improving the performance of governing boards*. Phoenix, AZ: American Council on Education/Oryx Press.

Chait, R. P., Ryan, W. P., & Taylor, B. E. (2005). *Governance as leadership: Reframing the work of nonprofit boards*. Hoboken, NJ: BoardSource/Wiley.

Chang, C. F., & Tuckman, H. P. (1990). Why do nonprofit managers accumulate surpluses, and how much do they accumulate. *Nonprofit Management & Leadership, 1*(2), 117–135.

Chan-Zuckerberg Initiative. (2017). *About*. Retrieved from https://chanzuckerberg.com/about

Charity Navigator. (2017a). *How do we rate charities?* Retrieved from https://www.charitynavigator.org/index.cfm?bay=content.view&cpid=1284

Charity Navigator (2017b). *How we are moving ahead*. Retrieved from https://www.charitynavigator.org/index.cfm?bay=content.view&cpid=4981

Chatel, A. (2015, March 12). 8 facts about the Girl Scouts' history you didn't know, in honor of the organization's 103rd birthday. *Bustle*. Retrieved from https://www.bustle.com/articles/68952-8-facts-about-the-girl-scouts-history-you-didnt-know-in-honor-of-the-organizations-103rd

Chen, C.-A. (2014). Nonprofit managers' motivational styles: A view beyond the intrinsic-extrinsic dichotomy. *Nonprofit and Voluntary Sector Quarterly, 43*(4), 737–758.

Chen, L., & Chen, J. (2011). The motivations and expectations of international volunteer tourists. *Tourism Management, 32*, 435–442.

Chhichhia, B. (2015, January 8). The rise of social stock exchanges. *Stanford Social Innovation Review*. Retrieved from https://ssir.org/articles/entry/the_rise_of_social_stock_exchanges

Child, C. D., & Grønbjerg, K. A. (2007, March). Nonprofit advocacy organizations: Their characteristics and activities. *Social Science Quarterly, 88*(1), 259–281.

Child, C. D., Witesman, E. M., & Braudt, D. B. (2014, July 17). Sector choice: How fair trade entrepreneurs choose between nonprofit and for-profit forms. *Nonprofit and Voluntary Sector Quarterly, 44*, 832–851.

Chipman, I. (2015, October 26). How the Habitat for Humanity CEO moved beyond houses. *Stanford Business*. Retrieved from https://www.gsb.stanford.edu/insights/how-habitat-humanity-ceo-moved-beyond-houses.

Choi, J. (2006). A motivational theory of charismatic leadership: Envisioning, empathy, and empowerment. *Journal of Leadership & Organizational Studies, 13*(1), 24.

Chuck, E. (2016, March 11). Wounded Warrior Project fires top two executives amid reports of lavish spending. *NBC News*. Retrieved from https://www.nbcnews.com/news/military/wounded-warrior-project-fires-top-two-executives-amid-reports-lavish-n536606

Clegg, S., Kornberger, M., & Pitsis, T. (2005). *Managing and organizations: An introduction to theory and practice*. Thousand Oaks, CA: Sage.

Cloninger, K. (2011). *Tough cookies: Leadership lessons from 100 years of the Girl Scouts*. Hoboken, NJ: Wiley.

Coe, C. K. (2011). *Nonprofit financial management: A practical guide*. Hoboken, NJ: Wiley.

Cohn, F. (2012, January). The ballad of NYCO. *Opera News*. Retrieved from http://www.operanews.com/Ballad_of_NYCO.html

Colinvaux, R. (2016). Nonprofits and advocacy. In E. T. Boris & C. E. Steuerle (Eds.), *Nonprofits and government: Collaboration and conflict* (3rd ed., pp. 191–215). Lanham, MD: Rowman & Littlefield/Urban Institute.

Collins, J. C. (2001). *Good to great: Why some companies make the leap … and others don't*. New York, NY: HarperCollins.

Collins, J. C. (2005). *Good to great and the social sectors: A monograph to accompany Good to Great*. New York, NY: Harper.

Collins, J. C., & Porras, J. L. (1994). *Built to last: Successful habits of visionary companies*. New York, NY: Harper Business.

Commission on Private Philanthropy and Public Needs. (1975). *Giving in America: Toward a stronger voluntary sector*. Washington, DC: Author.

Community Wealth Partners. (2013). *Social Transformation Lifecycle*. Retrieved from http://communitywealth.com/wp-content/uploads/2016/12/Community-Wealth-Partners-Social-Transformation-Lifecycle.pdf

Community Wealth Ventures (now Community Wealth Partners). (2001). *The community wealth seeker's guide*. Washington, DC: Author.

Community Wealth Ventures (now Community Wealth Partners). (2004). *Evaluating a social enterprise opportunity*. Washington, DC: Author.

Condon, S. (2012). Susan G. Komen reverses course, will keep funding Planned Parenthood. *CBS News*. Retrieved from http://www.cbsnews.com/8301-503544_162-57371169-503544/susan-g-komen-reverses-course-will-keep-funding-planned-parenthood/

Cone Communications. (2010, March 19). *Top ten types of cause promotions.* Retrieved from http://www.conecomm.com/top-10-types-of-cause-promotions

Cone Communications. (2017). *2017 Cone Communications CSR study.* Retrieved from http://www.conecomm.com/research-blog/2017-csr-study

Connolly, P., & Lukas, C. (2002). *Strengthening nonprofit performance: A funder's guide to capacity building.* Saint Paul, MN: Amherst H. Wilder Foundation and Grantmakers for Effective Organizations.

Coombs, W. T. (2007). Protecting organization reputations during a crisis: The development and application of situational crisis communication theory. *Corporate Reputation Review, 10,* 163–176.

Coombs, W. T. (2011). *Crisis management and communications.* Gainesville, FL: Institute for Public Relations. Retrieved from http://www.instituteforpr.org/crisis-management-and-communications/

Cooper, H. (2015, January 16). A presidential triple plea for Haiti fund. *New York Times.* Retrieved from http://www.nytimes.com/2010/01/17/world/americas/17prexy.html

Cooper, M. (2013a, September 26). For City Opera, the talk turns to a shutdown. *New York Times.* Retrieved from http://www.nytimes.com/2013/09/27/arts/music/city-opera-board-says-it-may-enter-bankruptcy.html

Cooper, M. (2013b, October 3). New York City Opera files for bankruptcy. *New York Times.* Retrieved from http://www.nytimes.com/2013/10/04/arts/music/new-york-city-opera-files-for-bankruptcy.html

Cooper, M. (2014, December 10). Tribute to Julius Rudel aims to aid City Opera. *New York Times.* Retrieved from http://artsbeat.blogs.nytimes.com/2014/12/10/tribute-to-julius-rudel-aims-to-aid-city-opera-revival/?_r=0

Cooper, M. (2015, January 20). Potential buyers of New York City Opera hold a bidding war in court. *New York Times.* Retrieved from http://www.nytimes.com/2015/01/21/nyregion/potential-buyers-of-new-york-city-opera-hold-a-bidding-war-in-court.html?_r=0

Cooper, M. (2016, December 30). New York City Opera, on the rebound with a boost from Bernstein. *New York Times.* Retrieved from https://www.nytimes.com/2016/12/30/arts/music/new-york-city-opera-leonard-bernstein-candide-preview.html?rref=collection%2Ftimestopic%2FNew%20York%20City%20Opera&action=click&contentCollection=timestopics&region=stream&module=stream_unit&version=latest&contentPlacement=10&pgtype=collection

Cooper, M., & Pogrebin, R. (2013, October 4). The frenzied last-act effort to save City Opera. *New York Times.* Retrieved from http://www.nytimes.com/2013/10/05/arts/music/the-frenzied-last-act-effort-to-save-city-opera.html

Copilevitz & Canter. (2017). *Working with commercial co-venturers.* Retrieved from http://www.copilevitz-canter.com/working-with-commerical-co-venturers/

Cordes, J., Dietz, N., Steuerle, C. E., & Broadus, E. (2017). New ways of creating social value: Hybrids. In E. T. Boris & C. E. Steuerle (Eds.), *Nonprofits and government: Collaboration and conflict* (3rd ed., pp. 263–290). Lanham, MD: Rowman & Littlefield and Urban Institute Press.

Corporation for National and Community Service. (2006, December). *Volunteer growth in America: A review of trends since 1974.* Retrieved from http://www.nationalservice.gov/pdf/06_1203_volunteer_growth.pdf

Corporation for National and Community Service. (n.d-a). *About the social innovation fund.* Retrieved from http://www.nationalservice.gov/programs/social-innovation-fund

Corporation for National and Community Service. (n.d-b). *Preparing for the budget process check in #2.* Retrieved from https://www.nationalservice.gov/sites/default/files/olc/moodle/fm_reparing_the_grant_budget_forc_ac/view764b.html?id=3202&chapterid=2054

Corporation for National and Community Service. (n.d.-c). *Volunteering and civic life in America.* Retrieved from https://www.nationalservice.gov/vcla/national

Council for Advancement and Support of Education. (2014, November 20). *Council for Advancement and Support of Education announces new president: Sue Cunningham will join education association* [Press release]. Washington, DC: Author. Retrieved from http://www.case.org/About_CASE/Newsroom/Press_Release_Archive/Council_for_Advancement_and_Support_of_Education_Announces_New_President.html

Council for Advancement and Support of Education. (n.d.). *International Initiatives.* Retrieved from http://www.case.org/About_CASE/International_Initiatives.html?site=desktop

Council on Foundations. (2018). *Summary and analysis of the final tax reform legislation.* Retrieved from https://www.cof.org/page/summary-and-analysis-final-tax-reform-legislation#contributions

Crary, D. (2017, October 13). It's Boy Scouts vs. Girl Scouts as BSA moves to admit girls. *Chicago Tribune.* Retrieved from http://www.chicagotribune.com/news/sns-bc-us—boy-scouts-vs-girl-scouts-20171012-story.html

Cravens, J., & Ellis, S. J. (2014). *The last virtual volunteering guidebook: Fully integrating online service into volunteer involvement.* Philadelphia, PA: Energize.

Critics question whether AG office demands will reform Hershey Trust. (2016, July 11). *Chronicle of Philanthropy.* Retrieved from https://www.philanthropy.com/article/Critics-Question-Whether-AG/237075

Crutchfield, L. R., & Grant, H. M. (2008). *Forces for good: The six practices of high-impact nonprofits.* San Francisco, CA: Jossey-Bass.

Crutchfield, L. R., & Grant, H. M. (2012). *Forces for good: The six practices of high-impact nonprofits* (2nd ed.). San Francisco, CA: Jossey-Bass.

Culhane, D. P. (2016, Spring). A first-class solution. *Stanford Social Innovation Review.* Retrieved from https://ssir.org/book_reviews/entry/a_first_class_solution

Daniels, A. (2014a, April 20). Nonprofit seeks a niche, and revenue, in helping Americans prevent diabetes. *Chronicle of Philanthropy.* Retrieved from http://philanthropy.com/article/Y-Seeks-Revenue-by-Helping/146101

Daniels, A. (2014b, April 20). YMCA sheds 'gym' image to focus more on youths and health. *Chronicle of Philanthropy.* Retrieved from http://philanthropy.com/article/YMCA-Sheds-Gym-Image-to/146115/?cid=pt&utm_source=pt&utm_medium=en

Dansereau, F., Graen, G. B., & Haga, W. (1975). A vertical dyad linkage approach to leadership in formal organizations. *Organizational Behaviour and Human Performance, 13,* 46–78.

Dees, J. G. (1998). Enterprising nonprofits. In *Harvard Business Review on Nonprofits* (pp. 135–166). Boston, MA: Harvard Business School Press. (Reprinted from *Harvard Business Review,* January/February, 1998)

Dees, J. G., & Anderson, B. B. (2006). Framing a theory of social entrepreneurship: Building on two schools of practice and thought. In R. Mosher-Williams (Ed.), *Research on social entrepreneurship: Understanding and contributing to an emerging field* (ARNOVA Occasional Paper Series, *1*(3), pp. 39–66).

Dees, J. G., Emerson, J., & Economy, P. (2001). *Enterprising nonprofits: A toolkit for social entrepreneurs.* New York, NY: Wiley.

Denhardt, R. B., Denhardt, J. V., & Aristigueta, M. P. (2016). *Managing human behavior in public and nonprofit organizations* (4th ed.). Thousand Oaks, CA: Sage.

Despard, M. R. (2017, June). Can nonprofit capacity be measured? *Nonprofit*

and Voluntary Sector Quarterly, 46(3), 607–626.

de Tocqueville, A. (1838). *Democracy In America.* New York, NY: G. Dearborn.

Dissension and fiscal troubles beset the Girl Scouts. (2013, June 23). *USA Today.* Retrieved from https://www.usatoday.com/story/news/nation/2013/06/23/girl-scouts/2450259/

Dixon, J., & Keyes, D. (2013, Winter). The permanent disruption of social media. *Stanford Social Innovation Review.* Retrieved from http://www.ssireview.org/articles/entry/the_permanent_disruption_of_social_media

Dollery, B. E., & Wallis, J. L. (2003). *The political economy of the voluntary sector.* Northampton, MA: Edward Elgar.

Donovan, D. (2012, September 30). New United Way USA leader to urge autonomous groups to work together. *Chronicle of Philanthropy.* Retrieved from https://philanthropy.com/article/New-United-Way-USA-Leader/156031

Douglas, J. (1983). *Why charity? The case for a third sector.* Beverly Hills, CA: Sage.

Douglas, J. (1987). Political theories of nonprofit organization. In W. W. Powell (Ed.), *The nonprofit sector: A research handbook* (pp. 43–54). New Haven, CT: Yale University Press.

Driessen, K. (2012, March 16). District opens new permanent-housing complex for homeless women. *Washington Post.* Retrieved from http://www.washingtonpost.com/local/district-opens-first-permanent-housing-complex-for-homeless-women/2012/03/14/gIQAtfLkGS_story.html

Drucker, P. (1990). *Managing the nonprofit organization: Principles and practices.* New York, NY: HarperCollins.

Duke Center for the Advancement of Social Entrepreneurship. (2008). *Developing the field of social entrepreneurship.* Retrieved from https://community-wealth.org/sites/clone.community-wealth.org/files/downloads/paper-case.pdf

Dunlop, D. (1993). Major gift programs. In M. J. Worth (Ed.), *Educational fund raising: Principles and practice* (pp. 97–116). Washington, DC: American Council on Education and Oryx Press.

Durand, C., & Cici, K. (2011, Fall/Winter). Four reason why not to use social media … and why to use it anyway. *Nonprofit Quarterly.* Retrieved from http://nonprofitquarterly.org/2011/12/20/four-reasons-why-not-to-use-social-media-and-why-to-use-it-anyway/

Durham, S. (2010). *Brandraising: How nonprofits raise visibility and money through smart communications.* San Francisco, CA: Jossey-Bass.

Dym, B., & Hutson, H. (2005). *Leadership in nonprofit organizations.* Thousand Oaks, CA: Sage.

Ebrahim, A. (2016). The many faces of nonprofit accountability. In D. O. Renz & Associates (Eds.), *The Jossey-Bass handbook of nonprofit leadership and management* (4th ed., pp. 102–124). Hoboken, NJ: Wiley.

Ebrahim, A., & Rangan, V. K. (2010, July 9). *The limits of nonprofit impact: A contingency framework for measuring social performance* (Harvard Business School Working Paper). Retrieved from http://hbswk.hbs.edu/item/6439.html

Echoing Green. (n.d.-a). *About Echoing Green.* Retrieved from http://www.echoinggreen.org/about/history

Echoing Green. (n.d.-b). *Work on purpose.* Retrieved from http://www.echoinggreen.org/work-on-purpose

Eckerd, A. (2015, June 1). Two approaches to nonprofit financial ratios and the implications for managerial incentives. *Nonprofit and Voluntary Sector Quarterly, 44*(3), 437–456.

Edgers, G. (2004, January 25). MFA's Monets: Dicey deal? *Boston Globe,* p. A1.

Edna McConnell Clark Foundation. (2017). *Grantee portfolio: Youth Villages.* Retrieved from http://www.emcf.org/our-grantees/our-grantee-portfolio/youth-villages/overview/

Egger, R. (2002). *Begging for change*. New York, NY: HarperCollins.

Eikenberry, A. M., & Kluver, J. D. (2004, March/April). The marketization of the nonprofit sector: Civil society at risk? *Public Administration Review*, 64(2), 132.

Eisenberg, P. (2011). Hershey School scandal underscores need for watchful governance. *Chronicle of Philanthropy*. Retrieved from https://www.philanthropy.com/article/A-Case-for-Nonprofit/157881

Elliott, J., & Sullivan, L. (2015, June 3). How the Red Cross raised half a billion dollars for Haiti and built six homes. *ProPublica*. Retrieved from https://www.propublica.org/article/how-the-red-cross-raised-half-a-billion-dollars-for-haiti-and-built-6-homes

Ellis, S. J. (2010). *From the top down: The executive role in successful volunteer involvement* (3rd ed.). Philadelphia, PA: Energize.

Emmons, G., Hanna, J., & Thompson, R. (2012, May 23). *Five ways to make your company more innovative*. Boston, MA: Harvard Business School. Retrieved from https://hbswk.hbs.edu/item/five-ways-to-make-your-company-more-innovative

Environmental Defense Fund. (2017). *Corporate donation policy*. Retrieved from http://www.edf.org/approach/partnerships/corporate-donation-policy

Erikson, E. (1959). *Childhood and society*. New York, NY: Norton.

European Commission. (2014). *Social innovation*. Retrieved from http://ec.europa.eu/growth/industry/innovation/policy/social/index_en.htm

Evans, M. G. (1970). The effects of supervisory behavior on the path-goal relationship. *Organizational Behavior and Human Performance*, 5, 277–298.

Ex-official at medical charity accused of $1.8-million theft. (2014, November 19). *Chronicle of Philanthropy*. Retrieved from http://philanthropy.com/blogs/philanthropytoday/ex-official-at-medical-charity-accused-of-1-8-million-theft/93573

Faulk, L., & Stewart, M. J. (2017, Spring). Evaluating whether targeted capacity building improves nonprofit financial growth. *Nonprofit Management & Leadership*, 27(3), 317–334.

Fernandez, B. (2015). *The chocolate trust*. Philadelphia, PA: Camino Books.

Fiedler, F. E. (1967). *A theory of leadership effectiveness*. New York, NY: McGraw-Hill.

Field, A. (2012, October 22). Ben & Jerry's, poster child for the B Corp movement, becomes a B Corp. *Forbes*. Retrieved from http://www.forbes.com/sites/annefield/2012/10/22/ben-jerrys-poster-child-for-the-b-corp-movement-becomes-a-b-corp/

Financial Accounting Standards Board. (1993, June). *Statement of financial accounting standards* (No. 116). Norwalk, CT: Author.

Fine, A. (2011, August 21). It's time to get serious about using social media. *Chronicle of Philanthropy*. Retrieved from http://philanthropy.com/article/Social-Media-Are-No-Longer/128749/

Fiscale, A., & Missoni, E. (2014). General coordination of responses to crisis situations. In E. Missoni & D. Alesani (Eds.), *Management of international institutions and NGOs* (pp. 181–202). New York, NY: Routledge.

Fischer, M. (2000). *Ethical decision making in fund raising*. Hoboken, NJ: Wiley.

Fisher, J. L. (1984). *Power of the presidency*. New York, NY: American Council on Education/Macmillan.

FitzGerald, K. (2013, June 26). *Successful mergers: Two CEOs talk shop* [Interview with Schroeder Stribling and Kelly Sweeney McShane]. Retrieved from http://meyerfoundation.org/successful-mergers-two-ceos-talk-shop

Flandez, R. (2012, March 6). Nature conservancy faces flap over fundraising deal to promote swimsuit issue. *Chronicle of Philanthropy*. Retrieved from http://philanthropy.com/article/Swimsuit-Deal-Causes-Flap-at/131084/

Flood, J., Minkler, M., Lavery, S., Estrada, J., & Falbe, J. (2015). The collective impact model and its potential for health promotion: Overview and case study of a healthy retail initiative in San Francisco. *Health Education and Behavior*, 42(5), 654–668.

Flynn, D., & Tian, Y. (2015, February 10). Nonprofit deaths, near deaths, and reincarnations: Part 1 of 5, Hull House. *Nonprofit Quarterly*. Retrieved from https://nonprofitquarterly.org/2015/02/10/nonprofit-deaths-near-deaths-and-reincarnations-part-1-of-5-hull-house/

Folino, L. (2010, February 18). The great leaders series: Ben Cohen and Jerry Greenfield, co-founders of Ben & Jerry's Homemade. *Inc.* Retrieved from http://www.inc.com/30years/articles/ben-and-jerry.html

Food Research and Action Center. (2016, June). *How hungry is America?* Retrieved from http://frac.org/wp-content/uploads/food-hardship-2016-1.pdf

Forbes, K. F., & Zampelli, E. M. (2014). Volunteerism: The influences of social, religious, and human capital. *Nonprofit and Voluntary Sector Quarterly*, 43(2), 227–253.

Forrer, J. J., Kee, J. E., & Boyer, E. (2014). *Governing cross-sector collaboration*. San Francisco, CA: Jossey-Bass.

Foster, W., & Bradach, J. (2005, February). Should nonprofits seek profits? *Harvard Business Review*, 83(2), 92–100.

Fouad, R. (2016, July 19). Charity and children suffer as Hershey's board fends off lucrative offer. *Chronicle of Philanthropy*. Retrieved from https://www.philanthropy.com/article/Opinion-CharityChildren/237175

4-H. (n.d.-a). *4-H history*. Retrieved from http://4-h.org/about/history/

4-H. (n.d.-b). *Grow true leaders*. Retrieved from http://4-h.org/get-involved/grow-true-leaders/

Fourth Sector Network. (2017). [Website]. Retrieved from http://www.fourthsector.net/

Fox, J. (2017, August 17). NACC votes for accreditation of nonprofit and philanthropic academic programs. *Nonprofit Quarterly.* Retrieved from https://nonprofitquarterly.org/2017/08/17/nacc-votes-accreditation-program-academic-degrees-nonprofit-philanthropic-studies/

Fox, R. C. (2014). *Doctors Without Borders: Humanitarian quests, impossible dreams of Médecins Sans Frontiéres.* Baltimore, MD: Johns Hopkins University Press.

Frechette, H. (2011, July 11). Aspire CoffeeWorks: A paradigm of social entrepreneurship. *Citizen Polity.* Retrieved from http://citizenpolity.com/2011/07/11/aspire-coffee-works-a-paradigm-of-social-entrepreneurship/

Fremont-Smith, M. R., & Cordes, J. (2004). *What the ratings revolution means for charities.* Washington, DC: Urban Institute.

Friedman, T. L. (2006). *The world is flat: The globalized world in the twenty-first century.* London, UK: Penguin Books.

Fritz, J. (2016, September 9). American social entrepreneurs from the 19th century to the 21st. *The Balance.* Retrieved from https://www.thebalance.com/social-entrepreneur-definition-history-2502509

Froelich, K. A. (1999, September). Diversification of revenue strategies: Evolving resource dependence in nonprofit organizations. *Nonprofit and Voluntary Sector Quarterly, 28*(3), 246–268.

Froelich, K., McKee, G., & Rathge, R. (2011). Succession planning in nonprofit organizations. *Nonprofit Management & Leadership, 22*(1), 3–20.

From risk management to risk leadership: A governance conversation with David O. Renz. (2017, Summer). *Nonprofit Quarterly, 24*(2), 14–18.

Frost, P. (2016, August 30). Why Mondelez gave up on acquiring Hershey. *Crain's Chicago Business.* Retrieved from http://www.chicagobusiness.com/article/20160830/NEWS07/160829839/why-mondelez-gave-up-on-acquiring-hershey

Frumkin, P. (2002). *On being nonprofit: A conceptual and policy primer.* Cambridge, MA: Harvard University Press.

Frumkin, P., & Imber, J. B. (2004). *In search of the nonprofit sector.* New Brunswick, NJ/London, UK: Transaction.

Gadsden, C. H. (2002, November 11). The Hershey power play. *Wealth Management.* Retrieved from http://wealthmanagement.com/asset-protection/hershey-power-play

Gainer, B. (2016). Marketing for nonprofit organizations. In D. O. Renz & Associates (Eds.), *The Jossey-Bass handbook of nonprofit leadership and management* (4th ed., pp. 366–395). San Francisco, CA: Jossey-Bass.

Gainer, B., & Moyer, M. S. (2005). Marketing for nonprofit managers. In R. D. Herman & Associates (Eds.), *The Jossey-Bass handbook of nonprofit leadership and management* (pp. 277–309). San Francisco, CA: Jossey-Bass.

Galafassi, N. (2013). Latin America. In P. Cagney & B. Ross, *Global fundraising: How the world is changing the rules of philanthropy* (pp. 59–87). Hoboken, NJ: Wiley.

Galaskiewicz, J., & Colman, M. S. (2006). Collaboration between corporations and nonprofit organizations. In W. W. Powell & R. Steinberg (Eds.), *The non-profit sector: A research handbook* (2nd ed., pp. 180–206). New Haven, CT: Yale University Press.

Gallagher, B. A. (2005, April 5). *Statement of Brian A. Gallagher, president and CEO United Way of America, United States Senate Committee on Finance* [Press release]. Alexandria, VA: United Way of America. Retrieved from http://www.finance.senate.gov/imo/media/doc/bgtest040505.pdf

Gallagher, L. (2001, August 6). Prairie Home commercial. *Forbes, 168*(3). Retrieved from http://www.forbes.com/forbes/2001/0806/054.html

Gammal, D. L. (2007, Summer). Before you say "I do." *Stanford Social Innovation Review, 5*(3), 47–51.

Gamwell, F. I. (1984). *Beyond preference: Liberal theories of independent association.* Chicago, IL: University of Chicago Press.

Gasparro, A., & Cimilluca, D. (2016, August 29). Mondelez drops offer for Hershey. *Wall Street Journal.* Retrieved from https://www.wsj.com/articles/snack-maker-mondelez-drops-pursuit-of-hershey-1472503081

Gazley, B. (2008). Beyond the contract: The scope and nature of informal government-nonprofit partnerships. *Public Administration Review, 68*(1), 141–154.

Gazley, B. (2015). The nonprofit sector labor force. In R. C. Kearney & J. Coggburn (Eds.), *Public human resource management: Problems and prospects* (6th ed., pp. 90–104). Thousand Oaks, CA: CQ Press.

Gazley, B. (2017). Theories of the nonprofit sector. In J. K. A. Word & J. E. Sowa (Eds.), *The nonprofit human resource management handbook* (pp. 15–28). New York, NY: Routledge.

Gazley, B., & Brudney, J. L. (2007). The purpose (and perils) of government-nonprofit partnership. *Nonprofit and Voluntary Sector Quarterly, 36*(3), 389–415.

Gifts that can warp a museum [Editorial]. (2001, May 31). *New York Times.* Retrieved from http://www.nytimes.com/2001/05/31/opinion/gifts-that-can-warp-a-museum.html

Girl Scouts launches $70 million STEM initiative. (2017, November 13). *Philanthropy News Digest.* Retrieved from http://philanthropynewsdigest.org/news/girl-scouts-launches-70-million-stem-initiative

Girl Scouts of the USA. (2011, August 24). *Anna Maria Chávez named chief executive officer of Girls Scouts of the USA* [Press release]. Retrieved from http://blog.girlscouts.org/2011/08/anna-maria-chavez-named-chief-executive.html

Girl Scouts of the USA. (2017, May 17). *Sylvia Acevedo named next chief executive officer of Girl Scouts of the USA* [Press release]. Retrieved from http://www.girlscouts.org/en/press-room/press-room/news-releases/2017/sylvia-acevedo-named-GSUSA-CEO.html

Girl Scouts of the USA. (n.d.). *Our history.* Retrieved from http://www.girlscouts.org/en/about-girl-scouts/our-history.html

Giving Pledge. (2018). [Website]. Retrieved from https://givingpledge.org/

Giving USA. (2016, June 23). *See the numbers—'Giving USA 2016' infographic.* Retrieved from https://givingusa.org/see-the-numbers-giving-usa-2016-infographic/

Glenn, B. (2007, January 18). Aspire of Illinois CEO. *Crain Communication.* Retrieved from http://www.chicagobusiness.com/article/20070118/NEWS01/200023520/aspire-of-illinois-ceo

GlobalGiving. (2017). *Our impact.* Retrieved from https://www.globalgiving.org/aboutus/impact/

Global Impact Investing Network (GIIN). (n.d.). *Impact investing.* Retrieved from http://www.thegiin.org/impact-investing/

Godfrey, E. (2017, October 18). How will the Boy Scouts' decision affect the Girl Scouts? *The Atlantic.* Retrieved from https://www.theatlantic.com/politics/archive/2017/10/how-will-the-boy-scouts-decision-affect-the-girl-scouts/543204/

Godfrey, J., & Schneiderman, J. (2013, October 10). Should New York City Opera board be held accountable? *Nonprofit Quarterly*, 15(12). Retrieved from https://nonprofitquarterly.org/governancevoice/23048-should-new-york-city-opera-board-be-held-accountable.html

Gose, B. (2005, January 6). America's charity explosion. *Chronicle of Philanthropy*, 17(6), 6–9.

Gose, B. (2006, October 26). Former financial officer faces charges in museum debt crisis. *Chronicle of Philanthropy*, 19(2), 17. Retrieved from http://philanthropy.com/premium/articles/v19/i02/02006201.htm

Grant Thornton. (2012). *2012 National board governance survey for not-for-profit organizations.* Chicago, IL: Author.

Greene, S. G. (2004, April 15). Hostile takeover or rescue? *Chronicle of Philanthropy*, 13(13), 24–27.

Greenleaf, R. K. (1977). *Servant leadership: A journey into the nature of legitimate power and greatness.* Ramsey, NJ: Paulist Press.

Greenwood, R. M., Stefanic, A., & Tsemberis, S. (2013). Pathways Housing First for homeless persons with psychiatric disabilities: Program innovation, research, and advocacy. *Journal of Social Issues*, 69(4), 645–663.

Grunfeld, D., & Lash, D. (2012, March 18). Komen's crisis came not from politics but from poor management decisions. *Chronicle of Philanthropy.* Retrieved from http://philanthropy.com/article/Don-t-Blame-the-Culture-Wars/131191/

Guidestar. (2009). *New York City Opera Form 990.* Retrieved from http://www.guidestar.org/FinDocuments/2010/132/974/2010-132974347-07353053-9.pdf

Guidestar. (2010). *New York Philharmonic Form 990.* Retrieved from http://www.guidestar.org/FinDocuments/2011/132/974/2011-132974347-0856fa0f-9.pdf

Guidestar. (2011). *Metropolitan Opera Association Form 990.* Retrieved from http://www.guidestar.org/FinDocuments/2011/131/624/2011-131624087-08604420-9.pdf

Guidestar. (2018). *National Taxonomy of Exempt Entities (NTEE) Classification System.* Retrieved from https://learn.guidestar.org/help/ntee-codes

GuideStar. (n.d.). *New York City Opera Inc.: The people's opera.* Retrieved from http://www.guidestar.org/organizations/13-2974347/new-york-city-opera.aspx

Guo, C., & Acar, M. (2005, September). Understanding collaboration among nonprofit organizations: Combining resource dependency, institutional, and network perspectives. *Nonprofit and Voluntary Sector Quarterly*, 34(3), 340–353.

Guo, C., & Saxton, G. D. (2014). Tweeting social change: How social media are changing nonprofit advocacy. *Nonprofit and Voluntary Sector Quarterly*, 43(1), 57–79.

Guo, C., & Saxton, G. D. (2016, Winter). Social media capital for nonprofits: How to accumulate it, convert it, spend it. *Nonprofit Quarterly*, 23(4), 10–16.

Habitat for Humanity International. (2017). *Habitat for Humanity: About.* Retrieved from http://www.habitat.org/how/about_us.aspx

Hager, M. A., & Flack, T. (2004, August). *The pros and cons of financial efficiency standards* (Brief No. 5). Washington, DC: Urban Institute/Indiana University Center on Philanthropy.

Haider, D. (2007, Summer). Uniting for survival. *Stanford Social Innovation Review*, 5(3), 52–55.

Haider, D. (2017, January 11). Nonprofit mergers: New study sees strategy and success. *Nonprofit Quarterly.* Retrieved from https://nonprofitquarterly.org/2017/01/11/nonprofit-mergers-look-contexts-indicators-success/

Haiti telethon haul put at $57 million so far. (2010, January 23). *MSNBC.* Retrieved from http://today.msnbc.msn.com/id/35023278/ns/today-entertainment/t/haiti-telethon-haul-put-million-so-far/

Hall, H. (2005, January 6). Fund-raising association clarifies stand on fees. *Chronicle of Philanthropy*, 17(6), 47.

Hall, H. (2006, July 20). Nonprofit-marketing experts outline hot trends, discuss challenges. *Chronicle of Philanthropy*, 18(19), 29.

Hall, H. (2007, November 1). Public radio network has a script for success. *Chronicle of Philanthropy*, 20(2).

Hall, H., & Perry, S. (2013, April 7). Girl Scouts' financial and leadership woes threaten 100-year-old group. *Chronicle of Philanthropy*. Retrieved from https://www.philanthropy.com/article/FinancialLeadership-Woes/155055

Hall, J. L. (2010). *Grant management: Funding for public and nonprofit programs*. Sudbury, MA: Jones & Bartlett.

Halloran, T. (2013, September 20). Defining nonprofit political activity through bright lines and safe harbors. *The Hill*. Retrieved from http://thehill.com/blogs/congress-blog/economy-a-budget/323461-defining-nonprofit-political-activity-through-brightl-lines-and-safe-harbors

Hammack, D. C. (1998). *Making the nonprofit sector in the United States*. Bloomington: Indiana University Press.

Handy, F., & Mook, L. (2010). Volunteering and volunteers: Benefit-cost analyses. *Research on Social Work Practice*, *21*(4), 412–420.

Hansmann, H. (1987). Economic theories of nonprofit organization. In W. W. Powell (Ed.), *The nonprofit sector: A research handbook* (pp. 27–42). New Haven, CT: Yale University Press.

Harlem Children's Zone. (2014). *Harlem Children's Zone: A national model for breaking the cycle of poverty with proven success*. Retrieved from https://hcz.org/wp-content/uploads/2014/04/FY-2013-FactSheet.pdf

Harlem Children's Zone. (2016). *Annual report*. Retrieved from http://hcz.org/wp-content/uploads/2016/12/HCZ-Highlights-2016.pdf

Harlem Children's Zone. (2017). History. Retrieved from http://hcz.org/about-us/history

Hatry, H. P. (2014). *Transforming performance measurement for the 21st century*. Washington, DC: Urban Institute.

Hauser, J. (2003, June). Organizational lessons for nonprofits. *McKinsey Quarterly*, *2003*(2), 52–59. Retrieved from http://dheise.andrews.edu/Content/leadership/comps/3a/4reflection/OrganizationalLessonsForNonprofits.htm

Hayes, C. L. (1998, May 22). Getting serious at Ben & Jerry's; Cherry Garcia and friends trade funky for functional. *New York Times*. Retrieved from http://www.nytimes.com/1998/05/22/business/getting-serious-ben-jerry-s-cherry-garcia-friends-trade-funky-for-functional.html?pagewanted=all&src=pm

Hayes, C. L. (2000, April 13). Ben & Jerry's to Unilever, with attitude. *New York Times*. Retrieved from http://www.nytimes.com/2000/04/13/business/ben-jerry-s-to-unilever-with-attitude.html?pagewanted= all&src=pm

Held, T. (2014, July 13). Charities like Facebook for rallying support but not much for fundraising. *Chronicle of Philanthropy*. Retrieved from https://philanthropy.com/article/Charities-Like-Facebook-for/150511

Helm, S. T. (2016). Social enterprise and nonprofit ventures. In David O. Renz & Associates (Eds.), The *Jossey-Bass handbook of nonprofit leadership and management* (4th ed., pp. 334–365). Hoboken, NJ: Jossey-Bass.

Herman, M. L. (2011). *Ready or not: A risk management guide for nonprofit executives* (2nd ed.). Leesburg, VA: Nonprofit Risk Management Center.

Herman, R. D. (2005). Conclusion. In R. D. Herman & Associates (Eds.), *The Jossey-Bass handbook of nonprofit leadership and management* (2nd ed., pp. 731–736). San Francisco, CA: Jossey-Bass.

Herman, R. D. (2016). Executive leadership. In D. O. Renz & Associates (Eds.), *The Jossey-Bass handbook of nonprofit leadership and management* (4th ed., pp. 167–187). San Francisco, CA: Jossey-Bass.

Herman, R. D., & Heimovics, D. (2005). Executive leadership. In R. D. Herman & Associates (Eds.), *The Jossey-Bass handbook of nonprofit leadership and management* (2nd ed., pp. 153–170). San Francisco, CA: Jossey-Bass.

Herman, R. D., & Renz, D. O. (2002). *Nonprofit organizational effectiveness: Practical implications of research on an elusive concept* (Occasional paper). Kansas City: University of Missouri-Kansas City, Henry W. Bloch School of Business and Public Administration.

Herman, R. D., & Renz, D. O. (2008). Advancing nonprofit organizational effectiveness research and theory: Nine theses. *Nonprofit Management and Leadership*, *18*(4), 399–415.

Hernandez, J. C. (2005, December 9). Educator is said to have rejected chancellor job. *New York Times*. Retrieved from https://www.nytimes.com/2010/12/10/nyregion/10canada.html

Hersey, P., & Blanchard, K. H. (1969). Life-cycle theory of leadership. *Training and Development Journal*, *23*, 26–34.

Hershey loses taste for Cadbury. (2010, January 22). *Forbes*. Retrieved from https://www.forbes.com/2010/01/22/hershey-cadbury-kraft-markets-equities-offer-withdrawn.html#1ede82127314

Herzberg, F. (1968). One more time: How do you motivate employees? *Harvard Business Review*, *46*, 36–44.

Hessenius, B. (2007). *Hardball lobbying for nonprofits: Real advocacy for nonprofits in the new century*. New York, NY: Palgrave/Macmillan.

Hirsch, L. (2017, October 13). Nestle US confectionery business draws attention from Hershey, others. *CNBC*. Retrieved from https://www.cnbc.com/2017/10/13/nestle-confectionery-business-draws-attention-from-hershey.html

History of transportation department: The Y line. (2005). Minneapolis: University of Minnesota Libraries, Kautz Family YMCA Archives. Retrieved from http://archives.lib.umn.edu/repositories/7/resources/868

Hochberg, E. (2002, August 8). Business ventures go beyond the bottom line. *Chronicle of Philanthropy*, *14*(20), 35.

Hochberg, E., & Wise, A. (2005, March 3). Don't give up on charity-run businesses. *Chronicle of Philanthropy*, 17(10), 49–50.

Hopkins, B. R. (2003). *Legal responsibilities of nonprofit boards*. Washington, DC: BoardSource.

Hopkins, B. R. (2005). *Nonprofit law made easy*. Hoboken, NJ: Wiley.

Hoque, F. (2014, June 4). How to create a culture of innovation. *Fast Company*. Retrieved from http://www.fastcompany.com/3031092/how-to-create-a-culture-of-innovation-in-the-workplace

Hosking, T. (2017, October 12). Why do the Boy Scouts want to include girls? *The Atlantic*. Retrieved from https://www.theatlantic.com/politics/archive/2017/10/why-did-the-boy-scouts-decide-to-accept-girls/542769/

House, R. J. (1976). A 1976 theory of charismatic leadership. In J. G. Hunt & L. L. Larson (Eds.), *Leadership: The cutting edge* (pp. 189–207). Carbondale: Southern Illinois University Press.

Howe, F. (2002). Nonprofit accountability: The board's fiduciary responsibility. In V. Futter (Ed.), *Nonprofit governance and management* (pp. 29–38). Chicago, IL: American Bar Association/American Society of Corporate Secretaries.

Howe, F. (2004). *The nonprofit leadership team: Building the board–executive director relationship*. San Francisco, CA: Wiley.

How nonprofit endowments performed. (2017, May 31). *Chronicle of Philanthropy*. Retrieved from https://www.philanthropy.com/interactives/endowments#id=table_0_2016

Hrywna, M. (2016, June 16). Wounded Warrior Project appoints decorated vet as CEO. *Nonprofit Times*. Retrieved from http://www.thenonprofittimes.com/news-articles/wounded-warrior-project-appoints-decorated-vet-ceo/

Hudson Institute. (2017). *Index of global philanthropy and remittances, 2016*. Washington, DC: Author. Retrieved from https://s3.amazonaws.com/media.hudson.org/files/publications/201703IndexofGlobalPhilanthropyandRemittances2016.pdf

Hudson, M. (2005). *Managing at the leading edge*. San Francisco, CA: Jossey-Bass.

Huget, J. J. (2010, May 4). Is buying KFC by the bucket a good way to fight breast cancer? *Washington Post*. Retrieved http://www.washingtonpost.com/wp-dyn/content/article/2010/04/30/AR2010043001971.html

Iaboni, R. (2013, October 1). New York City Opera sings the blues over finances, plans to file for bankruptcy. *CNN*. Retrieved from http://www.cnn.com/2013/10/01/us/new-york-city-opera/

Independent Sector. (2005). *Panel on the Nonprofit Sector: Strengthening transparency, governance, accountability of charitable organizations* (A final report to Congress and the nonprofit sector). Washington, DC: Author.

Independent Sector. (2007). *Principles for good governance and ethical practice: A guide for charities and foundations*. Washington, DC: Author.

Independent Sector. (2012). *Beyond the cause: The art and science of advocacy*. Washington, DC: Author.

Independent Sector. (2015). *Principles for good governance and ethical practice: A guide for charities and foundations*. Washington, DC: Author.

Independent Sector. (2016a). *America's nonprofit sector: Revenues*. Retrieved from https://www.independentsector.org/wp-content/uploads/2016/12/IS-Nonprofit-Revenues-2016.pdf

Independent Sector. (2016b, October 6). *Lobbying guidelines for private foundations*. Retrieved from https://www.independentsector.org/resource/lobbying-guidelines-for-private-foundations/

Independent Sector. (2016c, October 6). *Lobbying guidelines for public charities*. Retrieved from https://www.independentsector.org/resource/lobbying-guidelines-for-public-charities/

Independent Sector. (2017a). *Charting impact*. Retrieved from https://www.independentsector.org/resource/charting-impact/

Independent Sector. (2017b). *National value of volunteer time*. Retrieved from http://www.independentsector.org/volunteer_time

Ingram, R. T. (2015). *Ten basic responsibilities of nonprofit boards* (3rd ed.). Washington, DC: BoardSource.

Internal Revenue Service. (2013, July). *Form 990, Part VI—Governance, management, and disclosure: Frequently asked questions and tips*. Washington, DC: Author.

Internal Revenue Service. (2016). *"Substantially related" defined*. Retrieved from http://www.irs.gov/Charities-&-Non-Profits/Substantially-related

Internal Revenue Service. (2017a). *"Direct" and "grass roots" lobbying defined*. Retrieved from https://www.irs.gov/charities-non-profits/direct-and-grass-roots-lobbying-defined

Internal Revenue Service. (2017b). *Measuring lobbying activity: Expenditure test*. Retrieved from https://www.irs.gov/charities-non-profits/measuring-lobbying-activity-expenditure-test

Internal Revenue Service. (n.d.-a). *Exemption requirements—Section 501(c)(3) organizations*. Retrieved from https://www.irs.gov/charities-non-profits/charitable-organizations/exemption-requirements-section-501c3-organizations

Internal Revenue Service. (n.d.-b). *Social welfare organizations*. Retrieved from http://www.irs.gov/Charities-&-Non-Profits/Other-Non-Profits/Social-Welfare-Organizations

Internal Revenue Service. (n.d.-c). *U. museum retailing: UBIT issues*. Retrieved from https://www.irs.gov/pub/irs-tege/eotopicu79.pdf

InterSector Partners L3C. (n.d.). [Website]. Retrieved from http://www.intersectorl3c.com/l3c

IU's philanthropy school to be named for Lilly family. (2013, April 9). *Indianapolis Business Journal*. Retrieved from https://www.ibj.com/articles/40671-iu-s-philanthropy-school-to-be-named-for-lilly-family

James, E. (1987). The nonprofit sector in comparative perspective. In W. W. Powell (Ed.), *The nonprofit sector: A research handbook* (pp. 397–415). New Haven, CT: Yale University Press.

James, M. (2017, December 14). Disney buys much of Rupert Murdoch's 21st Century Fox in deal that will reshape Hollywood. *Los Angeles Times*. Retrieved from http://www.latimes.com/business/hollywood/la-fi-ct-disney-fox-sale-20171214-story.html

Javits, C. I. (2008). *REDF's current approach to SROI*. San Francisco, CA: Roberts Enterprise Development Fund.

Jensen, B. (2005, February 17). Housing group fires its founder. *Chronicle of Philanthropy*, *17*(9), 26.

Jensen, B. (2006, September 28). Grants to help charities improve operations are on the decline. *Chronicle of Philanthropy*. Retrieved from http://philanthropy.com/article/Grants-to-Help-Charities/57895/

Jensen, B. (2008, September 9). The controversy of charity endorsements of corporate products. *Chronicle of Philanthropy*. Retrieved from https://philanthropy.com/article/The-Controversy-of-Charity/192601

Jewell, J. (2005). New times, new leaders. *Christianity Today*, *49*(4), 24.

Johnson, E. M. (2006). *The Pension Protection Act of 2006 and nonprofit reforms*. Washington, DC: American Society of Association Executives, Center for Association Leadership.

Johnson, J. M., Piatak, J. S., & Ng, E. (2017). Managing generational differences in nonprofit organizations. In J. K. A. Word & J. E. Sowa (Eds.), *The nonprofit human resource management handbook* (pp. 304–322). New York, NY: Routledge.

Joslyn, H. (2004, January 8). Young people fuel demand for nonprofit study. *Chronicle of Philanthropy*, *16*(6), 6–10. Retrieved from https://www.philanthropy.com/article/Young-People-Fuel-Demand-for/164559

Joslyn, H. (2017, July 5). 4-H taps alumni and updates image to boost support. *Chronicle of Philanthropy*. Retrieved from https://www.philanthropy.com/article/4-H-Shows-How-an-Image-Update/240512

KaBOOM!. (2016). *Annual report*. Retrieved from https://media1.kaboom.org/app/assets/resources/000/002/201/original/KaBOOM!-Annual-Report-2016.pdf

KaBOOM!. (2017). *Our story*. Retrieved from http://kaboom.org/about_kaboom

KaBOOM!. (n.d.). *Play matters: A study of best practices to inform local policy and process in support of children's play*. Washington, DC: Author. Retrieved from http://kaboom.org/docs/documents/pdf/playmatters/Play_Matters_Case_Summaries.pdf

Kahn, C. (2014, July 31). As 'voluntourism' explodes in popularity, who's it helping most? *NPR*. Retrieved from http://www.npr.org/sections/goatsandsoda/2014/07/31/336600290/as-volunteerism-explodes-in-popularity-whos-it-helping-most

Kania, J., Hanleybrown, F., & Juster, J. S. (2014, Fall). Essential mindset shifts for collective impact. *Stanford Social Innovation Review*. Retrieved from http://www.ssireview.org/articles/entry/essential_mindset_shifts_for_collective_impact

Kania, J., & Kramer, M. (2011, Winter). Collective Impact. *Stanford Social Innovation Review*, *9*(1). Retrieved from https://ssir.org/articles/entry/collective_impact

Kania, J., & Kramer, M. (2013, January 21). Embracing emergence: How collective impact addresses complexity. *Stanford Social Innovation Review*. Retrieved from https://ssir.org/articles/entry/embracing_emergence_how_collective_impact_addresses_complexity

Kania, J., & Kramer, M. (2016, May 4). Advancing the practice of collective impact (Web log comment). *Collective Impact Forum*. Retrieved from https://collectiveimpactforum.org/blogs/51306/advancing-practice-collective-impact

Kaplan, R. S., & Norton, D. (1992). Using the balanced scorecard as a strategic management system. *Harvard Business Review*, *70*(1), 71–79.

Karnani, A. (2010, August 23). The case against corporate social responsibility. *Wall Street Journal*. Retrieved from http://www.wsj.com/articles/SB10001424052748703338004575230112664504890

Katz, D. (1955). Skills of an effective administrator. *Harvard Business Review*, *33*(1), 33–42.

Katz, D., & Kahn, R. L. (1966). *The social psychology of organizations*. New York, NY: Wiley.

Kearns, K. P. (2000). *Private sector strategies for social sector success*. San Francisco, CA: Jossey-Bass.

Kearns, K. P., Bell, D., Deem, B., & McShane, L. (2014). How nonprofit leaders evaluate funding sources: An exploratory study of nonprofit leaders. *Nonprofit and Voluntary Sector Quarterly* *43*(1), 121–143.

Kearns, K. P., Livingston, J., Sherer, S., & McShane, L. (2013). Leadership skills as construed by nonprofit chief executives. *Leadership & Organization Development Journal*, *36*(6), 712–727.

Kee, J. E., & Newcomer, K. E. (2008). *Transforming public and nonprofit organizations: Stewardship for leading change*. Vienna, VA: Management Concepts.

Kelly, H. (2017, December 28). Apple apologizes for slowing iPhone, drops battery prices. *CNN*. Retrieved from http://money.cnn.com/2017/12/28/technology/apple-battery-apology/index.html

Kelly, K. S. (1998). *Effective fund-raising management*. Mahwah, NJ: Erlbaum.

Kennicott, P. (2009, November 4). National Trust's chief retiring. *The Washington Post,* p. C12.

Kerlin, J. A., & Pollak, T. H. (2011). Nonprofit commercial revenue: A replacement for declining government grants and private contributions? *The American Review of Public Administration, 41*(6), 686–704.

Kerr, E. (2011, June 29). Three key moments define Bill Kling's legacy in public radio. *MPR News.* Retrieved from https://www.mprnews.org/story/2011/06/29/bill-kling-leaves-mpr

Kibbe, B. D. (2004). Investing in nonprofit capacity. In Grantmakers for Effective Organizations (Eds.), *Funding effectiveness: Lessons in building nonprofit capacity* (Chap. 1). San Francisco, CA: Wiley.

Kim, M., Pandey, S., & Pandey, S. K. (2017, April 4). Why do nonprofit performing arts organizations offer free public access? *Public Administration Review.* Retrieved from http://onlinelibrary.wiley.com/doi/10.1111/puar.12769/abstract

Kirkpatrick, K. T. (2007, Summer). Go ahead: Pop the question. *Stanford Social Innovation Review, 5*(3), 3–46.

Klintsov, V., & von Löhneysen, E. (2001). Shall we dance? *McKinsey Quarterly, 2001*(4), 6–9. Retrieved from https://www.questia.com/library/journal/1G1-80118067/shall-we-dance

Koenig, B. L. (2004). *Going global for the greater good: Succeeding as a nonprofit in the international community.* San Francisco, CA: Jossey-Bass.

Komen gifts plunged in year after Planned Parenthood flap. (2014, January 6). Retrieved from https://www.philanthropy.com/article/Komen-Gifts-Plunged-in-Year/221401

Komen has 'moved past' Planned Parenthood flap, leader says. (2014, July 21). Retrieved from http://philanthropy.com/blogs/philanthropytoday/komen-has-moved-past-planned-parenthood-flap-leader-says/88265

Koteen, J. (1997). *Strategic management in public and nonprofit organizations* (2nd ed.). Westport, CT: Praeger.

Kotter, J. P. (1996). *Leading change.* Boston, MA: Harvard Business School Press.

Kylander, N., & Stone, C. (2012, Spring). The role of brand in the nonprofit sector. *Stanford Social Innovation Review.* Retrieved from http://www.ssireview.org/articles/entry/the_role_of_brand_in_the_nonprofit_sector

LaBarre, P. (2006, November/December). How do you transform a 95-year-old organization? Ask the girls. *Merrill Lynch Leadership Magazine,* 44–50. http://www.mavericksatwork.com/pdf/labarre-girlscouts.pdf

Laidler-Kylander, N., & Stenzel, J. S. (2014, January 8). The brand IDEA. *Stanford Social Innovation Review.* Retrieved from https://ssir.org/articles/entry/the_brand_idea_managing_nonprofit_brands_with_integrity_democracy_and_affin

LaMonica, P. R. (2017, December 18). Sweet and salty! Hershey buys SkinnyPop maker. *CNN Money.* Retrieved from http://money.cnn.com/2017/12/18/investing/hershey-skinnypop-amplify-snack-brands/index.html

Lampkin, L. M., Winkler, M. K., Kerlin, J., Hatry, H. P., Natenshon, D., Saul, J., … & Seshadri, A. (2006). *Building a common outcome framework to measure nonprofit performance.* Washington, DC: Urban Institute. Retrieved from http://www.urban.org/sites/default/files/alfresco/publication-pdfs/411404-Building-a-Common-Outcome-Framework-To-Measure-Nonprofit-Performance.PDF

Lang, A. S., Eisig, W. D., Klumpp, L., & Ricciardella, T. (2017). *How to read nonprofit financial statements: A practical guide.* Hoboken, NJ: Wiley.

La Piana Consulting. (2018). *The collaborative map.* Retrieved from http://lapiana.org/insights-for-the-sector/insights/collaboration-and-strategic-restructuring/collaborative-map.

La Piana, D. (2008). *The nonprofit strategy revolution: Real-time strategic planning in a rapid-response world.* Saint Paul, MN: Fieldstone Alliance.

La Piana, D. (2010, Spring). Merging wisely. *Stanford Social Innovation Review, 8*(2), 28–33.

Larkin, E. D. (2002, November 28). A dangerous precedent for donors. *Chronicle of Philanthropy, 15*(4). Retrieved from https://www.philanthropy.com/article/A-Dangerous-Precedent-for/189125

Leap of Reason. (n.d.). [Website]. Retrieved from http://leapofreason.org/

Leap of Reason Ambassadors Community. (2018). *Performance Imperative Organizational Self-Assessment (PIOSA).* Retrieved from http://leapambassadors.org/products/piosa/?utm_source=lac+outreach+email&utm_campaign=bcf&utm_medium=email&utm_content=BCF+Message+41

Lee, M. (2010). The role of the YMCA in the origins of U.S. nonprofit management education. *Nonprofit Management and Leadership, 20*(3), 277–293.

Lee, Y. (2016, April 1). Comparison of job satisfaction between nonprofit and public employees. *Nonprofit and Voluntary Sector Quarterly, 45*(2), 295–313.

Lee, Y., & Wilkins, V. M. (2011). More similarities or more differences? Comparing public and nonprofit managers' job motivations. *Public Administration Review, 71*(1), 45–56.

Lenkowsky, L. (2015, December 3). Ending philanthropy as we know it: The charitable donation by the Facebook founder and his wife is radical—and not just because of the amount. *Wall Street Journal.* Retrieved from https://www.wsj.com/articles/ending-philanthropy-as-we-know-it-1449100975

Leonard, R. W. (2013). Nonprofit motivation behavior and satisfaction.

Journal of Business and Behavioral Sciences, 25(1), 81–93.

Leslie, K. (2017, June 19). Komen foundation's old Planned Parenthood flap haunts candidate in costly U.S. House race. *Dallas Morning News.* Retrieved from https://www.dallasnews.com/news/politics/2017/06/19/komen-foundations-old-planned-parenthood-flap-haunts-candidate-costly-us-house-race

Lester, P. (2016). Building performance systems for social service programs: Case studies in Tennessee. *IBM Center for the Business of Government.* Retrieved from http://www.businessofgovernment.org/report/building-performance-systems-social-service-programs

Letson, P. (2010, July 11). After helping Haiti at its worst, a need for economic development grows clearer. *Chronicle of Philanthropy.* Retrieved from https://www.philanthropy.com/article/Learning-Lessons-From-Haiti/160377?cid=cpfd_home

Letts, C. W., Ryan, W., & Grossman, A. (1997, March/April). Virtuous capital: What foundations can learn from venture capitalists. *Harvard Business Review,* 75(2), 36–44.

Letts, C. W., Ryan, W. P., & Grossman, A. (1999). *High performance nonprofit organizations: Managing upstream for greater impact.* New York, NY: Wiley.

Levine, H., & Zahradnik, A. (2012). Online media, market orientation, and financial performance in nonprofits. *Journal of Nonprofit & Public Sector Marketing,* 24(1), 26–42.

Levine, M. (2015, December 7). Chan Zuckerberg LLC: No tax breaks + no accountability = what exactly? *Nonprofit Quarterly.* Retrieved from https://nonprofitquarterly.org/2015/12/07/chan-zuckerberg-llc-are-no-tax-breaks-plus-no-accountability-good-for-the-public/

Leviner, N., Crutchfield, L. R., & Wells, D. (2006). Understanding the impact of social entrepreneurs: Ashoka's answer to the challenge of measuring effectiveness.

Research on Social Entrepreneurship [ARNOVA Occasional Paper Series, 1(3), 89–104]. Indianapolis, IN: Association for Research on Nonprofit Organizations and Voluntary Action. Retrieved from https://www.ashoka.org/en/atom/264

Lewis, N. (2002, February 21). Controversy over donor's role causes Smithsonian to lose $36.5 million. *Chronicle of Philanthropy,* 14(9), 16.

Levy, R. (2008). *Yours for the asking.* Hoboken, NJ: Wiley.

Libby, P. (2012). *The lobbying strategy handbook.* Thousand Oaks, CA: Sage.

Light, P. C. (2000). *Making nonprofits work: A report on the tides of nonprofit management reform.* Washington, DC: Brookings Institution.

Light, P. C. (2002). *Pathways to nonprofit excellence.* Washington, DC: Brookings Institution.

Light, P. C. (2004a, Spring). Capacity building and the national infrastructure to support it. *Nonprofit Quarterly,* 36–41.

Light, P. C. (2004b). *Sustaining nonprofit performance: The case for capacity building and the evidence to support it.* Washington, DC: Brookings Institution.

Light, P. C. (2011, May 15). Social entrepreneurs are visionaries—but not wizards. *Chronicle of Philanthropy.* Retrieved from http://philanthropy.com/article/Social-Entrepreneurs-Aren-t/127504/

Likert, R. (1967). *The human organization.* New York, NY: McGraw-Hill.

Liket, K. C., & Maas, K. (2015). Nonprofit organizational effectiveness: Analysis of best practices. *Nonprofit and Voluntary Sector Quarterly,* 44(2), 268–296.

Lilly Family School of Philanthropy at Indiana University. (2017). *Giving USA: See the numbers infographic.* Retrieved from https://givingusa.org/see-the-numbers-giving-usa-2017-infographic/

Lindsay, D., & Stiffman, E. (2017, January 4). Results are us: Efforts to measure

charity effectiveness by impact, not overhead, are growing. But how do you define impact? *Chronicle of Philanthropy.* Retrieved from https://www.philanthropy.com/article/Measuring-Charities-by-Impact/238776

Lipman, H. (2006, August 17). A record fund-raising feat. *Chronicle of Philanthropy,* 18(21), 2. Retrieved from http://www.philanthropy.com/premium/articles/v18/i21/21002201.htm

Lipman, H., & Williams, G. (2002, August 8). D.C. United Way's troubles cause concern elsewhere. *Chronicle of Philanthropy,* 14(20), 30.

Locke, E. A. (2000). Motivation by goal setting. In R. T. Golembiewski (Ed.), *Handbook of organizational behavior* (2nd ed., pp. 43–56). New York, NY: Marcel Dekker.

Locke, S. S. (2015, December). Saving Sweet Briar. *Currents* 41(9), 20–27.

Lohmann, R. A. (1992). *The commons.* San Francisco, CA: Jossey-Bass.

Lohmann, R. A. (2015). Voluntary action and new commons. In *Selected Works of Roger A. Lohmann.* Morgantown: West Virginia University/Skywriters Press. Retrieved from https://works.bepress.com/rogeralohmann/4/

Lovejoy, K., & Saxton, G. (2012, April 10). Information, community, and action: How nonprofit organizations use social media. *Journal of Computer-Mediated Communication,* 17(3), 337–353.

Lovejoy, M. (2017, November 15). National Trust for Historic Preservation to raise $25M to protect black history sites. *Nonprofit Quarterly.* Retrieved from https://nonprofitquarterly.org/2017/11/20/national-trust-historic-preservation-raise-25m-protect-black-history-sites/?utm_source=Daily+Newswire&utm_campaign=a780fc975a-EMAIL_CAMPAIGN_2017_11_17&utm_medium=email&utm_term=0_94063a1d17-a780fc975a-12425277

Lubell, S. (December, 2005). Katrina and heritage: Richard Moe, president of the

National Trust for Historic Preservation. *Architectural Record, 193*(12), 32.

Lyons, T. S., Townsend, J., Sullivan, A. M., & Drago, T. (2010, February). *Social enterprise's expanding position in the nonprofit landscape.* Retrieved from http://staging.community-wealth.org/sites/clone.community-wealth.org/files/downloads/paper-lyons.pdf

MacMillan, I. C. (1983). Competitive strategies for nonprofit organizations. *Advances in Strategic Management, 1,* 61–82.

Maddox, D. (1999). *Budgeting for not-for-profit organizations.* Hoboken, NJ: Wiley.

Make-a-Wish. (2017). *About us: Local and global structure.* Retrieved from http://wish.org/about-us/our-story/local-and-global-structure

Maloney, L. (2013, September 29). Do you think the fat lady has really sung? *Wall Street Journal.* Retrieved from https://www.wsj.com/articles/8216do-you-think-the-fat-lady-has-really-sung8217-1380505062

Martin, R. L., & Osberg, S. (2007, Spring). Social entrepreneurship: The case for definition. *Stanford Social Innovation Review, 28–39.*

Maryland State Department of Education. (2017). *SEED School of Maryland.* Retrieved from http://www.marylandpublicschools.org/programs/Pages/SEED-School/index.aspx

Maslow, A. H. (1954). *Motivation and personality.* New York, NY: Harper.

Massey, S. G., & Barreras, R. E. (2013). Introducing "impact validity." *Journal of Social Issues, 69*(4), 615–632.

Mattocks, R. (2008). *Zone of insolvency: How nonprofits avoid hidden liabilities and build financial strength.* Hoboken, NJ: Wiley.

MAXIMUS. (2018). Our philosophy. Retrieved from http://www.maximus.com/our-company/our-philosophy

Mazzola, J. (2017, October 12). No mergers, no boys: N.J. Girl Scouts not backing down. *NJ.com.* Retrieved from http://www.nj.com/news/index.ssf/2017/10/what_does_boy_scouts_change_mean_for_future_of_gir.html

McCambridge, R. (2012, January 11). Two years after Haiti's earthquake, the U.S. has delivered on only 30% of its pledge. *Nonprofit Quarterly.* Retrieved from http://www.nonprofitquarterly.org/philanthropy/19041-two-years-after-haitis-earthquake-the-us-has-delivered-on-only-30-of-its-pledge.html

McCambridge, R. (2015a, March 31). Virginia Claims Sweet Briar closing vote was precipitous, unwarranted and unlawful. *Nonprofit Quarterly.* Retrieved from https://nonprofitquarterly.org/2015/03/31/virginia-claims-sweet-briar-closing-vote-was-precipitous-unwarranted-and-unlawful/

McCambridge, R. (2015b, December 2). New Zuckerberg-Chan pledge a threat to democracy? *Nonprofit Quarterly.* Retrieved from https://nonprofitquarterly.org/2015/12/02/new-zuckerberg-chan-pledge-exceeds-all-of-americas-2015-charitable-giving/

McCambridge, R. (2016, Winter). Social media as an organizational game changer. *Nonprofit Quarterly, 23*(4), 6–9.

McCambridge, R. (2017, November 10). Repeal of Johnson Amendment: One step closer and another step worse. *Nonprofit Quarterly.* Retrieved from https://nonprofitquarterly.org/2017/11/10/repeal-johnson-amendment-one-step-closer-another-step-worse/

McCausland, C. (2008). Planting a SEED in Baltimore. *Baltimore Magazine.* Retrieved from http://www.baltimoremagazine.net/old-site/this-month/2008/07/planting-a-seed-in-baltimore

McClelland, D. C. (1961). *The achieving society.* New York, NY: Free Press.

McCormick, D. H. (2001). *Nonprofit mergers: The power of successful partnerships.* Gaithersburg, MD: Aspen.

McCoy, T. (2015, May 6). Meet the outsider who accidentally solved chronic homelessness. *Washington Post.* Retrieved from https://www.washingtonpost.com/news/inspired-life/wp/2015/05/06/meet-the-outsider-who-accidentally-solved-chronic-homelessness/?utm_term=.af3ab36c6b40

McCracken, J., & Brat, I. (2009, November 27). Hershey Trust seeks Cadbury-bid blessing. *Wall Street Journal.* Retrieved from http://online.wsj.com/article/SB100014240527487044988045745576009624712.html

McCurley, S. (2005). Keeping the community involved: Recruiting and retaining volunteers. In R. D. Herman & Associates (Eds.), *The Jossey-Bass handbook of nonprofit leadership and management* (2nd ed., pp. 587–622). San Francisco, CA: Jossey-Bass.

McCurley, S., & Lynch, R. (2006). *Volunteer management: Mobilizing all the resources in the community* (2nd ed.). Kemptville, ON, Canada: Johnstone Training and Consultation.

McDill, V. (2006, August). Preventing cultural catastrophe. *OAH Newsletter, 7.*

McGlone, P. (2016, August 16). Homeless art, lost jobs and low enrollment: Two years later, Corcoran's breakup still stings. *Washington Post.* Retrieved from https://www.washingtonpost.com/entertainment/museums/corcoran-breakup-deal-still-provokes-angry-feelings/2016/08/16/d6845300-581b-11e6-831d-0324760ca856_story.html?utm_term=.55620e9a526c

McGlone, P. (2017, July 6). Saving America's treasures. *Washington Post.* Retrieved from https://www.washingtonpost.com/graphics/lifestyle/smithsonian-kickstarter/?utm_term=.d2e132aecbaf

McGregor, D. (1960). *The human side of enterprise.* New York, NY: McGraw-Hill.

McKee, G., & Froelich, K. (2016). Executive succession planning: Barriers and substitutes in nonprofit organizations. *Annals of Public and Cooperative Economics, 87*(4), 587–601.

McKeever, B. (2015). *The nonprofit sector in brief 2015: Public charities, giving, and volunteering*. Washington, DC: Urban Institute. Retrieved from http://www.urban.org/research/publication/nonprofit-sector-brief-2015-public-charities-giving-and-volunteering

McKeever, B. S., Dietz, N. E., & Fyffe, S. D. (2016). *The nonprofit almanac* (9th ed.). Lanham, MD: Rowan & Littlefield/Urban Institute Press.

McKinsey & Company. (2001). *Effective capacity building in nonprofit organizations.* Washington, DC: Venture Philanthropy Partners. Retrieved from https://www.neh.gov/files/divisions/fedstate/vppartnersfull_rpt_1.pdf

McKinsey & Company. (2013). *The organizational capacity assessment tool (OCAT): 2.0* [Brochure]. Retrieved from http://mckinseyonsociety.com/ocat/

McKinsey & Company. (n.d.). *Our insights.* Retrieved from http://www.mckinsey.com/industries/social-sector/our-insights

McLaughlin, J. A., & Jordan, G. B. (2015). Using logic models. In K. E. Newcomer, H. P. Hatry, & J. S. Wholey (Eds.), *Handbook of practical program evaluation* (4th ed., pp. 62–87). Hoboken, NJ: Wiley.

McLaughlin, T. A. (2010). *Nonprofit mergers and alliances* (2nd ed.). Hoboken, NJ: Wiley.

McMillan, E. J. (2003). *Not-for-profit budgeting and financial management.* Hoboken, NJ: Wiley.

Médecins Sans Frontières. (2005, February 9). *MSF Greece reintegrated into the MSF international movement* [Press release]. Retrieved from http://www.msf.org/article/msf-greece-reintegrated-msf-international-movement

Médecins Sans Frontières. (2011, July 3). *MSF reforms its highest international governance structures* [Press release]. Retrieved from http://www.doctorswithoutborders.org/news-stories/press-release/msf-reforms-its-highest-international-governance-structures

Médecins Sans Frontières. (2016). *International activity report 2016—The year in review.* Retrieved from http://www.msf.org/sites/msf.org/files/msf_activity_report_2016_web.pdf

Médecins Sans Frontières (2017). *The MSF movement.* Retrieved from http://www.msf.org/msf-movement

Meeks, S. K. (2015, November 4). *PastForward 2015 preservation conference* [Keynote speech]. Retrieved from https://savingplaces.org/press-center/media-resources/pastforward-2015-keynote-speech#.WYHuPYjytPY

Meiksins, R. (2018, January 3). The impact of the Tax Cuts and Jobs Act on nonprofit salaries. *Nonprofit Quarterly.* Retrieved from https://nonprofitquarterly.org/2018/01/03/impact-tax-cuts-jobs-act-nonprofit-salaries/

Mendel, S. C. (2014, Winter). A field of its own. *Stanford Social Innovation Review, 12*(1), 61–62.

Mendel, S. C. (2016, April 5). [Review of the book *Governing cross-sector collaboration*]. *Nonprofit and Voluntary Sector Quarterly, 45*(4), 869–871.

Menon, U., & Tiwari, A. (2013). India. In P. Cagney & B. Ross (2013), *Global fundraising: How the world is changing the rules of philanthropy* (pp. 267–289). Hoboken, NJ: Wiley.

Metropolis Coffee Company. (2018). *About.* Retrieved from https://www.metropoliscoffee.com/

Meyer, M. W. (2002). *Rethinking performance measures: Beyond the balanced scorecard.* Cambridge, UK: Cambridge University Press.

Mildenberg, D. (2013, December 12). Private toll-road investors get low-risk deals from states. *Bloomberg Business News.* Retrieved from https://www.bloomberg.com/news/articles/2013-12-12/private-toll-road-investors-get-low-risk-deals-from-states

Miller, J. P. (1998, March 24). Public radio outlet reaps $120 million for direct marketer. *Wall Street Journal,* p. B9.

Miller, L. K., & Fielding, L. W. (1995, February 1). The battle between the for-profit health club and the "commercial" YMCA. *Journal of Sport and Social Issues, 19*(1), 76–107.

Milnes, S. E. (2015, February 2). Should New York City Opera just stay dead? *Daily Beast.* Retrieved from http://www.thedailybeast.com/articles/2015/02/02/should-new-york-city-opera-just-stay-dead.html#

Milton S. Hershey School. (2014). *About.* Retrieved from http://www.mhskids.org/about/

Milward, H. B., & Provan, K. G. (2016). A manager's guide to choosing and using collaborative networks. In J. S. Ott & L. A. Dicke (Eds.), *Understanding nonprofit organizations* (3rd ed., pp. 232–240). Boulder, CO: Westview.

Milway, K. S., Orozco, M., & Botero, C. (2014, March 6). Why nonprofit mergers continue to lag. *Bridgespan Group.* Retrieved from http://www.bridgespan.org/Publications-and-Tools/Strategy-Development/Why-Nonprofit-Mergers-Continue-to-Lag.aspx

Minkoff, D. C., & Powell, W. W. (2006). Nonprofit mission: Constancy, responsiveness, or deflection? In W. W. Powell & R. Steinberg (Eds.), *The nonprofit sector: A research handbook* (2nd ed., pp. 591–611). New Haven, CT: Yale University Press.

Minnesota Public Radio. (2017, April 13). *Minnesota Public Radio's Saint Paul headquarters to be named after founder, Bill Kling* [Press release]. Retrieved from https://www.mpr.org/press/2017/04/13/mpr-hq-to-be-named-after-founder-bill-kling

Minor, E. (2005, February 3). Habitat for Humanity volunteers urge reinstatement of founder and president. *Associated Press.* Retrieved from http://legacy.utsandiego.com/news/nation/20050203-0124-habitatfounder.html

Minzner, A., Klerman, J. A., Markovitz, C. E., & Fink, B. (2014). The impact of capacity-building programs on nonprofits: A random assignment evaluation. *Nonprofit and Voluntary Sector Quarterly*, 43(3), 547–569.

Mirabella, R. M. (2007, December). University-based educational programs in nonprofit management and philanthropic studies: A 10-year review and projections of future trends. *Nonprofit and Voluntary Sector Quarterly*, 36(4 Suppl.), 11S–27S.

Mirabella, R. M., & Young, D. R. (2012, Fall). The development of education for social entrepreneurship and nonprofit management: Diverging or converging paths? *Nonprofit Management and Leadership*, 23(1), 43–56.

Miriam's Kitchen. (n.d.). *More than a meal*. Retrieved from https://miriamskitchen.org/morethanameal/

Missoni, E. (2014a). International institutions: Classification and main characteristics. In E. Missoni & D. Alesani (Eds.), *Management of international institutions and NGOs: Frameworks, practices, and challenges* (pp. 13–48). New York, NY: Routledge.

Missoni, E. (2014b). International non-governmental organizations: Definitions, classification, and relation with the UN system. In E. Missoni & D. Alesani (Eds.), *Management of international institutions and NGOs: Frameworks, practices, and challenges* (pp. 49–76). New York, NY: Routledge.

Missoni, E. (2014c). Transnational hybrid organizations: Global public-private partnerships and networks. In E. Missoni & D. Alesani (Eds.), *Management of international institutions and NGOs: Frameworks, practices, and challenges* (pp. 77–102). New York, NY: Routledge.

Mitchell, G. E. (2012, February). The construct of organizational effectiveness: Perspectives from leaders of international nonprofits in the United States. *Nonprofit and Voluntary Sector Quarterly*, 42(2), 324–345.

Montgomery, D. (2012a, July 20). Corcoran gallery: Why don't donors give? *Washington Post*. Retrieved from https://www.washingtonpost.com/entertainment/museums/corcoran-gallery-why-dont-donors-give/2012/07/19/gJQAJkNGyW_story.html

Montgomery, D. (2012b, December 11). After months of turmoil, Corcoran to keep its home. *Washington Post*, p. A1.

Montgomery, D. (2013a, March 5). Wayne Reynolds, former Ford's Theatre chair, pitches to save the Corcoran. *Washington Post*. Retrieved from https://www.washingtonpost.com/entertainment/museums/wayne-reynolds-former-fords-theatre-chair-pitches-to-save-corcoran-gallery/2013/03/05/e4937706-85a5-11e2-999e-5f8e0410cb9d_story.html

Montgomery, D. (2013b, April 3). Corcoran, University of Maryland agree to explore partnership. *Washington Post*. Retrieved from https://www.washingtonpost.com/entertainment/museums/corcoran-university-of-maryland-agree-to-explore-partnership/2013/04/03/b2fb57d6-9c6b-11e2-9bda-edd1a7fb557d_story.html

Montgomery, D. (2014, February 19). Corcoran Gallery of Art and college agrees to takeover by the National Gallery of Art, GWU. *Washington Post*. Retrieved from https://www.washingtonpost.com/entertainment/museums/2014/02/19/a236132e-9994-11e3-b88d-f36c07223d88_story.html?utm_term=.27248027dcf4

Montgomery, D., & Judkis, M. (2014, August 18). Judge approves Corcoran Gallery of Art plan to partner with National Gallery, GWU. *Washington Post*. Retrieved from http://www.washingtonpost.com/lifestyle/style/judge-approves-corcoran-gallery-of-art-plan-to-partner-with-national-gallery-gwu/2014/08/18/18eefdbc-2326-11e4-8593-da634b334390_story.html

Mook, L., Maiorano, J., Ryan, S., Armstrong, A., & Quarter, J. (2015). Turning social return on investment on its head. *Nonprofit Management and Leadership*, 26, 229–246. doi:10.1002/nml.21184

More millennials value volunteering than previous generation did. (2015, January 5). *Philanthropy News Digest*. Retrieved from http://philanthropynewsdigest.org/news/more-millennials-value-volunteering-than-previous-generation-did

More scrutiny of decision to close Sweet Briar. (2015, March 18). *Inside Higher Education*. Retrieved from https://www.insidehighered.com/quicktakes/2015/03/18/more-scrutiny-decision-close-sweet-briar

More than food: Bill Shore's vision of sharing strength to fight hunger. (1998, Winter). *Penn Arts & Sciences*. Retrieved from http://www.sas.upenn.edu/sasalum/newsltr/winter98/shore.html

Morino, M. (2011). *Leap of reason*. Washington, DC: Venture Philanthropy Partners.

Mosher-Williams, R. (2018, Winter) The strength of social enterprise. *Stanford Social Innovation Review*. Retrieved from https://ssir.org/articles/entry/the_strength_of_the_social_enterprise

Moyers, R. L. (2011). *Daring to lead 2011* (Brief 3: The board paradox). San Francisco, CA: CompassPoint/Meyer Foundation. Retrieved from http://daringtolead.org/wp-content/uploads/Daring-Brief-3-080511.pdf

Moyers, R. L. (2012, February 27). Hull House collapse is a cautionary tale for boards and executives. *Chronicle of Philanthropy*. Retrieved from http://philanthropy.com/blogs/against-the-grain/hull-house-collapse-is-a-wake-up-call-for-boards-and-executives/28045

Moyers, R. L. (2013). *The nonprofit chief executive's ten basic responsibilities* (2nd ed.). Washington, DC: BoardSource.

Muchilwa, M. (2013). Africa. In P. Cagney & B. Ross (Eds.), *Global fundraising: How the world is changing the rules of philanthropy* (pp. 179–222). Hoboken, NJ: Wiley.

Mullins, L. (2012, December). Crisis at the Corcoran. *Washingtonian, 48*(3), 64–71.

Murray, S. (2016, Summer). Upgrading a network. *Stanford Social Innovation Review.* Retrieved from https://ssir.org/articles/entry/upgrading_a_network

Murray, V. (2010). Evaluating the effectiveness of nonprofit organizations. In D. O. Renz & Associates (Eds.), *The Jossey-Bass handbook of nonprofit leadership and management* (3rd ed., pp. 431–460). San Francisco, CA: Jossey-Bass.

Museums and money [Editorial]. (2001, May 31). *Washington Post,* p. A24.

Nanus, B., & Dobbs, S. M. (1999). *Leaders who make a difference: Essential strategies for meeting the nonprofit challenge.* San Francisco, CA: Jossey-Bass.

National Association of College and University Business Officers (NACUBO). (n.d.). *Uniform Prudent Management of Institutional Funds Act* (Summary). Retrieved from http://www.nacubo.org/Business_and_Policy_Areas/Endowment_Management/UPMIFA_Resources/UPMIFA_Summary.html

National Audubon Society. (2015, November 12). *Audubon names Chandra Taylor Smith its first vice president for diversity and inclusion* [Press release]. Retrieved from http://www.audubon.org/news/audubon-names-chandra-taylor-smith-its-first-vice-president-diversity-and

National Audubon Society. (n.d.-a). *About us.* Retrieved from http://www.audubon.org/about

National Audubon Society. (n.d.-b). *Audubon advocacy.* Retrieved from http://www.audubon.org/conservation/advocacy

National Center for Charitable Statistics. (n.d.). *Quick facts about nonprofits.* Retrieved from http://nccs.urban.org/statistics/quickfacts.cfm

National Council of Nonprofits. (2017a). *Interns: Employee or volunteer.* Retrieved from https://www.councilofnonprofits.org/tools-resources/interns-employee-or-volunteer

National Council of Nonprofits. (2017b). *Taking the 501(h) election.* Retrieved from https://www.councilofnonprofits.org/taking-the-501h-election

National Council of Nonprofits. (2018a). *Dashboards for nonprofits.* Retrieved from https://www.councilofnonprofits.org/tools-resources/dashboards-nonprofits

National Council of Nonprofits. (2018b, January 24). *Tax Cuts and Jobs Act, H.R. 1: Nonprofit analysis of the final tax law.* Retrieved from https://www.councilofnonprofits.org/sites/default/files/documents/tax-bill-summary-chart.pdf

National Council of Nonprofits. (n.d.-a). *Commercial co-ventures and cause related marketing.* Retrieved from https://www.councilofnonprofits.org/tools-resources/commercial-co-ventures-and-cause-related-marketing

National Council of Nonprofits. (n.d.-b). *Does your nonprofit need to have an independent audit?* Retrieved from https://www.councilofnonprofits.org/nonprofit-audit-guide/need-independent-audit

National 4-H Council. (2016, April 12). *Survey shows American youth feel today's leaders have a different agenda; they lack skills to lead themselves* [Press release]. Chevy Chase, MD: Author. Retrieved from http://4-h.org/media/survey-shows-american-youth-feel-todays-leaders-have-a-different-agenda-they-lack-skills-to-lead-themselves/

National Public Radio. (2013, October 7). *The fat lady sings for New York City Opera.* Retrieved from http://www.npr.org/templates/story/story.php?storyId=230126261

National Trust for Historic Preservation. (2008). *2008 annual report.* Washington, DC: Author.

National Trust for Historic Preservation. (2013). *2013 annual report.* Washington, DC: Author.

National Trust for Historic Preservation. (2014). *Reimagining historic sites: A vision for the future of National Trust historic sites.* Retrieved from http://forum.savingplaces.org/HigherLogic/System/DownloadDocumentFile.ashx?DocumentFileKey=90d52e1c-fb56-ff39-e75f-e38c9064b1c5

The nation's attic: Secret contracts, soaring salaries—they don't belong at the Smithsonian [Editorial]. (2006, April 24). *Washington Post,* p. A16.

Nations, D. (2017, May 30). What is social media? Explaining the big trend. *Lifewire.* Retrieved from https://www.lifewire.com/what-is-social-media-explaining-the-big-trend-3486616

NBC News. (2012). *Andrea Mitchell interviews Susan G. Komen's Nancy Brinker.* Retrieved from http://firstread.nbcnews.com/_news/2012/02/02/10303379-andrea-mitchell-interviews-susan-g-komens-nancy-brinker?lite

Nee, E., & Jolin, M. (2012, Fall). Roundtable on collective impact. *Stanford Social Innovation Review.* Retrieved from http://www.ssireview.org/articles/entry/roundtable_on_collective_impact

Neibauer, M. (2012, March 15). N Street Village moving homeless women into new apartments. *Washington Business Journal.* Retrieved from https://www.bizjournals.com/washington/blog/2012/03/n-street-village-moving-homeless-women.html

Nelson, L. A. (2012, June 26). Missing the mark on gainful. *Inside Higher Education.* Retrieved from http://www.insidehighered.com/news/2012/06/26/education-department-releases-data-gainful-employment-rule

Nelson, R. A., Kanso, A. M., & Levitt, S. R. (2007). Integrating public service and marketing differentiation: An analysis of the American Express Corporation's "Charge Against Hunger" promotion program. *Service Business, 1*(4), 275–293.

Network for Good. (2014). *The 2014 online fundraising survival guide.* Retrieved from http://www.fundraising123.org/files/2014%20Online%20Fundraising%20Survival%20Guide%20-%20March.pdf

Newcomer, K. E. (2008). Assessing performance in nonprofit service agencies. In P. D. Julnes, F. S. Berry, M. P. Aristigueta, & K. Yang (Eds.), *International handbook of practice-based performance management* (pp. 25–44). Thousand Oaks, CA: Sage.

Newcomer, K. E., Hatry, H. P., & Wholey, J. S. (2015). Planning and designing useful evaluations. In K. E. Newcomer, H. P. Hatry, & J. S. Wholey (Eds.), *Handbook of practical program evaluation* (4th ed., pp. 7–35). Hoboken, NJ: Wiley.

New Hope Housing. (2017). *New Hope Housing Strategic Plan 2013–2018*. Retrieved from http://www.newhopehousing.org/about/strategic-plan/

New York City Opera. (2013). The people's opera: New York City Opera's 2013–2014 season. *Kickstarter.* Retrieved from http://www.kickstarter.com/projects/1551842735/the-peoples-opera-new-york-city-operas-2013-2014-s

Nilsson, W., & Paddock, T. (2014, Winter). Social innovation from the inside out. *Stanford Social Innovation Review, 12*(1), 46–52.

Nobbie, P. D., & Brudney, J. L. (2003, December). Testing the implementation, board performance, and organizational effectiveness of the policy governance model in nonprofit boards of directors. *Nonprofit and Voluntary Sector Quarterly, 32*(4), 571–595.

Nolo. (2017). *Sexual orientation discrimination: Your rights*. Retrieved from http://www.nolo.com/legal-encyclopedia/sexual-orientation-discrimination-rights-29541.html

Nonprofit Academic Centers Council. (2018). [Website]. Retrieved from http://www.nonprofit-academic-centers-council.org/

Nonprofit Integrity Act of 2004: Summary of key provisions. (2004). Retrieved from http://ag.ca.gov/charities/publications/nonprofit_integrity_act_nov04.pdf

Northouse, P. G. (2016). *Leadership: Theory and practice* (7th ed.). Thousand Oaks, CA: Sage.

N Street Village. (2011, November 2). *N Street Village wins board leadership award* [Press release]. Retrieved from https://www.nstreetvillage.org/n-street-village-wins-board-leadership-award/

N Street Village. (2014). *Keeping our promise: The 40th anniversary capital campaign for N Street Village* [Brochure]. Washington, DC: Author.

N Street Village. (n.d.-a). *About the village*. Retrieved from http://www.nstreetvillage.org/about-the-village/

N Street Village. (n.d.-b). *July 1, 2015–June 30, 2016 annual report*. Retrieved from http://www.nstreetvillage.org/wp-content/uploads/2016/11/FY16-Annual-Report-FINAL.pdf

O'Donovan, D., & Flower, N. R. (2013, January 10). The strategic plan is dead. Long live strategy. *Stanford Social Innovation Review*. Retrieved from https://ssir.org/articles/entry/the_strategic_plan_is_dead._long_live_strategy

Ogden, T. (2008, July 21). Interview: United Way of America CEO Brian Gallagher. *Philanthropy Action*. Retrieved from http://philanthropyaction.com/articles/interview_united_way_of_america_ceo_brian_gallagher/

O'Neill, M. (2002). *Nonprofit nation: A new look at the third America*. San Francisco, CA: Jossey-Bass.

O'Neill, M. (2007, December). The future of nonprofit management education. *Nonprofit and Voluntary Sector Quarterly, 36*(4 Suppl.), 169S–176S.

O'Neil, M. (2014, November 16). An unexpected online success offers a blueprint for other nonprofits. *Chronicle of Philanthropy*. Retrieved from http://philanthropy.com/article/An-Unexpected-Online-Success/150023/

O'Neil, M. (2015a, September 28). $3-trillion U.N. development plan sets ambitious agenda for nonprofits. *Chronicle of Philanthropy*. Retrieved from https://philanthropy.com/article/3-Trillion-UN-Development/233451?cid= pt&utm_source=pt&utm_medium=en

O'Neil, M. (2015b, December 8). Americans' engagement with organizations wanes, report says. *Chronicle of Philanthropy*. Retrieved from https://www.philanthropy.com/article/Americans-Engagement-With/152055

O'Neil, M. (2017, December 15). Tax bill will not alter nonprofit nonpoliticking rule. *Chronicle of Philanthropy*. Retrieved from https://www.philanthropy.com/article/Nonprofits-Score-Rare-Victory/242065?cid=pt&utm_source=pt&utm_medium=en&elqTrackId=708cf2e4de2f4a048%E2%80%A6

Oostlander, J., Güntert, S. T., van Schie, S., & Wehner, T. (2014). Leadership and volunteer motivation: A study using self-determination theory. *Nonprofit and Voluntary Sector Quarterly, 43*(5), 869–889.

Osberg, S. R., & Martin, R. L. (2015, May). Two keys to sustainable social enterprise. *Harvard Business Review*. Retrieved from https://hbr.org/2015/05/two-keys-to-sustainable-social-enterprise

Oster, S. M. (1995). *Strategic management for nonprofit organizations*. New York, NY: Oxford University Press.

Oster, S. M., Massarsky, C. W., & Beinhacker, S. L. (Eds.). (2004). *Generating and sustaining nonprofit earned income*. San Francisco, CA: Jossey-Bass.

Ostrower, F., & Stone, M. M. (2010, September). Moving governance research forward: A contingency-based framework and data application. *Nonprofit and Voluntary Sector Quarterly, 39*(5), 901–924.

Ott, J. S. (2012). Perspectives on organizational governance: Some effects on government-nonprofit relations. In J. S. Ott & L. A. Dicke (Eds.), *The nature of the nonprofit sector* (2nd ed., pp. 249–256). Boulder, CO: Westview.

Ott, J. S., & Dicke, L. A. (Eds.). (2016). *The nature of the nonprofit sector* (3rd ed.). Boulder, CO: Westview.

Otterman, S. (2010, October 12). Lauded Harlem schools have their own problems. *New York Times*. Retrieved from http://www.nytimes.com/2010/10/13/education/13harlem.html?rref=collection%2Ftimestopic%2FCanada%2C%20Geoffrey&action=click&contentCollection=timestopics&region=stream&module=stream_unit&version=latest&contentPlacement=10&pgtype=collection

Overhead Myth. (2013). *Letter to the donors of America*. Retrieved from http://overheadmyth.com/letter-to-the-donors-of-america/

Page, A., & Katz, R. A. (2012, Fall). The truth about Ben & Jerry's. *Stanford Social Innovation Review, 10*(4), 39–43.

Pallotta, D. (2010). *Uncharitable: How restraints on nonprofits undermine their potential*. Lebanon, NH: Tufts University Press.

Pallotta, D. (2013). The way we think about charity is dead wrong. *TED Talk*. Retrieved from http://www.ted.com/talks/dan_pallotta_the_way_we_think_about_charity_is_dead_wrong?language=en

Pandey, S., Kim, M., & Pandey, S. K. (2017, Spring). Do mission statements matter for nonprofit performance? *Nonprofit Management and Leadership, 27*(3), 389–410.

Panepento, P. (2012, February 1). Social media fuel debate as big charity cuts off Planned Parenthood aid. *Chronicle of Philanthropy*. Retrieved from https://www.philanthropy.com/article/Social-Media-Fuel-Debate-as-a/227157

Pasquarelli, A. (2017, October 19). Bring it: The Girl Scouts are not worried about the Boy Scouts. *AdAge*. Retrieved from http://adage.com/article/cmo-strategy/girl-scouts-boy-scouts/310950/

Paton, R. (2003). *Managing and measuring social enterprises*. Thousand Oaks, CA: Sage.

Paton, R. (2007). Fundraising as marketing: Half a truth is better than nothing. In J. Mordaunt & R. Paton (Eds.), *Thoughtful fundraising: Concepts, issues, and perspectives* (pp. 29–37). New York, NY: Routledge.

Payton, R. L. (1988). *Philanthropy: Voluntary action for the public good*. New York, NY: Macmillan.

Pekkanen, R. J., & Smith, S. R. (2014). Nonprofit advocacy: Definitions and concepts. In R. J. Pekkanen, S. R. Smith, & Y. Tsujinaka (Eds.), *Nonprofits and advocacy: Engaging community and government in an era of retrenchment* (pp. 1–20). Baltimore, MD: Johns Hopkins University Press.

Peloza, J., & Steel, P. (2005). The price elasticities of charitable contributions: A meta-analysis. *Journal of Public Policy & Marketing, 24*, 260–272.

Peng, S., Pandey, S. K., & Pandey, S. (2015, February 16). Is there a nonprofit advantage? Examining the impact of institutional context on individual–organizational value congruence. *Public Administration Review*. Retrieved from http://onlinelibrary.wiley.com/doi/10.1111/puar.12357/pdf

Penn, S. (2015, June 9). Our cross to bear. *Huffington Post*. Retrieved from http://www.huffingtonpost.com/sean-penn/haiti-red-cross_b_7548084.html

Peregrine, M. (2012, February 19). Steps charity leaders can take to avoid "getting Komened." *Chronicle of Philanthropy*. Retrieved from http://philanthropy.com/article/article-content/130829/

Peregrine, M. (2013, May 16). Hershey Trust settlement shows what matters on board duties. *Chronicle of Philanthropy*. Retrieved from https://www.philanthropy.com/article/Hershey-Trust-Settlement-Shows/154841

Peregrine, M. (2015, June 23). Sweet Briar's remarkable reopening has lessons for all nonprofits. *Chronicle of Philanthropy*. Retrieved from https://www.philanthropy.com/article/Opinion-Sweet-Briar-s/231101

Perry, S. (2014, April 7). Despite attempts to boost volunteerism, rate hits a new low. *Chronicle of Philanthropy*. Retrieved from https://www.philanthropy.com/article/Despite-Attempts-to-Boost/153329

Peters, T. J., & Waterman, R. H. (1982). *In search of excellence*. New York, NY: Harper & Row.

Pettijohn, S. L. (2013). *Federal government contracts and grants for nonprofits* (Brief 01). Washington, DC: Urban Institute. Retrieved from https://www.urban.org/sites/default/files/publication/23671/412832-Federal-Government-Contracts-and-Grants-for-Nonprofits.PDF

Pettijohn, S. L., & Boris, E. T. (2013). *Contracts and grants between nonprofits and government*. Washington, DC: Urban Institute. Retrieved from https://www.urban.org/sites/default/files/publication/24256/412968-Contracts-and-Grants-between-Nonprofits-and-Government.PDF

Pfeffer, J. (2003). Introduction to the classic edition. In *External control of organizations: A resource dependence perspective* (Classic ed.). Palo Alto, CA: Stanford University Press.

Pfeffer, J., & Salancik, G. R. (1978). *The external control of organizations: A resource dependence perspective*. New York, NY: Harper & Row.

Pham, T. (2015). *A look at DC public charter school finances: Revenue and spending per student*. Washington, DC: Center for Budget and Policy Priorities/DC Fiscal Policy Institute. Retrieved from http://www.dcfpi.org/wp-content/uploads/2015/08/8.5.15-Revenue-and-Spending-Per-Student-TP-Final.pdf

Phillips, D. (2016a, January 27). Wounded Warrior Project spends lavishly on itself, insiders say. *New York Times*. Retrieved from https://www.nytimes.com/2016/01/28/us/wounded-warrior-project-spends-lavishly-on-itself-ex-employees-say.html

Phillips, D. (2016b, March 11). After complaints on Wounded Warrior Project, pressure from donors. *New York Times.* Retrieved from https://www.nytimes.com/2016/03/12/us/after-complaints-on-wounded-warrior-project-pressure-from-donors.html

Phills, J. A., Jr. (2005). *Integrating mission and strategy for nonprofit organizations.* New York, NY: Oxford University Press.

Phills, J. A., Jr., & Chang, V. (2005, Spring). The price of commercial success. *Stanford Social Innovation Review, 65–72.* Retrieved from http://www.ssireview.org/articles/entry/the_price_of_commercial_success

Phills, J. A., Jr., Deiglmeier, K., & Miller, D. T. (2008, Fall). Rediscovering social innovation. *Stanford Social Innovation Review.* Retrieved from http://www.ssireview.org/articles/entry/rediscovering_social_innovation/

Pidgeon, W. P., Jr. (2004). *The not-for-profit CEO: How to attain and retain the corner office.* Hoboken, NJ: Wiley.

Pierce, J. (2004). Habitat founder and board disagree on his retirement date. *Christian Century, 121*(20), 15.

Pioneer Human Services. (2017). *Manufacturing & assembly.* Retrieved from http://pioneerhumanservices.org/business/manufacturing/manufacturing-assembly/

Pogrebin, R. (2009, June 17). City Opera tries to hold off the ultimate finale. *New York Times.* Retrieved from http://www.nytimes.com/2009/06/18/arts/music/18city.html

Poiner, J. (2015, March 15). Is a boarding school for at-risk youth coming to Ohio? *Ohio Gadfly Daily.* Retrieved from https://edexcellence.net/articles/is-a-boarding-school-for-at-risk-youth-coming-to-ohio

Poister, T. H. (2015). Monitoring program outcomes. In K. E. Newcomer, H. P. Hatry, & J. S. Wholey (Eds.), *Handbook of practical program evaluation* (4th ed., pp. 108–136). San Francisco, CA: Jossey-Bass.

Poister, T. H., Aristigueta, M. P., & Hall, J. L. (2015). *Managing and measuring performance in public and nonprofit organizations* (2nd ed.). San Francisco, CA: Jossey-Bass.

Politically prominent Philadelphian accused of charity fraud. (2016, January 29). *Chronicle of Philanthropy.* Retrieved from https://www.philanthropy.com/article/Politically-Prominent/235092

Pollack, A. (2014, November 19). Deal by Cystic Fibrosis Foundation raises cash and some concern. *New York Times.* Retrieved from http://www.nytimes.com/2014/11/19/business/for-cystic-fibrosis-foundation-venture-yields-windfall-in-hope-and-cash.html?_r=0

Porter, M. E., & Kramer, M. R. (2011, January). Creating shared value. *Harvard Business Review.* Retrieved from https://hbr.org/2011/01/the-big-idea-creating-shared-value

Powell, W. W., & DiMaggio, P. J. (1991). *The new institutionalism in organizational analysis.* Chicago, IL: University of Chicago Press.

Preston, C. (2010, January 15). Social media aid efforts to help Haiti earthquake victims. *Chronicle of Philanthropy.* Retrieved from http://philanthropy.com/article/Social-Media-Aid-Efforts-to/63566/

Preston, C., & Wallace, N. (2011, January 6). Charities report slow progress in Haiti, despite $1.4 billion raised in a year. *Chronicle of Philanthropy.* Retrieved from http://philanthropy.com/article/Charities-Face-Struggles-to/125847/

A primer on risk management. (2007). Windsor-Salem, NC: HandsOn Northwest North Carolina. Retrieved from http://www.handsonnwnc.org/express/nccenteronriskmanagement.pdf

Prince, R. A., & File, K. M. (1994). *The seven faces of philanthropy.* San Francisco, CA: Jossey-Bass.

Public Relations Society of America. (n.d.). *About public relations.* Retrieved from http://www.prsa.org/AboutPRSA/PublicRelationsDefined/

Putnam, R. (1995, January). Bowling alone: America's declining social capital. *Journal of Democracy, 6*(1), 65–78.

Pynes, J. E. (2013). *Human resources management for public and nonprofit organizations* (4th ed.). San Francisco, CA: Jossey-Bass.

Q&A with Share Our Strength founder Billy Shore. (2015, September 9). *Williams Sonoma Taste.* Retrieved from http://blog.williams-sonoma.com/qa-with-share-our-strength-founder-billy-shore/

Rainey, H. G. (2014). *Understanding and managing public organizations* (5th ed.). San Francisco, CA: Jossey-Bass.

Raymond, J. (2009, October 13). Seeing red in pink products: One woman's fight against breast cancer consumerism. *Newsweek.* Retrieved from http://www.newsweek.com/seeing-red-pink-products-one-womans-fight-against-breast-cancer-consumerism-222566

Raynor, J. (2014, November 19). The return of capacity building. *Stanford Social Innovation Review.* Retrieved from http://www.ssireview.org/blog/entry/the_return_of_capacity_building

Regenovich, D. (2016). Establishing a planned giving program. In E. R. Tempel, T. L. Seiler, & D. F. Burlingame (Eds.), *Achieving excellence in fundraising* (4th ed., 259–290). San Francisco, CA: Jossey-Bass.

Rehberg, W. (2005, June). Altruistic individualists: Motivations for international volunteering among young adults in Switzerland. *Voluntas: International Journal of Voluntary and Nonprofit Organizations, 16*(2), 109–122.

Renz, D. O., & Herman, R. D. (2016). Understanding nonprofit effectiveness. In D. O. Renz & Associates (Eds.), *The Jossey-Bass handbook of nonprofit leadership and management.* (4th ed., pp. 274–292). Hoboken, NJ: Wiley.

Rich, C. (2014, October 15). 10 reasons for nonprofits to move to a revenue-driven model. *Forbes.* Retrieved from http://www.forbes.com/sites/yec/2014/10/14/10-reasons-for-nonprofits-to-move-to-a-revenue-driven-model/

Ridley-Duff, R., & Bull, M. (2016). *Understanding social enterprise: Theory and practice* (2nd ed.). London: Sage.

Robbins, K. C. (2012). The nonprofit sector in historical perspective: Traditions of philanthropy in the West. In J. S. Ott & L. A. Dicke (Eds.), *The nature of the nonprofit sector* (2nd ed., pp. 88–107). Boulder, CO: Westview.

Rockefeller Foundation gives $500,000 to develop "social" stock market. (2008, March 24). *Chronicle of Philanthropy*. Retrieved from http://philanthropy.com/blogPost/Rockefeller-Foundation-Gives/14716/

Rogers, J. L. (2006, April 16). Foundations are burning out charity CEOs. *Chronicle of Philanthropy, 18*(10), 45–46.

Romero, S., & Lacey, M. (2010, January 12). Fierce quake devastates Haitian capital. *New York Times*. Retrieved from http://www.nytimes.com/2010/01/13/world/americas/13haiti.html?_r=1

Ronquillo, J. (n.d.). Aspire: Building partnerships through social entrepreneurship and empowerment (E-case). *Hubert Project*. Retrieved from http://www.hubertproject.org/hubert-material/322/

Rose-Ackerman, S. (1996). Altruism, nonprofits and economic theory. *Journal of Economic Literature, 34*, 701–728.

Routhieaux, R. L. (2015). Shared leadership and its implications for nonprofit leadership. *Journal of Nonprofit Education and Leadership, 5*(3), 139–152.

Rudel, J. (2011, June 6). The people's opera, in peril. *New York Times*. Retrieved from http://www.nytimes.com/2011/06/07/opinion/07rudel.html

Ruiz, R. R. (2015, May 19). 4 cancer charities are accused of fraud. *New York Times*. Retrieved from http://www.nytimes.com/2015/05/20/business/4-cancer-charities-accused-in-ftc-fraud-case.html?_r=0

Rural Assistance Center. (2014). [Website]. *Rural Health Information Hub*. Retrieved from http://www.raconline.org/topics/federally-qualified-health-centers

Ryan, W. P., Chait, R. P., & Taylor, B. E. (2013, January 2). Problem boards or board problem? *Nonprofit Quarterly*. Retrieved from https://nonprofitquarterly.org/2017/05/08/problem-boards-or-board-problem/

Sabeti, H. (with the Fourth Sector Network Concept Working Group). (2009, September 9). *The emerging fourth sector: Executive summary*. Washington, DC: Aspen Institute. Retrieved from http://www.aspeninstitute.org/publications/emerging-fourth-sector-executive-summary

Sagawa, S., & Segal, E. (2000). *Common interest, common good: Creating value through business and social sector partnerships*. Cambridge, MA: Harvard Business School Press.

Salamon, L. M. (1999). *America's nonprofit sector: A primer* (2nd ed.). New York, NY: Foundation Center.

Salamon, L. M. (2012a). *America's nonprofit sector: A primer* (3rd ed.). New York, NY: Foundation Center.

Salamon, L. M. (2012b). *The state of nonprofit America* (2nd ed.). Washington, DC: Brookings Institution.

Salamon, L. (2014). The revolution on the frontiers of philanthropy: An introduction. In L. M. Solomon (Ed.), *The new frontiers of philanthropy* (pp. 3–88). New York, NY: Oxford University Press.

Salamon, L. M., Sokolowski, S. W., & Associates. (2004). *Global civil society: Dimensions of the nonprofit sector* (Vol. 2). Bloomfield, CT: Kumarian Press.

Sander, T. H., & Putnam, R. D. (2005, September 10). September 11 as civics lesson. *Washington Post*, p. A23.

Sandoval, T. (2016, August 17). Wounded Warrior sticks with accounting rules that drew fire. *Chronicle of Philanthropy*. Retrieved from https://www.philanthropy.com/article/Wounded-Warrior-Sticks-With/237487

Sandoval, T. (2017, May 24). Wounded Warrior Project chided in Senate report. *Chronicle of Philanthropy*. Retrieved from https://www.philanthropy.com/article/Wounded-Warrior-Project-Chided/240158

Sargeant, A. (2005). *Marketing management for nonprofit organizations*. New York, NY: Oxford University Press.

Sataline, S. (2011, October 16). From mergers that didn't stick, lessons emerge for other charities. *Chronicle of Philanthropy*. Retrieved from http://philanthropy.com/article/Avoiding-Messy-Breakups-/129370/

Sawhill, J., & Williamson, D. (2001). Measuring what matters most in nonprofits. *McKinsey Quarterly, 2001*(2), 16–25.

Schadler, B. H. (2015). *The connection: Strategies for creating and operating 501(c)(3)s, 501(c)(4)s and political organizations*. (3rd ed.). Washington, DC: Alliance for Justice.

Schambra, W. (2013, April 5). Charity Navigator 3.0: The empirical empire's death star? *Nonprofit Quarterly*. Retrieved from https://nonprofitquarterly.org/2013/04/05/charity-navigator-3-0-the-empirical-empire-s-death-star/

Schein, E. H. (2016). *Organizational culture and leadership: A dynamic view* (5th ed.). San Francisco, CA: Jossey-Bass.

Schervish, P. G. (2009). Beyond self-interest and altruism: Care as mutual nourishment. In *Conversations on Philanthropy* (Vol. 6, pp. 33–44). Alexandria, VA: DonorsTrust. Retrieved from http://www.conversationsonphilanthropy.org/wp-content/uploads/2009_entire_journal.pdf

Schervish, P. G., & Havens, J. J. (2001). The new physics of philanthropy: The supply-side vectors of charitable giving—Part 2: The spiritual side of the supply side. *CASE International Journal of Educational Advancement*, 2(3), 221–241.

Schmidt, S. (2018, May 9). Mormon Church breaks all ties with Boy Scouts, ending 100-year relationship. *Washington Post*. Retrieved from https://www.washingtonpost.com/news/morning-mix/wp/2018/05/09/mormon-church-breaks-all-ties-with-boy-scouts-ending-100-year-relationship/?utm_term=.cab7e66aeafe

Schwinn, E. (2007, May 17). Seven American Lung Association affiliates sever ties with national charity. *Chronicle of Philanthropy*. Retrieved from http://philanthropy.com/article/Seven-American-Lung-Associa/55124/

Schwinn, E. (2008, May 15). United Way of America outlines 10-year plan. *Chronicle of Philanthropy*. Retrieved from https://philanthropy.com/article/United-Way-of-America-Outlines/163103

Sciolino, E. (2001a, May 10). Smithsonian is promised $38 million, with strings. *New York Times,* p. A20.

Sciolino, E. (2001b, May 26). Smithsonian group criticizes official on donor contract. *New York Times,* p. A8.

Sciolino, E. (2001c, May 30). Citing differences, director of a Smithsonian museum resigns. *New York Times,* p. A20.

Scott, W. R. (1995). *Institutions and organizations*. Thousand Oaks, CA: Sage.

Scully, S. (2009, December 15). In Hershey's possible Cadbury bid, a school's fate. *Time*. Retrieved from http://www.time.com/time/printout/0,8816,1947492,00.html

SEED Foundation. (2017a). *History*. Retrieved from https://www.seedfoundation.com/history/

SEED Foundation. (2017b). *Our results*. Retrieved from https://www.seedfoundation.com/about/

Seelos, C., & Mair, J. (2012a, January). *What determines the capacity for continuous innovation in social sector organizations* (Rockefeller Foundation report). Stanford, CA: Stanford University Center on Philanthropy and Civil Society. Retrieved from http://www.christianseelos.com/capacity-for-continuous-innovation_PACS_31Jan2012_Final.pdf

Seelos, C., & Mair, J. (2012b, Fall). Innovation is not the Holy Grail. *Stanford Social Innovation Review*. Retrieved from https://ssir.org/articles/entry/innovation_is_not_the_holy_grail

Segal, D. (2016, July 30). Back-stabbing and threats of a 'suicide parachute' at Hershey. *New York Times*. Retrieved from https://www.nytimes.com/2016/07/31/business/dealbook/back-stabbing-and-threats-of-a-suicide-parachute-at-hershey.html

Seiler, T. L. (2016). Plan to succeed. In E. R. Tempel, T. L. Seiler, & D. F. Burlingame (Eds.), *Achieving excellence in fund raising* (4th ed., pp. 27–36). San Francisco, CA: Jossey-Bass.

Senge, P. M. (1990). *The fifth discipline: The art and practice of the learning organization*. New York, NY: Doubleday.

Senge, P. M. (1994). *The fifth discipline fieldbook: Strategies and tools for building a learning organization*. New York, NY: Currency.

Seo, M. G., Barrett, L. F., & Bartunek, J. M. (2004, July). The role of affective experience in work motivation. *Academy of Management Review*, 29(3), 423–439.

Sessa-Hawkins, M. (2015, September 9). Rupert Murdoch's 21st Century Fox buys National Geographic media. *PBS Newshour/The Rundown*. Accessed from http://www.pbs.org/newshour/rundown/national-geographic-fox-enter-profit-venture/

Seymour, H. J. (1966). *Designs for fund-raising*. New York, NY: McGraw-Hill.

Shapiro, T. R. (2016, April 8). For 4-H, a campaign to reach beyond corn fields and into cities. *Washington Post*. Retrieved from https://www.washingtonpost.com/local/education/for-4-h-a-campaign-to-reach-beyond-corn-fields-and-into-cities/2016/04/08/78e15436-fdae-11e5-9140-e61d062438bb_story.html?utm_term=.35a344b5a92a

Share Our Strength. (2011). *Facts on childhood hunger*. Retrieved from https://www.nokidhungry.org/sites/default/files/2011-childhood-hunger-facts.pdf

Share Our Strength. (2014). *Share Our Strength annual report 2013*. Retrieved from https://www.nokidhungry.org/annualreports/annual-2014/Annual-Report-2013.pdf

Share Our Strength. (2017). *About Share Our Strength*. Retrieved from https://www.nokidhungry.org/about-us

Share Our Strength. (n.d.). *No Kid Hungry 2016: A voice for kids: Share Our Strength's annual report*. Retrieved from https://www.nokidhungry.org/sites/default/files/2017-12/Annual-Report-2016.pdf

Share Our Strength Center for Best Practices. (n.d.). *No Kid Hungry case study: The partnership to end childhood hunger in Maryland*. Retrieved from http://bestpractices.nokidhungry.org/sites/default/files/resources/NKH%20Maryland%20Case%20Study.pdf

Shell, M. (2017, July 11). Why charities shouldn't start ignoring the ban on partisan politicking. *Chronicle of Philanthropy*. retrieved from https://www.philanthropy.com/article/Charities-Dont-Forget-About/240573

Shin, A. (2013, July 21). Gentrification in overdrive on 14th Street. *Washington Post*. Retrieved from http://www.washingtonpost.com/…entrification-in-overdrive-on-14th-street/2013/07/21/d07d344e-ea5b-11e2-a301-ea5a8116d211_story.html

Shin, S., & Kleiner, B. H. (2003). How to manage unpaid volunteers in organisations. *Management Research News*, 25(2/3/4), 63–71.

Shogren, E. (2011). BP: A textbook example of how not to handle PR. *NPR Morning Edition*. Retrieved from http://www.npr.org/2011/04/21/135575238/bp-a-textbook-example-of-how-not-to-handle-pr

Shoham, A., Ruvio, A., Vigoda-Gadot, E., & Schwabsky, N. (2006, September).

Market orientations in the nonprofit and voluntary sector: A meta-analysis of their relationships with organizational performance. *Nonprofit and Voluntary Sector Quarterly, 35*(3), 453–476.

Shore, B. (1999). *The cathedral within.* New York, NY: Random House.

Shore, B. (2013, September 24). A simple question but so hard to answer. *Chronicle of Philanthropy.* Retrieved from http://philanthropy.com/blogs/leading/2013/09/24/a-simple-question-but-so-hard-to-answer-what-is-success/

Shore, B., Hammond, D., & Celep, A. (2013, Fall). When good is not good enough. *Stanford Social Innovation Review.* Retrieved from http://www.ssireview.org/articles/entry/when_good_is_not_good_enough

Shrestha, L. B. (2006, August 16). *Life expectancy in the United States.* Washington DC: Congressional Research Service Report for Congress. Retrieved from https://www.everycrsreport.com/files/20060816_RL32792_8a7c7fa5bfd3890526d12d42c6df39faa5c67cfc.pdf

Silverman, L., & Taliento, L. (2006, Summer). What business execs don't know—but should—about nonprofits. *Stanford Social Innovation Review, 4*(2), 36–43.

Simmons, A. M. (2016, March 8). Haiti earthquake: $13.5 billion in donations, but is any of it working? *Los Angeles Times.* Retrieved from http://www.latimes.com/world/global-development/la-fg-global-haiti-recovery-story.html

Simon, J. G. (1987). Research on philanthropy. In K. W. Thompson (Ed.), *Philanthropy: Private means, public ends* (Vol. 4, pp. 67–87). Lanham, MD: University Press of America.

Simon, J. S. (2001). *The 5 stages of nonprofit organizations.* St. Paul, MN: Amherst H. Wilder Foundation.

Simonin, B., Samali, M., Zohdy, N., & Laidler-Kylander, N. (2016, May 19). Why and how do nonprofits work together? *Philanthropy News*

Digest, retrieved from http://philanthropynewsdigest.org/columns/the-sustainable-nonprofit/why-and-how-do-nonprofits-work-together

Sisco, H. F. (2012). Nonprofit in crisis: An examination of the applicability of situational crisis communication theory. *Journal of Public Relations Research, 24,* 1–17.

Skinner, B. F. (1953). *Science and human behavior.* New York, NY: Free Press.

Small, L. M. (2001, May 31). Mr. Smithson's was the first. *Washington Post,* p. A25.

Small, V. (2012, August 19). Charity Works: A match made in a recession. *Washington Post.* Retrieved from http://www.washingtonpost.com/...talbusiness/charity-works-a-match-made-in-a-recession/2012/08/19/333b6e36-e7db-11e1-936a-b801f1abab19_story.html

Smiley, D. (2014, January 28). SEED School of Miami to open as Florida's first public boarding school. *Miami Herald.* Retrieved from http://www.miamiherald.com/news/local/education/article1959729.html

Smith, D. H. (1991). Four sectors or five? Retaining the membership-benefit sector. *Nonprofit and Voluntary Sector Quarterly, 20*(2), 137–150.

Smith, S. R. (2012, September). Changing government policy and its implications for nonprofit management education. *Nonprofit Management and Leadership, 23*(1), 29–41.

Smith, S. R. (2016). Managing the challenges of government contracts. In D. O. Renz & Associates (Eds.), *The Jossey-Bass handbook of nonprofit leadership and management* (4th ed., pp. 536–561). Hoboken, NJ: Jossey-Bass.

Smith, S. R. (2017). Cross-sector nonprofit-government financing. In E. T. Boris & C. E. Steuerle (Eds.), *Nonprofits and government: Collaboration and conflict* (3rd ed., pp. 103–132). Lanham, MD: Rowman & Littlefield/Urban Institute Press.

Smithsonian Institution. (n.d.). *Working at the Smithsonian.* Retrieved from https://www.si.edu/OHR/workingsi_SE

Social Enterprise Alliance. (2017). *What is social enterprise?* Retrieved from https://socialenterprise.us/about/social-enterprise/

Solomon, D. S. (2016, July 5). Another Hershey deal may come unwrapped. Maybe it should. *New York Times.* Retrieved from https://www.nytimes.com/2016/07/06/business/dealbook/another-hershey-deal-may-come-unwrapped-maybe-it-should.html?_r=0

Sorting nonprofit risk and uncertainty [Special issue]. (2017, Summer). *Nonprofit Quarterly, 24*(2). Retrieved from https://nonprofitquarterly.org/2017/07/25/sorting-nonprofit-risk-and-uncertainty/

Sowa, J. E. (2009, December). The collaboration decision in nonprofit organizations: Views from the front line. *Nonprofit and Voluntary Sector Quarterly, 38*(6), 1003–1025.

Speckbacher, G. (2013, October). The use of incentives in nonprofit organizations. *Nonprofit and Voluntary Sector Quarterly, 42*(5), 1006–1025.

Standards for Excellence Institute. (2014). Standards for excellence®: An ethics and accountability code for the nonprofit sector (2nd ed.). Retrieved from http://standardsforexcellence.org/home-2/code/

Starr, K. (2012a, September 18). The eight-word mission statement: Don't settle for more. *Stanford Social Innovation Review.* Retrieved from https://ssir.org/articles/entry/the_eight_word_mission_statement

Starr, K. (2012b, December 11). Premature incorporation: Don't let it happen to you. *Stanford Social Innovation Review.* Retrieved from http://www.ssireview.org/blog/entry/premature_incorporation

State by state status of legislation. (2017). *Benefit Corporation.* Retrieved from http://benefitcorp.net/policymakers/state-by-state-status

Stebbins, R. A. (2009). Would you volunteer? *Social Science and Public Policy*, *46*, 155–159.

Steel, P., & Konig, C. (2006). Integrating theories of motivation. *Academy of Management Review*, *31*(4), 889–913.

Stein, L. (2016, April 11). Not just 'cows and plows': Century old 4-H rebrands. *Advertising Age*. Retrieved from http://adage.com/article/agency-news/4-h-rebrands-100-years-emphasize-stem-programs/303492/

Steiss, A. W. (2003). *Strategic management for public and nonprofit organizations*. New York, NY: Marcel Dekker.

Stelter, N. (2017, December 23). *Tax reform and charitable giving implications* (Web log comment). Retrieved from https://blog.stelter.com/2017/12/22/tax-reform-and-charitable-giving-implications/

Stengel, G. (2013, April 9). Nonprofit collaborations: Why teaming up can make sense. *Forbes*. Retrieved from https://www.forbes.com/sites/geristengel/2013/04/09/nonprofit-collaborations-why-teaming-up-can-make-sense/#3119e89c3985

Stephenson, A. (2013, Fall). Organizational identity and the rebranding of the YMCA. *Sociological Viewpoints*, *29*(1), 101–119.

Stern, M. (2011, April 2). *Real or rogue charity? Private health clubs vs. the YMCA, 1970–2010*. Paper presented to the Business History Conference annual meeting, St. Louis, MO. Retrieved from http://www.thebhc.org/sites/default/files/stern.pdf

Stevens, S. K. (2001). *Nonprofit lifecycles: Stage-based wisdom for nonprofit capacity*. Long Lake, MN: Stagewise Enterprises.

Stewart, J. B. (2013, October 11). A ransacked endowment at New York City Opera. *New York Times*. Retrieved from http://www.nytimes.com/2013/10/12/business/ransacking-the-endowment-at-new-york-city-opera.html?pagewanted=3&_r=0

Stiffman, E. (2016a, March 31). Nonprofit experts fear Dan Pallotta's efforts to defend charities' spending. *Chronicle of Philanthropy*. Retrieved from https://www.philanthropy.com/article/Nonprofit-Experts-Fear-Dan/235913

Stiffman, E. (2016b, May 27). 27% of groups scored by Charity Navigator will see ratings change. *Chronicle of Philanthropy*. Retrieved from https://www.philanthropy.com/article/27-of-Groups-Scored-by/236647

Stodgill, R. M. (1948). Personal factors associated with leadership: A survey of the literature. *Journal of Psychology*, *25*, 35–71.

Stolberg, G. S. (2015, June 23). Sweet Briar College is saved but is not yet in the clear. *New York Times*. Retrieved from https://www.nytimes.com/2015/06/24/us/sweet-briar-collegeis-saved-but-not-in-the-clear.html

Stone, P. C. (2016, August 5). Sweet Briar president: More than miracles needed to save small colleges. *Washington Post*. Retrieved from https://www.washingtonpost.com/news/grade-point/wp/2016/08/05/sweet-briar-president-pixie-dust-and-miracles-wont-save-small-colleges/?utm_term=.b54cdec7e27c

Strachan, M. (2015, April 28). Why did the NFL voluntarily give up its tax-exempt status? Experts weigh in. *Huffington Post*. Retrieved from http://www.huffingtonpost.com/2015/04/28/nfl-tax-exempt-status_n_7166020.html

Strauss, K. (2017, January 10). The 18 biggest charitable donations of 2016. *Forbes*. Retrieved from https://www.forbes.com/sites/karstenstrauss/2017/01/10/the-18-biggest-charitable-donations-of-2016/#72b5b0643abb

Strauss, V. (2017, June 14). Betsy DeVos delays 2 Obama-era rules designed to protect students from predatory for-profit colleges. *Washington Post*. Retrieved from https://www.washingtonpost.com/news/answer-sheet/wp/2017/06/14/betsy-devos-delays-2-obama-era-rules-designed-to-protect-students-from-predatory-for-profit-colleges/?utm_term=.a87a3177d04d

Stribling, S. (2014, June 17). *From the executive director: A "close-up" perspective* [Web log comment]. Retrieved from https://www.nstreetvillage.org/from-the-executive-director-a-close-up-perspective/

StriveTogether. (2017). *The network*. Retrieved from http://strivetogether.org/cradle-career-network

Strom, S. (2012, May 23). For Oreo, Cadbury, and Ritz, a new parent company. *New York Times*. Retrieved from http://www.nytimes.com/2012/05/24/business/mondelez-is-new-name-for-krafts-snack-foods-company.html

Stroup, S. S. (2012). *Borders among activists: International NGOs in the United States, Britain, and France*. Ithaca, NY: Cornell University Press.

Subaru of America. (2016, April 3). *Subaru of America partners with the National Park Foundation to celebrate National Park Service centennial* [Press release]. Retrieved from http://media.subaru.com/pressrelease/738/124/subaru-america-partners-national-park-foundation-celebrate-national

Sumariwalla, R. (1983). Preliminary observations in scope, size, and classification of the sector. In V. Hodgkinson (Ed.), *Working papers for the spring research forum: Since the Filer Commission* (pp. 433–449). Washington, DC: Independent Sector.

Svrluga, S. (2015, June 9). Va. Supreme Court says lower court erred in Sweet Briar case, sends it back, as advocates cheer. *Washington Post*. Retrieved from https://www.washingtonpost.com/news/grade-point/wp/2015/06/09/va-supreme-court-says-lower-court-erred-in-sweet-briar-case-sends-it-back-as-advocates-cheer/?utm_term=.aa0f7df584ce

Svrluga, S. (2016, July 12). A year after Sweet Briar was saved from closing, school leaders celebrate fundraising growth. *Washington Post*. Retrieved from https://www.washingtonpost.com/news/grade-point/wp/2016/07/12/a-year-after-sweet-briar-was-saved-from-closing-school-leaders-celebrate-fundraising-growth/?utm_term=.80e4504801c0

Tadena, N. (2016, April 11). 4-H looks to modernize brand beyond rural roots. *Wall Street Journal*. Retrieved from https://www.wsj.com/articles/4-h-looks-to-modernize-brand-beyond-rural-roots-1460402845

Taliento, L., Law, J., & Callanan, L. (2011). Introduction. In M. Morino, *Leap of reason* (pp. xvii–xxiii). Washington, DC: Venture Philanthropy Partners.

Tanguy, J., & Terry, F. (1999, December 12). *On humanitarian responsibility*. Retrieved from http://www.doctorswithoutborders.org/news-stories/op-ed/humanitarian-responsibility

Tatian, P. A. (2016, March 14). *Performance measurement to evaluation*. Washington, DC: Urban Institute. Retrieved from https://www.urban.org/research/publication/performance-measurement-evaluation-0

Tax Policy Center. (2016). *Key elements of the U.S. tax system*. Retrieved from http://www.taxpolicycenter.org/briefing-book/what-entities-are-tax-exempt-charitable-activities

Taylor, A. (2017, May 17). Hacking nonprofit collaboration. *Stanford Social Innovation Review*. Retrieved from https://ssir.org/articles/entry/hacking_nonprofit_collaboration

Taylor, B. E., Chait, R. P., & Holland, R. P. (1999). The new work of the nonprofit board. In *Harvard Business Review on nonprofits* (pp. 53–76). Boston, MA: Harvard Business School Press.

Teach for America. (2017). *About us*. Retrieved from https://www.teachforamerica.org/about-us

Thomas, A. (2017, April). *Two steps back: Haiti still reeling from Hurricane Matthew*. Washington, DC: Refugees International. Retrieved from https://static1.squarespace.

com/static/506c8ea1e4b01d9450dd53f5/t/58e56896414fb5affd68e857/1491429534724/2017.4.6+Haiti.pdf

Thomas, D. C. (2002). *Essentials of international management*. Thousand Oaks, CA: Sage.

Thompson, B. (2002, January 20). History for sale. *Washington Post*, pp. 14–22, 25–29.

3 causes the Y hopes will attract new members and new money. (2014, April 20). *Chronicle of Philanthropy*. Retrieved from https://philanthropy.com/article/3-Causes-the-Y-Hopes-Will/153255

Tomassoni, T. (2011, November 1). Two D.C. women's shelters to merge. *Washington Post*. Retrieved from http://www.washingtonpost.com/local/two-dc-womens-shelters-merge/2011/10/27/gIQAPhBddM_story.html

Tommasini, A. (2015, March 10). Julius Rudel gala benefits City Opera revival hopes. *New York Times*. Retrieved from http://www.nytimes.com/2015/03/11/arts/music/julius-rudel-gala-benefits-city-opera-revival-hopes.html?_r=0

Tough, P. (2008). *Whatever it takes*. New York, NY: Houghton Mifflin.

Trescott, J. (2006, December 16). Smithsonian deal with Showtime passes muster. *Washington Post*, p. C01.

Triner, S. (2013). Australia and New Zealand. In P. Cagney & B. Ross, *Global fundraising: How the world is changing the rules of philanthropy* (pp. 135–152). Hoboken, NJ: Wiley.

Trower, C. A. (2013). *The practitioner's guide to governance as leadership: Building high-performance nonprofit boards*. San Francisco, CA: Jossey-Bass.

Tugend, A. (2016, January 23). The Y embarks on its first national advertising campaign. *New York Times*. Retrieved from https://www.nytimes.com/2016/01/25/business/media/the-y-embarks-on-its-first-national-advertising-campaign.html

Union of International Associations. (2017). *The yearbook of international*

organizations. Retrieved from http://www.uia.org/yearbook

United Nations. (n.d.). *UN and civil society*. Retrieved from http://www.un.org/en/civilsociety/index.shtml

United Way of America. (1996). *Measuring program outcomes: A practical approach*. Alexandria, VA: Author.

United Way of America. (n.d.-a) *Our history*. Retrieved from https://www.unitedway.org/about/history

United Way of America. (n.d.-b). *Goals for the common good: The United Way challenge to America*. https://s3.amazonaws.com/uww.assets/site/Goals_for_the_Common_Good.pdf

University of Oxford. (2017). *Oxford Thinking: The campaign for the University of Oxford*. Retrieved from https://www.campaign.ox.ac.uk/the-campaign

Uo, M. T. (2013). Japan. In P. Cagney & B. Ross, *Global fundraising: How the world is changing the rules of philanthropy* (pp. 43–58). Hoboken, NJ: Wiley.

Van Til, J. (1988). *Mapping the third sector: Voluntarism in a changing social economy*. New York, NY: Foundation Center.

Van Til, J. (1992). Foreword. In R. A. Lohmann, *The commons: New perspectives on nonprofit organizations, voluntary action and philanthropy* (pp. iv–v). Retrieved from http://dlc.dlib.indiana.edu/dlc/bitstream/handle/10535/5310/TheCommons(Lohmann,1992).pdf?sequence=1&isAllowed=y

Van Til, J. (2000). *Growing civil society: From nonprofit sector to third space*. Bloomington/Indianapolis: Indiana University Press.

Voice of America. (2015, January 12). *Haiti still struggling 5 years after earthquake*. Retrieved from http://www.voanews.com/content/five-years-after-the-haitian-earthquake/2594607.html

Vroom, V. H. (1964). *Work and motivation*. New York, NY: Wiley.

Wachman, R. (2009, December 12). Hershey board and trust split over making bid for Cadbury. *The Guardian*. Retrieved from http://www.guardian.co.uk/business/2009/dec/13/hershey-trust-cadbury-bid

Wade, L. C. (2005). Settlement houses. In *The electronic encyclopedia of Chicago*. Chicago, IL: Historical Society. Retrieved from http://www.encyclopedia.chicagohistory.org/pages/1135.html

Wagner, J., Phillip, A., & Zauzmer, J. (2017, May 3). Trump to sign executive order making it easier for churches to support political candidates. *Washington Post*. Retrieved from https://www.washingtonpost.com/politics/trump-to-sign-executive-order-making-it-easier-for-churches-to-support-political-candidates/2017/05/03/a30294dc-3052-11e7-9dec-764dc781686f_story.html?utm_term=.47d5536ba92e

Wagner, L. (2004). Fundraising, culture, and the U.S. perspective. In L. Wagner & J. A. Galindo (Eds.), *Global perspectives on fundraising* (New Directions for Philanthropic Fundraising, No. 46; pp. 5–12). Hoboken, NJ: Wiley.

Wall, W. L. (1984, June 21). Companies change the ways they make charitable contributions. *Wall Street Journal*, pp. 1, 29.

Wallace, N. (2005, May 12). Bridging old divides. *Chronicle of Philanthropy*, 17(15), 31–34. Retrieved from http://philanthropy.com/article/Bridging-Old-Divides/56171/

Wallace, N. (2010a, March 7). Charity's "embedded" fund raisers work with local affiliates to secure big donations. *Chronicle of Philanthropy*. Retrieved from http://philanthropy.com/article/National-Charity-Embeds- F/64488/

Wallace, N. (2010b, May 25). Choosing wisely: The Nature Conservancy and BP. *Chronicle of Philanthropy*. Retrieved from https://philanthropy.com/article/Choosing-Wisely-the-Nature/193945

Wasserman, L. (2005). *Nonprofit collaboration & mergers: Finding the right fit. A resource guide for nonprofits.*

Milwaukee, WI: United Way of Greater Milwaukee.

Watson, M. R., & Abzug, R. (2016). Effective human resource management: Nonprofit staffing for the future. In D. O. Renz & Associates (Eds.), *The Jossey-Bass handbook of nonprofit leadership and management* (4th ed., pp. 597–638). San Francisco, CA: Jossey-Bass.

Weeks, L. (2015, June 2). How the YMCA helped shape America. *NPR*. Retrieved from http://www.npr.org/sections/npr-history-dept/2015/06/02/410532977/how-the-ymca-helped-shape-america

Weisbrod, B. A. (1975). Toward a theory of the voluntary non-profit sector in a three-sector economy. In E. S. Phelps (Ed.), *Altruism, morality, and economic theory* (pp. 171–195). New York, NY: Russell Sage.

Weisbrod, B. A. (1988). *The nonprofit economy*. Cambridge, MA: Harvard University Press.

Weisbrod, B. A. (2004, Winter). The pitfalls of profits. *Stanford Social Innovation Review*, 2(3), 40–48.

Weisenfeld, P. E. (n.d.). Successes and challenges of the Haiti earthquake response: The experience of USAID. *Emory International Law Review*. Retrieved from http://law.emory.edu/eilr/_documents/volumes/25/3/symposium/weisenfeld.pdf

Wei-Skillern, J., Austin, J. E., Leonard, H., & Stevenson, H. (2007). *Entrepreneurship in the social sector*. Thousand Oaks, CA: Sage.

Weisman, C., & Goldbaum, R. I. (2004). *Losing your executive director without losing your way*. San Francisco, CA: Jossey-Bass.

West, M. (2012a, February 2). Lessons from Hull House's collapse. *Chronicle of Philanthropy*. Retrieved from http://philanthropy.com/article/Lessons-From-Hull-House-s/130609/

West, M. (2012b, February 2). Some fear Hull House closure is an omen for struggling charities. *Chronicle of Philanthropy*. Retrieved from http://philanthropy.com/article/Collapse-of-Famous-Hull-House/130608/

West, M. (2012c, April 15). Red Cross makes shift to stabilize revenue and give local leaders a bigger voice. *Chronicle of Philanthropy*. Retrieved from http://philanthropy.com/article/Red-Cross-Gives-Local-Leaders/131508/

What is strategic communications? [Web log post]. (2011, March 16). *Institute for Dynamic Educational Advancement* Retrieved from http://www.idea.org/blog/2011/03/16/what-is-strategic-communications

White, G. B. (2015, December 3). Assessing Mark Zuckerberg's non-charity charity. *The Atlantic*. Retrieved from https://www.theatlantic.com/business/archive/2015/12/assessing-mark-zuckerbergs-non-charity-charity/418719/

Wilhelm, I. (2005, April 28). Fired Habitat founder establishes rival charity. *Chronicle of Philanthropy*, 17(4), 37.

Williams, G. (2006, September 28). A new report sheds light on nonprofit accountability practices. *Chronicle of Philanthropy*, 18(24), 59.

Witesman, E. M., & Fernandez, S. (2012, May 21). Government contacts with private organizations: Are there differences between nonprofits and for-profits? *Nonprofit and Voluntary Sector Quarterly*, 42(4), online first. Retrieved from https://doi.org/10.1177/0899764012442592

Wolf, T. (1999). *Managing a nonprofit organization in the twenty-first century*. New York, NY: Fireside.

Wolff, T. (2016, March 15). Ten places where collective impact gets it wrong. *Global Journal of Community Psychology Practice*, 7(1). Retrieved from http://www.gjcpp.org/en/resource.php?issue=21&resource=200

Wolverton, B. (2003, September 4). What went wrong? Board's actions at issue at troubled D.C. United Way. *Chronicle of Philanthropy*, 15(22), 27.

Wolverton, B. (2004, May 13). A new ear for nation's United Ways. *Chronicle of Philanthropy*. Retrieved from https://philanthropy.com/article/A-New-Era-for-Nations-United/164473

Wood, S. P. (2016, April 11). Interview: 4-H execs on the brand's renewed focus on youth empowerment. *Adweek*. Retrieved from http://www.adweek.com/digital/interview-4-h-rebrands-moves-past-a-sole-agrarian-harvest/

Word, J., & Carpenter, H. (2013). The new public service? Applying the public service motivation model to nonprofit employees. *Public Personnel Management, 42*(3), 315–336.

Worth, M. J. (1993). *Educational fund raising: Principles and practice*. Phoenix, AZ: Oryx Press/American Council on Education.

Worth, M. J. (2005). *Securing the future: A fund-raising guide for boards of independent colleges and universities*. Washington, DC: Association of Governing Boards of Universities and Colleges.

Worth, M. J. (2016). *Fundraising: Principles and practice*. Thousand Oaks, CA: Sage.

Worth, M. J. (2017a). *Advisory councils in higher education*. Washington, DC: Association of Governing Boards of Universities and Colleges.

Worth, M. J. (2017b). *Leading the campaign* (2nd ed.). Lanham, MD: Rowman & Littlefield.

Wyland, M. (2013, April 19). The merger that might have been: Sanford Health and Fairview Health Services. *Nonprofit Quarterly*. Retrieved from https://nonprofitquarterly.org/2013/04/19/the-merger-that-might-have-been-sanford-health-and-fairview-health-services/

Yankey, J. A., & Willen, C. K. (2005). Strategic alliances. In R. D. Herman & Associates (Eds.), *The Jossey-Bass handbook of nonprofit leadership and management* (pp. 254–274). San Francisco, CA: Jossey-Bass.

Yarnold, D. (2016, May 2). How technology transformed a legacy charity. *Chronicle of Philanthropy*. Retrieved from https://www.philanthropy.com/article/Opinion-How-Technology/236291

YMCA of the USA. (2014). *Delivering our cause: Strategic plan 2014–2017*. Chicago, IL: Author. Retrieved from http://s3.amazonaws.com/ymca-ynet-prod/files/organizational-profile/Delivering-Our-Cause-Strategic-Plan-Online.pdf

YMCA of the USA. (n.d.). *History*. Chicago, IL: Author. Retrieved from http://www.ymca.net

Young, D. R. (1983). *If not for profit, for what? A behavioral theory of the nonprofit sector based on entrepreneurship*. Lanham, MD: Lexington Books.

Young, D. R. (2006). *Corporate partnerships: A guide for the nonprofit manager*. Alexandria, VA: National Center on Nonprofit Enterprise.

Young, D. R. (Ed.). (2007). *Financing nonprofits: Putting theory into practice*. Lanham, MD: National Center on Nonprofit Enterprise.

Young, D. R. (2016a). Contract failure theory. In J. S. Ott & L. A. Dicke (Eds.), *The nature of the nonprofit sector* (3rd ed., pp. 121–125). Boulder, CO: Westview.

Young, D. R. (2016b). Government failure theory. In J. S. Ott & L. A. Dicke (Eds.), *The nature of the nonprofit sector* (3rd ed., pp. 126–128). Boulder, CO: Westview.

Young, D. R. & Casey, J. (2017). Supplementary, complementary, or adversarial? Nonprofit-government relations. In E. T. Boris & C. E. Steuerle (Eds.), *Nonprofits and government: Collaboration and conflict* (3rd ed., pp. 37–70). Lanham, MD: Rowman & Littlefield/Urban Institute Press.

Young-joo, L. (2016, April). Comparison of job satisfaction between nonprofit and public employees. *Nonprofit and Voluntary Sector Quarterly, 45*(2), 295–313.

Youth Villages. (2016). *Annual report*. Retrieved from http://www.youthvillages.org/Portals/0/PDFs/Program_Reports/2016AnnualReport.pdf

Youth Villages. (2017). [Home page]. Retrieved from http://www.youthvillages.org/

Yunus, M. (2007). *Creating a world without poverty: Social business and the future of capitalism*. Philadelphia, PA: Perseus.

Zietlow, J., Hankin, J. A., & Seidner, A. (2007). *Financial management for nonprofit organizations*. Hoboken, NJ: Wiley.

Index

Page numbers in *italics* indicate photos.

About the Author

Michael J. Worth is professor of nonprofit management in the Trachtenberg School of Public Policy and Public Administration at the George Washington University in Washington, DC. He teaches graduate courses related to the governance and management of nonprofit institutions and organizations and to philanthropic fundraising.

Dr. Worth served as vice president for development and alumni affairs at the George Washington University for 18 years and previously served as director of development at the University of Maryland. Earlier in his career, he was assistant to the president at Wilkes University and director of development at DeSales University. As vice president at the George Washington University, he planned and directed two major campaigns and provided support to the board of trustees. Dr. Worth has served as a member of the Commission on Philanthropy of the Council for Advancement and Support of Education (CASE) and as editor of the *CASE International Journal of Educational Advancement*, a peer-reviewed scholarly journal focused on the practice of institutional advancement in educational institutions.

He has written or edited various books, textbooks, and monographs, including *Public College and University Development* (1985); *The Role of the Development Officer in Higher Education* (1994); *Educational Fund Raising: Principles and Practice* (1993); *New Strategies for Educational Fund Raising* (2002); *Securing the Future* (2005); *Sounding Boards* (2008); *Nonprofit Management: Principles and Practice* (1st edition, 2009; 2nd edition, 2012; 3rd edition, 2013; 4th edition, 2017; 5th edition, 2019); *Foundations for the Future* (2012); *Leading the Campaign* (1st edition, 2010; 2nd edition, 2017); and *Advisory Councils in Higher Education* (2017).

Among other voluntary services, Dr. Worth has been a member of the board of directors of Miriam's Kitchen, an organization providing services to homeless individuals in Washington, DC, and a member of the advisory board of the Young Nonprofit Professionals Network, Washington, DC, chapter.

Dr. Worth consults widely on governance, management, and fundraising with colleges and universities, national associations and institutions, and nonprofit organizations in various fields and sectors.

He holds a BA in economics from Wilkes University, an MA in economics from American University, and a PhD in higher education from the University of Maryland.